LEGAL ENVIRONMENT OF BUSINESS

Second Edition

Susan A. Supina
University of St. Thomas

Susan J. Marsnik
University of St. Thomas

The publisher is not engaged in rendering legal or other professional advice, and this publication is not a substitute for the advice of an attorney. If you require legal or other expert advice, you should seek the services of a competent attorney or other professional.

© 2017 LEG, Inc. d/b/a West Academic
© 2022 LEG, Inc. d/b/a West Academic
    444 Cedar Street, Suite 700
    St. Paul, MN 55101
    1-877-888-1330

West, West Academic Publishing, and West Academic are trademarks of West Publishing Corporation, used under license.

Printed in the United States of America

ISBN: 978-1-64708-921-4

To our colleagues, past and present,
who shared guidance, support,
advice, and laughter.

— SJM and SAS

To Kevin Keatings

— SAS

Preface

No business topic is complete without an examination of legal and compliance issues. Whether it is accounting, management, human resources, or marketing, the law permeates business subjects. Learning and understanding relevant business laws can be challenging. This book addresses that challenge by emphasizing the most significant legal issues for each topic, explaining and clarifying the important aspects of applicable laws, and providing insight by discussing the laws in a comprehensive manner.

This text brings the legal environment of business to life for students. Each chapter starts with a clear statement of the Key Objectives to orient students to the general goals of the material that follows and to alert them to the topics they will be mastering in each chapter. Following the Key Objectives is a Chapter Overview that provides a general description of the topic and an Introduction that includes more detail and discusses any relevant societal, governmental, or legal considerations. Each chapter then breaks the material into manageable pieces, integrating the law with the relevant business activity.

The text covers the content for each chapter, while providing accessible and approachable tools for the undergraduate student to learn about legal methods, such as legal research, writing, and logic. Relevant terms that may be new to the students are highlighted and defined in each chapter. Sidebars, examples, and graphics reinforce the key points. In addition, each chapter contains content features to promote student learning and classroom engagement. These features include the following:

CASE BRIEFS AND EXCERPTS

This book uses both case excerpts and briefed cases to aid student understanding. The excerpts are simplified and condensed to focus on relevant issues, while the briefs follow the High Court Case Summaries model. Each brief focuses on the lesson to be learned from each decision. Including both types of case material lends more flexibility to instructors in courses with differing goals.

Each briefed case starts with a headline-style statement of the rule of the case, the name and citation, and an identification of the parties procedurally and practically. In *National Federation of Independent Business v. Sebelius* (Chapter 1), for instance, Sebelius is identified as the defendant and as Secretary of Health and Human Services and the National Federation of Independent Business is identified as the plaintiff and as a business interest group. Each time a party is referenced in the brief, the party is clearly flagged as plaintiff (P) or defendant (D) in the original case. Students then receive an overview with an "instant facts" description, the black-letter rule, and the procedural basis. With that grounding, the student proceeds to a lengthier version of the facts, the issue phrased as a yes/no question, and the court's decision. Pertinent legal concepts are presented and described using common English, with legal terminology clearly defined. Some briefs also include a short analysis and a glossary.

Case excerpts are also presented. Typically newer cases, these excerpts omit secondary issues, citations, and some case text. These changes provide a condensed and accessible version for undergraduates in the language of the court. The header conventions from the case briefs also appear for each excerpt to aid students.

For instructors wanting to assign students case briefing work, the prepared case briefs will provide strong examples, while the excerpts are ready for student analysis. To promote full understanding of the model and of case analysis, Chapter 1 discusses case briefing and shows how to brief a case. In this way, students are attuned to the model and may apply it themselves.

REVIEW QUESTIONS

Each chapter includes Review Questions for students to prepare individually or work through in class with instructor guidance.

DISCUSSION QUESTIONS

Discussion Questions range from hypotheticals to ethics dilemmas. They include variations on legal themes found in each chapter, and address common issues faced by businesspeople. They are suitable for group work or instructor-led conversations.

CAREERS IN THE LAW

Each chapter includes a section on legal careers. Most students are unfamiliar with legal jobs other than that of an attorney. For those who are interested in law, but do not wish to attend law school, these features illuminate the multitude of law-related options in the workplace.

VOCABULARY

Legal terminology is defined repeatedly to avoid confusion. Case briefs include short glossaries where new terms are introduced. The main text highlights legal references by bolding the word or phrase. The term is then defined in the text, and added to a glossary at the end of the chapter. Finally, for overall reference, all the terms in the book are gathered in a master glossary in the appendix.

ELECTRONIC RESOURCES

Supporting materials, including presentations, test banks, and hand-outs, are available at westacademic.com.

In addition to the features described above, this text includes:

- a broad selection of topics, including foundational issues, business formation, types of law, contracting, employment, and regulatory issues;

- numerous examples, case excerpts, sidebars, review materials, and exercises, with a focus on practical applications;

- several useful appendices, including those addressing primary law, key terms, and other aids;

- an accessible but non-patronizing language and tone aimed at undergraduates;

- newer cases and examples, while still including the seminal decisions found in most other business law texts; and

- graphics included throughout the text wherever appropriate or helpful.

This text's features stand out when compared to other introductory business law texts. As an entry-level textbook that focuses on clarifying and describing the implications of relevant laws and cases without over-simplification, it is an invaluable tool to provide the foundation for a business-law education and to act as a springboard for classroom discussions.

ACKNOWLEDGEMENTS

We owe a great debt of gratitude to the following professors and scholars who reviewed the first and second editions of this text and provided insights, edits, additions, and critiques. Their combined experience hammered, shaped, and finally polished this text into its current form. Their work was essential to the finished product.

Charlotte Alexander
Assistant Professor of Legal Studies
Department of Risk Management and Insurance
Georgia State University

Elizabeth Brown
Assistant Professor
Law, Taxation and Financial Planning
Bentley University

Brian Elzweig, J.D., LL.M.
Instructor of Business Law
Department of Accounting and Finance
University of West Florida

Dr. Michelle Evans
Associate Professor
Department of Political Science
Texas State University

Ryan C. Grelecki, J.D.
Clinical Assistant Professor of Legal Studies
Department of Risk Management & Insurance
J. Mack Robinson College of Business
Georgia State University

Lydie Louis
Professor of Finance
Hult International Business School

Karen E. Maull
Instructor
Smeal College of Business
Penn State University

David Orozco, J.D.
Associate Professor of Legal Studies
Dean's Emerging Scholar
College of Business
Florida State University

Alan Roline
Director of the MBA Program and Associate Professor of Business Law
Labovitz School of Business and Economics
University of Minnesota, Duluth

Kurt M. Saunders, J.D., LL.M.
Acting Chair & Professor
Department of Business Law
California State University, Northridge

Cindy Schipani
Merwin H. Waterman Collegiate
Professor of Business Administration
Professor of Business Law
Ross School of Business
University of Michigan

Dr. Laura L. Sullivan
Associate Professor
College of Business
Sam Houston State University

We gratefully acknowledge the International Association of Commercial Administrators and JAMS Alternative Dispute Resolution for granting permission to re-print the UCC Financing Statement and Comprehensive Arbitration Rules and Procedures, respectively. These materials will greatly enhance the learning experience for students nationwide.

We are enduringly grateful for the support, advice, and enthusiasm of our colleagues and friends from the Ethics & Business Law department of the Opus College of Business at the University of St. Thomas and further afield, without whom this work would not have been possible.

Dale Thompson
Professor
Opus College of Business
University of St. Thomas

Katherina Pattit
Dean
Herberger Business School
St. Cloud State University

Michael Garrison
Professor & Senior Associate Dean
Opus College of Business
University of St. Thomas

Kevin Ritchey
CEO
Legal Research Center, Inc.

Randall Holbrook
General Counsel & Managing Director-GRC
Legal Research Center, Inc.

We consider ourselves extremely fortunate to have worked with the West Academic team, who are remarkable for their patience, professionalism, and good humor. Our deep gratitude to all members of the team who helped create this edition, and special thanks to:

Sarah Bowser Agan
Acquisitions Editor
West Academic

Pamela Siege Chandler
Chief Content Officer & Publisher
West Academic

Laura Holle
Lead Publishing Specialist
West Academic

Tara Grosse
Graphic Designer
Orange Dream Designs

A Note to Students

If you have taken other business courses, you've probably already learned a little bit about the law. Every business topic involves legal issues, from financial filings required by the Securities and Exchange Commission to rules covering advertising claims. Studying business law independently places these topic-specific regimes into context.

This book is designed to provide that context. As a businessperson, your career will involve many decisions about business formation, operations, and cooperation. Each chapter in this book covers an area of major business decisions, and addresses the major legal issues raised by that concern. Learning how the law impacts business choices now will help you make informed decisions when those choices arise later.

The following features will help guide your reading:

- Key Objectives at the beginning of each chapter define the major concepts you should absorb from the text.

- The Chapter Overview sets the stage for detailed discussions that follow.

- Legal vocabulary is highlighted and defined as it appears, making ideas clearer.

- Practical examples show how the rules work in real life.

- Graphics and tables summarize critical information.

- Review questions help test whether you achieved the chapter's objectives.

- Discussion questions offer new ways to apply the chapter's lessons.

In addition, each chapter includes significant legal decisions to enhance your understanding and prepare you for classroom discussions. Some of these summaries are in the form of case briefs. Case briefs are how attorneys and law students outline decisions. They simplify legal terminology and cut to the core of the ruling.

The briefs used in this text focus on the lesson to be learned from each decision. Each brief starts with a headline-style statement of the rule of the case, the name and citation, and an identification of the parties in the case. Identifying the parties makes it easier to keep track of them and their role in the dispute. Each brief points out the central issue resolved by the court, how that issue was decided, and the court's reasoning for its decision. This model helps walk through a complex (and often lengthy) document to absorb its core message.

In addition to case briefs, each chapter also includes excerpts from cases. These are condensed and edited versions that give you the opportunity to work with the actual language of the court. This will help you to learn to read cases and to develop your critical thinking as you read and brief the cases.

The book also includes information on legal careers. It is not necessary to go to law school to work with the law. Many people are unaware of the variety of legal careers available. This book highlights many of those options.

With your instructor's guidance, this textbook will give you the foundation you need to make solid business decisions in the future.

Table of Contents

Preface v

A Note to Students xi

Chapter 1: Introduction to Law 1

KEY OBJECTIVES 1

CHAPTER OVERVIEW 1

INTRODUCTION 1

I. *The American Legal Structure* 2

    Legislative Branch 2

    National Federation of Independent Business v. Sebelius
    567 U.S. 519, 132 S. Ct. 2566, 183 L. Ed. 2d 450 (2012) 2

        Executive Branch 5

        Judicial Branch 7

    Marbury v. Madison
    5 U.S. (1 Cranch) 137, 2 L. Ed. 60 (1803) 10

II. *Sources of Law* 12

    Constitution 12

    Statutes 13

    Regulations 14

    Chevron v. Natural Resources Defense Council
    467 U.S. 837, 104 S. Ct. 2778, 81 L. Ed. 2d 694 (1984) 14

    Common Law 16

    Treaties and International Law 17

CHAPTER SUMMARY 18

Review Questions 18

Discussion Questions 20

CHAPTER 2: LAW AND ETHICS 23

KEY OBJECTIVES 23

CHAPTER OVERVIEW 23

I.   *Stakeholders* 23

II. *Stakeholder-Focused Ethics* 25

III. *Ethics in Business* 28

    Corporate Social Responsibility 29

    Business Roundtable 29

    Compliance & Ethics 30

    Legal Frameworks 32

    Committee on Legal Ethics v. Higinbotham
    342 S.E.2d 152 (W. Va. 1986) 32

    Professional Ethics 34

IV. *International Business Ethics* 34

V. *Ethics Online* 37

    Synopsis, Inc. v. AzurEngine Technologies, Inc.
    401 F. Supp. 3d 1068 (S.D. Cal. 2019) 37

        Acceptable Use of Online Resources 39

CHAPTER SUMMARY 39

Review Questions 40

Discussion Questions 41

Chapter 3: Litigation and Appeals 45

KEY OBJECTIVES 45

CHAPTER OVERVIEW 45

INTRODUCTION 45

I. *Civil and Criminal Law* 46

II. *Federal and State Court Systems* 51

    Federal Court System 52

    State and Federal Jurisdiction 53

    International Shoe Co. v. Washington
    326 U.S. 310, 66 S. Ct. 154, 90 L. Ed. 95 (1945) 54

    Asahi Metal Industry Co. v. Superior Court
    480 U.S. 102, 107 S. Ct. 1026, 94 L. Ed. 2d 92 (1987) 55

    Venue 57

III. *Foreign Legal Systems* 58

    Civil Law 58

    Bijuridical Systems 58

    Islamic Law 59

IV. *Legal Analysis* 59

    Case Format 59

    Reading the Law 60

    What Is the "Rule"? 63

    Mayo v. Satan
    54 F.R.D. 282 (1971) 64

    Is It Good Law? 65

CHAPTER SUMMARY 66

Review Questions 66

Discussion Questions 68

Chapter 4: Dispute Resolution ... 73

KEY OBJECTIVES ... 73

CHAPTER OVERVIEW ... 73

INTRODUCTION ... 73

I. *Litigation* ... 74

    Pleadings ... 74

    Conley v. Gibson
355 U.S. 41, 78 S. Ct. 99, 2 L. Ed. 2d 80 (1957) ... 77

    Discovery ... 78

        Depositions ... 79

        Interrogatories ... 79

        Requests for Admission ... 79

        Document Requests ... 80

    Motion Practice ... 82

        Motion for Summary Judgment ... 82

    Trial ... 82

    Post-Trial Motions ... 84

    Appeal ... 85

II. *Alternative Dispute Resolution* ... 87

    Negotiation and Settlement ... 88

    Mediation ... 89

    Arbitration ... 91

    Sanchez v. Nitro-Lift Technologies, LLC
762 F.3d 1139 (10th Cir. 2014) ... 93

    AT&T Mobility LLC (Defendant) v. Concepcion (Plaintiff)
563 U.S. 333, 131 S. Ct. 1740, 179 L. Ed. 2d 742 (2011) ... 94

    Other Kinds of ADR ... 95

III.	Avoiding Disputes	96
	Contract Negotiation	96
	Maintaining Business Relationships	98
	Cultural Issues	98

CHAPTER SUMMARY 99

Review Questions 100

Discussion Questions 101

CHAPTER 5: BUSINESS FORMS 105

KEY OBJECTIVES 105

CHAPTER OVERVIEW 105

INTRODUCTION 105

I.	*Unincorporated Forms*	105
	Sole Proprietorship	106
	Partnership	107
	Carlson v. Brabham 199 So. 3d 735 (Miss. App. 2016)	110
II.	*Limited Liability Forms*	111
	Limited Liability Partnerships	112
	Limited Partnerships	112
	Corporations	114
	C Corporations	116
	S Corporations	117
	Limited Liability Companies	118
	Non-Profit Corporations	119
	Public Benefit Corporations	119

III.	*Professional Forms*	120
	Partnership	120
	Professional Corporations	120
IV.	*Franchises*	121
V.	*Business Formation*	121
	Corporate Promoters	122
	Filing Obligations	123
	Tax Obligations	123
VI.	*Corporate Powers*	124
VII.	*Ongoing Management*	124
	Corporate Formalities	124
	Board of Directors	126
	Guth v. Luft, Inc. 5 A.2d 503 (Del. Ch. 1939)	127
	Corporate Officers	128
	Shareholders	128
	Piercing the Corporate Veil	128
	Shorter Brothers, Inc. v. Vectus 3, Inc. ___ So.3d ___, 2021 WL 2622054 (Ala. 2021)	129
VIII.	*Voluntary Dissolution*	130
	Succession Planning	131
	Mergers and Acquisitions	132
IX.	*Involuntary Dissolution*	133
	Bankruptcy	133
	Death of Key Member or Partner	134
CHAPTER SUMMARY		134

Review Questions 135

Discussion Questions 137

CHAPTER 6: CONTRACTS 141

KEY OBJECTIVES 141

CHAPTER OVERVIEW 141

INTRODUCTION 141

I. *Contract Formation* 141

   Offer 142

   Lucy v. Zehmer
   84 S.E.2d 516 (Va. 1954) 144

   Leonard v. Pepsico, Inc.
   88 F. Supp. 2d 116 (S.D.N.Y. 1999) 146

   Acceptance 148

   Consideration 150

   Hamer v. Sidway
   124 N.Y. 538, 27 N.E. 256 (1891) 152

      Promissory Estoppel 153

   Capacity 154

   Legality 155

II. *Contract Formalities* 157

   Written v. Oral Agreements 157

   Statute of Frauds 157

III. *Contract Enforcement and Performance* 159

   Enforcement: Genuineness of Assent 159

      Fraud/Misrepresentation 160

Mistake 162

Mutual Mistake 162

Raffles v. Wichelhaus
2 H. & C. 906, 159 Eng. Rep. 375 (Court of Exchequer 1864) 163

Unilateral Mistake 164

Scrivener's Error 165

Undue Influence 165

Genuineness of Assent/Duress 166

Contract Performance and Discharge 166

Breach of Contract 168

Remedies 171

Hadley v. Baxendale
9 Ex. 341, 156 Eng. Rep. 145 (1854) 172

U.S. for the use of Coastal Steel Erectors, Inc. v. Algernon Blair, Inc.
479 F.2d 638 (4th Cir. 1973) 176

Contract Torts 178

IV. *Sale of Goods Contracts (UCC)* 179

Bruel & Kjaer v. Suburban O'Hare Commission
969 N.E.2d 445 (Ill. App. 2012) 180

UCC Contract Formalities 182

UCC Contract Performance 183

UCC Contract Warranties 183

Express Warranties 183

Implied Warranties 184

Shaffer v. Victoria Station, Inc.
91 Wash. 2d 295, 588 P.2d 233 (1978) 185

Disclaimers 185

V. *Online Contracts* 186

CHAPTER SUMMARY 186

Review Questions 188

Discussion Questions 189

CHAPTER 7: CREDITOR-DEBTOR ISSUES 195

KEY OBJECTIVES 195

CHAPTER OVERVIEW 195

INTRODUCTION 195

I. *Truth in Lending* 196

    K/O Ranch, Inc. v. Norwest Bank of the Black Hills
    748 F.2d 1246 (8th Cir. 1984) 198

II. *Fair Debt Collection Practices* 199

III. *Fair Credit Reporting* 201

IV. *Article 9 Secured Transactions* 201

    Credit Bureau of Broken Bow, Inc. v. Moninger
    204 Neb. 679, 284 N.W.2d 855 (1979) 203

V. *Mortgage Foreclosure* 207

VI. *Bankruptcy* 208

    In Re: Advanced Vascular Resources of Johnstown, LLC
    590 B.R. 689 (Bank. W.D. Pa. 2018) 209

    Types of Bankruptcy 212

        Chapter 7 212

    Seror v. Lopez
    532 B.R. 140 (2015) 214

        Chapter 9 215

        Chapter 11 216

        Chapter 12 217

        Chapter 13 218

        Chapter 15 219

VII. *Receivership* 220

CHAPTER SUMMARY 221

Review Questions 222

Discussion Questions 223

CHAPTER 8: TORTS AND PRODUCTS LIABILITY 227

KEY OBJECTIVES 227

CHAPTER OVERVIEW 227

INTRODUCTION 227

I. *Negligence* 228

    Duty of Reasonable Care 228

    Breach of the Duty of Reasonable Care 229

    Causation 229

        Intervening Event 230

Palsgraf v. Long Island R.R. Co.
248 N.Y. 339, 162 N.E. 99 (1928) 231

    Damages 233

    Professional Malpractice Actions 233

    Res Ipsa Loquitur 234

    Negligence Per Se 235

    Defenses to Negligence Cases 235

II. *Intentional Torts* 236

    Fraudulent Misrepresentation 236

    Interference with Contractual Relations 237

    Interference with Prospective Business Advantage 238

Defamation 238

    Actual Malice 241

    Trade Libel/Product Disparagement 243

III. *Strict Liability* 243

IV. *Products Liability* 244

    Negligence 245

    Strict Liability 245

Arbogast v. A.W. Chesterton Co.
197 F. Supp. 3d 807 (D. Md. 2016) 246

    Warranty 246

Wallace v. Tri-State Assembly, LLC, and Amazon.com LLC
157 N.Y.S.3d 438 (N.Y. App. Div., 1st Dep't 2021) 247

    Types of Defects 248

        Manufacturing Defects 248

        Design Defects. 249

        Warning Defects 249

        Improper Packaging 249

Sheats v. The Kroger Company
336 Ga. App. 307, 784 S.E.2d 442 (2016) 250

V. *Defenses to Product Liability* 251

    Assumption of Risk 251

Puckett v. The Plastics Group, Inc.
561 Fed. Appx. 865 (2014) 252

    Comparative Fault 253

R.J. Reynolds Tobacco Co. v. Sury
118 So. 3d 849 (Fla. Dist. Ct. App. 2013) 254

    Modification/Substantial Change 255

Rix v. General Motors
723 P.2d 195 (Mont. 1986) 255

Abnormal Uses/Product Misuse 256

Pitman v. Ameristep Corporation
208 F. Supp. 3d 1053 (E.D. Mo. 2016) 257

VI. *Damages* 257

Compensatory Damages 258

Anderson v. Sears, Roebuck & Co.
377 F. Supp. 136 (E.D. La. 1974) 258

Punitive Damages 259

CHAPTER SUMMARY 259

Review Questions 260

Discussion Questions 262

CHAPTER 9: INTELLECTUAL PROPERTY 267

KEY OBJECTIVES 267

CHAPTER OVERVIEW 267

INTRODUCTION 267

I. *Copyright* 268

Copyright on Creative Works 269

Proving Copyright 272

Registering Copyrights 272

Copyright Infringement 274

Fleischer Studios, Inc. v. A.V.E.L.A., Inc.
654 F.3d 958 (9th Cir. 2011) 275

Fair Use 276

Authors Guild v. Google, Inc.
804 F.3d 202 (2d Cir. 2015) 277

Batiste v. Lewis
976 F.3d 493 (5th Cir. 2020) 279

II. *Trademark* 280

Abercrombie & Fitch Co. v. Hunting World, Inc.
537 F.2d 4 (2d Cir. 1999) 283

Other Distinctive Marks 284

Trade Dress 285

Trademark Use and Registration 286

Mattel, Inc. v. Walking Mountain Productions
353 F.3d 792 (9th Cir. 2003) 286

Dilution 289

Protecting Trademarks 290

New Kids on the Block v. News America Publishing, Inc.
971 F.2d 302 (9th Cir. 1992) 291

Fair Use 292

III. *Patents* 293

Utility Patents 293

O'Reilly v. Morse
56 U.S. 62, 15 How. 62, 14 L. Ed. 601 (1854) 294

Design Patents 295

Plant Patents 295

Bowman v. Monsanto Co.
569 U.S. 278, 133 S. Ct. 1761, 185 L. Ed. 2d 931 (2013) 296

Securing a Patent 297

IV. *Trade Secrets* 298

Protecting Trade Secrets 300

V. *International Protection* 301

VI. *Enforcing Intellectual Property Rights* 303

  Civil Infringement or Misappropriation 303
   Copyright Infringement 303
   Trademark Infringement 305
   Patent Infringement 306
   Trade Secret Misappropriation 307
VII. *Licenses and Assignments* 307
  Pros and Cons 308
   Pros 308
   Cons 308
  Contractual Safeguards 309
   Description of the Property 309
   The Grant 309
   Payment 309
   Accounting 310
   Dispute Resolution 310
VIII. *Intellectual Property and Technology* 310
  Increased Enforcement Challenges 310
  Protection of Technical Intellectual Property 311

CHAPTER SUMMARY 311

Review Questions 312

Discussion Questions 313

CHAPTER 10: AGENCY 317

KEY OBJECTIVES 317

CHAPTER OVERVIEW 317

INTRODUCTION 317

I.	Creating an Agency Relationship	318
II.	Duties and Liabilities	321

    MDM Group Associates, Inc. v. CX Reinsurance Company Ltd.
    165 P.3d 882 (Colo. Ct. App. 2007) 321

    Vicarious Liability 325

    Faragher v. City of Boca Raton
    524 U.S. 775, 118 S. Ct. 2275, 141 L. Ed. 2d 662 (1998) 326

    Employer Liability for Negligence 327

    Principal Liability for Agent Malfeasance 327

    Edgewater Motels, Inc. v. Gatzke
    277 N.W.2d 11 (Minn. 1979) 328

    Negligent Hiring and Retention 330

III.	Scope of Authority	331
IV.	Actual and Apparent Authority	333

    Rogers v. Mashantucket Pequot Gaming Enterprise
    6 Mash. Rep. 374 (Mashantucket Pequot Tribal Court 2016) 334

V.	Termination	337

    Lapse of Time 337

    Act of the Parties 337

    Operation of Law 338

CHAPTER SUMMARY 339

Review Questions 339

Discussion Questions 341

CHAPTER 11: EMPLOYMENT 345

KEY OBJECTIVES 345

CHAPTER OVERVIEW 345

INTRODUCTION 345

I. *Employment Relationship* 345

    At-Will Employment 346

    Pine River State Bank v. Mettille
    333 N.W.2d 622 (Minn. 1983) 347

    Independent Contractor 348

    Weiss v. Loomis, Sayles & Company, Inc.
    97 Mass. App. Ct. 1 (2020) 349

II. *Employer Responsibilities* 351

    Minimum Wage 352

    Overtime Pay 352

    Mandated Benefits 352

    Family and Medical Leave 353

    Other Leaves 353

        Paternity/Maternity Leave 353

        Military Service Leave 354

        Sick Leave 354

        Vacation Leave and Holidays 354

        Jury Leave 355

III. *Termination of Employment* 355

    Severance Pay 355

IV. *Employee Protection Laws* 355

    Anti-Discrimination Laws 355

    Title VII 356

    Oncale v. Sundowner Offshore Services, Inc.
    523 U.S. 75, 118 S. Ct. 998, 140 L. Ed. 2d 201 (1998) 357

Desert Palace, Inc. v. Costa
539 U.S. 90, 123 S. Ct. 2148, 156 L. Ed. 2d 84 (2003) 359

Age Discrimination 360

Mallon v. Frostburg State University
2021 WL 4215331 (D. Md. 2021) 360

Disability Discrimination 363

Employee Safety 363

Workers' Compensation 365

Disability Insurance 366

Affirmative Action 367

Fisher v. University of Texas
579 U.S. 365, 136 S. Ct. 2198, 195 L. Ed. 2d 511 (2016) 368

Protection for Terminated Workers 368

    Health Insurance Continuation 368

    Unemployment Compensation 369

    WARN Act 369

V. *Immigration and Employment* 369

    Permanent Resident Status 369

    Temporary Work Visas 374

    Work Permits 374

VI. *Labor Organization* 374

    Collective Bargaining 375

    Right to Work Laws 377

CHAPTER SUMMARY 377

Review Questions 378

Discussion Questions 379

Chapter 12: Business Topics ... 385

KEY OBJECTIVES ... 385

CHAPTER OVERVIEW ... 385

INTRODUCTION ... 385

I. *Investor Relations* ... 385

    Accountants and Auditors ... 388

    Financial Reporting ... 389

    Internal Controls ... 390

    Criminal Penalties ... 391

II. *Antitrust Laws* ... 392

    Sherman Act ... 392

Coronavirus Reporter v. Apple Inc.
2021 WL 5936910 (N.D. Cal. 2021) ... 393

U.S. v. Paramount Pictures
334 U.S. 131, 68 S. Ct. 915, 92 L. Ed. 1260 (1948) ... 397

    Clayton Act ... 398

III. *International Business Transactions* ... 400

    Transportation Risk and Costs ... 401

    Harmonized Tariff Schedule ... 404

St. Paul Guardian Insurance Company v. Neuromed Medical Systems & Support
2002 WL 465312 (S.D.N.Y. 2002) ... 405

Toy Biz, Inc. v. U.S.
24 C.I.T. 1351 (2000) ... 408

    Trading Areas ... 409

CHAPTER SUMMARY ... 411

Review Questions ... 411

Discussion Questions ... 413

Chapter 13: Regulatory Programs 415

KEY OBJECTIVES 415

CHAPTER OVERVIEW 415

INTRODUCTION 415

I. *Administrative Procedure Act* 416

    Fund for Animals, Inc. v. Rice
85 F.3d 535 (11th Cir. 1996) 417

II. *Advertising and Marketing* 419

    POM Wonderful, LLC v. Federal Trade Commission
777 F.3d 478 (D.C. Cir. 2015) 420

    Deceptive Trade Practices 422

    State Deceptive Practices Law 424

III. *Labelling and Packaging* 425

IV. *Consumer Protection Laws* 426

    Consumer Sales 427

        Telemarketing 427

        "Cooling Off" Periods 427

        Plain Language 428

        Unconscionability 428

    Consumer Health and Safety 429

        Warranties 429

V. *Investor Protection* 430

    Federal Securities Regulation 431

        Securities Act of 1933 431

        Securities Exchange Act of 1934 432

        Trust Indenture Act 432

Affiliated Ute Citizens v. United States
406 U.S. 128, 92 S. Ct. 1456, 31 L. Ed. 741 (1972) 432
    Investment Company Act 433
    Investment Advisers Act 433
    Sarbanes-Oxley Act 433
    Dodd-Frank Wall Street Reform and Consumer Protection Act 434
    Jumpstart Our Business Startups Act (the "JOBS Act") 434
  Consumer Financial Protection Bureau 434
  State Securities Law 436
VI. *Environmental Protection* 436
  Federal and State Environmental Laws 437
  Air Quality Rules 438
  Water Quality Rules 439
Rapanos v. United States
547 U.S. 715, 126 S. Ct. 2208, 165 L. Ed. 2d 159 (2006) 439
  Waste Management 441
  Toxic Substances 442
    Pesticides 443

CHAPTER SUMMARY 443

Review Questions 444

Discussion Questions 445

CHAPTER 14: CRIMINAL LAW 451

KEY OBJECTIVES 451

CHAPTER OVERVIEW 451

INTRODUCTION 451

I.	*Basic Principles of Criminal Law*	451
	Mens Rea	452
	General Intent Mens Rea	452
	Specific Intent Mens Rea	453
	Actus Reus	455
	Elements	456
	Search and Seizure	458
	Sentencing	462
	Commonwealth v. Almonor 482 Mass. 35, 120 N.E.3d 1183 (2019)	463
II.	*Inchoate Crimes*	465
	Attempt	466
	Solicitation	467
	Conspiracy	467
III.	*"White-Collar" Crimes*	469
	Fraud	469
	Fountain v. U.S. 357 F.3d 250 (2d Cir. 2004)	471
	Embezzlement	472
	Insider Trading	473
	Federal Criminal Statutes	474
	Antitrust Laws	475
	Immigration Control and Reform Act (ICRA)	475
	Racketeer Influenced and Corrupt Organizations Act (RICO)	475
	Foreign Corrupt Practices Act (FCPA)	475
	Other Crimes	476

IV. *Corporate Criminal Liability* 476

New York Central & Hudson River Railroad Co. v. United States
212 U.S. 481, 29 S. Ct. 304, 53 L. Ed. 613 (1909) 477

Commonwealth v. Pi Delta Psi, Inc.
211 A.3d 875 (Pa. Super. Ct. 2019) 479

Sentencing 480

Fines 480

Restitution 480

Probation 481

Confiscation of Property 481

Involuntary Dissolution 481

CHAPTER SUMMARY 481

Review Questions 482

Discussion Questions 484

Appendices 489

1. Constitution of the United States 491

2. Amendments to the Constitution 501

3. Sarbanes-Oxley Act of 2002 (Selected Provisions) 509

4. Delaware General Corporate Law (Selected Provisions) 517

5. JAMS Comprehensive Arbitration Rules & Procedures 543

6. Sample Corporate Bylaws (eBay, Inc.) 567

7. Business Law Glossary 597

Index 615

LEGAL ENVIRONMENT OF BUSINESS

Second Edition

1 Introduction to Law

KEY OBJECTIVES:

▶ Explain how the branches of government interact and create laws.
▶ Describe the sources of laws regulating business and business transactions.
▶ Explain how court decisions become legal precedents.

CHAPTER OVERVIEW

Before you can meaningfully engage in the study of business, you must understand the laws that govern business activities and relationships. This chapter provides a broad overview of the United States legal system and its impact on business transactions. This foundation sets the stage for the rest of the chapters in this book.

INTRODUCTION

When Lao Tzu philosophized that "a journey of a thousand miles begins with a single step," he certainly did not have the United States legal system in mind. The quote is as applicable to the U.S. legal system as it was to any facet of ancient Chinese culture.

The journey to the American legal system as we know it today began with the implementation of the English **common law** by the 13 original colonies. It continued with the ratification of the United States Constitution in 1789. Ratification of the Constitution put our legal system on the path to where we are today. While the path includes many twists and turns, most of our system can be traced back to our Constitution.

The U.S. Constitution is divided into seven articles. Articles I, II, and III establish three branches of the federal government: the legislative, executive, and judicial branches. Each branch is powerful in its own way, but power is checked by the other branches. This system helps prevent one person or small group from dominating the American people. This concept is referred to as the **separation of powers**. Next, in Articles IV and V, the Constitution identifies specific matters over which the federal government has exclusive control, leaving all other matters to the discretion of the individual state governments. Dividing power between the national and state governments is a concept referred to as **federalism**. The U.S. Constitution makes clear in Article VI that federal law

COMMON LAW:
Law developed through court decisions over time rather than through constitutions or codes.

SEPARATION OF POWERS:
Giving legislative, executive, and judicial powers of government to separate bodies of the government.

FEDERALISM:
Governmental system that shares power between national and state governments.

is superior to state law, in what is referred to as the "Supremacy Clause."

While the U.S. Constitution is helpful for understanding the structure of the federal government, it is important to note that each state has its own governmental structure. While many state structures are similar to the federal structure with separate branches of government, there are differences from state-to-state. The differences are often minor. The overview in this chapter mainly addresses the federal government's structure.

I. The American Legal Structure

The United States is governed through the cooperation of three distinct branches: the legislative branch, which makes the laws; the executive branch, which enforces the laws; and the judicial branch, which interprets the laws. Each branch is discussed in more detail below.

Legislative Branch

Article I of the Constitution grants legislative powers to Congress and lists the specific matters over which Congress can legislate. These **enumerated powers** include matters that pertain to the United States as a whole, such as issuing money, collecting taxes, spending for the general welfare, regulating trade between states, granting patents and copyrights, and immigration.

While Congress makes liberal use of its power over these matters, the taxing and spending clause is particularly useful to federal legislation. The following brief summary of a Supreme Court case (called a "brief"), *National Association of Independent Business v. Sebelius*, focuses on a legal challenge to the Affordable Care Act. The U.S. Supreme Court considered whether the law was permitted under the Constitution's taxation clause.

> **ENUMERATED POWERS:**
> Specific identified powers reserved only for the federal government.

THE PATIENT PROTECTION AND AFFORDABLE CARE ACT'S INDIVIDUAL MANDATE IS CONSTITUTIONAL, BUT THE MEDICAID EXPANSION IS NOT

National Federation of Independent Business v. Sebelius
(Business Group) v. (Secretary of Health and Human Services)
567 U.S. 519, 132 S. Ct. 2566, 183 L. Ed. 2d 450 (2012)

INSTANT FACTS:
The National Federation of Independent Business (P) brought suit against Sebelius (D) as a representative of the government, claiming that (1) the mandate in the Patient Protection and Affordable Care Act that individuals purchase health insurance exceeded Congress's power under the Constitution, and (2) the requirement that states expand their Medicaid programs or lose all federal funding was also unconstitutional. The Act was enacted under the Spending Clause of the Constitution.

BLACK LETTER RULE:
The legitimacy of Spending Clause legislation depends on whether a state voluntarily and knowingly accepts the terms of such programs, and when Congress threatens to terminate other grants as a means of pressuring the states to accept a Spending Clause program, the legislation runs counter to this nation's system of federalism.

PROCEDURAL BASIS:
Appeal from an order of the Eleventh Circuit Court of Appeals holding the Patient Protection and Affordable Care Act unconstitutional in part.

FACTS:
Congress enacted the Patient Protection and Affordable Care Act in 2010. The Act aimed to increase the number of Americans covered by health insurance and to decrease the cost of health care. The mandate of the Act requires most Americans to maintain at least minimal health care coverage or be charged a penalty—a "shared responsibility" payment. The Act also expanded the scope of the Medicaid program, increasing the number of low-income individuals to whom states must provide health insurance coverage. A consortium of businesses took legal action against the government opposing these provisions.

ISSUE:
Did Congress have the power under the Constitution to enact the challenged provisions of the Patient Protection and Affordable Care Act of 2010?

DECISION AND RATIONALE:
(Roberts, C.J.) Yes and no. With regard to the individual mandate, the power of Congress to regulate interstate commerce does not include the power to compel individuals to become active in commerce by purchasing a product. In our system, Congress has limited powers, and other powers are reserved to the states. The facets of governing that touch on citizens' daily lives are normally administered by the states. The Constitution authorizes Congress to "regulate Commerce with foreign Nations, and among the several States, and with the Indian Tribes." This Congressional power to regulate commerce presupposes the existence of some commercial activity to be regulated. Cases dealing with Commerce Clause powers have always described those powers as reaching an "activity."

The individual mandate does not regulate existing activity; instead, it compels individuals to become active in commerce by purchasing a product. Construing the Commerce Clause to permit Congress to regulate individuals precisely because they are doing nothing would open a new and potentially vast domain to congressional authority. The Government (D) argues that sickness and injury are unpredictable but unavoidable, and so the uninsured as a class are active in the market for health care. The mandate merely regulates how individuals pay for that active participation. The phrase "active in the market for health care" has no constitutional significance. An individual who bought a car two years ago and who may buy another in the future is not "active in the car market."

The Government (D) also argues that Congress has the power under the Necessary and Proper Clause to enact the individual mandate because it is an integral part of a comprehensive scheme of economic regulation. The Necessary and Proper Clause gives Congress the power to enact provisions incidental to an enumerated power, and conducive to its beneficial exercise. The Clause is merely a declaration that the means of carrying into execution the enumerated powers of Congress are included in the grant. We have been very deferential to Congress's determination that a regulation is "necessary." But we have also carried out our responsibility to declare unconstitutional those laws that undermine the structure of government established by the Constitution.

Applying these principles, the individual mandate cannot be sustained under the Necessary and Proper Clause as an essential component of the insurance reforms. Each of our prior cases upholding laws under that Clause involved exercises of authority derived from a granted power. The individual mandate vests Congress with the extraordinary ability to create the necessary predicate to the exercise of an enumerated power. Such a conception of the Necessary and Proper Clause would allow Congress to reach beyond the natural limit of its authority and draw within its regulatory scope those who otherwise would be outside of it.

Having concluded that the individual mandate is invalid under the Commerce Clause, we must next consider the Government's (D) argument that the individual mandate is a valid exercise of

Congress's taxing powers. Here, we agree with the Government (D). Congress has broad authority to levy taxes, and there is no constitutional basis to hold that an individual is exempt from taxation due to his or her inactivity. Although the Commerce Clause does not give Congress the authority to regulate inactivity that burdens commerce, the Constitution does not provide the same guarantee with regard to taxation.

The power to tax is limited to the power to require an individual to pay money into the Federal Treasury. The shared responsibility payment has the functional characteristics of a tax, rather than a penalty. For most Americans, the amount that will be due will be far less than the price of insurance. The payment is collected by the Internal Revenue Service through the normal means of collecting revenue, except that the Service may not use criminal prosecutions to collect payments. The payments here will collect revenue, but they are also intended to influence conduct, by expanding health insurance coverage. Taxes that encourage conduct are nothing new. Every tax is in some measure regulatory, in that a tax interposes an economic impediment to the activity taxed. The fact that the law requiring the payments seeks to shape decisions about whether to buy health insurance does not mean that it cannot be a valid exercise of the taxing power.

Turning to the Medicaid issue, the legitimacy of Spending Clause legislation depends on whether a state voluntarily and knowingly accepts the terms of such programs. When Congress threatens to terminate other grants as a means of pressuring the states to accept a Spending Clause program, the legislation runs counter to this nation's system of federalism. The Medicaid expansion fails to pass muster under this principle.

Congress may use its spending power to create incentives for States to act in accordance with federal policies, but when pressure turns into compulsion the legislation runs contrary to our system of federalism. Permitting the federal government (D) to force the states to implement a federal program threatens the political accountability key to our federal system. State officials will bear the brunt of public disapproval, while the federal officials who devised the program may remain insulated from the ramifications of their decision. This is not a danger when a State has a legitimate choice whether to accept the federal conditions in exchange for federal funds.

The federal government (D) claims that the Medicaid expansion is merely a modification of the existing program because the states agreed that Congress could change the terms of Medicaid when they signed on in the first place. Although Congress's power to legislate under the Spending Clause is broad, it does not include surprising participating states with post-acceptance or "retroactive" conditions. We have no need to fix a line where persuasion gives way to coercion. It is enough that wherever that line may be, the Act is surely beyond it.

Affirmed in part, reversed in part.

ANALYSIS:
The Commerce Clause portion of this opinion generated much debate about its implications for Congress's legislative authority. Some commentators see it as a substantial limitation, if not a rollback, of Congressional authority. Others have noted that the Court ultimately upheld this unusual method of regulating the market, albeit on other grounds.

The shared responsibility payments are called "penalties" in the Act. It is not clear why Congress, which so carefully framed the payments to have the attributes of a tax, refused to call them a tax. It has been suggested that this was a failure of political courage. Congress simply did not want to open itself to the criticism that it was levying new taxes.

The dissenters (not included here) argued that the payments cannot be upheld as a tax because Congress did not "frame" them as such. This argument says that the law must be struck down even if the Constitution permitted Congress to enact it, because Congress used the wrong labels.

CASE VOCABULARY:
CAPITATION:
A tax levy that is a fixed sum per person, without regard to any other factors.

MEDICAID:
A federal-state cooperative program providing medical care to low-income individuals. The program is administered by the states in compliance with federal criteria, and is funded jointly by the state and federal governments.

The United States Congress has 535 members and numerous additional employees who provide support services to the members. Congress is divided into two parts, the Senate and the House of Representatives.

Each state elects two senators. Thus, the Senate has 100 members. The number of senators changes only if a new state is added or one is removed. Senators are elected to six-year terms, in even years, with approximately one-third of Senate seats up for election in any even year. There is no limit to the number of terms a senator may serve.

The House of Representatives currently has 435 voting members. The number of members is based on population, with roughly one representative seat for every 710,000 individuals. Therefore, states have differing numbers of representatives in the House. For example, California, with a population of over 39 million, has 53 members representing it in the House. North Dakota, in contrast, has only one member due to its population of roughly 760,000. Representatives are elected to two-year terms, in even years. This means that the composition of the House can change drastically during each even-year election, since every seat is up for election. There is no limit to the number of terms a representative may serve.

CABINET:
The most senior appointed officers of the executive branch of government, nominated by the President and confirmed by the Senate.

The federal legislature's primary duty is to make laws, but it has additional powers. For example, declarations of war must be passed in both the House and Senate. Congress determines how many seats there are in the United States Supreme Court. Presidential appointments of federal judges must be confirmed through a simple majority vote of the Senate.

With so much power over laws resting with the legislative branch, it is easy to understand why corporations and lobby groups interact so closely with elected members. While corporations and unions are banned from contributing directly to candidates for federal office, many corporations find individuals within the organization to donate and then present those donations together through "bundling." Meanwhile, lobbyists often form political action committees (PACs) to contribute to candidate campaigns. PACs can also conduct fund-raisers for candidates.

Executive Branch

Article II of the Constitution calls for a president to serve as chief executive for the country and to enforce the laws passed by Congress. The president is elected every four years in even years. The president is limited to two full terms in office. The Constitution requires the president to be at least 35 years old, to be a natural-born citizen of the United States, and to have resided in the United States for at least fourteen years.

The Constitution leaves great discretion to the president to assemble a team, or **cabinet**, to assist in enforcing the laws of the land.

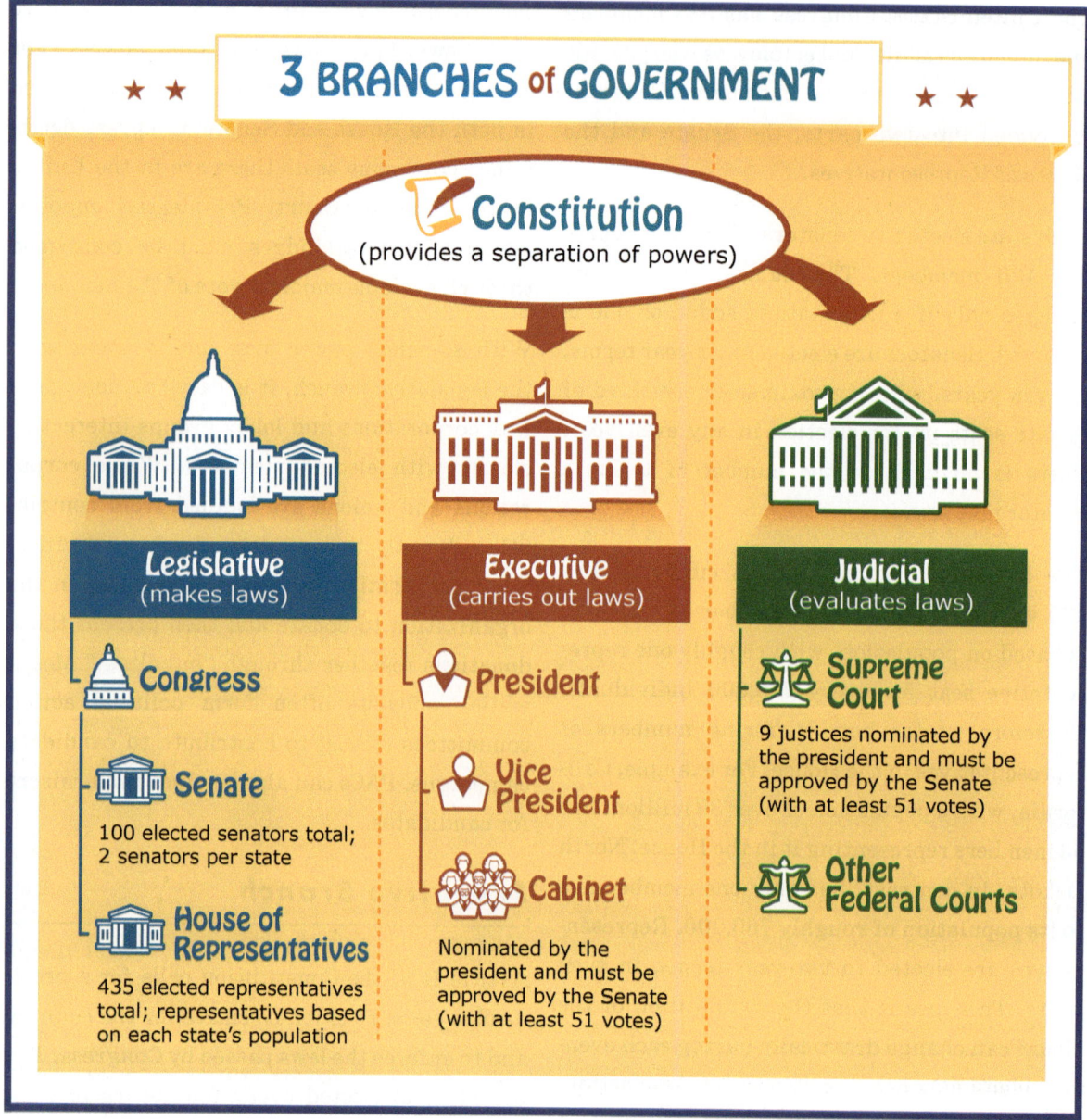

In general terms, that cabinet includes the vice president and the heads of fifteen executive departments:

- Secretary of Agriculture
- Secretary of Commerce
- Secretary of Defense
- Secretary of Education
- Secretary of Energy
- Secretary of Health and Human Services
- Secretary of Homeland Security
- Secretary of Housing and Urban Development

- Secretary of the Interior
- Secretary of Labor
- Secretary of State
- Secretary of Transportation
- Secretary of Treasury
- Secretary of Veterans Affairs
- Attorney General

Over the years, the team has grown to include large executive departments, agencies, boards, commissions, and committees. As a result, more than four million employees now work under the executive branch. This part of the government enforces laws on a day-to-day basis.

The president holds veto power over federal legislation. After Congress passes a bill, the president must sign or veto the bill within ten days. To prevent the president from using the veto power excessively, Congress may override a veto with a two-thirds majority vote from both the House and the Senate. The presidential veto and legislative override are good examples of the Constitution's checks and balances.

Presidents also have the power to issue executive orders. An executive order is an instruction issued by the president to direct executive agencies to act in a specific way. Executive orders can also set policy for the executive branch.

> As one example, on April 27, 2021, President Biden signed an executive order raising the minimum wage for federal contract workers to $15 per hour, effective 2022.

The president has the power to recognize (or not recognize) foreign governments. The president can enter into agreements with foreign governments through official treaties that require Senate approval or through executive orders, which may require Congressional approval. The Constitution recognizes that foreign relations are best handled at the federal level because of their impact on national security, the national economy, and other national concerns. For example, Alaskan gun retailers might like to import guns from Russia if they were less expensive and could be delivered quickly to municipal docks. But the federal government would likely have national security and health concerns if Russian ships could dock and unload guns without inspections. And gun producers (and their employees) in the United States would likely suffer if Alaskans started buying cheaper guns from Russia. This is just one example of the wisdom in leaving foreign relations in the hands of the federal government.

Judicial Branch

Article III of the Constitution establishes a Supreme Court of the United States and allows Congress to establish lower federal courts. Each federal (and state) court has its own specific **jurisdiction**. Jurisdiction is the legal power to hear a case.

> **JURISDICTION:**
> The legal power of a court to hear a case.

CONSTITUTION

LEGISLATIVE BRANCH

CONGRESS

Senate · House of Representatives

- Architect of the Capitol
- United States Botanic Garden
- Government Accountability Office
- Government Printing Office
- Library of Congress
- Congressional Budget Office

EXECUTIVE BRANCH

PRESIDENT · VICE PRESIDENT

EXECUTIVE OFFICE OF THE PRESIDENT

- White House Office
- Office of the Vice President
- Council of Economic Advisers
- Council on Environmental Quality
- National Security Council
- Office of Management And Budget
- Office of National Drug Control Policy
- Office of Policy Development
- Office of Science And Technology Policy

JUDICIAL BRANCH

SUPREME COURT

- United States Courts of Appeals
- United States District Courts
- Territorial Courts
- United States Court of International Trade
- United States Court of Federal Claims
- United States Court of Appeals for the Armed Forces
- United States Tax Court
- United States Court of Appeals for Veterans Claims
- Administrative Office of the United States Courts
- Federal Judicial Center
- United States Sentencing Commission

The Supreme Court decides disputes between states. The Supreme Court and federal courts have jurisdiction over disputes between citizens of different states and disputes involving non-U.S. citizens. The federal courts also decide cases where a party claims their federal legislative or Constitutional rights or protections have been withheld. These matters are said to involve a **federal question**.

The Supreme Court also holds the power to decide the **constitutionality** of laws. In an early decision, *Marbury v. Madison,* the Supreme Court held that it cannot order a government official to take a specific action. While the decision seems to limit the Court's power, the decision established that the Court has the power to determine what laws mean and to eliminate laws that conflict with the U.S. Constitution.

Federal judges are appointed by the president, and confirmed with a simple majority vote of the Senate. A federal judge is appointed for life, but Congress may impeach and remove a federal judge in extreme circumstances.

> **FEDERAL QUESTION JURISDICTION:**
> Case with alleged violations of the U.S. Constitution, federal laws, or federal treaties.
>
> **CONSTITUTIONALITY:**
> Whether a law or government action agrees with the Constitution.

FEDERAL COURTS HAVE AUTHORITY TO REVIEW ACTS OF CONGRESS AND THE EXECUTIVE BRANCH AND TO INVALIDATE ACTS THAT VIOLATE THE CONSTITUTION

Marbury v. Madison
(Judicial Appointee) v. (Secretary of State)
5 U.S. (1 Cranch) 137, 2 L. Ed. 60 (1803)

INSTANT FACTS:
Marbury (P) was a last-minute judicial appointee of outgoing President Adams, whose commission was not delivered to him before Adams left office; Jefferson, the incoming President, declined to deliver the commission.

BLACK LETTER RULE:
Where the Constitution, as interpreted by the Supreme Court, conflicts with the laws or actions of the other branches of government, the Supreme Court may declare such laws or actions unconstitutional and invalid.

PROCEDURAL BASIS:
Direct claim to the Supreme Court asking for mandamus commanding delivery of a judicial commission.

FACTS:
William Marbury (P) was appointed as a justice of the peace at the very end of John Adams' presidency. Thomas Jefferson, the incoming president, chose to disregard the appointments because formal commissions had not been delivered before the end of Adams' term. Marbury (P) and others

took their case to the Supreme Court, seeking a writ of mandamus [order directing that an official perform an act] that would order Madison (D), Jefferson's Secretary of State, to deliver the commissions.

ISSUE:
(1) Does Marbury (P) have a right to the commission? (2) If so, and if that right has been violated, does Marbury (P) have a legal remedy? (3) Is the legal remedy a writ of mandamus issuing from the Supreme Court?

DECISION AND RATIONALE:
(Marshall, J.) (1) Yes. As soon as the President signs the commission and the Secretary of State affixes the seal of the United States, the appointee has a vested legal right in the commission. To withhold the commission violates this legal right.

(2) Yes. The government of the United States is one of laws and not of men, and the law must afford a remedy for violation of a vested legal right. Where a duty is assigned to the head of a government department by the Legislature, and individual rights depend on performance of that duty, an individual who is injured has a right to a remedy.

(3) No. The answer to this question depends on (a) the nature of the writ applied for [mandamus], and (b) the power of the Supreme Court. (a) A mandamus is a proper remedy in this case. The Secretary of State was directed by law to do an act affecting the rights of individuals, and mandamus is the only appropriate remedy for violation of these rights. (b) By the Judiciary Act of 1789, the Supreme Court has the power to issue writs of mandamus to any persons holding office in the United States. However, this statute conflicts with Article III of the Constitution, which does not grant original jurisdiction to the Supreme Court over cases involving executive officers. This in turn creates a conflict between Congress and the Constitution. Either the Constitution is supreme, or it is on a level with ordinary legislative acts, and is alterable whenever Congress pleases. The idea of a written constitution is that it forms the fundamental and paramount law of the nation, and an act in conflict with the constitution must be void.

It is emphatically the province and duty of the judiciary to say what the law is. If two laws conflict, the court must decide the case conformably with the Constitution. Also, the Constitution itself gives the judiciary jurisdiction over "all cases arising under the Constitution," supporting the Court's power to invalidate laws in conflict with the Constitution. The judge swears to discharge his duties in conformity with the Constitution, and according to the laws of the United States. In the Supremacy Clause of Article IV, the Constitution itself is first mentioned, and the laws of the land that are granted recognition are those made pursuant to the Constitution. Writ of mandamus denied.

ANALYSIS:
Marbury has been widely criticized, although the doctrine of judicial review is now indisputably established. Most scholars, if not in agreement with Chief Justice Marshall's arguments, generally concur that Marshall's opinion in Marbury was shrewd and courageous.

Some argue, however, that Marshall's assertions were statements of authority rather than arguments for authority. For example, one scholar has pointed out that the statement that it is the assigned duty of the Supreme Court to interpret the Constitution raises the question of why the judiciary's interpretation should trump the congressional interpretation. Also, just as the Court took an oath to uphold the Constitution, every government official takes a similar oath.

It is important to recognize that the Court's opinion in Marbury reads the Constitution as setting the upper limits of the Supreme Court's jurisdiction. Thus, the Court could decline to grant Marbury relief by invalidating a statute on the grounds that it unconstitutionally expanded the Court's appellate jurisdiction.

CASE VOCABULARY:
VESTED RIGHT:
A right that is unconditional, that cannot be taken away from a party.

WRIT OF MANDAMUS:
A writ requiring a lower court or government official to perform some duty or act.

II. Sources of Law

Laws come from constitutions, statutes, treaties, regulations, and court decisions. There are federal and state versions of each, except that treaties only exist at the federal level. Constitutions, statutes, treaties, and regulations form a body of *enacted laws*, while court decisions either interpret those laws or create new laws. Each type of law carries weight based on its source.

The Hierarchy of Laws

Sometimes different laws conflict with each other. In those cases, laws generally give way to more fundamental provisions. This list starts with the Constitution as the supreme law of the land, and continues through to state common law, which usually applies only to matters within that state.

- U.S. Constitution
- Federal statutes and treaties
- Federal administrative agency regulations
- Federal common law
- State constitutions
- State statutes
- State agency regulations
- State common law

ENACTED LAWS:
Laws adopted by a legislative or administrative body.

Constitution

Article VI establishes that the U.S. Constitution is the supreme law of the land. No other law, regardless of the source, may conflict with the U.S. Constitution.

The Constitution not only governs the federal government's structure and powers, it also lists specific rights for individuals. The Bill of Rights, which was added to the U.S. Constitution in 1791, included ten amendments. The original ten amendments guarantee freedom of speech and religion, the right to peaceably assemble, the right to bear arms, protection from unreasonable searches and seizures, and the right to fair proceedings in civil and criminal cases, among other protections. Later amendments added more rights and protections. The Twenty-sixth Amendment, for example, gave eighteen-year-old citizens the right to vote.

Each state has its own constitution, as well. State constitutions establish the structure of the state's government, but they otherwise vary greatly. State constitutions may deal with the matters that the U.S. Constitution has left for states to regulate. State constitutions may also include provisions similar to those in the U.S. Constitution, but cannot contradict it.

> State constitutions may give their residents additional rights and protections beyond those guaranteed by the U.S. Constitution. For example, some state constitutions provide a right to education within the state—a right that does not appear in the supreme law of the land.

Statutes

Statutes are laws passed by federal or state legislators. At the federal level, members of the House or Senate begin the legislative process by introducing a proposed law as a bill. The bill is assigned to a committee, which discusses and studies the bill. If the committee finds the proposed law viable, they send it to the rest of the House or Senate, depending on where the bill started. The House or Senate debates and votes on the bill. The version voted upon may be far different than the originally proposed bill due to amendments the committee and House or Senate make.

If a simple majority of representatives or senators vote for the bill, it is passed and is sent to the other branch of Congress, where it is put through the same process of committee study, debate, amendment, and vote. Here again, a simple majority voting in favor passes the bill. Because the bill is amended separately by the House and Senate, the final versions may differ. Therefore, the two versions are sent to a committee with both House and Senate members to create a final version. The final version is again voted on by both the House and Senate, requiring a simple majority vote from each. Once Congress approves a bill, the president has ten days to either approve the bill or veto it.

States pass laws using procedures that are usually defined in the state constitution and are often similar to the federal process. In addition, counties, cities, towns, and villages pass laws. These laws are generally called "ordinances." Ordinances deal with very localized issues and only apply in their area. They cannot conflict with state or federal law.

State statutes cannot conflict with federal statutes, but states face many issues not regulated by federal law. There are comparatively few federal crimes, so states create most of the criminal laws. State statutes can enhance protections offered by federal statutes, just as state constitutions can offer more protection than the U.S. Constitution.

One example of this can be seen by comparing the federal Civil Rights Act of 1964 with state statutes. The Civil Rights Act made it illegal for employers to discriminate against someone based on race, color, religion, national origin, or sex. In 1976, Michigan passed the Elliott-Larsen Civil Rights Act, which prohibits discrimination based on religion, race, color, national origin, sex, *age*, *height*, *weight*, or *marital status*. Thus, Michigan guarantees protection for all the groups protected by the federal law, *plus* additional categories not in the Civil Rights Act.

> If a Michigan employee believes he was discriminated against at work because of his weight, does he sue based on the U.S. Civil Rights Act or the Michigan law? Answer: Michigan. If the employee believes he was discriminated against based on religion, does he sue based on the federal or state act? Answer: Both!

STATUTES:
Written laws passed by a legislative body.

Regulations

At the federal level, the executive branch (led by the president) upholds the law. Because the president cannot personally enforce the thousands of laws enacted by Congress, the president relies, in part, on administrative agencies to enforce laws. For example, if Congress passes a new law limiting the amount of pollution manufacturing plants can put into the air, then the Environmental Protection Agency (EPA) generally acts on the president's behalf to enforce the law. To do so, the EPA has been given the power to write procedures and guidelines for enforcing the law, so long as they do not conflict with the law. For example, the EPA may set a schedule for routine testing that the manufacturing plants must follow, and the EPA may determine that suspected violators will be heard first in an administrative hearing rather than in a federal district court. The case of *Chevron v. Natural Resources Defense Council*, provides an excellent example.

State regulatory agencies work in much the same way. Building on the previous example, California may enact even stricter air pollution limits. In other words, all states must follow the federal law, but each state is free to give its citizens *more* protection than the federal law. California's state environmental protection agency will develop procedures to enforce the state's air pollution laws.

SUPREME COURT DEMANDS DEFERENCE TO AGENCIES' STATUTORY CONSTRUCTION

Chevron v. Natural Resources Defense Council
(Environmental Protection Agency [and Polluters]) v. (Environmentalists)
467 U.S. 837, 104 S. Ct. 2778, 81 L. Ed. 2d 694 (1984)

INSTANT FACTS:
When the EPA interpreted the Clean Air Act to allow polluting factories to add new equipment while keeping pollution levels constant, environmentalists claim the Act should be interpreted to reduce pollution.

BLACK LETTER RULE:
If an agency's interpretation of its enabling statute is challenged, (i) reviewing courts must first independently determine if the statute clearly requires or forbids the agency's interpretation, then, (ii) if the statute is ambiguous, courts must uphold the agency's interpretation if it is a permissible construction of the statute.

PROCEDURAL BASIS:
In suit challenging agency's interpretation of statute, appeal from declaration for plaintiffs.

FACTS:
The Clean Air Act's (CAA) 1977 Amendments required polluters to obtain a state permit before constructing any "new or modified stationary sources" of air pollution. Obtaining the permit required abating new pollution stringently. The Environmental Protection Agency (EPA) (D) promulgated a rule interpreting the statutory phrase "stationary source" to include all polluting devices within a single plant. Thus, under EPA's (D) "bubble policy," factories could add a new pollutant, or increase emissions from an existing one, without obtaining a permit, if the addition/

increase did not increase the factory's total emissions, e.g., by replacing a broken polluting machine with a new one, or increasing emissions from one machine but reducing emissions from another.

Environmental lobby Natural Resources Defense Council (NRDC) (P) challenged EPA's (D) interpretation as unlawful, contending "source" means each polluting device. At trial, the Court of Appeals held for NRDC (P), finding the CAA indicated no Congressional opinion about the EPA's (D) "bubble policy," and finding NRDC's (P) interpretation served the CAA's goals better. EPA (D) appealed.

ISSUE:
If an agency's statutory mandate is ambiguous, may a court overturn the agency's construction of that statute upon finding it is not the best interpretation?

DECISION AND RATIONALE:
(Stevens, J.) No. If an agency's interpretation of its enabling statute is challenged, (i) reviewing courts must first independently determine if the statute clearly requires or forbids the agency's interpretation. Then, (ii) if the statute is ambiguous, courts must uphold the agency's interpretation if it is a permissible construction of the statute.

When courts review an agency's construction of the statute it administers, they must do so in two stages. First, if the court determines Congress spoke directly on the precise issue, then it must follow Congress' intent. But if the court determines the statute is silent or ambiguous on the issue, then it must determine whether the agency's interpretation is a permissible construction of the statute. If so, the court must uphold that interpretation, even if the court feels the agency's interpretation is not the only one, or not the best one.

Courts, upon finding Congressional ambiguity, cannot simply impose their own construction of the statute. Congress delegated to agencies the right to interpret the statutes they administer, and courts must give considerable deference to agencies' interpretation. This is because (i) judges are not experts, (ii) statutes' language often reflects a political choice or compromise, which courts should not upset, and (iii) when Congress delegates policymaking to Executive agencies, that is a political choice by elected officials, which should not be disturbed by the (unelected) judiciary.

Here, the Court of Appeals erred. First, it found, correctly, that the statutory language was ambiguous and the legislative history was unilluminating. Next, however, it failed to consider whether the EPA's (D) construction was permissible, and instead improperly imposed its own reading. Reversed.

ANALYSIS:
In Chevron, the Supreme Court sets the standard for courts' review of agencies' interpretations of their enabling statutes. It is a landmark case, and the most-cited decision in administrative law. Chevron requires courts to analyze agencies' statutory interpretations very deferentially; not surprisingly, in practice agencies prevail seventy-one percent of the time.

Chevron reconciles the longstanding Marbury v. Madison doctrine—that courts are the final interpreters of statutes—with more recent concerns about judges trampling Congress's delegation and overriding administrators' expertise, by its "Chevron two-step" approach. First, the courts may interpret the statute using their independent judgment, to decide whether the statute clearly demands one construction. But if the court decides it does not, then it must review the agency's interpretation with great deference.

CASE VOCABULARY:
ABATEMENT:
Reduction.

Common Law

Courts in the United States have two roles creating and interpreting **common law**, and interpreting and applying enacted, or codified, laws. Common law is law developed only through court decisions. It is said to be **uncodified**, meaning there is no statute or code that formally establishes the law. Some parts of today's common law started in court decisions from centuries ago.

> Many well-known legal rules come from court decisions. For example, police "read rights" when they arrest a suspect. The right to remain silent and other rights come from the Constitution, but the requirement that police inform an arrested person of those rights was set in *Miranda v. Arizona*, a Supreme Court case. The case name is used when people refer to "Miranda warnings" or ask if a person was "Mirandized."

COMMON LAW:
Judicial decisions that create a body of law over time.

UNCODIFIED LAW:
Rules taken from custom and precedent rather than statutes.

STARE DECISIS:
Legal principle that directs courts to follow precedents.

PRECEDENT:
An earlier court decision regarded as a guide to be considered in similar, subsequent cases.

The doctrine of **stare decisis** means that lower courts must uphold, or follow, decisions reached by higher courts of appeal or the Supreme Court. Once a legal principle is established in a court decision, it is said to be a **precedent**. Courts generally follow or build on their own precedents in later cases involving the same types of issues. Stare decisis is not an absolute rule, however. Courts may overturn their own precedents (although not those of higher courts).

> In 1976, the U.S. Supreme Court decided that the Fair Labor Standards Act could not apply to state or local government employers. *National League of Cities v. Usery*, 426 U.S. 833. The Act established a minimum wage, among other protections, so state and local governments were exempted from those rules. Nine years later, the Supreme Court reversed its position in *Garcia v. San Antonio Metropolitan Transit Authority*, 469 U.S. 528. A reversal in such a short timeframe is unusual.

Over the decades, many common law rules have been codified. In other words, legislatures have enacted statutes to take the place of common law or supplement it in some way.

Constitutions and statutes can be vague or incomplete. No one can predict every situation that might arise. Whenever statutes remain unclear, courts may determine what the legislature intended and what the law means.

When a court decides these issues, it sets a standard for future, similar cases. This standard is called **precedent**. If the decision is made

> The First Amendment to the Constitution guarantees free speech. But does that mean individuals may say *anything*? May you claim a product you sell will cure cancer if it does not really cure cancer? May you publish an article stating that your neighbor is a murderer if she has not murdered anyone? The answer, of course, is no. Those statements go too far, and may injure others. Since the Bill of Rights became part of the Constitution, courts have established limits on free speech, creating common law on the issue.

in a federal appeals court, for example, then the courts below it must abide by that decision on future cases. Likewise, if the U.S. Supreme Court decides a matter, then all federal courts below it must follow that decision when deciding future cases (as well as state courts that need to apply federal law). Because they help to define the enacted laws, precedents carry the same weight as the laws themselves.

Treaties and International Law

Treaties are agreements with foreign nations. Only the federal government may enter into treaties. Official treaties are proposed by the president and ratified by the Senate. Because treaties are passed in much the same way as federal statutes, they hold the same weight.

International law typically applies to how governments act rather than how organizations and individuals behave within a country. Generally, countries voluntarily agree to the rules that govern their relationships with other countries on various issues, which are spelled out in treaties adopted by those countries. Common international law topics are admiralty law, international criminal law, and humanitarian law. Businesses are interested in laws concerning trade and intellectual property rights, and may lobby their governments to work on these issues with other nations.

Some international law involves regional agreements, such as the treaties that created and govern within the European Union. The rules in those agreements can carry more weight than a member nation's own laws in much the same way that federal law may carry more weight than a state's law.

An example of how international law can impact international business is illustrated by the work of the International Maritime Organization (IMO). The IMO was created by a treaty and it acts as a specialized Agency of the United Nations. It regulates shipping, focusing on safety, environmental impact, cooperation, and security. Currently 175 nations participate. Participating countries follow the rules in the treaty that created the IMO. The IMO rules affect the processes and costs of transporting goods overseas.

Many international agreements seek to facilitate international business. The Convention on Contracts for the International Sale of Goods, for instance, helps businesses gain predictability and fair outcomes in their international transactions.

CHAPTER SUMMARY

It is crucial for everyone who engages in business to have some understanding of the law. Law and business complement each other. Business activities take place within a framework of laws. Likewise, many aspects of our legal system are put in place to reflect our business culture.

The American legal system is the product of many different factors. It is based on English common law, reflecting the early heritage of the United States. The authority of the government—and the division of powers between states and the federal government—reflects a historic commitment to federalism. Our constitutional government exists as a guard against unchecked, arbitrary power. New laws and regulations are made, and old ones repealed, reflecting changing social and political concerns. As the country and the business environment change, changes, so too will our laws change.

CAREERS IN THE LAW

Because business and the law are so intertwined, there are many jobs within companies that have a strong legal focus but don't require a law degree. For example, you might work as a contract administrator or specialist. While the complexity of the job may differ depending on the company, a contract administrator will review and manage the company's contracts for consistency and compliance with company policies and legal obligations. International trade compliance is another option. In this position, an individual might work on maintaining records needed to prove compliance with import or export regulations, such as tracking exports of products that could be used as weapons. If you are interested in working in these well paid positions, explore options and requirements in positions posted in major job search engines.

Review Questions

Review question 1.
What is the role of the Constitution in American law? What are enumerated powers? Checks and balances? How do state constitutions differ from the U.S. Constitution?

Review question 2.
What are the three branches of government in the United States? What are their different roles? Which branch does the president belong to? Which branch do government agencies belong to? The police?

Review question 3.
What is the president's cabinet? Why is the cabinet important? What role does it play? How is the Senate involved in staffing the cabinet?

Review question 4.
What does the Constitution say about the Supreme Court? Federal courts? What is the role of the Supreme Court? How did the case of Marbury v. Madison change constitutional law in the United States?

Review question 5.
What two bodies make up the U.S. Congress? How many members are in each body? How is that number established? What terms may different members serve, and how many may they serve?

Review question 6.
What is the difference between a bill and a law? Describe the legislative process of creating a statute. What role does the president play in formalizing a bill?

Review question 7.
When do presidential elections take place? How often do they occur? How long is a presidential term? How many terms may a president serve?

Review question 8.
What is the common law? What is its source? Why does the United States follow the common law tradition?

Review question 9.
What is a precedent? How long does it remain in effect? What does a precedent require of judges? What does stare decisis mean?

Review question 10.
What is an executive order? Who may make an executive order at the federal level? At the state level?

Review question 11.
What is the Bill of Rights? When was it created? How many rights did it originally have? What is its function?

Discussion Questions

Question 1:

You are a U.S. Representative. Together with partners across the aisle, you have drafted a bill to provide grocery vouchers to college students who are spending more than 50% of their individual or family income on tuition, fees, books, and school materials. The so-called "Brain Food" bill has passed the House of Representatives and is headed to the Senate. The president held a press conference today saying that he does not like the idea. "Where's the food for newly returned veterans?" he says. You understand that some senators are echoing those comments with their constituents.

> What could happen to the bill in the Senate? What must happen there for the bill to move on to the next step?
>
> What if the Senate makes amendments to the bill that are inconsistent with your original goals for the legislation?
>
> How could the bill be blocked even if the Senate passes it?

Question 2:

Suppose that the bill in Question 1 becomes law, even though many people are still opposed to the measure.

> Now that the bill is part of federal law, how will the provisions be put into action?
>
> How can the new law be challenged? Is it possible for the challenges to kill the law?
>
> What do you think of this process? Is it too cumbersome? Too much red tape? A good way to incorporate everyone's input?
>
> What do you think of the zero-sum game argument that the president uses against the bill in this scenario?

Question 3:

U.S. Representatives and Senators have different term lengths, but can serve as many terms as they are elected for. By contrast, the president may only serve two terms.

> Do you think that the difference in approach helps the governing process? Why or why not?

> Are the term lengths for each office appropriate, given that the legislative process can take years?

> If the country wanted to make a change to these term lengths, how could that change be made?

Question 4:

Unlike the term lengths and limits discussed in the last question, federal judges are appointed for life (or until they choose to retire).

> The U.S. Supreme Court has nine justices. This number is traditional, and not required by the Constitution. Considering the life terms that justices serve, is this a good number of members for the Supreme Court?

> Other federal judges are also appointed for life. These appointments can be very political. What are the drawbacks of life terms? The advantages?

Question 5:

In Chaplinsky v. New Hampshire, 315 U.S. 568 (1942), a man was arrested for loudly insulting religion and a public official in the street. The law barred intentionally insulting speech from being used in a public place. The man challenged the constitutionality of the state law under which he was arrested, arguing that it harmed the First Amendment's right to free speech. While noting the importance of free speech, the U.S. Supreme Court upheld the law, saying that "fighting words"—those words that tend to incite an immediate breach of the peace—are not protected by the First Amendment. They add no value to public discourse, the Court said, and any benefit they do have is outweighed by the state's interest in public order. Apply this precedent to the following scenarios.

The Westboro Baptist Church is known nationally for its offensive protests at the funerals of soldiers and other public events. Their signs claim that "God hates" U.S. troops, Jews, Muslims, and LGBTQ people, among others. The signs also make other inflammatory claims. Are these protest signs "fighting words"? Should local communities enforce or even enact laws against that type of speech?

Charlotte is walking on the sidewalk and accidentally cuts off Bill. Bill tells her to watch where she's going. Charlotte says, "Wow, you are a major jerk!" As she walks away, Bill hits Charlotte in the back of the head. Bill says that Charlotte's comment amounted to fighting words, so he was justified in hitting Charlotte. Is he correct? Was Charlotte's statement protected by the First Amendment?

Question 6:

Regulations are created by administrative agencies under authority from legislation. Regulations have the force of law.

> Should Congress be able to delegate this level of authority to unelected officials? Why or why not?

Question 7:

The common law system means that court decisions add to the body of law. "Civil law" systems are typical in much of the world. In civil law countries, courts still apply and interpret statutory law, but the decisions do not become precedents. Instead, the decisions only apply to their particular situation.

> What are the pros and cons of a common law system? A civil law system?

> Which system makes more sense for the judiciary in your view? Why?

Question 8:

Federal and state laws both affect business operations. Companies that do business in multiple states must keep track of requirements in each jurisdiction.

> Is this a valid argument against federalism as a system? Why or why not?

> What are the benefits of federalism in a geographically large country? The disadvantages?

2 LAW AND ETHICS

KEY OBJECTIVES:
- ▶ Explain the differences between law and ethics.
- ▶ Describe how law and ethics intersect.
- ▶ Analyze business scenarios using ethics concepts.

CHAPTER OVERVIEW

What are ethics? Ethics are standards of behavior determining how we respond in specific situations. Simply put, ethics are a code of conduct. In business, ethics act as the legal, fair, and thoughtful ways businesses interact with **stakeholders**.

Where do ethics come from? Just like individuals have choices in how they conduct themselves, so do businesses. Both individuals and businesses are regulated by laws. Often, the laws create the "ground floor" for individual and business conduct. If basic legal responsibilities are not met, civil or criminal legal action can follow.

You probably strive to conduct yourself somewhat better than the minimum required by law. You may try to be kind to others or to "give back" to the community. There is no law saying you must act considerately toward others, volunteer in your community, or donate to charity, but you may choose to do so. This may be because you like being nice. It might be because you hope your good behavior will cause others to like you, respect you, or even hire you. It may be because you have a sense of obligation to do your part for the common good.

Businesses are also encouraged to operate with principles above the minimum required by law. Businesses may choose to pollute less than the law allows, pay above the minimum wage, or donate some of their profits to good causes. Some business leaders are driven toward good behavior by a sense of social responsibility, while other businesses try to appeal to investors, customers, and other stakeholders by having a track record of ethical behavior. Many ethics topics are covered in detail in the chapters that follow. This chapter provides a general overview of business ethics.

STAKEHOLDER: an individual or organization that is affected by a business's activities

SHAREHOLDER: an individual or organization that holds shares (stock) in a company

I. Stakeholders

In October 2001, Enron, at the time one of the biggest American companies, was caught hiding billions of dollars in business losses and debt from **shareholders**. After the world found out about Enron's true financial status, its executives were disgraced and the company declared bankruptcy within two months. Shareholders lost enormous amounts of money and thousands of employees lost their jobs and retirement savings. In addition to the loss of over $70 billion of investor money within Enron, the scandal also bankrupted Enron's auditing firm, Arthur Andersen LLP, which had been implicated in Enron's fraud. In all, over 90,000 people lost their jobs as a direct result of the scandal. Enron's and Arthur Andersen's downfall provided a very public and far-reaching example of the harm that can occur when a company is unethical in its dealings.

Obviously, business owners, executives, and investors hold a financial "stake" in a business, but a business has many other stakeholders as well. The word "stakeholder" in this context is just what it sounds like: those who hold a stake in a business's successes, failures, and conduct. Its customers and employees stand to benefit or gain from the business's performance, and so do its suppliers and others it does business with. On a larger scale, the communities where the business conducts its trade are also stakeholders in the business's performance, not only in terms of profits (or losses), but also in the way it conducts business.

> Stakeholders include those most connected with an organization. Shareholders and employees are stakeholders as well. But "stakeholder" extends much wider to anyone affected by a business's activities.

Many of the consequences of the Enron collapse emanated directly from the scandal, but everyone who was affected by the event was a "stakeholder." In the wake of Enron's and Arthur Andersen's bankruptcies, not just employees and shareholders experienced losses. Family members also suffered, as did small businesses that relied on Enron and its employees for revenue. Communities and neighborhoods lost residents who moved to new jobs. Arthur Andersen's other clients needed to find new accountants and auditors. The government lost tax revenue. The ripple effects are still being felt today.

Stakeholders do not only suffer bad outcomes, though. If a business behaves legally and ethically, stakeholders share in the good effects of that behavior.

Ethical actions can have an impact on business success. Suppose a business owns and leases commercial property. If that business is known for its high ethical standards, it is likely to attract good tenants with similar values. On the other hand, if a commercial property company has low ethical standards, over time it will develop a poor reputation in the business community. Once a business has this bad reputation, it will be less likely to attract strong tenants. The company will instead attract tenants who could have a negative impact on the community and the surrounding businesses.

By the same token, good ethical standards can be a competitive differentiator in the marketplace. Increasingly, consumers take an interest in what businesses stand for and how they interact with their communities. Ethical companies stand out from the crowd, and are

> **Example:** Patagonia is an outdoor gear and clothing retailer. Since its beginnings, the company has been known for its commitment to environmentalism and good employment practices. Among its innovations is a repair service to reduce the clothing waste stream. Patagonia also created the "1% for the Planet" program, through which it gives one percent of its sales to protect and restore the natural environment. While these programs could reduce profits, they also show the company's stance on issues important to consumers. Patagonia attracts customers who appreciate its strong environmental record.

well-placed to bring in customers with similar values and concerns.

Reviewing stakeholder interests is a useful way to help determine whether a particular decision is correct and ethical. As you work through this chapter, consider ways in which a business's ethics might impact stakeholders in the community, in either a positive or negative way. For example, might an ethical business recruit and keep different types of employees than an unethical business? What about the businesses that buy from or sell to an ethical versus unethical business? Can you think of other contexts where a business's ethics might impact the community?

II. Stakeholder-Focused Ethics

Ethics professor Ken Goodpaster developed a useful analytical model for ethical decision making. His model includes four ethical approaches, called the "four avenues," that can help businesspeople make the best decision in a given situation. By using each of the "avenues" to consider a possible decision, it is possible to gain deeper understanding of how the decision could impact various stakeholders.

The four avenues are:

1. Interests
2. Rights
3. Duties
4. Virtues

The basic idea behind the *Interests Avenue* is deciding whether an action or policy is ethical is based solely on its consequences and the only consequences that really matter are the interests of the parties impacted. In other words, ethics is about the harms and benefits to identifiable stakeholders. In other words, this avenue considers the possible consequences of a proposed decision to determine how to achieve the greatest good for the greatest number of stakeholders. The "good" that can be achieved is any benefit to a stakeholder, including money, happiness, or well-being. In a business setting, there is a tendency to prioritize revenue, but other goods are also be valuable to consider. The critical issues in interest based analysis are how will this action benefit or harm stakeholders and which action will result in the greatest good to the greatest number, or minimize harm.

The central idea behind the *Rights Avenue* focuses is not maximizing interest satisfaction, but on protecting stakeholder rights. There are two broad categories of rights: rights one has by virtue of belonging to a group, including rights to opportunities or social justice; and rights that a basic to all human beings, like a right to choice, autonomy, life, free speech, or self-development. These ethical rights may coincide with legal rights, but they are not the same. A rights based ethical analysis may even consider more basic issues of fairness, such as the right not to be lied to. Stakeholders might not have a defined civil or legal right in a given situation, but they might have a basic moral right. While the consequence of the decision is the most important factor in interest based analysis, with rights based analysis it is the intentions of the actor that lead to the action, rather than the consequences, that are most important.

> An easy way to remember the Four Avenues is "DRIVE": Duties, Rights, Interests, and Virtues: Ethics!

Using the Four Avenues in Decision-making

Suppose you own a small pharmacy. You have not sold tobacco products in the past, but you are considering adding them. You will need to eliminate some products stocked near the cash registers in order to have room for cigarette racks. While tobacco use is down overall, the products have a better profit margin than the items they would displace, and your business has been struggling financially. You think that the new products will bring in more customers who might otherwise not come into the store; it will also make shopping at your store more efficient for existing customers who use tobacco.

Before you make the decision, apply the Four Avenues model.

- *Step 1: Identify the stakeholders*
  The stakeholders include your existing customers and your employees. The supplier for the products you will need to eliminate is also a stakeholder. What other stakeholders can you identify? Once you have identified the stakeholders, determine which are the most important and be able to articulate why.

- *Step 2: Apply the Interests Avenue*
  Look at your list of stakeholders and determine the interests that each stakeholder has in the potential decision. Existing customers may have an interest in accessing the products that you would eliminate if you were to add tobacco products, for instance. The supplier has an interest in keeping your business. Work through all the stakeholders, keeping in mind that some may have multiple interests.

  When you are finished, determine whether the decision or the status quo supports more stakeholder interests. The key questions to consider are whose interests matter the most?

When considering your action, ask whether it will benefit or harm the stakeholders. Under the Interests Avenue, the ethical choice is the one that minimizes harms or provides the greatest good for the greatest number of stakeholders.

- *Step 3: Apply the Rights Avenue*
  Return to your list, and identify each stakeholder's rights in the circumstances. The existing supplier does not have a right to your business, but could be said to have a right to be dealt with fairly. Employees might be concerned about their rights if they were to violate tobacco sale rules. Consider the rights of each stakeholder carefully and ask whether the action you are considering is fair in the circumstances. Does it affirm or threaten basic rights? Remember that it is your intentions, rather than the consequences of your actions, that matter most in the Rights Avenue.

- *Step 4: Apply the Duties Avenue*
  Under duty based analysis, consider how your decision values community and at what level. Do you have a duty to avoid selling products that are detrimental to the health of the community? Do you owe your employees a duty concerning whether tobacco products are sold or not? What are those duties. Does the decision uphold fidelity in relationships with your current suppliers? Again, review your results to see which decision is the better option under this avenue focusing on your intentions rather than the consequences of the action you choose.

- *Step 5: Apply the Virtues Avenue*
  Consider your decision in terms of whether it supports integrity and your character development. For example, foregoing the more lucrative tobacco products may support the strengthening of the virtues of courage or compassion for other human beings. On the other hand, adding a more profitable product may be the prudent, or wise choice, because it will allow you to take better care of your employees. Consider this question in light of which virtue is most important and how the decision it supports serves the stakeholders.

- *Step 6: Review the Results and Decide*
  Review the ethical outcomes you identified for each avenue. Sometimes, the avenues will point to a uniform result, but often times each avenue will lead you to a different ethical result. And, those results may be in conflict. It is your job to use the results to create a result that you can justify: a result that leads to a moral insight. By tracing the results and finding the option that best supports stakeholders or character development, you will have completed a thorough analysis, and you will select the most ethical decision from the options.

  Sometimes, this process will lead you to consider a new option. If this is the case, run through the avenues with the new option to determine whether it is a better choice.

The ethical choice in the *Duties Avenue* is the one that fulfills a duty or responsibility to communities or groups, rather than to individuals. This famous line from President Kennedy's inaugural address captures the essence of duty based thinking: "Ask not what your country can do for you, ask what you can do for your country." The "duties" in this avenue are commitments, responsibilities, or other behavior owed to the community. While ethical duties may overlap with legal duties, they are separate and may require additional obligations. Common ethical duties include: duties of fidelity, to keep promises; duties of trust, requiring that we uphold our obligations to groups; duties of reparation to those we have hurt through wrongful conduct; duties of fairness that require respect for other's rights or fair sharing of goods; duties of self improvement; and duties of non-maleficence to not harm or injure others. As with the Rights Avenue analysis, what matters is the intention of the decision maker, not the consequences of the action. In addition, often times duties and rights will correspond. For example, if an individual has a right to privacy, another person has a duty to protect that right as a member of the community.

The focus of the *Virtues Avenue* is ethical decision making that develops and reinforces habits of the heart and character traits. In the case of organizations, the focus is on culture. The focus might also be on *avoiding* certain habits, vices, or cultures that could corrupt the decision maker. The focus here is on the traits of the individual making the decision. This avenue is not only for individual stakeholders but stakeholder groups as well. Organizations can reinforce or cultivate good or bad behavior inside or outside of the organization through their decisions. Examples of virtues include prudence (wisdom), temperance (restraint), courage, justice or fairness, selflessness, and compassion. The key question to ask is whether the decision support integrity or character development in the decision maker, or promote the development of an ethical culture in the organization.

> **CAREERS IN THE LAW**
>
> Corporate social responsibility has grown beyond self-regulation into industry norms, best practices, and legal standards. CSR departments often work with the compliance and legal teams in an organization. CSR jobs have a wide variety of responsibilities. If you have experience in community outreach, writing, social media, or project management, you will be able to find a role in corporate social responsibility. Look into this growing field of opportunity.

The more often you use this ethics model, the easier it will be to fully consider all perspectives before making the best possible decision in the circumstances. Practice will build the ability to make difficult decisions in an ethical way.

III. Ethics in Business

For most of U.S. history, businesses were expected to follow the law, but not to demonstrate ethics. This understanding was summed up by economist Milton Friedman in the 1970s, who wrote, "There is one and only one social responsibility of business—to use its resources and engage in activities designed to increase its profits so long as it stays within the rules of the game, which is to say, engages in open and free competition without deception or fraud."

More recently, though, the corporate world started emphasizing ethics. This shift is the result of changing public opinion, industry thought leadership, and legal guidance.

Corporate Social Responsibility

There have been many efforts to regulate ethics, but it remains largely a voluntary endeavor. The government would be hard-pressed to enforce mandatory community service on businesses, for example.

Corporate social responsibility (CSR) refers to business efforts to be good "corporate citizens" through charitable and service activities in the larger community. CSR is voluntary and requires resources of time and money. Despite these costs, most large businesses have sizeable CSR programs.

CSR has a range of benefits to many parties. Stakeholders, customers, and the general public may all benefit from gifts to the community or volunteer time from a company's employees. The company enjoys a heightened reputation for good works and additional public exposure. Now that consumers expect more from businesses, CSR is an important business program.

> Founded in 1974, the Ronald McDonald House Charities is a non-profit organization that provides housing and support for families with critically ill children. McDonalds gives a portion of every Happy Meal purchase to the charity. McDonalds also pursues sustainability initiatives and workplace readiness programs, among other initiatives.

Business Roundtable

The Business Roundtable (businessroundtable.org) is an association made up of Chief Executive Officers of major American corporations. The group's goal is to promote public policies that support a strong economy and opportunity for U.S. workers. Founded in 1972, the Business Roundtable (BRT) became known for standing behind pro-corporate policies, such as reduced tax rates for corporations and fewer obligations to organized labor. These positions were consistent with building shareholder value (that is, maximizing the return on shareholder investments).

In 2019, however, BRT published a surprising recommendation. The Statement on the Purpose of a Corporation represented a departure from previous policy letters. The document changed the organization's focus from shareholders to stakeholders, stating, "Each of our stakeholders is essential. We commit to deliver value to all of them, for the future success of our companies, our communities and our country." The Statement emphasized ethical practices and environmental sustainability.

Press releases and reporting about the Statement noted the seeming departure from BRT's traditional positions. But according to Jamie Dimon, CEO of JPMorgan Chase & Co., "[I]nvesting in workers and communities is the only way to be successful over the long term."

Some minimized this shift as a ploy to offset growing anti-corporate sentiment, but other commentators supported the change. "Times change," Fortune magazine noted. The public expects more transparency and public commitment from corporations now than in prior decades. Increasingly, consumers change their buying habits and employees change their jobs based on corporate ethics. The BRT change in focus demonstrates the popular demand for ethical practices.

Compliance & Ethics

The federal government elevated the importance of ethical corporate cultures as a way for businesses to reduce the likelihood of regulatory and legal violations. Guidance provided by the government gives businesses credit for prioritizing an ethical environment, which can reduce penalties for legal violations.

The United States Sentencing Guidelines provide standards for criminal sentencing. Most criminal prosecutions are against individuals, who can be penalized through prison terms and personal fines. But organizations such as corporations may also break the law. In that case, courts look to the U.S. Sentencing Guidelines for Organizations, a set of standards aimed specifically at wrongdoing by organizations.

There are several ways that a court can penalize an organization: it can be barred from government contracts, subjected to third party oversight, and even dissolved. But the most common way to sanction a corporation is to levy fines against it. The Sentencing Guidelines provide that penalties start with the "base" penalty for the particular illegal activity, modified by the organization's "culpability score."

> While a company cannot be jailed, corporations face many other possible penalties. For example, when the U.S. Department of Justice found that a Chicago area tax preparation service was filing falsified returns for clients, the tax service was ordered to disgorge over $33,000 in money made by filing the illegal returns. The service was also barred from preparing federal tax returns in future, and the owner prevented from ever owning or running federal tax preparation services again. These types of consequences are severe, because they stop business owners from continuing in their field of experience and knowledge. The severity reflects the aggravating factor of the owner's involvement in the wrongdoing.

The base penalty arises from the seriousness of the crime. The prosecutors look to the type of illegal activity, the money gained by that activity, and the financial harm caused to others, and choose the greatest of the three. The formula for corporate penalties for criminal acts given in the U.S. Sentencing Guidelines for Organizations is:

(The base penalty for the illegal action) x (The organization's culpability score) =

(The organization's sentence or settlement)

As with individual criminal defendants, organizations may have positive features that may reduce the criminal penalty, or negative issues that could increase it. These are referred to as mitigating and aggravating factors. Mitigating factors reduce an organization's culpability score, while aggravating factors increase it.

Organizational "character"—ethics in action at an organization—can weigh in a company's favor. The mitigating factors for an organization include:

- An effective compliance and ethics program at the company.

- Acceptance of responsibility by the organization.

- Cooperation with investigators.

- Self-reporting of criminal activity or evidence.

On the other hand, there are several aggravating factors that weigh against a company. Each of the factors suggest that the organization lacked strong values. These factors include:

- Organizational tolerance of illegal activity.

- Lack of cooperation with the investigation.

- History of prior offenses or violations of court orders.

- Involvement of executives in wrongdoing.

Taken together, these mitigating and aggravating factors make up the organization's culpability score. More aggravating factors will mean that the organization's penalty will be higher, while mitigating factors, such as pursuing a compliance and ethics program, will reduce the penalty. In this way, the Sentencing Guidelines encourage corporations to promote ethics throughout the organization.

An "effective" compliance and ethics program does not necessarily need to have uncovered criminal activities. Instead, a company will receive credit for a program that follows the "Seven Pillars":

1. Written Policies and Procedures: The program is documented so that it can be researched and followed.

2. High-Level Oversight: Senior executives and the board are involved in the program, and a person with authority leads the effort.

3. Communication and Education: The organization communicates its policies and trains its employees on the program.

4. Monitoring and Auditing: The organization regularly reviews and updates the program to improve its impact.

5. Reporting and Investigating: Employees feel empowered to raise concerns, and the company follows up on possible violations.

6. Enforcement and Discipline: The organization enforces the program at all levels, and establishes incentives for compliance.

7. Remediation: If or when the program misses an issue, the organization corrects the problem and updates the program.

This guidance has led to many companies establishing compliance and ethics programs. The goal of these programs may be both preventative (aimed at avoiding legal wrongdoing) and protective (designed to reduce government penalties should legal wrongdoing occur). As these programs became more common, the idea of ethical business culture has become an expectation.

Legal Frameworks

In response to the Enron and Arthur Andersen scandals, as well as other similar scandals that quickly followed, Congress passed a federal act to improve the state of business ethics in the United States. The act is most commonly called the Sarbanes-Oxley Act of 2002 (SOX). By legislative standards, this act was drafted, passed, and enacted very quickly, on July 30, 2002. Here are the highlights:

1. Auditors must be wholly independent and federally registered, and must use approved standards in auditing. This provision protects investors and shareholders by making sure they get accurate information about a company's financial health.

2. Senior executives are personally responsible for providing accurate financial reports. Before this provision, bad business practices did not make people worry about jail sentences because businesses could not be sent to jail. With this provision, senior executives pay close attention to following the rules because they can go to jail if they do not.

3. Corporate officers and executives must disclose stock transactions to prevent insider trading. The Securities Exchange Commission (SEC) has the power to regulate these disclosure, investigate suspected violations, and to punish violators.

4. Market analysts must disclose any conflicts or financial interests. People invest based

---

ATTORNEY'S FAILURE TO FILE PERSONAL INCOME TAX RETURNS IS ALSO A BREACH OF PROFESSIONAL ETHICS

Committee on Legal Ethics v. Higinbotham
(Disciplinary Panel v. Attorney)
342 S.E.2d 152 (W. Va. 1986)

This is a disciplinary action against William H. Higinbotham, a West Virginia attorney, filed by the Committee on Legal Ethics (Committee) of the West Virginia State Bar. Higinbotham was charged with a violation of DR 1–102(A)(6) of the West Virginia Code of Professional Responsibility. The basis of the charge was his failure to file federal income tax returns.

Higinbotham was charged [with] violating Section 7203 of the Internal Revenue Code for willful failure to file federal income tax returns for calendar years 1977 through 1980[.] [H]e pleaded guilty [to] willful failure to file a federal income tax return for 1978 [and] was convicted upon his plea of guilty, was fined $10,000, and was sentenced to a prison term of one year [of which] he served five months[.] [A] presentence investigation report revealed that he had failed to file federal income tax returns for nine consecutive years from 1975 through 1983.

In his answer to the statement of charges, Higinbotham admitted all the factual allegations, but denied that his failure to file federal income tax returns and his conviction constituted a violation of the Code of Professional Responsibility.

In explaining why he failed to file a federal income tax return for 1975, he said: "Gentlemen, I took on an amount of work and paid attention to it rather than doing those things for myself that I should have." . . . The subcommittee found "no mitigating circumstances excusing or explaining the failure to file a Federal Income Tax Return[.]" The subcommittee also viewed the failure to file returns for nine years as an aggravating factor. Consequently, it was recommended he be suspended from the practice of law for six months.

> A violation, by a member of the bar, of willful failure to file federal income tax return has been held to be unethical and unprofessional conduct in violation of Canons 29 and 32 of the Code of Professional Ethics. It is undisputed that Higinbotham engaged in illegal conduct which clearly and forcefully reflects on Higinbotham's fitness to practice law. The willful failure to file an income tax return constitutes a violation of DR 1–102(A)(6) of the Code of Professional Responsibility.
>
> He contends, however, that the recommended discipline is too severe, citing the following circumstances: incarceration for five months during which he was unable to practice law; imposition of $10,000 fine; loss of associates in his law practice leading to increased workload; and cooperation with the Internal Revenue Service in resolving his tax difficulties. He also relies on *Committee on Legal Ethics v. Scherr*, where this Court imposed a one-month suspension for a similar violation.
>
> In *Scherr*, an attorney who [failed to file an income tax return] was charged by the Committee on Legal Ethics with an ethical violation involving moral turpitude and recommended the attorney's suspension for one year. We distinguished between the felony of evading or defeating the payment of taxes from the misdemeanor of willfully failing to file a tax return, and we concluded that the misdemeanor offense did not involve moral turpitude. We reached this conclusion by viewing the accused attorney's reputation and the deaths of his wife, mother, and father as mitigating circumstances. Nevertheless, we also concluded that the accused attorney was subject to discipline [and] we suspended Scherr from the practice of law for one month.
>
> In disciplinary proceedings, this Court, rather than endeavoring to establish a uniform standard of disciplinary action, will consider the facts and circumstances, including mitigating facts and circumstances, in determining what disciplinary action, if any, is appropriate[.] We do not consider Higinbotham's imprisonment and fine to be mitigating factors. These are punishments imposed by the criminal justice system and have no bearing on the appropriateness of disciplinary action undertaken to vindicate the high standards of professional conduct to which attorneys must adhere. His overburdened law practice is somewhat mitigative but is far outweighed by the aggravated circumstance of his failure to file tax returns for nine consecutive years.
>
> Where a lawyer has pleaded guilty to a charge of willful failure to file a federal income tax return and it also appears that said lawyer has failed to file federal income tax returns for a period of nine consecutive years, and has thereby violated DR 1–102(A)(6) of the Code of Professional Responsibility, a six-month suspension from the practice of law is an appropriate disciplinary sanction. We therefore adopt the recommendation of the Legal Ethics Committee.

in part on analysts' recommendations. Investors should know if the analyst stands to make money by convincing people to invest in a specific company.

5. Companies and employees face penalties if they destroy records in the face of an investigation.

6. Whistleblowers, that is, employees who report their employers of suspected SOX violations, are protected from retaliation.

SOX had a huge impact on many aspects of business ethics. You will learn more about additional legal guidelines in the following chapters. Some of those laws cover truth in advertising and labelling; intellectual property rights; and employment discrimination; consumer protection; and embezzlement.

There is no law dictating how companies carry out their ethical obligations. Rather, companies comply in various ways based on a number of factors. Some industries are heavily regulated. Businesses involved in those industries may have staff, or entire departments, specifically assigned to ensure the company follows the rules. These employees may be compliance officers, general counsels, or staff attorneys. Smaller companies may use consultants to monitor their business activities. And very small businesses may leave it up to officers or managers to ensure the rules are followed.

Professional Ethics

In some organizations, ethics rules apply to everyone in a particular role. These jobs are often referred to as "professions." The professions traditionally included doctors, lawyers, and clergy members. Now, more jobs that require a high level of training so that the public may put its trust in those individuals to meet a particular standard of care often have ethical codes. Professional boards set licensing standards and maintain and enforce ethics codes on individuals in those jobs. If an individual breaches those rules, they may lost the right to continue in their role, temporarily or permanently.

Some positions that have these requirements include accountants, architects, attorneys, medical doctors, dentists, and professional engineers. The legal profession has a particularly long history of ethics oversight. The rules that apply to attorneys can even apply to activities outside of their employment, as the following case demonstrates.

IV. International Business Ethics

Businesses in the United States routinely conduct business with foreign companies and countries. The United States imports more goods than it exports. As a result, it is common to buy products locally that originated or contain parts from other countries. Look at the packaging for any consumer product—it is likely to show that the product was made overseas.

Just as the United States sets corporate standards through laws, other countries create business laws that establish ethical rules. Because each country has its own needs, issues, and values, these provisions can vary widely. Many countries have little or no regulation of business practices.

It would be useful to have universal business standards in place. Businesses and consumers around the world would know what to expect when dealing with a foreign company. Companies would be in similar competitive positions if they were all following the same standards. But there are two major obstacles to creating such a universal code:

1. Acceptable behavior varies greatly from country to country. No one would be able to agree on what the standards should be.

2. No country would be able to punish another country for violating such standards. Without enforcement, the standards would not work.

Three notable attempts to find universal standards include the United Nations International Labour Organization, the Foreign Corrupt Practices Act of 1977, and the Organisation for Economic Co-Operation and Development Anti-Bribery Convention.

First, in 1919, the United Nations (UN) launched the International Labour Organization (ILO) to promote the rights of workers by encouraging living wages, employment opportunities, social

Foreign Corrupt Practices Act: High Penalties and International Reach

The following excerpts from a 2019 U.S. Department of Justice press release shows just how expensive bribery can be. FCPA penalties and settlements can be extremely large. Also, the U.S. often coordinates with other countries to investigate bribery, which makes the practice difficult to hide. If a foreign company is publicly traded on a U.S. stock exchange, it can be prosecuted in the United States. Individual employees and executives who are involved can be prosecuted separately and receive prison terms, as shown here.

TechnipFMC Plc and U.S.-Based Subsidiary Agree to Pay Over $296 Million in Global Penalties to Resolve Foreign Bribery Case

TechnipFMC plc (TFMC), a publicly traded company in the United States and a global provider of oil and gas services, and its wholly-owned U.S. subsidiary, Technip USA, Inc. (Technip USA), have agreed to pay a combined total criminal fine of more than $296 million to resolve foreign bribery charges with authorities in the United States and Brazil. TFMC is the product of a 2017 merger between two predecessor companies, Technip S.A. (Technip) and FMC Technologies, Inc. (FMC). The charges arose out of two independent bribery schemes: a scheme by Technip to pay bribes to Brazilian officials and a scheme by FMC to pay bribes to officials in Iraq. Technip USA and Technip's former consultant pleaded guilty today in connection with the resolution.

"Today's charges demonstrate not only the capabilities of the FBI personnel who investigate international corruption, but the successful results of strong partnerships in the international community," said Assistant Director Johnson. "In attempting to cheat the system, Technip violated the FCPA. Through the collaboration and dedicated efforts of the FBI and our foreign partners, Technip is being held accountable for perpetrating illegal schemes and justice is served."

"This case shows the FBI will continue to work tirelessly to hold those accountable who treat corruption and bribery as a common business practice," said Acting Special Agent in Charge Dayoub. "Today's agreement is the culmination of the hard work of the FBI and Department of Justice and our international partners."

TFMC entered into a deferred prosecution agreement with the Department in connection with a criminal information filed today in the Eastern District of New York charging the company with two counts of conspiracy to violate the anti-bribery provisions of the Foreign Corrupt Practices Act (FCPA). In addition, Technip USA pleaded guilty and was sentenced on a one-count criminal information charging it with conspiracy to violate the anti-bribery provisions of the FCPA. Pursuant to its agreement with the Department, TechnipFMC will pay a total criminal fine of over $296 million, including a $500,000 criminal fine paid by Technip USA. As part of the deferred prosecution agreement, TechnipFMC committed to implementing rigorous internal controls and to cooperate fully with the Department's ongoing investigation.

In connection with the scheme to bribe Brazilian officials, Technip's former consultant also pleaded guilty in the Eastern District of New York to a one-count criminal information charging him with conspiracy to violate the FCPA. He is awaiting sentencing.

> According to admissions and court documents, beginning in at least 2003 and continuing until at least 2013, Technip conspired with others, including Singapore-based Keppel Offshore & Marine Ltd. (KOM) and their former consultant, to violate the FCPA by making more than $69 million in corrupt payments and "commission payments" to the consultant, companies associated with the consultant and others, who passed along portions of these payments as bribes[.] In addition, Technip made more than $6 million in corrupt payments to the Workers' Party in Brazil and Workers' party officials in furtherance of the bribery scheme.
>
> The admissions and court documents also establish that beginning by at least 2008 and continuing until at least 2013, FMC conspired to violate the FCPA by paying bribes to at least seven government officials in Iraq, including officials at the Ministry of Oil, the South Oil Company and the Missan Oil Company, through a Monaco-based intermediary company in order to win secure improper business advantages and to influence those foreign officials to obtain and retain business for FMC Technologies in Iraq.

protections, protection of workers in foreign countries, and job training. Membership is open to UN member countries that accept the invitation to join the ILO. To date, 187 countries participate, which is all but six of the UN member countries.

The ILO has a constitution and passes declarations regarding ethical employment practices. The problem the ILO faces is enforcement. Each country participates voluntarily, and can withdraw at any time. Additionally, each country can choose to adopt or reject each declaration the ILO passes. Even when a country accepts a declaration, the ILO has little power to discipline the country if it fails to follow guidelines. Because enforcement is difficult, the ILO is not considered a truly effective solution to the problem of exploited workers.

In the United States, Congress was concerned that U.S. companies with foreign operations were bribing government officials to gain an unfair business advantage. In response to these concerns, Congress passed the Foreign Corrupt Practices Act of 1977 (FCPA). That act gave the Securities Exchange Commission and the Department of Justice the power to prosecute U.S. businesses engaged in bribery of foreign officials.

American business leaders feared the FCPA would make them less competitive against foreign companies that could, and often were expected to, use bribes to land business deals. This again led to discussions on the need for a universal solution.

The result was the Organisation for Economic Co-Operation and Development (OECD) Anti-Bribery Convention, which took effect in 1999. Countries that joined the Convention agreed to pass legislation that outlawed bribery among businesses headquartered in their countries. But because only about twenty percent of countries are members, the OECD Convention is not a viable universal solution to bribery.

V. Ethics Online

Compared to other technological advancements, the internet dramatically changed the lives of average citizens in record time. In a country where legislation can take years to pass, this creates a problem for protecting users from privacy risks, scams, and having their ideas and their work used inappropriately. To a very large extent, we all use the internet at our own risk. In an ideal world, people would use the same ethical standards online that they use in other aspects of their lives. Civil society dictates we should not use hate speech, or use private information without permission. But feeling anonymous tempts some into behaving badly. Thus,

---

COPYRIGHT PIRACY IS STILL AGAINST THE DIGITAL MILLENIUM COPYRIGHT ACT IF ACCESS IS OBTAINED IN ANOTHER COUNTRY

Synopsis, Inc. v. AzurEngine Technologies, Inc.
(Software Maker v. Competitor)
401 F. Supp. 3d 1068 (S.D. Cal. 2019)

Synopsys is one of the world's leading producers of Electronic Design Automation ("EDA") software, which are tools used by microchip manufacturers to design, verify, and simulate the performance of electronic circuits. [These] tools that are the result of "hundreds of millions of dollars of investment as well as years of Synopsys' time."

Synopsys permits access to its tools only through customized licenses that grant the purchaser limited rights. Synopsys employs strict controls that monitor and limit access in accordance with each licensee's specific terms.

Beginning in June 2019, Synopsys' monitoring programs detected "call-home data" indicating that individuals associated with AzurEngine—a company with no current license from Synopsys—had impermissibly accessed its EDA software. According to Synopsys, this call-home data indicates that AzurEngine has used counterfeit license keys to circumvent Synopsys' software protections more than 15,000 times. For its part, AzurEngine says it believed it had permission to access Synopsys software because its Chinese business partner "purported to provide AzurEngine with valid licensed access to the Synopsys software."

Synopsys claims that AzurEngine's unauthorized use of its software constitutes a violation of the Digital Millennium Copyright Act ("DMCA"). It seeks a temporary restraining order enjoining AzurEngine from further accessing its software.

[To receive a temporary restraining order] Synopsys must establish "that [it] is likely to succeed on the merits, that [it] is likely to suffer irreparable harm in the absence of preliminary relief, that the balance of equities tips in [its] favor, and that an injunction is in the public interest." Each of these factors is met here.

To prevail on its claim for relief under the DMCA, Synopsys must prove that (1) its software included a technological measure that effectively controls access, (2) AzurEngine circumvented that technological measure, and (3) the Synopsys software that AzurEngine accessed is a work protected under the Copyright Act.

First, Synopsys' software "effectively controls" access to its suite of EDA software. The software will not run without the licensee "checking out" a license key from a server that is designed to only grant such keys to approved licensees. Every court to consider the issue has found that similar methods of license-control satisfy the "effectively controls" requirement of the DMCA, and this Court does too.

Synopsys has also plausibly demonstrated that AzurEngine circumvented its controls through the use of counterfeit license keys. These counterfeit keys work by effectively tricking the company's license-control systems into thinking AzurEngine is a licensed user. As discussed above, Synopsys' "call-home data" indicates that individuals associated with AzurEngine have circumvented its license-control system at least 15,000 times, which is 14,999 more times than would be necessary to find a violation of the DMCA.

AzurEngine's responses on this point are unavailing. It argues, for example, that its use of Synopsys software was authorized because one of its business associates—an unnamed "Chinese business partner"—had "purported to provide AzurEngine with valid licensed access to the Synopsys software at issue in this case." But even if it were true that AzurEngine had a valid license, that would not allow the company to use counterfeit keys to circumvent Synopsys' software protections. Even "lawful purchasers" must establish that they had specific "authorization to circumvent" in order to avoid DMCA liability. Because Synopsys has shown that AzurEngine likely circumvented its license-control systems, it is irrelevant that AzurEngine believed it had a license to use the software.

Finally, Synopsys likely owns the copyrights to its EDA software, including the specific tools at issue in this case. Much of Synopsys' EDA software is protected by a registered copyright, which is prima facie evidence of lawful ownership over the code. And if that weren't enough, almost all novel software code constitutes a creative, original work of authorship that is automatically protected under the Copyright Act.

[T]he Court concludes that Synopsys is likely to succeed on the merits of its DMCA claim. Largely conceding this, AzurEngine's opposition instead focuses on the red herring of extraterritoriality. Specifically, it argues that although it is a California-based company with engineers operating in the United States, the access to Synopsys' software occurred through its servers in China. Since the "access" technically occurred abroad, AzurEngine argues that enjoining its behavior would violate the rule against applying United States law extraterritorially.

But . . . there is plainly no extraterritoriality problem here. The conduct—gaining access to copyrighted works by circumventing technological access controls—"occurred in the United States," and thus application of the DMCA to AzurEngine's U.S.-based circumventions "involves a permissible domestic application [of the DMCA] even if other conduct occurred abroad."

AzurEngine's argument has also been flatly rejected by numerous courts. Were its argument correct, "large-scale criminal copyright pirates could avoid United States copyright liability simply by locating their servers outside the United States." But that's not the law. Because it's undisputed that AzurEngine's alleged DMCA violations occurred "at least in part[ ] in the United States," its extraterritoriality defense fails.

[The Court also found that Synopsis would suffer irreparable harm if the temporary restraining order were not granted and that the order was in the public interest.]

IT IS SO ORDERED.

the internet has created many hazards, and it is as yet unclear what combination of responses is appropriate.

Among the most pressing issues related to online ethics are privacy concerns. There have been some federal attempts to protect users from a loss of privacy, but problems persist. Because states may create laws that offer greater protection than federal laws provide, some states have introduced stricter privacy provisions to fill in gaps from federal statutes. California was the first state to enact an omnibus privacy law that gave its residents ownership over their personal information. This law gave Californians more rights over how their information is used, and regulates business practices around that information. In 2020, the California privacy law was strengthened. By January 1, 2023, a company doing business in California must comply with more stringent retirements. A business that buys, shares, receives, or sells personal information of 100,000 or more Californians in a year, and meets certain revenue requirements, is subject to the California law, even if it is not located in California. The new law also provides for the creation of the California Privacy Protection Agency responsible for enforcing the law. This stricter regime may prove to be a model for other states or even national legislation.

Acceptable Use of Online Resources:

Every day millions of bits of copyrighted material are used inappropriately and without permission. These works are protected by copyright laws, but the internet makes it easy for the materials to be "lifted," and difficult for the offenders to be caught. In the United States, federal protection of these electronic materials generally falls under the Digital Millennium Copyright Act of 1998. The act serves many purposes, including:

- Criminalizing the production and distribution of technologies intended to steal or use copyrighted material.
- Making "hacking" into protected material illegal.
- Imposing strict penalties for internet copyright infringement.
- Exempting internet service providers from being prosecuted for content their customers post or distribute in violation of the law.

Among other features, the Digital Millenium Copyright Act requires internet service providers to immediately remove material when someone claims that material is copyrighted protected.

Many defenses have been levelled against the law, but as the following case shows, courts tend to reject these arguments when they appear to be excuses for what amounts to theft.

CHAPTER SUMMARY

Although this textbook focuses on business law, a grounding in ethics enhances the understanding of law and business. Further, the increasing focus on ethical business operations links ethics and law. Creating an ethical workplace is now a best practice.

Stakeholder analysis and use of different ethical perspectives improves business decision-making. Incorporating these practices into an ongoing compliance and ethics program is an excellent way to reduce time out of legal compliance. It can also foster a more productive and competitive organization.

Increasingly, businesses are expected to behave ethically. Alongside this expectation, the law is incorporating ethical standards. As business activities become more transparent, businesspeople must learn to be accountable to the public and its desire for ethical corporate behavior. They must also be aware of how ethical standards can apply to businesses in a wider context.

Review Questions

Review question 1.
What is the difference between ethics and law?

Review question 2.
What is a stakeholder? A shareholder? How do the groups overlap and differ?

Review question 3.
What are the "four avenues"? How are they used to examine potential decisions? What is their focus?

Review question 4.
What is compliance? How does it relate to ethics? What is a culpability score? How can a corporation's approach to its operations help mitigate legal problems? Aggravate legal problems?

Review question 5.
What is corporate social responsibility? How does CSR benefit customers and stakeholders? The corporation itself?

Review question 6.
What is the Business RoundTable? What was unusual about its 2019 statement on the purpose of a corporation? How does the statement reflect changes in the culture?

Review question 7.
What is the Sarbanes Oxley Act and how does it relate to business ethics?

Review question 8.
How does U.S. law deal with international ethical issues? What international organizations seek to harmonize approaches to common ethical questions?

Review question 9.
What are professional ethics codes? When do they apply? Why do some jobs have ethics codes and others do not?

Review question 10.
What ethical questions are raised by use of personal information on the internet? By the copying and use of internet-posted materials?

Discussion Questions

Question 1:

Describe a scenario where ethics and law are both important to a business.

> If ethics are not required, why should businesses be concerned about them?

> Do the ways in which ethics and law matter to a business differ?
> In what ways?

Question 2:

Identify the businesses you admire the most. They may be restaurants that you like or retailers that you purchase from.

> Do these businesses have a reputation for ethical behavior?

> Does that reputation affect your admiration for those businesses?
> Why or why not?

Question 3:

Under the Federal Sentencing Guidelines for Organizations, an ethical corporate culture may reduce penalties levied against a company for illegal actions.

> What do you think of an "ethical corporate culture" mitigating a company's misdeeds?

> Should efforts to avoid problems count for the company, or should penalties be absolute regardless of the circumstances?

Question 4:

Federal sentencing guidelines also allow for harsher punishments for companies if senior executives were involved in wrongdoing or if the company has a history of violations.

> Do these "aggravating factors" make sense in counterpoint to the mitigating factors raised in the prior question?

> Why would the involvement of senior executives count more heavily against an organization than that of other employees?

Question 5:
Think about jobs you have held.

> Did you feel that you or your co-workers were treated fairly by your manager or by the company? If so, did their behavior demonstrate personal or professional ethics? Why or why not?
>
> If you felt you or your co-workers were treated unfairly, can you point to specific ethical failures?
>
> What should management have done differently?

Question 6:
The so-called "golden rule" is to do unto others as you would have done to yourself.

> How applicable is the "golden rule" in a business context?
>
> Is there such a thing as behaving ethically toward your competitors?
>
> Would such behavior be advisable from a business perspective?

Question 7:
Imagine a department with a manager and four employees. One of the employees, Chris, has children, and regularly needs to leave early or miss work to attend teacher conferences or medical appointments. Pat is a member of the National Guard, and sometimes needs to be out of work to train or serve. The other two employees, Sasha and Lin, feel as if they are always required to "pick up the slack" whenever Chris or Pat needs to be out of the office. All the employees make about the same amount of money; they are all on salary, so no one receives overtime pay or necessarily loses wages if they need to be out.

> How can the department manager ethically deal with the different needs of these four employees?
>
> Compare your solution with others. How do the solutions differ? What considerations did others take into account that you did not?

Question 8:

The French philosopher and author Albert Camus said, "A man without ethics is a wild beast loosed upon this world."

> What distinguishes personal ethics from professional ethics? Does it make sense for personal failures of judgment to affect a person's professional license?

> Why are some jobs ("professions") like medicine, law, and accounting subject to additional ethics codes? Are professional ethics codes something that should apply to more types of work? Why or why not?

Question 9:

The United States generally does not "legislate" ethics.

> Should it? If yes, who would determine the standards and how?

> Are other communities (such as social groups or organizations) within the United States more reliant on ethical behavior? If so, is that an advantage to those groups?

3

LITIGATION AND APPEALS

KEY OBJECTIVES:
▸ Describe the progress of a case through trial and appeals.
▸ Explain the differences between criminal and civil cases.
▸ Brief appeals cases for deeper understanding.

CHAPTER OVERVIEW

This chapter examines how cases move through the court system. Different types of cases take different paths, but there are many commonalities. Trial courts are a shared first step, for example. Here, you will learn about the different courts and their powers, as well as the options available to the parties in a case.

Understanding how litigation, prosecution, and appeals work means that businesspeople can make better decisions about legal issues. Accordingly, this chapter shows how to analyze an appeals court decision to help determine why the decision is significant and how it affects business operations.

INTRODUCTION

In the United States, there are two major court systems: state and federal. Both systems have trial courts, and both systems have appeals courts that hear disputes over the trial court result. While these systems work in parallel, decisions from both could ultimately lead to the U.S. Supreme Court, which chooses which cases to hear from the federal and state court systems.

Courts have different jurisdictions, or powers to hear cases. Rules on jurisdiction direct which court should preside over different types of cases. For instance, there are specialist courts, such as bankruptcy courts, that only hear cases of a certain type. There are also rules for whether a case should proceed in state or federal court, and where the correct court is located.

Whether at the state or federal level, trials for civil issues (disputes between private parties that are typically resolved with monetary damages) and for criminal matters (in which the government prosecutes an individual to seek punishment) have many similarities. They both involve a judge, and they can both have juries. Both civil and criminal cases involve witnesses and evidence brought in the courtroom. But, there are important differences. It is more difficult to achieve a criminal conviction than to win in a civil case. The system sets a higher bar for conviction than for payment of private damages.

Disputes between parties can be resolved through lawsuits. Business-related disagreements include issues such as trademark infringements, failed contracts, and wrongful termination of an employee. These civil matters all follow similar rules for trial and appeal.

I. Civil and Criminal Law

The U.S. legal system includes both civil and criminal law. "Civil law" deals with disputes between private parties, such as contract matters or personal injury cases. Criminal law is more familiar as the way the federal and state governments prosecute and punish individuals who commit crimes.

Civil and criminal cases are heard in both federal and state courts. They are similar in some ways, but there are important differences.

Civil claims start when a **party**, which can be a person, group, corporation, or government body, believes another party has injured them or will injure them in the future. The injury can be physical, financial, or even emotional in some cases. To seek compensation, the injured party brings a lawsuit against the other party. The process starts with the injured party filing a claim in court, called a **complaint**. When a complaint is filed, the filing party becomes the **plaintiff**. The party against whom the complaint was filed is the **defendant**.

The complaint must include two things:

1. An explanation for why the court has the authority to decide the case, and
2. A short description telling why the injured party deserves to win.

The short description included in the original complaint must name a **cause of action** for the claim. A cause of action is a fact or set of facts

> The same action may lead to both civil and criminal cases. In 1995, a jury found former football player O.J. Simpson not guilty of the murders of his ex-wife, Nicole Brown Simpson, and her friend, Ronald Goldman. Later, the victims' families brought civil claims against Mr. Simpson for wrongful death in state court. In 1997, jurors concluded that Mr. Simpson caused the deaths and should pay $33.5 million in compensation to the families. The change in outcomes is due to the different **burden**, or degree of proof, needed to win a civil case rather than a criminal case. A criminal case must be proved "beyond a reasonable doubt" while a civil matter is decided by a "preponderance of the evidence"—a much lower bar.

BURDEN OF PROOF:
Amount of proof needed to prove one's case.

CIVIL CLAIMS:
Lawsuit to remedy a private legal dispute.

PARTY:
Plaintiff or defendant in a civil case. The state or defendant in a criminal case.

COMPLAINT:
First document filed with a court by a party that claims legal rights against another party.

PLAINTIFF:
Party starting civil legal action against another party.

DEFENDANT:
Party accused or defending in a legal action.

that gives the plaintiff the legal right to seek judgment against the defendant. There are far too many civil causes of action to list here, but some common ones include:

- Breach of Contract
- Negligence
- Defamation
- Patent Infringement
- Trespass

Each cause of action has a set of elements that the plaintiff must prove to win. The elements are like pieces of a puzzle, and all of the pieces must be proven for the plaintiff to win. The burden is on the plaintiff, who must prove each element by a preponderance of the evidence. Loosely, this means the plaintiff must show that it is more likely than not that the defendant is responsible. Essentially, more than half of the evidence must support the plaintiff.

Once a complaint is filed, the case is assigned to a judge who has no personal interest in the case. The defendant has twenty days to respond to the complaint. Defendants may ask that the judge dismiss the case because the complaint did not adequately state a cause of action. This is referred to as filing a motion to dismiss. Or defendants might respond by stating the reasons they do not believe the plaintiff should win. This is called filing an answer.

No two lawsuits are the same. Each side can file motions for a variety of reasons. A motion is simply a formal request to the court. For example, the defendant might think the injury was someone else's fault, and file a motion asking that another defendant be added to the case. Or one party might think the other party is not complying with the court's orders and may file a motion to "compel" compliance. This type of motion requests that the court demand the other party follow a request, such as producing documents or other evidence. The court controls this part of the process through a scheduling order, which tells the parties when certain parts of the case must be completed, including a deadline for filing motions.

An important part of the schedule is the discovery process. This is a time when the two sides can ask each other to turn over or share records and other possible evidence. For

CAUSE OF ACTION:
Fact(s) that enable a party to bring legal action against another party.

ELEMENTS:
Parts of a crime or legal action that each must be proven.

PREPONDERANCE OF THE EVIDENCE:
More than half of the evidence.

MOTION TO DISMISS:
Party's request to end a legal action.

ANSWER:
Response to a complaint.

DISCOVERY PROCESS:
The process by which the parties to a lawsuit obtain information from each other and from witnesses.

example, suppose a woman injured in a car accident sues the driver of the car that hit her vehicle. The other driver might think the accident was the woman's fault, because she was not paying attention. The driver might want to ask the woman to provide her cell phone record for that day, to see if she might have been talking on the phone or texting at the time of the accident. The driver's lawyer would make a discovery request for those records. Discovery is also the time when the two sides might interview witnesses, and even each other.

While this process sounds simple, there are often disputes over whether one side should have to provide all the things the other side is asking for. These disputes often cause delays and might require a hearing with the judge to iron out disputes. By the end of the discovery process, it is possible that the information collected can lead the parties to want to settle their dispute. If not, the parties prepare for trial.

Whether there is a jury involved in the trial depends on what the plaintiff seeks to achieve. A plaintiff seeking money is generally entitled to a jury trial. But when a plaintiff asks for an **injunction**, which is a court order requiring the defendant to stop doing something, the judge decides the case without a jury.

Trials typically begin with the plaintiff, and then the defendant, giving opening statements. These statements are designed to set the stage for trial, in an effort to prepare the judge or jury to hear the evidence as it fits into the big picture.

Plaintiffs must then call witnesses and present evidence to prove the elements of their cases. After the plaintiff questions a witness, called **direct examination**, the defendant may ask follow-up questions, called **cross-examination**. This process might go back and forth, with the plaintiff asking additional questions (re-direct) and the defendant following up (re-cross).

When the plaintiff has called all its witnesses, it is the defendant's turn to call witnesses and present evidence that supports his version of events or legal theories. The process is repeated, with defendant conducting direct examination of the witnesses and plaintiff conducting cross-examination. There is also an opportunity for re-direct and re-cross examination.

When each side is done presenting evidence and testimony, each makes closing arguments, starting with the plaintiff. The case is then turned over to the judge or jury to decide. When the judge or jury gives its decision, it is deciding in favor of one party or the other.

If either party is not satisfied with the decision in the case, she may start the appeal process. In an appeal, a party is claiming that an error

INJUNCTION:
Court order for a party to do or not to do a specific thing.

DIRECT EXAMINATION:
Examination of a witness by the party that called the witness to testify.

CROSS EXAMINATION:
Examination of a witness that has already testified in a court proceeding, conducted by the other side.

in either procedure or in the judge's interpretation of the law that took place in the trial court. Some common reasons for appeals are that judges did not allow evidence that could have helped that party, or that the jury was given the wrong instructions for deciding the case.

Appeals are heard by appellate courts. In the federal court system, trials are generally held in one of the many federal district courts, and those decisions may be appealed to the circuit court of appeals. If either party remains dissatisfied after the appeal, she may ask the United States Supreme Court to correct the claimed errors. Most state court systems largely follow the same process, with a trial court and two levels of appellate courts.

With all these steps and variables, it is easy to understand why it often takes years before a lawsuit is finally over. It is also easy to understand why judges tend to encourage parties to settle their disputes without a trial.

The criminal law system is similar to the civil law system in many ways, but there are also important differences:

- The party who starts a criminal proceeding is a **prosecutor**, not a plaintiff. The prosecutor works for the local, state, or federal government and represents the people served by that government. Crimes are wrongs against the nation, state, or municipality and its people. Civil cases involve wrongs against or between private parties. The party being charged with a crime is still called the defendant.

- When a defendant loses a criminal case, the defendant is **convicted** while a losing party in a civil case is liable (held responsible) to pay monetary damages.

- Convictions in criminal cases can result in loss of freedom, voting privileges, and other rights, depending on the crime.

- Lawyers are sometimes provided free of charge for criminal defendants, unlike in most civil cases.

- In a criminal case, the defendant cannot be forced to testify in any way that might help the prosecutor prove the case.

- The burden of proof for a criminal conviction is proof *beyond a reasonable doubt*, which is much more difficult to prove than the civil preponderance-of-the-evidence burden. Judges and attorneys have struggled for generations to explain beyond a reasonable doubt clearly.

PROSECUTOR:
Public official who starts legal proceedings against another, usually for a crime.

CONVICTION:
Declaration of guilt for a criminal charge.

MISDEMEANOR:
Minor wrong-doing.

FELONY:
A crime more serious than a misdemeanor, usually punishable by more than one year's imprisonment.

Crimes are divided into **misdemeanors** and **felonies** based on how serious the possible punishment can be. Misdemeanors are crimes where the worst possible penalties are fines or up to one year in jail. Felonies are crimes with maximum possible penalties of more than a year in prison.

Usually, the criminal process starts when police or federal agents arrest a suspected criminal and accuse the suspect of committing a specific crime. Prosecutors review the police report and evidence, decide if there is enough evidence to charge the suspect, and decide what crime or crimes the evidence supports. If charges are filed, the defendant hears the charges at a first court appearance, called an **arraignment**. During the arraignment, the defendant enters a plea of guilty or not guilty.

> A common understanding of "beyond a reasonable doubt" is that the prosecution's evidence must show that no other logical explanation can be concluded from the facts except that the defendant committed the crime, thereby overcoming the presumption that a person is innocent until proven guilty. A better definition of "beyond a reasonable doubt" is that it is the evidence presented by the prosecutor in a criminal trial proves the defendant's guilt to such a degree that no reasonable doubt could exist in the mind of a rational, reasonable person.

If the plea is not guilty, the judge decides whether to keep the defendant in jail while awaiting trial or let the defendant remain free while awaiting trial. The judge may decide the defendant can remain free without paying anything, or the judge might require the defendant to pay an amount of money before being released. The idea behind collecting a fee is to ensure that the defendant returns for the trial. The money paid is forfeited if the defendant does not return for trial. The defendant may also request a free lawyer during the arraignment.

The next step in the criminal process is a preliminary hearing. In some cases, a **grand jury** might be asked to listen to the prosecutor's evidence and determine whether there is enough to continue with the case. In other cases, a judge will hear the prosecutor's evidence and determine whether the case should continue. If the judge or grand jury permits it, the case moves forward and is set for a trial date. Time is given for the defendant, usually through a lawyer, to review the evidence against the defendant. The defense may interview witnesses and collect evidence that tends to show it is less likely that the defendant committed the crime. This process is very similar to discovery in civil cases, with

ARRAIGNMENT:
Court proceeding calling a party to court to answer a criminal charge.

GRAND JURY:
A panel of citizens who examine accusations in a criminal case to determine if the case should go forward.

PLEA AGREEMENT:
Agreement in a criminal case between prosecutor and defendant by which defendant agrees to plead guilty to a particular charge in return for some deal from the prosecutor.

the exception that the defendant never has to speak to the prosecutor about the case.

Another similarity to civil cases is that criminal cases often settle at this stage. In criminal cases, this is called reaching a **plea agreement**. If an agreement is reached, the defendant will change the plea to guilty for the crime charged or for a less serious crime if the defendant and prosecutor agree. The defendant then accepts a penalty that both sides have agreed on. The judge must approve the plea agreement and make sure the defendant understands the rights he is giving up by pleading guilty.

If the case proceeds to trial, the process is similar in many ways to a civil trial. The prosecutor gives the first opening statement, followed by the defense. The prosecutor calls witnesses and presents evidence to prove each element of the alleged crime. The defense can cross-examine the witnesses and challenge the evidence the prosecutor wants to present. The defense may then call its own witnesses and offer evidence that tends to show it is less likely the defendant committed the crime, to raise a reasonable doubt, or that there were circumstances that justified the defendant's actions, such as self-defense.

The defendant may or may not take the stand to testify. In other words, a defendant is not obligated to say anything in her own defense, and the jury is instructed that this silence may not be held against the defendant. In fact, a defendant is not required to present any evidence or witnesses at his trial. The burden is completely on the prosecutor to prove that the defendant committed the crime. The jury must presume the defendant is innocent unless the prosecutor proves every element of the crime beyond a reasonable doubt.

When both sides are done presenting evidence, the prosecutor and then the defense counsel give closing arguments. The judge then gives jurors instructions about the elements of the crime and the burden of proof the prosecutor must meet (beyond a reasonable doubt). The jury then discusses the case privately and comes to a decision. If the defendant has declined the right to a jury, the judge decides whether the prosecutor has proven the case.

If the defendant is found guilty, the judge will later impose a sentence, which may include jail or prison time, and usually requires the defendant to pay a variety of costs and penalties, as well. A defendant may appeal a criminal conviction or sentence using much the same procedure as in civil cases. With rare exceptions, a prosecutor may *not* appeal if the defendant is found not guilty.

As a business student, you may feel that the civil legal process is the only one that will impact your career. That is not true. Corporations can break the law, and officers or employees can be charged with a variety of business related crimes like tax evasion, money laundering, embezzlement, and bribery.

II. Federal and State Court Systems

Earlier in this chapter, you learned that there are both federal and state court systems. You learned that only some claims can be heard in

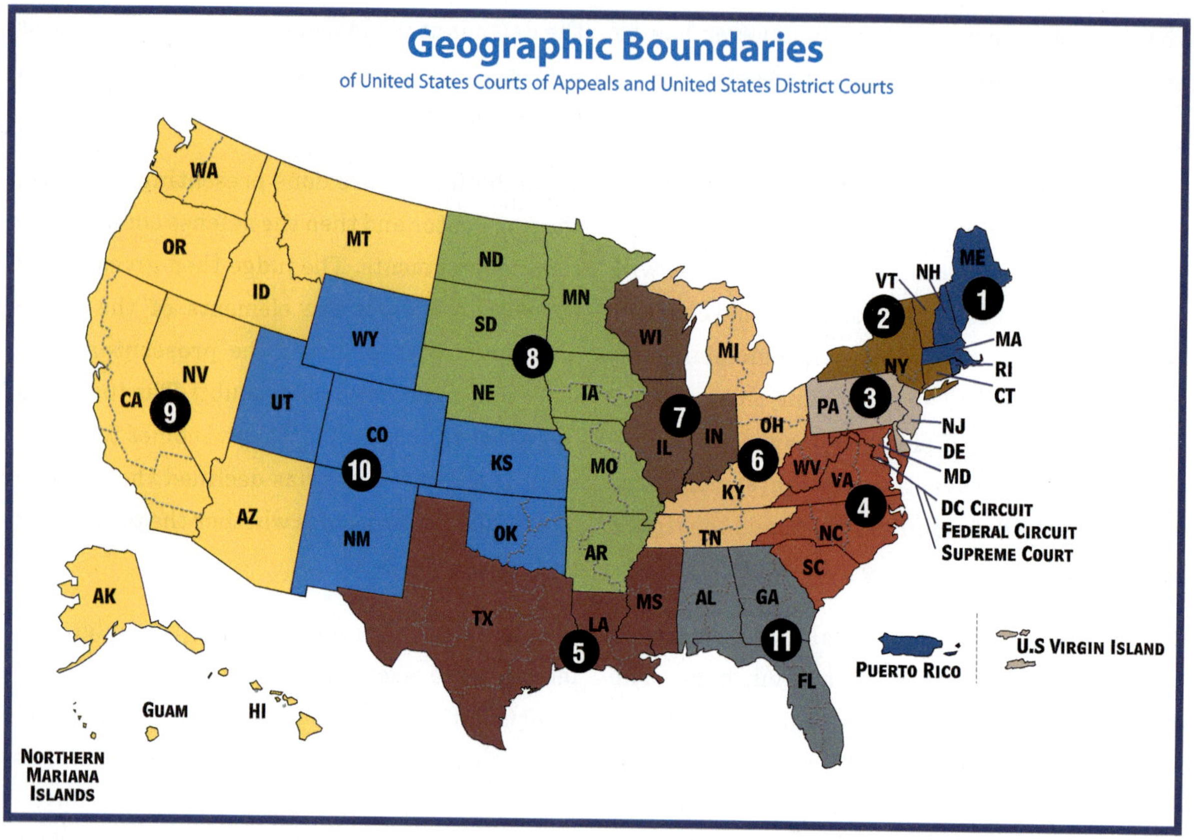

Geographic Boundaries
of United States Courts of Appeals and United States District Courts

federal courts, while others must be heard in state courts. You learned that states may structure their court systems in a way that best meets the state's needs, although many states use structures quite similar to the federal court structure. We will now look more closely at those federal and state court systems.

Federal Court System

The U.S. Constitution only created the U.S. Supreme Court. Congress was given the authority to create lower federal courts as needed. Today, the U.S. Supreme Court is assisted by 13 federal appellate courts and 94 federal district courts.

> A party who wants the Supreme Court to hear a case submits a petition for **certiorari** to the Court. The petition is a request for the Court to take the matter. If the Supreme Court agrees to review the case, it grants a writ of certiorari. Some state supreme courts also use certiorari to manage the cases they accept. Federal circuit courts or appeal and some state appeals courts take appeals "as a matter of right," meaning that they do not screen out cases prior to reviewing their merits.

CERTIORARI:
A higher court's acceptance of a case from a lower court for review.

Many cases based on federal causes of action are first filed in federal district courts. They may be appealed in the corresponding federal appellate court. As a last resort, the matter can be appealed again, to the U.S. Supreme Court. The appealing party submits what is called a petition for a **writ of certiorari** that asks the Supreme court to review the case. But the U.S. Supreme Court accepts very few cases. Some factors that may influence whether the Supreme Court accepts a case include whether the case raises an important constitutional issue or whether the case presents a legal problem that different federal courts of appeal have interpreted differently. A U.S. Supreme Court decision is the final word on the matter.

State and Federal Jurisdiction

Plaintiffs in civil actions are faced with a decision when they file a complaint: where to file the action. Most claims can be filed in state courts.

> **PERSONAL JURISDICTION:**
> Power of a court over the defendant in a case.
>
> **SUBJECT MATTER JURISDICTION:**
> Authority of a court to decide a case of a particular type.
>
> **SUFFICIENT CONTACTS:**
> Enough connection between a non-resident defendant with the location where a legal case is filed to give a court there personal jurisdiction over that defendant.

But sometimes a plaintiff may prefer to file in a federal court. This decision may be because the issues are primarily based on federal law, or a plaintiff may feel he will have a better outcome in federal court.

Other times, a plaintiff may file in state court, but the defendant might want the case to be heard in a federal court instead. In those circumstances, the defendant may ask the state court to transfer the case. While many claims based on federal law may be brought in either state or federal court, certain federal claims can only be heard in federal court. When bringing a claim in federal court, the plaintiff must show that the federal court has both **personal jurisdiction** over the defendant and **subject matter jurisdiction** over the legal claim. Personal jurisdiction means that a court has the power to make a ruling against a particular person or organization. Subject matter jurisdiction is the power to hear cases only involving particular issues. A family court could hear a divorce or custody case, for instance, but could not preside over a business-to-business contract dispute. Only federal courts may hear patent infringement cases or law suits in which the United States is a defendant.

Personal jurisdiction is usually easy to show for individual people. Any federal court in the state where a person resides has personal jurisdiction over that person. For cases involving a corporation as the defendant, there are two easy ways to show personal jurisdiction: (1) the business was incorporated in the state where the court is located; or (2) the corporation's primary place of business, or headquarters, is in the state where the court is located. But there are other ways to

CONTINUOUS, SYSTEMATIC CONTACTS WITH A STATE SUBJECT A DEFENDANT TO JURISDICTION

International Shoe Co. v. Washington
(Delaware Corporation) v. (State Taxing Authority)
326 U.S. 310, 66 S. Ct. 154, 90 L. Ed. 95 (1945)

INSTANT FACTS:
The State of Washington (P) sought to recover unemployment compensation fund contributions from International Shoe Co. (D). Even though it employed salespeople in Washington, International Shoe (D) argued that it was not subject to jurisdiction in Washington.

BLACK LETTER RULE:
A corporation is subject to jurisdiction in any state with which it has "minimum contacts," so that the exercise of jurisdiction is consistent with notions of "fair play and substantial justice."

PROCEDURAL BASIS:
Certiorari to review a decision of the Washington Supreme Court upholding jurisdiction over International Shoe (D).

FACTS:
International Shoe (D), a manufacturer and seller of shoes, was a Delaware corporation with its principal place of business in St. Louis, Missouri. International Shoe (D) had no office in Washington and made no contracts for sale or purchase of merchandise there. At one point, International Shoe (D) employed eleven to thirteen salesmen who resided in Washington (P) but reported to sales managers in St. Louis. The salesmen solicited orders from prospective buyers, which orders were transmitted to St. Louis, where they were processed and the products were shipped.

The State of Washington (P) required employers to contribute a certain percentage of wages to its unemployment compensation fund. Because International Shoe (D) did not pay into the fund, the State (P) issued a notice of assessment. International Shoe (D) moved to set aside the assessment because it was not a Washington corporation. The workers' compensation appeal tribunal denied the motion and ruled that the Commissioner was entitled to recover unpaid workers' compensation contributions. After subsequent appeals, the decision was affirmed by the Washington Supreme Court, which held that the continuous solicitation of orders in Washington by the defendant's in-state salesmen sufficiently demonstrated that International Shoe (D) did business in the state.

ISSUE:
Is it consistent with due process to subject a nonresident defendant to jurisdiction in a state where the defendant is not present, but with which it has minimum contacts?

DECISION AND RATIONALE:
(Stone, C.J.) Yes. No longer is a party's physical presence in a state necessary to establish personal jurisdiction. Instead, a defendant may fairly be subject to personal jurisdiction, even if it is not physically present in a particular state, if it has certain "minimum contacts" with the state.

Determining whether jurisdiction is proper depends on the nature and quality of the defendant's contacts with the forum state. A defendant's single or isolated activity in a state is not enough to subject it to suits that are not connected with those activities. Conversely, if a defendant's conduct in a state is continuous and systematic, the defendant is subject to suits that are not related to those activities. To the extent a defendant exercises the privilege of conducting activities within a state, the defendant enjoys the benefits and protections of the law of that state and must accept the potential for suits to arise against them.

In this case, International Shoe's (D) activities in Washington (P) were neither irregular nor casual. They were systematic, continuous, and gave rise to a large volume of interstate business. The obligation to pay into the unemployment compensation fund arose directly from International Shoe's (D) activities in the state. These activities created sufficient ties with Washington (P) so as to make it reasonable to subject International Shoe (D) to jurisdiction there. Affirmed.

CASE VOCABULARY:

LONG-ARM STATUTE:
A statute providing for jurisdiction over a nonresident defendant who has had contacts with the territory in which the statute is in effect.

MINIMUM CONTACTS:
A nonresident defendant's forum-state connections, such as business activity or actions foreseeably leading to business activity, that are substantial enough to bring the defendant within the forum-state court's personal jurisdiction without offending traditional notions of fair play and substantial justice.

SELLING A PRODUCT INTO THE STREAM OF COMMERCE IS NOT ENOUGH TO IMPOSE JURISDICTION OVER A MANUFACTURER

Asahi Metal Industry Co. v. Superior Court
(Japanese Manufacturer) v. (California Trial Court)
480 U.S. 102, 107 S. Ct. 1026, 94 L. Ed. 2d 92 (1987)

INSTANT FACTS:
Victim of motorcycle accident brought suit in California court against Taiwanese tire tube maker, who cross-claimed against Japanese manufacturer of the tire tube valve assembly.

BLACK LETTER RULE:
The defendant must purposefully avail himself of the forum by more than just putting a product into the stream of commerce with the expectation that it will reach the forum state; however, such conduct is enough to satisfy the minimum contacts requirement.

PROCEDURAL BASIS:
Writ of Certiorari to the Supreme Court of California for its reversal of the Court of Appeal's writ of mandate directing the Superior Court to quash service of summons on cross-complaint for indemnification in action for damages for negligence.

FACTS:
In September 1978, Gary Zurcher and his wife, Ruth Ann Moreno, were in a serious motorcycle accident that left Ruth dead and Gary seriously injured. He claimed that the accident had been caused when the rear wheel of his motorcycle suddenly lost air and exploded, sending the motorcycle out of control and into a tractor. Zurcher filed suit in Solano County, California, where the accident had occurred, alleging that the tire, tube, and sealant of his motorcycle were defective. He named as one of the defendants Cheng Shin Rubber Industrial Co., Ltd., the tire tube's Taiwanese manufacturer. Cheng Shin in turn filed a cross-claim—for indemnification in the event it was found liable—against Asahi Metal Industry Co., Ltd. (D), the Japanese manufacturer of the tire tube's valve assembly.

Zurcher eventually settled out of court with Cheng Shin, leaving Cheng Shin's cross-claim against Asahi (D) as the sole remaining issue to be tried. Asahi (D) argued that California could not exert jurisdiction over it, since Asahi lacked sufficient contacts with the state. Asahi (D) did not do business in California and did not import any products into California itself. Rather, it sold its valve assemblies to Cheng Shin and various other tire manufacturers. The sales to Cheng Shin took place in Taiwan, and the valve assemblies were shipped to Taiwan. Cheng Shin bought valve assemblies from other manufacturers as well. Sales to Cheng Shin accounted for a very small fraction of Asahi's (D) annual income—usually less than 1–2%.

Asahi (D) claimed that it had never contemplated that it might be subject to suit in California because of sales to Cheng Shin in Taiwan, but Cheng Shin claimed that Asahi (D) had been told and definitely knew that its products were being sold in California.

The trial court found that Asahi (D) could be subjected to California's jurisdiction. The Court of Appeal disagreed. Unfortunately for Asahi (D), the Supreme Court of California overruled the Court of Appeal, finding that Asahi's (D) intentional act of putting its products into the "stream of commerce" with the awareness that they might wind up in California was enough to justify California's exercise of jurisdiction. Asahi (D) proceeded to the U.S. Supreme Court.

ISSUE:
To establish minimum contacts with a state, is it enough to put a product into the stream of commerce, with the expectation that it will reach the forum state?

DECISION AND RATIONALE:
(O'Connor, joined by Rehnquist, Powell, and Scalia) No. It is not sufficient, for purposes of establishing that the defendant has minimum contacts with the forum state, to show that the defendant has intentionally placed its products into the stream of commerce—even if the defendant had the expectation in doing so that its products would reach the forum state. Something more, in addition to placing products in the stream of commerce, is necessary to establish minimum contacts between the defendant and the forum state.

Foreseeability alone is insufficient as a basis for jurisdiction. It is not enough that Asahi (D) might have been able to guess that some one or more of its products might eventually find its way into the state of California. Asahi (D) must have performed some act showing that it deliberately intended to take advantage of that state's market or laws. This does not mean that Asahi (D) could only invoke California's jurisdiction by importing its products directly. Cheng Shin's actions in importing Asahi's (D) products could qualify, provided that Asahi (D) took additional actions indicating its intent, such as, for instance, advertising or marketing its product in California, or deliberately designing its product to conform to regulations or laws unique to California, or providing a means for California users of its products to receive technical help or advice.

Since Asahi (D) has done nothing to indicate a deliberate wish on its part to see its products in California or to exploit the California market, it cannot be said to have the requisite minimum contacts with the state.

The minimum contacts analysis is not the only reason why California cannot exercise jurisdiction. There is still the matter of "traditional notions of fair play and substantial justice." Even if minimum contacts existed between Asahi (D) and California, it would be fundamentally unfair to require Asahi (D) to defend itself there. California's interest in this matter—the welfare of its citizens—was put to rest, for the most part, when Zurcher settled. The dispute is not just between two non-residents of California, but two nonresidents of the U.S. Given the rather extreme inconvenience necessitated by defending a suit in a distant forum and a foreign legal system, it would be unreasonable and unfair for California to exercise jurisdiction over Asahi (D) in this matter. Reversed and remanded.

ANALYSIS:
The Court unanimously held in this case that the California state court could not constitutionally exercise jurisdiction over Asahi (D). The Court followed a two-step analysis it had developed in its previous decisions. First, inquiry was made into the sufficiency of Asahi's (D) contacts with the forum state, and then those contacts were examined in light of fairness considerations to determine if the exercise of jurisdiction would be reasonable. Asahi's (D) mere awareness that the valve assemblies it sold to Cheng Shin eventually would end up in California was not sufficiently purposeful to establish minimum contacts.

CASE VOCABULARY:
INDEMNIFICATION:
Reimbursing another party for financial losses or damages, or an agreement to indemnify against losses or damages.

show personal jurisdiction over a corporation, as well. A pivotal case, *International Shoe Co. v. State of Washington Office of Unemployment Compensation and Placement*, introduces the concept of **sufficient contacts**. This is the idea that a corporation that knowingly does a great deal of business in a specific state may be sued in the federal courts in that state.

To show personal jurisdiction over a defendant, the plaintiff must show that the defendant has contact with the place where the federal court is located. It must be fair to require the defendant to appear in a court in that location. In *Asahi Metal Industry Co., Ltd. v. Superior Court of California, Solano County*, the U.S. Supreme Court determined that asking the defendant, a Japanese manufacturer, to appear in a California federal court was unreasonably inconvenient for the defendant, and that other, less burdensome options were available. Of course, a defendant can consent, or agree to, personal jurisdiction in a particular court.

After showing that the court has personal jurisdiction over the defendant, the plaintiff must show that the court has subject matter jurisdiction over the claim. In other words, the plaintiff must show that the legal claim belongs in federal court or state court. Federal courts may hear cases only if they are based on **diversity jurisdiction** or a **federal question**, including questions involving the U.S. Constitution. Diversity jurisdiction applies when no plaintiff and no defendant to a lawsuit are from the same state, or when one party is from another country. Federal questions are those that claim federal rights or protections are being withheld. These may include claims that challenge whether a law conflicts with the U.S. Constitution. In most cases not involving diversity or federal questions, state courts may be used. As previously mentioned, federal courts have exclusive subject matter jurisdiction over some federal cases such as disputes over government contracts, patent and copyright infringement, and veterans' benefits.

Venue

After a plaintiff has shown both personal *and* subject matter jurisdiction, she must show that the specific federal court is the correct **venue** for the case. Although the concepts of jurisdiction and venue are similar, they are treated separately by the courts, and they have different purposes, as well. Jurisdiction refers to a court's legal authority over parties to a lawsuit. It would not be fair for a court to impose liability on a party who had absolutely no connection to the geographic area where the court sits. For such parties, the court has no personal jurisdiction.

Venue is the geographic location of a particular court. For example, Minnesota has three locations with federal courts. The case could be venued in Minneapolis, St. Paul, or Duluth. Venue refers to a set of rules that considers the convenience of one court over another. Generally, a case is in the proper venue if it is filed in a federal district court where either (1) the defen-

> **DIVERSITY JURISDICTION:** Court case with parties from different states or with a foreign party.
>
> **VENUE:** Residence of defendant or place where most events leading to a legal claim took place.

dant resides, or (2) most of the events that led to the lawsuit took place. If neither is true, venue is proper in any district court that has personal jurisdiction over the defendant. The parties may agree on venue.

III. Foreign Legal Systems

In chapter one, we learned about the common law system in the United States. In addition to the legal systems that we have already discussed, considering today's international business climate, understanding that foreign legal systems can be substantially different than the United States. Many countries use components of more than one system. Because today's business students will interact in global markets, it is important for you to recognize that other countries have their own way of doing business. You will be accountable under another country's legal system if you choose to do business there. Many countries follow the common law system, including Great Britain and countries, like the United States, that are former colonies, including Australia, New Zealand, India and Pakistan.

Civil Law

Civil law is a system where only formal statutory codes are used by judges to decide cases. (In this context, "civil law" describes a legal system in a foreign country; it has a different meaning than "civil law" disputes between private parties in the U.S. system.) Foreign civil law systems rely on comprehensive codes, as well as constitutions, as their legal authority. This system grew from ancient Roman law, and forms the basis for legal systems in Continental Europe, such as France, Spain, and Portugal, and areas once colonized by those countries.

Civil law systems are also often found in countries with historical or current socialist or communist ties. Legal codes in those countries have been revised to include principles associated with Socialism and Communism. Some examples include Russia and Cuba. China and Japan also have civil law systems. And unlike the rest of the United States, the Louisiana state legal system is based on civil law.

One of the primary practical differences between civil law and common law is the role that lawyers and judges play. In common-law countries, like our own, lawyers serve as advocates, building a case and presenting it to a judge, who serves as more of a referee or arbiter. In civil law systems, judges have a more active, investigative role than judges in common law jurisdictions. They may ask the parties questions or direct the appointment of expert witnesses. Another practical difference is that, unlike the common law, there is no stare decisis. A court decision binds only the parties to the case and other courts are not required to follow it as precedent.

Bijuridical Systems

Some countries have legal systems that include more than one category. The Canadian system, for example, stems from English common law concepts. But Quebec uses a French civil law system in most civil matters. Therefore, Canada is referred to as a bijuridical system. In the United States, Louisiana also follows a French civil law model. India's legal system, too, is of a much bigger picture. And although each case is very important to the *parties*, it is even more important to the rest of us. In a common law system, each case in which the judge interprets law builds on previous cases. The judges consider more than just the parties to a lawsuit, as each case builds on the ones before it in defining the law.

When reading cases, then, you need to keep the bigger picture in mind: how does this case help shape the law considering everything else we know about the law?

An efficient and effective way to help you to understand as you read cases includes writing a case brief. This is a standardized way of summarizing the most important parts of the case. So let's look at an actual court decision, identify the parts of the decision, and examine the case brief. In fact, the cases in this book are presented in the form of case briefs. You should look at some of the actual opinions, though, to gain practice in reading cases effectively.

The somewhat humorous case of *Mayo v Satan* includes a short discussion of a concept we covered earlier in this chapter, personal jurisdiction, as well as some other legal issues.

So, what happened here? The plaintiff, Mr. Gerald Mayo, attempted to sue Satan (and his "staff") for putting obstacles in the plaintiff's way and causing him problems. In this case, though, the court was not asked to decide whether the defendant had actually done what Mayo alleged. Instead, the case addressed a preliminary procedural matter: was Mayo allowed to bring the suit at all?

Many courts include a syllabus in their decisions. And in many other cases, the publisher will include a syllabus even when the court does not. The syllabus can be an excellent starting point when reading a case because it summarizes very briefly the key issues and holdings in the case. Having this information before reading the case gives you an advantage: you know what to look for. You can read the case with an eye toward understanding the basis for the court's holding, and understanding the nuances of the court's reasoning.

The syllabus in the Mayo case does a nice job of summarizing the most relevant parts of the case: Mr. Mayo wants to bring a civil-rights suit against the devil; the court said no, for three reasons: personal jurisdiction, problems with a class-action suit, and no way to notify Satan about the suit. Now read the syllabus carefully, with this summary in mind. Do you see how this will help you as you read the rest of the case?

Moving on to the opinion itself, you can see that the court states the legal issue in the first sentence of the opinion: "Plaintiff . . . prays for leave to file a complaint . . ." Plaintiff is asking the court's permission (or "leave") to sue Satan. Unfortunately, not all courts make it this easy to find the issue! The first sentence also identifies some of the statutes that are relevant to whether the court has jurisdiction.

The rest of the first paragraph, along with the second paragraph, gives background facts. The court could have gone into detail about the specific ways in which Satan allegedly interfered with the plaintiff's life, but those details are not be relevant to whether the plaintiff should be allowed to sue. Courts will often include legally

54 F.R.D. 282

United States District Court, W. D. Pennsylvania.

UNITED STATES ex rel. Gerald MAYO

v.

SATAN AND HIS STAFF.

Misc. No. 5357.

Dec. 3, 1971.

Civil rights action against Satan and his servants who allegedly placed deliberate obstacles in plaintiff's path and caused his downfall, wherein plaintiff prayed for leave to proceed in forma pauperis. The District Court, Weber, J., held that plaintiff would not be granted leave to proceed in forma pauperis who in view of questions of personal jurisdiction over defendant, propriety of class action, and plaintiff's failure to include instructions for directions as to service of process.

Prayer denied.

Opinion

MEMORANDUM ORDER

WEBER, District Judge.

Plaintiff, alleging jurisdiction under 18 U.S.C. § 241, 28 U.S.C. § 1343, and 42 U.S.C. § 1983 prays for leave to file a complaint for violation of his civil rights in forma pauperis. He alleges that Satan has on numerous occasions caused plaintiff misery and unwarranted threats, against the will of plaintiff, that Satan has placed deliberate obstacles in his path and has caused plaintiff's downfall.

Plaintiff alleges that by reason of these acts Satan has deprived him of his constitutional rights.

We feel that the application to file and proceed in forma pauperis must be denied. Even if plaintiff's complaint reveals a prima facie recital of the infringement of the civil rights of a citizen of the United States, the Court has serious doubts that the complaint reveals a cause of action upon which relief can be granted by the court. We question whether plaintiff may obtain personal jurisdiction over the defendant in this judicial district. The complaint contains no allegation of residence in this district. While the official reports disclose no case where this defendant has appeared as defendant there is an unofficial account of a trial in New Hampshire where this defendant filed an action of mortgage foreclosure as plaintiff. The defendant in that action was represented by the preeminent advocate of that day, and raised the defense that the plaintiff was a foreign prince with no standing to sue in an American Court. This defense was overcome by overwhelming evidence to the contrary. Whether or not this would raise an estoppel in the present case we are unable to determine at this time.

If such action were to be allowed we would also face the question of whether it may be maintained as a class action. It appears to meet the requirements of Fed. R. of Civ. P.23 that the class is so numerous that joinder of all members is impracticable, there are questions of law and fact common to the class, and the claims of the representative party is typical of the claims of the class. We cannot now determine if the representative party will fairly protect the interests of the class.

We note that the plaintiff has failed to include with his complaint the required form of instructions for the United States Marshal for directions as to service of process.

For the foregoing reasons we must exercise our discretion to refuse the prayer of plaintiff to proceed in forma pauperis.

It is ordered that the complaint be given a miscellaneous docket number and leave to proceed in forma pauperis be denied.

irrelevant detail anyway, though, so this is something to watch out for.

In the third paragraph, the court states its holding: Mr. Mayo's request is denied. It is helpful when a court starts with the conclusion like this, but you can also skip ahead to see how the court resolved the issue. Here, of course, you already knew the answer because the syllabus provided it. Reading a case can be a bit like putting a jigsaw puzzle together. It is far easier if you can see a picture of the final product while you're working on the puzzle. In the same way, if you know the court's holding, the rest of the decision can be easier to understand.

At this point, you may be wondering what "in forma pauperis" means. The law is filled with Latin terms that lawyers have become used to and that some would call "legalese." Regardless, it is important to stop when you come across a term you do not understand and look the term up. This is easy, since you can find the definitions of terms easily on the Internet. *In forma pauperis* mean "in the manner of a pauper." Practically speaking, it means that Mr. Mayo wants the court to waive the costs of filing his lawsuit. Although interesting, it is not relevant to the legal issue: whether Mr. Mayo will be allowed to sue.

The third paragraph next identifies and then explains the court's first reason for denying Mr. Mayo's request: even if Satan *has* violated Mr. Mayo's civil rights, the court cannot tell if it has personal jurisdiction over Satan. (You may want to go back and quickly review personal jurisdiction.) The court gives three reasons. First, Mr. Mayo did not include an address for Satan.

Second, the court could not find any other cases in the district where Satan was a party, so that too suggests he does not live in the jurisdiction. Third, the court found an unofficial account of a New Hampshire case where Satan was a plaintiff, which could affect this case. In other words, Mr. Mayo did not give the court enough information to allow it to conclude that it has personal jurisdiction over Satan.

In the next paragraph, the court theorizes that even if the court allows Mr. Mayo to file the suit, there are so many potential plaintiffs with the same claims against Satan, that the case might have to be tried as a class-action suit. The court even goes through the requirements for a class-action suit. But the last sentence of the paragraph explains why this is a problem: a class action requires someone to represent everyone else who has similar claims against the same defendant. The court does not have enough information to decide whether Mr. Mayo could do this. This is the second reason the court will not allow Mr. Mayo to file the suit.

Finally, in the fifth paragraph of the opinion, the court notes that Mr. Mayo was required to include instructions to the U.S. Marshal to be able to deliver the complaint to the defendant. He failed to include those instructions. This is the third reason the court will not allow him to file the suit.

What Is the "Rule"?

Unfortunately, you will not usually find a sentence in court decision that starts with, "The rule is . . ." It often takes careful reading to find, and then to understand, the rule from a case.

The rule from the case is not the same as the holding, although they are closely connected. The holding is the answer to the issue. Will Mr. Mayo be allowed to sue? No.

The rule is what judges and lawyers can take from the case to help guide future decisions and future representation of clients. Here, we can formulate a rule from the court's holding and reasoning.

The court here held that Mr. Mayo could not file suit for three reasons. It is difficult to tell, though, whether a future plaintiff could sue Satan if, for example, he overcame one of the three reasons. Consider this: what if Mr. Mayo's application to the court had made clear that he would be an excellent class-action representative? Would the other two reasons be enough to preclude that next plaintiff from filing suit? Probably, but this is the sort of question that might be argued later.

First, presume that any one of the court's reasons was enough. In that case, we could formulate three rules:

A PLAINTIFF MAY NOT PROCEED IF THE COURT CANNOT DETERMINE WHETHER IT HAS PERSONAL JURISDICTION OVER THE DEFENDANT, WHETHER THE PLAINTIFF CAN ADEQUATELY REPRESENT THE INTERESTS OF THE CLASS, AND HOW THE DEFENDANT IS TO BE SERVED

Mayo v. Satan
(Private Individual) s. (Evil Entity)
54 F.R.D. 282 (1971)

INSTANT FACTS:
Mayo (P) attempted to sue Satan (D) for violating Mayo's (P) civil rights by interfering with his life.

BLACK LETTER RULE:
A court must have personal jurisdiction to hear a case.

PROCEDURAL BASIS:
Civil rights action.

FACTS:
Mayo (P) attempted to file a civil-rights action, *in forma pauperis*, against Satan and his staff (D) for causing Mayo (P) misery, making threats against Mayo (P), deliberately placing obstacles in Mayo's (P) path, and causing Mayo's (P) downfall.

ISSUE:
May the court hear a case against Satan?

DECISION AND RATIONALE:
(Weber, District Judge) No. (1) A plaintiff may not proceed in a lawsuit if the court does not have personal jurisdiction over the defendant. The court noted that P had not provided an address for D, and that the court was unable to find any other case in the jurisdiction in which D was a party. (2) A plaintiff may not proceed in a lawsuit if that suit is likely to become a class action, and the court cannot determine whether the plaintiff can adequately represent the interests of the entire class. (3) A plaintiff may not proceed in a lawsuit if he fails to give instructions in his complaint that would allow the U.S. Marshal to serve the defendant. Application denied.

CASE VOCABULARY:
IN FORMA PAUPERIS:
"in the manner of a pauper"; being excused from paying court costs and fees.

1. A plaintiff may not file a lawsuit where the record lacks enough information for the court to determine whether it has personal jurisdiction over the defendant.

2. A plaintiff may not file a lawsuit where the suit will likely be a class action and the court cannot determine whether the plaintiff will fairly represent the interests of the class.

3. A plaintiff may not file a lawsuit where the complaint does not include service-of-process instruction to the U.S. Marshall, as required.

Alternatively, we might identify a single rule: A plaintiff may not file suit where the court cannot determine whether it has personal jurisdiction over the defendant, where the suit is likely to result in a class action and the court cannot determine whether the plaintiff will adequately represent the class, and where the plaintiff fails to include the required instructions to the U.S. Marshal in his complaint.

The rule, then, helps guide the legal community, including future plaintiffs. And if Mr. Mayo wants to try again, he will need to overcome at least the three obstacles listed by the court.

Now that we have identified the important parts of the Mayo v. Satan case, you can see how the parts come together in the case brief. In practice, writing the case brief is an ongoing process. You will understand the case better as you try to reduce its parts to writing. As you gain a better understanding, you will be able to refine the case brief.

Is It Good Law?

A critical question when reading cases is whether the case is "good law." In other words, does anyone need to follow this case? It has been said that the law is a living, breathing thing. And while the courts try to achieve stability in the law, each new case still clarifies the law a bit. A new case may expand or limit the reach of the law, create an exception, create or change the

CAREERS IN THE LAW

As courts decide cases, the decisions appear in many sources, including published books and online services. Publishers hire lawyers to make the cases more understandable. For example, many cases are published with explanatory notes. Cases published by Thomson Reuters in print and on Westlaw also include Key Numbers, an indexing system that sorts cases into more than 400 topics and more than 98,000 legal issues. Lawyers read the cases, analyze the opinions, and assign the appropriate Key Numbers to help other lawyers find cases for issues they are researching. Many lawyers find this kind of non-traditional work an attractive employment option.

For non-lawyers, the court system offers many career opportunities. Court reporters are essential to making the official record in each case. Their training on specialized stenograph machines is in high demand. Bailiffs also work directly in the courtroom, administering oaths, managing juries, handling evidence, and keeping order. Other professionals, such as translators and managers, keep the system running.

way a word or phrase is defined, or overturn the existing law all together.

Because of this, it does no good to thoroughly understand a case, only to find out that later cases (or later statutes or rules) have changed the law, and that a case no longer carries any weight.

The methods of determining whether a case is still good law are outside the scope of this book. But you should be aware of this important detail when reading cases in the future.

CHAPTER SUMMARY

The information in this chapter will help businesspeople appreciate the issues to be resolved in any court matter. Whether the case is a criminal or civil matter, the jurisdiction, standard of proof, and possible outcomes of a case are important details to understand. With this knowledge, businesses can be more thoughtful and strategic about how to manage their legal concerns.

The ability to read and understand an appeals case by producing a brief is a benefit to a businessperson. Many find cases too legalistic to understand, but with the information provided in this chapter, most will be able to navigate through "legalese" to see why a case is important. As a common law country, appeals court decisions in the United States can change the law, and the business environment.

For businesses, most legal issues will be civil matters. Because jurisdiction can be an area of dispute, many attorneys and businesspeople seek to manage the risk and potential cost of a jurisdictional disagreement through their contracts with other parties. The next chapter discusses some of the options that businesses can pursue.

Review Questions

Review question 1.
What are the three levels of federal courts? What happens at each level? How do these levels correspond to state courts?

Review question 2.
What is a plaintiff? A defendant? A prosecutor?

Review question 3.
What are the Federal Rules of Civil Procedure? When do they apply? What do they help regulate?

Review question 4.
How can a federal case end up in the Supreme Court? A state case? Is there an automatic right of appeal to the Supreme Court? To any other appellate court?

Review question 5.
What are the parts of a court decision? What information is contained in each part?

Review question 6.
What is the difference between civil law and criminal law? Why might a defendant be found not guilty in a criminal trial, but liable for damages in a civil trial about the same incident?

Review question 7.
What are some of the documents filed in a civil case? Who files each one? What happens if one party does not respond to a filing by the other party?

Review question 8.
What is the difference between a misdemeanor and a felony? Why is this difference important to the defendant?

Review question 9.
What is the general order of events in a court trial? What is the jury's role? How does the job of the trial court differ from the responsibilities of an appellate court?

Review question 10.
What is jurisdiction? Who determines whether a court has jurisdiction? When might a case be brought in state court versus federal court? What happens if the parties disagree about jurisdiction?

Review question 11.
What is the rule of an appeals decision? Why is the rule important?

Review question 12.
What is "civil law" as a legal system? How is it different from common law? How is it different from a civil trial or civil issue in U.S. courts?

Review question 13.
What are the sections of a case brief? What is shown in each section? What level of court issues decisions that can be briefed?

Discussion Questions

Question 1:

Chris and Simu argue over who has the better car. Chris becomes angry and punches Simu, breaking his nose. Simu calls the police and Chris is arrested. The police know Chris because he has been arrested locally in the past. The county attorney decides to prosecute Chris for assault and battery. At trial, Chris provides evidence that Simu was holding a wrench during the argument, and Chris believed that Simu was about to attack him with the wrench, so his punch was defensive. The jury acquits Chris.

> What standard of proof did the prosecution have? How does the self-defense claim affect that standard?
>
> The prosecutor has discretion to determine which cases to pursue in criminal trials. What factors might the county attorney consider when deciding whether to prosecute this case?
>
> Who does this criminal trial benefit?

Question 2:

Refer back to the prior question. Suppose that Simu has unpaid medical bills from his injury, so he decides to sue Chris for battery.

> Is Simu more likely to prevail than the prosecutor? Why or why not?
>
> What type of trial is this? Why is it allowed even though this incident was already before a court?
>
> What will Simu receive if he wins? How is that outcome different from the criminal trial?

Question 3:

Supergood Inc. sells imported towels and bed linens online. Supergood is headquartered in Florida, but sells all over the country. It owns distribution warehouses in New York, Texas, and Illinois. It recently started talking to contractors in California about building a warehouse there, but has not made an agreement for that work as yet.

Supergood sells some towels that were treated with an antifungal spray before export. Supergood was not aware of the spray treatment, but several towel buyers have a severe allergic reaction to the spray residue when they use the towels. Several buyers sue for medical expenses.

> Suppose some of the buyers who sue are located in New York. Where could they sue Supergood and why?
>
> What about buyers in California?
>
> What about buyers in Michigan?
>
> Suppose that a few buyers are in Canada. Where would they sue and why?

Question 4:
Refer back to the prior question. Supergood wants to sue its supplier for the reactions to the spray.

> Where can Supergood sue the supplier?
>
> Can Supergood sue in any of the locations given in the prior question? Why or why not?

Question 5:
Larry lives in Minnesota, but works in Wisconsin. He drives to Wisconsin every day, where he works. One morning after he has crossed into Wisconsin, he is distracted and collides with a Wisconsin-registered vehicle, injuring Betty, the driver. Her damages in medical expenses and other costs are $48,000. Larry does not have car insurance.

> Where can Betty sue Larry?
>
> Should she sue in state or federal court? In which level of court?
>
> Betty hears about higher damages awards being granted by juries in Iowa to car crash victims. Iowa borders both Minnesota and Wisconsin. Should Betty be able to move her case to Iowa? Why or why not?

Question 6:

Elek is arrested for car theft in a city that has been plagued by frequent similar crimes and carjackings. The local prosecutor told the media that she was going to "throw the book" at anyone arrested for car-related thefts.

> What are the next steps in the process for Elek?
>
> What would Elek's attorney want to know about the alleged crime?
>
> What might Elek's attorney request if Elek's case is brought to trial?

Question 7:

The U.S. court system is adversarial. The idea is that having each side represented by an attorney who will contest and challenge the position of the other side, with a neutral judge making rulings, will tend to reveal the true state of affairs and lead to a fair resolution. By contrast, alternative dispute resolution techniques tend to focus on cooperation and reaching consensus between parties in dispute.

> What do you think of the adversarial court system?
>
> Would a collaborative model be preferable? Why or why not?

Question 8:

The following is an excerpt from a U.S. Supreme Court decision (citations are omitted). Brief the case. Does the decision raise any issues for private businesses that manage properties, such as shopping malls?

> Board of Airport Commissioners v. Jews for Jesus, Inc.
> 482 U.S. 569 (1987)
>
> The issue presented in this case is whether a resolution banning all "First Amendment activities" at Los Angeles International Airport (LAX) violates the First Amendment.
>
> On July 13, 1983, the Board of Airport Commissioners (Board) adopted Resolution No. 13787, which provides, in pertinent part:
>
> NOW, THEREFORE, BE IT RESOLVED by the Board of Airport Commissioners that the Central Terminal Area at Los Angeles International Airport is not open for First Amendment activities by any individual and/or entity[.]

Respondent Jews for Jesus, Inc., is a nonprofit religious corporation. On July 6, 1984, Alan Howard Snyder, a minister of the Gospel for Jews for Jesus, was stopped by a Department of Airports peace officer while distributing free religious literature[.] The officer warned Snyder that the city would take legal action against him if he refused to leave as requested. Snyder stopped distributing the leaflets and left the airport terminal.

Jews for Jesus and Snyder then filed this action[.] [They] contended that the resolution was facially unconstitutional under Art. I, § 2, of the California Constitution and the First Amendment to the United States Constitution because it bans all speech in a public forum[.] [T]he Court of Appeals concluded. . .the resolution was unconstitutional on its face under the Federal Constitution. We granted certiorari[.]

Under the First Amendment overbreadth doctrine, an individual whose own speech or conduct may be prohibited is permitted to challenge a statute on its face because it also threatens others not before the court—those who desire to engage in legally protected expression but who may refrain from doing so rather than risk prosecution or undertake to have the law declared partially invalid. A statute may be invalidated on its face, however, only if the overbreadth is "substantial." [T]here must be a realistic danger that the statute itself will significantly compromise recognized First Amendment protections of parties not before the Court for it to be facially challenged on overbreadth grounds.

On its face, the resolution at issue in this case reaches the universe of expressive activity, and, by prohibiting all protected expression, purports to create a virtual "First Amendment Free Zone" at LAX. [T]he resolution expansively states that LAX "is not open for First Amendment activities by any individual and/or entity". . . The resolution therefore does not merely reach the activity of respondents at LAX; it prohibits even talking and reading, or the wearing of campaign buttons or symbolic clothing. Under such a sweeping ban, virtually every individual who enters LAX may be found to violate the resolution[.] We think it obvious that such a ban cannot be justified . . . because no conceivable governmental interest would justify such an absolute prohibition of speech. We conclude that the resolution is substantially overbroad [and] hold that the resolution violates the First Amendment.

4 DISPUTE RESOLUTION

KEY OBJECTIVES:
- ▶ Explain the process through which a dispute is resolved in the court system, and the advantages and disadvantages of litigation.
- ▶ List the key features, advantages, and disadvantages of various methods of alternative dispute resolution.
- ▶ Recognize the ways in which commercial parties attempt to avoid or plan for future business disputes.

CHAPTER OVERVIEW

At some point in time, most businesses will find themselves in some kind of dispute. In this chapter, we examine the available options for resolving those disputes. Although the business will most likely work with an attorney, it is important to understand the options and your role in the process. We begin with an overview of litigation, the formal process of resolving a dispute using the court system. After that, we explore a number of methods of alternative dispute resolution. In addition to learning about the key features of each method of dispute resolution, it is important to understand the advantages, disadvantages, and reasons why a business party might choose a particular method. We also consider several ways in which a commercial player can attempt to avoid, or at least minimize, potential business disputes. Finally, we discuss contract provisions commonly used by business parties to address dispute resolution issues before a dispute even arises.

INTRODUCTION

Although parties often have high expectations and the best of intentions, many business deals and relationships do not work out as the parties hope. Any number of circumstances may lead to a dispute between business parties. A business may disagree with another company regarding the terms of the agreement between them. A customer or employee may bring a lawsuit against the company. A corporation may need to file a lawsuit to protect its interest in proprietary information.

When a business dispute arises, there are many ways to try to resolve the dispute. The most informal way to resolve a dispute is through negotiation. The most formal is using the court system. This form of resolution, litigation, is often slow, time-consuming, unpredictable, and expensive. In some circumstances, though, it may be the best option for parties to protect their interests. The parties may prefer to use the court system because they want a formal decision issued by a court of law. A formal decision may influence other cases or have more impact on the parties' behavior going forward. Sometimes, when a business is sued, it may be the only option available.

Often, the parties are looking for a faster, more cost-effective, and less public way to resolve disputes. In that situation, the parties may agree to **Alternative Dispute Resolution**, also known as **ADR**. There are several types of ADR, and each has its own advantages and disadvantages.

In this chapter, we examine formal dispute resolution through the court system as well as the various methods of alternative dispute resolution. We also consider ways in which a party can attempt to avoid disputes, and how parties might address the dispute resolution process through their business agreements before a dispute arises.

I. Litigation

Litigation is the process of resolving a dispute through a lawsuit in the court system. It is both the most formal and the most public way to settle a business dispute. In litigation, the parties to the lawsuit present their claims, arguments, and evidence to a judge or jury. The plaintiff is the person who files the lawsuit: the defendant is the person being sued. After the jury (or sometimes the judge) decides the case, the court issues a judgment, a decision on the parties that the parties must legally follow. Procedural rules control how the process works, and different rules apply to state and federal courts.

In the United States, litigation is an adversarial process. The plaintiff and the defendant are represented by attorneys advocating for their respective positions. Each side presents its best case, and each side has an opportunity to point out problems with the version presented by the other side, then the jury or judge must determine the truth. The goal of the process is to reach a decision in favor of one of the parties (*i.e.*, is the defendant liable to the plaintiff and, if so, how much money does the defendant owe the plaintiff in damages). Litigation has winners and losers. If the goal of the parties is to reach a compromise as a solution, litigation is not the answer.

> In the American court system, except in special circumstances, each party must pay their own attorneys' fees and costs in litigation, even if they win the case. In many countries, the party who loses the law suit pays both side's lawyers.

ALTERNATIVE DISPUTE RESOLUTION:
Any means of settling disputes without litigation.

LITIGATION:
The process of resolving a dispute through a lawsuit initiated in the court system.

PLEADINGS:
Documents filed with the court by the parties to a lawsuit. Pleadings include the complaint, answer, and counterclaims.

COMPLAINT:
A document filed by the party initiating a lawsuit which contains a brief summary of the alleged facts of the case, the claims the party is alleging, and a statement of the relief desired from the other party.

Pleadings

In a standard lawsuit, the initial documents filed by the plaintiff or defendant with a court are called the **pleadings**. The document that starts the litigation process is the **complaint**.

The complaint is a document explaining why the court has the power to hear the case, the alleged facts of the case, the legal claims against the other party, and the relief sought against the other party. The person who files the complaint is called the **plaintiff**. The party being sued is called the **defendant**.

After filing the complaint with the court, the plaintiff must serve the defendant with a copy of the complaint and a summons which are usually hand-delivered to the defendant. The summons informs the defendant of the lawsuit, in which court it will be heard, and that she must respond to the complaint within a certain number of days. Service of process is the special procedure used to ensure that the summons and complaint and other court documents are properly delivered.

As soon as the defendant receives the summons and complaint, it is best to contact a lawyer immediately, since responding to the complaint is time sensitive. The defendant may respond to the complaint in several ways.

- In most cases, the defendant files a pleading called an **answer**. In the answer, the defendant admits or denies the facts alleged in the complaint. The answer also states the legal defenses upon which the defendant will rely.

- The defendant may also file a **counterclaim**. A counterclaim is a related lawsuit involving the same basic facts that is brought by the defendant against the plaintiff. For example, if Pinnacle Company sues Radd Inc. for breach of contract, Radd Inc. may file a counterclaim against Pinnacle arguing that Pinnacle breached the implied covenant of good faith and fair dealing.

- As another option, the defendant may file a motion to dismiss. A motion to dismiss asks the court to dismiss the case outright. Motions to dismiss typically argue that the complaint does not state a valid legal claim that the court can resolve on any set of proven facts, that the court lacks the power to hear the case, or that the defendant was not properly served with the complaint. If the court grants the motion, the plaintiff may be allowed to file an amended complaint to fix whatever deficiency existed in the original complaint.

What happens if the defendant does not respond in one of these ways? For defendants, doing nothing is a poor choice. If a defendant does

PLAINTIFF:
The party who files a complaint to initiate a lawsuit against another party.

DEFENDANT:
The party who is being sued in a litigation.

ANSWER:
A written pleading filed by a defendant to respond to a complaint filed by a plaintiff in a lawsuit.

COUNTERCLAIM:
A claim asserted by the defendant against the plaintiff in a lawsuit.

UNITED STATES DISTRICT COURT
SOUTHERN DISTRICT OF INDIANA
INDIANAPOLIS DIVISION

CP PRODUCTIONS INC.,)
    Plaintiff,)
)
vs.) 1:12-cv-00808-JMS-DML
)
GERALD L. GLOVER, III,)
    Defendant.)

FINAL JUDGMENT

For the reasons set forth in the Court's contemporaneously entered Order, the Court now enters **FINAL JUDGMENT** in favor of Plaintiff and against Defendant and taxes costs in favor of Plaintiff and against Defendant for a total amount of **$151,425**. This figure includes:

1. Statutory damages of $150,000;
2. Attorneys' fees of $1,000; and
3. Costs of $425.

03/26/2013

[signature]

Hon. Jane Magnus-Stinson, Judge
United States District Court
Southern District of Indiana

Distribution via ECF only:

Matthew Edward Dumas
HOSTETTER & O'HARA
matt@hostetter-ohara.com

Distribution via U.S. Mail:

Gerald L. Glover, III
5846 Hartle Drive
Indianapolis, IN 46216

AN EXAMPLE OF A FEDERAL TRIAL COURT JUDGMENT

DISMISSAL IS APPROPRIATE ONLY IF NO SET OF FACTS CAN SUPPORT A CLAIM

Conley v. Gibson
(Black Employees) v. (Union Officers)
355 U.S. 41, 78 S. Ct. 99, 2 L. Ed. 2d 80 (1957)

INSTANT FACTS:
Black employees brought a class action against a union and its officers for not representing them or protecting their labor contract job and seniority rights.

BLACK LETTER RULE:
A complaint should not be dismissed for failure to state a claim unless it appears beyond doubt that the plaintiff can prove no set of supporting facts that would entitle him or her to relief.

PROCEDURAL BASIS:
Certiorari to review a dismissal of the complaint.

FACTS:
Conley and other Black employees (P) brought a class action against a union, its local, and its officers, alleging federal Railway Labor Act violations. The complaint alleged that the plaintiffs were employees of the Texas and New Orleans Railroad in Houston and members of Local 28 of the Brotherhood of Railway and Steamship Clerks. A collective bargaining contract between the railroad and the union gave the members seniority and job rights. The railroad purported to abolish the jobs of the Black employees, but, in reality, white employees filled most of the jobs and the few Black employees hired back lost seniority. Despite the plaintiffs' requests, the union did not protect them against the discharges and refused to give them protection comparable to that given to white employees, thereby violating the union's duty of fair representation under the Railway Labor Act. Gibson and other union officers (D) moved to dismiss on the grounds that the National Railroad Adjustment Board had exclusive jurisdiction over the claims, that the railroad had not been joined as an indispensable party, and that the complaint failed to state a claim upon which relief could be granted. The trial court dismissed on the exclusive jurisdiction ground and the Fifth Circuit Court of Appeals affirmed.

ISSUE:
Should a complaint be dismissed for failure to state a claim upon which relief may be granted only if the plaintiff cannot prove a set of facts that would entitle him or her to relief?

DECISION AND RATIONALE:
(Black, J.) Yes. A complaint should be dismissed only if there is no doubt that the plaintiff cannot prove a set of facts entitling him to relief. Here, the complaint alleged that the plaintiffs were wrongfully discharged by the railroad and that the union refused to protect their jobs or to help them with their grievances because they were Black. If proven, these allegations constitute a manifest breach of the union's statutory duty to represent fairly and without discrimination all bargaining unit members. Once a bargaining agent undertakes to represent a bargaining unit, it must represent in good faith and without discrimination all employees in the unit. The Federal Rules of Civil Procedure do not require a complaint to set forth specific facts to support general allegations of discrimination; the rules require only a "short and plain statement of the claim" that will give the defendant fair notice of the claim and the grounds upon which it rests. Following the simple guide of Rule 8(f) that "all pleadings shall be so construed as to do substantial justice," the complaint adequately sets forth a claim and gives the defendants fair notice of its basis. Pleading is not a game of skill in which one misstep of counsel may be decisive. Reversed.

ANALYSIS:
Conley is the leading case on pleading requirements under the Federal Rules of Civil Procedure. In *Conley*, the Supreme Court clearly demonstrates the liberality with which the Federal Rules of Civil Procedure approach pleading. The Court rejects two distinct arguments raised by the defendants: that no cause of action exists under the Railway Labor Act and that the complaint contains insufficient factual detail. In reaching its conclusion, the Court also dismissed the defendants' contention that the National Railroad Adjustment Board had exclusive jurisdiction and that the railroad was an indispensable party.

> **CASE VOCABULARY:**
> **CLASS ACTION:**
> A lawsuit in which a single person or a small group of people represents the interests of a larger group.

> *Example:* CP Productions sued Glover for copyright infringement, claiming that Glover had downloaded CP Productions' copyrighted work via torrent. Glover did not respond to the lawsuit. The federal district court entered a default judgment against Glover for the maximum amount allowed by law for copyright violations ($150,000), plus attorney fees, and court costs. *CP Productions Inc. v. Glover*, 1:12-cv-0080-JMS-DML (S.D. Ind. March 26, 2013).

not respond after receiving valid notice of the lawsuit, the court will enter a **default judgment** against the defendant. A default judgment is a binding ruling in favor of the plaintiff. The default judgment grants the plaintiff the damages sought against the defendant. When served with a lawsuit, an individual or company should act quickly to avoid defaulting.

Discovery

If the complaint makes a valid claim and the case continues, the parties will engage in **discovery**. Discovery is the process by which the parties in a lawsuit obtain information from each other and from witnesses. In discovery, each party requests information, documents, records, and testimony from the opposing party. Each party must respond to the requests for information and documents, locate the requested information, and produce relevant documents and other information to the other side. The purpose of discovery is to allow the parties to obtain evidence that helps their case, to make the parties aware of evidence in favor of the opposing party's position, and to narrow the questions to be decided during trial.

Special court rules apply to the discovery process. The rules define the types of information that may be requested and limit the information that must be produced. The discovery rules also govern the conduct of the parties and their attorneys during discovery. Only information relevant to the case, or likely to lead to the discovery of relevant information, must be produced to an opposing party. If a party believes that requested information is not relevant, his attorney may ask the court to deny

> **DEFAULT JUDGMENT:**
> A binding judgment entered by a court if the defendant does not respond to the plaintiff's complaint.
>
> **DISCOVERY:**
> The process by which the parties to a lawsuit obtain information from each other and from witnesses.

the request. If the court deems the information relevant, the party must produce it. If the party still refuses to do so, the requesting party's attorney may ask the court to compel the other party to produce the information. This illustrates that the process of discovery can be difficult, drawn out, and expensive.

There are different discovery tools your lawyer may use. And, as a party to the lawsuit, you will work closely with your lawyer to make certain you appropriately respond to discovery requests.

Depositions: During discovery, a party may request to take the deposition of a party or witness who has information relevant to the case. A deposition is the sworn testimony of a party or witness and is similar to providing testimony at trial. At the deposition, the party or witness answers questions asked by the attorneys for both sides in the case. The party or witness answer under oath, and a court reporter takes down everything that is said. The attorneys use depositions to obtain information for the case and to see how witnesses would perform if they were required to testify in court.

Interrogatories: Interrogatories are written questions sent to the other party. The responding party works with its attorney to prepare written answers to the questions. The answers are made under oath. Interrogatories may only be directed to parties. Unlike a deposition request, interrogatories may not be issued to witnesses who are not parties in the case.

> One party might issue the following interrogatories to the other party:
>
> INTERROGATORY NO. 1: Describe in detail the nature of Defendant's business.
>
> INTERROGATORY NO. 2: Identify all agreements and/or contracts between Plaintiff and Defendant.
>
> INTERROGATORY NO. 3: Describe the transactions covered by the first contract between Plaintiff and Defendant.
>
> The full list of interrogatories may go on for many pages, depending on the complexity of the case.

You can see from the sample interrogatories that they can be broad. The attorney will work to ensure that the questions are answered properly, revealing only as much information as is necessary and taking care to avoid answering in a way that could be used against the party in court. But they must be careful, because the court may penalize a party who fails to answer interrogatories.

Requests for Admission: Parties may also issue requests for admission. Requests for admission ask the opposing party to admit or deny facts about the case. The purpose of

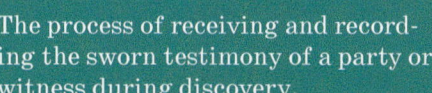

DEPOSITION:
The process of receiving and recording the sworn testimony of a party or witness during discovery.

INTERROGATORIES:
A written set of questions served by a party to a lawsuit to an opposing party during discovery. The responding party prepares written answers under oath.

In a breach of contract dispute, the plaintiff might send the following requests for admission to the defendant:

> REQUEST NO. 1: Admit that Defendant and Plaintiff entered into the Contract for Services on May 19, 2005.
>
> REQUEST NO. 2: Admit that Defendant failed or refused to pay all of the invoices issued by the Plaintiff for services provided under the Contract.

As with interrogatories, there may be many requests issued to a party.

Document requests are a different type of litigation tool, but they look very similar. A party seeking documents or records might make the following requests to the other party:

> REQUEST No. 1: Provide any and all agreements/contracts between Plaintiff and Defendant dated May 19, 2005.
>
> REQUEST No. 2: Provide all documents, including electronic documents, relating to or discussing the May 19, 2005 agreement.

requests for admission is to determine a set of facts upon which the parties agree and to avoid spending time trying to prove those facts in the courtroom.

Document Requests: Document requests are another tool used in discovery. The attorney will write the request for documents and records in the possession of the opposing party in a way to ensure that the appropriate information is provided. The request can be made for information in all mediums, including paper or electronically stored documents and audio and video recordings.

Electronic evidence has become an important part of discovery and includes all electronic documents, emails, voice mails, tweets, blogs, social media posts, files, and records. Computers and other electronic devices record a lot of information, such as who created a file and when it was created, modified, or accessed which may be very relevant to the dispute. These items are often referred to as **electronically stored information (ESI)**. Parties often find the information in and about the files, such as when a document was created or viewed, provides

REQUESTS FOR ADMISSION:

A written set of questions or statements served by a party to a lawsuit on an opposing party or witness during discovery in an effort to determine agreed-upon facts. The responding party must deny or admit each statement in writing.

DOCUMENT REQUESTS:

A written request for documents, electronically stored information, or other items issued during discovery to an opposing party.

METADATA:

Information about electronic files describing how, when, and by whom a particular set of data was collected, and how the data is formatted.

ELECTRONICALLY STORED INFORMATION (ESI):

Data or information that is stored in electronic format, including documents, emails, voice mails, tweets, blogs, social media posts, files, and other records.

Discovery Tools	
Tool	*Description*
Depositions	The process of receiving and recording sworn testimony of a party or witness. Attorneys for all parties in the case may ask questions of the deponent.
Interrogatories	Written questions submitted to the other party. The responding party must provide written answers under oath.
Requests for Admission	Written statements submitted to the other party in an effort to determine agreed-upon facts. The responding party must admit or deny each statement.
Document Requests	Written requests for records, documents, and other information, including electronically stored information, to be produced by the opposing party.

information useful to their case. Discovery rules require the parties to preserve documents and electronically stored information that may be relevant to the lawsuit if they reasonably anticipate litigation.

Several other types of information may be added to the process through discovery. For instance, scientific publications or expert reports created by third parties may provide critical information relevant to the case. Police records or reports may be important to the plaintiff or the defendant, even though the case is not a criminal matter. In short, any information relevant to the case may be part of the discovery process—including information gathered or created after the original complaint was filed.

Discovery is expensive. It takes time and costs money. The parties' attorneys may spend substantial billable time dealing with discovery requests and conducting depositions. It may also take a long time to locate, retrieve, and review documents requested by the other party. Attorney fees are not the only costs. The parties will have to devote substantial time to the discovery process: time that would otherwise be spent on their business. And, the parties may need to hire a specialist to assist them in retrieving, reconstructing, and reviewing electronically stored information. Depending on the circumstances, hundreds of thousands, if not millions, of electronic files from multiple locations around the country may need to be reviewed for a single case.

Motion Practice

Throughout litigation, the parties may file motions. A **motion** is a request to the judge to make a decision about some issue in the case. Some types of motions are frequently mentioned in legal dramas, such as:

- A motion to treat a witness as hostile (if granted, the attorney has greater leeway in the format of questions to the witness at trial).

- A motion to suppress evidence (an attorney may argue that certain evidence does not tend to prove a point, or that it is more inflammatory than relevant so that it might overly influence a jury).

- A motion to subpoena a witness (a party may ask the court to require that an absent witness appear in court for questioning by issuing an enforceable legal order—a subpoena—for the witness's presence).

As noted in a previous section, the defendant may file a motion to dismiss the case. Motions are also frequently filed during the discovery process. The parties may disagree on whether certain documents or information are relevant to the case and must be produced, whether documents may be withheld because of attorney-client privilege, or whether a party has completely responded to discovery requests. When such a dispute arises, a party may file a motion with the court asking the judge to resolve the issue.

Motion for Summary Judgment: When discovery has concluded, a party might file a motion for summary judgment. In a motion for **summary judgment**, the party is asking the court to decide the case without a trial. The court may consider the evidence gathered to that point, including sworn statements and documents obtained during discovery. Summary judgment may only be granted if there are no undisputed material, or important, facts in the case. The judge will apply the law to the facts and the evidence. The motion for summary judgment will be granted only if there is one clear result based on those settled facts. The advantage to summary judgment can be that that the case is decided without the time and cost of proceeding through the trial.

Trial

If a case goes to trial, the parties present their arguments, evidence, and witnesses to the finder of fact. The finder of fact is either a jury or the judge. On television and in movies, trials are almost always heard by a jury. The jurors attend the trial and make decisions about the facts of the case. For instance, in a negligence

---

MOTION:
A request to the judge to make a decision on an issue in a lawsuit.

SUMMARY JUDGMENT:
A judgment entered by the court deciding the case in favor of one party or the other based on application of the law to the available evidence, but without a full trial.

> **Example:**
>
> Parties to lawsuits often find that the opposing party is not eager to comply with discovery requests. A motion to compel discovery in a hypothetical case look something like the example below; it would be up to the court to grant or deny the motion.
>
> The Plaintiff, Aza Inc., by its attorney, Hugh Hugherson, moves for an Order compelling the Defendant, Bizz Corp., to promptly produce all outstanding discovery, and states grounds as follows:
>
> 1. That discovery in the form of Interrogatories and Request for Production of Documents was served on Defendant in this case on December 15, 2015.
>
> 2. That on April 1, 2016, Plaintiff requested by letter to Defendant's counsel that Answers to the Interrogatories and Requested Documents be promptly supplied.
>
> 3. That on September 1, 2016, Plaintiff requested by letter to Defendant's counsel that Answers to the Interrogatories and Requested Documents be promptly supplied.
>
> 4. That to this date, Plaintiff has not received either Answers to the Interrogatories or Requested Documents from Defendant in this matter.
>
> Wherefore, the Plaintiff moves for an Order compelling the Defendant to produce complete Answers and all of the Requested Documents within 15 days.
>
> Hugh Hugherson, Esq.

lawsuit before a jury, the jurors determine whether the defendant failed to act with reasonable care in the circumstances. The judge is responsible for the legal decisions in the case, including whether or not to grant motions. The judge also issues the decision in the case based on the jury's findings of fact.

Actually, civil juries hear relatively few cases. If the parties consent, a judge can hear the case as the finder of fact. The judge will also make legal determinations in the case. Using the judge as the finder of fact expedites the process because no jury needs to be selected for the trial. There is also no need for lengthy deliberations among jurors regarding the facts.

In a jury trial, the parties must choose a jury. **Voir dire** is the process of questioning potential jurors in order to determine who will serve on the jury. The purpose of *voir dire* is to ask prospective jurors questions that might expose conflicts of interest or bias for or against the plaintiff or defendant. Out of the pool of potential jurors, lawyers for each side will eliminate individuals whom they believe cannot fairly judge the facts of the case. When the pool is narrowed down to enough individuals to make up the jury, or when the attorneys have used all their opportunities to eliminate potential jurors, the remaining candidates are sworn in as the jury.

Once the jury is sworn in, the plaintiff presents his case first. During the plaintiff's case, the defendant may object to the evidence presented. The defendant may also cross-examine the plaintiff's witnesses.

After the plaintiff's case, outside the presence of the jury, the defendant may make a motion for a **directed verdict**, also referred to as a motion for **judgment as a matter of law** in federal courts. This motion asks the judge to issue a verdict in favor of the defendant because the plaintiff has not presented enough evidence to justify an decision in the plaintiff's favor. If the judge grants the motion, the trial is over and the defendant wins. If the judge denies the motion, the defendant then presents its evidence, to which the plaintiff's attorney can object, and its witnesses, whom the plaintiff's attorney can cross-examine. After the defendant's case, the attorneys present closing arguments.

The judge then instructs the jury regarding the law applicable to the case. The jurors go to the jury room to deliberate and reach a verdict in favor of one of the parties. The jury may also need to decide on the amount of damages if they find one of the parties liable. After the jury has left the courtroom, either side can also move the court for a directed verdict or judgment as a matter of law.

Post-Trial Motions

Once the jury issues a verdict, the parties may file post-trial motions. One type of post-trial motion is a motion for **judgment notwithstanding the verdict (JNOV)**, also called a judgment as a matter of law in federal court. In a motion for JNOV, the requesting party asks the court to set aside the jury's verdict and enter judgment in her favor. It is rare for a judge to

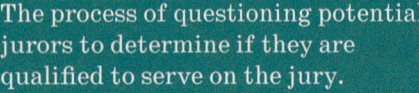

VOIR DIRE:
The process of questioning potential jurors to determine if they are qualified to serve on the jury.

DIRECTED VERDICT:
A ruling in a lawsuit entered by the trial judge after a determination that a reasonable jury could not reach a different conclusion.

JUDGMENT NOTWITHSTANDING THE VERDICT:
A judgment entered by the trial judge which reverses a jury verdict because the judge finds that there was no factual basis for the verdict or it was contrary to law.

set aside a jury verdict. A judge will only do so if no reasonable jury could have reached that verdict based on the evidence presented at trial.

A party may also file a **motion for a new trial**. In this motion, the party is asking the judge to set aside the jury verdict and hold a new trial. A motion for a new trial may be granted for a number of reasons. If the judge believes the jury made a mistake or returned an excessive verdict, if new evidence was brought forward, if an attorney or jurors behaved improperly, if the judge made a mistake when instructing the jury, or if other errors occurred, the motion may be granted, and the litigation process would begin again.

Appeal

Either party may **appeal** the verdict or the judge's decision on motions filed during the case if they are unhappy with the result. A party must have sufficient legal grounds to challenge the verdict or ruling and will work with their lawyer to determine whether an appeal is likely to be successful. The appealing party must show that the trial judge made appealable error and can meet the appropriate standard of review. There are three primary categories of decisions that may be reviewed on appeal and each has its own standard. Findings of fact are reviewable for clear error. This means that the court of appeal may not set aside a jury's findings of fact unless they are clearly erroneous. Even if the appellate court may have reviewed the evidence differently, they cannot set aside the findings of fact if they are plausible. This is because the trial judge or jury had the opportunity to see and judge a witness' credibility. A judges conclusion of law can be reviewed *de novo*, which means that the court of appeal can review a legal decision, such as whether to grant a motion for summary judgment, without giving weight to the trial court's decision. This is because courts of appeal are responsible for correcting errors interpreting the law and for developing precedent. If a party decides to appeal, that party must file the appeal within a specified number of days. The appealing party must file a notice of appeal with the trial court where the case was decided. The appealing party is called the **appellant** or **petitioner**. The opposing party is called the **appellee** or **respondent**.

The appellant files the appeal with the appropriate appellate court. Appellate courts at the state level can include courts of appeal and state supreme courts.

APPEAL:
Review of a trial court decision by a higher court.

APPELLANT OR PETITIONER:
The party who files an appeal of a court decision.

APPELLEE OR RESPONDENT:
The party responding to an appeal filed by the other party.

> Most states call their top appellate court the state's supreme court, but New York and Maryland's top appellate courts are both called the Court of Appeals.

On appeal, the case is presented to and decided by a judge or a panel of judges. The appellant must provide the appellate court with a copy of the trial court record of the case. The record includes a copy of the trial transcript, all documents and motions filed in the trial court, and orders issued by the trial court. The appellate court may only consider evidence contained within the record. Each party files a **brief**. A brief is a party's written legal argument. The appellant's brief summarizes of the facts of the case, the issues being appealed, the applicable law, and the reasons that the trial court decision should be reversed. The appellee files an answering brief setting forth its opposing arguments and why the trial court's decision was correct. Sometimes, someone who was not a party to the case will file an *amicus curiae*, or friend of the court brief, providing legal arguments favoring either the appellantt, appellee, or neither party.

After the parties have filed their briefs, the court reviews the documents and hears **oral argument**. At the oral argument, the attorneys present their cases orally to the appellate judges and answer questions from the judges. After oral argument, the appellate judges confer

> **BRIEF:**
> A written legal argument submitted to the court.
>
> **ORAL ARGUMENT:**
> Spoken presentation of arguments to the appeals court by attorneys for the parties appearing in person.

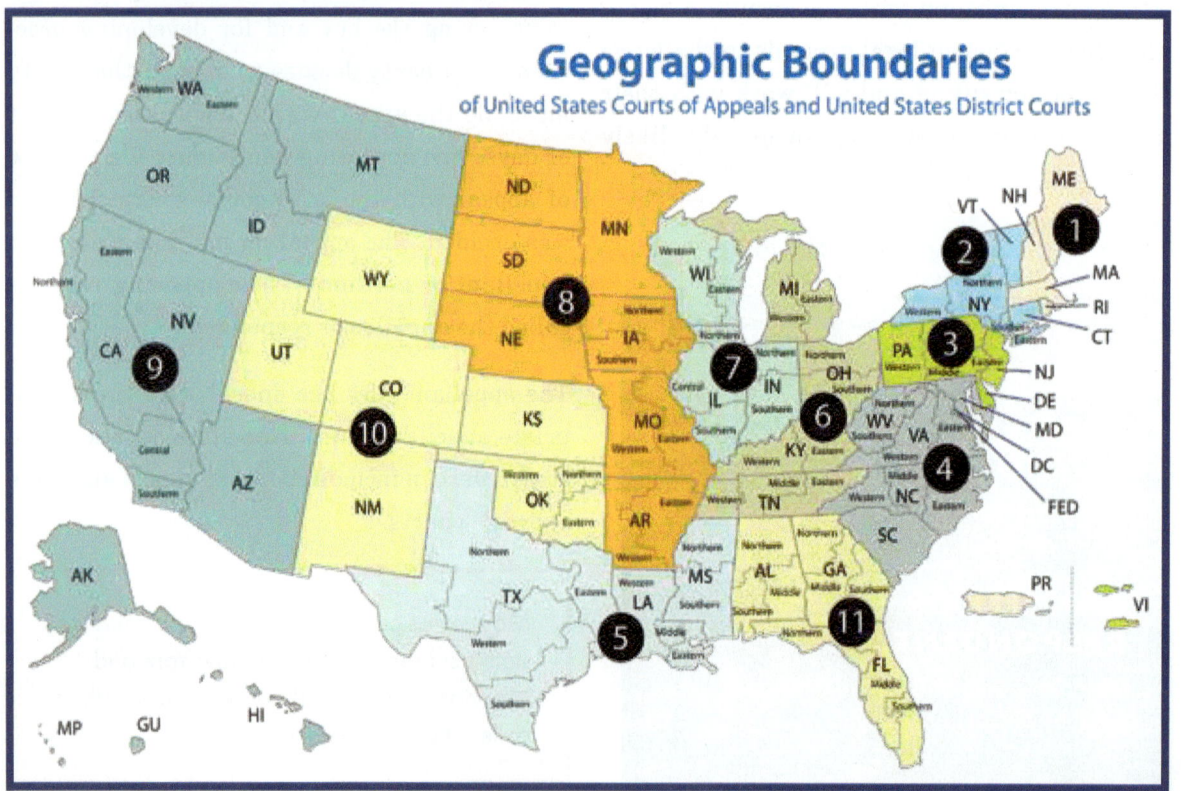

and then issue a written opinion. The appellate court may take one of the following actions: **affirm** (uphold) or **reverse** the trial court decision in whole or in part, **modify** the decision, or **remand** (send back) the case to the trial court to re-hear the case taking into account the appellate court's decision.

The losing party on appeal may **petition** to the highest state or federal court. The highest court of a state is usually called the **supreme court** (although both New York and Maryland call this court the "Court of Appeals"). The petition sets out reasons why the lower court made a mistake interpreting and important area of law and asks the supreme court to review the case to fix the mistake so that the law will be clear. The supreme court decides which cases it will review. A party does not have the right to have its case heard by the supreme court. In fact, only a small percentage of petitions are granted by state supreme courts or by the U.S. Supreme Court.

If a petition for review is granted, the parties must file new briefs and present oral arguments before the supreme court panel. The supreme court may affirm, reverse, modify, or remand the decision.

SUPREME COURT:
The highest appellate court in a jurisdiction.

WRIT OF CERTIORARI:
Permission to have a case heard by the U.S. Supreme Court that is given by the Court in response to a petition by the appealing party.

For federal cases, appeals from federal trial courts are heard by the federal circuit courts. If a party wishes further review after losing at the state supreme court or the federal circuit court, the party must file a petition for a **writ of certiorari** with the U.S. Supreme Court. The U.S. Supreme Court only hears cases after (1) all other appellate options for the issue have been exhausted, and (2) the Court grants a writ of certiorari meaning that it will hear the case. While some say that they will "take it all the way to the Supreme Court," the U.S. Supreme Court only hears cases that it chooses to review. For most parties, there is no right to be heard by the Supreme Court.

Once all of these avenues for appeal have been exhausted, or petitions denied, the case is concluded.

II. Alternative Dispute Resolution

The entire litigation and appellate process can go on for several years. Each separate part of the process can take many months, or even years. The process can also be slow because the courts must work through a heavy load of cases. For these and other reasons, parties are increasingly using Alternative Dispute Resolution ("ADR") to resolve business disputes. ADR may provide time and cost savings, although it can still be expensive. ADR also gives the parties more control over the process, allows for creative solutions, and may help preserve their business relationship. We now look at the various types of alternative dispute resolution available to business entities and individuals.

The Litigation Process

- Plaintiff initiates lawsuit by filing a complaint with the court
- Defendant responds by filing an answer, counterclaim, or motion to dismiss
- The parties engage in discovery process
- The parties may file motions related to discovery or other issues
- The parties engage in voir dire process to determine jurors for trial
- Plaintiff's attorney gives his opening statement to the jury
- Defendant's attorney gives her opening statement to the jury
- Plaintiff's attorney presents his case to the jury; defendant cross-examines witnesses
- Defendant may move for a directed verdict
- Defendant's attorney presents her case to the jury; plaintiff cross-examines witnesses
- Parties present closing arguments
- Jury deliberates and returns verdict
- Judge may consider post-trial motions filed by the parties, such as a motion for a new trial, or motion for judgment notwithstanding the verdict
- Losing party may appeal if there are legal grounds to be decided on appeal
- If appealed, the parties must submit briefs to the appellate court

Negotiation and Settlement

At any point during the litigation process, or even before litigation has begun, the parties may decide to deal with the case outside of court. The parties will discuss the issues to determine whether there is a way to resolve the problem. This process of informal dispute resolution between the parties is called **negotiation**. The goal of negotiation is to **settle** the case by reaching an agreement on how to resolve the dispute. Negotiation to solve the business problem is often a good place to start prior to filing a case in court or arbitration. It gives the parties an avenue to amicably settle their differences and to preserve what could be a valuable business relationship. While not a formal type of alternative dispute resolution, negotiation leading to settlement is a very common alternative to litigation. Negotiations can take place at a meeting of the parties, by phone, email, or other means. The parties' attorneys may not even be involved in these conversations. If the negotiations are successful, the parties will agree to a settlement. If the settlement is reached prior to a law suit being filed, it may take the form of a new agreement or contract terms between the parties. If it is after a law suit has begun, the defendant may agree to pay a sum of money in exchange for the plaintiff dismissing the case.

Sometimes, the parties may even negotiate a settlement after a verdict, if one party plans to appeal the trial court's judgment. In that situation, the parties may agree to a payment of some part of the damages awarded in exchange for agreeing not to file an appeal. A settlement may take many forms, depending on the circumstances and remedies sought by the parties.

The parties typically sign a written settlement agreement stating the terms agreed to between them. After the parties have signed the agreement, it becomes a legally binding contract.

Settlement agreements usually will not include a statement concerning whether one party was liable or not. Many settlement agreements are confidential and the parties agree to not disclose the terms to which they have agreed.

A large majority of lawsuits today end in settlement. Parties choose settlement for a variety of reasons. Parties may wish to resolve the dispute quickly, rather than waiting years for litigation to conclude. Extended litigation may require corporate employees or business owners to spend a lot of time dealing with a case. If so, the lawsuit may distract the owner and employees from the ongoing work of the business. The parties may also wish to avoid the expense and uncertainty of trial.

Reputation may be another reason to settle. The parties may prefer settlement to avoid the public nature of litigation. Documents or other evidence produced for trial may reveal embarrassing details or facts about the parties, or may otherwise harm a party's public image. Furthermore, the adversarial nature of litigation often permanently damages the relationship between the parties. If the parties value the business relationship, a negotiated settlement is often the best choice. For all of these reasons and others, negotiation and settlement is a popular option for many parties involved in business disputes.

Mediation

In **mediation**, the parties to a lawsuit work with a neutral third party, or **mediator**, to help them reach a resolution. It may be useful to think of meditation as using a neutral person to help

> **NEGOTIATION:**
> A method of alternative dispute resolution in which the parties, either with or without their attorneys, work to reach a resolution.
>
> **SETTLE/SETTLEMENT:**
> Agreed final resolution of a dispute outside of court.

the parties negotiate a settlement. The form of the mediation process takes can change from one mediation to another. Although the parties are free to adopt any rules they wish for mediations, various ADR organizations provide rules and can help the parties select a mediator. Popular organizations providing mediation services include the American arbitration Association (AAA), Judicial Arbitration and Mediation Services, Inc. (JAMS), and for international disputes, the International Chamber of Commerce (ICC). Typically, the mediator meets with each party separately and then meets with the parties jointly. Each party usually presents to the mediator a brief summary of the facts, evidence, and argument in support of their position. The mediator is likely to explain to each party what he views as the strengths and weaknesses of each side's position. The mediator tries to help the parties find common ground and a resolution to which both parties can agree.

The mediator does not issue a decision regarding the case. Rather, if the mediator has been successful helping the parties to resolve their issue, there may be a settlement agreement, much the same as that in a negotiated settlement. Mediation does not require the parties to settle the case (although they may agree to be bound by the mediator's recommendation). Generally, because the parties are involved in finding a solution to the conflict, mediation should be less adversarial and contentious than litigation. As such, mediation is particularly useful in disputes between parties in long-term business relationships, such as business partners or employers and employees.

If the parties agree to the process, they may voluntarily attempt mediation at any time. In some instances, a court may require the parties to attempt mediation or some other form of ADR during the pre-trial stages of litigation. Although the parties are not required to reach a settlement in court-mandated mediation, they must cooperate in good faith with the mediation process.

Even before the COVID-19 pandemic, some disputes were resolved through online mediation, a form of online dispute resolution (ODR). In online mediation, the process is completed through the internet and electronic technologies, such as video-conferencing and electronic sharing of documents. There are many advantages to online mediation. It can be much less expensive and give the parties more flexibility, since they are not required to travel to meet for mediation. The costs are also lowered because there is no need to pay for a meeting location. ODR, including online mediation, is successful and widely used. By some estimates, 60 million disputes between traders on Ebay are solved every year through ODR.

Typically, the parties will share the cost of mediator fees. In some circumstances, such as where one party has more resources than the other, one party may agree to pay all mediation fees. The parties may agree to any related

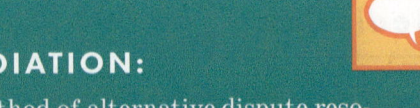

MEDIATION:
A method of alternative dispute resolution in which the parties work with a neutral third party, a mediator, in an attempt to reach a settlement.

details about the mediation, including, but not limited to, who the mediator will be and where the mediation will take place.

Arbitration

Arbitration is another form of alternative dispute resolution. Arbitration requires a contract between the parties who agree to have their disputes decided a neutral third party, the **arbitrator**. Because parties arbitrate by agreement, they have a great deal of flexibility in determining many factors, including which rules will govern the proceedings and where the dispute will be heard. The parties may agree to use a panel of three arbitrators rather than a single decision maker. The arbitrator's decision is called an **award**. Arbitration is similar to litigation in a number of ways. It is an adversarial proceeding in which each side presents its case. It is typically less formal than litigation with fewer avenues to discovery. Typically, the arbitration award is binding on the parties in the way a litigation judgment is binding. But, the parties may agree to engage in nonbinding arbitration.

It is difficult to successfully appeal an arbitration award because court review of an arbitration award is more limited than review of a court decision. An arbitration award will only be set aside or modified for a few reasons, such as the arbitrator engaged in serious misconduct or exceeded his authority by deciding an issue outside the scope of the arbitration agreement, or the award violates public policy.

Parties to an arbitration will typically choose a set of arbitration rules that will apply. There are different arbitration providers, like the American Arbitration Association (AAA) that provide rules for how the arbitration will proceed. At an arbitration hearing, the parties usually give opening statements and present evidence and witnesses to the arbitrator, as they could in a trial. But, arbitration is usually less formal than a court proceeding. The procedural and evidence rules are often more relaxed during arbitration than in court. Certain types of evidence that may not be allowed in a court proceeding may be permitted in an arbitration. The discovery process in arbitration is usually limited and less burdensome than in litigation.

Parties generally choose arbitration because the process is typically faster and less expensive than trial. Often, the finality of the decision and limited ground to appeal are seen as a benefit. Parties may also prefer that arbitration because unlike litigation, which is a public event, arbitration is private and between the parties. Unlike a court case that could be reported in the news, arbitration may be kept confidential. Another possible advantage of arbitration is that the parties typically select the arbitrator or panel who will decide the case.

> **ARBITRATION:**
> A method of alternative dispute resolution in which the parties present their case to one or more neutral parties, called arbitrators, who issue a binding decision on the parties.
>
> **AWARD:**
> The final decision of the arbitrator in an arbitration proceeding.

It is possible to choose an arbitrator with expertise in the particular issue in the case, like residential real estate or international contracts. In some circumstances, the parties may prefer litigation to arbitration because they prefer to have a jury decide the case, they wish to have a public record of the case, they want a judicial decision on a particular aspect of the law, or they want the ability to formally appeal the decision.

> Because the parties choose to arbitrate by contract, they are free to choose *ad hoc* arbitration, where they make up the rules. Most businesses would choose institutional arbitration. There are a number of mediation and arbitration organizations that provide rules for ADR, help the parties find mediators and arbitrators, and provide venues where the cases can be heard. AAA and JAMS are two examples.

Parties may agree to arbitrate a dispute at any time after the dispute has arisen, even after the dispute is already in litigation. In many instances, though, the parties agree to arbitrate any future disputes between them before any dispute occurs. Commercial contracts often include an **arbitration clause**. An arbitration clause states that if a dispute arises, the parties will resolve the dispute through binding arbitration. An agreement to binding arbitration means that the parties give up their day in court. This type of arbitration, agreed to by the parties in a contract, is often referred to as private arbitration.

> **Sample Arbitration Clause**
>
> The arbitration organizations will have sample arbitration clauses that anyone can use. What follows is the AAA's standard clause: "Any controversy or claim arising out of or relating to this contract, or the breach thereof, shall be settled by arbitration administered by the American Arbitration Association in accordance with its Commercial Arbitration Rules. The arbitration hearing shall take place in _____, before a single arbitrator."

The parties to arbitration may decide which disputes an arbitrator may decide. The AAA clause above is appropriate if the parties want the arbitration to decide everything. Some arbitration clauses limit arbitration to only certain types of disputes between the parties. For instance, an arbitration clause might state that "all employment disputes" must be submitted to arbitration. The arbitration clause may indicate that the parties split the cost of arbitration, or state that the losing party pays the costs. The written agreement will determine this issue. However, if the parties don't decide this in their agreement, the arbitration rules they have chosen provide the answer. For example, the AAA Commercial Arbitration Rules require each party to pay for its own witnesses, while all other expenses, including the arbitrator's compensation and expenses, are split

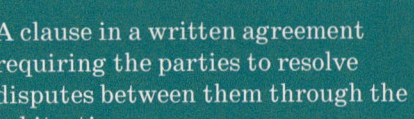

ARBITRATION CLAUSE:
A clause in a written agreement requiring the parties to resolve disputes between them through the arbitration process.

ARBITRATION CLAUSES ARE ENFORCEABLE IN EMPLOYMENT CONTRACTS

Sanchez v. Nitro-Lift Technologies, LLC
762 F.3d 1139 (10th Cir. 2014)

INSTANT FACTS:
Employers moved to compel employees to submit the dispute to arbitration to resolve employees' claim for overtime wages.

BLACK LETTER RULE:
Arbitration clauses are valid and enforceable contract clauses, unless the provision denies one party a substantive right provided by statute.

FACTS:
Nitro-Lift is a corporation in the business of servicing oil rigs. The plaintiffs were employees of Nitro-Lift who worked in Oklahoma. At the start of employment with Nitro-Lift, the employees signed a "Confidentiality/Non-Compete Agreement." That agreement contained an arbitration clause stating that "any disputes" between Nitro-Lift and the employee "shall be settled by arbitration by a single arbitrator . . . conducted in Houston, Texas."

The employees filed suit in federal court, claiming the company failed to pay overtime wages in violation of the Fair Labor Standards Act. The company responded by filing a motion to compel arbitration. The employer company argued that the employees were required to submit their claims to arbitration under the arbitration clause in the Confidentiality Agreement. The employees argued that their dispute did not fall within the scope of the arbitration clause and that the clause was unfair to them because they did not agree to arbitration, they were not given an opportunity to read the clause, and enforcement of the clause would cause them to incur substantial costs. The trial court denied the company's motion, finding that the overtime claim was outside the scope of the clause because the clause was contained in the Confidentiality Agreement and did not apply to claims unrelated to that agreement. The company appealed that decision.

ISSUE:
Is an arbitration clause enforceable against employees in a dispute regarding violations of the Fair Labor Standards Act?

DECISION AND RATIONALE:
Yes. On appeal, the court reversed the trial court decision. The court noted that the Federal Arbitration Act states that arbitration agreements are valid and enforceable, and that federal policy favors arbitration. The court also utilized a three-part test to determine whether the clause was broad or narrow, and whether the dispute at issue fell within the purview of the clause. The court determined that the clause was very broad, and in light of the presumption in favor of arbitrability, the dispute fell within the broad scope of the clause.

The appellate court also remanded the case to the trial court to determine whether the clause was enforceable because it required costs to be borne by the losing party or split between the parties, which contradicts the FLSA's provision providing fees only to a prevailing plaintiff, not a prevailing defendant.

ANALYSIS:
Although courts were originally skeptical of and disfavored arbitration, this decision demonstrates the courts' significant change in attitude toward arbitration following passage of the Federal Arbitration Act. Even though the parties were not of equal bargaining power, the clause was contained in a Confidentiality Agreement, and the employees claimed not to have read the clause, they were still bound to its terms by signing the agreement. This case is also important because it shows how the interplay with other contract provisions may affect the enforceability of an arbitration clause. Here, the provision regarding attorneys' fees, which might seem to be an independent issue, could render the arbitration clause unenforceable with respect to this claim.

between the parties. Compare that with the ICC rules for international arbitration which gives the arbitrator the power to decide which party will pay the costs of arbitration, or how those costs will be split.

Private arbitration agreements will be governed by both state arbitration laws and the Federal Arbitration Act (FAA). Historically, some courts were hostile to arbitration agreements, preferring that disputes remain in the courts. The FAA provides that commercial arbitration agreements "shall be valid, irrevocable, and enforceable, save upon such grounds as exist in law or in equity for the revocation of any contract." This means that unless there is fraud, unconscionability, or other reason to not enforce the clause, the courts will uphold the arbitration agreement.

As with mediation, online arbitration is a form of ODR. It can be advantageous in that the parties may participate from anywhere in the world. Even before the COVID-19 epidemic, there had been a rise in online arbitrations, particularly in international commercial disputes. Many of

---

THE FEDERAL ARBITRATION ACT PRE-EMPTS STATE ARBITRATION RULES

AT&T Mobility LLC (Defendant) v. Concepcion (Plaintiff)
(Cellular Service Company) v. (Cell Service Customer)
563 U.S. 333, 131 S. Ct. 1740, 179 L. Ed. 2d 742 (2011)

Justice Scalia delivered the opinion of the Court.

Section 2 of the Federal Arbitration Act (FAA) makes agreements to arbitrate "valid, irrevocable, and enforceable, save upon such grounds as exist at law or in equity for the revocation of any contract." We consider whether the FAA prohibits States from conditioning the enforceability of certain arbitration agreements on the availability of classwide arbitration procedures. In February 2002, Vincent and Liza Concepcion entered into an agreement for the sale and servicing of cellular telephones with AT&T Mobility LCC (AT&T). The contract provided for arbitration of all disputes between the parties, but required that claims be brought in the parties' "individual capacity, and not as a plaintiff or class member in any purported class or representative proceeding." The agreement authorized AT&T to make unilateral amendments, which it did to the arbitration provision on several occasions. The version at issue in this case reflects revisions made in December 2006, which the parties agree are controlling.

The revised agreement provides that customers may initiate dispute proceedings by completing a one-page Notice of Dispute form available on AT&T's Web site. AT&T may then offer to settle the claim; if it does not, or if the dispute is not resolved within 30 days, the customer may invoke arbitration by filing a separate Demand for Arbitration, also available on AT&T's Web site. In the event the parties proceed to arbitration, the agreement specifies that AT&T must pay all costs for nonfrivolous claims; that arbitration must take place in the county in which the customer is billed; that, for claims of $10,000 or less, the customer may choose whether the arbitration proceeds in person, by telephone, or based only on submissions; that either party may bring a claim in small claims court in lieu of arbitration; and that the arbitrator may award any form of individual relief, including injunctions and presumably punitive damages. The agreement, moreover, denies AT&T any ability to seek reimbursement of its attorney's fees, and, in the event that a customer receives an arbitration award greater than AT&T's last written settlement offer, requires AT&T to pay a $7,500 minimum recovery and twice the amount of the claimant's attorney's fees.

The Concepcions purchased AT&T service, which was advertised as including the provision of free phones; they were not charged for the phones, but they were charged $30.22 in sales tax based on the phones' retail value. In March 2006, the Concepcions filed a complaint against AT&T in

> the United States District Court for the Southern District of California. The complaint was later consolidated with a putative class action alleging, among other things, that AT&T had engaged in false advertising and fraud by charging sales tax on phones it advertised as free.
>
> In March 2008, AT&T moved to compel arbitration under the terms of its contract with the Concepcions. The Concepcions opposed the motion, contending that the arbitration agreement was unconscionable and unlawfully exculpatory under California law because it disallowed classwide procedures. The District Court denied AT&T's motion. It described AT&T's arbitration agreement favorably, noting, for example, that the informal dispute-resolution process was "quick, easy to use" and likely to "promp[t] full or . . . even excess payment to the customer without the need to arbitrate or litigate"; that the $7,500 premium functioned as "a substantial inducement for the consumer to pursue the claim in arbitration" if a dispute was not resolved informally; and that consumers who were members of a class would likely be worse off. Nevertheless, relying on the California Supreme Court's decision in *Discover Bank v. Superior Court* (2005), the court found that the arbitration provision was unconscionable because AT&T had not shown that bilateral arbitration adequately substituted for the deterrent effects of class actions.
>
> The Ninth Circuit affirmed, also finding the provision unconscionable under California law as announced in the *Discover Bank* [case]. It also held that the *Discover Bank* rule was not preempted by the FAA because that rule was simply "a refinement of the unconscionability analysis applicable to contracts generally in California." In response to AT&T's argument that the Concepcions' interpretation of California law discriminated against arbitration, the Ninth Circuit rejected the contention that " 'class proceedings will reduce the efficiency and expeditiousness of arbitration' " and noted that " '*Discover Bank* placed arbitration agreements with class action waivers on the exact same footing as contracts that bar class action litigation outside the context of arbitration.' "
>
> The "principal purpose" of the FAA is to "ensur[e] that private arbitration agreements are enforced according to their terms." This purpose is readily apparent from the FAA's text.
>
> Contrary to the dissent's view, our cases place it beyond dispute that the FAA was designed to promote arbitration. They have repeatedly described the Act as "embod[ying] [a] national policy favoring arbitration," and "a liberal federal policy favoring arbitration agreements, notwithstanding any state substantive or procedural policies to the contrary."
>
> California's *Discover Bank* rule interferes with arbitration. [. . .] Because it "stands as an obstacle to the accomplishment and execution of the full purposes and objectives of Congress," California's *Discover Bank* rule is preempted by the FAA. The judgment of the Ninth Circuit is reversed, and the case is remanded for further proceedings consistent with this opinion.
>
> It is so ordered.

the domestic and international arbitration institutions have provided guidance for using videoconferencing for hearings and have support staff with expertise to help the parties.

Other Kinds of ADR

Although negotiation, mediation, and binding arbitration are the traditional forms of ADR, a number of other types of ADR may also be used. Some states may require litigation parties to use **judicial arbitration**. The decision is not binding on the parties unless a party fails to reject the decision within a certain amount of time. In a **mini-trial**, the parties present their arguments to a third party who issues an advisory opinion setting forth the third party's conclusion as to how a court would decide the case. The opinion is not binding on the parties.

Many of these other types of ADR are a combination of the three main forms of ADR. For example, in **binding mediation**, the parties attempt mediation. If the parties cannot reach agreement, they must follow a binding decision issued by the mediator. Similarly, in **mediation-arbitration**, the parties attempt to mediate the case. If they cannot resolve the dispute, the dispute is then submitted to arbitration.

> **JUDICIAL ARBITRATION:** Arbitration that is required by a statute, court, court rule, or regulation, but is not binding on the parties.
>
> **MINI-TRIAL:** A method of alternative dispute resolution in which the parties present their arguments to a third party who issues an advisory opinion.
>
> **BINDING MEDIATION:** A method of alternative dispute resolution in which the parties attempt mediation, but if they do not reach an agreement, they agree to follow a binding decision issued by the mediator.
>
> **MEDIATION-ARBITRATION:** A method of alternative dispute resolution in which the parties attempt to mediate the case, and if they do not resolve the dispute, the dispute is then submitted to arbitration.
>
> **SUMMARY JURY TRIAL:** A method of alternative dispute resolution in which the parties engage in a short mock trial and a jury issues a non-binding verdict. The purpose is to encourage the parties to settle the case based on the verdict result.

In some federal courts, the courts are using **summary jury trials** as another type of alternative dispute resolution. The summary jury trial is essentially a mock trial in which the parties present their case to a jury. The jury issues a verdict, but the verdict is not binding on the parties. The parties are required to attend negotiations following the summary jury trial.

III. Avoiding Disputes

Even for the most prepared business parties, disputes among entities, partners, customers, employees, and individuals are inevitable. Dispute resolution, in any form, can be a difficult, expensive, and unpleasant experience. Thus, many commercial parties look for ways to avoid, or at least minimize, potential disputes in their business relationships.

Contract Negotiation

Most business relationships are governed by contracts setting forth the actions to be taken or avoided by both parties. Through the process of negotiation, the parties propose contract terms and agree to or reject terms proposed by the other party. Business parties should take care in preparing commercial agreements. The agreement should be in writing and clearly state, in detail, what each party is expected to do. Disputes often arise when agreements do not clearly describe expectations and consequences. To avoid future misunderstandings or disagreements, the contract should avoid vague or confusing terms that are subject to multiple interpretations.

Summary of Alternative Dispute Resolution Methods

Type of ADR	Key Features
Negotiation	• Parties work together to resolve dispute • Attorneys may or may not be involved • Purpose is to reach a settlement
Mediation	• Third party neutral works with parties • Purpose is to reach a settlement
Arbitration	• Parties present evidence, witnesses, and arguments to arbitrator(s) • Arbitrator is neutral third party • Arbitrator(s) issue a binding award • Limited ability to appeal the decision
Mini-Trial	• Parties present evidence, witnesses, and arguments to a third party • Third party issues advisory opinion
Summary Jury Trial	• Parties present evidence, witnesses, and arguments to a jury • Jury issues nonbinding verdict • Parties must attempt mediation

It is often difficult for the parties to imagine the need to end the relationship when a business relationship is just beginning. A well-written contract will provide terms regarding termination of the relationship. Circumstances change and businesses frequently need to modify their business relationships. A clear and thorough contract can help make business transactions and transitions proceed smoothly.

The parties must also consider areas of possible conflict. Although it is impossible to anticipate every potential scenario, the contract should address how the parties will handle common situations that might arise. For example, the contract might state what happens if one party fails to pay an invoice on time, which is a common and foreseeable occurrence.

Business contracts frequently include a dispute resolution a **choice of forum** clause that specifies where the lawsuit must be filed in the event of a dispute. Another form of forum selection is the arbitration clause, in which the parties agree to resolve disputes through arbitration. If arbitration is selected as the forum, the parties may chose the **situs**, or place in which the arbitration will occur.

Other frequently used contract terms provide guidance should litigation occur. The parties might agree to attempt mediation before one of them may file a lawsuit or arbitration.

The parties may also include a **choice of law clause** in their contract, agreeing in advance that the law of a particular state or country will govern the dispute. Lawyers, who understand the requirements of different jurisdiction's laws, will be instrumental in this process. Including a choice of forum and choice of law clause in the contract is a good idea. It can save time and makes the place where the dispute will be settled more predictable.

Maintaining Business Relationships

While it may seem obvious, many business parties overlook the importance of maintaining a good working relationship after a deal is in place. In addition to other benefits, maintaining strong business relationships with partners and associates can address issues before they become full-blown disputes. Parties may wish to hold regular status or "check-in" meetings to address any issues that have arisen during the course of doing business. The purpose of these meetings is to keep the lines of communication open and to work through small issues. The goal is to avoid large-scale disputes that require expensive or extensive dispute resolution efforts.

Cultural Issues

In today's world, business is a global enterprise. Businesses engage in commercial activity with business entities, partners, suppliers, vendors, employees, and customers in all

> The perception of time and its value vary widely from culture to culture. American businesspeople are often interested in "getting to work" when negotiating in other countries. But their negotiating partners may value the time learning about negotiating partners and their businesses. In Mexico, the relationship is critical to a business deal, and an American urge to skip social events to focus on business may sink the deal.
>
> In some cultures, the need for consensus may slow the negotiation process. For instance, Chinese companies tend to involve more team members in decisions, and may bring more people than expected to meetings. Because consensus is an important aspect of decision-making in China, reaching an acceptable solution for all parties is critical. Other cultures might bring multiple negotiators, but have one leader who can make faster decisions.
>
> Cultural and other issues can also influence how parties will solve a dispute, although globalization is minimizing the difference. Nevertheless, in some Asian Pacific countries with cultures stressing harmony and compromise, mediation may be the preferred method for resolving disputes.
>
> Because many countries will not enforce litigation judgments from other countries, but will enforce arbitration awards, international arbitration is a good choice.

parts of the globe. This means that commercial entities routinely work with people from all different cultures. In addition to cultural norms varying from country to country, business practice and laws can differ greatly as businesses move around the world. For instance, in some cultures, a party may say "yes" to indicate acknowledgement or understanding. In other cultures, "yes" indicates agreement or acceptance. Likewise, some cultures tend to use unwritten handshake agreements in their business dealings. They may be suspicious of exhaustive written agreements. In other places, the parties prefer a written agreement detailing the business relationship.

When conducting business with parties in a different country, it is useful to gain a basic understanding of the culture there. On some occasions, commercial entities hire an advisor who has knowledge and experience working in a particular country to assist them with their business relationships. In the event of a dispute, cultural differences may become very important. If the parties decide to use a method of ADR involving a third party, such as a mediator or arbitrator, the parties may achieve best results by selecting a third party who has an understanding of the parties' cultural backgrounds as well as the particular kind of business dispute.

CHAPTER SUMMARY

Engaging in business is not a solo activity. It necessarily involves communication, collaboration, and competition with other businesses and individuals. This constant interaction with others presents many opportunities for disputes to arise. An understanding of the available methods of dispute resolution is therefore critical for everyone in the business world.

When a dispute happens, business parties have many options to consider. In some circumstances, the parties may choose the formal litigation process to resolve a dispute. Increasingly, however, parties are looking for alternatives to the often lengthy and expensive litigation process. Several methods of alternative dispute resolution, including negotiation, mediation, arbitration and forms of online dispute resolution, are frequently used by business parties to address disputes outside of the courtroom. Depending on the circumstances, these ADR methods may be less expensive, provide a quicker result, preserve the business relationship, and allow the parties more control over the resolution process.

CAREERS IN THE LAW

Trained mediators provide an important service to parties that want to resolve a dispute. While many arbitrators are attorneys or retired judges, mediators fill a different space in dispute resolution. Mediators work with parties to find a way forward. A mediator's role is more collaborative than the job of an arbitrator, who actually rules on the issue. Instead, mediators work directly with the parties to reach an agreement on the underlying dispute. The work involves a great deal of care and diplomacy. Mediators need not hold a law degree, but they usually must complete 20 to 40 hours of state-mandated training to work in mediation. Mediation jobs are in demand. If you are interested in mediation, check with the National Association of Certified Mediators to learn more.

Review Questions

Review question 1.
What are the different ways that a case may end up at the U.S. Supreme Court? How does a party bring a case before the Court? What are the Court's responsibilities to parties appealing a case?

Review question 2.
A plaintiff starts a lawsuit by filing a complaint. How may the defendant respond? What do the different types of responses achieve? What is the outcome if the defendant does not take action when served with a lawsuit? Would this result change if the defendant said that she had not received notice of the lawsuit?

Review question 3.
What are some reasons that a party might make a motion to the court? What are some different types of motions, and what are their desired outcomes? Which types of motions might occur in discovery or pre-trial? Which motions might be made at trial? How can a granted motion end a lawsuit?

Review question 4.
What happens during the discovery process? What tools can the parties use? How could one party use discovery strategically to force settlement? How could the court control discovery requests?

Review question 5.
What are the main types of alternative dispute resolution? What are the advantages of each? The disadvantages? Which appeals to you most and why?

Review question 6.
What is negotiation and settlement? At what points in the process might negotiation and settlement occur? What is the goal of negotiation and settlement?

Review question 7.
What are the major differences between mediation and arbitration? Why might parties choose each one?

Review question 8.

How do mediations and arbitrations proceed? What additional parties are involved? How might the parties to a dispute agree on mediators or arbitrators?

Review question 9.

How does planning for disputes improve business relationships? What are the potential consequences of not including dispute resolution in a contract?

Review question 10.

What issues relating to dispute resolution do business parties often address in their business contracts? What factors go into selecting a form of dispute resolution prior to a dispute? Do you think dispute resolution choices could be a negotiating point when drafting a contract? Why or why not?

Discussion Questions

Question 1:

Bigg Company is in the business of making processors for electronic devices. Hypo-Corporation purchases one million processors from Bigg Company each year for use in Hypo Corporation's cell phones. The parties negotiate and sign an agreement governing this deal. This is one of many deals between the two companies, which have been doing business together for 10 years.

Last year, a dispute arose between the two companies. Bigg Company claims that Hypo Corporation did not pay for 10,000 of the processors, and Hypo claims that it did not pay because that batch of processors was defective.

> Is litigation a good option for the parties to resolve this dispute? Why or why not?

> What other dispute resolution methods might the parties consider? What are the advantages and disadvantages of other methods?

Question 2:

Assume that under the terms of the contract in the prior question, the parties agreed to resolve all disputes through binding arbitration. Earlier this year, this dispute was decided through arbitration, with an award issued in favor of Bigg Company. Hypo Corporation is unhappy with the arbitrator's decision.

>Can Hypo Corporation appeal the award?

>Does the corporation have any other recourse?

Question 3:

Finally, assume that under the terms of the contract, the parties agreed to mediation. The parties submitted to mediation, and the mediator proposed a solution. Hypo Corporation does not like the mediator's solution.

>What steps should Hypo Corporation take now?

>What happens to the dispute as a result?

Question 4:

Proprietor Pete owns a coffee shop in a small town. He hires two employees to work at the shop. One day, a customer trips over a rug on the shop floor and suffers second degree burns from spilling coffee on himself in the process. The customer believes Pete is at fault for the burn and threatens to sue him.

Two weeks prior, a different customer, Ferlin, who is the father of Pete's best friend, also tripped over the rug. Ferlin emailed Pete to make him aware of the hazard, but Ferlin was not injured and does not plan to make a claim against Pete. Pete forwarded that email to one of his employees, including a disparaging comment about Ferlin's clumsiness. That employee was working at the time of the burn incident.

>Should Pete consider resolving the dispute before the customer files a complaint? Why or why not?

>If so, what type of dispute resolution methods might Pete prefer? Which one might the customer want? Why?

>What are the risks to Pete's business for each dispute resolution type in this scenario?

Question 5:

Large Bank provides savings and checking accounts, debit cards, credit cards, and counseling services to its customers. Large Bank's customer agreement, signed by all customers who use any of the services listed above, contains an arbitration clause requiring "all disputes between the parties be submitted to arbitration."

Large Bank's sales associates were tasked with selling additional accounts to Large Bank's existing customers. Sales associates were required to meet rigorous sales quotas for the additional accounts. To meet those quotas, many sales associates began creating accounts in a customer's name, even though the customer was unaware of the account and did not agree to the additional account.

After learning about the fraudulent accounts, a number of customers sued Large Bank in court. Large Bank brought a motion to compel arbitration, arguing that the customers were bound by the arbitration clause in the customer agreement signed by the customers when they originally agreed to services provided by Large Bank.

> Does the dispute have to be decided by arbitration?
>
> Is it better for the customers to litigate the case through the court system or to agree to arbitration even if they are not bound by the clause? What about Large Bank?
>
> What other options can the parties consider for resolving the dispute?

Question 6:

Wiser and Bayer had a personal and business relationship for 15 years. After they broke up, Wiser changed the locks to a townhouse that Wiser owned but Bayer lived in while Bayer was in town.

Bayer sued Wiser and two of Wiser's employees; she prepared the complaint without an attorney in order to save money. Her complaint alleged that Wiser promised her the townhouse and financial support indefinitely, even if their relationship ended. She also claimed that some of her property had been removed from the townhouse. Her complaint included seven different claims, including fraud, conversion, and breach of contract. The document is long and rambling, and isn't formatted like a legal complaint.

You are Wiser's attorney. Wiser visits your office and says that he can't tell what defendant Bayer intended for which of her seven claims. He also says there was no financial support agreement. Wiser thinks the complaint is "bogus" and unprofessional, and he doesn't think he needs to respond to it.

> What options are open to Wiser? What course of action do you recommend?

See Bower v. Weisman, 639 F. Supp. 532 (S.D.N.Y. 1986).

Question 7:

Fence & Enclosure Solutions, LLC, enters into a contract with Huzzah Doggy Day Care, Inc. Huzzah operates pet day care centers and long-term care kennels around the United States. The contract gives the exclusive right to supply fence components, crates, and kennel parts to Huzzah. After one year, Huzzah wants to end the contract, which contains no terms about dispute resolution or terminating the contract. Huzzah says that too many dogs are escaping, and Fence & Enclosure's products are to blame. Fence & Enclosure disagrees, and wants the contract to continue.

> Without a dispute resolution clause, what are Fence & Enclosure's options for enforcing the contract?

> Can Fence & Enclosure pursue any type of alternative dispute resolution at this point? If so, how?

Question 8:

Acme Corp. sued Coyote Inc. for breach of contract. The contract provided for litigation if the parties had a dispute. The entire litigation process took 18 months and substantial attorney fees for both sides. Acme Corp. won at trial, and was awarded $2.8 million in damages. Coyote Inc. cannot afford that amount, and wants to appeal the judgment. However, Coyote's attorneys say that the company is unlikely to prevail on appeal.

> What are Coyote's options at this point?

> Suppose that Acme determines that Coyote will be unable to pay the awarded damages. What are Acme's options?

> Suppose Coyote appeals and wins. What happens next?

5 BUSINESS FORMS

KEY OBJECTIVES:
- ▶ Learn the different forms of business organization.
- ▶ Describe the advantages and disadvantages of each form.
- ▶ State the importance of corporate formalities.

CHAPTER OVERVIEW

This chapter covers business forms such as corporations, partnerships, and limited liability companies. "Business forms" refers to how a company is owned and operated. It also deals with how to maintain the advantages of a chosen business form.

In this chapter, we will look at the different types of business forms. Each has different rules for its formation, and rules regarding the rights and obligations of the business owners. We will also consider differences in how various business forms are managed and maintained. We will also discuss the advantages and disadvantages of each form. There is no perfect business form for all purposes, but knowing about every form will help you make informed decisions about the best form for a particular situation.

INTRODUCTION

Choosing the form of a business is one of the most important decisions to be made when starting a business. The business form chosen will affect a business's taxes, how it pays its workers, and its liability for debts and injuries. It will even affect the ability of the business to continue operating if one or more of the owners leaves.

In any situation, the answer to the question, "What form of business should I choose?" will be, "It depends." There is no ideal business form that will meet every business's needs. Each form has its advantages and disadvantages. Selecting a form is a matter of deciding which one best meets the greatest concerns of the owners, while presenting the most acceptable or manageable disadvantages.

I. Unincorporated Forms

An unincorporated business may seem like the ultimate in simplicity. No incorporation means less paperwork, and fewer formalities to manage. Creating an unincorporated business is almost too easy. In fact, it is safe to say that a large percentage of unincorporated businesses are owned by people who do not even realize they are operating an unincorporated business. They have chosen the business form by not choosing a form. There are two types of unincorporated business: sole proprietorships and partnerships.

> A musician who plays at weddings for a fee, or a freelance writer who is paid for publication in several magazines could both be considered sole proprietors.

Sole Proprietorship

A **sole proprietorship** is the simplest form of business. Sole proprietorships are owned by one person (the proprietor) and they have no separate identity from the proprietor. The proprietor personally owns not only the business, but also all of the business assets. For example, a contractor operating as a sole proprietor might own a truck and tools in her own name. Because proprietors act as individuals, they are personally responsible for all business property, debts, and liabilities. All income or losses of the business are reported on the proprietor's individual income tax return.

The personal liability for business debts is the main reason most businesspeople will not choose a sole proprietorship as their business form. Even if a debt or obligation is incurred for the benefit of the proprietor's business, she is still personally responsible. All of her personal assets are at risk, as they would be with any personal debt.

While many become sole proprietors just by doing business on their own and not incorporating, others are attracted to the form because of its simplicity. There is no registration required, no internal agreements to prepare, and all decisions are made by the proprietor. In theory, a sole proprietorship can conduct any kind of business. A sole proprietor may not have co-owners, but can have employees.

> In a sole proprietorship, employee wages are the proprietor's personal responsibility.

There is very little to be done when forming a sole proprietorship. The proprietor must obtain any licenses or permits for the type of business he intends to conduct. If the proprietor will be

SOLE PROPRIETORSHIP: An unincorporated business owned entirely by one person.

Example: Tanya works for a large corporation. She goes to school part-time and gets her CPA license. While she is looking for an accounting job, she decides to earn some extra money by doing tax returns and general accounting work for neighbors and small businesses. Tanya has business cards printed and sets up a website for her accounting business, but she does not incorporate. She gives one of her clients some bad advice about deducting medical expenses, and the client has to pay a substantial penalty to the IRS. The client sues Tanya for malpractice, and obtains a judgment. Tanya does not have malpractice insurance, so her (former) client garnishes her wages from her corporate job. Since Tanya is a sole proprietor, her personal wages can be claimed by creditors.

> An assumed name certificate is sometimes referred to as a "d.b.a.," which stands for "doing business as." The assumed name certificate may require publication of notice in a newspaper.

doing business under any name other than her legal name, most states require filing paperwork with the state to acquire an assumed name certificate.

Once those minimal formalities are accomplished, the person will be legally considered a sole proprietor. This is true even if the sole proprietor is unaware of her status.

Ending a sole proprietorship is even simpler: the proprietor just stops doing business. Because all debts are the personal responsibility of the proprietor, and because all assets already belong to her, there is no formal "winding up" process to dissolve a sole proprietorship.

Filing federal income taxes is straightforward because sole proprietorships are considered "pass-through" entities. Being a pass-through entity means that the profits and losses are passed *directly through the business* to the proprietor and are taxed on the proprietor's individual tax returns. Unlike other forms of business, the proprietor is not required to file a separate business tax report. Instead, the proprietor will list business information on Schedule C of their individual tax return. The ability to report business earnings on the individual tax return allows the proprietor to avoid taxation at both the corporate and individual level, saving costs on accounting and filing. The business will be taxed at the personal income rate, not at the corporate tax rate. For this reason, the overall tax rate of sole proprietorships is very low compared to other business entities.

The drawback of being a sole proprietor, however, is that there is no legal separation between the proprietor and the business. The means the proprietor is personally responsible for all liabilities, including business debts. If a business creditor seeks repayment from the sole proprietorship, the proprietor's personal assets such as his personal bank accounts, home, and other personal property, may be at risk.

Partnership

A **partnership** is an unincorporated business association made up of two or more owners who team up to do business. The partnership is created by the partners' joining forces to make a profit. A partnership is a separate legal entity, but the partners and the partnership are not completely separated from one another.

PARTNERSHIP: An association of two or more persons for the purpose of carrying on a business for profit.

> The discussion in this section of the chapter is about general partnerships, which are an unregistered business form. Other types of more formal registered partnerships are dealt with later in this chapter.

The minimal separation of the partnership from the partners has two consequences. First, the partnership is not subject to federal income taxes. Like sole proprietorships, partnerships are considered pass-through entities where profits and losses flow to the individual partners. Each partner is taxed on her share of partnership income, and each partner is allowed to claim a share of partnership losses as a deduction, but the partnership itself pays no federal income tax. Therefore, the partnership is often effectively subject to a lower tax rate than corporations. The partnership does retain income-tax related responsibilities, however. The partnership must file an informational return that sets out each partner's share of income and losses. The shares are determined by the agreement of the partners, but the allocation must reflect the partnership's actual financial performance.

Remember that this exemption from income taxation refers only to federal income taxes. Partnerships are subject to other taxes, including sales and property taxes. Some states and communities also have business activity taxes that apply to unincorporated entities, and that are calculated on the receipts from business income.

> New York City levies a tax of 4% on the taxable income of an unincorporated business.

> Partners must pay tax on their share of partnership income even if they do not actually receive any money from the partnership.

The second consequence of a general partnership is that partners are personally liable for all business debts and liabilities in their entirety. This liability is called **joint and several liability**, meaning that each member of the partnership is liable for all of the partnership debts. The partnership provides no legal protection. If a debt or liability is incurred in the scope of the partnership's business, each individual partner is liable. Likewise, this liability for partnership debt extends to all partners, even if the debt arose from the actions of a single partner.

JOINT AND SEVERAL LIABILITY: Liability that applies both to a group and to the individual members of the group personally.

Example: Jonas and Willie are partners in a maritime consulting business. While on his way to a meeting with a client, Jonas, who is alone and driving his own car, drives through a traffic light and hits another vehicle. Willie and Jonas are both liable for any injuries caused.

> Apple, Google, and Microsoft all started as partnerships, but incorporated soon after starting to do business.

The personal liability of partners is a significant drawback of the partnership form. Many businesses start as partnerships but are incorporated later, when the business begins to develop.

Forming a partnership is a simple matter. All that is required is for two or more people to associate to carry on a business for profit as co-owners. There is no requirement that there be a complex agreement, or even that there should be a written agreement. The partners do

> The "people" forming a partnership may be individuals, corporations or limited liability companies, or any other type of business entity.

not have to use the term "partnership," and it is not necessary that a partnership is intended. A legally sufficient partnership agreement can just be a few words between the partners.

Many partnerships operate without having a formal partnership agreement in place. Others will have formal agreements that do not cover many situations that will come up during the

> Uniform acts are created by legal thinkers and then adopted by state legislatures that think the acts are useful. Sometimes, though, a state may choose to change something in the uniform act, meaning that the precise rules can vary slightly from state to state.

course of a partnership's operation. In that situation, a law known as the Uniform Partnership Act (UPA) comes into play. The UPA was first adopted in 1914, and is updated as needed. The UPA is the default law regarding partnerships. Most of the law's provisions apply to partnerships that do not have a formal agreement among the partners.

In the absence of any other agreement, the UPA provides for equality between the partners. Each partner has an equal say in the management of the partnership, and each partner has the right to an equal share of the partnership profits. Each partner also has the legal right to make contracts that will bind the partnership.

If partners do not want strict equality between themselves in any area, their partnership agreement may divide things up according to the partners' wishes. Partners generally have the right to operate the partnership according to their own preferences. A partnership agreement can be drafted to reflect those preferences.

Example: Maggie is a web designer. Although she is good at the visual aspects of web design, she is not confident of her ability to write the copy on the site. She asks her friend Kayla to join her in her business. "We work together, and just split everything 50-50." Kayla agrees. Maggie and Kayla have formed a partnership.

DETERMINING WHETHER A PARTNERSHIP EXISTS DEPENDS ON THE CONDUCT OF THE PARTIES

Carlson v. Brabham
(Girlfriend) v. (Boyfriend)
199 So. 3d 735 (Miss. App. 2016)

INSTANT FACTS:
Carlson (P) claimed that she and Brabham (D) had a business partnership.

BLACK LETTER RULE:
The three main questions that are considered when deciding whether a partnership exists are the intent of the parties, the control of the business, and profit sharing.

FACTS:
Carlson (P) and Brabham (D) became romantically involved and began living together in 2004. Before their relationship, Brabham (D) owned and operated Brabham Logging. When Brabham (D) started seeing Carlson (P), she encouraged him to incorporate the business. Carlson (P) set up a meeting with an attorney for the purpose of incorporating the business. The incorporation papers listed Brabham (D) as the president of the business, and Carlson (P) as the secretary, treasurer, and agent for service of process.

After Longhorn Logging had operated for several years, the Mississippi Secretary of State administratively dissolved it for failing to file articles of incorporation and issue stock. Longhorn Logging ceased operations as a viable business after September 2007.

When Carlson (P) and Brabham (D) ended their relationship, Carlson (P) wanted a share of Longhorn Logging. She filed a complaint for an equitable distribution, claiming that she was in a partnership with Brabham. The Chancellor found in favor of Brabham (D).

ISSUE:
Was there a partnership?

DECISION AND RATIONALE:
(Griffis, P.J.) No. The three main questions that are considered when deciding whether a partnership exists are the intent of the parties, the control of the business, and profit sharing. Brabham (D) and Carlson (P) did not enter into any written agreement to form a partnership, so the court must look at the circumstances surrounding the relationship to determine intent. Brabham (D) testified that Carlson (P) had some administrative responsibilities. Nonetheless, Carlson (P) completed multiple state forms naming Brabham (P) as the sole owner of Longhorn Logging. Carlson (P) did not prove that the parties intended to enter into a partnership agreement for Longhorn Logging.

The second factor is control. Outside of administrative functions, Carlson (P) did not control any aspect of the business. The control factor goes in Brabham's (D) favor.

Of the three factors, profit sharing is the most important one in determining whether a partnership exists. The chancellor found that Carlson (P) met the profit-sharing factor because Brabham (D) used his income from Longhorn Logging for the couple's expenses. According to Longhorn Logging's profit and loss detail, Carlson (P) received checks for bookkeeping services. Only Brabham (D) received dividends, even though Longhorn Logging did not properly issue dividends. This distinction strongly implies that Longhorn Logging did not consider Carlson a partner in the business. Affirmed.

ANALYSIS:
The original intent of the parties seems to have been creation of a corporation. A partnership was never intended or attempted. In hindsight, Carlson (P) could best have protected herself by making sure that stock in Longhorn was issued to her.

CASE VOCABULARY:
CHANCELLOR:
The judge presiding over a court of chancery, or equity.

> **Example:** Norma and Max are architects who have formed a partnership. Their agreement does not limit either partner's authority to make contracts. One day, Norma tells Max that she thinks they have all the business they can handle right now, and they should focus on their existing work. The next day, without Norma's knowledge, Max commits the partnership to design indoor swimming pools for a chain of hotels. The partnership is obligated to honor this agreement.

> **Example:** Norma and Max have written their partnership agreement to provide for a division of partnership income. Fifty percent of the income from architectural work goes to the partnership for overhead and the salaries of assistants, and the remaining half would be divided between the partners in proportion to the work done to earn the income. The partnership is paid $10,000 for the work done to design one indoor swimming pool. The partnership receives $5,000. Norma's role in the project was limited to reviewing Max's final design. She estimates that she did 10% of the work. Norma receives one-tenth of the partners' share, or $500, and Max receives the remainder.

A comprehensive partnership agreement may include the following:

- Name of the partnership,
- Contributions of cash, property, or services required of each partner,
- How profits and losses are to be allocated,
- How partnership authority is delegated,
- How new partners are admitted to the partnership, and
- What happens when one partner wants to withdraw, or is incapable of continuing in the business.

II. Limited Liability Forms

For most businesspeople, the main reason not to do business as an unincorporated entity is the personal liability of the business owners. Every business is going to be liable for something, whether it is a contract, a personal injury, or taxes. Shielding oneself from personal liability is an important concern when deciding which business form to choose.

> **LIMITED LIABILITY PARTNERSHIP:**
> A partnership in which partners are not personally liable for partnership debts or obligations. Identified by the initials "LLP."

Limited Liability Partnerships

In the last section, we talked about general partnerships, which are unregistered associations of people in business together. Other partnerships are more formal. A **limited liability partnership** (LLP) removes one of the main drawbacks of doing business in a partnership: the personal liability of the partners. An LLP functions in the same way as a general partnership, but the personal liability of the partners is either limited or eliminated.

In most states, there are no special requirements to be met before an LLP may be formed. The partnership merely files a declaration or statement with either state or local authorities. The declaration states that, as of the date of the filing, the partnership will be a limited liability partnership. After that filing, most states require that an LLP include the initials "LLP" as a part of its name. While some states limit the partnerships that may become LLPs to partnerships of professionals such as lawyers, architects, or accountants, most states allow any partnership to file an LLP declaration.

The limitation on liability will also vary from state to state. Under the Uniform Partnership Act, LLP partners are not liable for any partnership obligations or liabilities. Most states have adopted this limitation. Some states, however, have a more restrictive liability limitation. In those states, partners are shielded from liability only for negligence claims, such as personal injury lawsuits. There is no shield from liability for contract claims, or claims for intentional acts.

A partnership's status as an LLP does not make any difference to how the partnership is treated for income tax purposes. Income and losses still "pass through" to the partners who then report this information on their individual tax returns. The only significant difference between an LLP and a general partnership is the limitation of liability.

Limited Partnerships

All businesses need money. They need money to start up, and they need money to operate. A potential business person who does not have money of her own may seek investors to

> In some states, some professions can only form a professional limited liability partnership. Professional limited liability partnerships use the initials "PLLP" at the ends of their names.

Example: Alice, Jimmy, and Harriet are partners in a real estate brokerage that is set up as an LLP. Alice has been skimming profits from real estate sales by altering the figures on real estate documents. In most states, Jimmy and Harriet are not personally liable for Alice's thefts. In states that provide limited liability only for negligent acts, however, Alice and Jimmy are liable for the debts caused by Harriet's thefts, as is Harriet.

contribute money and to share in the profits of the new business. Investors, however, will often have a say in how the business is operated. To limit the role of the investor of the operation of a business, a business person may form a **limited partnership** (LP).

An LP is similar to a general partnership, in that it is an association for the purpose of doing business. As with a general partnership, there is no income taxation of the LP. Distributions are taxed individually to each partner. The difference lies in the functions of the partners.

There are two sets of partners in a limited partnership: general partners and limited partners. There must be at least one of each type of partner, although it is most common for an LP to have one general partner, and several **limited partners**. The **general partner** is responsible for the operation of the business of the LP. A general partner may be an individual, a corporation, or another type of entity. The general partner also has unlimited personal liability for the debts and liabilities of the LP.

The limited partners usually do not take any part in the operation of the business; in fact, in many states, limited partners are barred from

> **LIMITED PARTNERSHIP:**
> A type of partnership in which one or more of the partners (the limited partners) is liable only to the extent of the amount of money that he has invested.
>
> **GENERAL PARTNER:**
> In a limited partnership, the party who operates the business. Note that a "general partner" is not connected to the idea of a "general partnership."
>
> **LIMITED PARTNERS:**
> A partner in a limited partnership who receives a share of the profits, but whose personal liability for partnership debts is limited to her investment in the limited partnership.

> As another layer of liability protection, the general partner may be a corporation. The corporate form further limits liability for the general partner's role in the organization. For instance, a corporation's debts belong to the corporation, and generally are not enforced against the people who started it. If a corporate general partner faces debts for the partnership, collection may be limited to the resources held by that corporation.

Example: Max, a theatrical producer, forms an LP to finance his next production. He is the general partner, and he finds 10 investors who are willing to be limited partners. Max raises $250,000 from the limited partners. The costs of the production are more than Max anticipated, so he gets a $150,000 personal loan from a bank to cover the remaining costs. Unfortunately, the production is a flop, and closes after six days. The limited partners have lost their contributions, but that is the only amount they have lost. Max is personally liable for the $150,000 loan.

active participation. The limited partner invests money, and shares in any profits or losses of the LP. The liability of a limited partner for partnership debts is limited to the amount of his contribution or investment. Most states require LPs to register with the state authorities.

As with other types of partnerships, limited partnerships are considered pass-through entities requiring that all partners individually report and pay taxes on their share of the profits. The limited partners, however, do not have to pay self-employment taxes, because they are not active in the business and draw no wages. For this reason, their share of partnership income is not considered "earned income" under the self-employment tax. Because the general partner is actively involved with the partnership, the general partner's share of partnership income is considered earned income subject to the self-employment tax.

Corporations

While terms such as "partnership," or even "company," are often used to describe different types of businesses, a **corporation** is most properly thought of as a type of business form.

Corporations are creatures of state law. For many purposes, they are regarded as legal "persons." Although they have a legal existence, there is no physical "thing" that one can point to and say it is the corporation. The only tangible parts of a corporation are the property that it owns, and the people who own it or who work for it.

> Most state corporation laws are modeled on the Delaware General Corporation Law. Delaware has a reputation for having corporation-friendly laws and a thriving business environment. Selections from the Delaware General Corporation Law are included in the Appendix.

A corporation is owned by its **shareholders**. You may also know the older term "stockholder," which means the same thing. Shareholders measure their ownership interest according to the number of **shares** they own of a corporation's **stock**. Stock represents partial ownership of a company. Every corporation must have at least one shareholder.

CORPORATION:
A legal entity formed under the laws of a state to do business.

SHAREHOLDER:
The owner of all or part of a corporation.

SHARE:
One of a number of equal parts into which the stock of a corporation is divided.

STOCK:
A proportional part of the ownership of a corporation. Stock grants its owner the right to vote on the management of the corporation.

DIVIDENDS:
The distribution of profits to shareholders or members.

> **Example:** Outside investors have launched a bid to take over the Veruko Corporation. The directors of Veruko fight the takeover attempt by issuing 10,000 shares of Class B stock. Each share of Class B stock has three votes, while the pre-existing stock has only one vote per share. The extra votes give management enough control to defeat the takeover attempt.

> Mark Zuckerberg, the founder of Facebook, holds "Class B" shares in the company. Facebook's Class B stock carries voting rights worth ten times the voting rights of regular Facebook shares. That means that Class B shareholders can control the company while owning less than a majority of the overall shares.

Ownership of stock usually gives shareholders the right to vote on the management of the corporation. Stock may be divided into different classes with different voting rights. For example, preferred stock gives its owner a superior right to **dividends** from the corporation, but the owner has no voting rights. Corporations have also issued stock with enhanced voting rights to fight takeover attempts.

The laws of each state determine how a corporation comes into being. In some states, a corporation exists when **articles of incorporation** (a form giving basic information about the business) are filed with the appropriate state office. In other states, a corporation does not exist until property or cash is exchanged for shares of stock.

One of the main features of the corporate business form, and the main reason it is attractive to businesspeople, is the limitation of liability for shareholders. Because a corporation is its own entity, shareholders have limited personal liability for the debts or liabilities of the corporation. If a corporation is run properly, and all of the formalities of running a corporation are followed, the personal liability of shareholders is limited to the value of their investments in the corporation. Other assets of the shareholder are not at risk.

> Yia owns shares in Above Lighting, Inc., a light fixture manufacturer. He paid $10/share for 100 shares. Above Lighting runs into financial trouble and closes down, leaving several employees unpaid. Yia loses his $1,000 investment, but the unpaid employees cannot ask him to contribute to their unpaid wages. As a shareholder, Yia has no personal liability for the company's debts.

Corporations have a perpetual existence, unless the articles of incorporation say that the corporation will last for only a limited time. A corpo-

ARTICLES OF INCORPORATION: The document filed with the state for the formation of a corporation.

ration will continue to exist, and be able to do business, as long as formalities are followed and the required filings are made. In theory, a corporation could last forever.

C Corporations

Corporations are subject to federal income tax, unless they are able to take advantage of an exception. A **C corporation** (named for Subchapter C of the Internal Revenue Code) is subject to corporate income tax. All corporations are C corporations unless they qualify for a Subchapter S exemption.

One of the disadvantages of a C corporation is "double taxation." Shareholders in C corporations are required to pay income tax on any dividends received from the corporation. These dividends are taxable even though the corporation has already paid tax on the same profits. In that

> One of the oldest corporations currently operating in the United States is Caswell-Massey, a personal-care products maker founded in 1752.

sense, the same money has been doubly taxed. This taxation effect is unique to C corporations.

Most major corporations are C corporations despite double taxation. There are major advantages to the C corporation form. There are few limits on investment, which means that C corporations can use more techniques to raise capital. The investment flexibility means that C corporations can be publicly traded. C corporations also have more flexibility in how they use capital because profits and losses do not all need to be taxed at the individual level every year as with pass-through forms. These added benefits offset the double taxation issue for many companies.

C CORPORATION: A corporation that is subject to the federal corporate income tax. All for-profit corporations are C corporations, unless they qualify as an S corporation.

Example: Lonnie is the CEO and sole shareholder of Subrido, Inc., a C corporation. In 2014, Subrido earned a profit of $50,000, all of which is to be paid to Lonnie. Subrido must pay federal income tax on the profit, and Lonnie must pay income tax when he receives the dividend.

Example: In 2015, Subrido earned a profit of $75,000. Lonnie decides not to pay himself a dividend, but to put the profits towards building a new building for Subrido's headquarters. Subrido must pay corporate income tax on the profits. Lonnie did not receive any income, so he does not have to pay income tax on the profits.

> **Example:** Roberto owns 60% of the stock in Gelkis Manufacturing Co., and Diego owns the remaining 40%. Gelkis is an S corporation. In 2014, Gelkis makes a profit of $100,000. Only one-quarter of the profits are distributed, and the remainder is to be retained to keep up the company's cash reserves. Roberto receives $15,000, and must pay federal income tax on $60,000. Diego receives $10,000, and must pay tax on $40,000.

S Corporations

Some corporations choose to opt out of Subchapter C tax treatment. These companies take advantage of Subchapter S, a federal income tax law that allows corporations to pass profits through to shareholders. The corporation pays no income tax, but shareholders pay on their proportional share of the company's income. The corporation is taxed like a partnership, but still has the limited liability of a corporation. Such a corporation is known as an **S corporation**.

A corporation will not be treated as an S corporation unless the corporation qualifies for a Subchapter S election. In order to qualify, the corporation must:

- Be incorporated in the United States,
- Have only individuals who are U.S. citizens or resident aliens as shareholders,
- Have no more than 100 shareholders,
- Have only one class of stock, and
- File an election with the IRS that says the corporation will be an S corporation.

To keep S corporation status, the company cannot later violate any of these requirements. This rule limits the amount of investment an S corporation can raise, and prevents S corporations from being publicly traded.

Financial institutions, insurance companies, and domestic international sales corporations may not be S corporations.

Shareholders of S corporations pay income tax on a proportionate share of the profits, even if those profits are not paid out to them. This treatment avoids double taxation experienced by C corporations, but can complicate plans to use money for business development rather than distributing profits. Shareholders dislike paying personal income tax on money that is retained by the business.

> **S CORPORATION:** A corporation that meets certain qualifications and that has chosen to be taxed as a partnership.
>
> **LIMITED LIABILITY COMPANY:** A hybrid business organization that combines the liability protection for owners of a corporation, with the pass-through taxation of a partnership. Identified by the initials "LLC."

Limited Liability Companies

A **limited liability company** (LLC) is a hybrid business entity. It has the attributes of both a corporation and a partnership, but is in a class by itself. An LLC provides its members with the same limited liability protection as the shareholders of a corporation enjoy. For tax purposes, however, an LLC is treated as a partnership. The profits pass through directly to the LLC's members.

Like corporations and partnerships, LLCs are entities separate from their members. They come into existence when **articles of organization** are filed with the state authority. The articles of organization are analogous to the articles of incorporation filed for a corporation.

LLCs have many of the same attributes as corporations, even though the terminology differs. For example, LLCs do not have shareholders. "**Members**" play a role similar to shareholders, but they have a right to distribution of the profits. Similarly, LLCs are operated by a **board of governors**, rather than a board of directors. Despite these differences, LLCs are similar to corporations, and courts generally use rules that apply to corporations to resolve cases involving LLCs.

There are some significant differences between corporations and LLCs. Most states allow LLCs more flexibility in how they are organized and managed. The members and governors have fewer legal formalities to follow, and less paperwork to complete to maintain their limited liability status.

> The lack of federal tax rules for LLCs does not affect the members' protection against personal liability.

The most important difference is in the tax treatment. Federal income tax law does not recognizes LLCs, so there is no tax payable on their income. An LLC is treated as a partnership if there are multiple members, or as a sole proprietorship if there is only one member. An LLC does not pay taxes even if it would not qualify as an S corporation if it were incorporated.

This non-recognition leads to a tax problem for LLC members who are also active in the busi-

> The self-employment tax is an additional amount due for FICA (Social Security and Medicare). Ordinarily, employers pay half of this tax, but the self-employed must pay the whole amount.

ARTICLES OF ORGANIZATION:
The document filed with the state for the formation of a limited liability company.

MEMBER:
The owner, or one of the owners, of a limited liability company.

BOARD OF GOVERNORS:
Individuals elected to act as representatives of members in running a limited liability company.

ness. Because they are recognized as either sole proprietors or partners, any wages paid to the members is treated as self-employment income. This means that members must pay the self-employment tax. The members of an LLC can avoid this issue by having the LLC elect to be treated as a corporation for tax purposes. If the LLC qualifies as an S corporation, the pass-through taxation of profits is continued, but members are regarded as employees. The LLC will be able to pay the employer's share of the FICA tax.

Non-Profit Corporations

Business corporations are formed with the intention or expectation of making a profit. A **non-profit corporation** is one that is formed for a purpose other than making money. It may be formed for charitable, educational, social, or recreational purposes.

Non-profits do not have shareholders. They may have members, but the members have no ownership interest. Non-profits are generally subject to the same rules regarding directors and by-laws, except that many states require the non-profit to designate a CEO and a treasurer.

Not all non-profits are tax-exempt. Under the Internal Revenue Code, a tax-exempt corporation is one formed for a specific charitable purpose. A non-charitable organization would not receive the tax exemption. A tax-exempt entity may not have political advocacy as a substantial part of its activities. If a tax-exempt non-profit involves itself in promoting a particular candidate, for example, it may lose its tax-exempt status.

Public Benefit Corporations:
Most states allow for the creation of public benefit corporations. A **public benefit corporation** is a business corporation that has a dual purpose: to make a profit and to work to improve social or environmental issues. The management and the board of a public benefit corporation must consider both goals when taking action.

A public benefit corporation may make a profit, but is not required to maximize investor gain. That means that the company can use resources on both business goals and social or environmental projects without being challenged by shareholders. Because public benefit corporations are intended to make a profit, they receive no special tax benefits.

Public benefit corporations are often called "B corps." Actually, a "Certified B Corporation" is a related but different concept. Public benefit corporations and other entities may become certified by B Lab, a private organization. Certification recognizes a company's ongoing work on social and environmental goals. A public benefit corporation does not need to be

> **NON-PROFIT CORPORATION:**
> A business organization formed to serve some public purpose, rather than to make a profit for investors.
>
> **PUBLIC BENEFIT CORPORATION:**
> A corporation that has a public or social purpose in addition to the purpose of earning a profit for shareholders.

certified, although many famous public benefit corporations choose to pursue and maintain the certification.

III. Professional Forms

Businesses formed to practice a profession are normally governed by the same rules as businesses formed for any other purpose. A profession is a type of work that requires a high level of education and maintains ethical standards for undertaking the work. Professions are usually licensed and require individuals to prove their qualifications by taking an exam. Doctors and lawyers are engaged in professions, as are architects, accountants, and professional engineers. State laws often limit the types of business forms that can be operated by people in a profession. These limits are designed to decrease the amount of liability protection that individuals in a profession receive by starting a business. By limiting liability protection, clients can recover higher damages from professionals who fail them.

Partnership

Traditionally, a partnership is the preferred business form for professionals. A partnership of professionals operates under the same legal rules as any other partnership. Professionals, however, have the additional concern of malpractice. If a partner commits a negligent act in the course of his professional practice, all of the partners are liable. It does not matter if none of the other partners participated in the negligence, or that the negligent partner was working on his own. The nature of the partnership is that all of the partners are liable for all liabilities of the partnership.

The possibility of malpractice liability leads many professionals to choose an LLP (or, depending on the state, a PLLP). The LLP allows the partners to keep the benefits of a partnership, but individual partners are shielded from liability for acts they did not commit. If a partner is found to have committed professional misconduct, the responsibility will remain with the guilty partner. The other partners will not be disciplined unless they participated in the misconduct.

Professional Corporations

A professional corporation (PC) is another type of business form for the professions. All of the shareholders in a PC must be authorized to practice their profession and the corporation must be engaged in that specific profession.

Professional corporations allow shareholders to limit their liability for malpractice of other shareholders. They may also qualify for Subchapter S status.

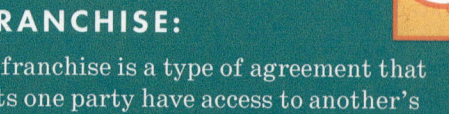

> **FRANCHISE:**
> A franchise is a type of agreement that lets one party have access to another's proprietary knowledge, processes, and trademarks in order to sell a product or provide a service.

> Ethical rules for some professionals, such as lawyers, limit the business forms that can be used. These limits are designed to protect clients.

IV. Franchises

A *franchise* is not, strictly speaking, a separate business form. Instead, it is a licensing agreement. The agreement grants one person (the franchisee) the right to operate a business using a trademark owned by another person (the franchisor).

Franchises offer several advantages for both parties. The franchisor gets the ability to operate his business in multiple locations without having to be directly involved in the day-to-day operation of each location. The franchisee gets the opportunity to run a business with some degree of independence, with the added advantage of being able to rely on the franchisor's goodwill and marketing efforts. In addition, some franchisors offer a high degree of support in the operation of the franchised business.

> The largest franchise restaurant, by number of locations, is Subway, with over 37,000 locations. The largest in terms of revenue is McDonald's. Pokémon is the world's largest media franchise, with an estimated $100 billion in annual global revenues.

Franchising is regulated largely by the federal government, through the Federal Trade Commission. While the terms of a franchise agreement are left to negotiation between the franchisor and franchisee, the FTC regulates the disclosures that must be provided to a prospective franchisee. The franchisee must receive a Franchise Disclosure Document before signing the franchise agreement, or before paying any money.

The Franchise Disclosure Document requires franchisors to provide audited financial statements. In addition, the Disclosure must include information about other franchisees in the territory, an estimate of franchise revenues, and an estimate of the franchisor's profitability. State law may require additional disclosures.

The franchise agreement itself will set out the terms of the relationship between the franchisor and franchisee. An agreement may provide for a high degree of supervision by the franchisor, calling for regular inspections. Franchise agreements commonly limit the products that may be offered by a franchisee, and some even restrict a franchisee's operating hours (for example, stating that the franchisee may not be open for business on Sundays).

> A franchise allows a small business to benefit from a proven business model, trademarks, and brand recognition.
> The franchisee is usually an LLC or an S corporation formed to operate the franchise. The franchisor is usually a C corporation.

V. Business Formation

Deciding which business form to use is the first step. It is also surprisingly difficult, with all the different factors that go into the decision. The next step, forming the business, is not always as difficult as it may seem.

As noted above, forming a sole proprietorship is very simple. Starting a sole proprietorship scarcely counts as "business formation" at all. A sole proprietor just starts doing business without forming a partnership, and without incorporating.

A partnership is also simple to form, but it can be difficult to do well. For general partnerships, it is easy to agree to associate as partners, thus meeting the legal definition of a "partnership." Without a well-crafted partnership agreement, however, most partnerships will eventually run into problems. Disputes will arise about everything from sharing start-up expenses, to a partner needing time off or even leaving the business. Limited partnerships and other registered partnership forms also benefit from a partnership agreement to help the business run smoothly.

Corporations and LLCs are somewhat more complicated to form, although the process is not as complex as one might think. Since both types of businesses are formed by making a filing with the state, it is important to pay attention to all of the legal requirements, and be sure that they are followed exactly. On the other hand, the formalities are not difficult to learn and follow. Virtually every state allows online filing to form corporations and LLCs,

Corporate Promoters

A **corporate promoter** is a person who develops and organizes a new business venture. He may be promoting his own business, or he may be engaged in promoting business ventures for others. Promoters handle matters related to a corporation or LLC before it is formed, although their activities, such as soliciting investors, may continue after the company is formed.

A promoter may make contracts for a company before the company is formed. A promoter who makes a contract like that is personally liable on the contract, unless otherwise agreed. If the company adopts the contract after the company is formed, the company is also liable. The promoter remains personally liable unless the company makes a new contract. Companies are usually not liable to promoters for payment for services rendered, or for reimbursement for expenses incurred unless the company expressly agrees after it is formed.

A corporate promoter stands in a **fiduciary** relationship to both the new company and its present and prospective owners. This fiduciary relationship continues until the promotion plan has been accomplished. Usually, this will be when the company has been established and an independent board takes charge. As a fiduciary, a promoter must act with the utmost good faith. She must fully disclose to them all material facts involved in the promotion. She may not benefit by any secret profit or advantage gained at the expense of the company or its owners.

CORPORATE PROMOTER:
A person who solicits investors for a corporation before it is formed.

FIDUCIARY:
A person who has the duty to act for another with total good faith, trust, and honesty.

Filing Obligations

Both corporations and LLCs start by filing articles with the state corporate authority. Usually, this is the secretary of state's office. The articles are normally a simple form, asking for basic information, such as the company's name, address, and the name and address of the person doing the filing. The name of the company must be distinct from others in the state. The state may refuse a corporate name that is too similar to an existing business name to avoid confusion in the marketplace. In that case, the new business can simply choose an alternative name. Articles may be filed online, or a hard copy may be filed.

> The name of a corporation must end in "Co.," "Corp.," "Ltd.," or some other word or abbreviation that shows the company is a corporation. The name of an LLC must end in the initials "LLC."

Filing articles of organization or incorporation is not the end of the filing requirements. Most states require annual filings. The annual filing shows that the corporation still exists.

If the required filings are not made, a company will lose its status as a company "in good standing." The specific consequences of losing good standing will vary by state, but typically, losing good standing means that the company no longer exists. It will not be able to bring lawsuits in court, and it probably will lose the right to its tradename. In some cases, the shareholders or members of the former company could be held personally liable for business liabilities.

Tax Obligations

Corporations and LLCs have tax filing obligations, even if the company itself does not have to pay any tax.

A C corporation must file an annual income tax return. A return must be filed even though the corporation had no income to be taxed. Of course, the corporation must pay any tax that is due.

An S corporation is not liable for federal income tax. An LLC is liable only if it chooses to be taxed as a C corporation. In either case, the business still must make a filing with the Internal Revenue Service. The filing summarizes each shareholder's or member's shares of the company's income or deductions and credits. The form is nearly as detailed as a regular income tax return. Shareholders and LLC members are likewise required to file their own personal income tax returns.

> For an S corporation, the filing is IRS Form 1120S. An LLC that is being treated as a partnership for tax purposes files Form 1065.

TRADENAME:
The name under which a business operates.

> **Example:** A non-profit corporation is formed to operate a hospital. After a few years, the hospital corporation opens an elementary school for children in the neighborhood. The formation of the school is *ultra vires*.

VI. Corporate Powers

Corporations and LLCs exist by virtue of state laws. These laws may limit the activities and powers of a company. Modern corporate law imposes some limits on the activities of companies. A corporation may not engage in banking business without special permission from state or federal regulators, for instance. Apart from limitations such as these, a company is free to decide on the business it will conduct.

A company seldom makes a formal declaration of the business it will engage in. At one time, corporations were required to state in the articles of incorporation what the business would specifically do. Most incorporators met this requirement by saying that the corporation was being formed to conduct "any lawful business."

A corporation that did something outside of its powers was said to be acting *ultra vires*.

State corporate and LLC laws now provide that a company is being organized for any lawful purpose unless the articles provide otherwise. The prohibition against acting *ultra vires* is largely obsolete. It now only applies to non-profit or charitable organizations.

VII. Ongoing Management

Businesses don't run themselves. After a company is formed, there are two aspects to the ongoing management of the business. The first aspect is doing business; that is, doing whatever the business does to make money. The second is following all of the legal requirements for operating the type of business form chosen.

Corporate Formalities

In order for a corporation to exist, certain rules must be observed. Unless an exception applies, all corporations, of whatever size, must follow the same rules. These rules on business maintenance are usually referred to as "corporate formalities." They include requirements from annual meetings and shareholder communications to board membership and management powers.

While state law sets out the formalities to be followed, the corporation is usually given some

---

ULTRA VIRES:
An action outside the legal ability of an entity to perform.

BY-LAWS:
The rules and regulations adopted to govern the operation of a corporation.

OPERATING AGREEMENT:
The rules and regulations adopted to govern the operation of a limited liability company.

leeway to decide the specifics of those formalities. These decisions are set out in the corporate **by-laws**. In an LLC, the comparable document is the **operating agreement**. By-laws are the internal rules of a corporation. Usually, state laws do not require a corporation to file its by-laws with the state, or even to have by-laws in place. It is, however, very difficult to run a corporation without by-laws.

By-laws address many topics. If there are special qualifications for being a director, those qualifications need to be in the by-laws. If there is no limitation, anyone can be a director of a corporation. Some corporations, however, may want to place a limit on who may be a director. The limitation may be that the director must be a shareholder. Corporate by-laws may include such a rule.

By-laws may also include a buy-sell agreement. A buy-sell agreement is a limitation on how stock is disposed of, or sold. The agreement may provide that, before stock is sold, the shareholder must offer it to the other shareholders at the same price. This prevents ownership of a small corporation from being too widely dispersed.

The main corporate formality addressed by by-laws is the requirement that a company have regular meetings. Shareholders and the **board of directors** must meet regularly. These meetings are typically separate, even if the directors and the shareholders are the same person. The by-laws will set out when a shareholders' meeting must be held. It will say when and where the directors' meeting is held. Provisions will often be made for special meetings, held in between regular meetings. Other topics, such as the quorum required for a shareholders' or directors' meeting, or the notice required for a special meeting, will also be included.

Many states have recognized that all of these formalities are a burden on smaller corporations. All of the formalities are required of all corporations, of whatever size, so a one-person corporation would be required to hold two annual meetings of herself: one as shareholder, one as director. Instead of requiring smaller corporations to go through this ritual, states have allowed some corporations, called closely-held or close corporations, to have one combined shareholders' and directors' meeting.

The states that allow skipping formalities have different criteria for the corporations that will qualify. The most common qualifications are:

- The directors and the shareholders are the same people,

- The corporation is the only business of the shareholders (it is not an investment), and

- There is no ready market for stock in the corporation.

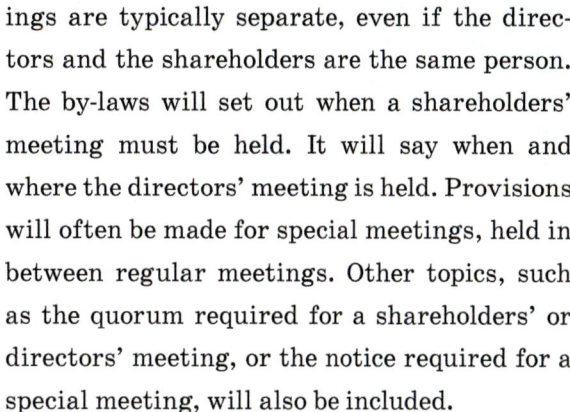

BOARD OF DIRECTORS: Individuals elected to act as representatives of shareholders in running a corporation.

> *Example:* Simio, Ltd. operates child-care centers. Simio wants to expand its operations into a new area. Corwin, a director of Simio, owns property in that area that would be suitable for the company's purposes. Corwin tells the other directors about his interest in the property, and offers it to Simio for sale. Corwin has not breached his duty of loyalty.

> *Example:* Corwin learns of Simio's expansion plans. His cousin owns a property in the area that would be suitable. Corwin buys a half-interest in the property from his cousin at a steeply discounted price. The cousin, pretending to act on his own, negotiates a sale of the property to Simio, giving Corwin a healthy profit. Corwin has breached his duty of loyalty.

Board of Directors

The board of directors is responsible for high-level oversight of the corporation. The board acts through meetings. Depending on the corporate by-laws, these meetings may be virtual, in person, or even in writing.

Directors have a duty of loyalty to the corporation. This means that they must act in the best interests of the corporation. A director may not take unfair advantage of her position as a director. If she does business with the corporation, she must disclose her interest to the other directors.

Directors are expected to stay informed about the corporation's business. While they are not expected to be masters of every detail, they must at least have a general idea of what is going on with the business. Directors should also seek outside help, such as legal or financial advice, as needed.

If the board or an individual director makes a mistake that harms the business, shareholders may wish to take action against them. A legal principle called the "business judgment rule" holds that directors are in the best position to make decisions about business matters. Because of this rule, courts will usually defer to the superior knowledge and business experience of the directors, even when there has been a bad outcome. Shareholders can punish bad directors by voting them off the board at the next shareholder meeting.

Directors of publicly-traded corporations have additional requirements. These requirements are imposed by the Sarbanes-Oxley Act. The Act

> It is common for corporations to designate a person to act as corporate secretary, to keep charge of corporate records and to maintain the minutes of corporate meetings. Maintaining meeting minutes is an important corporate formality.

CORPORATE OFFICERS MUST GIVE BUSINESS OPPORTUNITIES TO THEIR CORPORATIONS AND NOT TO THEMSELVES

Guth v. Luft, Inc.
(Officer) v. (Corporation)
5 A.2d 503 (Del. Ch. 1939)

INSTANT FACTS:
Guth took a business opportunity for his family's business rather than give it to the company he served as president. The companies handled similar products.

BLACK LETTER RULE:
If a business opportunity is presented to a corporate officer or director in his representative capacity, the law will not permit him to take the opportunity for himself.

FACTS:
Guth (D) was an officer of Luft, Inc. (P), a candy and syrup company. Luft (P) was primarily a retail operation, but also ran a wholesale business. Guth (D) and his family owned Grace Company, a manufacturer of soft drink syrups. Guth (D) was unhappy at the prices Luft (P) was paying for Coca-Cola syrups, and wanted to negotiate with Pepsi instead. Pepsi was declared bankrupt in 1931, but a representative made an agreement with Guth (D) to secure Pepsi's secret formula and trademarks from the bankruptcy court and to form a new company to manufacture Pepsi Cola. Guth (D) proceeded with this plan, and did not offer the opportunity to Luft (P). Luft (P) assisted in the endeavor and was repaid; however, Luft (P) did not own any shares in the new company. Guth's (D) private plan was to unseat Coca-Cola in Luft (P) retail outlets.

ISSUE:
May a corporate officer take a business opportunity for personal gain rather than give it to the corporation?

DECISION AND RATIONALE:
No. When an officer or director is acting in a representative capacity for the corporation, he may not take the opportunity for himself, assuming:

1. The corporation is financially able to undertake it;
2. The opportunity is in the line of the corporation's business and is of practical advantage to it; and
3. The opportunity is one in which the corporation has an interest or a reasonable expectancy.

In this case, Luft (P) was financially capable of undertaking the opportunity. The Pepsi product was in line with Luft's (P) business, and the company had a reasonable expectation that the opportunity would be presented to it by Guth (D).

ANALYSIS:
The so-called "Guth Corollary" states that if an officer or director is in his individual capacity, he may take the opportunity as long as he does not steal corporate assets in the effort. The opportunity must not be essential to the corporation or be one that the corporation has an interest in. The difficult factual question is whether an officer or director is acting in his representative or individual capacity in any given case.

says that directors certify the accuracy of financial reports. Directors must also put internal controls to ensure compliance into place. Publicly-traded companies must also comply with any Securities and Exchanges Commission (SEC) regulations. Compliance with SEC regulations and reporting requirements is mandatory for all public companies. Any company that does not meet these requirements may be fined heavily, disqualified from public trading, and even face an enforcement action by the SEC.

Corporate Officers

Corporate officers are employees of the corporation. They have specific management authority, delegated to them by the board of directors. For most corporations, officers are not legally required.

Corporate officers handle day-to-day business operations, while the board focuses on longer-term and high-level planning. Corporate officers are subject to the control of the board of directors.

Shareholders

Shareholders are the owners of the corporation. They act by voting at meetings. Shareholders may agree among themselves on how to vote, and a shareholder agreement may be enforced by petitioning a court for specific performance. Shareholders may also delegate their voting to a substitute or proxy.

Shareholders have three functions:

- To elect the board of directors,
- To approve corporate by-laws, and
- To approve organic changes, such as a merger or dissolution of the corporation.

A shareholder has no direct management role, unless she is also an officer or director. Shareholders express their opinions about the management of a corporation through the directors they elect.

> The term "piercing the corporate veil" refers also to piercing the liability protection of an LLC. Generally, the same rules are followed.

Piercing the Corporate Veil

One of the main reasons for forming a corporation or an LLC is the liability protection for the owners. Shareholders or members are not liable for actions of their companies, even if there is only one shareholder or member, and even if that one shareholder or member is the sole director or governor, and the sole employee, of the company. That protection, however, has its limits. The liability protection may be set aside in the situation known as **piercing the corporate veil**.

Piercing the corporate veil will happen when the owners do not treat a company as a separate entity. Instead, the business and the individual act as if they are interchangeable. The legal outcome of piercing is that an aggrieved person may sue a director, officer, or member of a corporation or limited liability company personally in addition to suing the business. That means that

PIERCING THE CORPORATE VEIL: The legal process by which corporate shareholders or LLC members may be held liable for the debts or obligations of a corporation or LLC.

individuals could end up personally responsible for paying damages to a plaintiff. The most common reasons courts will allow the veil to be pierced are:

- **Failure to follow corporate formalities.** Failing to hold annual shareholder or directors' meetings, or neglecting to keep adequate records, makes it appear as though the owners themselves have disregarded the corporate form. While by-laws are not a legal requirement in most states, they provide the best plan for making sure corporate formalities are followed.

BROTHERS WHO FORMED COMPANY BUT COULD NOT PROVE THAT THE COMPANY HAD A SEPARATE EXISTENCE MAY BE PERSONALLY LIABLE FOR DEBT

Shorter Brothers, Inc. v. Vectus 3, Inc.
(Truck Purchaser) v. (Delivery Company)
___ So.3d ___, 2021 WL 2622054 (Ala. 2021)

Vectus 3, Inc., sued Shorter Brothers, Inc., and its owners for breaching an asset-purchase agreement and related claims. In doing so, Vectus asked the trial court to pierce Shorter Brothers' corporate veil—that is, hold Shorter Brothers' owners personally liable for the company's actions. The trial court granted complete relief to Vectus and awarded it damages[.] We affirm the trial court's judgment.

Vectus operated FedEx Ground delivery routes for several years before its owner decided to sell its assets. Brothers Joseph Shorter and Jason Shorter expressed interest in purchasing those assets. In March 2018, Joseph and Jason filed a certificate of formation in the Jefferson Probate Court to form Shorter Brothers.

Shorter Brothers entered into an asset purchase agreement ("the Agreement") with Vectus in October 2018. In the Agreement, Shorter Brothers agreed to purchase the rights to Vectus's contract with FedEx Ground and nine delivery trucks for $400,000 at the closing scheduled for October 31, 2018. [The] Shorter Brothers planned to finance with a loan. Because of concerns that Shorter Brothers would not obtain financing by closing, the parties provided [a] financing contingency in the Agreement [through which Shorter Brothers would pay the loan and rental fees until financing was secured]. Shorter Brothers failed to obtain financing [and it] ceased making any payments after June 2019.

The trial court then entered summary judgment and awarded $400,000 to Vectus—an amount equal to the purchase price under the Agreement. The defendants contend that the trial court erred by entering summary judgment in favor of Vectus and holding Joseph and Jason personally liable for Shorter Brothers' actions. We disagree.

The defendants do not contest the trial court's summary judgment on the breach-of-contract, conversion, or unjust-enrichment claims. Rather, they argue that the trial court should not have pierced Shorter Brothers' corporate veil. It is well established that "a corporation is a legal entity existing separately from its shareholders." Thus, "[p]iercing the corporate veil is not a power that is lightly exercised."

Vectus advanced an alter-ego theory. To establish that an entity is the alter ego of its owners, " '[t]he dominant party must have complete control and domination of the subservient corporation's finances, policy and business practices so that at the time of the attacked transaction the subservient corporation had no separate mind, will, or existence of its own.' " The defendants concede this element. But "mere domination cannot be enough for piercing the corporate veil." Rather, "[t]here

> must be the added elements of misuse of control and harm or loss resulting from it." Thus, we have held that an alter-ego theory of piercing the corporate veil is viable where
>
>> "a corporation is set up as a subterfuge, where shareholders do not observe the corporate form, where the legal requirements of corporate law are not complied with, where the corporation maintains no corporate records, where the corporation maintains no corporate bank account, where the corporation has no employees, where corporate and personal funds are intermingled and corporate funds are used for personal purposes, or where an individual drains funds from the corporation."
>
> The evidence submitted with Vectus's summary-judgment motion shows that Shorter Brothers' shareholders—Joseph and Jason—did not observe the corporate form and that their misuse of the corporate form left Vectus with little recourse. As the trial court noted, in response to Vectus's request for "corporate documents," the defendants failed to produce copies of any bylaws, operating agreement, shareholder agreement, corporate minutes, or other documents to support that Shorter Brothers had a separate corporate existence and was not the mere "instrumentality or alter ego" of Joseph and Jason. Further, the defendants' discovery responses indicate that Shorter Brothers had little, if any, financial records at that time. The defendants likewise said in discovery responses that Shorter Brothers had employees; yet they produced no information about employee numbers, roles, or duties.
>
> The defendants did not timely produce any admissible evidence to refute the assertions in Vectus's summary-judgment motion. On appeal, the defendants point to documents attached to Vectus's summary-judgment motion. Specifically, they cite Shorter Brothers' certificate of formation, the Agreement, and Shorter Brothers' Form 1099-MISC from 2018 to refute Vectus's alter-ego theory. But those documents fail to provide "substantial evidence" that Shorter Brothers had a corporate existence separate from Joseph and Jason. The certificate of formation merely shows that Shorter Brothers exists as a legal entity—a fact no one disputes. And while entering into contracts may, in some circumstances, indicate that an entity has a separate corporate existence, the Agreement is the only contract to which the defendants point.
>
> In sum, Vectus made a prima facie showing that Joseph and Jason operated Shorter Brothers as their instrumentality or alter ego. The defendants failed to timely produce substantial evidence—or any evidence, for that matter—revealing the existence of a genuine issue of material fact. Thus, the trial court did not err by piercing Shorter Brothers' corporate veil. Affirmed.

- **Continuous undercapitalization.** If a corporation does not have enough funds to operate, that means it is not a stand-alone enterprise. It is the alter ego of the owners.

- **Commingling funds.** This is perhaps the most common reason a corporate veil will be pierced. Business owners do not pay themselves a salary, but just help themselves to money as they need it. There is no separate business bank account, and company funds are used to pay personal expenses of the owners. The company is the alter ego of the owners, and its legal existence can be ignored.

There is a strong presumption against piercing the corporate veil. In order to allow it, courts require proof of very serious misconduct.

VIII. Voluntary Dissolution

Although a corporation or LLC could, in theory, exist forever, most will eventually come to an end. Estimates vary, but corporate "lifespans" are shorter than in the past, with estimates putting the average length from 10 to 15 years. The end may come voluntarily, as a result of a decision by the owners. The end may also be involuntary.

State laws provide for the orderly termination of corporations and LLCs. These laws set out the procedure to be followed before a corporation may be officially considered to have closed. These laws primarily protect creditors of the closing business. If a corporation goes out of business with unpaid debts, the creditors (most of whom will have had nothing to do with the corporation going out of business) will have no one left who is obligated to pay the debts.

Under most state laws, the procedure for voluntarily dissolving a corporation or LLC is as follows:

- **Shareholder/member vote.** The shareholders or members of the company must vote in favor of dissolution. The vote to dissolve must have been on the agenda for the meeting before the meeting takes place.

- **Notice of intent to dissolve.** The notice must be filed with the state authority that is in charge of business registrations.

- **Stop doing business.** While existing contracts may be fulfilled, the dissolving company must refrain from soliciting or accepting new business.

- **Collect assets.** The assets of the company are used to pay creditors. Anything remaining is distributed to shareholders. All of the assets of the company need to be collected before the company may officially dissolve.

- **Pay creditors.** Creditors are given notice of the dissolution and given a time within which they may make a claim for payment. The notice may be written and sent directly to creditors, or published in a newspaper. Once all claims are paid, the company certifies payment.

- **Distribute assets.** Any remaining assets are distributed to the shareholders, in proportion to their ownership.

> Stock is property, and it could be subject to division in a divorce, or seizure by creditors. Many buy-sell agreements provide for a buy-out in those situations.

Succession Planning

"Succession planning" involves arrangements for how to keep a business running if a key shareholder or member withdraws from the

Example: The by-laws of the Yokai Corp. provide that the stock of a deceased shareholder may be repurchased by the corporation at the directors' option. Shareholder Jane dies, leaving as her sole heirs her wife Cynthia and their son Roger. Cynthia has no interest in joining the business, and Roger is only twelve. The other shareholders of Yokai secure an appraisal of Jane's shares, and purchase the stock for that price from Jane's estate.

business. The withdrawal may be voluntary (retirement or accepting a new job) or involuntary (death or disability). Smaller, closely-held companies are especially vulnerable to disruption when a key member or shareholder leaves. Succession planning allows the business to stay in operation after such a departure.

Succession planning can take many forms, depending on the company. Many companies, large and small, have life insurance policies on key employees. Those policies provide funds to the business to help it adjust to operations after the death of a key member or shareholder.

Another succession planning tool is the buy-sell agreement. A buy-sell agreement usually says that a shareholder who wants to sell her stock must first offer it to the other shareholders at the same price. Many agreements also provide for a buy-out in the event a shareholder dies, or is otherwise forced to leave the company.

Mergers and Acquisitions

Mergers and acquisitions are transactions that involve some combination of two or more companies.

A **merger** involves two or more companies combining into one company. In practice, there is usually one company that "survives" the merger. The management of the survivor company is installed as the management of the new company. In many cases, the new company may operate under the survivor's name.

Most state laws provide that a merger must be approved by a majority of the shareholders. By-laws may provide that a larger majority must approve a merger.

An **acquisition** is when one company, or a group of investors, buys all or nearly all of the assets or stock of a corporation. Sometimes, these are "friendly" takeovers. A friendly takeover is one that has been approved by the management of the corporation being acquired. The board should move forward with a takeover when it is in the best interests of the shareholders.

A hostile takeover is one that does not have the approval of management. In a hostile takeover, the acquiring party may have made an offer for a friendly takeover that was refused. There

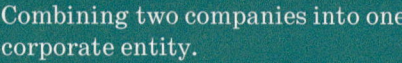

MERGER:
Combining two companies into one corporate entity.

ACQUISITION:
The purchase of a corporation by another entity or group of investors.

Example: The Flechette Group is interested in acquiring the Anderson Department Store Co. Flechette makes an offer to the board of Anderson, but the offer is refused. Flechette then offers Anderson shareholders the chance to sell their stock for $15 per share. The current market price fluctuates between $12 and $13.50 per share. Flechette has made a tender offer.

> **Example:** Instead of buying Anderson stock from shareholders, Flechette buys stock on the open market. The principals of Flechette soon accumulate 30% of the stock. Along with some dissident shareholders, Flechette is able to vote in new directors on the board of Anderson. The new directors approve the takeover by Flechette. Flechette's takeover is the result of a proxy fight.

are two types of hostile takeovers. In a tender offer takeover, shareholders are offered a price for their stock that is higher than the current market price. It is up to individual shareholders to decide whether to accept or reject this offer.

The other type of hostile takeover is a proxy fight. In a proxy fight, the acquiring party purchases enough stock to vote to replace the management of the board with one receptive to a takeover.

Mergers and acquisitions may raise regulatory concerns. If the companies involved are large, for instance, the government may be concerned about creating a monopoly that would reduce competition.

IX. Involuntary Dissolution

Not all corporations end voluntarily. Involuntary dissolution can happen for a number of reasons. A corporation may neglect to make the required filings, and lose its status as a corporation in good standing, for example.

In some states, shareholders may bring a court action to force dissolution of a corporation. An action for dissolution is allowed when the board of directors is deadlocked. A deadlock renders the corporation legally incapable of doing anything. Some states also allow an action for dissolution when the majority of shareholders are taking actions that are harmful to the rest of the shareholders.

Bankruptcy

Bankruptcy is not always the death knell for a corporation. A Chapter 11 bankruptcy, for example, is meant to restructure the company and put it in good (or, at least better) financial shape. Chapter 11 contemplates the continuation of the business. A Chapter 7 bankruptcy, however, will result in the end of the business. The business is liquidated, and any assets are sold off.

In some circumstances, creditors may petition for an involuntary bankruptcy of a company. The petition may request either a Chapter 7 or Chapter 11. A petition for an involuntary bankruptcy may be brought if:

- There are unsecured claims of more than $15,775, or secured claims of at least $15,775 more than the value of the collateral securing them,

- These claims are undisputed,

- The company is generally not paying its debts, and

- The petition is brought by at least three creditors, if there are 12 or more creditors, having undisputed claims totaling more than $15,775. If there are fewer than 12 creditors, one creditor with claims totaling more than $15,775 may bring the petition.

An involuntary bankruptcy petition does not automatically result in a bankruptcy. The court is asked to declare that the company should be in bankruptcy. Until the court makes such an order, the company may continue to function normally.

Death of Key Member or Partner

Many small businesses depend on one or two key people for the bulk of their income. A company may in fact consist of only one key person. If that person dies, the business will likely stop.

Succession planning, as discussed above, may help to keep a business afloat if a key person dies. However, that may not be the case, especially if the key person was the only person involved. In that case, it will be necessary to take steps to dissolve the business.

> Under the original version of the Uniform Partnership Act, a partnership dissolved on the death or withdrawal of a partner unless the partnership agreement provided otherwise.

CAREERS IN THE LAW

Many turn to law firms to incorporate a business, but it might not be a lawyer who does the work. Setting up businesses is often handled by paralegals in a law firm. Paralegals have special training in the law, but they do not go to law school (the same way that paramedics know a lot about medical treatment but do not go to medical school). Paralegals can also work in corporate legal departments or in other areas of law. Some paralegals receive training through approved programs, or even major in paralegal studies, but others are trained by their employers (they are usually called legal assistants). A paralegal or legal assistant works directly with lawyers and may manage projects or meet with clients. Paralegal work is in demand and is well paid. If you are interested in the law and you are a detail-oriented person who can manage competing priorities, paralegal work might be for you.

CHAPTER SUMMARY

There is no "ideal" business organization. Each type presents distinct advantages and disadvantages. Choosing one type over another is a matter of deciding which advantages are most important, and which disadvantages can be tolerated. A good choice means understanding the pros and cons, and knowing how you can work with them.

A sole proprietorship is the most informal type of business. While it requires no formalities to start or operate, it is also the type of business that carries the greatest risk of personal liability. A general partnership is also simple, depending as it does on the agreement between the partners. The partners, however, continue to bear the risk of personal liability for business debts or obligations. Limited liability partnerships will generally take away this risk. Limited liability companies and corporations also protect the owners of the business from personal liability. There are formalities associated with corporate business models that must be followed in order to benefit from liability protections.

Choosing a business form is an ongoing obligation, and observing the requirements of each form is an essential responsibility for businesspeople.

Review Questions

Review question 1.
What are the two types of unincorporated and unregistered businesses? How are they formed? May they be formed unintentionally, and if so, how? What are the advantages and disadvantages of these forms?

Review question 2.
Define "limited partnerships" and "limited liability partnerships." How does each differ from a general partnership? Who manages the business for each type? Why would a business choose a partnership form over a limited liability company or other corporate form?

Review question 3.
What is the role of the board of directors? What legal doctrine protects directors from liability? What is the difference between a director and a shareholder? What do shareholders of a corporation do?

Review question 4.
What is a limited liability company? Why is it a popular business form? What are its advantages and disadvantages?

Review question 5.
What is the difference between a C corporation and an S corporation? What types of businesses are more likely to choose one or the other? What are the advantages and disadvantages of each forms? What elements would disqualify a business from being an S corporation?

Review question 6.

How does a non-profit corporation differ from a corporation or LLC? Are all non-profits exempt from taxes, and why or why not? What is the difference between a non-profit and a public benefit corporation? Between a corporation and a public benefit corporation? What is a B corporation?

Review question 7.

How are the various business forms taxed? What forms are pass-through entities? Which one involves double taxation? What are the pros and cons for each taxation model?

Review question 8.

What documents are generally required to start a corporation? What is the process? What actions must a business take to remain an active corporation?

Review question 9.

What is a corporate promoter? What are the promoter's responsibilities? Under what circumstances could the promoter become personally responsible for money spent promoting the business?

Review question 10.

What is piercing the corporate veil? What are the consequences of piercing the veil? How can businesses avoid the problem?

Review question 11.

What are the voluntary and involuntary ways that a company can be dissolved? What is the process for voluntary dissolution? What are the circumstances that could lead to involuntary dissolution?

Review question 12.

What is succession planning and why is it important? What advantages does it have for a small business? For a business's customers and creditors?

Review question 13.

What is the difference between a Chapter 7 bankruptcy and a Chapter 11 bankruptcy? When does it make sense for a business to choose bankruptcy? What are the consequences, if any, for the business owners?

Discussion Questions

Question 1:

Tariq and Levi are physicians. They decide to combine their medical practices and form a partnership. A partnership agreement is prepared. One clause in the agreement calls for each partner to contribute $10,000 towards the initial start-up costs of the partnership. Tariq and Levi both sign the agreement, but paying the money cannot happen until the next day, when they will be able to open a partnership bank account. The next day, before he has a chance to pay the money, Levi performs a minor surgical procedure on a patient he has been treating for several years. He overlooks a notation in the patient's record that she cannot be given a certain anesthetic, and that anesthetic is ordered. The patient suffers a severe reaction and is permanently injured.

> If the patient sued for malpractice, would Tariq be liable for Levi's malpractice? Why or why not?

> What additional legal factor could change the answer to the first question?

Question 2:

Arthur is the CEO and sole member of an LLC. The company has moved out of its offices and relocated to Arthur's home, while owing four months' rent on its former offices. The company is doing business only sporadically, because Arthur is, as he puts it, "practicing for retirement." The little money that does come in to the company is deposited into Arthur's personal checking account, and the company bank account was closed three months ago. Some favored suppliers of the company are paid occasionally by Arthur's personal check. Charlie, the former landlord of the company, threatens to sue the company for unpaid rent. Arthur tells him to go ahead: "There's no money there for you to get."

> What is the legal doctrine that allows members to be held liable for unpaid LLC debts?

> In this case, can Charlie hold Arthur personally liable for the unpaid rent? Why or why not?

Question 3:
Refer back to the last question. Suppose Charlie sues both Arthur and his LLC. Documents produced during discovery show that Arthur has held regular meetings of the board of governors, and has documented all of those meetings.

> Does this fact affect Charlie's ability to hold Arthur personally liable? Why or why not?

Question 4:
Chyna operates a small retail business as a sole proprietor. She would like the business to involve more of the family. Chyna is married to Chris, who is a naturalized US citizen. Chyna's Irish mother-in-law Brighid lives with Chyna and Chris for several months a year, and lives the rest of the year in Ireland. Because many of the items sold by the business are from Ireland and sourced by Brighid, Chyna also wants her to have a stake in the business. Chyna wants to avoid double taxation.

> What business form do you recommend? Why?

> Are there business forms that will not work for Chyna? What are the problems with those forms?

Question 5:
You and two colleagues have decided to go into business together. You will have no other employees at first. You have been friends since you were children.

> What business form would you choose? Why would you choose that one?

> Explain the steps involved in creating that business form.

> What are the main disadvantages of that business form?

> What concerns do you have about starting a business with friends? How can you deal with those concerns?

Question 6:
Sue decides to work as a distributor for a vitamin and supplement company. The company takes orders online and sends the orders in Sue's area to her. She packages and hand-delivers or mails the pills. She decides to work as a sole proprietorship because she is the whole business and she does not intend to add employees.

Sue is driving to deliver an order. She uses the family car. She hits a pedestrian in a crosswalk when she was checking her text messages. What is Sue's liability to the pedestrian?

One of Sue's customers has an extreme allergic reaction to one of the supplements and ends up in a vegetative state. Sue does not do anything with the supplements other than deliver them. What is Sue's potential liability to the customer?

It is tax season. What are Sue's tax obligations for her business venture?

Question 7:

The Takei family runs a jewelry shop. It is a true "mom and pop" business, started by Mr. and Mrs. Takei 40 years ago. Their only child, Glen, does the bookkeeping for the business in his spare time. The company is organized as an LLC with the couple as owners. Mrs. Takei is the jewelry maker, and Mr. Takei is the salesman and manager. They have some part-time employees, who are mostly unrelated college students.

Mrs. Takei dies, leaving the shop with nothing to sell when the stock runs out. What should Mr. Takei do?

Mr. Takei dies. Glen quits his day job and becomes the salesperson. What happens to the business when Mrs. Takei dies?

Mr. and Mrs. Takei decide to divorce. Mr. Takei wants to cash out the business. Mrs. Takei wants to keep going. Glen wants to take over the business when Mrs. Takei retires. How can these issues be resolved? What advance planning would have been helpful?

Question 8:

Gigi's Gardens is a landscaping business set up as a corporation with five shareholders: CEO Gigi, Gigi's sister, Gigi's father, Gigi's spouse, and Gigi's nephew. All of the shareholders are also employees; the corporation also hires seasonal workers as needed. The corporation operates out of a rented garage, and owns a truck and several pieces of heavy equipment.

Is Gigi's Gardens probably an S corporation or a C corporation? Which would be the best option?

> Suppose Gigi becomes a social media influencer and becomes a reality show star on HGTV. The business grows dramatically to include retail goods sold at major retailers. Do you recommend any change to the corporate tax model? Why or why not?

6 Contracts

KEY OBJECTIVES:
- Describe the rules for formation of a contract.
- List the consequences of a breach of contract.
- Explain sales contracts under the Uniform Commercial Code (UCC).

CHAPTER OVERVIEW

Contracts are a fundamental part of all business relationships and transactions. In this chapter, you will learn about the basics of contract law you will need in your everyday life and in business, including how contract are performed and rules for contract performance. You will also learn about what remedies are available if someone breaches a contract. Many different laws govern contracts. This chapter focuses on the general common law rules and also considers the law of sales contracts as set out in the Uniform Commercial Code (UCC). Finally, we will review some of the special issues that relate to online contracts.

INTRODUCTION

Contracts are fundamental to business. Almost every transaction, deal, or relationship in business hinges on some kind of contract. It has been said that the greatest privilege we have in business is the "right" to be sued over a contract, because that right is the assurance that the contract will be performed. The ability to make contracts, and the confidence that the contract will be enforced, is an essential part of our economy.

What is a contract? Ask that question of five people, and you might get six different answers. Most of those answers will be at least partially true. We all have some intuitive understanding of what a contract is, even if we don't know the complete legal definition.

The most common answer you will hear when you ask what a contract is will probably say that a contract is some kind of promise. You may also hear that a contract is an agreement. While those answers are not wrong, they are not entirely correct. All contracts are promises, and all contracts are agreements, but not all promises or agreements are contracts. The full answer goes a little further, and says that a contract is a promise or agreement that has some legal consequences if the promise is not kept, or the agreement is not followed.

What is special about a contract? What turns a promise into something that can be enforced in court? A contract is a promise that must contain certain elements. If all of the elements are present, the promise becomes a contract.

I. Contract Formation

Contracts can be very complex undertakings, involving millions of dollars and taking years to perform. They can also be extraordinarily simple: if you downloaded a movie last night or bought a cup of coffee this morning, you made and performed a contract. Under the common law of contract in the U.S., every **contract** requires four elements: Agreement, or mutual assent (offer and acceptance); consideration; capacity; and legality. If all of these elements are not present, the promise may not form a valid contract or may not be enforcible.

Mutual assent is one of the fundamental requirements for forming a valid contract. It is made up of an offer and an acceptance indicating that the parties intended to make a contract. One party, the **offeror**, must make an offer and another party, the **offeree**, must accept the offer in order for there to be an agreement.

Although some describe this element as a "meeting of the minds," what is important is not what each party subjectively was thinking at the time, but whether a reasonable person would find an offer had been made and accepted. This is called the **objective theory of contracts.**

> **OFFER:**
> A proposal to make a contract.
>
> **OFFEREE:**
> The person to whom an offer is made.
>
> **OFFEROR:**
> The person who makes an offer.
>
> **CONTRACT:**
> A legally enforceable promise.

Offer

An **offer** is a proposal made by the **offeror** inviting another party to make a contract on certain terms. The offer is a promise to do, or to refrain from doing, some specified thing.

There are three requirements under the common law for a valid contract:

1. the offer must indicate the **offeror** intends to be bound by its terms;

Example: Ruth mentions to her friend Bo that she is planning on looking for a new apartment. Bo replies "Don't bother looking. I have a great apartment in a building I own. It's yours if you want it." Bo does not mention the address of the apartment, or how much rent he would expect Ruth to pay. Bo has not made an offer to Ruth.

Example: Bo tells Ruth he has a one-bedroom apartment available in his building at 5691 Second Avenue, and the rent is $900/month. He says he is willing to give her a one-year lease that he will write up. The written lease form contains additional terms that oblige the tenant to pay all of her own utilities. Bo has made an offer to Ruth, even though all of the terms of the lease were not stated in the offer.

> *Example:* Matt owns a neighborhood tavern. He has the habit of complaining constantly about how miserable he is running the bar, and how he wishes he could get out of the business. One day, during one of his complaining sessions, he concludes with the statement, "And the next person who gives me $5 has bought himself a bar!" The context of the statement shows that Matt is not making a serious offer.

> *Example:* Matt has decided to retire from operating the bar, and concentrate on another business he owns. He wants to turn the bar over to his son Bob. Matt does not want to give him the business, because he thinks it would sound better for Bob to have purchased the bar "for an undisclosed amount." Matt offers to sell it to him for $1. Matt has made a valid offer. The low price for the sale, in the context in which it was offered, makes it a serious offer.

2. the offer must be reasonably definite or certain, so that a person in the place of the **offeree** know what they would be agreeing to and a court can determine what was agreed to; and

3. the offer must be communicated to the offeree.

These make sense. To be effective, the offeree must understand that an offer has been made.

The context and circumstances under which the offer is made must lead a reasonable person to believe that accepting the offer would lead to a valid contract. Whether a statement indicates intent to make an offer and enter into a contract is usually clear from the context. Statements that are obviously jokes or made in a situation where they are not believable will not be considered offers.

An offer will be valid even if all of the details of the potential contract are not included. It is enough that the essential terms are communicated. The omitted details can be learned from other sources or sometimes implied. For example, if a price is not specified in a sale of goods contract, the law will imply the market price of the goods at the time and place of sale.

In order to be effective, an offer must be understood by the offeree to be an offer. The offeree must say or do something that manifests his intention to make an offer. Mere statements of intention, or a general willingness to do something, will not be an offer. Offers to negotiate or solicitations of bids are likewise not offers.

The offer must be communicated to be effective. If the offeree never receives the offer, it is not valid. If the offer goes missing in the mail, for instance, it is not a valid offer.

Normally, advertisements are not offers but are considered to be invitations to make an offer to buy. There is an exception to this rule for adver-

ASSENT OF PARTY TO A CONTRACT MAY BE ESTABLISHED BY CONDUCT

Lucy v. Zehmer
(Farm Buyer) v. (Farm Seller)
84 S.E.2d 516 (Va. 1954)

On Saturday December, 20, 1952, [Lucy encountered the Zehmers at a restaurant]. Lucy asked Zehmer if he had sold the Ferguson farm and Zehmer replied that he had not. Lucy had tried to buy the Ferguson farm from Zehmer about eight years ago, but the deal fell apart because it wasn't in writing. Lucy said, "I bet you wouldn't take $50,000.00 for that place." Zehmer replied, "Yes, I would too; you wouldn't give fifty." Lucy said he would and told Zehmer to write up an agreement to that effect. Zehmer took a restaurant check and wrote on the back of it, "I do hereby agree to sell to W. O. Lucy the Ferguson Farm for $50,000 complete." Lucy told him he had better change the wording to "we" because Mrs. Zehmer would have to sign it too. Zehmer then tore up what he had written, wrote 'We hereby agree to sell to W. O. Lucy the Ferguson Farm complete for $50,000.00, title satisfactory to buyer. He walked over to his wife. She initially refused to sign, but Zehmer told her that he "was just needling him [Lucy], and didn't mean a thing in the world, that I was not selling the farm." Both of the Zehmers testified that when Zehmer asked his wife to sign he whispered that it was a joke so Lucy wouldn't hear and that it was not intended that he should hear. Both the Zehmers signed the back of the check. The discussion leading to the signing of the agreement, lasted thirty or forty minutes. Lucy suggested the provision for having the title examined and Zehmer made the suggestion that he would sell it "complete, everything there."

When Zehmer refused to honor the agreement, Lucy for specific performance. The trial court sided with the Zehmers and Lucy appealed.

The defendants insist that the evidence was ample to support their contention that the writing sought to be enforced was prepared as a bluff or dare to force Lucy to admit that he did not have $50,000; that the whole matter was a joke; that the writing was not delivered to Lucy and no binding contract was ever made between the parties.

In his testimony Zehmer claimed that he 'was high as a Georgia pine, ' and that the transaction 'was just a bunch of two doggoned drunks bluffing to see who could talk the biggest and say the most.' That claim is inconsistent with his attempt to testify in great detail as to what was said and what was done. It is contradicted by other evidence as to the condition of both parties, and rendered of no weight by the testimony of his wife that when Lucy left the restaurant she suggested that Zehmer drive him home. The record is convincing that Zehmer was not intoxicated to the extent of being unable to comprehend the nature and consequences of the instrument he executed, and hence that instrument is not to be invalidated on that ground.

The appearance of the contract, the fact that it was under discussion for forty minutes or more before it was signed; Lucy's objection to the first draft because it was written in the singular, and he wanted Mrs. Zehmer to sign it also; the rewriting to meet that objection and the signing by Mrs. Zehmer; the discussion of what was to be included in the sale, the provision for the examination of the title, the completeness of the instrument that was executed, the taking possession of it by Lucy with no request or suggestion by either of the defendants that he give it back, are facts which furnish persuasive evidence that the execution of the contract was a serious business transaction rather than a casual, jesting matter as defendants now contend.

If it be assumed, contrary to what we think the evidence shows, that Zehmer was jesting about selling his farm to Lucy and that the transaction was intended by him to be a joke, nevertheless the evidence shows that Lucy did not so understand it but considered it to be a serious business transaction and the contract to be binding on the Zehmers as well as on himself. The very next day he arranged with his brother to put up half the money and take a half interest in the land. The day after that he employed an attorney to examine the title. The next night, Tuesday, he was back at Zehmer's place and there Zehmer told him for the first time, Lucy said, that he wasn't going to sell and he told Zehmer, 'You know you sold that place fair and square.' After receiving the report from his attorney that the title was good he wrote to Zehmer that he was ready to close the deal.

Not only did Lucy actually believe, but the evidence shows he was warranted in believing, that the contract represented a serious business transaction and a good faith sale and purchase of the farm.

In the field of contracts, as generally elsewhere, 'We must look to the outward expression of a person as manifesting his intention rather than to his secret and unexpressed intention. 'The law imputes to a person an intention corresponding to the reasonable meaning of his words and acts.'

The mental assent of the parties is not requisite for the formation of a contract. If the words or other acts of one of the parties have but one reasonable meaning, his undisclosed intention is immaterial except when an unreasonable meaning which he attaches to his manifestations is known to the other party. The law, therefore, judges of an agreement between two persons exclusively from those expressions of their intentions which are communicated between them. An agreement or mutual assent is of course essential to a valid contract but the law imputes to a person an intention corresponding to the reasonable meaning of his words and acts. If his words and acts, judged by a reasonable standard, manifest an intention to agree, it is immaterial what may be the real but unexpressed state of his mind. . . . So a person cannot set up that he was merely jesting when his conduct and words would warrant a reasonable person in believing that he intended a real agreement.

The complainants are entitled to have specific performance of the contracts sued on. The decree appealed from is therefore reversed and the cause is remanded for the entry of a proper decree requiring the defendants to perform the contract in accordance with the prayer of the bill.

Reversed and remanded.

> A solicitation of bids for a large project is a request for offers. The responses sent in by potential vendors are the offers, which the soliciting company can choose to accept or not.

tisements that are clear and definite, and that make an explicit offer. An advertisement makes an offer if it leaves nothing open for negotiation, or is not a solicitation for more offers (such as, an offer to buy a product).

Unless the offer says otherwise, an offer will remain open for a "reasonable time." The definition of a reasonable period of time will depend on the circumstances of the offer. It may also depend upon the usages of the trade or community in which the offer was made. As a rule, the offerer may "revoke" (cancel) the offer, at any time before it is accepted. Revocation occurs when the offeror informs the offeree that she no longer intends to make a contract. Alternately, an offer is revoked when the offeror does something inconsistent with an intention to enter into the contract with the offeree. One example would be selling the property to someone else when the offeree knows about the transaction. Revocation is effective when the offeree receives it.

Example: A department store runs an advertisement in a newspaper saying that it will sell a black lapin (rabbit fur) stole worth $139.50 for $1 to the first customer in line on Saturday morning. The advertisement was an offer. *Lefkowitz v. Great Minneapolis Surplus Store, Inc.*, 251 Minn. 188, 86 N.W.2d 689 (1957).

ADVERTISEMENTS ARE NOT OFFERS

Leonard v. Pepsico, Inc.
(High School Student) v. (Soft Drink Company)
88 F. Supp. 2d 116 (S.D.N.Y. 1999)

INSTANT FACTS:
Leonard (P) claimed that an advertisement was an offer for a sale of a fighter jet.

BLACK LETTER RULE:
An advertisement is not transformed into an enforceable offer merely by a potential offeree's expression of willingness to accept the offer.

FACTS:
Pepsico (D) ran a promotion that offered branded merchandise in exchange for "Pepsi Points." The points were obtained by buying Pepsi products, or the points could be purchased directly for $0.10 each. Leonard (P) saw a television commercial advertising the promotion. The commercial showed various items of merchandise, along with the number of points needed to obtain the item ("T-Shirt 75 Pepsi Points," or "Shades 175 Pepsi Points"). The commercial also showed a teenager riding to school in a Harrier fighter jet. The caption on that part of the advertisement read "Harrier Fighter 7,000,000 Pepsi Points." The commercial also said to see Pepsico's (D) printed catalog for further details. The catalog did not list a Harrier jet as being available under the promotion.

Leonard (P) raised $700,000 to buy the 7 million Pepsi Points. When he submitted his points to Pepsico (D) and said that he expected to receive a Harrier jet, Pepsico (D) turned him down. Leonard (P) sued for breach of contract, and Pepsico (D) moved for summary judgment.

ISSUE:
Did the television commercial constitute a valid offer?

DECISION AND RATIONALE:
(Wood, J.) No. An advertisement is not transformed into an enforceable offer merely by a potential offeree's expression of willingness to accept the offer. While a "clear and definite" advertisement that leaves nothing for negotiation may be an offer, there are several reasons why the advertisement in this case does not meet the criteria for an offer.

First, the commercial cannot be regarded in itself as sufficiently definite, because it specifically reserved the details of the offer to the catalog. Second, even if the catalog had included a Harrier Jet among the items that could be obtained, the advertisement merely urged consumers to accumulate Pepsi Points and to refer to the catalog to determine how they could redeem them. The commercial sought a reciprocal promise.

The court finds that no objective person could reasonably have concluded that the commercial actually offered consumers a Harrier Jet. If it is clear that an offer was not serious, then no offer has been made: In light of the obvious absurdity of the commercial, the court rejects Leonard's (P) argument that the commercial was not clearly in jest. Summary judgment for Pepsico (D) granted.

ANALYSIS:
This case did not put an end to the use of the Harrier jet in the Pepsi Points promotion. Pepsico (D) updated the commercial to say that the price would be 700 million Pepsi Points.

A Harrier jet is a fighter that can take off and land vertically. At the time of this case, a Harrier cost around $23 million. Federal law would have required stripping a jet of its ability to take off and land vertically before it could have been sold to a civilian.

If the terms of the offer state that it will remain open for a specified time, in many cases, the offeror may still revoke the offer. The law provides exceptions to the rule. For example, the UCC has special rules for a "firm offer" for the sale of goods. A firm offer works as follows: The merchant offering the goods puts the offer in a signed writing saying that the offer will remain valid for a certain amount of time (not exceeding three months). The merchant's writing makes the offer irrevocable.

> An offer contained in an **option contract** must remain open for the time stated in the contract. An option contract is a separate contract that promises to keep an offer open.

The offeree also has the power to terminate the offer by rejecting it. Rejection can be communicated by either words or actions. Once the offer has been rejected, it no longer exists. If an offeree changes their mind after acceptance, it is too late. The offer has been accepted.

An offeree may also make a **counteroffer** if they do not like the terms of the original offer. In essence, a counteroffer is a rejection of the original offer that replaces it with a new offer. If the offeree is really interested in the subject matter of the offer, it is necessary to make sure to use conditional language to keep the offer alive. For example, if a seller offers to sell a car for $10,000 and the buyer wants to negotiate, the buyer should ask, "Would you be willing to accept $9,500?" The question will keep the offer alive. If the buyer were to say, "I'll give you $9,500," then the buyer has given a counteroffer. Suppose the seller refuses the $9,500 counteroffer and the buyer says, "Fine, I'll give you $10,000." In that case, the seller is under no obligation to accept the new offer to buy at that price.

In addition to actions taken by the offeror or offeree, the offer will terminate by operation of law if any of the following occur:

- lapse in time,
- death or incapacity of either party,
- destruction of the contract's subject matter, or
- supervening illegality.

A lapse of time can destroy an offer if a reasonable amount of time has passed. If either party dies or is judged to be insane, the offer dies, too, unless it is an irrevocable offer. Likewise, the offer is terminated if the particular subject matter of the offer is destroyed. For example, if a breeder has offered to sell a particular race horse to you and the horse is in a terrible accident and has to be put down before you accept, the offer is also dead.

A supervening illegality means that after the offer is made, but before it can be accepted, the law changes so that it is not longer legal to enter into that kind of contract. This might happen in an international contract in which the government makes it illegal to import a product. If the offer is for such a product, the company could not legally fulfill the contract. In that case, the supervening illegality would terminate the offer.

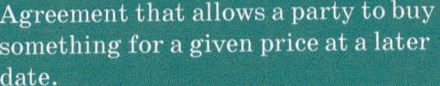

OPTION CONTRACT: Agreement that allows a party to buy something for a given price at a later date.

COUNTEROFFER: A response to an offer that proposes different or additional terms.

Acceptance

Acceptance is the second component of mutual assent. Without acceptance, there is no contract because there has been no agreement. A contract is created the moment the offer has been accepted. The default rule in the United States is called the "mailbox rule." Under this rule, the offer is accepted and the contract formed at the time the acceptance is communicated or dispatched, whether by mail, overnight courier, or email. Under this rule, the acceptance is valid the moment it is sent, regardless of whether the offeror ever receives it. Acceptance changes an offer into a statement of the terms of a contract.

> **ACCEPTANCE:**
> Agreeing to the terms of an offer.

Example: The Flugel Street Business Association wants to sponsor an Independence Day fireworks display for the community. On May 15, a representative of the Association contacts the Susquehanna Pyrotechnic Company, asking for a quote. The next day, the Company responds with an offer to put on the show for $5,000. The Association does not make a decision until July 3, when they phone the Pyrotechnic Company to say that the offer is accepted. The acceptance was not communicated in a reasonable time, so it is ineffective as an acceptance.

Example: Kris is interested in hiring someone to dig drainage ditches on her property. Fred submits an offer to do the job for $10,000. Fred has a number of other jobs pending, so he needs to be very certain of his commitments. His offer therefore says that "your acceptance of this offer must be received in writing in my office no later than September 10." On September 9, Kris telephones Fred saying that she intends to accept his bid, but would like to know when he will be able to start. Fred tells her that he will be able to start the next week. Kris says that's fine, but sends no additional communication to Fred. Kris has not accepted the offer.

Example: Instead of saying that written acceptance "must be received," Fred's offer says "please send your acceptance to me no later than September 10." Kris's phone call on September 9 would probably be a valid acceptance because Fred did not specify acceptance by writing.

> Some courts use the expression "meeting of the minds" or "mutual assent" to refer to the acceptance of an offer.

In order to be effective, the acceptance must be communicated to the offer or by words or actions indicating an intent to be bound by the terms of the offer. The unspoken or uncommunicated intention to accept has no effect. In other words, silence is typically not an acceptance.

If the offer does not set a time limit for acceptance, the acceptance must be sent within a reasonable time. "Reasonable" is determined according to the circumstances of each situation. A late acceptance is considered a counteroffer.

As a general rule, the acceptance must accept the exact terms of the offer. This is known as the "mirror image" rule. Any changes or additional terms become a counteroffer.

A counteroffer starts the process all over again. The original offeror becomes the new offeree, and her acceptance is needed to form a contract. No contract is formed if the acceptance includes additional terms. Note that the Uniform Commercial Code has changed this rule for

Example: A newspaper offers home delivery for $10 per week, and Ivan takes out a subscription. The price increases to $11 per week the next year, and Ivan continues to pay. In late November of this year, the newspaper sends a note to subscribers saying that the subscription price will increase on January 1. If Ivan does not cancel his subscription, the newspaper is justified in assuming that he has accepted the offer for the higher price because of prior dealings between the parties.

Example: After a heavy snowfall, Brian texts his neighbor Tommy to ask if Tommy can shovel the snow from his sidewalk. Brian says he will pay Tommy $15 if he does this job. Tommy does not reply to the text, but goes outside and shovels the walk. Tommy has accepted Brian's offer.

Example: Tommy is outside shoveling his own sidewalk when Brian sends his text. Tommy does not see the text, because he has left his phone inside, but decides to shovel Brian's sidewalk anyway, as a neighborly gesture. Because Tommy did not receive Brian's offer, there can be no acceptance and there is no contract. Brian is not obligated to pay Tommy $15 when he later receives the text.

acceptances of offers for the sale of goods, which will be discussed later in this chapter.

The offeror has the control over the terms of the offer, so she may set out the time, place, or manner of acceptance. If the offer includes requirements for the acceptance, those requirements must be followed. The question of whether an offer states a requirement for a method of acceptance, or merely a preference or suggestion, is sometimes open to interpretation. If the terms of the offer are clear and definite, then those terms must be followed. If the offer is silent on the subject, acceptance may be communicated in any reasonable manner.

In most cases, silence is not acceptance. There are four exceptions to this general rule:

- Where goods are delivered under circumstances that make it clear they are not sent as a gift, and the goods are not rejected,
- When the offeree takes or retains offered property, or acts in a way inconsistent with the offeror's ownership,
- When the offeror says that silence will be acceptance, or
- When the prior dealings of the parties make it clear that the offeree intends for silence to be acceptance.

Acceptance may also be made by performing the contract. The performance must be in a way that shows it is intended as acceptance of the offer.

Consideration

In the United States, **consideration** is a key ingredient that must be added to an offer and acceptance to make a contract. Without consideration, a contract is just an unenforceable promise to make a gift.

Consideration is explained in many different ways. It can best be thought of as something that you bargain for and that you give in return for something else. It is the reason, or the motive, for entering into the contract. Something of value has to flow from each party to the other.

The things exchanged do not have to have monetary value. Mutual promises may be consideration, as long as the promises are something that is possible for each party to do. Actually doing something that a person is not otherwise required to do may be consideration.

Similarly, not doing something that a person has the right to do may also be consideration. This type of consideration is referred to as a legal detriment. The detriment does not mean that a person's promise is harmful or disadvantageous to them. The "detriment" could, in fact be something helpful or beneficial. It is also not important that the person receiving the performance gets no benefit from the doing or not-doing of the action. The key requirement is

CONSIDERATION:
A bargained for exchange; a legal detriment entered into as an exchange.

Example: Lou goes into a grocery store and takes a can of lima beans off the shelf. He gives the cashier $1.50 (the price marked on the can) and takes the lima beans out of the store. There was a contract to sell the lima beans. The consideration was the payment of $1.50 in exchange for the beans.

Example: Eric tells his nephew Nick that he will pay him $1,000 if he gets a "decent" haircut and has his beard trimmed. Nick goes immediately to his barber and has his beard trimmed to a half-inch. He also has his man-bun cut off. Nick's haircut and beard trim are legal detriments, and are Nick's consideration for a contract with his uncle.

Example: Eric never tires of telling Nick how much he disapproves of his appearance. Nick goes for a haircut and beard trim, hoping that Eric will be favorably impressed and offer him a job at the business he owns. The haircut and beard trim are not consideration, since they are not in exchange for any promise by Eric.

that what is done, or not done, is an exchange for something.

A "moral obligation," meaning a promise to do something because it is the right thing to do, is not consideration. Promising to do something that is already required is also not consideration. There is no legal detriment in doing something a person is already required to do. If there is a dispute about a person's legal obligations, however, doing what would be required under that obligation may be consideration. In those cases, the legal detriment is not in doing the act, but in refraining from contesting the obligation to do it.

If there is an exchange, the adequacy of the consideration is not important. As long as there is an exchange, it does not matter that the value of one party's performance is disproportionate to the value of the other party's.

> Disproportionate values may be evidence of some other defect in the contract, such as fraud. There is some truth in the phrase "too good to be true."

This is referred to as the "peppercorn" theory of consideration. Under this theory, even a single peppercorn can be valid consideration for a contract. Written contracts often are drafted to recite some nominal consideration as adequate and sufficient. "Adequacy" refers to the question of whether the amount of consideration is

FORBEARANCE OR GIVING UP SOME LEGAL RIGHT IS GOOD CONSIDERATION TO SUPPORT A PROMISE

Hamer v. Sidway
(Assignee of Right of Nephew) v. (Executor of Uncle)
124 N.Y. 538, 27 N.E. 256 (1891)

INSTANT FACTS:
William E. Story Sr. (D) promised his nephew, William E. Story Jr. (P), that he would pay William Jr. $5,000 if William Jr. would refrain from drinking, using tobacco, swearing, and gambling, until William Jr. was 21 years of age, which William Jr. did.

BLACK LETTER RULE:
The party who abandons some legal right in the present or limits his legal freedom of action in the future as an inducement for a promise, gives sufficient consideration to create a legally binding contract.

PROCEDURAL BASIS:
An appeal from the Supreme Court reversing the trial court judgment that awarded judgment for Hamer (P), the assignee, against Sidway (D), the executor.

FACTS:
On March 20, 1869, William E. Story, Sr. (D) promised William E. Story, Jr. (P) that if William Jr. would refrain from drinking, using tobacco, swearing, and playing cards or billiards for money until William Jr. became 21 years of age, William Sr. would pay him $5,000. On January 31, 1875, after William Jr. (P) had become 21 years old, William Jr. wrote his uncle, William Sr. (D), and informed him that he had performed his part of the agreement and was entitled to the $5,000. William Sr. (D) wrote his nephew back and stated that "I have no doubt but you have, for which you shall have five thousand dollars as I promised you." However, William Sr. insisted that William Sr. continue to keep the money in the bank for William Jr. until William Jr. was capable of making good decisions about the use of the money, when he would then receive the $5,000 with interest. William Jr. (P) agreed to these terms. On January 29, 1887, William Sr. (D) died without having paid William Jr. (P) the $5,000 and interest. William Jr.'s right was subsequently assigned to Hamer, the plaintiff, who sued William Sr.'s executor, Sidway, the defendant in this action.

ISSUE:
Is forbearance to do that for which one has a legal right to do sufficient consideration to support a promise made to induce the forbearance?

DECISION AND RATIONALE:
(Parker) Yes. A valuable consideration in the sense of the law may consist either in some right interest, profit, or benefit accruing to the one party, or some forbearance, detriment, loss, or responsibility given, suffered, or undertaken by the other. The forbearance does not have to benefit the promises or a third party, or have any substantial value to anyone. It is enough that something is promised, done, forborne, or suffered by the party to whom the promise is made as consideration for the promise made to him. William Jr. (P) used tobacco, occasionally drank liquor, and he had a legal right to do so. He abandoned these rights for a period of years upon the strength of William Sr.'s (D) promise that for such forbearance William Sr. would give him $5,000. It is not of any legal importance whether or not the forbearance benefitted William Sr. (D). The judgment of the Supreme Court is reversed and the special term judgment for plaintiff, Hamer, is affirmed.

ANALYSIS:
The waiver of the legal right in this case was clearly induced by the promise of the uncle. The court pointed out that the consideration given may in fact have benefitted the nephew even more than the uncle. However, the degree of benefit is not measured by the court to determine the validity of a contract. The determining factor is that William Sr. (D) "bargained" for the surrender of William Jr.'s (P) legal right to drink alcohol, use tobacco, and gamble. The abandonment of these rights may have saved William Jr. (P) money or contributed to his health, nevertheless this same abandonment, when bargained for, is sufficient consideration to uphold the promise.

> **Example:** When Khalid and Marta get divorced, the final decree orders Khalid to sign ownership of their house to Marta within 90 days. In return, Marta is to transfer some mutual funds owned by the parties to Khalid. When Marta asks Khalid for the deed to the house, Khalid requests an additional $5,000. In return, he will sign over the house. Khalid's promise to sign over the house is not consideration since there is already a legal obligation to sign over the deed.

> **Example:** After 90 days, Khalid learns that Marta liquidated some of the mutual fund shares to pay for the divorce lawyer. Khalid claims he is no longer obligated to sign he house over, but says he will do it if Marta pays him $5,000 as compensation for the liquidated shares. In this case, Khalid's consideration is his agreement to refrain from contesting his obligation to sign over the house.

a fair exchange. As noted, the adequacy of the consideration is not important and a court will not interfere if one party made a bad deal. The "sufficiency" of consideration is different from the adequacy. Sufficiency is the question of whether the consideration was in fact delivered as promised. If the consideration is not paid, or a promise is not performed, this is a "failure" of consideration. A failure of consideration means that the consideration was, for some reason, not transferred. Some courts have held that a written contract that says that consideration was paid creates a presumption that it was paid. Unless there is contrary proof, the court will say that consideration was paid and not consider the issue further.

> **PROMISSORY ESTOPPEL:**
> Legal doctrine converting a promise to a contract if injustice would otherwise result.

Promissory Estoppel: There is an exception to the rule that a contract requires an exchange of consideration. That exception is known as **promissory estoppel** (also called "detrimental reliance" in some courts). Promissory estoppel lets a promise not made as a part of an exchange substitute for an exchange of consideration. It

> **Example:** Leo and Molly own a house that they rent to tenants. When their son Stephen graduates from college, they want to let him have the house. They sell him the house for $10. The $10 is sufficient consideration for the sale.

> *Example:* An agreement to buy a house says that the promise is made "for $1 and other good and valuable consideration." Unless the seller can show that there was no real payment of consideration beyond the recitation, a court will acknowledge that there was consideration paid.

> *Example:* Toya, a wealthy business person, announces that she is making a $1 million gift to the local opera company. Toya makes this announcement at a press conference at which she shares the stage with the opera's director and two of its star performers. The opera company decides that the promised gift will allow it to commission a new work, so it arranges to pay and pays a well-known composer $500,000 for two new operas. Toya, however, does not follow through on her gift. The opera company may be able to enforce her promise on the basis of promissory estoppel. The company will be able to recover the amount it paid the composer in reliance on Toya's promise.

arises in contexts where there is traditionally no bargain made for performance.

Promissory estoppel will make a promise legally binding when:

- There is a promise,
- The promise is of a type that would induce a person to do something, or not to do something,
- The promise does induce that action or inaction, and
- It is necessary to enforce the promise in order to avoid an injustice.

Promissory estoppel makes a promise enforceable even when there is no agreement.

Capacity

Capacity refers to a person's legal ability to make a contract. If a person does not have capacity, they are legally incapable of making a binding agreement. Any contract entered into by a person without legal capacity will be voidable.

There are several reasons for concluding that a person does not have legal capacity. One is mental defect or illness. If a person has a mental defect that prevents them from understanding the nature and consequences of their actions, a contract they enter into will be voidable. The mental defect must be so substantial that the person does not understand they are making a contract. Sometimes, a person will have a court ruling legally documenting that they do not have capacity. It does not

CAPACITY: The legal ability to make a contract.

> *Example:* Rhea is in a car accident and suffers severe head trauma. The trauma has affected her mentally, so that her doctor has concluded that she has the mental abilities of a 10-year-old child. Billy, an aspiring filmmaker, has Rhea sign an agreement that allows Billy to make an "inspiring" documentary about Rhea and how she has managed her injuries. Rhea probably does not have the capacity to make such an agreement and her legal guardians could declare the contract void.

matter that the person who makes the contract does not know of the mental defect.

A person who is voluntarily intoxicated may also be found to lack capacity. In those cases, a contract will be voidable only if the other party either caused the intoxication, or knew or had reason to know of the extent of the inability to act reasonably. This test applies only to voluntary intoxication, or people who are impaired after taking "recreational" drugs. A person who was intoxicated involuntarily, or who is taking medication that affects their thought processes, are treated as having a mental impairment.

It is assumed that an adult will have legal capacity. A minor, defined as a person under the age of majority (generally 18), does not have capacity, however intelligent or sophisticated she may be. The minor's lack of capacity is different from other forms of incapacity. Contracts made by minors are unenforceable against the minor at the minor's option. This is true even if the minor misrepresented his age when making the contract. The minor, or the minor's guardian, may choose to enforce the contract against the other party. Minors may also be obligated to pay for necessities of life (food, shelter, or clothing) that are sold to them.

If a minor disaffirms a contract, or declares that he will no longer be bound by it, any property sold to him under the contract is returned to the seller. If the contract is for services, or if property sold cannot be returned, some courts have held that the minor must pay the reasonable value of the property or services received.

Legality

One of the basic principles of contract law is the idea of freedom of contract. This freedom is subject to the limitation that a contract cannot

> *Example:* Reggie is 17 years old, and lives in a state where the age of majority is 18. He wants to throw a birthday party for his girlfriend, so he tells a caterer he is 18, and hires the caterer to supply food for the party. After the party, Reggie does not pay, and the caterer tries to collect from him. Reggie may disaffirm the contract, and avoid paying the full price, but he still may be liable for the value of the food supplied.

be made for an illegal purpose. A contract that calls for someone to do something illegal is void and not enforceable.

Any contract that violates a criminal statute, such as theft, forgery, or embezzlement, is unlawful. Statutes make other kinds of bargains illegal, as well. For example, usury laws set the maximum amount of interest that may be charged. These rates are primarily regulated at the state level. Because rates can vary from one state to another and may not apply to all kinds of loans, usury laws can be confusing. The interest rate will depend upon the kind of loan and, in some cases, where the lender is headquartered. National banks are allowed to charge the highest interest rate in the state in which they are incorporated to customers in states that might otherwise require lower rates. As a result, many credit card companies are based in states that do not have limits interest rates for credit card customers. The agreement should identify which state's law applies and what the interest rate will be.

All states have regulations restricting gambling contracts. These laws prohibit various kinds of wagers, games, or bets that rely on chance. Some states prohibit social gambling, such as betting on card games or tournament pools. Other states allow state-run lotteries, commercial or tribal casinos, or sports betting. Most states allow charitable gambling, such as casino nights or raffles, to raise money for good causes, although these options are highly regulated. What may be legal in one state could be illegal in another state.

State licensing statutes require certain professional and tradespeople to be licensed by the state. Doctors, lawyers, electricians, plumbers, hairdressers, and real estate agents are among the positions that states regulate through licensing. The consequences of hiring an unlicensed worker can have consequences for both the worker and the person contracting for services. For example, in most jurisdictions, a license is required to do heating and air conditioning work. The licensing statute may state that a contract to do such work by a person who is unlicensed is not enforceable. The heating and air conditioning work is not illegal, but doing it without a license is and the consequence to the unlicensed worker is that they may not be paid.

Example: Kenneth offers Dana 10 grams of cocaine if she will do some electrical work on his house. Dana agrees. Since cocaine is an illegal drug, this contract is not legally enforceable.

Example: Tura lives in a state in which the legal age for buying liquor is 18. When she turns 18, she orders several cases of wine for a party she intends to give in three months. A month after Tura places her order, the state legislature meets and raises the legal drinking age to 21. The contract to buy the wine is now illegal and may not be enforced.

It is possible that the performance of a contract could become illegal after the agreement was made. In that case, the supervening illegality excuses performance. The contract was legal when made, but may not be enforced because performance would now be illegal.

II. Contract Formalities

The power of contract is that it memorializes the relationship between the parties and its terms govern that relationship. The contract should provide clear guidance to everyone involved what they are supposed to do. When interpreting the contract, the idea is to give effect to the intent behind the making of the contract. In other words, what did the parties agree to? When there are disputes about who is to do what, or when they are supposed to do it, the courts look for some evidence from which the intent of the parties can be deduced.

Written v. Oral Agreements

One of the common misunderstandings that people have about contract law is that a contract is not valid if it is not in writing. This simply is not true. Most contracts do not have to be in writing to be enforceable. Your purchase of a cup of coffee in the morning is a valid contract, yet it is not in writing. A verbal agreement that has all of the elements of offer, acceptance, consideration, capacity, and legality will, with some exceptions, form a valid and binding contract.

There are exceptions to the general rule that a contract need not be in writing. Unless a contract falls into one of these exceptions, however, an oral contract is still valid and enforceable.

Note that, while some contracts are not enforceable unless they are in writing, the reverse is not true. There is no species of contract that is unenforceable if it is in writing. Written contracts have the advantage of making it easier to prove what the parties intended to accomplish by their agreement.

Statute of Frauds

There are some exceptions to the general rule. Some types of contracts must be in writing or they are unenforceable. The **Statute of Frauds** says that certain types of contracts will not be enforced unless there is a writing memorializing the contract.

STATUTE OF FRAUDS:
A law that states that certain types of contract are not enforceable unless they are in writing.

Example: In 1984, a jury in Cook County, Illinois, found that the McDonald's Corporation breached a "handshake" non-written agreement with the Central Ice Cream Co. to distribute Central's "Triple Ripple" ice cream cones for 20 years. The jury awarded damages of $52 million. The case later settled for $15.5 million.

Nowadays, the Statute of Frauds has little, if anything, to do with fraud. The Statute of Frauds requires certain categories of contracts to be in writing, or they cannot be enforced in court. The original version of the Statute was enacted in England, in the 17th century. Before that time, testimony in contract lawsuits was given by hired experts. These experts would testify to whatever the party hired them wanted to hear, regardless of whether it was true. In order to prevent this type of fraud on the courts, the Statute was enacted to require written evidence of the terms of certain types of contracts. The Statute, or variations on the Statute, has been adopted in almost every U.S. jurisdiction.

The Statute of Frauds traditionally requires the following types of contracts to be in writing:

- Contracts in consideration of marriage, such as **antenuptial agreements**,

- Contracts that, by their terms, cannot be performed within one year,

- Contracts to sell an interest in land,

- Contracts by an executor of an estate to pay an estate debt with the executor's own money,

- Contracts for the sale of goods (not services) for $500 or more, and

- Suretyship agreements to answer for or guarantee another person's debts.

> Most law students are taught to remember Statute of Frauds contracts through the mnemonic "MY LEGS" (marriage, year, land, executor, goods over $500, and sureties).

Several other statutes or regulations may require a written agreement in order to be effective. For example, a transfer of a copyright must be in writing, regardless of the price or value of the transfer.

In order to satisfy the terms of the Statute, a written contract must have been signed by

ANTENUPTIAL AGREEMENTS: A pre-marital contract in which the parties agree on issues like the disposition of property after death or dissolution of the marriage.

Example: In order to clear the title to some property owned by their family, Delta is willing to transfer her interest in the property to her brother Billy. She sends him a letter that says "I agree to sell you my interest in the property our parents owned at 123 Sycamore Street, Hometown City, for $1." She signs the letter with her full name. The letter meets the requirements of the Statute of Frauds. If Delta had only promised Billy she would sell him her interest in the property orally, that promise would not be enforceable.

> **Example:** Quan places a telephone order for 1,000 reams of printer paper for his office. The paper costs $8/ream. It is to be shipped in two equal lots of 500 reams each. After the first lot is delivered, Quan concludes he ordered too much paper. He tells the seller he will not take any more, and because there was no written contract, he is not bound to pay for the paper that was delivered. Because the seller has partially performed the oral contract by sending the first lot, so Quan must pay for the paper delivered.

the party against whom the contract is being enforced. The signature can be any symbol intended to show agreement. It does not need to be handwritten.

Courts have created exceptions to the requirements of the Statute of Frauds. If a party agrees that a contract was formed, she may not claim that the Statute bars enforcement. Partial performance of a verbal agreement will also take the contract outside the Statute of Frauds.

A contract will also be taken outside the Statute of Frauds if there has been reliance on a verbal promise. The reliance must have been reasonable, meaning the promise relied upon must have been the kind that would be expected to induce a person to act, or not to act, in a certain manner. Enforcement of the promise will be granted only to avoid injustice. In deciding if enforcement is necessary to avoid injustice, courts look at:

- The availability and adequacy of other remedies,
- The nature of the action or inaction in relation to the remedy sought,
- The extent to which the action or inaction corroborates the evidence that a promise was made,
- The reasonableness of the action or inaction, and
- The extent to which the inaction or action was foreseeable.

The proof necessary to show reliance is difficult. Courts are reluctant to find reliance that justifies the enforcement of an oral contract, out of fear that such a finding could make the Statute of Frauds meaningless.

III. Contract Enforcement and Performance

Contract analysis does not end with formation. Once the contract is in place, it must be enforced. This section considers various events that can impact whether the contract will be enforced and what happens if one or both parties does not perform their obligations. Formation of a contract is not the last stage. Now, the contract must be performed. If it is not performed, it must be enforced.

Enforcement: Genuineness of Assent

It is possible that the elements of a contract may appear to have met the requirements of offer and acceptance, consideration, capacity, and legality and all the appropriate rules on formation appear to have been followed, but the agreement is still not enforceable. The key here is that even though everything appears to be correct, there may be no actual "meeting of the minds." A court may refuse to enforce a contract if one or more of the parties did not or could not agree to its terms. Something present in the transaction has negated mutual assent.

Fraud/Misrepresentation: When there is a misrepresentation in a contract or the making of the contract, one party is not getting what he bargained for. A party has made an agreement, but it is not the agreement that he thinks he has made. A contract may be void or voidable if it is tainted by fraud.

Two kinds of contractual fraud bear closer examination: fraud in the factum and fraud in the inducement.

Fraud in the factum, which is sometimes called fraud in the execution or fraud in the making, results when an innocent party is given false information that makes them sign something without realizing it is a contract. It involves deceit in the subject matter of the contract. For example, a son tell his blind father to sign a piece of paper, saying that it is a letter to the bank when it is actually a legal document changing the father's will. It may also occur when a document is forged or when the terms of the contract are changed without knowledge or approval. Such contracts are void.

Fraud in the inducement occurs when an innocent party is tricked into entering into a contract because they are misled as to important facts underlying the agreement. Such an agreement is voidable at the option of the innocent party. Fraud in the inducement requires a **material misrepresentation**. "Material" means that it concerns something that is important to the innocent party's decision to enter into the contract. The misrepresentation could be a false

> **MATERIAL MISREPRESENTATION:**
> A misrepresentation of an important fact that would induce a reasonable person to make an agreement.

Example: Jean operates an antique store. She has a set of dishes for sale. The dishes are actually inexpensive dishes made to have what the manufacturer considers a "retro" look. Nevertheless, Jean tells two potential buyers that the dishes were featured in a photo shoot in the November 1965 issue of an interior design magazine. The first buyer, Pedro, is just interested in buying dishes that match his dining room's color scheme. The misrepresentation is not material. The second buyer, Jasmine, has told Jean that she is looking for authentic dishes for a recreation of a mid-1960s home she is doing for a television program. The misrepresentation is material as to Jasmine.

> **Example:** Pat hires Capital Roofing to repair hail damage and to re-roof the house. Without Pat's knowledge, Capital Roofing changes the amount owed on the contract to three times the agreed to price. This is fraud in the factum and renders the contract void.

> **Example:** Pat wants an experienced company to repair hail damage and to re-roof the house. Pat hires Capital Roofing because the owner of says the company has been in business for fifteen years. In actuality, Pat's roof is the company's first job and the roofers cause substantial damage. This could be fraud in the inducement, because deceit was used to prompt Pat to sign the contract. The contract could be voidable.

statement, but it could also be omitting information when there is a legal disclosure duty.

A fraudulent misrepresentation is one that is made with the intention of inducing reliance. It was also made with the knowledge that it was false, or without knowing whether it was false.

The innocent party must prove justifiable reliance on the fraudulent statement in order to void a contract based on a misrepresentation. The reliance must be justifiable under the circumstances, meaning that it must be reasonable for the innocent party to have relief for the material misrepresentation or omission. Whether the reliance is reasonable is based on a number of factors including age, education, experience, and relative expertise of the parties. Reliance is more likely to be deemed reasonable if the person

> **Example:** Arvid is a professor of art history at a university. He is a well-known expert on 20th century American painting. His neighbor Margot is thinking of buying a painting he owns. Arvid tells her it is an original Jackson Pollack. In fact, the painting is just a student's effort to make a painting that looked like a Pollack. Margot buys the painting. Her reliance on Arvid's misrepresentation was reasonable.

> **Example:** Instead of being an art history professor, Arvid is an engineer who knows nothing about art, and does not claim any special knowledge. When Margot asks if the painting is a Pollack, he shrugs and says "Sure, I guess so." Margot's reliance on that statement would not be reasonable.

> **Example:** Ed has owned horses for several years. His niece Jodi wants to buy one of his horses. He tells her that one particular horse is a nice choice for a beginner, because he is gentle and docile. The horse is actually spirited and hard for Jodi to handle. Ed's opinion that the horse was a "nice choice" was a misrepresentation on which Jodi reasonably relied.

making the false statement has some expertise in the field. For example, it is more reasonable to rely on a jeweler's statement that an engagement ring contains a real diamond than it may be to rely on a description from a private seller on an app.

A statement of opinion ("This is the finest car on the market today") will generally not be considered a misrepresentation. The exception to this rule is when the opinion has, or purportedly has, some factual basis, and the person expressing the opinion has, or claims to have, superior knowledge. In that situation, reliance on the opinion may be found justified.

Mistake

We all make mistakes. Some mistakes can affect the validity of a contract.

The type of mistake that will affect a contact is a mistake of facts. It is a mistaken belief that is not in accord with the facts as they exist at the time of making the contract. This is not the same as an error in judgment (for example, deciding that goods are worth the price being charged). It is also not a prediction that does not come true (for example, artwork that does not appreciate in value as predicted). Finding that there was a mistake of fact can make a contract void. It can also be the basis for **reforming**, or rewriting, the contract.

Mutual Mistake: A mutual mistake of facts can make a contract voidable by the party to the contract who is adversely affected. There are four conditions that must be met before a contract is voidable for mutual mistake:

- The mistake must relate to the facts in existence at the time the contract was made,

REFORMATION: Rewriting a contract to conform to the terms of the parties' agreement.

> **Example:** Ivy meets with Bjorn to finalize an agreement to sell a painting. The painting is being stored at Ivy's vacation home. While the discussion is going on, the vacation home and the painting are destroyed by fire. Neither Ivy not Bjorn know of this until after they sign the sales agreement. The contract may be voided for mutual mistake.

COURT VOIDS A CONTRACT THAT HINGED ON AN AMBIGUOUS TERM

Raffles v. Wichelhaus
(Cotton Seller) v. (Cotton Buyer)
2 H. & C. 906, 159 Eng. Rep. 375 (Court of Exchequer 1864)

INSTANT FACTS:
Two parties to a cotton transaction disagree as to the exact identity of a ship named in their contract.

BLACK LETTER RULE:
A contract can be voided if it contains an ambiguous term which was, in fact, interpreted differently by the parties.

PROCEDURAL BASIS:
Decision of the Court of Exchequer on a breach of contract action.

FACTS:
Raffles (P) agreed to sell Wichelhaus (D) 125 bales of cotton which were supposed to arrive in England by ship. Wichelhaus (D) agreed to pay for the cotton after it arrived from Bombay on a ship called Peerless. Neither party to the contract knew it at the time, but there were two ships called Peerless which sailed from Bombay. One ship sailed in October. The second ship sailed in December. Unfortunately, each party had a different ship in mind for the transaction. Raffles (P) thought that the Peerless which sailed in December was the agreed upon ship. When that ship arrived in England, Raffles (P) attempted to complete the transaction. Wichelhaus (D), however, refused to accept delivery or to pay for the cotton since he had expected the other Peerless. Raffles (P) subsequently sued Wichelhaus (D) for breach of contract. Wichelhaus's (D) plea followed and Raffles (P) demurred. The court then rendered its opinion.

ISSUE:
Can a specific contract term be interpreted according to a party's subjective interpretation of that term?

DECISION AND RATIONALE:
(Mellish) Yes. Raffles (P) and Wichelhaus (D) did not make it clear that the Peerless was a particular ship sailing on a particular date. When it turned out that there were actually two different ships named Peerless, a latent ambiguity was exposed in the contract. In that event, the court can hear parol evidence in order to establish that there was an actual subjective disagreement between the parties. Since there was no consensus ad litem, there is no contract. Since there is no contract, Raffles (P) has no right to sue for its breach. The action will be dismissed and judgement entered in favor of Wichelhaus (D).

ANALYSIS:
Note that the rule of law announced by the court is meant for the exceptional case. Usually, courts require the objective intent of the parties to govern the interpretation of a contract. Occasionally, though, a crucial term in the contract is subject to differing interpretations. If the parties actually interpreted an ambiguous term in different ways, the contract can be voided.

CASE VOCABULARY:

AD LITEM:
Ad litem means "for the purposes of the suit."

COURT OF EXCHEQUER:
A trial level court which existed until 1873. Its jurisdiction was subsequently turned over to the Exchequer Division and then the Queen's Bench Division of the High Court of Justice.

DEMURRER:
A demurrer is a means of attacking a party's pleading. In essence, the attacker argues that the pleading need not be answered because it is insufficient or defective in some manner. There are a variety of different demurrers, some of which are still recognized. The modem equivalent of a general demurrer is a request for dismissal under Federal Rule of Civil Procedure 12 (b) (6). A

> request under 12 (b) (6) alleges that the opposing party fails to state a claim for which relief can be granted.
>
> **PAROL EVIDENCE:**
> Oral or verbal evidence. In contract law, "parol evidence" refers to evidence of agreements outside of the written agreement. Parol evidence is generally not admissible when it would alter or contradict the terms of a written agreement.

- The mistake relates to a basic assumption both parties made at the time of making the contract,

- The mistake has a material effect on the contract, so that the contract is severely unfair and enforcement would be unjust, and

- The party who is asking to void the contract did not assume the risk of mistake.

Assuming the risk of mistake means not investigating the facts when given the opportunity or obligation to do so, or acting with the knowledge that the party does not know the essential facts.

Unilateral Mistake: If only one party is mistaken about a fact, it may be possible to void a contract. Relief for a unilateral mistake will be granted if the non-mistaken party first shows:

- The mistake must relate to the facts in existence at the time the contract was made,

- The mistake relates to a basic assumption both parties made at the time of making the contract,

- The mistake has a material effect on the contract, so that the contract is severely unfair and enforcement would be unjust, and

- The party who is asking to void the contract did not assume the risk of mistake.

In addition, the non-mistaken party must also show either:

- The other party knew or had reason to know of the mistake, or

- The mistake makes the contract unconscionable.

> A unilateral mistake of fact could be the result of misrepresentation.

> *Example:* Virgil is visiting his friend Pete, and sees what looks like an expensive guitar. Virgil tells Pete that the guitar is a collector's item, and offers $1,000 for it. Pete knows that the guitar is an inexpensive knock-off he bought the week before, but accepts the offer of $1,000. He does not tell Virgil that the guitar is a recent copy, but he also has not told him that it is a collector's item. The contract is voidable for unilateral mistake.

> **Example:** Emma agrees to sell her house to Jaynie. The negotiations for the sale were done in a serious of e-mails, all referring to the house at 70 Willow Street, and the sale price as $350,000. When the final purchase agreement is written up and signed, the address of the property is given as 80 Willow Street, and the sale price as $359,000. The contract may be reformed to reflect the true agreement between Emma and Jaynie.

Scrivener's Error: Errors can be made getting the actual agreement down on paper. These are referred to as scrivener's errors. They are not the product of a mistake of facts or misrepresentation.

A scrivener's error does not mean a contract can be voided. Instead, the written instrument will be reformed to reflect what the parties intended when they made the contract.

Undue Influence

Undue influence will make a contract voidable. Undue influence is found when improper persuasion causes a person to enter into an unfair contract. Undue influence means that the person's assent was not the product of their own free will.

There are two types of undue influence. The first type involves a person taking advantage of someone else's weakened state of mind. The "weakened state of mind" is not necessarily the result of incapacity, but comes from circumstances that make a person unable to make sound decisions. The person who takes advantage of that weakness knows of the vulnerability, and exploits it to her advantage. Undue influence may result from emotional or psychological pressure to receive something that person might otherwise not give to them. An example might be a caregiver convincing their elderly client to disinherit her children who live in another state and to leave all the money to the caregiver instead.

The other type of undue influence comes from a fiduciary relationship. When a person has placed their trust and confidence in another person, and that person receives an unfair

> A will may also be contested for undue influence, in circumstances similar to those that will void a contract.

> **Example:** Jorge's wife has just died in childbirth, along with the baby she was carrying. Jorge is devastated with grief. Frieda, a neighbor who knows of Jorge's mental state, offers to buy some jewelry owned by Jorge's late wife for one-tenth of the actual value of the jewels. Jorge agrees, not paying much attention to Frieda's offer. The sale of the jewelry could be voided for undue influence.

> **Example:** Luci has been Marco's attorney for many years. She has been a close adviser on many business and personal legal matters. One day, during a casual conversation, Luci remarks that she might be interested in moving from her house to a condominium. Marco offers to sell her a condominium unit he owns for the same price that he paid for it 10 years ago. This is significantly less than the market value of the unit. Luci agrees to the purchase. The contract may be set aside for undue influence because of the fiduciary relationship between Luci and Marco.

advantage from a contract with the person who trusts him, the contract may be set aside for undue influence. It is not necessary to show that the fiduciary tried to take advantage of the relationship.

Genuineness of Assent/Duress

There is also no genuine assent if the agreement was the product of **duress.** Duress traditionally meant inducing agreement by means of a threat of bodily or physical harm. In recent years, courts have expanded the definition of duress to include any wrongful or unlawful act. The wrongful or unlawful act must be a kind that leaves the threatened person no reasonable alternative but to comply. The threatened wrongful or unlawful act does not need to be physical harm. Economic duress may also constitute the kind of threat that will justify voiding a contract.

Contract Performance and Discharge

Once an enforceable contract is made, it is up to the parties to perform the contract. Every contract carries with it an implied duty of good

DURESS: Inducing agreement by means of a threat or wrongful act.

> **Example:** Dale supplies heating oil to several businesses; she is the only local heating oil seller. One local business is a new restaurant owned by Shadi. While discussing a contract for heating fuel sales, Dale mentions that her son Jake has just opened a new bakery, and is looking for commercial accounts. Shadi says that he is satisfied with the bakery his restaurant uses now. Dale says "Yeah, that's okay. I just don't know how you're going to make it through the winter if you can't heat your place." Shadi takes the hint, and signs a contract to buy bread from Jake. The contract is the product of duress, and is voidable.

faith and fair dealing. That duty has two parts. The first is to perform, or make reasonable efforts to perform, the contractual duties. The second is the duty not to interfere with the other party's performance.

Performance of a contract is often made subject to certain conditions. A condition may give rise to a contractual duty of it occurs, or if it does not occur. The happening or non-happening of a condition may also excuse performance. Conditions may be express, implied in fact, or constructive.

An express condition is one that is stated explicitly in the contract. Express conditions are created by the language used by the parties in making their contract. For example, many real estate contracts are conditional upon a satisfactory report from a property inspector or upon financing for the buyer. If there is an express condition in a contract, courts will usually require that the condition fully occurs before any contract duty is created or excused.

Implied-in-fact conditions are not set out expressly. The contract terms make it clear that the parties intended that something must happen before a duty would arise. The absence of express language does not defeat the finding that there is a condition.

Constructive conditions are found when duties are not expressed as conditions, but it is evident that a condition was intended. For instance, in a restaurant, the server brings the order and the diner eats before paying, but there is a constructive condition that the meal will be paid for at the prices shown on the menu.

Example: Alice signs a contract to buy a new car from Zippy Motors, if she can obtain financing. Alice has second thoughts after leaving the dealership, and decides she doesn't want the car after all. She does not apply for a loan. Alice has breached her duty of good faith.

Example: Alice applies for a loan at a bank located out-of-state. She knows that the bank will not be willing to lend to someone so far away. Alice has breached her duty of good faith.

Example: Alice applies for a car loan at her local bank. The Zippy Motors salesman is angry that she is not trying to arrange financing through him. When the bank calls to verify the car being purchased, the salesman says he has no record of Alice ever trying to buy a car from Zippy. Zippy has breached its duty of good faith.

Example: Life insurance contracts promise to pay the beneficiary a certain sum of money. They are obligated to do this only when the insured dies. The death of the insured is an express condition for payment to the beneficiary.

Example: Grace agrees to print 1,000 t-shirts for Louise. Louise is to give Grace a copy of the logo she wants printed on the shirts. There is a condition implied-in-fact that Louise must furnish the logo before Grace is obligated to perform.

Example: At a newsstand, Lyle picks up a newspaper and approaches the cashier. The cashier looks at the newspaper, and says "a dollar twenty-five, please." Lyle pays him $1.25 and leaves with the newspaper. Payment of $1.25 was a constructive condition of Lyle getting possession of the newspaper.

Breach of Contract

Broadly speaking, a breach of contract is when one party to a contract does not perform their duties under the contract. Breaches are classified as either **material** or **minor**. The distinction between the two is important for deciding what the non-breaching party may do in response to the breach.

A material breach is one that goes to the very essence of the agreement. It deprives the non-breaching party of the benefits under the contract that she bargained for. A material breach will render the contract irreparably broken. The non-breaching party may declare the contract to be at an end, and sue the breaching party for damages. The non-breaching party has no further obligations under the contract.

A minor breach is one that still allows the non-breaching party to have the benefits of the agreement. Although there has not been strict compliance with every term of the contract, the non-breaching party may not declare the contract to be over. She must continue her obligations under the contract, but may sue for damages for the breach.

When deciding if a breach is material or minor, courts look at the following factors:

MATERIAL BREACH:
A breach of contract that deprives the non-breaching party of the value of the contract.

MINOR BREACH:
A breach of contract that allows the non-breaching party to have the benefits of the agreement.

- The benefit received by the non-breaching party,

- Whether the non-breaching party can be adequately compensated for the breach,

- The extent of the breaching party's performance,

- The hardship to the breaching party,

- The negligent or willful behavior of the breaching party, and

- The likelihood that the breaching party will complete the contract.

A breach of contract may occur before the performance was supposed to happen. This is known as an **anticipatory breach**. An anticipatory breach happens when a party notifies another that he will not be able to perform the contract. It may also happen when one party has reason to doubt that the contract will be performed, and asks for reassurance of performance but does not receive it. The contract is breached as of the notification or failure to receive assurances.

> Determining the exact date of the breach is necessary to determine when the statute of limitations begins to run.

ANTICIPATORY BREACH: Informing a party that a contract will be breached before the breach takes place.

Example: Rufus hires Daria to do an extensive remodeling job on his house. The contract requires that Daria install a new bathroom with a whirlpool bath. It also requires that Daria leave the premises in a "neat and clean" condition every day. The work is to be done by October 15, and Rufus will make payment in full.

Unfortunately, Daria does not finish the bathroom by October 15; in fact, it looks like she has barely started the job. This is a major breach of the contract, and Rufus may declare the contract ended. He is not required to pay Daria, and may bring suit for damages.

Example: Daria finishes the job on schedule. As Rufus inspects the job, he notices that Daria and her workers have left fast-food wrappers from their lunch under one of the bushes in his yard. This is a minor breach of the contract. Rufus may not cancel the contract, but he may recover damages for the cost of cleaning up.

> **Example:** Franny's band is hired to play at a New Year's Eve Party given by Al. In early December, Al sees a report that two members of Franny's band have left, and that the band may not be performing any more. He writes to Franny, asking if she will in fact be able to play as agreed. If Franny does not reply, or is unable to say that the band will perform, Al may treat the contract as breached.

If a party does not perform his contractual obligations, his failure may still be excused. There may be defenses that can be raised to a claim of breach of contract. Some of these defenses, such as illegality, lack of capacity, mistake, or misrepresentation, have already been discussed. These defenses say, essentially, that no contract was truly made due to the circumstances, or the situation of the parties. There are other defenses that acknowledge the existence of a valid contract, but note that there is a reason why performance should be excused.

One such defense is impossibility. Impossibility may be raised when something happens after the making of the contract that makes the performance either pointless, or impossible. The thing that happens must not be the fault of the party seeking to be excused. Non-occurrence of the event must have been a basic assumption when the contract was made.

Another defense is frustration of purpose. This defense is available to the buyer in a contract. If the buyer had a specific purpose for the transaction at the time of contracting, and the seller knew of that purpose, then the buyer is excused if the purpose is later thwarted in an unforeseen way beyond the buyer's control.

Another defense is **accord and satisfaction**. Accord and satisfaction is when performance, or a substitute for performance, has been found adequate. This may be a compromise of a claim, or just an agreement to accept an alternate performance.

ACCORD AND SATISFACTION: Accepting performance, or a substitute for performance, as adequate.

> Performance will not be excused merely because performance is more difficult that originally believed.

> **Example:** Richard hires Joanna to sing at the opening of his new dinner theater. The night before the opening, a fault in the electrical wiring starts a fire, and the theater burns down. Performance of the contract is impossible, so Joanna's non-performance is excused.

> *Example:* Jack agrees to rent a vintage car in two weeks. He tells the car's owner that the car will be used to drive in a local parade scheduled the day that the rental starts. The week of the parade, a tornado knocks down several trees along the parade's route. The town cancels the parade. Jack's purpose is frustrated, and he is not liable for the rental.

> *Example:* Tina agrees to customize Graydon's car for $2,500. When the job is done, Graydon discovers that he does not have enough money to pay her. Tina agrees to take Graydon's valuable stamp collection instead of cash. Her acceptance of the stamp collection is an accord and satisfaction.

Remedies

Remedies are the legal consequence for not keeping the promises of a contract. The term "remedy" is significant. The goal is to fix something that is wrong. They are not meant as a penalty, or as a deterrent to future misconduct.

DAMAGES:
A sum of money awarded as compensation for a breach of contract.

EXPECTATION DAMAGES:
The monetary value of the benefit that would have been received if the contract had been performed as agreed.

GENERAL DAMAGES:
The harm that normally flows form a breach of contract.

SPECIAL DAMAGES:
Damages that occur due to the special circumstances of a particular contract.

The typical remedy for breach of contract is an order to pay a sum of money to the non-breaching party. This is referred to as an award of **damages.** The award of damages is limited to the damages caused by the breach. Punitive or exemplary damages are not usually allowed in contract cases. The purpose of contract damages is compensation to the non-breaching party, to put that party in the same financial position as if the contract had not been breached. There are five types of contract damages.

Expectation damages equal the monetary amount of the benefit that would have been received if the contract had been performed as agreed. This amount is reduced by the amount that is saved by reason of the non-breaching party not being required to perform.

Expectation damages are further divided into **general** and **special** damages.

General damages are those that a contracting party would imagine being liable for if she breached the contract. In the example above, Noelle should realize that she would be liable for

> **Example:** Jesse is hired to pave the parking lot at an office building owned by Noelle. The job is to be done on Saturday, and Jesse will be paid $10,000 for the job. On Wednesday, Noelle tells Jesse that she does not want the job done after all, and that Jesse should just forget it. Because he will not be doing the job, Jesse will not have to pay $5,000 for workers that day, and will not have to pay $2,500 for materials. In a breach of contract suit, Jesse's damages will be $2,500.

> Expectation damages must be proven with a high degree of certainty. Courts do not permit an award of speculative damages.

the monetary loss to Jesse. Special damages are not ones that would ordinarily be anticipated. They may be recovered only if the breaching party was aware that there were special facts or circumstances that would cause these damages.

There may be contracts where the expectation damages are too difficult to prove. The damages awarded in those cases will be **reliance damages**. Reliance damages are the amount that the non-breaching party spent to perform the contract, in reliance on the other

> **RELIANCE DAMAGES:** The amount that the non-breaching party spent to perform the contract, in reliance on the other party's performance.

PARTY INJURED BY A BREACH OF CONTRACT CAN ONLY RECOVER THOSE DAMAGES THAT MAY REASONABLY BE CONSIDERED AS ARISING NATURALLY FROM THE BREACH, OR AS HAVING BEEN CONTEMPLATED BY THE PARTIES IN ADVANCE AS A LIKELY RESULT OF THE BREACH

Hadley v. Baxendale
(Mill Operators) v. (Delivery Service)
9 Ex. 341, 156 Eng. Rep. 145 (1854)

INSTANT FACTS:
Baxendale failed to deliver a broken mill shaft for Hadley on time, and the delay prevented Hadley from reopening the mill on time.

BLACK LETTER RULE:
A party injured by another party's breach of contract can only recover those damages that may fairly and reasonably be considered either as arising naturally, or as may reasonably be supposed to have been in the contemplation of both parties, at the time the contract was made, as the probable result of such a breach of the contract.

PROCEDURAL BASIS:
Rule nisi for new trial in action for damages for breach of contract of carriage.

FACTS:

The Hadleys (P) operated a mill in Gloucester. This mill had to be shut down on May 11, 1854, when the crankshaft of the steam engine which ran the mill became broken. The Hadleys (P) arranged to have the manufacturers of their (P) engine make a replacement one based on the pattern of the broken shaft. To accomplish this, a representative of the Hadleys (P) went to Baxendale (D) at Pickford & Co., a well-known carrier [delivery and transport] business, on May 13. This representative told the Baxendale's (D) clerk that the Hadleys' (P) mill was stopped, and that the shaft must be sent immediately to the manufacturers at Greenwich. The clerk assured the Hadleys' (P) servant that it could be delivered in a day.

The next morning, Baxendale (D) took the shaft and was paid to deliver it to Greenwich. This delivery was delayed by Baxendale's (D) neglect. As a result, the completion of repairs and the reopening of the mill were delayed by five days. In that time, the Hadleys (P) were compelled to pay wages. The Hadleys (P) claimed they (P) also lost wages totaling £300 [pounds] and sought judgment for that amount.

Baxendale (D) claimed these damages were too remote, and that liability should not be found. The jury awarded £25 in damages to the Hadleys (P). Baxendale (D) appealed.

ISSUE:

Should the measure of damages awarded to a party who is injured by a breach of contract be limited to only those damages that are not considered remote by the parties?

DECISION AND RATIONALE:

(Alderson) Yes. A party injured by another party's breach of contract can only recover those damages that may fairly and reasonably be considered either as arising naturally, or as may reasonably be supposed to have been in the contemplation of both parties, at the time the contract was made, as the probable result of such a breach of the contract. In other words, if the special circumstances under which a contract is made are described by one party to another, it follows that both sides are aware of these special circumstances. Thus, any damages caused by a breach would have been reasonably contemplated by the parties.

The measure of those damages would be the amount of injury which would ordinarily follow from such a breach under these circumstances. If, however, a party that breaches the contract did not know of these special circumstances, then he or she could only be presumed to have knowledge of the kind of injury that would result generally from a breach. This is because parties with knowledge of special circumstances regarding a contract could very well provide for them. It would be unfair for this advantage to be taken away from such parties by presuming otherwise.

Here, the Hadleys' (P) servant only told Baxendale's (D) clerk at the time the contract was made that the mill shaft was broken, and that the Hadleys (P) operated that mill. It is unclear how these circumstances could reasonably show that the mill's profits would be stopped if the delivery of the shaft to the manufacturer were unreasonably delayed. Baxendale (D) had no idea of whether the Hadleys (P) had an extra shaft at the mill, or whether the steam engine was otherwise defective. Ordinarily, a miller sending an engine shaft to a third person by a common carrier would not result in a loss of profits and a stopped mill.

The special circumstances here that would lead to such a situation were never communicated to Baxendale (D). Therefore, the loss of profits in this case cannot reasonably be considered such a consequence of the breach of the contract as could have been fairly and reasonably contemplated by both parties when they made this contract. The jury should not have taken the loss of profits into consideration when measuring damages. A new trial is necessary in this case. Rule absolute.

ANALYSIS:

Consequential damages are affected by the circumstances under which the contract was made, such as the amount of information provided by one party to another. The court here said the loss of profits for the mill could not have been in Baxendale's (D) "contemplation" because he (D) did not know if Hadley (P) had an extra mill shaft, if the mill engine was otherwise faulty, etc. This "contemplation" requirement imposed on the recovery of breach of contract damages was more severe than the test for substantial or proximate cause used in actions for tort or breach of warranty. Shortly after the Hadley decision, it appeared that both English and American courts would transform this contemplation test into an even stricter one. Some courts supported the idea that a party could not be held liable for consequential damages unless that party had made a "tacit agreement" to assume that particular risk when making the contract. Fortunately, this restrictive test has not survived to this day, and is explicitly rejected in the comments to the UCC. The modern trend has been to define the test as one of "foreseeability." A party must only have been given notice of facts that made a loss foreseeable to be held liable.

CASE VOCABULARY:
COMMON CARRIER:
A business that offers its services to the public for transportation of people, goods, or messages.

NOLLE PROSEQUI:
A formal declaration that a prosecutor or plaintiff will "no longer prosecute" a particular case.

RULE ABSOLUTE:
A rule which commands that an order be forthwith enforced.

Example: Noelle hires Jesse to pave the parking lot of her building for $10,000. Jesse does not show up to do the job as promised, and Noelle has to hire a different contractor for $12,000. The additional $2,000 is recoverable by Noelle as general damages. The cost of hiring a substitute should have been within Jesse's contemplation when he made the contract.

The substitute is not able to pave Noelle's parking lot until two weeks after Jesse was supposed to do it. This means that Noelle was not able to rent her parking lot to a visiting carnival, an event that would have paid her $5,000. Jesse is not liable for the additional $5,000 in special damages unless Noelle had made him aware of the carnival rental at the time the contract was made.

Example: Cheryl agrees to remodel Del's house. Del agrees to pay for the work in stages. When the first payment is due, Del announces that she doesn't have the money to pay for the complete job. Cheryl should stop further work, and pursue Del for breach of contract. If she continues to work, she will not be able to recover damages for the work done after Del tells her the contract will not be fulfilled.

The "American Rule," requires each party to bear her own litigation costs. The "English Rule" holds that the losing party bears the litigation costs for both sides. The English Rule does not just apply in England; it is the most common means of splitting litigation costs in the Western world.

party performing her obligations. Reliance damages may not exceed the amount that would have been paid under the contract.

Restitution damages are awarded when there was no legal contract. They are appropriate in situations in which one party has partially performed his obligations, and the other

> **Example:** Mavis has been hired as the manager of a new band. Her contract says that she will receive 10% of the receipts for each concert that she books. Mavis books concerts in four different cities, traveling to each one to inspect concert venues. She also spends money for internet and phone access, as well as on printing promotional materials. Before the first contract, the band members have a falling out and split up. Mavis does not know what the receipts from each concert could have been, because the band was new and an unknown quantity. Mavis may not recover her expectation damages, but she may recover what she spent to perform her contractual duties.

> **Example:** Meg makes a verbal agreement with Jo to buy $1,000 worth of yarn, to resell in Meg's craft shop. After half of the yarn is delivered, Meg says she doesn't want the rest. The contract is within the Statute of Frauds, so Jo may not sue for breach of contract. Jo may, however, sue for restitution for the value of the benefit conferred on Meg.

party has received a benefit from that performance. Restitution damages for the value of the performance rendered are ordered to avoid unjust enrichment.

Liquidated damages are damages fixed by the contract. The limitation on liquidated damages is that they must be reasonable. Liquidated damages are used in cases where it is hard to know in advance what the damages for a breach of contract could be.

Interest will be awarded when the breach is the failure to pay a specific sum of money at a specific time. Interest is generally not awarded in other types of breach of contract cases.

The contract remedy that may seem the most intuitive is also the one that is awarded the least. **Specific performance** is an order from the court to do what the contract obligates you to do. It is ordered in cases in which an award of money will not be adequate compensation. The most common cases in which specific performance will be ordered are:

- A contract for the sale of something unique. The non-breaching party cannot

> **RESTITUTION DAMAGES:**
> Damages awarded when there was no legally enforceable contract.
>
> **LIQUIDATED DAMAGES:**
> Damages fixed by the contract.
>
> **SPECIFIC PERFORMANCE:**
> An order from the court to do what the contract obligates the person to do.

QUANTUM MERUIT AVAILABLE AS AN ALTERNATIVE TO BREACH OF CONTRACT

U.S. for the use of Coastal Steel Erectors, Inc. v. Algernon Blair, Inc.
(Representative of Subcontractor) v. (Contractor)
479 F.2d 638 (4th Cir. 1973)

INSTANT FACTS:
Coastal Steel (P) brought suit to recover the value of labor and equipment supplied, but the trial court denied recovery under the contract.

BLACK LETTER RULE:
When a contract is breached, the non-breaching party may sue for the value of the performance provided.

FACTS:
Blair (D) contracted with the U.S. Navy for the construction of a hospital. Blair (D) then contracted with Coastal (P) for services and to supply equipment for that contract. Coastal started to perform its obligations, supplying cranes for handling and placing steel. Blair (D) refused to pay for crane rental, maintaining that it was not obligated to do so under the subcontract. Coastal (P) then terminated its performance.

The district court found that the subcontract required Blair (D) to pay for crane use and that Blair's (D) refusal to do so justified Coastal's (P) termination of performance. The court then found that under the contract the amount due Coastal (P), less what had already been paid, totaled approximately $37,000. The court also found that Coastal (P) would have lost more than $37,000 if it had completed performance. Holding that any amount due Coastal (P) must be reduced by any loss it would have incurred by complete performance of the contract.

ISSUE:
Was Coastal (P) allowed to recover for the value of its services?

DECISION AND RATIONALE:
(Craven, J.) Yes. When a contract is breached, the non-breaching party may sue for the value of the performance provided. It is an accepted principle of contract law that the non-breaching party has the option to forego any suit on the contract and claim only the reasonable value of his performance. Coastal (P) has, at its own expense, provided Blair (D) with labor and the use of equipment. Blair (D) retained these benefits without having fully paid for them. On these facts, Coastal (P) is entitled to restitution in *quantum meruit*. The impact of *quantum meruit* is to allow a non-breaching party to recover the value of services provided to the defendant irrespective of whether he would have lost money on the contract and been unable to recover in a suit on the contract.

The measure of recovery for *quantum meruit* is the reasonable value of the performance. It is not diminished by any loss which would have been incurred by complete performance. The contract price may be evidence of reasonable value of the services, but it does not measure the value of the performance or limit recovery. The standard for measuring the reasonable value of the services rendered is the amount for which such services could have been purchased at the time and place the services were rendered. Reversed and remanded.

ANALYSIS:
Quantum meruit literally means "as much as he deserves." Coastal (P) may have come out better because of the breach of contract, because its recovery is measured by the value of services rendered, instead of considering the position it would have been in if the contract had not been breached. Coastal (P) may recover the value of its services, but the value is not measured by the contract price.

CASE VOCABULARY:
QUANTUM MERUIT:
An equitable doctrine that allows a party to recover the actual value of goods and services rendered, even in the absence of an enforceable contract. The goal is to prevent unjust enrichment of a party.

> **Example:** Fred wants to buy a house as a graduation gift for his nephew Reginald. The farm Fred grew up on has been redeveloped into a residential community, Mitching Hill. Although all of the houses in Mitching Hill look identical, Fred identifies number 42 as being on the site of a fond memory from his childhood. He signs a contract to purchase number 42. The next day, the developer calls him and says he will not sell him number 42, as he wants to keep that house as a model. The developer says he can purchase number 41 or 43, instead. Fred refuses. A court may order specific performance of the contract to sell number 42 because every piece of real estate is considered completely unique under the law.

remedy her loss by buying an identical item from another seller.

- A contract for the sale of land. Every parcel of real estate is deemed unique and irreplaceable by similar properties.

- Shareholder voting agreements. It is hard, if not impossible, to calculate the monetary loss from such a breach.

There are a number of reasons specific performance is not ordered more frequently. The main reason is that courts do not want to be put in the position of supervising a party's performance. When the contract is a sales contract, performance is easy and quick. If the contract requires more extensive performance, such as a construction contract, a court that ordered specific performance would have to go beyond ordering performance, but would have a continuing role of making sure performance was adequate.

Damages such as pain and suffering or emotional distress are usually not foreseeable, so are not recoverable in a contract action. In addition, a person's attorney's fees incurred in enforcing a contract are not recoverable unless the contract specifically provides.

When a contract has been breached, the non-breaching party must take reasonable steps to minimize, or mitigate, her damages. A wronged party cannot maximize damages by

> **Example:** Stock photo licensing contracts call for the user of a picture to pay a flat fee to use a picture for a certain purpose. The contracts often have liquidated damages clauses that set damages at a certain multiple of the contract price, such as five times the price. Violating the terms of a photo license could cause substantial damages if, for example, the photo is used in a way that generates a large profit. It may also cause minimal damage. The probable damages cannot be estimated when the contract is made, so liquidated damages are included in the contract.

> **Example:** Toni agrees to repair Bal's roof, but Toni fails to show up. Bal allows the roof damage to increase, with water damage from a subsequent storm creating a much bigger job. Bal's rationale is that it is Toni's problem now. But if Bal could have mitigated the later damage through achievable measures (such as throwing a tarp over the roof or using buckets to catch leaks), she will not be able to claim damages from Toni for those repairs.

allowing property to be harmed or otherwise increasing costs when it is reasonably possible to avoid it.

Contract Torts

The usual definition of a tort is that it is a civil wrong that is not a breach of contract. This definition is not entirely correct. There are tort actions that involve a breach, or potential breach, of contract.

Interference with contract is the most important contract/tort action. In order to prove a claim of interference with contract, the aggrieved party must prove the following facts:

- The existence of a valid contract,
- The defendant knew of the existence of the contract,
- The defendant intentionally did something to interfere with the contract, and
- The aggrieved party was damaged by the defendant's actions.

Note that the lawsuit for interference with contract is not brought against the contracting party, although they may be liable for a breach of contract. Note also that the tort does not prevent legitimate competition, provided existing contracts are respected.

> **Example:** Sonya owns a bar that buys its beer from Kipele Distributors. Her contract with Kipele runs until the end of the year. In July, Toshi, a sales representative for Tulala Wholesalers, visits Sonya's bar. He tells her that if she switches distributors now, he can save her 20% on the cost of beer. Sonya agrees, and cancels her contract with Kipele. Kipele may sue Sonya for breach of contract, and may also sue Tulala for interference with contract.

> **Example:** Sonya's contract with Kipele has a clause that says it may be renewed at the end of the year. Toshi tells her that if she doesn't renew, but switches to Tulala, she will save 20%. Sonya does not renew her contract with Kipele. Kipele may not sue for interference with contract.

> **Example:** Jeffrey is accused of embezzling money from his employer. He makes an agreement with Joe, a writer, that Joe write a book to show Jeffrey's innocence. As Joe researches his book, he becomes convinced that Jeffrey is guilty. He writes the book in a way that details the arguments for Jeffrey's guilt. Jeffrey may sue Joe for breach of contract and fraud.

Some situations may support an action for tort and contract. When misrepresentation is involved, a party may bring a tort action for fraud, and may seek to declare the contract void. Contract claims have also been held to be the basis for claims under deceptive or unfair trade practice laws.

IV. Sale of Goods Contracts (UCC)

The most common type of contract probably is contracts for the sale of goods. "Goods" are tangible, movable items, such as books, laptops, and pens. The category also includes business-to-business sales (things like production equipment, tools, and servers). It does not include intangibles such as intellectual property, accounts, or services, or immovable real estate (land and the structures permanently attached to the land). Any time we buy an item at our local store, we are making this kind of contract. It is such a commonplace transaction that we seldom give it any thought.

The rules we have discussed so far in this chapter have mostly been common law rules. The law governing the sale of goods is Article 2 of the Uniform Commercial Code (UCC). Article 2 has been adopted in nearly all U.S. jurisdictions. It is meant to make the laws governing the sale of goods uniform across the nation. Most of the rules in Article 2 build on common-law contract rules, with some adaptations.

There are two important points about on Article 2 to remember. First, Article 2 deals only with sales of goods. It does not cover the sale of real estate. Article 2 also does not cover the sale of services.

> If a contract is for the sale of both goods and services, such as a contract for both parts and labor, Uniform Commercial Code Article 2 applies if the goods are the essence of the contract.

The second point is that some of the rules in Article 2 are limited to contracts between or with **merchants.** For purposes of Article 2, a merchant is someone who regularly deals in goods of the kind at issue. It does not mean an individual or business that makes an occasional or casual sale of property.

> **MERCHANT:** Under Article 2 of the UCC, a person who regularly deals in goods of a kind.

MIXED CONTRACTS ARE CONTRACTS FOR GOODS WHEN THE SERVICES ARE MEANINGLESS WITHOUT THE CONTEMPLATED GOODS

Bruel & Kjaer v. Suburban O'Hare Commission
(Radar Equipment Seller) v. (Airport Commission)
969 N.E.2d 445 (Ill. App. 2012)

Plaintiff, Bruel & Kjaer, a supplier of noise-monitoring and radar equipment and systems, appeals the judgment of the circuit court of Du Page County dismissing its complaint against defendant, the Suburban O'Hare Commission, on the ground that plaintiff's complaint was filed outside the four-year statute of limitations that applies to the sale of goods pursuant to a contract under the Uniform Commercial Code (UCC).

In February 1999, plaintiff entered into an agreement with defendant and the Village of Bensenville. Plaintiff agreed to provide certain equipment and services to defendant in exchange for a single payment of $227,000. [. . .] Plaintiff also agreed to "deliver, assemble, install, test and make fully operational such Equipment and System F.O.B. at the MCI Tower, Bensenville, Illinois, or other site designated" by defendant. Plaintiff further warranted, under paragraph 5 of the agreement, that "all Equipment and services furnished and/or delivered hereunder will be delivered, installed and operated in a workmanship like manner and that the design of the System is fit for the purposes therein purchased."

The agreement also set forth a service component. In paragraph 2, an annual servicing agreement was referenced. Paragraph 3(j) provided that plaintiff would "provide all software adjustments necessary to insure" that the software for the systems would be accessible to all the member communities of defendant. Exhibit A to the agreement enumerated the work to be provided by plaintiff in upgrading the existing passive radar to Long-Range PAS SUR, upgrading the software as necessary, and setting forth terms of additional free services to be offered to defendant as a "most favored customer" by plaintiff and its subcontractor.

Plaintiff alleged that it provided the equipment and systems, which were accepted and used by defendant. In January 2002, plaintiff submitted a formal approval document and invoice for the $227,000 price specified in the agreement. Plaintiff alleged that defendant did not pay this first invoice, so it again invoiced defendant for the purchase price.

In June 2004, following repeated invoicing, defendant paid plaintiff $50,000 toward the purchase price set forth in the agreement. Thereafter, despite further invoices plaintiff sent to defendant, defendant did not pay any more money toward the purchase price.

On November 12, 2010, plaintiff filed its complaint for breach of the agreement. Defendant filed a motion to dismiss, arguing that plaintiff's complaint was untimely under the four-year statute of limitations in section 2–725 of the UCC. Plaintiff countered that the UCC statute of limitations was not applicable, because the contract was predominantly for the provision of services and not the sale of goods. Plaintiff argued that, instead, the 10-year statute of limitations governing written contracts set forth [elsewhere] applied to its action.

In support of its response, plaintiff included an affidavit by Imram Mohamed, a support engineer on the project. Mohamed outlined the time that was spent developing new software and upgrading existing software for the equipment and systems. Mohamed averred that, as a result of these efforts, the software "in no way constituted a pre-developed, stock product." Mohamed compiled a chart, which was attached to the affidavit, that purported to show the number of days spent developing the software and whether that development was for newly developed software or for customizing an existing application. The chart further indicated that the customization and development work was "typically done for each noise monitoring system" plaintiff installs. According to Mohamed's chart, plaintiff spent 52 days creating newly developed software, 37 days customizing software from an existing application for this project, and 72 days of combined work, consisting of "New/Customized application[s]," for a total of 161 days working on software for the project. Mohamed averred that, "[w]ithout the services to develop the software, and without the services to install and support the upgrade," defendant would not have been able to obtain the information it was seeking.

On appeal, plaintiff argues that the predominant purpose of the agreement was the provision of services to defendant, so the 10-year limitations period should apply rather than the 4-year period of section 2–725 of the UCC. Plaintiff also argues that, in the alternative, Mohamed's affidavit evidences the existence of disputed issues of material fact regarding the predominant purpose of the agreement, which should have precluded the dismissal of its complaint.

This appeal concerns whether section 2–725 of the UCC or section 13–206 of the Code should apply to the subject matter of the agreement between the parties. Article 2 of the UCC applies only to transactions in "goods" and "goods" are defined as "all things, including specially manufactured goods, which are movable at the time of identification to the contract for sale". A contract for services is not a transaction in goods and is not covered by Article 2 of the UCC. Where a contract mixes the sale of goods and the provision of services, the applicability of Article 2 of the UCC is determined by the " 'predominant purpose' " test. Under this test, if the contract is predominantly for goods and only incidentally for services, Article 2 of the UCC will apply. If the contract is predominantly for services and only incidentally for goods, Article 2 of the UCC will not apply.

In determining whether a contract is predominantly for goods, a court will review the contractual language relating to the design, installation, or delivery of an identifiable and tangible object. E.g., *Bob Neiner Farms, Inc. v. Hendrix*, 141 Ill.App.3d 499, 501–03, 95 Ill.Dec. 784, 490 N.E.2d 257 (1986) (the builder provided a standardized structure and placed it on the buyer's site, and the builder was not in the business of providing individualized design and construction services; the court held this to be a contract for goods); *Yorke v. B.F. Goodrich Co.*, 130 Ill.App.3d 220, 223, 85 Ill.Dec. 606, 474 N.E.2d 20 (1985) (contract called for provision of plastic pellets to make vinyl siding; the defendant provided consulting services in exchange for the plaintiff's continued purchase of pellets; the court held this to be a contract for goods); *Meeker v. Hamilton Grain Elevator Co.*, 110 Ill.App.3d 668, 671, 66 Ill.Dec. 360, 442 N.E.2d 921 (1982) (contract used terms like seller and purchaser, charged a sales tax, referred to grain bins as the equipment being sold, and did not refer to the labor of the installation; court held this to be a contract for goods). With these principles in mind, we turn to the facts of this case.

In this case, the agreement referred to the parties as "buyer" (defendant) and "seller" (plaintiff). The object of the contract was the upgrade of tangible equipment, being components of noise-monitoring systems and radar systems. In addition, the contract provided that, "[u]pon final payment [plaintiff] shall deliver to [defendant] a Bill of Sale for the Equipment and System free and clear of any and all liens and encumbrances." We note that the UCC defines a "sale" as "the passing of title from the seller to the buyer for a price." Thus, the contract appeared by its language to contemplate a sale of goods via the passing of title from plaintiff to defendant for the equipment and systems that were the object of the agreement.

In addition, the agreement provided that plaintiff was to deliver and install the goods: plaintiff agreed to "deliver, assemble, install, test and make fully operational such Equipment and System, F.O.B." Further, "[t]he Equipment and System shall be delivered and installed F.O.B. * * * with all freight and cargo to be paid by Seller." "F.O.B." is an abbreviation for "free on board," a term used in transactions in tangible goods, and is defined in the UCC. Plaintiff also promised to provide various services "in consideration" of defendant's purchase of the equipment and systems. Thus, the terminology employed by the agreement called for the sale of goods rather than the provision of services.

This is also seen by noting that defendant was to make a single payment of $227,000 after plaintiff had delivered and installed the equipment, rather than multiple payments based on time and type of service. Further, there was no breakdown in the price between the cost of the equipment and the cost of the labor needed to make it operational. For all these reasons, then, we hold that the agreement provided for the sale of goods, with any specified services being only incidental to the sale of goods.

This can also be seen when approached from a different angle. Plaintiff supplies certain tangible widgets to buyers along with sufficient services to make the widgets operable. In the absence of the widgets themselves, the services to make them operable would be meaningless and without value.

Affirmed.

UCC Contract Formalities

Article 2 does not alter the general rule that a contract is created when an offer is accepted, and the agreement is supported by consideration. But the rule regarding the form of the acceptance is updated to reflect actual business practices. Recall that, under the common law, acceptance must mirror the offer: it is just saying "yes" to the offer, with no additional terms or conditions. Under Article 2, however, an acceptance may be effective even if it contains additional or different terms from those of the offer. The acceptance with additional or different terms is good unless the acceptance is expressly conditioned on accepting the additional or different terms.

This change from the common law helps businesses maintain contractual relationships. The UCC rule reflects the realities of business practice. One business might send an order to another company. The recipient company might send back a confirmation or invoice, or simply ship goods with paperwork. The original order and the subsequent documents are likely to include different terms and conditions in the fine print. These differences are unlikely to be checked closely in an active business. They are also unlikely to cause problems most of the time. Occasionally, however, the variations in the terms and conditions in the documents will cause a dispute.

This type of dispute is referred to as a "battle of the forms." In a battle of the forms, the various documents issued in a transaction are compared to determine which terms and conditions "win." In other words, battle of the forms rules determine which parts of the fine print in which documents apply to the specific sale.

If the acceptance contains terms different from the terms of the offer, those terms do not become a part of the contract. If the contract is between merchants, additional terms become a part of the contract unless:

- The offer says expressly that acceptance must be limited to the terms of the offer,
- The additional terms materially alter the contract, or
- The offering party has given notification of her objection to the additional terms, or notice of her objections is given within a reasonable time.

Unless the offer says otherwise, acceptance may be made "in any manner and by any medium reasonable in the circumstances."

Article 2 contains a version of the Statute of Frauds. The UCC version of the Statute says that contracts for the sale of goods for more than $500 must be in writing. There are exceptions to the writing requirement for the following:

- A written confirmation between merchants that is not objected to within 10 days after it is received,
- Contracts for specially manufactured goods not suitable for sale to others,
- Contracts for which payment for the goods has been made and accepted,
- Contracts for goods which have been received and accepted, and

- Admissions made in pleadings, testimony, or otherwise in court.

UCC Contract Performance

Performance of a sales contract under Article 2 follows rules similar to the common law rules for performance of a contract. The main difference between Article 2 and the common law is that a court construing a sales contract will supply "missing" terms for a contract. If the parties have neglected to include terms, the courts are allowed to add reasonable terms for:

- Price of the goods,
- Time for delivery,
- Place for delivery (the seller's place of business), and
- Time for payment (when the buyer receives the goods).

These terms are just placeholders. The courts will not substitute terms in a contract if the parties have already included the terms.

Article 2 does not provide a default term for the quantity of goods under a contract. The quantity must be included in the contract. This figure could be expressed in any way that makes sense for the item (number of individual units, number of cases including a set quantity of units, a measurement of a bulk good, or other appropriate quantity). Parties can also agree to an output contract without a specific quantity ("buyer will purchase all the units that seller can produce in a year") or a requirements contract ("buyer will purchase all the units from seller that buyer will need in a year"). These two options are allowed because the general quantity is roughly known and will become clear by the end of the given time period.

UCC Contract Warranties

Article 2 imposes requirements for warranties on goods sold by merchants. These warranties are valid unless they are effectively disclaimed.

Express Warranties

Express warranties are created by the seller, and communicated to the buyer. There is no need to use specific terms ("warranty" or "guarantee"). A warranty is created when the seller makes a statement of fact or promise about the goods to the buyer relating to the goods that becomes part of the basis of the bargain. Such a statement creates an express warranty that the goods will conform to the affirmation or promise. A description of the goods which is part of the basis of the bargain creates an express warranty that the goods conform to the description. Finally, a sample or model that is part of the basis of the bargain creates an express warranty that the goods will conform to the sample or model.

> **Example:** A golf ball manufacturer makes a claim in its advertising that its new golf ball will travel 15% further than the manufacturer's other models. An express warranty has been created.

The term "basis of the bargain" is not defined in Article 2. Courts have held that any affirmation of fact becomes part of the "basis of the bargain." Other courts have required some showing that the buyer relied on the statements before they can be said to be part of the basis of the bargain.

Statements of opinion, or "**puffery**," will not create a warranty.

Implied Warranties

Implied warranties are created by operation of law when a merchant sells goods. They are operative unless they are explicitly disclaimed. The warranties that are created are:

- Merchantability: a warranty that the goods will pass without objection in the trade, or function as well as other goods of that type.

- Fitness for a particular purpose: if the seller has reason to know the buyer's particular purpose for buying the goods, and also knows that the buyer is relying upon the seller to select or recommend suitable goods for that purpose goods, then there is a warranty that the goods will meet the particular purpose for which the buyer intends to use them.

- Non-infringement: a warranty that the goods will not infringe upon a rightful claim of any third party.

- Title: a warranty that the seller owns the goods and will transfer good title to the buyer.

- Freedom from Encumbrances: a warranty that the goods are free of any liens, security interests or other encumbrances.

PUFFERY:
Minor exaggeration when selling goods.

Example: A salesperson at an electronics store tells a customer that a certain home video system "will make you feel like you're sitting in the front row of your favorite movie theater." The statement is just puffery, so no warranty is created.

Example: A toaster purchased at an appliance store has an implied warranty that it will function as an acceptable toaster.

Example: A designer goes to an electronics store to buy a computer to use in his design business. The salesperson listens to her questions, and recommends a particular model. There is an implied warranty that the computer is suitable for use in a design business.

U.C.C. ARTICLE 2 WARRANTIES APPLY TO SALES OF FOOD AND DRINK IN RESTAURANTS

Shaffer v. Victoria Station, Inc.
(Restaurant Patron) v. (Restaurant)
91 Wash. 2d 295, 588 P.2d 233 (1978)

INSTANT FACTS:
Shaffer (P) sued for breach of warranty when a restaurant wine glass broke in his hand.

BLACK LETTER RULE:
The serving for value of food or drink to be consumed either on the premises or elsewhere is a sale, and Article 2 warranty provisions apply.

FACTS:
Shaffer (P) ordered a glass of wine at the Victoria Station restaurant (D). When he took his first or second sip, the wine glass broke in Shaffer's (P) hand. He alleged that this caused him permanent injury. Shaffer (P) brought suit against Victoria Station (D) based upon three theories: negligence, breach of implied warranty under the Uniform Commercial Code, and strict liability. Prior to trial, Shaffer's (P) attorney indicated that he could not prove negligence, and wished to submit the case to the jury on the grounds of breach of warranty and strict liability. The court ruled the case sounded in negligence alone, and granted Victoria Station's (D) motion for dismissal.

ISSUE:
Could Shaffer (P) bring suit for breach of warranty?

DECISION AND RATIONALE:
(Dolliver, J.) Yes. The serving for value of food or drink to be consumed either on the premises or elsewhere is a sale, and Article 2 warranty provisions apply. The U.C.C. states that a warranty that goods shall be merchantable is implied in a contract for their sale if the seller is a merchant with respect to goods of that kind. It is our opinion that, when the Code states "the serving for value of food or drink to be consumed either on the premises or elsewhere is a sale" and that such food and drink must be "adequately contained, packaged, and labeled as the agreement may require", it covers entirely the situation in this case. Shaffer (P) ordered a glass of wine from Victoria Station (D). Victoria Station (D) sold and served the glass of wine to Shaffer (P) to be consumed by him on the premises. The wine could not be served as a drink nor could it be consumed without an adequate container. The drink sold includes the wine and the container both of which must be fit for the ordinary purpose for which used. Shaffer (P) alleges the drink sold wine in a glass was unfit and has, therefore, stated a cause of action. Reversed.

ANALYSIS:
The analysis in this case turns on the definition of what is being sold. The sale is not of the wine glass. Instead, the court says the sale is of wine contained in the glass. The defect was in the packaging of the wine, not in the wine itself.

Disclaimers

Implied warranties can be disclaimed, or excluded, by the parties. In order to disclaim the warranties of merchantability or fitness for a particular purpose, the disclaimer must be in a "conspicuous" writing. If the seller wants to disclaim the warranty of merchantability specifically, the disclaimer must explicitly include the word "merchantability." Disclaimers that include words such as "as-is" or "with all faults" will disclaim all implied warranties.

> Since express warranties are direct representations by the seller, they cannot be disclaimed. It would not make any sense for a seller to explicitly guarantee a level of quality or performance for a product, and then to say, "Oops, didn't mean that!" This logical inconsistency aside, sellers do sometimes attempt to disclaim express warranties.

V. Online Contracts

Here's a news flash: more and more business is being done online. Electronic commerce has many advantages, but there are issues with online contracting. The rules about contract formation contemplated people meeting face-to-face and documenting the resulting agreement down on paper. When contracts are negotiated by electronic communications between people who may never meet in person, the old requirements of signed written agreements become problematic.

Contract law has made some adaptation to electronic commerce. The adaptations do not change any substantive rules about the elements of a contract. Instead, the new rules set parameters for contracts entered into online.

State contract laws generally provide that an exchange of e-mails will satisfy the requirement that a contract be in writing. Most states have also enacted the Electronic Signatures in Global and National Commerce Act (E-Sign Act). That Act provides that in most cases, a signature, contract, or other record relating to a transaction may not be denied legal effect solely because it is in electronic form. A contract is not invalid solely because an electronic signature or electronic record was used to form the contract.

CHAPTER SUMMARY

A contract is a special type of promise. It is a promise that has five elements: offer, acceptance, consideration, capacity, and legality. The offer is a proposal to make a contract, and acceptance is agreeing to that proposal. Consid-

> *Example:* Marla wants to sell her vacation home. She e-mails Cindy, a friend from college:
>
> (Marla) I am selling my vacation condo in Rehoboth Beach. Are you interested in buying it? It's where we stayed last summer. 2 bedrooms, 2 baths, close to the beach.
>
> (Cindy) Maybe. How much?
>
> (Marla) $234,000.
>
> (Cindy) Yes, we'll take it.
>
> The sales contract meets the requirements of the Statute of Frauds.

eration is the exchange of something that makes the promise a contract, and not just an unenforceable promise to make a gift. Capacity is the legal ability to make a contract, while legality is the requirement that the promises made are to do something allowable under law. However simple or complex a promise may be, all five elements must be present in order to make it a contract.

Unlike most other promises we make ("I'll call you tomorrow"), there are consequences if a promise in a contract is not kept. These consequences are intended to put both parties to the contract in the position they would have been in had the contract not been breached. The most common way of doing this is for a court to order the payment of damages sufficient to cover the loss caused by the breach. Alternately, the non-breaching party may be reimbursed for the cost of her performance, or for the value of her performance. The goal is to make the non-breaching party whole.

> **CAREERS IN THE LAW**
>
> People with a good business education, a head for detail, and an interest in contracts should consider contract management. Contract managers are not usually lawyers, but they coordinate writing, review, and finalization of contract documents for their organizations. They help develop budgets and timelines for contracted work, and perform contract and service reviews, working with cross-disciplinary teams. Contract managers also make sure that personnel are aware of existing contract requirements and that critical documentation and due diligence work is available for review. Many industries use contract managers, from health care to real estate, as well as all levels of government. Contract management is a growth field, with excellent compensation and good opportunities for advancement.

Review Questions

Review question 1.
What is offer and acceptance? Why are they critical to contract formation?

Review question 2.
When is silence acceptance of an offer? How else may an offer be accepted? What is a firm offer?

Review question 3.
Define "consideration." Why is consideration important to contracts? Consideration is usually monetary, but what are some other examples of valid consideration?

Review question 4.
What are capacity and legality? How do these concepts affect contract creation?

Review question 5.
What is "undue influence?" What is "duress?" How does the law address contracts that are the result of either undue influence or duress?

Review question 6.
What is promissory estoppel? When does it apply? What are the possible outcomes?

Review question 7.
How might misrepresentation or fraud affect contracting? What are the different types of misrepresentation? Does misrepresentation or fraud always end the contract?

Review question 8.
What does "UCC" stand for? How do state law and the UCC work together? What Article of the UCC deals with the sale of goods?

Review question 9.
How does the UCC differ from common law on contracts for the sale of goods? What is the battle of the forms? What rules determine which form defines the contract?

Review question 10.
What type of damages are typical in a contract dispute? What is the goal of contract damages? What types of damages are not appropriate for contract cases?

Review question 11.

What are liquidated damages? How would you measure them? What is the difference between liquidated damages and damages you might win in a lawsuit?

Review question 12.

What law requires certain contracts to be put in writing? What are some types of sales that must be in writing? Is there ever a good situation to conclude a contract without any written evidence?

Review question 13.

What is an accord and satisfaction? How does it differ from specific performance?

Review question 14.

What are warranties? What is the difference between an express and implied warranty? What are the most common implied warranties and their requirements? How are they disclaimed?

Review question 15.

What is the E-Sign Act? How does the Act improve online business transactions?

Discussion Questions

Question 1:

Beverly, a local newspaper publisher, has established a scholarship fund. The scholarship will pay for all of the expenses of the recipient's college education, including all of the student's living expenses. In return, the student who receives the scholarship must agree to work for Beverly's newspaper three years after earning a degree. After reviewing many applications, Beverly sends a letter to Kyle offering him the scholarship. Kyle responds by sending an e-mail that says only "Sounds great! Thanks!"

> Is there a valid contract here? Why, or why not?

> Assuming that there is a contract, is it the type of contract that has to be put into writing? Why, or why not?

> After Kyle earns his degree, he gets a job offer from a local advertising

agency. The ad agency would pay significantly more than the job with Beverly's newspaper. It would also offer more responsibility and chance for advancement. If Kyle were to accept the ad agency's offer, and he is found to have breached his contract with Beverly, what damages would he have to pay? Be specific.

Question 2:

Jacob goes to a building supply store to buy a nail gun. He asks Leah, the salesperson, which one she recommends. Leah asks what Jacob wants the gun for, and he says he is building a new shed in his backyard. Leah tells him that the Nailz-it-Good 3000 will suit his needs. Jacob buys the nail gun and takes it home. The Nailz-it-Good 3000 is actually designed for light jobs for crafters, not for carpentry. It cannot drive nails into the wood Jacob is using, and it falls apart after an hour of attempted use.

Is this a breach of the implied warranty of merchantability? Why or why not?

If there were a warranty of fitness for a particular purpose, would there be a breach of that warranty here? Why or why not?

Question 3:

Refer back to the facts of Question 2. Suppose Jacob takes the nail gun back to the store and demands a refund. An employee of the store looks in the box and finds a small piece of paper under one of the flaps. The piece of paper says "The Nailz-it-Good 3000 is sold AS IS, with no warranty."

Is this enough to disclaim any warranties? Why or why not?

Question 4:

Two local softball teams, the East Side Storks and the West Side Siroccos, have an intense, even bitter, rivalry. The rivalry has gone so far that the managers of the teams have a "peace conference." At the conference, it is agreed that the Storks would not wear their team jackets on the west side of town (called "Sirocco territory"), and the Siroccos would not wear their team jackets on the east side of town.

Is there a valid contract? If so, what is the consideration for the contract?

Suppose a Stork were to wear his jacket while in Sirocco territory. If there were a valid contract between the Siroccos and the Storks, what damages would the Siroccos be able to claim?

Question 5:

Suppose that the teams agree to rent softball fields for their games. The teams agree orally that one team (the Storks) will rent the fields and pay for them, but that the Siroccos will repay the Storks for half the rental fees. The Storks enter into a written rental agreement for softball fields for the teams' games.

> If the Siroccos do not pay, can the Storks enforce either contract? Can the Storks rescind the rental agreements in that case?

> If the Siroccos do not show up for a game, may the Storks rescind the rental agreement for that particular date?

Question 6:

Helena has just opened a new business as a wedding planner. She hears that her cousin Chin is planning on getting married. Helena wants to establish a name for herself in the business, so she offers to do the job for half of the usual fee, which will almost cover Helena's expenses. Chin and his fiancée Alex accept the offer. Two days before the wedding, Chin calls Helena and tells her that she can stop work right now, and that Helena's services will not be used as planned.

> Chin claims he does not need to pay, because the wedding planning was to be a gift, and that there was no consideration for a contract. Is this claim correct? Why or why not?

> Suppose there is a valid contract, but Chin has cancelled it because he and Alex have decided to elope instead of having a formal wedding. What damages may Helena claim?

> The wedding was cancelled because Alex is in the Army Reserve, and her unit was called up and sent overseas on active duty. Is Helena entitled to claim any damages? Why or why not?

Question 7:

Alex and Chin have an argument a month before the wedding and break up. Chin handled all of the wedding arrangements, and all of the contracts are in his name.

> How do you suppose wedding vendors protect themselves against this common eventuality?

> Will Chin be able to sue Alex for any of the costs that he might have to bear from the wedding contracts?

Question 8:

Denis is a consultant. He sees a request for proposals from a major company in a trade magazine. Denis wants the business, but does not think he can do it on his own. He contacts Polly about taking care of some of the work. They talk about the project, and Polly agrees that, if Denis gets the business, she will take care of half the work for $50/hour. Denis will pay Polly's fees to her out of the company's payments to him. Denis bids on the work. The company sends a letter saying that Denis can have the project, but only if he reduces his bid by 20%. Denis accepts, and then tells Polly that he can only pay her $40/hour.

> Identify the offers, counter-offers, and acceptances in this scenario.

> If Polly is unwilling to work for the decreased rate, is her dispute with Denis or with the company? Why?

> What is a practical way that Denis can accept the business and satisfy Polly's rate requirement?

Question 9:

Sanjay is a high school student. He really wants a motorcycle, so he arranges to buy his parents' neighbors' motorcycle over time. He makes a payment every week. About halfway through the payments, Sanjay decides he doesn't want a motorcycle, and wants to rescind the contract.

> Identify the issues that will arise in this scenario. How are they likely to be decided?

Question 10:

Harvey calls his sister Hayley and says, "I could really use your help. How about you come work for me in Denver? The job pays twice what you are getting in Des Moines." Hayley quits her job in Des Moines, breaks her apartment lease, and rents a place in Denver. She pays to have her stuff moved. On her first day of work, Harvey says, "I spoke too soon. I don't have the funds to pay for this position."

> Is there a contract between Harvey and Hayley?

> If not, is there a way that Hayley might still be able to claim damages from Harvey? Why or why not?

Question 11:

Suppose in the last question, Harvey sent Hayley an employment contract before she quit her prior job. Hayley types in her name on the PDF of the contract and sends it back.

> Is Hayley bound to the contract? Why or why not?

Question 12:

PD Health, Inc., a health food retailer, orders kradom supplements from Herbs Almighty Co. After Herbs Almighty produces and packages the kradom, but before it can ship the supplements, the Drug Enforcement Agency illegalizes kradom.

> What are the parties' rights and responsibilities in this case?

> Suppose that PD Health received the shipment, but hadn't unpacked it yet, and that the DEA only outlawed kradom sales in health food stores. What are the parties' rights and responsibilities now?

7 CREDITOR-DEBTOR ISSUES

KEY OBJECTIVES:
▶ Explain the main laws relating to debt collection.
▶ Outline the major consumer lending laws.
▶ Describe the workings of bankruptcy and receivership.

CHAPTER OVERVIEW

This chapter covers debtor and creditor relationships. The relationship starts when a **creditor** agrees to lend money or sell goods on credit (payment over time) to another. The person receiving credit or buying the goods is the **debtor.** This chapter will review the rules creditors are required to follow to treat debtors fairly when they apply for and use credit. We will also look at the laws that limit how a creditor may collect a debt. Finally, the chapter will consider what happens when a debtor cannot or will not pay a creditor.

INTRODUCTION

It is no exaggeration to say that the modern economy runs on credit. Herbert Hoover called credit "the lifeblood of business, the lifeblood of prices and jobs." Credit is an efficient way to facilitate purchases while making sure payments are made and received to cover those purchases.

Generally, the terms of a credit agreement are left to the parties to decide. There are some limits on this general rule. For example, lenders may not discriminate based on race or gender. There are also limits on how credit is extended. If a person takes a loan to buy a car, the law does not limit how much can be borrowed, but it does require you receive good information about the loan. It also says that the creditor must tell the debtor how much it will cost to repay the debt. If everyone receives accurate information about the loan, then the details of the transaction are up to the parties.

The theory behind credit is one thing. In the real world, credit is meaningless without payment. In order to make sure credit works, there must be a way of enforcing debts. When a person borrows to buy a car, the credit agreement generally provides that the car would be the collateral for the loan. Collateral secures the loan, and can be reclaimed by a creditor if the debtor fails to pay. The possibility of legally taking the car back is one way for the bank to feel confident that it would be paid. The law

CREDITOR:
A person to whom money is owed. In bankruptcy law, a "creditor" has or may have a claim against the debtor's property.

DEBTOR:
A person who owes money. In bankruptcy law, the "debtor" is the person or entity that files a bankruptcy petition.

also provides ways that creditors can recover if debtors fail to pay on mortgages or credit cards. For any of these methods, though, there is a possibility that the debtor will not have enough money to satisfy all debts. Bankruptcy and receivership are designed to distribute funds to creditors as fairly as possible while protecting debtors' rights.

I. Truth in Lending

The Truth in Lending Act (TILA) is a federal law that applies to consumer finance. TILA is basically a disclosure law. Its goal is to protect consumers in credit transactions by making sure they know as much as possible before agreeing to take on debt. TILA does not dictate the substance or terms of a credit agreement. It just says that those terms have to be set out clearly and conspicuously.

TILA only protects borrowers or debtors who are "natural" persons. A natural person is a human individual, and not a "legal" person like a business or non-profit. Other entities, like corporations or partnerships, are not protected by the law. On the other side of the transaction, the disclosure requirements of TILA only apply to companies who lend money, sell on credit, or arrange for the extension of credit in the ordinary course of business.

TILA covers only certain types of loans to consumers. The law applies to installment agreements that require four or more payments. Only loans or credit that are primarily for personal, family, or household purposes must include TILA disclosures. This includes student loans, but only those from private lenders. TILA does not apply to business or agricultural loans. TILA also does not cover unsecured loans for over $50,000, or to credit extended by a securities broker.

TILA disclosures give consumers information that helps them shop for the best loan terms. All lenders must use the same format to make the disclosures, so it is easier to compare terms. This innovation results in better credit decisions and more competition among lenders serving consumers.

Regulation Z sets forth TILA's disclosure requirements. Under Regulation Z, a TILA disclosure must include the following items.

- The Annual Percentage Rate (APR) of the loan.
- The amount financed, or how much is being borrowed.
- The finance charge, meaning the total dollar amount of interest and fees that will be charged if every payment is made on time.
- The total amount of all payments.
- The number of payments.
- The amount of each scheduled payment.

UNSECURED:
A debt is unsecured if there is no collateral guaranteeing the debt. Most credit cards are unsecured.

- The right of rescission (cancellation of the agreement).
- Late fees.
- Whether the borrower will have to pay a penalty if all or part of the loan is repaid ahead of schedule.

A TILA disclosure must be given to the borrower before the loan agreement is final.

Depending on the type of credit that is being extended, other disclosures may be required. For example, a bank that issues a credit card must to give notice of changes in the interest rate it charges.

TILA gives borrowers rescission rights. **Rescission** is the right to cancel the entire transaction. A borrower may rescind a credit agreement within three days of signing it. Within that three-day window, a borrower may rescind for any reason, as long as the rescission is in writing. After three days though, rescission is allowed only if the TILA disclosures were not correct.

> Note that rescission does not mean that the borrower gets to keep the money without paying it back. Any money that was paid to the borrower must be returned.

RESCISSION: Cancellation of an agreement. The parties to the agreement are put back to where they were before the contract was made.

TILA's disclosure provisions are well known, but the law also protects consumers in other ways. An amendment to TILA prohibits credit card companies from sending customers unsolicited cards. Lenders that violate this rule face serious penalties. In 2016, Wells Fargo Bank was penalized $185 million for opening credit card and bank accounts without customers' knowledge. Employees would open new accounts for existing customers, then close the new unauthorized accounts. In all, there were approximately 1.5 million bank accounts and 565,000 unauthorized credit card accounts opened. Wells Fargo also agreed to refund $2.6 million in fees that were improperly charged.

TILA also contains protections against fraudulent use of credit cards. Customers may not be billed for unauthorized charges on unsolicited cards. A customer's liability for unauthorized charges is legally limited to $50 per card before the cardholder gives notice that a card was lost. TILA's provisions also set out ways to resolve disputes between customers and credit card companies.

An important part of TILA is the Equal Credit Opportunity Act (ECOA). The ECOA says that a person may not be denied credit solely because of his race, religion, national origin, color, gender, marital status, age (provided he is of legal age, usually 18), or because he receives public assistance.

> While the federal ECOA does not ban discrimination based on sexual orientation, a state's law may protect people on this basis.

LOANS TO RANCHERS DO NOT QUALIFY FOR CONSUMER PROTECTION PROVISIONS OF THE TRUTH IN LENDING ACT

K/O Ranch, Inc. v. Norwest Bank of the Black Hills
(Ranch) v. (Bank)
748 F.2d 1246 (8th Cir. 1984)

From February of 1979 through 1983, the Olsons and their corporation, K/O Ranch, borrowed various sums in 31 separate transactions [. . .] to finance the operation of the K/O Ranch. The Norwest loans were secured by livestock, feed, and equipment used for farming operations. [Other] loans were secured by livestock and a real estate mortgage. The Olsons are in default on their payments[.]

On March 6, 1984, the Olsons filed this action in the District Court, alleging that Norwest [. . .] failed to comply with the general disclosure requirements of the Truth in Lending Act, and the right-of-rescission disclosure requirement of the Act. On its own motion, the District Court dismissed the action for failure to state a claim upon which relief could be granted. This appeal followed.

A. *The Agricultural Purpose Exemption*

The purpose of the Truth in Lending Act is to provide consumers with meaningful disclosure of credit terms to promote the informed use of credit and to protect consumers from unfair credit practices. Currently, the Act exempts from coverage "[c]redit transactions [regardless of amount] involving extensions of credit primarily for business, commercial, or agricultural purposes." Prior to October 1, 1982, [the Act] exempted from coverage loans obtained "primarily for agricultural purposes in which the total amount to be financed exceeds $25,000."

Twenty-five of the thirty-one loans are excluded from coverage by the Act's agricultural-purpose exemption. It is clear from the complaint that all of the loans involved in this action were made for agricultural purposes. The Olsons state that they are "members of the greatest industry in this nation, American Agriculture." Exhibits list the collateral for most of the loans as livestock, feed, and equipment used in farming. The exhibits also include agricultural financing statements and an application for a disaster loan [. . .] due to drought. In addition, the first count of the complaint names the agricultural loan officer of Norwest as an individual defendant, and he is listed as the bank officer on all but two of the Norwest promissory notes. Because the loans were made for agricultural purposes, they are, with a few exceptions, clearly exempt from coverage under the agricultural-purpose exemption. Six of the thirty-one loans involved in this action were consummated prior to October 1, 1982, and involved amounts less than $25,000. Only these loans are not subject to the agricultural-purpose exemption.

B. *The Corporate Maker Exemption*

As noted above, the purpose of the Truth in Lending Act is to protect consumers involved in credit transactions. The Act characterizes a consumer transaction as "one in which the party to whom credit is offered or extended is a natural person, and the money, property, or services which are the subject of the transaction are primarily for personal, family, or household purposes." Moreover, the Act provides that it does not apply to "[c]redit transactions involving extensions of credit . . . to organizations." The term "organization" is defined by the Act to include corporations.

Two of the six loans which are not within the agricultural-purpose exemption were made to K/O Ranch, Inc., and are therefore exempt from the coverage of the Act under the corporate-maker exemption of [the Act].

C. *The Time Limitations of the Act*

The Olsons' action as to the remaining four loans is barred by the time limitations of the Act [which] provides a one-year period of limitations for actions for violations of the general disclosure requirements of the Act. This Court has interpreted this section to mean that the period of limitations begins to run when credit is extended through the consummation of the transaction without the proper disclosures. None of the four remaining loans was consummated within the one-year period preceding institution of this action and, with regard to these loans, the action is clearly time-barred.

> ### D. *The Right of Rescission*
>
> Finally, the Olsons' complaint alleges that they have a right to rescind the loans under section 1635 of the Act. This section provides a right of rescission as to consumer-credit transactions in which the security interest is the consumer's principal place of residence. Assuming that the mortgages which secure some of the loans involve the Olsons' current or intended place of residence, the Olsons are still not entitled to rescind. As previously stated, the Act exempts credit transactions for agricultural purposes. The Act also exempts loans to corporations. Thus, the Olsons are not entitled to rescind the twenty-seven loans which are exempt from the coverage of the Act under the agricultural-purpose or corporate-maker exemptions.
>
> As noted above, four of the loans involved in this action do not come within either the agricultural-purpose or corporate-maker exemption. However, none of these loans is secured by the Olsons' principal place of residence as required[.] Therefore, the Olsons are not entitled to rescind these loans. Thus, the Act's right of rescission is not applicable to any of the loans involved in this action.
>
> We have carefully reviewed the complaint and conclude that these claims, which are unsupported by any factual allegations, were properly dismissed. Accordingly, the judgment of the District Court is affirmed.

A creditor may not consider those factors when a person applies for credit, although a creditor may ask about them as a way of helping to enforce anti-discrimination laws. Providing that information is voluntary for applicants. Immigration status may be considered to decide if the credit applicant will be in the U.S. long enough to repay the debt.

If an applicant meets a lender's standards for income and creditworthiness, the lender must grant credit on the same terms as other qualifying customers. The applicant may not be charged a higher interest rate, and the creditor may not require a co-signer if other customers would not be required to have one.

II. Fair Debt Collection Practices

With credit comes the possibility that the debt will not be repaid. Creditors base their decisions on the odds that an applicant will pay a debt. If a debtor fails to make payments, creditors will take steps to collect the unpaid balance.

In most states, the law puts few limits about how a creditor may collect a personal debt. If a creditor can avoid criminal acts, such as making physical threats or harassing another person, debt collection by an individual creditor is mostly unregulated.

The same is true for business-to-business debts. In a commercial setting, the creditor and debtor are free to conduct and resolve their debts as they see fit.

When it comes to consumer debt, however, collection is strictly regulated. In that situation, collection is regulated by a federal law known as the Fair Debt Collection Practices Act (FDCPA). The FDCPA applies to debts primarily for personal, household, or family purposes that are being collected by a third party. To fall within the Act, the third-party collector must be regularly engaged in debt collection activities. The third party is typically a collection agency or an attorney.

The FDCPA gives debt collectors three areas of compliance:

- Identifying as a debt collector,
- Telling the debtor that she has the right to contest the debt, and
- Not harassing the debtor, making false statements, or contacting others about the debt.

Identification means that the collector must let the debtor know that he is attempting to collect a debt. Communications from the collector are required to say that the contact is part of a debt collection effort.

The collector must tell the debtor of the right to contest the debt. Collector take care of this requirement by sending a validation notice. The notice must be sent within five days of the collector's first contact with the debtor. The notice provides the debt amount and identifies the original creditor for the debt. The notice gives instructions for the debtor to contest the debt. The debtor must contest the debt within 30 days of the notice. If she does not do so, it is assumed that the amount of the debt is not contested.

Most complaints of FDCPA violations involve collections harassment. Harassment includes contacting a debtor early in the morning or late at night. It also includes calling a debtor at work if she has asked not to be contacted there, making threats, or using harsh or abusive language. Collectors are also not allowed to make false statements or to misstate the amount of the debt. The FDCPA also bars attempts to collect a debt that is too old to be enforced, or to collect from someone who is not liable for the debt.

> According to the Consumer Financial Protection Bureau, 40% of the complaints against debt collectors in 2015 concerned attempts to collect a debt no longer owed.

Finally, collectors have only a limited right to contact a third party about a debt. They may contact another person only to verify an address or to locate a person.

A collector who violates the FDCPA may be sued for damages. A debtor may recover actual damages caused by the violation, such as lost wages. The debtor may also collect statutory damages of up to $1,000. Statutory damages are fixed financial awards established by legislation.

IDENTIFICATION:
A collector must disclose that he is trying to collect a debt when contacting the debtor.

VALIDATION NOTICE:
A notice to a debtor from a collector providing information on the debt, including the total and the creditor, as well as how to contest the debt.

STATUTORY DAMAGES:
Damages that are fixed by statute. They are awarded without considering what the actual loss was.

III. Fair Credit Reporting

Credit reports contain information used to decide if a person should receive credit. The agencies and bureaus that issue credit reports only publish information they receive from others; they are not required to investigate the accuracy of the information. This system leads to the possibility that data in a credit report may be inaccurate. The Fair Credit Reporting Act (FCRA) protects consumers from incorrect credit reporting.

The FCRA covers credit reporting bureaus and organizations that use credit reports or provide credit information. In certain circumstances, prospective employers and insurance companies may use a credit report as part of their evaluation processes. The information that makes up the reports is mainly provided by banks and other creditors. If there is a breach of the FCRA by any of these entities, a consumer can sue for damages and costs. If the violation was deliberate, the plaintiff can recover punitive damages as well.

The FCRA gives consumers the right to access their credit files. While a reporting bureau is not required to tell a person if his credit is "good" or "bad," a consumer does have the right to see his credit score. A "credit score" is a number assigned to a person that is the result of a calculation designed to predict that person's creditworthiness. The major credit reporting agencies each allow consumers to view their report annually. Consumers can also go to annualcreditreport.com, a site established by the three agencies to coordinate consumer access under the law.

The FCRA contains substantial consumer protections. Consumers must be notified when their credit information has been used against them. For example, when a person is denied a new credit card because of negative information in a credit report, he has a right to be informed. Consumers may also dispute inaccurate or outdated information in a credit file. Inaccurate, incomplete, outdated, or unverified information must be removed. Credit reporting agencies must remove negative information from a credit report after seven years, with some exceptions. Personal bankruptcies remain on a report for ten years.

The Fair Credit Reporting Act prompts credit reporting agencies and organizations that use or report credit information to make sure they are acting legally. Amendments during this century benefit consumers by improving access to credit reports, which can reveal FCRA violations. Agencies and creditors have developed more careful practices to avoid FCRA lawsuits and damages, resulting in better credit information overall.

IV. Article 9 Secured Transactions

There is never any guarantee that a debt will be paid. Some creditors protect themselves that by requiring **collateral** (a right to property in exchange for credit). Collateral may be taken by

> Credit reporting formulas are proprietary trade secrets developed by credit reporting agencies.

the creditor if the debtor fails to meet payment obligations. Collateral protects the creditor in two ways. First, the risk of losing the collateral gives debtors more incentive to pay the debt. If the debtor still defaults, the creditor can minimize its losses by taking the collateral and selling it to cover the debt.

Transactions with credit secured by collateral are referred to as "secured transactions." Secured transactions are governed by Article 9 of the Uniform Commercial Code (UCC).

> Article 9 of the UCC has been adopted in all 50 states, the District of Columbia, the U.S. Virgin Islands, and Puerto Rico.

COLLATERAL:
Property or goods used to guarantee payment of an obligation.

PERSONAL PROPERTY:
Any property other than real estate. Also called "personalty."

ATTACHMENT:
Creation of a security interest that may be enforced against the debtor.

AUTHENTICATION:
Formal proof of a security agreement, such as a signed document.

PERFECTION:
Filing of a security interest paperwork with the government to provide notice of the creditor's right to the security.

Article 9 applies when the collateral is **personal property**, which is most property other than real estate. A creditor can enforce a security interest against a debtor if it is attached to the collateral. **Attachment** occurs when three requirements have been met.

First, value must be given to support the security interest. A secured transaction is a form of contract, so something of value must be exchanged for the security interest, just as contracts must be supported by consideration.

Second, the person giving the security interest must have the legal right to use the property for collateral. This usually means that the person giving the security interest is the owner, or has the legal authority to act on behalf of the owner (for example, an officer of the corporation that owns the collateral).

Third, a security agreement is authenticated. **Authentication** means that the agreement was signed, or there was some other proof of making the agreement. There must be some proof that the property was used as collateral as a part of an agreement. This agreement must adequately identify the collateral to be used.

The attachment of the security interest to the collateral gives the creditor the power to enforce the interest against the debtor. Normally, the creditor and the debtor are the only parties involved, but there are situations when additional parties have rights that bear on the security interest. A debtor may want to use the same collateral to secure debts from other creditors, for instance. This often occurs when the collateral has a high value.

To protect the interests of secured creditors and potential secured creditors, Article 9 provides for **perfection** of security interests. Perfection involves filing a security interest with a government office to make the interest a matter of public record.

Although perfection is a routine part of most secured transactions, it is not required in order to create a security interest. Perfection notifies anyone outside the original transaction that the property is collateral. Knowing that a particular piece of property is—or is not—already collateral for another transaction can help a potential creditor decide whether to extend credit against the property.

With limited exceptions, perfection requires the creditor to take certain steps. The most common exception is for **purchase money security interests** in consumer goods. A purchase money security interest arises when the collateral was purchased with the money from the debt (for example, when the retailer finances the purchase of a large appliance). Those security interests attach and are perfected automatically.

Other security interests require filing a financing statement with the state government. The "financing statement" is the document required for perfection of a security interest. Creditors typically use a pre-printed version of a standardized document called a "UCC–1." The UCC–1 asks for basic information, such as the names and addresses of the parties to the transaction. The legal name of the debtor is very important. The records of perfected security interests are filed by the debtor's name. If the name listed on the statement is inaccurate or incomplete, future creditors could miss the statement.

The financing statement will also list the collateral that is covered by the statement.

> **PURCHASE MONEY SECURITY INTERESTS:**
> A security interest in property that is purchased by means of the debt, such as a car purchase loan secured by the car itself.

> The UCC–1 form requires minimal information. The amount of the debt is not required.

UNPERFECTED SECURITY INTERESTS DO NOT OVERRIDE OTHER CLAIMS

Credit Bureau of Broken Bow, Inc. v. Moninger
(Lien Holder) v. (Truck Owner)
204 Neb. 679, 284 N.W.2d 855 (1979)

INSTANT FACTS:
Moninger (D) told a deputy who was seizing his truck that the Bank (D) had a security interest in the truck.

BLACK LETTER RULE:
Verbal notice of an unperfected security interest does not prevent a prior creditor from seizing the collateral.

FACTS:
On October 20, 1977, the Credit Bureau of Broken Bow (P) won a default judgment against Moninger (D) for $1,518.27. On May 16, 1978, Moninger (D) renewed a loan he had with Broken Bow State Bank (D). Part of the collateral was to be a pickup truck Moninger (D) owned. There was no written security agreement.

On June 27, 1978, the Credit Bureau (D) obtained a writ of execution for the unpaid part of its judgment. The lien was given to the Sheriff for execution. A deputy looked at the motor vehicle records, and did not see any liens recorded on Moninger's (D) pickup. The deputy found Moninger (D), served him with the papers for execution, and told him that he was executing on the pickup. Moninger (D) the deputy that there was money borrowed from the Bank (D) against the pickup, and that the Bank (D) had title to the vehicle. The deputy then "grabbed ahold of the pickup." He then said "I execute on the pickup for the County of Custer." The deputy did not take possession of the truck, nor did he ask for the keys.

On July 10, the Bank (D) and Moninger (D) entered into a security agreement on the truck. The agreement was filed, and notation of the security interest was made on the truck's title. The truck was seized by deputies on July 13, and sold at a sheriff's sale. The sheriff asked the court to decide how the proceeds from the sale should be distributed. The court held that the Bank's (D) security interest was perfected on July 10, and that the sheriff had notice of the lien on July 7, 1978. The court also held that the Bank's (D) lien was prior to the Credit Bureau's (P) lien. The court ordered that the proceeds of the sheriff's sale should be paid to the Bank (D).

ISSUE:
Does verbal notice of a security interest make that interest prior to other liens?

DECISION AND RATIONALE:
(Brodkey, J.) No. Verbal notice of an unperfected security interest does not prevent a prior creditor from seizing the collateral. An unperfected security interest is subordinate to the rights of a lien creditor without knowledge of the security interest and before it is perfected. The Credit Bureau (P) became a lien creditor on July 7, 1978 when the sheriff levied on the vehicle. Notice by a debtor to the deputy was not sufficient. The Credit Bureau (P) was a lien creditor without knowledge of the security interest the Bank (D) claimed in the truck. The Bank (D) did not perfect its security interest in the vehicle until July 10, 1978, when it filed a security agreement entered into on that date. The Credit Bureau (P) thus has prior rights to the proceeds of the sheriff's sale.

The levy was valid, even though the deputy did not take physical possession of the truck. The deputy asserted his dominion over the truck, and exerted control over it. Reversed.

ANALYSIS:
If the court had held that telling the deputy that the Bank (D) had a security interest in the truck was sufficient notice, would the laws requiring recording of a security interest have any meaning? A security interest is recorded to give the public notice. It also leaves no room for doubt that notice was sufficient, instead of having a court dispute about who said what to whom, and when.

CASE VOCABULARY:

EXECUTION:
An order allowing the seizure another person's property to enforce a money judgment.

LEVY:
The act of taking property to satisfy a judgment.

LIEN:
A claim on someone else's property that is made to enforce a debt.

LIEN CREDITOR:
A person who claims a lien on someone else's property.

The completed financing statement is filed with a public office. In many states, the secretary of state is responsible for recording financing statements. In some states, creditors may be able to file the statement at the county level.

The purpose of perfecting a security interest is to give notice to potential creditors. The perfected interest is notice that there is another claim on the collateral. When there are multiple security interests on the same collateral, there may be a question of priority. Priority decides which creditor's security interest will be satisfied first. Generally, security interests have priority according to the date of perfection. A security interest perfected on September 1 will have priority over an interest in the same collateral perfected on September 15. Both will have priority over an interest perfected on October 1. Therefore, it is best for a creditor to perfect a security interest as soon as possible.

Once a debt is paid, the debtor may request the creditor issue a "termination statement." The termination statement shows that the creditor's security interest claimed on this collateral has been released. It is usually the debtor's responsibility to file a statement; filing makes the termination a matter of public record.

REPLEVIN:
A court order, or writ, deciding who is entitled to physical possession of particular personal property. Replevin does not decide who the legal owner of the property is, only who is entitled to possess it.

If the debt is not paid, the creditor's remedy is repossession of the collateral that secured the debt. Repossession of collateral must not breach the peace. Many states bar a repossessor from entering private property without consent. Physical assault is prohibited.

If the person in possession of the collateral will not surrender it peacefully, the repossessor may go to court and seek an order of **replevin.** A replevin order will state who is entitled to possession of the property in question.

> Creditors often hire repossession professionals to reclaim the collateral. Car repossessions are common, but specialized companies also repossess boats and airplanes.

When collateral is repossessed, it is sold in a "commercially reasonable manner." There is no firm definition of a "commercially reasonable" sale. It will depend on many circumstances, such as the nature of the collateral. Normally, a better price can be realized if a sale is widely advertised and potential buyers have time to reach the sale. On the other hand, it will cost money to store the collateral. While the cost of storing automobiles or construction equipment may be relatively low, perishable goods or livestock will come with high costs prior to sale. It is better to sell that type of collateral quickly, both to minimize the storage fees or to avoid losses to the collateral.

The proceeds of the collateral sale are applied to the costs of conducting the sale, such as advertising or auctioneer fees, and then to the debt. If

> A UCC Financing Statement allows creditors to formalize their agreements with debtors.

UCC FINANCING STATEMENT
FOLLOW INSTRUCTIONS

A. NAME & PHONE OF CONTACT AT FILER (optional)

B. E-MAIL CONTACT AT FILER (optional)

C. SEND ACKNOWLEDGMENT TO: (Name and Address)

THE ABOVE SPACE IS FOR FILING OFFICE USE ONLY

1. DEBTOR'S NAME: Provide only one Debtor name (1a or 1b) (use exact, full name; do not omit, modify, or abbreviate any part of the Debtor's name); if any part of the Individual Debtor's name will not fit in line 1b, leave all of item 1 blank, check here ☐ and provide the Individual Debtor information in item 10 of the Financing Statement Addendum (Form UCC1Ad)

OR
- 1a. ORGANIZATION'S NAME
- 1b. INDIVIDUAL'S SURNAME | FIRST PERSONAL NAME | ADDITIONAL NAME(S)/INITIAL(S) | SUFFIX
- 1c. MAILING ADDRESS | CITY | STATE | POSTAL CODE | COUNTRY

2. DEBTOR'S NAME: Provide only one Debtor name (2a or 2b) (use exact, full name; do not omit, modify, or abbreviate any part of the Debtor's name); if any part of the Individual Debtor's name will not fit in line 2b, leave all of item 2 blank, check here ☐ and provide the Individual Debtor information in item 10 of the Financing Statement Addendum (Form UCC1Ad)

OR
- 2a. ORGANIZATION'S NAME
- 2b. INDIVIDUAL'S SURNAME | FIRST PERSONAL NAME | ADDITIONAL NAME(S)/INITIAL(S) | SUFFIX
- 2c. MAILING ADDRESS | CITY | STATE | POSTAL CODE | COUNTRY

3. SECURED PARTY'S NAME (or NAME of ASSIGNEE of ASSIGNOR SECURED PARTY): Provide only one Secured Party name (3a or 3b)

OR
- 3a. ORGANIZATION'S NAME
- 3b. INDIVIDUAL'S SURNAME | FIRST PERSONAL NAME | ADDITIONAL NAME(S)/INITIAL(S) | SUFFIX
- 3c. MAILING ADDRESS | CITY | STATE | POSTAL CODE | COUNTRY

4. COLLATERAL: This financing statement covers the following collateral:

5. Check only if applicable and check only one box: Collateral is ☐ held in a Trust (see UCC1Ad, item 17 and Instructions) ☐ being administered by a Decedent's Personal Representative

6a. Check only if applicable and check only one box:
☐ Public-Finance Transaction ☐ Manufactured-Home Transaction ☐ A Debtor is a Transmitting Utility

6b. Check only if applicable and check only one box:
☐ Agricultural Lien ☐ Non-UCC Filing

7. ALTERNATIVE DESIGNATION (if applicable): ☐ Lessee/Lessor ☐ Consignee/Consignor ☐ Seller/Buyer ☐ Bailee/Bailor ☐ Licensee/Licensor

8. OPTIONAL FILER REFERENCE DATA:

FILING OFFICE COPY — UCC FINANCING STATEMENT (Form UCC1) (Rev. 04/20/11)   International Association of Commercial Administrators (IACA)

UCC FINANCING STATEMENT (UCC-1), USED BY PERMISSION OF INTERNATIONAL ASSOCIATION OF COMMERCIAL ADMINISTRATORS (IACA.ORG) there are any funds remaining, it is paid to the debtor. If the proceeds of the sale aren't enough to pay the debt, the debtor remains liable for the difference. The difference between the amount of the proceeds and the amount of the debt is called a "deficiency." A creditor may still pursue a debtor for this remaining debt, but after the sale, the debt is no longer secured by collateral.

V. Mortgage Foreclosure

Article 9 applies only to agreements to use personal property as collateral. If **real estate** is the collateral for a debt, the transaction is called a mortgage. Real estate is land and objects attached to the land, such as houses and other permanent improvements. As in an Article 9 secured transaction, a mortgage enforces a debt by giving the lender the right to take the collateral: the pledged real estate.

A mortgage, or mortgage loan, is usually used to finance a real estate purchase, and is secured by that real estate. A mortgage can also be taken out on real estate that the borrower already owns, and the money can be used for any purpose. In this way, the borrower can use the equity from real estate to pay down other debts or to start a business, for example.

The mortgage loan is paid back in installments, usually over a period of several years.

> **REAL ESTATE:**
> Land, structures permanently attached to land, and legal interests in land.

The regular payment includes principal and interest. The payments in the early years of a mortgage are typically credited more heavily toward interest on the loan, with the proportion of the payment going more toward principal as the loan ages.

> The mortgagor (borrower) is the legal owner of the property. Her ownership is subject to their mortgage.

If a borrower (the "mortgagor") defaults on a mortgage, the lender (the "mortgagee") takes possession of the property by "foreclosure." Foreclosure is governed by state law. While every state's laws will be slightly different, foreclosure usually follows a similar procedure.

> There were approximately 2.9 million foreclosure filings in 2010, the peak year for foreclosures. By 2020, foreclosure filings fell to under 215,000.

Before a foreclosure may start, the mortgagee notifies the mortgagor. The notice allows the borrower mortgagor time to cure the default, and bring the mortgage payments current. Some states may also require mortgagees and mortgagors to try to reach an agreement to avoid foreclosure. These state laws require mediation between mortgagees and mortgagors for mortgages on residential property. If a settlement cannot be worked out, the foreclosure action will proceed.

A traditional mortgage is foreclosed through a judicial proceeding. An action is filed with the appropriate court, and the mortgagor is served with court documents. If the mortgagor does not answer or enter a defense, the mortgagee will receive a default judgment. A default judgment will allow the mortgagee to proceed with the foreclosure.

A judgment does not give the mortgagee the right to immediate possession. Instead, the mortgaged property is sold at a public auction. Notice of the sale is published in a newspaper. The mortgagor also receives a copy of the notice, or the notice is posted on the property.

Before the sale, the mortgagor may **redeem** the mortgage. The mortgage is redeemed if the mortgagor pays the full amount of the mortgage balance. Many states' laws also give the mortgagor a period of time to redeem the mortgage after the sale. Post-sale redemption requires paying the amount of the successful bid for the property.

As in the case of secured transactions, the owner-mortgagor may be responsible for any deficiency between the amount owed the mortgagee and the amount realized by the foreclosure sale. The deficiency total may be raised by additional tax, advertising, and sale costs. The mortgagee may seek payment of the deficiency, but the debt is no longer connected to the property after the foreclosure sale. Therefore, the deficiency amount is more difficult to collect.

VI. Bankruptcy

Bankruptcy law serves many purposes. For individuals and families, it offers a fresh start by removing an unmanageable debt load. For businesses, bankruptcy can be a valuable tool for reorganizing and putting a business back on track. For local governments, bankruptcy can help avoid financial ruin.

Bankruptcy has a long, if checkered, history in American law. Before the Constitution was ratified, bankruptcy was left up to the states. Each state had the power to make (or not make) its own rules. This decentralized system caused problems for national commerce. As one commentator stated at the time, states could use "almost infinite" rules and standards. These differences could cause issues between states, including unfair variations in outcomes for similarly situated debtors in different jurisdictions.

When the Constitution was adopted in 1789, the drafters included a clause in Article I, section 8 that gave Congress the power to enact "uniform laws on the subject of bankruptcies throughout the United States." There seems to have been little debate or controversy about this clause. The drafters of the Constitution may have thought the reasoning was obvious. In Federalist Papers No. 42, James Madison said only that the "power of establishing uniform laws of bankruptcy is so intimately connected with the regulation of commerce, and will prevent so

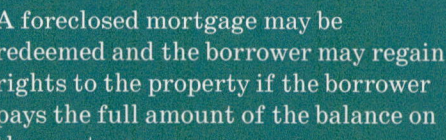

REDEEM/REDEMPTION: A foreclosed mortgage may be redeemed and the borrower may regain rights to the property if the borrower pays the full amount of the balance on the mortgage.

LIMITED LIABILITY COMPANY MEMBER CANNOT UNILATERALLY FILE FOR BANKRUPTCY AGAINST THE TERMS OF THE OPERATING AGREEMENT

In Re: Advanced Vascular Resources of Johnstown, LLC
(Bankruptcy Proceeding of Limited Liability Company)
590 B.R. 689 (Bank. W.D. Pa. 2018)

Samir Hadeed, M.D. and Johnstown Heart and Vascular Center, Inc. have moved to dismiss the above captioned bankruptcy case [arguing] that this chapter 11 filing is an *ultra vires* filing due to lack of consent by the owners of the "Majority Interest" of the units in the Debtor (which is a limited liability company).

The United States Supreme Court long ago opined that with respect to corporations, the entity vested with "the power of management" has the requisite authority to file a bankruptcy petition. Courts have also held in the corporate context that if a bankruptcy petition is filed by persons lacking the "power of management," the bankruptcy case must be dismissed for want of legal authority to do so. This precept of law operates in all corporate cases, including in those cases filed by a limited liability company.

The question before the Court is whether it was proper for the Debtor to file the instant bankruptcy case when one of its equity holders—Johnstown Heart and Vascular Center, Inc. ("JHVC")—did not consent to its filing?

The Debtor and JHVC do not dispute that the governance of the Debtor is set forth in the corporate document entitled: *Advanced Vascular Resources of Johnstown, LLC Operating Agreement* (the "Operating Agreement"). [. . .] Specifically, Section 4.1 of the Operating Agreement assigns the "full power and authority . . . to manage the business and affairs of [the Debtor] to the "Manager," which in-turn is initially defined as AVR Management, LLC. [. . .] Section 4.1 of the Operating Agreement sets forth instances where the "Manager" lacks authority to act on behalf of the Debtor "without first obtaining written approval of the holders of a Majority Interest of the Class A Units" of the Debtor.

One instance where the Manager lacks the capacity to act without the express written consent of the holders of the "Majority Interest of the Class A Units" is when the "Manager" desires to: *commence any action or proceeding seeking liquidation, dissolution, reorganization or other relief [on behalf of the Debtor] under any bankruptcy, insolvency or other similar law . . .*

The term "Majority Interest" is defined in the Operating Agreement as being "Class A Members that, taken together, hold more than sixty six percent (66%) of the aggregate of all Percentage Interests of Class A Members entitled to act or vote on such matter." [. . .] Schedule I to the Operating Agreement lists as "Class A Members" both Advanced Vascular Resources, LLC and JHVC. Schedule I further indicates that JHVC holds a Class A interest in the amount of fifty-five percent (55%) and that Advanced Vascular Resources, LLC holds a forty-five percent (45%) interest.

Relying upon this equity structure, JHVC contends that the Debtor lacked the requisite authority to commence the instant bankruptcy case because JHVC never consented to the bankruptcy filing and never ratified it. Specifically, JHVC contends that absent JHVC's express written consent, the Debtor's bankruptcy filing is *ultra vires* due to the Debtor's failure to obtain approval from the Debtor's "Majority Interest" holders[.]

The alleged Debtor does not dispute JHVC's construction of the Operating Agreement generally. Instead, the Debtor contends that JHVC does not hold a 55% Class A Membership interest in the Debtor. Rather, the Debtor contends that JHVC holds a mere 3% interest and that Advanced Vascular Resources, LLC holds a 97% interest.

In support of its efforts to re-allocate member interests, the alleged Debtor further concedes that Schedule I reflects a 55% membership allocation to JHVC, but nonetheless argues that Schedule I "is not reflective of the parties' intent and with other provisions of the Operating Agreement."

More particularly, the Debtor argues that a "Counterpart Signature Page" to the Operating Agreement contemplates that JHVC was required to make an initial payment or capital contribution of

$480,000 as a pre-requisite to it obtaining its 55% interest. [. . .] The Debtor contends that JHVC only contributed a mere $36,000 upon execution of the Operating Agreement. As such, the Debtor contends that JHVC's interest is limited to 3% and not 55%[.]

A court should not conclude that a contract is ambiguous merely because the parties disagree about its proper interpretation. Whether a contract is ambiguous is determined according to an objective, reasonable-person standard and is a question of law. Words are to be given their ordinary meaning and should not be "tortured" to impart ambiguity where none exists.

Thus, in order for the Operating Agreement to be rendered ambiguous as argued by the Debtor, it must first be objectively reasonable to read the Operating Agreement as making the allocation to JHVC of a 55% Class A Membership interest contingent on the full payment of a $480,000 capital contribution. The Court, however, does not find this to be the case.

The Court reaches this conclusion because the Operating Agreement itself makes express reference to JHVC's capital contribution of $36,000 and states unequivocally [. . .]: <u>Capital Contributions: Capital Account Balances</u>. *Johnstown Heart & Vascular Center, Inc. shall contribute $36,000 of its Capital Contribution upon execution of this Agreement, and the remaining amount his Capital Contribution obligation shall be deemed to be contributed as described in Section 6.1.3.* As this language recognizes, JHVC was permitted to contribute only $36,000 upon execution of the agreement, and the remaining sums were "deemed" by the parties to have been contributed by JHVC. These provisions are plain and unambiguous. They are also not unreasonable in light of other provisions of the Operating Agreement.

Indeed, these provisions make sense as the agreement itself provides that JHVC expressly agreed to permit Advanced Vascular Resources, LLC to have the lion's share of distributions of the company's profits until the "Recovery Date," which is the date distributions total $1.2 million. This $1.2 million figure also equals the total amount of initial aggregate capital contributions by the Debtor's members as set forth in Schedule I to the Operating Agreement.

In addition, the plain text of Section 3.2 of the Operating Agreement states that "[t]he Percentage Interests of each Class A Member shall be as set forth on Schedule I . . ." The use of the word "shall" is unequivocal and demonstrative of the fact that JHVC was granted a 55% member interest.

In rendering its decision today, the Court also notes that the Debtor cites to several pieces of extrinsic evidence in support of its claim that JHVC's member interest should be re-allocated to a 3% interest. [. . .] Delaware law, however, commands that no extrinsic evidence may be used to "interpret the intent of the parties, to vary the terms of the contract or to create ambiguity." The evidence cited by the Debtor is therefore inadmissible parol evidence.

For all of these reasons, the Court finds that the Debtor's bankruptcy filing is *ultra vires* and must be dismissed.

many frauds where the parties or their property may lie or be removed into different States, that the expediency of it seems not likely to be drawn into question."

> Although bankruptcy is a federal law and is mentioned in the Constitution, there is no constitutional right to bring a bankruptcy action.

Bankruptcy courts are units of the U.S. district court. There is one in each federal judicial district. All bankruptcies are court proceedings, but they usually do not involve trials or lengthy hearings. Judicial decisions in a bankruptcy case may be appealed to the federal district court.

There are six different types of bankruptcies allowed under federal law. While each type of case works on different assumptions, there are certain aspects that they have in common.

Bankruptcy terminology is consistent from case to case. A person or company who starts a bankruptcy action, or who has a bankruptcy action started against them, is called the **debtor**. The debtor's property is called the **estate**, or the bankruptcy estate. The people who are owed money by the debtor, or who have some kind of monetary claim against the debtor, are the **creditors**. A bankruptcy case is administered by a **trustee**, or administrator. A trustee's role is to manage the estate for the protection of the creditors. Trustees are appointed by the bankruptcy court.

All bankruptcy cases start the same way. A case starts when a **petition** is filed with the bankruptcy court clerk. A petition may be filed by a debtor or, in some cases, by a creditor.

When the petition is filed, the debtor must file additional documents:

- Schedules, or lists, of all assets and liabilities,
- Schedules of income and expenditures,
- Statement of financial affairs, and
- Statement of unexpired leases and **executory contracts** (a contract that has not been fully performed).

Different types of bankruptcy cases may call for additional documents to be filed.

The third common point is the stay. As soon as a petition is filed, an **automatic stay** goes into effect. The automatic stay is a legal stop on most efforts at collecting debts from the debtor. There are several exceptions to the stay:

- Child support or spousal support (alimony) collection,
- Criminal actions,
- Dissolution of marriage or divorce actions,
- Domestic violence actions,
- Tax collection,
- Wage withholding to repay a loan from a retirement account, and
- Evictions, if the landlord already has a judgment against the tenant, or if the eviction is for endangerment or drug abuse.

TRUSTEE:
A person appointed to hold or manage property for another. In bankruptcy law, a person appointed to oversee the case.

PETITION:
In bankruptcy law, the documents that ask the court for relief under the Bankruptcy Act.

EXECUTORY CONTRACTS:
An agreement that is not yet fully performed on both sides.

AUTOMATIC STAY:
An order from the Bankruptcy Court that stops all collection efforts against a debtor. The automatic stay goes into effect as soon as a bankruptcy case is filed.

> **Example:** Alan used his herd of dairy cattle as the collateral for a loan. He filed a bankruptcy petition. The bank became concerned that Alan would be unable or unwilling to take care of his cows. The bank may move the court for an order allowing it to repossess the herd.

A creditor may ask the court to have the automatic stay lifted. Secured creditors may file a petition for relief from the stay if the debt is not being paid. If a creditor stops making payments on her car loan, for instance, the lender may ask the court for permission to repossess the car. A secured creditor may also request the court to lift the stay if the creditor is not adequately protected. This means that the collateral for the debt is at physical risk of being damaged or destroyed and is not adequately insured.

Finally, in every bankruptcy case, the court holds a meeting of creditors. The debtor must attend this meeting. The debtor is placed under oath, and asked questions about her financial affairs. The trustee may ask the questions, but creditors may also speak. The meeting gives creditors a chance to hear directly from the debtor without having to make the discovery requests used in most court proceedings.

Types of Bankruptcy

The different types of bankruptcy cases are referred to by chapter numbers that refer to sections of the federal bankruptcy law. The chapter number indicates what kind of relief the debtor is seeking. In each case, the final outcome will depend on the facts of each individual case.

Many creditors believe that if a debtor files bankruptcy, they have little to no chance of recovering the money still owed. That is true in many cases, but not in all. If a creditor files a claim for payment when the debtor files for bankruptcy, it is possible to receive some payment. Creditors in a Chapter 7 case will receive payment if the estate has assets that are not **exempt** (protected from creditors by law). Creditors who file claims in Chapter 11, 12, or 13 cases, however, will receive at least partial payment of their debts.

Chapter 7

Chapter 7 is what most people think of when "bankruptcy" is mentioned. It is also referred to as a "liquidation," because the property of the estate that is not exempt is liquidated, or sold. The proceeds of the liquidation are paid to the creditors who have made claims. There is no other plan for repayment of creditors.

Chapter 7 bankruptcy may be filed by individuals or married couples. Chapter 7 may also be

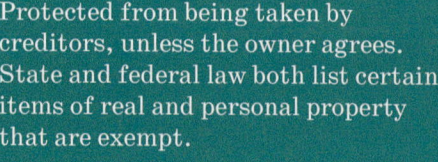

EXEMPT: Protected from being taken by creditors, unless the owner agrees. State and federal law both list certain items of real and personal property that are exempt.

filed by a business entity, such as a corporation, limited partnership, or an LLC. An entity that files Chapter 7 goes out of business after the bankruptcy process, because all of its assets will be gone.

The end result of a successful Chapter 7 bankruptcy will be **discharge** of the debts. Discharge means that the debtor is no longer liable for that debt. While the discharged debtor no longer needs to pay, the debt does not disappear. Co-signers or guarantors of a debt will still be responsible. There are also several types of debts that cannot be discharged:

- Certain taxes or customs duties,
- Debts incurred through fraud or false statements,
- Debts from embezzlement or larceny,
- Alimony or child support,
- Damages for willful or malicious injury to another person,
- Fines or penalties owed to the government,
- Damages due to operating a vehicle while intoxicated, or
- Debts not listed on the debtor's schedules.

Student loan debts are not dischargeable unless not discharging the loan would cause an "undue hardship." Discharges of student loans due to undue hardship are very rare.

Discharge of debts will be denied if the debtor does not cooperate with the trustee or fails to produce adequate records.

Discharge will also be denied if the debtor makes false statements during the bankruptcy proceedings.

If there is doubt about whether a debt is dischargeable, a creditor may file an action in the bankruptcy court. The purpose of the action will be to decide if a debt is dischargeable. It is up to the creditor to prove that a particular debt cannot be discharged and must therefore be repaid. Bankruptcy courts tend to resolve doubts in favor of debtors.

There is no minimum or maximum amount of debt to qualify for Chapter 7. The only limitation is that a Chapter 7 petition may abuse the bankruptcy system. Concerns that Chapter 7 was too easy to file, and let too many irresponsible debtors walk away from debt, led to new legal requirements for debtors.

> It is estimated that 62% of consumer bankruptcies include medical debt. Medical debt is now the largest source of consumer debt in the United States.

As part of these reforms, debtors must pass a means test before they can file Chapter 7. Under the means test system, abuse of the system is presumed unless the debtor has a monthly income less than the median income for a

DISCHARGE:
A debt is discharged when the debtor is no longer liable for paying it.

DEBTORS WHO DO NOT COOPERATE WITH THE TRUSTEE WILL BE DENIED A DISCHARGE

Seror v. Lopez
(Trustee) v. (C.D. Cal.)
532 B.R. 140 (2015)

INSTANT FACTS:
Seror (P) objected to Lopez's (D) Chapter 7 discharge for failure to provide financial records.

BLACK LETTER RULE:
A debtor's failure to turn over estate property and records will justify denying a Chapter 7 discharge.

FACTS:
Lopez was the debtor in a Chapter 7 proceeding. Lopez filed her schedules and statement of financial affairs ("SOFA"), but asserted her Fifth Amendment privilege against self-incrimination on some of the important questions in her SOFA. Lopez invoked her privilege with respect to questions about her income, and certain business losses. Lopez (D) also claimed the privilege about other business records, a gambling debt, and a claim she had against another person. She also claimed she was unable to turn over other books and records, because she had sold all of her electronic office equipment and could not reproduce them. An agreement was reached for her to turn over some records, but Lopez (D) failed to turn over any records. Seror (P) brought an action objecting to her discharge, saying that Lopez (D):

- Failed to keep or preserve records,
- Withheld records, and
- Failed to explain the loss of estate assets.

ISSUE:
Should Lopez (D) be denied a discharge?

DECISION AND RATIONALE:
(Tighe, J.) Yes. A debtor's failure to turn over estate property and records will justify denying a Chapter 7 discharge. A debtor must present sufficient written evidence to let creditors reasonably ascertain the debtor's present financial condition and to follow the debtor's business transactions for a reasonable period in the past. Although Lopez (D) eventually provided many records, she did it in a way that would slow the proceedings down and thwart any real understanding of her finances. While Seror (P), as Trustee, has the duty to investigate Lopez's (D) financial affairs, the information about her assets must come primarily, if not entirely, from her. Seror (P) cannot conjure it out of thin air.

Lopez (D) correctly argues she cannot be denied a discharge for invoking her Fifth Amendment privilege against self-incrimination. But exercising her privilege against self-incrimination did not excuse Lopez (D) from cooperating with Seror (P) and does not protect Lopez (D) from being denied a discharge. Discharge denied.

ANALYSIS:
The reason for denying Lopez (D) a discharge is her failure to cooperate. It was not because her debts were non-dischargeable.

CASE VOCABULARY:

FIFTH AMENDMENT PRIVILEGE:
The rule set out in the Fifth Amendment to the U.S. Constitution that no person "shall be compelled in any criminal case to be a witness against himself." The privilege applies in any type of proceeding, so that a person may decline to answer questions if her answer could lead to criminal charges.

household of her size in her state. The median monthly income is published by the U.S. Census Bureau. If a debtor has an income higher than the median, she can still file Chapter 7 if her monthly income after paying living expenses is not enough to pay off at least part of her unsecured debt. If she does have enough to pay, her case will be converted to a Chapter 13.

All Chapter 7 debtors, regardless of income, must certify that they have attended an approved credit counseling session.

Chapter 9

Chapter 9 is a financial reorganization for municipalities. A municipality includes cities, towns, or villages, as well as counties, school districts, taxing districts, and publicly-owned utilities. A state is not a "municipality."

To file for bankruptcy, a municipality must be **insolvent**. A municipality is insolvent if it is not paying its debts. Insolvent can also mean that the municipality is unable to pay its debts as they come due.

Reorganization may include delaying the time when a debt becomes due or reducing the principal or interest of a debt. It may involve taking out a new loan to refinance a debt. The Bankruptcy Act does not require liquidation of any of a municipality's assets, but a voluntary sale of some assets may be part of a reorganization plan.

Municipal bankruptcies are very politicized. As a result, in Chapter 9 cases, bankruptcy courts typically focus strictly on approving the petition, confirming a reorganization plan, and making sure the plan is put into effect.

INSOLVENT:
The inability to pay debts.

> **Example:** The largest Chapter 9 bankruptcy, in terms of both the amount of money involved ($18–20 billion) and the size of the municipality (population 700,000), was the city of Detroit. The Emergency Financial Manager appointed by the state to oversee Detroit's finances filed a Chapter 9 petition on July 18, 2013. The city worked out a restructuring plan, and exited bankruptcy on December 10, 2014.

> **Example:** Interstate Stores operated several chains of discount stores. In the mid-1970s, the company filed Chapter 11 bankruptcy, and closed or sold its poorly performing units. The company then concentrated on its strongest component, the children's retailer Toys "R" Us. Once a retail powerhouse, Toys "R" Us declared bankruptcy and closed all its U.S. locations in 2018.

Sometimes, municipalities avoid bankruptcy by the thinnest of margins. In 1975, New York City came within hours of defaulting on its bills, and started the process for filing bankruptcy. A last-minute agreement by the city teachers' union to invest pension funds in city bonds made the filing unnecessary.

Chapter 11

Chapter 11 is a reorganization. Although individuals are allowed to file Chapter 11, it is mostly used by businesses. A Chapter 11 bankruptcy allows a business to restructure itself to become profitable. The restructuring can involve selling off part of the business, renegotiating debt, or cancelling contracts. The goal is survival as a business, not liquidation.

Chapter 11 bankruptcies use the same terminology as other types of bankruptcy, with one major exception. A debtor that files a Chapter 11 bankruptcy is officially known as the **debtor in possession**. Unlike a Chapter 7 debtor, the debtor in a Chapter 11 case does not turn assets over to the trustee. The debtor in possession is responsible for keeping the business running during the Chapter 11 proceedings. The debtor is required to perform most of the functions of a trustee. These duties include accounting for property, examining and objecting to claims, and filing required reports. The debtor is also responsible for filing tax returns and reports that the court might require, such as a final accounting.

An entity that files Chapter 11 files the same documents with the petition as other debtors. In addition, the debtor must file a written disclosure statement and a plan of reorganization. The disclosure statement sets out information about the assets, liabilities, and business affairs of the debtor. The disclosure statement is the main source of information that creditors have to make an informed judgment about the reorganization plan. In order for the case to move forward, the statement must be approved by the court after a hearing.

Creditors may object to the disclosure statement. The most common objection is that the statement does not have enough detail for creditors to make an informed decision about the reorganization plan. Details that the courts expect to see include a listing of assets and liabilities, the circumstances that caused the debtor to file for bankruptcy, and the source for the information in the statement. The statement should also include a summary of the reorganization plan.

When the judge approves the disclosure statement, a date is set for voting on the plan of reorganization. The plan of reorganization (the "plan") is the debtor's proposal for restructuring the business and paying creditors. Most debtors must file the plan within 120 days of filing the petition. If the debtor qualifies as

> **DEBTOR IN POSSESSION:** A Chapter 11 bankruptcy debtor over the term of the Chapter 11 process.

> Since 1979, U.S. airlines have filed over 150 Chapter 11 reorganizations.

"small business" (a company with less than $2 million in debt), the debtor has 60 additional days to file its plan.

If the plan is not filed on time, any creditor may file a proposed plan for the debtor. In either case, a plan will not go into effect unless it is approved by the court.

Chapter 11 encourages close participation by all creditors. Creditors can vote on approving a plan, but their involvement goes deeper than voting. It is common for creditors to become involved with the plan. In many cases, creditors negotiate a plan with the debtor before the petition is filed. After the petition, the court will seek input from creditors before taking or approving any action. Unsecured creditors may participate in the case through a creditor's committee appointed by the court. That committee is made up of the seven largest unsecured creditors. It participates in crafting the plan, but the committee also consults on administration of the case, and reviews the debtor's operation of the business.

Every Chapter 11 plan is different, and is tailored to meet the circumstances and needs of each case. All creditor claims must be classified according to their size and type. The plan will direct how each debt classification will be treated. Creditors holding the same debt classification must be treated consistently.

> A collective bargaining agreement may be rejected only if the debtor has tried to negotiate with the union. The debtor may modify the agreement if the change is essential for business continuation.

When creating a plan, debtors have some power to decide how each creditor classification will be treated. Employees may be terminated, and assets may be sold off. Contracts that have not been completed may be accepted as they are, rejected, or renegotiated.

Some creditors may receive less than full value for their claims. Others may have the value of their claim reduced. Claims that will not be paid in full are called "impaired" claims. Creditors with impaired claims are allowed to vote on the reorganization plan submitted by the debtor.

After a vote is taken on the plan, the court will conduct a confirmation hearing to determine whether to confirm the plan. A plan may be approved if it is:

- Feasible,
- Proposed in good faith, and
- In compliance with all of the provisions of the Bankruptcy Code.

If the creditors vote down a plan that meets all of the legal requirements, the court may still approve the plan over their objections of the creditors. To do this, the court must find that the plan does not discriminate unfairly and is fair and equitable with respect to each dissenting class of impaired claims. This process is colorfully known as "cram down."

Chapter 12

Chapter 12 bankruptcy applies to family farmers or commercial fishers. This chapter allows farmers and fishers to make a plan to repay their debts. Chapter 12 debtors must have a regular income, and more than half of that income must come from farming or commercial fishing.

A Chapter 12 plan usually lasts from three to five years. It will not go into effect unless it is approved by the bankruptcy court. The court will approve a plan that is feasible. The plan must also meet the legal requirements for a Chapter 12 plan:

- Priority claims must be paid in full, unless the priority creditor agrees otherwise, and
- Secured creditors must be paid at least as much as the value of their collateral.

If the original debt was scheduled to be paid off in more than three to five years, the debtor may continue with that schedule as long as any past due payments are made up during the plan.

Unsecured, non-priority debts will be discharged if the plan calls for all of the debtor's **disposable income** to be applied to plan payments, and if the creditors would receive at least as much as they would in a Chapter 7 bankruptcy. "Disposable income" is any income not needed for the maintenance or support of the debtor or dependents, or for making payments needed to operate the debtor's business.

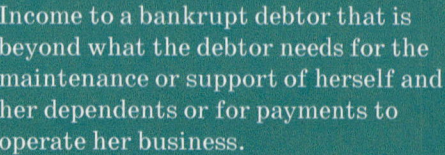

DISPOSABLE INCOME:
Income to a bankrupt debtor that is beyond what the debtor needs for the maintenance or support of herself and her dependents or for payments to operate her business.

Chapter 13

Chapter 13 bankruptcy is for individuals or married couples with mostly household or consumer debt. It is often called a "wage earner's plan," because it allows debtors with a regular income to repay all or part of their debts. Chapter 13 differs from a conventional repayment plan, because the plan is always under the supervision of the Bankruptcy Court.

A Chapter 13 petition may be filed by an individual or a married couple. The petition includes the same documents as are filed in other bankruptcies, but the debtor must also file proof that he has received credit counseling, along with a copy of any debt repayment plan achieved through credit counseling. The debtor must also file evidence of any payment from employers received within 60 days of filing, a statement of monthly net income, and a statement of any expected increase in income or expenses that may come up after the petition is filed. The court must also be informed interests in federal or state qualified education or tuition accounts. Finally, the debtor must provide the trustee with a copy of his tax return for the most recent tax year, and tax returns filed after the petition is filed.

Chapter 13 has an automatic stay provision for co-debtors. Unless the court says otherwise, a creditor may not try to collect a consumer debt from any individual who is liable along with the debtor (typically a spouse). This special stay applies even if the co-debtor has not filed a bankruptcy petition.

The debtor must file a repayment plan no later than 14 days after the petition is filed. The plan must provide for payments of fixed amounts to the trustee on a regular basis. The trustee then distributes the funds to creditors who have filed valid claims according to the terms of the plan.

A Chapter 13 plan must pay priority claims in full unless a particular priority creditor agrees otherwise. If the claim is for a child or spousal support obligation, payment in full is required unless the debtor contributes all disposable income to a plan lasting five years.

For secured claims, the debtor may keep the collateral (such as a car) if the plan provides that the creditor will receive at least the item's value. Unsecured claims do not have to be paid in full if the debtor will pay all her disposable income over the plan's life, and as long as unsecured creditors receive at least as much under the plan as they would have received in a Chapter 7 liquidation.

A Chapter 13 plan must be approved by the bankruptcy court. The debtor must start making payments on the plan within 30 days after filing the petition, even if the plan has not yet been approved by the court. If the court confirms the plan, the trustee will start to distribute funds to creditors. If the plan is not approved, the debtor may file a modified plan, or convert the case to a Chapter 7 liquidation.

Plans stay in effect for three to five years after filing the petition. The Chapter 13 debtor is entitled to a discharge after all of the plan payments have been made if:

- All domestic support obligations have been paid,
- The debtor has not received a discharge in a prior case filed within a certain time, and
- The debtor has completed an approved course in financial management.

The discharge will release the debtor from all debts provided for by the plan.

Federal law strongly prefers that individuals who file bankruptcy file under Chapter 13, rather than Chapter 7.

Chapter 15

Chapter 15 deals with bankruptcies across international borders. Chapter 15 has two purposes. The first is to allow a trustee to act in a foreign country if a debtor has assets over-

> **Example:** Octaviar, an Australian company, was the subject of insolvency proceedings in Australia. Octaviar had legal claims against various parties in the U.S. It deposited a $10,000 retainer with a law firm to pursue those claims. The claims and the retainer met the legal requirement of property in the U.S. Octaviar was eligible for Chapter 15 relief recognizing the Australian proceeding. *In Re Octaviar Administration Pty. Ltd.*, 511 B.R. 361 (Bankr. S.D.N.Y. 2014).

seas. The second is to recognize a foreign bankruptcy proceeding for a debtor that has property in the United States. A representative appointed in a foreign proceeding would be allowed to handle the debtor's assets in the U.S.

> In 2020, Cirque du Soleil, an acrobatic performance company founded in Canada, filed to restructure using Chapter 15 due to losses from COVID-19.

Chapter 15 is a relatively recent addition to bankruptcy law. It was added in 2005 to improve how bankruptcies were handled when international assets are involved. The changes allow U.S. and foreign courts to coordinate more effectively. Still, Chapter 15 bankruptcies are rare, with only 130 cases in 2019.

VII. Receivership

Receivers are appointed by a court to oversee a business. A receiver can be appointed for any one of a number of functions. He may be acting solely to liquidate a business, or he may be working towards restructuring the business to make it profitable again. Alternatively, he may be attempting to stabilize the business to find a buyer to take it over.

RECEIVER: A person appointed by a bankruptcy court to oversee a business.

Receiverships may be ordered when a company engages in wrongdoing. In mid-2012, for instance, Zeek Rewards ran an investment program that was based on an online auction service. For $1, a buyer got a chance to bid on heavily discounted items. Investors were recruited to promote the auction site. In theory, an investor would make money as she signed up more investors to promote the auctions. Auction profits were shared with all of the investors in the line.

Zeek Rewards was operated as a Ponzi scheme, in which new investments were used to fund pay-outs to more senior investors. Federal regulators shut the company down in 2012, after it had raised money from approximately a million users worldwide. The U.S. District Court appointed a receiver to marshal and preserve the company's assets. The receiver distributes those assets to those who lost money by investing in Zeek Rewards. According to the receivership website, zeekrewardsreceivership.com, by 2020, the receivership was able to return 81 percent of claimants' money.

Receivership is different from bankruptcy in several ways. First, while bankruptcy is a federal matter, receivership can be either state or federal. Federal receivership typically is limited to federally-regulated businesses, such as banks or securities brokerages. Second, receivership is almost always involuntary. A receiver is appointed after or during a court case. Third, a company in receivership does not enjoy the protections of bankruptcy law, unless the receiver is appointed as a part of a bankruptcy. This means that there is no automatic stay of debts. In receiverships, debts are not discharged at the end of the case.

CHAPTER SUMMARY

Extending credit is a carefully regulated process. The decision about who gets credit is mostly left to the discretion of the creditor. That discretion must be exercised in a proper manner. At the same time, creditors are allowed to take steps to help ensure payment of debts. The most common step taken is obtaining a security interest in property as collateral. Security interests generally give the creditor the right to repossess and sell the collateral.

Bankruptcy is another facet of creditor-debtor relations. Bankruptcy could involve a liquidation and discharge of a debtor's obligations, or it could be a restructuring of a business. For individuals, bankruptcy could be a simple, court-supervised repayment plan. The goal of bankruptcy is a fresh start for the debtor, and protection for the creditors.

CAREERS IN THE LAW

Most banking careers involve legal issues to some extent. In the credit area, though, loan officers are especially critical to a bank or financial institution's legal compliance and smooth credit operations. A mortgage loan officer (also referred to as a mortgage loan originator) works directly with commercial and residential buyers who need mortgages. The officer works with the buyer on the credit application and determines what loan program is appropriate for the transaction. The loan officer works with underwriters, appraisers, and other professionals to finalize the deal.

Mortgage loan officers do not need specific degrees, but, like attorneys, they must be licensed by the state where they work. The federal Secure and Fair Enforcement for Mortgage Licensing Act of 2008 requires pre-license training, criminal and credit background checks, and federal and state license exams. This licensing requirement ensures that loans are given and administered according to all legal requirements without discrimination. Mortgage loan originators are well-compensated and highly regarded in their institutions.

Review Questions

Review question 1.
What disclosure does Regulation Z govern? What is the goal of the disclosure, and why is it important for creditors and debtors?

Review question 2.
What is the difference between a secured and an unsecured loan? Does this difference matter for purposes of the Truth in Lending Act? What types of loans are not covered by TILA?

Review question 3.
Who is protected by the Equal Credit Opportunity Act? Who is not?

Review question 4.
What debts does the Fair Debt Collection Practices Act cover? Who is regulated by the FDCPA? What are the law's major requirements?

Review question 5.
What types of organizations are governed by the Fair Credit Reporting Act? What consumer rights are guaranteed by the FCRA? What can consumers do if there are problems in their credit reports?

Review question 6.
What types of transactions does UCC Article 9 cover? What is needed for a secured transaction? How does a security interest attach? How does a creditor perfect a security interest? What is a UCC–1? What are the requirements for repossession?

Review question 7.
What is a foreclosure? How does a foreclosure differ from a repossession? What are the steps in the foreclosure process? What is redemption? What happens if there is a deficiency after a foreclosure sale?

Review question 8.
Who can declare bankruptcy under Chapters 7, 11, 12, and 13? How do the chapters differ? What happens in a reorganization? What are the advantages and disadvantages of bankruptcy for a business? For an individual?

Review question 9.

In what circumstances will a court appoint a receiver? What is the goal of a receivership? How is it different from bankruptcy?

Review question 10.

What are the practical consequences of debt default for an unincorporated business? What types of businesses have legal obligations to debtors? What are those obligations?

Discussion Questions

Question 1:

Jorge and Luis have decided to buy their uncle's restaurant supply business. Their father, who works as an engineer, agrees to lend them half of the money they will need. He has them sign an agreement to repay the loan in 12 monthly installments. He does not give them TILA disclosures. Four days after signing the agreement, Luis learns that his wife is pregnant. He decides it is a bad time for him to take on the financial risk of running a business, so he wants to get out of the loan agreement.

> Under TILA, can the loan agreement be rescinded? Why or why not?

> Suppose that, instead of borrowing the money from his father, Luis borrowed his share of the money from his credit union. Would your answer be the same? Why or why not?

Question 2:

Andre and Caitlin go to their bank to apply for a loan to buy a new car. Andre has been married twice before, and this is Caitlin's second marriage. They meet their bank's credit and income requirements, but the loan officer who reviews the application has heard that spouses who have been married more than once before are at a higher risk of getting a divorce than other couples. A divorce could make it less likely that the loan would be repaid. Andre and Caitlin are approved for a loan, but have to pay 0.5% more interest than other borrowers.

> Is this an ECOA violation? Why, or why not?

What if this were the first marriage for both, but Caitlin is a new immigrant to the United States and does not yet have a green card? Could the loan officer take that status into consideration?

Question 3.

Howie runs a neighborhood bar. Although he does a good business, Howie is far from the most efficient manager around. He has neglected to pay state and federal income taxes for the past two years, and two different liquor wholesalers refuse to do business with him, due to unpaid bills. To stay open, Howie has taken to buying supplies at a local retail liquor store. This violates city ordinances, and the city is demanding he pay a penalty or his bar will be shut down. Howie is considering filing bankruptcy.

What chapters of bankruptcy can Howie file? Explain the differences between each chapter.

Suppose Howie is operating his bar as a sole proprietor, and he is personally liable for the bar's debts. If he files a Chapter 7 bankruptcy, would any of the debts be discharged? If so, which ones?

Question 4.

Jasdeep is a 20-year-old college student who works as a department assistant. As compensation for this work, she receives an hourly wage and 10 percent rebate on her tuition for the semester. Due to an administrative error, Jasdeep receives a 20 percent rebate on her tuition. When the department discovers the error, it contacts Jasdeep at her permanent address to seek repayment. Jasdeep is on vacation when the letter arrives, and her mother calls the department to see what the problem is. The department secretary tells Jasdeep's mother that she has to make the repayment, because she is legally responsible for Jasdeep as long as she is a full-time student. Jasdeep's mother refuses to pay. Over the next three days, the secretary calls Jasdeep's mother 12 times at odd hours to pursue payment.

Is Jasdeep's mother responsible for the debt?

May the department secretary pursue Jasdeep's mother for the debt? May the secretary contact Jasdeep? Are there any limits on how the secretary may pursue either person? If so, why?

Question 5.

Chang & Daughter LLC is a small business that earns most of its revenues through retail sales. Chang & Daughter sells its products at local craft fairs and farmer's markets. During the summer, their primary income is from the sale of fresh fruit and eggs that the company produces on a small farm plot it financed just outside of the city. The rest of the year, Chang & Daughter relies on sales of fragrant soaps, which accounts for just over half of the company's annual income. The soaps look handmade and contain dried herbs and flowers, but Chang & Daughter imports the soaps from China. After one of the better craft fairs loses its space, sales fall dramatically. Chang & Daughter start a website, which is starting to produce sales, but it is not yet keeping pace with payments on the farm plot. Chang & Daughter management starts considering a reorganization to stay in business.

> What chapter is most applicable to Chang & Daughter's needs?
>
> Is a reorganization a good idea, or should the company liquidate and start over? Does the company have another practical option?
>
> Suppose Chang & Daughter start to produce soaps using herbs and flowers they raise on their plot. They replace half of the imports with their own product. Do these facts change your answers to the prior questions? If so, how?

Question 6.

Dante runs a furniture store. His brother Dallas is a debt collector. Dante asks Dallas to work on collecting some of the bad debt held by the business. Dallas calls Zach, a customer, about money he owes on a sofa. Dallas decides to start the call by checking on how Zach likes his purchase, acting as if he is calling from the store. When Dallas finally asks about the debt, though, Zach says he can't pay right now. "Well, keep in mind that Dante has a problem keeping his temper in check," Dallas says before hanging up.

> What laws apply to Dallas's collection activities?
>
> What mistakes did Dallas make in his call with Zach? What should he have done instead?

How would your answers change if Dallas was a salesperson for the store and was following up with Zach about payments?

Question 7.

The local music store sells Tad a guitar on credit. The store fills out a financing statement and files it with the state. Tad's full legal name is Tadworth Emerson-Schmuttly, but the store knows him as Tad Schmuttly, and uses that name on the form. Tad stops making payments on the guitar, and the store manager seizes the guitar when he sees it backstage at a local festival.

Is the name discrepancy a problem in this repossession? Why or why not?

When did the store perfect its interest in the guitar? How?

Suppose Tad used the guitar as collateral on a different loan before it was repossessed. Was the repossession acceptable in that case?

Question 8.

Wyatt buys a house in a foreclosure auction. About a week after moving in, he comes home to find a note in the mail from the prior owner, Winona. The note reads, "I came up with the money, so I'm getting the house back. You need to move out, sorry." Wyatt asks you what's going on. He says he bought the house fair and square.

What right is Winona exercising? What expenses and amounts will she need to cover?

What if the note was postmarked a year after the auction?

What compensation will Wyatt receive, if any?

8

TORTS AND PRODUCTS LIABILITY

> **KEY OBJECTIVES:**
> ▶ Explain when a party may be liable for its negligent conduct.
> ▶ List intentional torts relevant to business entities.
> ▶ Outline how a business may be liable for defective products it created, distributed, or sold to customers.

CHAPTER OVERVIEW

People and businesses interact constantly. Through the course of those activities, some actions result in harm to others. The law attempts to balance the rights of citizens to go about their business with the rights of those who are harmed by another's actions.

TORT:
A wrongful act resulting in harm to another person.

TORT CASE:
A lawsuit brought by an injured party seeking compensation from the wrongdoer.

PLAINTIFF:
The party who initiates a lawsuit; the injured party who seeks compensation from a tortfeasor.

TORTFEASOR:
An individual who commits a wrongful act that injures another person.

DEFENDANT:
The party who responds to a lawsuit initiated by another party; the defendant is the party whom the plaintiff alleges engaged in a tort.

This balancing process is handled through tort law. A **tort** is a wrongful act resulting in harm to another person. Tort law attempts to provide compensation to those who have been injured as a result of another's negligent, reckless, or intentional actions. Tort liability also influences behavior; the possibility of a lawsuit can deter harmful activity.

In this chapter, we take a look at negligence claims and the elements that must be proven to hold a party liable for unintentional conduct. Next, we review the various intentional torts, with a focus on the intentional torts that are particularly relevant to business parties and entities. Finally, we discuss the ways in which a business party can be liable for defective products sold in the marketplace.

INTRODUCTION

In simple terms, a tort is a wrongful act that causes harm to another party. The person who was harmed, referred to as the **plaintiff**, may bring a lawsuit against the person who committed the wrongful conduct. The person who caused the harm is called the **tortfeasor**, or the **defendant**. A tort action seeks some compensation or other remedy for the party who was injured. Typically, the harmed party will seek money compensation, called **damages**. A tort lawsuit is filed in civil court. Criminal penalties, such as imprisonment, are not available in civil court.

The law recognizes a variety of torts. These torts are based on the varying types of conduct that may cause harm to another party. To recover money or other remedies, the plaintiff must prove elements, or requirements, specific to each tort. Broadly speaking, torts can be divided into three categories: (1) negligence (non-intentional torts); (2) intentional torts; and (3) strict liability torts. We examine all three of these types of torts below. Furthermore, of particular interest in the business world, a business entity may be liable for any defective products it sells to consumers. **Products liability** is a specific type of tort that is based on principles governing general tort law.

> **DAMAGES:**
> Money compensation awarded to the injured party in a lawsuit.
>
> **PRODUCTS LIABILITY:**
> A manufacturer or seller's liability for a defective product created by the manufacturer and sold to the public.
>
> **NEGLIGENCE:**
> The failure to act as a reasonably prudent person would act in the same circumstances.
>
> **REASONABLE PERSON:**
> The legal standard by which a person's conduct is measured in a negligence action. A party must act as a reasonable person would act in the same circumstances.

I. Negligence

One of the most common types of torts is a **negligence** action. A negligence tort results from a party's unintentional conduct. This means that the party did not intend or want to cause harm, but acted without enough care to avoid that outcome.

A party acts negligently when it fails to act the way an ordinary, reasonable person would act in the same circumstances. A party may act negligently in many different ways, and negligence lawsuits may arise from a variety of situations. Car accidents, slip and fall accidents, and medical malpractice claims are examples of negligence torts.

Businesses may be liable for negligence, just like individuals. A business owes a duty of care to its employees and its customers. A business entity is also responsible for the actions of its employees, who may be negligent in the performance of their work duties.

In a negligence lawsuit, the plaintiff must prove four elements: (1) a duty of reasonable care; (2) breach of that duty; (3) causation; and (4) resulting damages.

Duty of Reasonable Care

The basic idea underlying a negligence tort is that each person owes a duty to others to exercise reasonable care in their actions. This standard does not require every person to be perfect at all times. Instead, each person is expected to act as a "**reasonable person**" would act in the same circumstances.

> **Example:** Consider a negligence lawsuit arising from a slip and fall accident. The customer was shopping in the produce section of a grocery store when he stepped on a strawberry that had fallen on the floor. The customer fell and hurt his shoulder. The strawberry had been on the floor for over two hours at the time the customer stepped on it. The customer sues the grocery store for negligence. The jury would consider whether a reasonable grocery store would have cleaned up the strawberry within two hours.

The "reasonable person" is a fictitious concept. In a negligence case, the jury (or in some cases, the judge) must decide what a reasonable person would have done in the circumstances. The jury might consider customs in the local community or rules provided by statute to determine what is reasonable in a certain situation.

Because the standard depends on the circumstances, it varies for each situation. If the jury considers a claim against a developmentally disabled adult, for instance, the jury must consider what a reasonable person with that disability would do in the circumstances. If the case involves a claim for negligence against a professional, such as a doctor or attorney, the standard of care reflects that person's status as a professional. The professional must act as a reasonable person in that profession or trade would act in that situation.

Breach of the Duty of Reasonable Care

A party breaches the duty of care when she fails to act as a reasonable person would in the same circumstances. The party may breach the standard of care through an action (leaving the floor wet and soapy at a retail store) or by an omission (failing to dry the floor or put up warning signs that the floor could be wet). Look at the example about the strawberry on the floor. In that example, assume that the jury concludes that a reasonable "person" (i.e., a reasonable grocery store) would clean up any fallen produce within two hours. If the jury also concludes that the grocery store did not clean up the strawberry for at least two hours on the day the customer slipped and fell, then the defendant will be considered to have breached the duty of care.

> Many states have enacted statutes called dram shop acts. These laws make a bar owner or bartender liable if a customer becomes intoxicated and injures another person. The bar owner or bartender is liable because he provided the alcohol. Some states also hold social hosts liable if they provide alcohol to someone who injures another party.

Causation

The plaintiff must prove that the defendant's actions were the cause of the plaintiff's injuries. Causation is usually discussed as two concepts:

cause-in-fact ("but-for") causation and **proximate cause**. Both types of causation must be present for a defendant to be held responsible.

Under cause-in-fact causation, the defendant is only liable if the harm would not have occurred "but-for" the defendant's actions. The issue that the court must consider becomes, "Would the harm have occurred but for the defendant's action? Would the injury have occurred without the defendant's actions?"

Under the concept of proximate cause, the defendant is liable only if the type of harm that occurred was a foreseeable result of the defendant's actions. If the type of harm that occurred was not reasonably foreseeable, then the defendant cannot be responsible. The law finds it unfair to hold a person liable for risks that were unforeseeable.

Intervening Event: In some cases, the defendant may be able to show an intervening event caused or contributed to the plaintiff's injury. This event may happen at the same time as the defendant's act, or may take place after the original incident. Sometimes, the defendant may be able to show that the intervening event

> **CAUSE-IN-FACT:**
> The action that caused an injured party's injury. It is also referred to as but-for causation.
>
> **PROXIMATE CAUSE:**
> The main or legal cause of an injury.

Example: In the strawberry slip and fall case mentioned above, the customer would not have been injured if the store had cleaned up the strawberry. In other words, but for the store's failure to clean up the strawberry, the customer would not have fallen and injured his shoulder. The customer could show that the store's failure was a cause-in-fact of the injury.

Example: Consider the strawberry slip and fall case again. To establish proximate causation, the customer must show that it was reasonably foreseeable that a customer might fall and be injured from a strawberry on the floor. If harm to the customer was a foreseeable result of the store's failure to clean up the strawberry, the customer can show proximate causation. If, however, some unpredictable chain of events occurs as a result of the strawberry on the floor, the proximate cause requirement would not be satisfied. For example, if a customer accidentally kicks the strawberry out into the parking lot, where a dog eats it and has an allergic reaction, leading it to bite a passing pedestrian, the pedestrian's injuries were not foreseeable from the store's failure to pick up the strawberry.

A DEFENDANT IS ONLY LIABLE FOR DAMAGES TO A PLAINTIFF TO WHOM THE DEFENDANT FORESEEABLY OWES THE DUTY OF CARE

Palsgraf v. Long Island R.R. Co.
(Passenger) v. (Railroad)
248 N.Y. 339, 162 N.E. 99 (1928)

INSTANT FACTS:
Palsgraf (P) sued Long Island R.R. Co. (D) ("the railroad") for the injuries sustained when a package fell out of the hand of one of the train passengers and exploded.

BLACK LETTER RULE:
A defendant owes a duty of care only to those plaintiffs who are in the reasonably foreseeable zone of danger.

PROCEDURAL BASIS:
Appeal in action in negligence for recovery of damages.

FACTS:
Palsgraf (P) was standing on the platform of the train station when a man jumped on an already-moving train. The man was being pulled in by an employee of the railroad (D), when an unmarked package containing firecrackers fell out of his hand. When the package fell, the firecrackers within it exploded, and the shock of the explosion threw down scales many feet away from the explosion. The scales fell on Palsgraf (P) injuring her. Palsgraf (P) sued the railroad (D) for her injuries. The trial court and the Appellate Division ruled in favor of Palsgraf (P). The railroad (D) appeals.

ISSUE:
Does a defendant owe a duty of care only to those plaintiffs who are in the reasonably foreseeable zone of danger?

DECISION AND RATIONALE:
(Cardozo, C.J.) Yes. A defendant owes a duty of care only to those plaintiffs who are in the reasonably foreseeable zone of danger. In this case, the conduct of the railroad employee (D) was not negligent at all with respect to Palsgraf (P). No one was on notice that the package contained explosives which could harm a person so far removed.

In every negligence case, before negligence of the defendant can be determined, it must be found that the defendant owed a duty to the plaintiff, and that the defendant could have avoided the injury to the plaintiff, had he observed this duty. The plaintiff in a negligence case may sue in her own right only for a wrong personal to her. The orbit of the danger or risk as disclosed to a reasonable person would be the orbit of the duty. Thus, a plaintiff must show a wrong to herself, or a violation of her own rights, but not a "wrong" to anyone.

In this case, there is no indication in the facts to suggest to the most cautious mind that the wrapped package would explode in the train station. Even if the guard had thrown the package intentionally, he would not have threatened Palsgraf's (P) safety, so far as appearances could warn him. Thus, liability cannot be greater where the act of the guard was unintentional or inadvertent. Reversed.

DISSENT:
(Andrews, J.) Where an act threatens the safety of others, the doer is liable for all its proximate consequences, even when the injury is to one who would generally be thought to be outside of the radius of danger. It is important to inquire only as to the relation between cause and effect. Due care is a duty imposed on each member of the society to protect others in the society from unnecessary danger, and not just to protect A, B, or C. Negligence involves a relationship between a man and his fellows, but not merely a relationship between man and those whom he might reasonably expect his act would injure. Everyone owes to the world at large the duty of refraining from those acts which may unreasonably threaten the safety of others. If such an act occurs, not only has he wronged those to whom harm might reasonably be expected to result, but also those whom he has in fact injured, even if they may be thought of as outside the zone of danger.

ANALYSIS:
This case deals with the question of causation in terms of the plaintiff. In other words, to whom does a defendant owe a duty of care? According to the majority opinion written by Cardozo, the defendant only owes a duty of care to those individuals who are within the foreseeable zone of danger. Thus, according to the majority opinion in this case the plaintiff, who was standing far away from the explosion, is not entitled to damages even though she was injured. According to the dissent, however (the famous Andrews dissent), every plaintiff is a foreseeable plaintiff. Thus, regardless of how far or how near or how unforeseeable, any individual is entitled to recover for his/her damages which resulted from the defendant's negligent conduct.

When dealing with the issue of proximate causation, we must not only ask whether the injury to the plaintiff was proximately caused by the defendant's negligence, but also whether the plaintiff was a foreseeable plaintiff to whom the defendant owed a duty of care.

CASE VOCABULARY:
ATTENUATE:
To lessen or weaken.

CONFLAGRATION:
A great destructive burning or fire.

FORESEEABILITY:
The foreseeability of the consequences of a defendant's actions depend on the balancing between the likelihood of risk and the magnitude of damages flowing therefrom.

INVASION:
An encroachment upon the rights of another.

PROXIMATE CAUSE:
The type of cause which in the natural and continuous sequence unbroken by any new independent cause produces an event, and without which the injury would not have occurred.

---

breaks the chain of causation. If the intervening event is unforeseeable, that event may relieve the defendant of liability. In that situation, the event is called a superseding cause. If the intervening event is foreseeable, however, the defendant remains liable.

Example: Return again to the strawberry on the floor. Suppose a person slipped on the strawberry and fell, hitting her head. After returning home, suppose that the injured person felt like she had been through enough that day, and did not want to inject her regular required insulin dose. If the person later dies of diabetic issues from not taking her insulin, that would be an intervening cause of her death. The slip and fall would not be the reason she died, so the strawberry left on the floor, while negligence, would not be the cause of the person's death.

> **Good Samaritan Laws**
>
> After a person has been injured, other individuals often stop to help the injured party. These individuals may be trained medical professionals, or simply concerned citizens who do not have any specialized knowledge. These individuals are sometimes referred to as Good Samaritans, based on a biblical story about people who are willing to stop and help others. What if the person who stops to help is negligent when helping and makes the injuries worse? In the past, the injured party could sue the individuals who had stopped to help. Society recognized that it was not good public policy. If an individual could be liable for stopping to help an injured person, Good Samaritans were discouraged from helping others. Thus, most states passed Good Samaritan laws. These laws state that a person who is injured may not sue someone who stops to help them.

Damages

In a negligence claim, plaintiffs must also show that they incurred some loss. Without harm to the plaintiff, there is no reason to pursue a negligence lawsuit. Consider the strawberry slip and fall case discussed above. Imagine that the customer briefly slipped on the strawberry, but regained his footing and did not suffer any injury. In that circumstance, the plaintiff did not suffer any harm. There would be no negligence lawsuit.

If a plaintiff proves the defendant breached the duty of care and caused harm, the plaintiff may recover money damages. Damages are provided to compensate the plaintiff for losses. Depending on the case, damages may be awarded to compensate for physical injuries, damage to property, lost wages, medical expenses, pain and suffering, humiliation, and embarrassment.

> Originally, a tort suit was only available to persons who had been injured. If a party died as a result of another party's action, the lawsuit died with the person. This discrepancy allowed a party to avoid liability where a party's injuries were severe enough to cause death of the victim. Eventually, the law recognized the unfairness of that doctrine. Today, all states have statutes recognizing wrongful death actions. A wrongful death suit is brought by the surviving family members of a person who has died. Wrongful death actions allow the family members to recover damages for the injuries they suffer from the family member's death.
>
> A closely related type of action is a survival action. Survival actions are brought for damages suffered by the victim between the time of the injury and the time of death. Damages in survival actions are not paid directly to the family members, but are paid to the victim's estate.

Professional Malpractice Actions

A lawsuit claiming negligence against a professional, such as a doctor or lawyer, is one type of negligence tort. A professional malpractice claim is similar to a standard claim for negligence. The plaintiff must prove the same basic

> **Example:** Paula, a 75-year-old woman, went to see her doctor because she had a sore throat. She told the doctor the sore throat had persisted for three months. Paula's medical history form indicated that she smokes heavily. The doctor looked in her throat and sent her home, believing it was only a virus that would clear up soon. After the sore throat continued for another five weeks, Paula went back to the doctor. This time, the doctor ran additional tests and discovered that Paula had throat cancer. By the time the cancer was detected, it was too late for Paula to undergo treatment and she died two months later. Paula's family sues the doctor for malpractice, claiming that he should have discovered the cancer when Paula first visited him. The jury will consider whether the doctor acted as reasonable doctor would have acted in the same situation. The parties will likely present the testimony of experts who understand the needed skills and knowledge for a doctor.

elements: a duty, breach of duty, causation, and damages. In this context, though, the professional must act as a reasonable person in that profession would act. The knowledge and expertise of a reasonable member of that profession is considered as part of the standard of care. A jury does not have expertise in every profession. Therefore, the jury considers the testimony of experts who describe how a reasonable doctor, lawyer, or other professional would act.

Res Ipsa Loquitur

As stated above, in negligence cases, the plaintiff must typically show that the defendant's conduct was negligent. In some circumstances, the plaintiff is unable to show what the defendant did. The plaintiff may not have any evidence to demonstrate what happened. In some unique situations, though, it is clear that the defendant must have caused the harm. If certain elements are met, negligence may be presumed under the doctrine of **res ipsa loquitur**.

Res ipsa loquitur is a Latin phrase meaning "the thing speaks for itself." Negligence may be presumed where (1) the defendant had exclusive control of whatever caused the injury, and (2) it is the type of accident that would not have happened without negligence.

RES IPSA LOQUITUR: Meaning "the thing speaks for itself," this legal principle allows negligence to be presumed when (1) a defendant had exclusive control of the circumstances under which someone was injured, and (2) the incident would not normally occur without negligence.

NEGLIGENCE PER SE: A doctrine under which negligence is proven through the defendant's violation of a statute or regulation designed to prevent the type of injury that occurred.

Consider this example: a farm worker walks past a barn. The hayloft door (a door above the ground to access the barn's upper level) is open. As the worker walks past the barn, a barrel falls out of the hayloft door and hits the worker. Everyone at the farm claims to have been elsewhere. Even though the worker cannot show exactly what happened, the farm owner may be liable under res ipsa loquitur. The owner had control of the barn, and there is no way that a barrel falls out of an open hayloft unless someone was not taking due care.

If the court finds that the case presents the type of situation to which res ipsa loquitur applies, then the defendant must prove he was not negligent.

Negligence Per Se

Sometimes, a party's conduct is considered negligent, without examining what a reasonable person would do. If someone violates a statute or ordinance, that violation might be **negligence per se**. For negligence per se to apply, the statute must be designed to prevent the type of injury that occurred and set out clear rules of conduct.

Defenses to Negligence Cases

Even if a defendant has engaged in a negligent act, the defendant might not always be liable for damages. In some circumstances, the defendant can show a defense exists. The defenses to negligence generally focus on the plaintiff's conduct. For instance, if a plaintiff is negligent himself, his negligence may reduce or prohibit the recovery of damages under the doctrine of comparative negligence. If a plaintiff assumes the risk of an activity, the plaintiff also might not recover against the defendant.

Example: Big Building Co. is constructing a high rise building. A load of bricks is on the roof of the building. The load of bricks falls and injures Emilio, who was walking on the sidewalk below. The bricks were in Big Building's control and it is the type of accident that occurs only with negligence. Big Building is liable for Emilio's injury even if no one saw the load fall.

Example: Sal was fishing in a boat at night. Another boat on the water collided with Sal's boat. Sal was thrown from the boat and drowned. Otto, the operator of the other boat, did not use running lights. A local regulation requires all watercraft to use running lights from sunset to sunrise. The regulation is designed to prevent collisions between boats at night. Otto's violation of the running light regulation could be considered negligence per se.

II. Intentional Torts

An **intentional tort** occurs when the person who acts wrongly intends to perform the action. The person who performs the act does not need to intend the harm that resulted. The defendant only needs to intend his action.

> "Intentional" does not mean that the tortfeasor had any ill or harmful motive. The term refers to the intention to undertake the action, not its consequences.

INTENTIONAL TORT: A civil wrong causing harm to another that results from a party's intentional act.

FRAUDULENT MISREPRESENTATION: A false statement made with the intention to induce the other person's reliance on the statement.

There are many types of intentional torts. Assault, trespass, fraud, defamation, invasion of privacy, nuisance, and interference are all considered intentional torts. Several intentional torts are particularly relevant to business relations. These torts are discussed below.

Fraudulent Misrepresentation

A misrepresentation is a false or untrue statement. A **fraudulent misrepresentation** occurs when the party making the statement knew the statement was false, or made the statement recklessly without knowing whether it was true or not. The defendant must intend for the plaintiff to rely on the false statement. To prove a fraud claim, a plaintiff must show that all of the following are true:

- The defendant intentionally misrepresented a material fact.
- The plaintiff relied on that misrepresentation.
- The plaintiff was harmed by the misrepresentation.

Example: Denny surprises his friend Jan by jumping out at him while wearing a monster mask. Jan has a heart condition, and the scare causes Jan to have a heart attack. Denny committed an intentional tort, even though he did not intend for Jan to have a heart attack.

Example: As part of its efforts to expand its business, ABC Company seeks a loan from National Bank. In its application, ABC Co. submits misleading financial statements to National Bank. Relying on those statements, National Bank provides the loan to ABC Co. ABC Co. defaults on the loan. National Bank may sue ABC Co. for fraud.

> **Example:** Business Inc. is planning a major transaction this quarter. Business Inc. tells its accountant, Amy Numbers, about the upcoming transaction, but does not ask her for any tax advice about the transaction. Based on a new IRS regulation, however, Amy knows that Business Inc. will owe a large tax bill based on the transaction. Amy does not inform Business Inc. of the tax liability. Business Inc. may be able to sue Amy for failing to tell them about the tax liability because of her relationship with the company.

The false statement must appear to relate to a material fact. A material fact is a fact that is important to the other party's decision.

The false statement must be a statement of fact. A party cannot be liable for a statement of opinion or puffery. Puffery is an exaggerated statement about a product or service. Puffery is stated in vague, but complimentary terms. Puffery is considered to be the speaker's opinion and not a representation of fact about the product's actual qualities or capabilities. A statement from a car salesperson that "this is the best car on the lot" is puffery. It is the salesperson's opinion and not independently verifiable. The statement that "this car has passed all safety tests and contains anti-lock brakes" is a statement of fact. Its truth can be independently confirmed. If the statement of fact is false, the speaker may be liable for misrepresentation.

In some circumstances, a party can also be liable for keeping quiet when they know a material fact that the other party does not know. If there is a special relationship of trust between the parties, one party has a duty to speak.

Interference with Contractual Relations

Many business relationships involve a contract between two parties. If another party interferes with that contractual relationship, they may be liable for interference. The tort of **interference with contractual relations** allows a plaintiff to recover damages if a defendant causes one of the contracting parties to breach the contract. The elements of an intentional interference with contractual relations claim are (1) a valid contract between plaintiff and another party; (2) defendant knew about the contract; (3) defendant acted to interfere with the contract; (4) the contract was breached or disrupted; and (5) damages resulted.

To be liable, the defendant must have known about the contract. The interference must be the kind of conduct that falls outside the scope of fair competition. General advertising or marketing of products and services does not constitute interference.

INTENTIONAL INTERFERENCE WITH CONTRACTUAL RELATIONS: The tort that occurs when a person intentionally harms the plaintiff's contractual or business relationship.

> *Example:* Andrews Company and Breyerson Corp. have a contract. Andrews supplies Breyerson with a heating element for an industrial oven that Breyerson manufactures. Breyerson pays $5/unit for 10,000 units/year. Colby Co. is Breyerson's main competitor. Colby's CEO goes to Andrews and convinces Andrews to sell all the heating elements it produces to Colby for $9/unit. Andrews breaches the contract with Breyerson to accept this higher-paying agreement. Colby might be liable to Breyerson for tortious interference because Colby caused Andrews to breach its supply contract with Breyerson.

> *Example:* Company X would like to hire Best Band to perform at its annual employee appreciation party on June 10. Company X offers to pay Best Band $15,000 for its performance. Unbeknownst to Company X, Best Band had already agreed to perform at a different event on June 10. Best Band has a contract with Promotional Events, Inc., to perform at the other event for $5,000. In light of the higher amount of money offered by Company X, Best Band breaches the contract to perform at the other event. Promotional Events, Inc., does not have a claim for wrongful interference with contractual relations against Company X because Company X was unaware of Best Band's prior commitment.

Interference with Prospective Business Advantage

A party also may not interfere where two parties are currently in negotiations, but have not yet signed an agreement. This tort is called **interference with prospective business advantage**. To prove this claim, a plaintiff must show that (1) the plaintiff had an economic relationship with another party; (2) the defendant knew about the relationship; (3) the defendant acted to disrupt the relationship; (4) the relationship was disrupted; and (5) the plaintiff incurred damages.

> **INTENTIONAL INTERFERENCE WITH PROSPECTIVE ECONOMIC ADVANTAGE:** The tort that occurs when a person intentionally harms the plaintiff's business relationship that was likely to have economic benefit for the plaintiff.

Defamation

In the United States, the Bill of Rights provides for freedom of speech. Although the right is broad, it is not well-understood by most people. Many are unaware that there are a number of

> **Example:** Bill owns a small accounting firm. His office has a contract to buy its office supplies from Paper Clips, Inc. Office Store Co. is a competitor of Paper Clips, Inc. Office Store Co. creates an aggressive new advertising campaign offering deep discounts on office supplies. Bill sees the advertising and decides to break his contract with Paper Clips and buy supplies from Office Store Co. Paper Clips, Inc., cannot sue Office Store Co. for interference because general advertising does not constitute wrongful interference.

> **Example:** Company XYZ rents office space from Larry Landlord. Company XYZ's lease with Larry Landlord will expire in two months. A new office building is being constructed by Barry Builder across the street. Larry Landlord knows that Company XYZ has been in negotiations with Barry Builder regarding a possible lease of office space in the new building. Larry does not want to lose Company XYZ as a tenant. Larry contacts a friend of his who works for the city permit office. Larry pays his friend to delay approval of the new building. Larry's friend interferes with the approval process so that the new building will not be available to lease for another eight months. Given the long delay until the building will be ready, Company XYZ decides to renew its lease in Larry's building. Barry Builder may sue Larry Landlord for interfering with the relationship between Barry Builder and Company XYZ.

restrictions on free speech. One such limit on that right is that a person may not make false statements about another person if that statement harms the other person's reputation.

The tort of **defamation** holds the speaker liable for a false statement that damages a person's reputation. To hold a speaker liable, the statement must be a statement of fact, the statement must be published, and the false statement must harm another person's reputation. Written defamation is called **libel**. Spoken defamation is called **slander**.

Defamation law distinguishes between statements of fact and statements of opinion. In order to be defamatory, a statement must be a statement of fact, rather than an opinion. Because a

DEFAMATION:
A false statement that damages the other party's reputation.

LIBEL:
A written false statement that damages another person's reputation.

SLANDER:
A spoken false statement that damages another person's reputation.

> **Example:** During an interview with a large financial news publication, Ernie Executive, CFO of Company X, is asked about the company's poor performance. Ernie Executive states that "Company X's CEO is the worst CEO ever." That statement is opinion and cannot be defamatory.
>
> On the other hand, if Ernie Executive states that "Company X's CEO lied about the financial status of Company X during his press conference last week and falsified several documents submitted to the SEC." Here, the statement can be verified as true or false. If false, the statement may be slanderous if the CEO suffers reputational damage as a result.

> **Example:** After an argument with his co-worker John, Ryan goes to his desk and writes a letter to a local newspaper. In the letter, Ryan states that John, a high-ranking executive at the company, submitted false expense reports for reimbursement and lied during his deposition in a lawsuit against the company. Ryan saves the letter, but does not send it. Several hours later, Ryan has second thoughts, and deletes the letter. Because the statement was never communicated to a third party, the statement was not published.
>
> Assume instead that Ryan drafted an email making the same statements. Ryan sends the email to his business unit comprised of 25 employees. This could be considered publication of the statement.

statement of opinion cannot be deemed true or false, a party cannot be liable for an opinion.

Truth is a defense to defamation. If the statement is a true statement, the speaker cannot be liable.

To be published, a statement does not need to be written in a book or professionally published. In the law of defamation, publication means that the statement was communicated to another person. A statement is published if it is stated to a third party or otherwise made public. A statement may be published through magazines, television, email, blogs, websites, and social media, or verbal statements. Publication may be established even where someone overhears defamatory statements.

A person claiming defamation must also show the statement damaged his reputation. As an example, the plaintiff might show that he lost his job, could not obtain work, or was rejected by social groups and family members. If the plaintiff already had a negative reputation in the community, he may have a difficult time proving damage to his reputation from the defendant's statement.

In a few circumstances, statements are "privileged" and cannot support a defamation claim, even if the statements are false statements of fact. For instance, witnesses who testify to a false statement in court cannot be sued for defamation. Likewise, legislators cannot be sued for defamation for statements made in the legislative chamber. Some jurisdictions recognize an employer privilege for statements made during an employee review. Good faith statements made by credit review agencies may also be privileged.

Actual Malice

The law of defamation makes a distinction between public figures and private figures. Public figures must meet a higher standard to prove a defamation claim. Public officials and figures must prove the elements stated above, and that the defendant acted with **actual malice**. "Actual malice" means that the person who made the statement knew it was false, or was reckless about the truth and did not care if the statement was true or not. In other words, a public figure cannot sue for defamation where the speaker made an honest mistake about the facts.

> **ACTUAL MALICE:**
> The standard of proof required of public figures in a defamation case. The public figure must show that the defendant knew the statement was false or acted with reckless disregard as to whether the statement was false or not.

> Actual malice is a difficult, but not impossible, standard to meet. In one recent case, Jesse Ventura, the former wrestler and governor of Minnesota, brought a defamation action against Chris Kyle. The late Chris Kyle was a former Navy SEAL and author of American Sniper, a book that was later made into a movie. In the book, Kyle described an incident with Ventura. Kyle claimed Ventura made derogatory statements about Navy SEALs and the two engaged in a brawl. Ventura, a former SEAL, denied making the statements and said the incident did not occur. Ventura argued the story ruined his reputation in the Navy SEAL community. Because Ventura is a public figure, he was required to show that Kyle acted with actual malice. The jury awarded $500,000 to Ventura on the defamation claim. After an appeal, the case eventually settled on undisclosed terms.

Example: A reporter for a large newspaper is writing a story about the governor. One of his sources tells him that the governor embezzled money from the company he worked for prior to running for office. The reporter has doubts about the truth of that statement because the source has provided false information in the past. The reporter did not check or try to verify the statement, but included it his story anyway. The reporter acted with actual malice.

The actual malice requirement originally applied only to statements about public officials. The purpose behind the requirement was to protect citizens' rights to criticize the people who govern. The actual malice requirement has now been extended to all public figures who have access to the media or have placed themselves in the public eye. Private persons do not need to prove actual malice. Private persons must show that the defendant was negligent in making the false statement.

Intentional Torts Relevant to Business Parties

Intentional Tort	Description
Fraudulent Misrepresentation	• Defendant makes a false statement about a material fact relied upon by the plaintiff • Defendant knew the statement was false or was reckless about the truth • Statement must be a statement of fact, not opinion
Intentional Interference with Contractual Relations	• Defendant interferes with a contractual relationship between other parties • Defendant must know about the contract
Intentional Interference with Prospective Business Advantage	• Defendant interferes with a business relationship between other parties • No contract or formal agreement is in place • Defendant must know about the negotiations or prospective relationship
Defamation	• Defendant makes a false statement about the plaintiff that damages the plaintiff's reputation • Public officials and public figures need to prove the higher standard of actual malice
Trade Libel/Product Disparagement	• Defendant makes a false statement about the quality of a business's services or products

> **Example:** ABC Company and XYZ Corporation are competitors. Both companies produce and sell cameras. ABC Company recently stated that XYZ Corporation began installing poor quality lenses on its cameras without notifying customers. If untrue, ABC Company's statement might constitute product disparagement if XYZ loses business as a result.

Trade Libel/Product Disparagement

Trade libel is a type of defamation related to businesses. Trade libel is also referred to as product disparagement. Trade libel is a defamatory statement about the quality of a business's services or products. The purpose behind this tort is to maintain fair competition among businesses.

This type of defamation is similar to the general claim for defamation discussed above. In trade libel, the statement must state a fact about a business's services or products. As with the general defamation claim, it must be a statement of fact and cannot be an opinion. The statement also must be published. Further, the statement must damage the business's reputation. To show damage, the plaintiff must present proof that the statement resulted in lost business or profits.

III. Strict Liability

In a few limited circumstances, someone can be liable for a tort even though that person was not negligent or otherwise at fault. When a party is held liable without negligence or fault, it is called strict liability. Strict liability applies to a few situations where the party is engaging in an inherently dangerous or hazardous activity. If a party is engaging in an inherently dangerous activity, the party may be liable even if they took all reasonable steps to avoid injury to others.

Examples of hazardous activities that might result in strict liability include keeping a wild animal, storage or transportation of flammable materials or explosives, blasting in a populated area, and emission of toxic fumes. Sometimes a court might consider where the activity is taking place to determine if the activity is merely dangerous, or inherently dangerous. For instance, blasting that occurs in a remote area might not be considered inherently dangerous. However, because of the risk to people living and working in the area, blasting to demolish a building within a city will be considered inherently dangerous.

> **TRADE LIBEL:**
> A defamatory statement about the quality of a business's services or products. It is also referred to as product disparagement.
>
> **STRICT LIABILITY:**
> The imposition of liability on a party without a showing of fault.

> **Example:** XPLO Corp. provides fireworks shows for special events. Its driver was hauling a large truck of fireworks to Smallville for its Centennial celebration fireworks show. While the truck was in the parking lot of a restaurant during transit, several of the fireworks went off, causing the entire truckload to explode. Several restaurant patrons were injured from the blast. XPLO could be strictly liable for the patrons' injuries because the hauling of explosives is an inherently dangerous activity.

Types of Torts

Type of Tort	Key Features
Negligence	• Defendant did not act as a reasonably prudent person in the circumstances
Intentional Torts	• Defendant intended his conduct, but not necessarily any harm • Does not require evil or harmful intent
Strict Liability	• No fault required on behalf of Defendant • Defendant engaged in inherently dangerous activity

Three elements must be established for a defendant to be strictly liable:

1. The defendant engaged in an inherently dangerous activity.
2. The inherently dangerous act caused something bad to happen to the plaintiff.
3. The plaintiff suffered harm from the resulting injury.

IV. Products Liability

Millions of products are bought and sold every day. Sometimes a product may harm a customer or another person. If a person is injured from a product with a defect, they may sue the parties responsible for the product. The entities involved in the supply chain of a product can all be liable for defective products. This includes the companies who manufacture, wholesale, and sell the product.

Each claim for products liability must describe the basis for liability on behalf of the company and the type of defect the product contains. In addition to showing the injury caused by a product, a plaintiff must show that (1) the manufacturer or other entity is liable for the product, (2) the product contained a defect, (3) the defect proximately caused the injury, and (4) the plaintiff suffered compensable damages.

There are several possible theories of liability by which a company may be responsible for a product. Like other tort actions, a products liability claims were historically based on negligence on behalf of the manufacturer or other entity. Modern products liability imposes strict liability on manufacturers. Products liability may also be based on breach of warranty. Depending on when and where a case is brought, a manufacturer or other party may be liable for a product if the business was negligent, if the entity created a defective or dangerous product, or if the manufacturer breached a warranty.

Negligence

A negligence claim may be brought in a number of different circumstances. For many years, claims for products liability were based on the manufacturer's negligence in making the product. The same elements required in a standard negligence action were required in products liability cases. The standard of care in this instance was that of a reasonable manufacturer of similar products. In other words, a manufacturer must have exercised a standard of care that was reasonable for those who manufactured similar products. The plaintiff needed to show that the manufacturer did not act like a reasonable manufacturer when it made the product.

The injured party also needed to show that they were injured and that the injury would not have happened without the manufacturer's negligence. In short, a claim for negligence with regard to products was the same as any other negligence claim. The same elements needed to be proved, with the only variation being the product's role in the injury.

Strict Liability

Under modern tort law, sometimes a party may also be liable even without negligence or proof of fault. As noted above, strict liability applies when a party engages in an inherently dangerous activity. Strict liability also applies to modern products liability. If a manufacturer creates a product that is unreasonably dangerous, the manufacturer may be strictly liable for injuries resulting from the product. Thus, the manufacturer may be liable for a defective product even if the manufacturer was not negligent in making that product defective.

As the complexity of products has increased over time, it has often become difficult for injured parties to show that the manufacturer of a product had acted negligently. However, it did not seem fair to deny relief to people who were injured by products created by a manufacturer. Therefore, as a matter of public policy, the law holds that manufacturers may be strictly liable for the defective products they create. While negligence claims focused on the manufacturer's conduct, strict liability focuses on the product itself.

ASBESTOS IS A DEFECTIVE PRODUCT THAT RAISES MANUFACTURER LIABILITY FOR INJURIES CAUSED BY THE PRODUCT

Arbogast v. A.W. Chesterton Co.
(Electrician) v. (Asbestos Products Manufacturer)
197 F. Supp. 3d 807 (D. Md. 2016)

INSTANT FACTS:
Electrician sued manufacturers, distributors, and installers of products containing asbestos.

BLACK LETTER RULE:
The manufacturer of a defective product may be liable for its negligence or in strict liability if the plaintiff can show the defective product caused the plaintiff's injury.

FACTS:
An electrician brought a products liability claim against the manufacturers of various products containing asbestos. The electrician claims he breathed in asbestos that was released into the air, causing his mesothelioma. The suit alleged liability on the basis of negligence and strict liability.

ISSUE:
Were manufacturers liable for asbestos in their products?

DECISION AND RATIONALE:
Yes. The court stated that a manufacturer may be strictly liable for a defect that existed when the product left the defendant's control and the defect makes the product unreasonably dangerous. The court noted that strict liability is essentially a version of negligence per se. Manufacturers may also be liable for failing to warn consumers about the dangers of asbestos. However, the electrician could not prove exposure to asbestos from many of the specific products. Thus, summary judgment was entered in favor of most of the defendants.

ANALYSIS:
This case focuses on the plaintiff's need to demonstrate causation. Even though it was clear that asbestos was dangerous, the plaintiff still needed to show he was exposed to the asbestos products. Without that showing, the plaintiff could not recover for the defective product, even if the product was dangerous.

Warranty

A **warranty** is a promise or guarantee to another party. In the commercial world, companies often provide a warranty about the products they make and sell. A warranty promises to the consumer that the product is of good quality, or that the product will operate safely for the purposes for which the product was intended. If a manufacturer provides a written statement of warranty, that is an express warranty.

If no express warranty is provided by the manufacturer, the law may find that a warranty is implied. That warranty is referred to as implied warranty. With respect to the sale of goods, the law implies a **warranty of merchantability**. This means that the manufacturer promises that the product is in good working order and can safely

> **WARRANTY:**
> A promise or guarantee to a consumer.
>
> **WARRANTY OF MERCHANTABILITY:**
> A promise from the manufacturer that the product is in good working order and can safely be used for the purposes stated on the label.

> *Example:* Mike recently purchased a new coffee pot made by Sunrise Ventures. One morning, Mike brews a pot of coffee. When he goes to pour a cup of coffee, the handle separates from the pot and the coffee pot falls to the ground. The coffee pot shatters and hot coffee splashes on Mike, causing severe burns on his feet and legs. An expert examines the coffee pot and determines that one of the screws needed to securely attach the handle to the pot was not included. The missing screw is a manufacturing defect.

ONLINE RETAILER IS NOT RESPONSIBLE FOR INJURIES FROM PRODUCT SOLD BY A THIRD PARTY THROUGH ITS WEBSITE UNDER WARRANTY THEORY

Wallace v. Tri-State Assembly, LLC, and Amazon.com LLC
(Injured Bicyclist) v. (Assembly Service and Online Retailer)
157 N.Y.S.3d 438 (N.Y. App. Div., 1st Dep't 2021)

Plaintiff sustained injuries when the handlebars of an electric bicycle his father purchased for him through Amazon.com loosened while he was riding it and caused him to fall. Nonparty Eshion, a China based company, listed the bicycle for sale on Amazon.com. At the time of purchase, plaintiff's father [chose] a service option to have the bicycle assembled. Tri-State Assembly (Tri-State), which offers its services for sale on Amazon.com and is an Amazon approved service provider, assembled it.

[P]laintiff asserted claims against defendants [Tri-State and Amazon] for negligence and breach of the implied warranties of fitness and merchantability. Plaintiff alleged that Amazon and its agents were careless and negligent in the assembly and sale of the bicycle; in assembling, distributing and selling a product unfit for public use; and in making, assembling, distributing and selling a product that collapsed under normal use. [The lower court] granted Amazon's motion for summary judgment dismissing the complaint. For the reasons stated below, we affirm.

The Uniform Commercial Code clearly provides that implied warranties only extend to sellers (*see* UCC 2–314 [1]; 2–315). Plaintiff's breach of warranty claim fails because Amazon submitted sufficient documentary evidence and unrefuted affidavits from its representatives to establish prima facie that it did not sell, manufacture, distribute or assemble the bicycle.

The supporting affidavits indicate that third-party sellers such as Eshion are responsible for all aspects of their sales, such as setting a price, describing the product being sold, and offering any warranties. In this case, Eshion sold the bicycle and shipped it directly to plaintiff. At no time was the bicycle ever in Amazon's possession or control, nor did it ever obtain title to the bicycle (*see* UCC 2–106 [1]). Further, when placing orders all Amazon.com users agree to its *Conditions of Use*, wherein Amazon disclaims all warranties for products sold by third-party sellers.

Moreover, Amazon did not impliedly warrant the assembly service Tri-State offered for sale. Plaintiff improperly alleged . . . that issues of fact existed as to whether Amazon properly vetted Tri-State to ensure its competency and that it maintained insurance as required by agreement between Amazon and Tri-State. Despite not being a party to that agreement, plaintiff argued that Amazon breached its duty to obtain proof of insurance from Tri-State and thus provided him with third-party services from an uninsured vendor. The motion court properly declined to entertain this newly alleged theory of liability for which plaintiff offered no supporting authority.

This Court similarly declines plaintiff's invitation to fashion an equitable remedy effectively extending implied warranties to nonsellers because he has no other means of recovery. In support, plaintiff cites to *Bolger v. Amazon.com, LLC,* 53 Cal. App. 5th 431, 438, 267 Cal.Rptr.3d 601 (Ct. App., 4th Dist. 2020). There, the California Court of Appeal reversed an award of summary judg-

> ment to Amazon finding that Amazon could be held strictly liable for defective products third-party vendors sell on its website. Its holding rested on the notion that under the circumstances presented, Amazon was a pivotal part of the distribution chain that brought the product at issue to the plaintiff consumer. . . . Plaintiff's reliance on *Bolger* is misplaced [because] *Bolger* involved a strict products liability claim, which plaintiff does not allege.
>
> [T]he US District Court for the Southern District of New York cited state and federal case law from around the country and noted "an emerging consensus against . . . holding Amazon strictly liable for defective products sold on its website." Subsequently . . . the US District Court for the Eastern District of New York described "the issue of whether Amazon can be held strictly liable for defects in the products that consumers purchase from third-party vendors through Amazon's online marketplace" as "a developing area of law"[.] The court noted that "[w]hile many courts that initially considered the issue found in Amazon's favor, some more recent cases have reached different results, with appeals on a few of these cases still pending"[.]
>
> Nonetheless, the Eastern and Southern District Courts of New York did not expand the chain of liability. Rather, both applied New York law and found that Amazon could not be held liable under the theories of strict products liability or breach of warranty. . . . Central to both courts' analyses was the undisputed fact that at no time did Amazon ever obtain title to the products in question and, rather than being viewed as a distributor, "Amazon is better characterized as a provider of services"[.]
>
> Against this backdrop, there is simply no authority that would enable this Court to create a remedy based upon equitable principles as plaintiff urges. To do so would unjustifiably contradict settled New York law limiting liability for breach of warranty to sellers and parties within the manufacturing, selling, or distribution chain. Amazon is neither, as it merely provided the website plaintiff's father used to purchase the bicycle from an independent third-party seller and have it assembled by an independent third-party assembler.
>
> Accordingly, the judgment of the Supreme Court, New York County dismissing the complaint against [Amazon] should be affirmed.

be used for the purposes stated on the label. If a product does not work as it is supposed to, the manufacturer may be liable for breach of warranty on the product.

Types of Defects

A product may contain one of several types of defects that raise strict liability against the manufacturer and other parties. A problem in the manufacturing or design process, or the manner in which a product is packaged, might create a defective product. Furthermore, a manufacturer's failure to warn consumers about the dangers of a product can be a defect. There are three main types of product defects: (1) a manufacturing defect; (2) a design defect; and (3) a warning defect. Improper packaging may also be an issue.

Manufacturing Defects: A **manufacturing defect** is a defect that occurs in the manufacturing process. These defects may involve poor-quality materials or poor workmanship. When there is a manufacturing defect, only a few manufactured items are defective. The design itself and the manufacturing process are generally fine. The issue usually affects just one or comparatively few finished items.

> **MANUFACTURING DEFECT:**
> A product defect that occurs in the manufacturing process due to poor workmanship or poor quality materials.

> When a manufacturing defect occurs in auto manufacturing, the defective vehicle is often referred to as a "lemon." State statutes called "lemon laws" give car buyers who end up with a lemon a way to recover from car companies and dealers.

Design Defects: **Design defects** are defects in the product design. A product may be inherently dangerous or useless, even if manufactured properly, because the design is flawed. With design defects, every item manufactured is defective because the design itself is flawed and makes the finished product dangerous.

DESIGN DEFECT:
A defect in the design of the product that makes the product dangerous or useless.

> A manufacturer does not owe a duty to warn about obvious risks, but manufacturers tend to include many warnings to avoid liability. This approach to risk management sometimes leads to warnings some consider excessive. For instance, it is typical for clothes irons to come with a warning that they should not be used on clothes when the user is wearing them.

Warning Defects: Some products require clear instructions or warnings so consumers can use them safely. If such a product did not have clear instructions or warnings, and if that factor led to injury, then the consumer might have a products liability case. If a manufacturer fails to provide a warning about the dangers, it could be liable for its failure to warn consumers.

Improper Packaging: Manufacturers must take care to use safe packaging for their prod-

Example: Consider Mike and the coffee pot incident described above. Assume that the handle was originally attached with the intended screws. However, the expert determines that the handle was made of a lightweight plastic that cannot support the weight of the coffee pot when it is filled with coffee. The weak handle is a design defect.

Example: Rainbow Corp. manufactures aerosol paint cans. The aerosol cans are pressurized and contain highly flammable propellants. If the aerosol cans are exposed to flames or high temperatures, the cans can explode or create a fire. Rainbow Corp. knows about the flammability of its aerosol cans, but does not include a warning on its paint cans. Walt purchases a Rainbow Corp. aerosol can. Walt uses the paint can to paint a sign and then sets it down next to the space heater in the garage. After a few minutes, the can explodes, leaving Walt with serious injuries. Walt sues Rainbow Corp. for its failure to include a warning about the flammability of the aerosol cans.

ucts. A product may be considered defective if the package it comes in is not safe. The packaging includes plastic wrapping, boxes, cans, bottles, and other containers in which products are packaged and shipped. Some types of packaging can create an obvious risk, such as a glass bottle that may shatter, or an aluminum can that can cut. A defect in packaging is typically treated as a defect in the product itself.

In products liability, the packaging is treated as a product. The package may have a design flaw or become defective due to a problem in the manufacturing process. For instance, improper packaging may cause harm because it is not

---

LIABILITY FOR DEFECTIVE PRODUCT ONLY EXISTS IF THE DEFECT AROSE WHILE THE PRODUCT WAS IN THE DEFENDANT'S CONTROL

Sheats v. The Kroger Company
(Shopper) v. (Grocery Store)
336 Ga. App. 307, 784 S.E.2d 442 (2016)

Brenda Sheats sued The Kroger Co. and Clayton Distributing Company, Inc. ("Clayton"), asserting claims based upon product liability and res ipsa loquitur.

Sheats was shopping at a Kroger grocery store in Athens. Sheats took a cardboard package containing several glass bottles of Red Rock Golden Ginger Ale off of a shelf and placed it in her cart. Sheats then lifted a second pack off the shelf. As she did so, the bottom of the package opened up, all of the glass bottles fell to the floor, and they broke. At least one bottle struck Sheats' left foot, injuring her.

According to the manager . . . the glue on one side of the bottom of the package failed to stay glued to the other flap. [The manager] observed that one of the outside bottom flaps was cleanly separated from the other, inside bottom flap, and the glue was only stuck to one flap.

After leaving Kroger, Sheats went to a hospital emergency room. She was subsequently diagnosed with a blood clot in her left big toe and had to have surgery to remove the toenail. Sheats had to wear a protective shoe for two months after her surgery. Additionally, her toenail failed to grow back correctly.

In its order, the trial court ruled that Sheats had failed to establish an essential element of [her res ipsa loquitur claim], i.e., that the package had been under Kroger's exclusive control. The elements of the doctrine of res ipsa loquitur are: (1) an injury which ordinarily does not occur in the absence of someone's negligence; (2) the injury must be caused by an agency or instrumentality within the defendant's *exclusive control*; and (3) the injury was not caused by any voluntary action or contribution on the part of the plaintiff. "Res ipsa loquitur should be applied with caution and only in extreme cases, and is not applicable when there is an intermediary cause which could have produced the injury."

Here, the trial court properly concluded that the package had not been in Kroger's exclusive control because the undisputed evidence showed that the package had been placed on a display shelf and was readily accessible to other customers. Accordingly, the trial court properly granted summary judgment to Kroger on Sheats' res ipsa loquitur claim.

Sheats' product liability claim was based upon allegations that Kroger negligently sold a defective and unsafe product and failed to warn customers of the defect. Sheats presented evidence showing that the bottom of the package opened up when she lifted it off the shelf. Sheats is unable to prove, however, that the package opened because of an original manufacturing defect, as opposed to some other cause, such as mishandling during delivery or while stocking the shelf. Consequently, the trial court did not err in granting summary judgment to Kroger on Sheats' product liability claim.

Judgment affirmed in part.

Types of Defects

Type of Defect	Description
Manufacturing Defect	• Product contains a defect from the manufacturing process • Product may have been poorly constructed or made out of subpar materials
Design Defect	• Product was not properly designed • The flaw in the design caused the product to be dangerous or useless
Failure to Warn	• The manufacturer failed to warn consumers about non-obvious risks of the product
Improper Packaging	• Packaging of a product was ineffective or caused injury to the plaintiff

properly designed to safety transfer the products contained in the package. Likewise, something might happen during the manufacturing process, such as an improper seal, which makes the package defective.

Packaging may be designed to make a product tamper-resistant. For example, manufacturers have created child-proof caps for medicine bottles. This type of packaging was created as a way to avoid possibly liability where a child obtains access to pills or other medicine that could be harmful to the child.

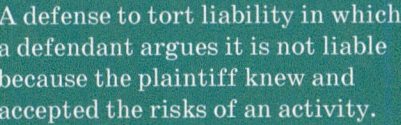

ASSUMPTION OF RISK:
A defense to tort liability in which a defendant argues it is not liable because the plaintiff knew and accepted the risks of an activity.

V. Defenses to Product Liability

Even where a manufacturer or other entity is responsible for a defective product, the manufacturer may not be liable if a defense to liability applies. The defenses in a products liability case typically focus on the behavior of the plaintiff user.

Assumption of Risk

Assumption of the risk is one possible defense to tort actions. It is particularly useful in cases of products liability. Assumption of risk focuses on the plaintiff's conduct. In a products liability case, if a plaintiff assumes the risk posed by a product, the defendant is not liable for injury.

To prove assumption of the risk, the defendant must show that the plaintiff knew of the hazard and continued to use the product anyway.

One can assume the risks of an activity expressly or impliedly. An express assumption of risk occurs when an individual signs an agreement or other document agreeing to assume the risks. Assumption of risk may also be implied from an individual's conduct. If the risk of a product is known to the individual, but she chooses to use the product anyway, assumption of risk is implied.

> *Example:* Amir decides to go skydiving to celebrate his birthday. He signs up for a skydiving session with Sky High Co. Helpful Harnesses Inc. manufactures the parachute and harnesses used for skydiving, and provided to users by Sky High Co. At an orientation session, Sky High explains the risks of skydiving and tells the divers that Sky High Co. and Helpful Harnesses Inc. are not responsible for any equipment malfunctions. Amir chooses to go ahead with his skydiving session. It could be argued that Amir assumed the risk through his actions. He was aware of the risks, but decided to use the equipment anyway.
>
> Now assume that Sky High Co. requires Amir to sign a waiver of liability before his skydiving session. The waiver states that skydiving has inherent dangers, and that Sky High Co. and Helpful Harnesses Inc. cannot guarantee safety. Amir agrees not to sue Sky High Co. or Helpful Harnesses Inc. if he is injured. By signing the waiver, Amir expressly assumes the risks of using the skydiving equipment.

A CONSUMER WHO KNOWS THE RISKS OF A PRODUCT CANNOT HOLD THE PRODUCT'S MANUFACTURER LIABLE

Puckett v. The Plastics Group, Inc.
(Gasoline Container User) v. (Container Manufacturer)
561 Fed. Appx. 865 (2014)

INSTANT FACTS: Consumer sued manufacturer of gasoline can, claiming the can contained design defects, the manufacturer failed to warn of dangers, and that the manufacturer was negligent.

BLACK LETTER RULE: The manufacturer of a product is not liable where the consumer knows the risks of using the product in the manner in which it was used.

FACTS: The consumer splashed gasoline from a gasoline can onto a fire. Vapors inside the gasoline can ignited, the can exploded, and the consumer was severely burned. The consumer's products liability suit claimed the gasoline can was defectively designed and the manufacturer failed to warn consumers about the danger of exploding vapors.

ISSUE:
Did the consumer assume the risks of using a gasoline can near open flame?

DECISION AND RATIONALE:
Yes. The consumer showed that a small screen can be installed in the nozzle of a gasoline can to reduce the risk of exploding vapors. However, the side of the gasoline can contained a warning about the risk of exploding vapors. Although the consumer did not read that warning, he knew that gasoline was flammable. The consumer was not aware that vapors in the can could explode in the way they did, but his actions showed that he knew it was risky to pour gasoline on a fire. The court held that the consumer assumed the risk of his injury because he knew the risk of combining gasoline and fire. The consumer does not need to know the exact series of events which lead to the injury. If the consumer has an understanding of the general risk involved, they assume the risk by engaging in the activity.

ANALYSIS:
This is an example of implied assumption of risk. The consumer's conduct, by exercising caution in using gasoline around the fire, showed that he appreciated a risk involved when using gasoline and fire. This case demonstrates that a general understanding of the risk involved in an activity is sufficient to assume the risk of the activity. Even though the product could have been designed to reduce the danger, the consumer's knowledge and acceptance of the risk prevented any liability by the manufacturer.

Comparative Fault

Everyone in society owes a duty to exercise reasonable care to avoid harm to others. This includes a duty to use reasonable care to avoid harm to oneself. In the past, most courts applied the doctrine of **contributory negligence**. Under this rule, if an injured party was at fault in any way for the incident causing harm, the injured party could not recover anything. The jury would consider the amount of fault of the injured party. If the jury determined that the injured party was only 1% at fault, the injured party could not recover anything.

Today, most jurisdictions apply the doctrine of **comparative negligence**. Comparative negligence considers the extent of fault of both parties. The jury allocates fault to both parties. For instance, the jury might determine that the plaintiff is 30% at fault and the defendant is 70% at fault. The defendant would be responsible for only 70% of the damages determined by the jury. Under a modified approach, some jurisdictions do not allow a plaintiff to recover damages if their fault is higher than the level of defendant's fault.

> **CONTRIBUTORY NEGLIGENCE:**
> A doctrine under which a plaintiff may be barred from recovering damages because the plaintiff was partially at fault for the accident or injury.
>
> **COMPARATIVE NEGLIGENCE:**
> A doctrine under which a plaintiff's recovery of damages may be reduced by the amount of negligence attributed to the plaintiff.

> *Example:* Troy was driving his ATV when he noticed the temperature light flashing. The ATV was manufactured by Outdoor Sports Co. The instruction manual stated that drivers should stop the vehicle and shut the engine off when the temperature light is blinking. The light came on because a hose in the engine was defective when the ATV was sold. Troy did not read the instruction manual and ignored the temperature light. Troy continued driving the vehicle. An electrical fire in the ATV caused Troy serious harm. Troy's failure to read the manual and his failure to deal with the flashing temperature light could be considered by the jury. If the jury finds Troy was 25% at fault, he may recover only 75% of his damages against Outdoor Sports Co.

STRICT LIABILITY CASES DO NOT REQUIRE CONSIDERATION OF COMPARATIVE NEGLIGENCE

R.J. Reynolds Tobacco Co. v. Sury
(Tobacco Company) v. (Estate of Deceased Smoker)
118 So. 3d 849 (Fla. Dist. Ct. App. 2013)

INSTANT FACTS:
The son of a smoker, as personal representative of the smoker's estate, brought a claim against tobacco companies.

BLACK LETTER RULE:
Comparative negligence does not apply to products liability claims based on strict liability and fraud.

FACTS:
The smoker died from lung cancer resulting from nicotine addiction. At trial, the jury concluded that the cigarette manufacturers were liable for placing a defective product, cigarettes, into the market. The jury determined the smoker was also contributorily negligent because of his decision to smoke the cigarettes. The smoker was found to be 60% negligent and each of the two tobacco companies was 20% negligent. The jury found the smoker's son suffered $1 million in damages.

ISSUE:
Should the products liability damage award be reduced based on the level of fault attributable to the plaintiff?

DECISION AND RATIONALE:
No. In this case, the plaintiff alleged negligence as well as several intentional torts (fraud, fraudulent concealment, and civil conspiracy) against the tobacco companies. The jury found the tobacco companies were negligent and strictly liable, and also engaged in fraud. The court held that comparative negligence did not apply because the action was based on intentional conduct in addition to negligence. Comparative negligence applies only to negligence actions.

ANALYSIS:
In this case, a large percentage of fault was attributable to the smoker himself. However, because the tobacco companies also engaged in intentional behavior, the companies were responsible for the entire damage award. The decision demonstrates that it is wise for a plaintiff to consider all possible theories of liability against a defendant. A plaintiff's claim may be vulnerable to a defense under one theory of liability that may not be available under other types of claims.

Modification/Substantial Change

Modification is a potential defense if a product has been changed since it left the defendant's hands. In a products liability case, the plaintiff must show that the product was defective when it left the defendant's control. If the product was changed or modified before it injured the plaintiff, then the defendant may not be liable. A product can be changed in many ways. For instance, modification may be shown if safety guards are removed or if nonstandard parts are installed on the product. To establish modification, the defendant must prove the original design, how the product was changed, and that the change caused the plaintiff's injuries.

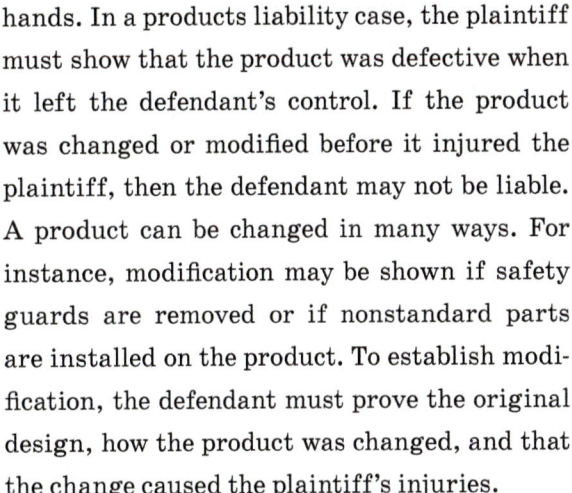

MODIFICATION:
A defense to products liability by which the defendant argues it should not be liable for the defective product because the plaintiff modified the product.

Example: Mark is using a table saw to cut wood for furniture he is making. The table saw was made by Woodchuck Inc. The saw came with a pre-installed blade guard to protect a user's hands. Mark removed the guard because he felt the guard made it hard for him to see the wood cuts. While cutting the wood for the furniture, Mark slices his finger and sues Woodchuck Inc. Woodchuck Inc. could argue the removal of the blade guard was a substantial change to the saw and that the removal of the guard caused Mark's injuries.

ALTERATIONS TO PRODUCTS MAY DEFEAT STRICT LIABILITY

Rix v. General Motors
(Driver) v. (Car Manufacturer)
723 P.2d 195 (Mont. 1986)

INSTANT FACTS:
A driver was injured when his vehicle was hit from behind by a GMC vehicle.

BLACK LETTER RULE:
The manufacturer of a defective product may be strictly liable for a design defect or a manufacturing defect, unless the product was altered.

FACTS:
A man was injured when the vehicle he was driving was hit from behind by a GMC vehicle. The man sued GMC for products liability. The parties agreed that brake failure caused the accident. However, GMC claimed the product was altered after it left GMC's control, and the alteration relieved it of any liability.

ISSUE:
Did alteration of the vehicle prevent liability on behalf of the manufacturer for defective brakes?

DECISION AND RATIONALE:
Maybe. To establish strict liability, the plaintiff must show the vehicle's brake system was defective, the defect caused the injury, and the defect is traceable to the product. Slight alteration does not negate the manufacturer's liability for a design defect because wear and tear does not change the product's design. The availability of an alternative design is one of a number of factors considered in determining whether a design defect exists. In this case, the instructions to the jury were incorrect, and the case was remanded for a new trial.

ANALYSIS:
This case provides a clear description of the distinction between manufacturing and design defects. The court's discussion also demonstrates how the modification defense may apply differently to a design defect and a manufacturing defect. While alteration of the product may affect liability for manufacturing defects, insubstantial alterations do not affect design defects because the alterations do not change the product's original design. Design defects examine the design at the time the product left the defendant's control.

Abnormal Uses/Product Misuse

A person may use a product to do something other than what the product was made to do. For example, a person may use an electric knife as a letter opener. If a person uses the product for a different purpose or in a way that it was not intended, the manufacturer may not be liable for product defects. This is referred to as **product misuse**.

PRODUCT MISUSE:
A defense to products liability in which the defendant argues the plaintiff used the product for an abnormal purpose.

A manufacturer must expect or anticipate some misuse of its products. Product misuse is either foreseeable or unforeseeable. If a party misuses a product in a way that is foreseeable, the manufacturer may still be liable. On the other hand, if a party misuses a product in an unforeseeable manner, the manufacturer may have a defense to liability. In some states, product misuse is a complete defense. If the plaintiff misused the product, they cannot recover anything against the defendant. In other states, the plaintiff's misuse reduces the amount of compensation.

Example: Tony is remodeling his home. He is replacing the tile flooring. He realizes he does not have a pry bar to lift up the old tiles. Tony decides to use a screwdriver to lift the old tiles. As Tony is lifting the tiles, the plastic handle on the screwdriver breaks and Tony is injured. The screwdriver was manufactured by ABC Tool Corp. At the time the screwdriver left ABC Tool Corp.'s control, the handle was defective because it was made from poor quality materials. If the use of a screwdriver as a pry bar is a foreseeable misuse of the screwdriver, ABC Tool Corp. may be liable for Tony's injuries. If Tony's use of the screwdriver is not foreseeable, that product misuse may reduce or prevent liability for ABC Tool Corp.

FORESEEABLE MISUSE OF A PRODUCT DOES NOT EXCLUDE MANUFACTURER LIABILITY

Pitman v. Ameristep Corporation
(Hunting Guide) v. (Strap Manufacturer)
208 F. Supp. 3d 1053 (E.D. Mo. 2016)

INSTANT FACTS: The manufacturer of ratchet straps claimed that a hunting guide's misuse of straps negated its liability for the guide's fall from a tree stand when the strap failed.

BLACK LETTER RULE: Products liability depends on whether the product is dangerous during reasonably anticipated use of the product, which includes objectively foreseeable misuse.

FACTS: A hunting guide fell from a tree stand after the ratchet straps he used to attach the stand to the tree failed. The guide had not read the warning label with the strap, but the experts agreed the strap was appropriate for use with tree stands. The guide originally installed the strap with a tree stand in September 2010, where he left it until January 2011. The strap was then stored indoors until inspected and re-installed. The guide installed the strap with the tree stand without wearing a safety harness. After installation, the strap failed and the guide fell from the tree. The guide claimed both design and manufacturing defects existed in the strap. The manufacturer claimed that leaving the strap attached to a tree stand outdoors for an extended period caused it to fail.

ISSUE: Did the plaintiff's misuse of the product eliminate the ratchet strap manufacturer's liability for the product's failure?

DECISION AND RATIONALE: Maybe. A design defect is one that makes the product unreasonably dangerous. When reviewing a design defect case, the focus should be on the reasonably anticipated use of the product rather than on the potential harm it could cause. Reasonably anticipated use includes objectively foreseeable misuse and abnormal use. A manufacturing defect exists when there is a problem during manufacturing of the specific item in question. This type of defect depends on whether the product is in its intended condition. In either circumstance, however, wear to the product over time is relevant, and excessive wear may be the true cause of the accident rather than a defect. The trial court will need to decide whether or not that was the case.

ANALYSIS: The guide also brought a claim for failure to warn, arguing that the manufacturer had not adequately notified him of the dangers posed by the product during normal use. One issue was whether the warnings should have included how to inspect a ratchet strap to ensure it is still safe. What is a reasonable line to draw for product warnings?

ABNORMAL USE: A defense to products liability actions by which a defendant argues it is not responsible for harm caused by the product because the plaintiff used the product for an unforeseeable purpose.

VI. Damages

The purpose of a tort lawsuit is to recover compensation for the injuries resulting from the defendant's conduct. In some circumstances, however, a defendant may be required to pay other damages as punishment.

Compensatory Damages

In most tort lawsuits, the injured party is seeking money compensation, called damages. The damages meant to compensate the party for the injuries suffered are called **compensatory damages**. In most negligence-based tort suits, a successful party can recover compensatory damages only. Compensatory damages do not provide the injured party with a windfall. Rather, compensatory damages are designed to pay the party back for expenses incurred as a result of the party's injuries.

Compensatory damages may be awarded for expenses related to physical and emotional injuries. Depending on the case, a party might

COMPENSATORY DAMAGES:
A sum of money awarded to the injured party in a lawsuit to compensate for expenses incurred as a result of the injuries.

Large personal injury awards can be misleading. A large monetary sum may need to fund the plaintiff's medical expenses for life. Such awards may seem like windfalls, but actually must be carefully managed.

JURY-AWARDED COMPENSATORY DAMAGES WILL BE UPHELD IF REASONABLY SUPPORTED BY EVIDENCE

Anderson v. Sears, Roebuck & Co.
(Burn Victims) v. (Heater Manufacturer)
377 F. Supp. 136 (E.D. La. 1974)

INSTANT FACTS:
A woman and her daughter were severely burned when a heater caused a fire at their home.

BLACK LETTER RULE:
A jury's determination of compensatory damages will not be overturned if the amount is reasonably based on the evidence.

FACTS:
A woman and her daughter were severely burned when a heater caused a fire at their home. The family sued the manufacturers of the heater for negligent installation, maintenance, and repair of the heater. The jury found in favor of the family and awarded $2 million in damages. On appeal, the defendants argue that plaintiffs were awarded an excessive amount of damages.

ISSUE:
Did the jury award the plaintiffs an excessive amount of damages?

DECISION AND RATIONALE:
No. The court found that the damage award was not excessive. Injured plaintiffs may recover damages for the following types of injury: past physical and mental pain, future physical and mental pain, future medical expenses, loss of earning capacity, and permanent disability. The evidence supported the amount of damages awarded by the jury.

ANALYSIS:
If a damages award is within the scope of the evidence presented on the amount of damages, the award is likely to stand. Courts do not like to second guess a jury's determination of damages.

receive damages for pain and suffering, disfigurement, loss of reputation, medical expenses, and lost wages.

Punitive Damages

In some circumstances, a party may receive **punitive damages** in addition to compensatory damages. While compensatory damages take care of the plaintiff's monetary losses, punitive damages are meant to punish the wrongdoer. Punitive damages are available only in cases involving egregious conduct. Egregious conduct typically requires an intentional act by the defendant. Because negligence cases typically do not involve intentional conduct punitive damages are generally not available in negligence actions.

Where punitive damages are available, juries have occasionally granted extremely high figures. In one famous case, *Liebeck v. McDonald's Restaurants*, a customer spilled hot coffee on herself, and was injured badly enough to require skin grafts. In 1994, a New Mexico jury awarded a plaintiff $160,000 in compensatory damages, but $2.7 million in punitive damages against McDonald's. (An appeals court later reduced the award.) The case opened a national debate about punitive damages.

The U.S. Supreme Court considered punitive damages in *State Farm Mutual Automobile Insurance Co. v. Campbell*, 538 U.S. 408 (2003). The Court held that the Due Process Clause of the Fourteenth Amendment prevents disproportionate punitive damage awards. The Court said it would be unfair for potential defendants to have no notice of the potential monetary penalty that would result from their actions. Punitive damages should be based on the egregiousness of the conduct, but generally should not be more than 10 times the compensatory award.

CHAPTER SUMMARY

Tort law provides a framework for injured parties to recover compensation from the parties who caused the injury. This applies to all actors in business just as it applies to individuals in their personal lives. In the business world, all entities and their employees must take care to act prudently in their actions with others. Furthermore, many commercial entities find that they may be liable, even without any negligence or fault, if a product they produce or sell contains a defect. Thus, it is important for

PUNITIVE DAMAGES:
A sum of money awarded to the injured party in a lawsuit to punish the wrongdoer for his actions.

CAREERS IN THE LAW

Many careers touch on tort law in one way or another. For businesses, those who design, document, create, and test products are essential to reducing the risk of products liability lawsuits. Product design, assembly, and packaging are also important to legal risk management. Technical writers prepare clear owner's manuals and instructions, and quality control professionals test products to ensure that they are safe. Almost every step in design, manufacturing, documentation, and packaging has a direct relationship with legal issues.

all parties involved in business to understand the rules governing negligence, intentional torts, strict liability, and products liability. A thorough understanding of the principles guiding tort law recovery can help commercial entities to establish appropriate business practices and reduce organizational liability.

Review Questions

Review question 1.
What is the difference between negligent and intentional torts? How does an injured person seek tort damages?

Review question 2.
What entities can commit a tort and be held liable for damages? If the answer different for negligent and intentional torts?

Review question 3.
What is the reasonable person standard? How does it apply in negligence cases? How can the standard vary?

Review question 4.
What is malpractice? How does the reasonable person standard relate to malpractice liability?

Review question 5.
What is the difference between slander and defamation? What is meant by the term "actual malice"? Is there a constitutional defense to either slander or defamation? Why or why not?

Review question 6.
What is an example of puffery? How is puffery different from fraud? How can you tell the difference?

Review question 7.
What are the different types of product defects? What defenses might a manufacturer assert in a products liability case?

Review question 8.
What is the difference between a manufacturing defect and a design defect? How can packaging flaws cause liability?

Review question 9.
Why are product instructions and warnings important? What should they provide to the consumer?

Review question 10.
What are the elements of an interference with contract claim? How is this tort different from a breach of contract case? Why is there a difference in how the two issues are treated legally?

Review question 11.
If an employee commits a tort at work, is the employer liable? What information is needed to determine if an employer may be responsible for an employee's torts?

Review question 12.
What types of damages are available to parties who have been injured? What is the difference between compensatory and punitive damages? What are the goals of each type of damage award?

Review question 13.
What happens if a tort plaintiff was also negligent? Is the plaintiff barred from recovery?

Review question 14.
In what circumstances would a defendant have strict liability for injuries? For strict liability, do the defendant's behavior or intentions help or harm the defense?

Review question 15.
What is res ipsa loquitur? What does a plaintiff need to prove to recover on a res ipsa loquitur claim?

Review question 16.
What is proximate cause? Why is it important? What types of causation are necessary for tort liability? In what circumstances might causation be too remote to raise liability?

Discussion Questions

Question 1:

Trina is competing in the Tri-City Triathlon. When she registered for the event, Trina signed a waiver. The waiver noted that participants assumed the risk of collisions with other participants. The organizer of the triathlon, Fun Sports, purchases a drone to use at the event. Earl, an employee of Fun Sports who has never used a drone before, uses the drone during the triathlon to take photos of the event for Fun Sports to post on their website for marketing. While Earl is operating the drone, the drone gets tangled in power lines. The blades of the drone sever one of the power lines. The line falls to the ground and hits Trina, who suffers severe burns. The incident also causes a power surge, which releases sparks and flames from a power line three blocks away. The sparks and flames burn a man, Pablo, walking below the power lines. Earl says the drone started acting erratically right before the incident.

> Does Trina have a tort claim against Fun Sports? If so, what type of tort?
>
> Does Pablo have a tort claim against Fun Sports?
>
> Can Fun Sports sue the drone manufacturer for a product defect?

Question 2:

Coach Chris is a very popular basketball coach at Northeast Southwest University. He is under contract to coach at NSU for the next three years. The terms of the contract were disclosed in a press release issued by the college. Coach Chris was approached by two men looking to establish a professional basketball team for the state of Hawaii, called the Hawaii Hornbills. Coach Chris has been discussing the possibility of leaving his job at NSU to become the head coach of the Hornbills. Alfred, a friend of Coach Chris, overhears him talking about the Hornbills job offer to his wife. Alfred is a prominent business owner, and he is a huge supporter of the basketball team. Alfred and does not want Coach Chris to take the Hawaii job. That night, hoping to dissuade the Hornbills from hiring Coach Chris, Alfred posts on social media that he and his family vacationed in Hawaii several years ago with Coach Chris and his family. Alfred includes a video in which Coach Chris says he hates Hawaii. In the video, Coach Chris also says "the only good thing about Hawaii is that the people understand basketball better than NSU fans." The video goes viral.

Upon seeing the video, the Hornbills tell Coach Chris that they will not hire him to coach the Hornbills. After public outrage, NSU fires Coach Chris two weeks later. In response, Coach Chris conducts an interview in which he says "Alfred is not a friend. He is a traitor who does whatever he can to get what he wants. He has engaged in insider trading and his company defrauded the public. The government should conduct an investigation." Someone told Coach Chris that Alfred traded stocks based on inside information, but Coach Chris was not involved in the transaction.

> Could Alfred be liable for a tort? If so, which one(s)?
>
> Could Coach Chris be held liable for a tort? If so, which one(s)?

Question 3:

Mika buys a new smart phone. The phone was designed and manufactured by Pyro Phones. One week after purchasing the phone, Mika drops the phone and cracks the screen. He purchases a replacement screen online and installs the screen on the phone. Two months later, Mika is using the phone when the battery overheats. The phone starts on fire and burns Mika's hands.

> Does Mika have a cause of action against Pyro Phones?
>
> Can Pyro Phones assert any defenses against Mika's claim?

Question 4:

Bob works as a farm laborer. He is known for goofing around on the job to make people laugh. One day, while walking with his co-worker Patricia, Bob starts flapping his arms like a chicken to emphasize the punch line of a joke. Patricia moves to give Bob flapping room, and is hit by a swinging pulley that normally hangs above the door of the barn.

> Does Patricia have a tort claim against Bob? Against the farm? Against the pulley manufacturer?
>
> What type of claims does Patricia have against each party? What elements are present for any identified tort claims?

Question 5:

Kellogg USA has been sued several times because plaintiffs claim they were misled by the company. Specifically, the plaintiffs charge that they believed Froot Loops contained actual fruit. The cases are routinely dismissed.

>Why do courts dismiss these cases?

>Is the product name misleading?

>If a case went to trial, what defenses would make sense for Kellogg?

Question 6:

Akash is a window cleaner. He purchases a new, taller ladder and uses it on a job. A customer asks Akash to paint his commercial building. The ladder won't reach high enough for part of the job. Akash decides to put the ladder on the roof of the building next door and lean the ladder across the gap to complete the job. He falls from the ladder and is injured. He would like to sue because the ladder's packaging did not say that he should not use the ladder in that specific way.

>What type of defect is Akash claiming?

>What defenses could the ladder manufacturer use against Akash's suit?

>Should the ladder manufacturer change its packaging?

Question 7:

Shirley has cosmetic surgery to reduce a large scar near her ear. The surgeon cuts a nerve to Shirley's face, which causes her mouth to droop on that side of her face. The damage is not repairable. Shirley wants to sue the surgeon for negligence. The surgeon says that Shirley signed a consent form that listed possible side effects, including cut nerves.

>What will Shirley need to show to prevail in her case?

>How is this case different from a standard tort matter?

>Suppose that Shirley had a condition that made nerve damage more likely following surgery, and she disclosed this information to the surgeon. How would that change the case?

Question 8:
Lili does not like the president of the small company where she works. She tells a friend that the president is "a big jerk." Lili also dislikes the U.S. president, so she says that he is a big jerk as well. "He probably kicks puppies in his spare time," she adds.

    Has Lili committed a tort against the company president? Why or why not?

    Has Lili committed a tort against the U.S. president? Why or why not?

Question 9:
Latoya runs a bar. One of the regulars comes in earlier than usual and already intoxicated. The bartender serves the regular one drink, but then Latoya says to cut him off. The regular becomes angry and leaves. He drives away, and hits a bicyclist as he pulls out of the parking lot.

    Who is liable to the bicyclist?

    What defenses are available to the various parties?

Question 10:
Quincy received a personal injury settlement after a car accident in which they were injured and their car was heavily damaged. Quincy was out of work for quite a while because of the injuries. Quincy's spouse had to cut back his work hours to care for them, and they had to hire home health care for several months. The home health care aide accidentally stepped on Quincy's pet chameleon, killing it.

    What type of damages did Quincy probably receive in the settlement?

    What types of injuries would the damages cover?

Question 11:
Harold runs a horse-and-carriage tour of a local park. The traffic laws say that horse-pulled vehicles must have a reflective orange hazard triangle on the back, but Harold says that it detracts from the carriage and makes it less romantic-looking. A car rear-ends Harold's carriage and seriously injures the passengers.

    Who may be liable to the passengers?

    Why might each party identified in the last question be liable?

Question 12:

Cara is 12. She is driving a golf cart on the local course, which is allowed by the course rules. While Cara is looking at her phone, she hits another golfer.

How will the reasonable person standard apply in this case?

Under what circumstances might Cara have a defense against the other golfer?

9

Intellectual Property

KEY OBJECTIVES:

▶ Distinguish between copyright, trademarks, patents, and trade secrets.

▶ Explain the need to protect intellectual property interests.

▶ Identify how intellectual property owners may license or assign their rights.

CHAPTER OVERVIEW

This chapter covers intellectual property, which is often the most valuable asset a company owns. Intellectual property is a form of intangible property that may originate from an idea or creative impulse. It can protect an invention, a song, or an advertising slogan. Although the intellectual property may be in a physical object, like the copyright in this textbook, it is not a physical thing. Instead, intellectual property is a right, or a set of rights, to control how a creation or invention is used.

In this chapter, we will consider the various types of intellectual property, including how to recognize those rights and how to protect them. Finally, the chapter will discuss how to allow others to make use of intellectual property through licensing.

INTRODUCTION

Millions of people now subscribe to streaming services to access music and tv. Indeed, many students choose Spotify® to access millions of songs, and Hulu® to watch streaming movies and television programs. This everyday scenario involves three kinds of intellectual property rights. You pay a subscription fee for streaming services, because the music and videos you access through these services are protected by copyright. The names of the bands who recorded the songs and the streaming services, brand names are all trademarks. The smartphone or tablet on which you consume the content might involve thousands of patents. And, if you are drinking a Dr. Pepper® soft drink as you watch your movie, a fourth type of intellectual property comes into play: the recipe for Dr. Pepper is a trade secret. The brand names for soft drinks like "Coca Cola" and "Dr. Pepper" are also trademarks.

Intellectual property serves a number of purposes. In the U.S. and across the globe, copyrights, trademarks, and patents are valuable commercial assets. Legal protection makes it profitable to create and invent. For many creators and inventors, their intellectual property is also a way of having their creative or inventive efforts recognized. Trademarks are valuable assets to the owner of the goods or services, but also provide important information to consumers about the source and quality of the products and services they consume. Trade secret law recognizes the value of keeping business information confidential, either temporarily or permanently. Intellectual property covers a lot of different areas, and affects virtually every type of business.

Understanding intellectual property law is important not only for the protection and commercial development of your own ideas, but to make sure that you do not run afoul of someone else's rights.

There are four main types of intellectual property: copyrights, trademarks, patents, and trade secrets. Each type protects different interests.

I. Copyright

Copyright law has a long history in the United States. The Constitution gives Congress the power to

> promote the Progress of Science and useful Arts, by securing for limited Times to Authors and Inventors the exclusive Right to their respective Writings and Discoveries.

Copyright strikes a balance between the author and society. In exchange for granting authors the exclusive rights to exploits their creative works, society benefits from the expansion of knowledge and the arts (what in the 18th century was the "Progress of Science"). The first federal copyright law was the Copyright Act of 1790, passed in the second session of Congress. It allowed copyright protection for any "map, chart, book or books" authored by a U.S. citizen. Copyright protection was for 14 years, and could be extended for 14 more.

Over time, copyright law has expanded a great deal in terms of what can be protected and for how long. Copyright now protects photographs, movies, sound recordings, architecture, digital works, and some aspects of computer software. Copyright law has adapted to new technology. And, U.S. law has changed to include global norms.

All of these changes are made within the same constitutional framework as the 1790 Act: securing exclusive rights to authors, for limited times. There are two important concepts contained in that sentence. First, copyright gives "exclusive" rights. When a person owns the copyright in a work, she is said to have a "bundle of rights." This bundle is made up of the right to do the following:

- Make copies of a work,
- Distribute copies,
- Create **derivative works**,
- Display the work publicly, if it is a visual work,
- Perform it publicly, if it is a script or written music, and
- Transmit the work by broadcast, webcast, or any other means.

It is important to remember that these rights belong exclusively to the owner of the copyright. She is the only one who gets to decide how, or whether, a work is used.

> **DERIVATIVE WORK:**
> A work based on another work. Examples of derivative works include adaptations or sequels.

The second concept is that the time of the exclusive rights is limited. All copyrights will expire after a period of time. Since the first copyright act, the length of protection has successively increased and how long an author receives protection depends on when a work was created. Generally, if a work was created after 1978, copyright protection will last for the lifetime of the author, plus 70 years, with no renewal. The copyright term will be shorter for a work created by an employee in the scope of their employment. These works made for hire receive protection for 95 years from the date they are published or 120 years from the date they are created, whichever comes sooner.

Copyright on Creative Works

Every time you doodle on a piece of paper or your tablet, or take a selfie or photo of your friends, you are the **author** of a creative work protected by copyright.

Since 1989, when the U.S. joined the Berne Convention for the Protection of Literary and Artistic works, copyright protection is automatic on creation of an eligible work. This means that there is nothing formal you have to do to receive full copyright protection in the U.S. (and 178 other Berne Convention countries). You do not have to register, and you do not have to put any notice on your work, in order to enjoy copyright protection (although there are good reasons to register with the U.S. Copyright Office and to put a copyright notice on your work). In most cases, the individual who creates the work is both the author and owner of the copyright. If it is a work made for hire, the law considers the employer both the author and the owner of the copyright. The author may or may not be the owner of the actual work created. If you frame the doodle and give it to your professor, you don't own the physical object of the drawing any more, but you still own the copyright.

The only real limitation on this rule is that the work must qualify for copyright protection, or be copyrightable. Under U.S. copyright law, a work qualifies for copyright protection if it is an

> original work[ ] of authorship fixed in any tangible medium of expression, now known or later developed, from which they can be perceived, reproduced, or otherwise communicated, either directly or with the aid of a machine or device.

AUTHOR:
In copyright law, the creator of a copyrightable work.

Example: A photographer took a picture of a statue in a cemetery. He has created an original work that is entitled to copyright protection. The photographer's right extends only to his photograph. The statue itself has its own copyright. *Leigh v. Warner Brothers,* 212 F.3d 1210 (11th Cir. 2000).

The "originality" requirement has two parts. First, there must be some small amount of creativity and it must be created independently by the author. It does not mean complete novelty or uniqueness. It just means that the work was created independently, and that there was some "spark" of creativity. Two people taking a photo at the same time of the same tree will each have met the threshold requirement for originality.

While copyright protects entire works, there are some elements of a work that cannot be protected. Using one of these elements without permission would not constitute copyright infringement. The non-copyrightable parts of a work include:

- Titles (although a title may be protected by trademark law),
- Ideas,
- Facts,
- Quotations,
- Slogans (which may be protected by trademark law),
- Natural elements, such as the coloring of a horse,
- Public domain material, or
- Scènes à faire, which are common elements or devices used in a particular type of work (for example, star-crossed lovers whose parents are feuding).

Works that are based on another work (so-called "derivative" works) are considered original, and entitled to copyright protection. The owner of the original work has the exclusive right to create derivative works, but may authorize or license others to do so. For example, if a writer authors a successful novel, she may grant a license to Netflix to make a movie version. The movie will have its own copyright. The protection for the derivative works is separate from the protection given to the original work. The protection for the derivative work only applies to the new additions. It does not give the author of the derivative any copyright in the original work, if the original copyright is held by another person.

The **author** is the creator of the original work and is typically the owner, unless there is a

WORK FOR HIRE:
A work that was either created by an employee within the scope of her employment, or that was commissioned for a special purpose with the written agreement that it would be work-for-hire. Copyright authorship and ownership for a work-for-hire automatically vests in the employer or person who commissioned the work.

Example: Steven is authorized to translate a series of popular mystery novels from Swedish into English. Steven is the author of the English translation. He cannot claim copyright in the untranslated Swedish works. An unauthorized translation would be a copyright violation.

written agreement whereby the author transfers ownership to someone else. The author of a work may be an individual, or there may be multiple authors. If a work is **work made for hire**, the author is the employer, not the individual employee who created the work. In some cases, certain kinds of works created by an independent contractor, can qualify as a work made for hire if it is one of the kinds of works listed in the statute and the creator agrees in writing.

> Works created by the U.S. government, or by U.S. government employees within the scope of their employment, are not eligible for copyright protection. The government could, however, purchase the copyright in a work produced by someone else.

"Fixed in any tangible medium of expression" is a requirement that a work be physically recorded by some means. This allows the work to be recorded, so there is some way of knowing what is protected. For example, dance moves are creations, but they are not tangible. The choreography may, however, be protected by copyright if there is a diagram made of the moves. The other, and probably more important, purpose of the "fixed in any tangible medium of expression" requirement is to make clear that copyright protection will not be given to abstract ideas. Instead, only the expression of those ideas will be protected. Many different authors may use the same basic idea for their works (think zombie apocalypse), but it is how that basic idea is expressed that gets the protection.

The copyright statute lists the kinds of creative works that can be protected. However, not all works can be protected. Copyright cannot protect "any idea, procedure, process, system, method of operation, concept, principle, or discovery, regardless of the form in which it is described, explained, illustrated, or embodied in such work." This means that copyright expression cannot be extended to works such as:

- Blank forms,
- Recipes,
- Mathematical proofs,
- Scientific theories,
- Historical facts, or
- Business methods.

Even if a type of work is not copyrightable, there may be expression attached to it, or closely associated with it, that could be protected. For example, the historical facts related to the battle at Gettysburg during the Civil War cannot be protected by copyright. But, the actual words used to describe the battle in a history book will be protected by copyright. Remember, the copy-

> *Example:* In one of her cookbooks, the late Julia Child published a recipe for Caesar salad. She also told the story of how and where the salad was popularized (in Mexico, not Italy). The recipe is not copyrightable, but her telling of the story behind the recipe is.

right will not extend to the non-copyrightable parts of the work, but only to the actual expression or words chosen by the author.

Proving Copyright

It is very easy to get copyright in a work: copyright is automatic for creative expression. Proving that you have copyright is a different matter. The question of proof can come up in many different situations. Suppose you post a picture you have taken online, and then you learn that someone has used it without your permission. This could be an infringement of your copyright. In order to do anything about it, you have to show that you own the copyright.

One of the best ways of proving copyright is the copyright notice. The copyright notice is not required for works published or created since March 1, 1989. An author will have a valid copyright without the notice, but the notice can help prove ownership.

> If a work was published before 1978 without a copyright notice, there was no copyright on the work. If the work was published between 1978 and 1989, and notice was not put on within five years of publication, there was no copyright. Since 1989, no notice is required for protection.

The notice still is important. It tells anyone who sees a work that it is indeed protected by copyright. It also lets them know who the owner of the copyright is.

Notice is also important because it can defeat a claim of innocent infringement. Innocent infringement occurs when a person who uses a work without permission is able to make a claim that she didn't know it was copyrighted work. An innocent infringer still must pay damages for copyright infringement, but the damages are less than what an intentional infringer would pay.

The copyright notice itself is very simple. It consists of:

- The letter "C" in a circle (©), the word "copyright," or the abbreviation "Copr.,"
- The year the work was first published, and
- The name of the owner of the copyright.

The notice should be placed on publicly distributed copies so that it can be visually perceived, directly, or with the aid of a device. It must be on the copy in a manner and location that gives reasonable notice of the claimed copyright.

Registering Copyrights

If an author has a valid copyright in a work without registering it, then why bother regis-

Example: Mayra has made a video of herself singing. At the end of the video, she includes a copyright notice in small letters. The notice is visible for only a second. The notice is sufficient.

tering? After all, it takes time and costs money. What's the point?

Since 1989, registration is no longer a legal requirement for copyright protection, but it is still important. First, registration is *prima facia* evidence that you are the owner of the copyright in the work. It is evidence that can be rebutted, but if there is no other evidence introduced, the registration will be conclusive proof.

Second, the registration is public notice of who claims ownership. Copyright records are open to the public for searching. Records since 1978 are available online. They may be searched by name, title, keyword, registration number, or document number. Records for registrations before 1978 are only partially online, and a full search would have to be done in the federal Copyright Office in Washington, D.C.

Third, registration is required for U.S. copyrighted works, even though copyright protection attaches immediately. There are substantial benefits to registering withing three months of creating the work. Doing so means that the copyright owner could get enhanced damages, attorney fees, and cost from the infringer.

Registration is a very simple process. It may be done electronically (the preferred method), or by sending hard copies of the required documents to the U.S. Copyright Office in Washington, D.C. The process is also not as expensive as many might fear. As of January 2022, the registration fees range from $45 to $65 for online registration, and $125 for paper registration. There are three steps for registering copyright: application, payment, and deposit of copies.

> The "poor person's copyright" strategy of mailing a copy of a work to oneself via certified mail, and leaving the envelope unopened, is not a substitute for registration. The only effect it may have is as evidence of when a work was created.

Application involves filling out a form. The form asks for information about the author of the work, and about the work itself. The applicant must give the title of the work, a description of the type of work that it is (for example, musical recording, audio-visual work, or one of several other options), and the name of the author. If the work is based on another work, that must be included in the application. The application form also asks if the work has been published.

Payment of the filing fee is required when the application is submitted. If the application is

Example: A band issued an album on vinyl, with elaborate cover art. The band registered its copyright in the songs on the album, but never submitted the cover art for registration. A designer later used some of the more distinctive images from the cover art for a separate project, without the band's permission. The band was not entitled to sue for infringement, because the art was not registered. *Jefferson Airplane v. Berkeley Systems, Inc.*, 886 F. Supp. 713 (N.D. Cal. 1994).

online, it is much like making payment for any online purchase.

Deposit of copies means that two copies of the work are submitted. The copies may be sent electronically or by mail. Some works may have photographs sent in, instead of physical copies of the work.

After the application for registration is submitted, the Copyright Office examines the application. The examination looks to see if all of the legal requirements for the application have been met. The examination determines whether the work is copyrightable. The examination does *not* compare the work with other registered copyrights.

If the application is denied, the applicant may ask for an internal review by the Copyright Office. After the review process, an applicant whose registration is still refused may be bring a court action. A person whose application is denied may bring an infringement action without appealing the refusal.

Copyright Infringement

Putting the copyright notice on work and registering copyright can provide important protections. They are preventative measures and, as with all preventative measures, there will be times when they don't work. Other measures will have to be taken. The "other measures" take the form of a lawsuit for copyright infringement.

The law defines "infringement" as the "violation" of the exclusive rights of the owner of a copyright. "Violation" means exercising one of these rights without the permission of the owner. An infringement can be unintentional, as in cases where the infringer had a good faith belief that the work was **public domain**. A valid claim of infringement can be made even if the infringement did not cause any financial damage to the copyright owner.

The essence of an infringement lawsuit is a claim for unauthorized use, or copying, of the copyrighted work. Only the owner of a particular right is entitled to sue for copyright infringement. The owner is either the author of the work, or a person who bought or licensed some or all of the rights in the copyrighted work. While it is not conclusive proof, the listing of an owner's name on the registration certificate issued by the Copyright Office will be strong evidence of ownership.

An infringement lawsuit requires proof that the material taken, or copied, was actually protected by copyright. If the part that was taken is public domain, there is no infringement, even if there was copying.

A work enters the public domain in one of two ways. An author or owner may dedicated the work to the public domain, by making an explicit statement that they reserve no rights and has no limits on use.

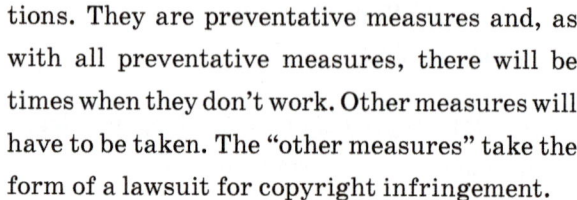

PUBLIC DOMAIN:
Work that cannot be copyrighted. An old copyright may have expired, or the author or owner of the work has made an explicit designation that the work is public domain. The term also refers to U.S. Government works that cannot be copyrighted.

A PERSON WHO CLAIMS INFRINGEMENT MUST PROVE OWNERSHIP OF THE COPYRIGHT

Fleischer Studios, Inc. v. A.V.E.L.A., Inc.
(Copyright Licensor) v. (Competing Licensor)
654 F.3d 958 (9th Cir. 2011)

INSTANT FACTS:
Fleischer (P) claimed ownership in all the rights to the character Betty Boop.

BLACK LETTER RULE:
The plaintiff in an infringement action bears the burden of proving copyright ownership.

FACTS:
The character Betty Boop was developed in 1930, and all rights in the character and films were sold to Paramount. Paramount transferred its rights in the films only to UM & M, and the rights were resold multiple times, until Fleischer (P) purchased them. Fleischer (P) licensed the Betty Boop character for use in toys, dolls, and other merchandise. A.V.E.L.A. (D) also licensed Betty Boop merchandise. The copyright under which A.V.E.L.A. (D) licensed its products is based on vintage posters featuring Betty Boop's image that A.V.E.L.A. (D) had restored. Fleischer (P) claimed that it owned the exclusive rights to the Betty Boop character. A.V.E.L.A. (D) claimed that Fleischer (P) had not proven its exclusive ownership of the copyright. The district court entered judgment for A.V.E.L.A. (D).

ISSUE:
Was Fleischer (P) the holder of the entire copyright?

DECISION AND RATIONALE:
(Kagan, J.) No. The plaintiff in an infringement action bears the burden of proving copyright ownership. Fleischer has not met this burden. When Paramount sold copyrights to UM & M, the transfer included only the rights to the films. The rights to the character were excluded from the sale.

The licensee of a copyright work obtains only partial copyright privileges. Under the doctrine of indivisibility, a licensee of a copyright may not copyright a work in the licensee's name. Affirmed.

ANALYSIS:
The court and all of the parties agreed that the character Betty Boop was separately copyrightable. Fictional characters are protected by copyright apart from the works they appear in if the character is highly developed and distinctive. Stock characters are not protectable.

> Creative Commons licensing is not the same as public domain. Although a Creative Commons license does not require payment, there still are requirements that must be followed to use a work. These non-monetary requirements are legally enforceable.

A work enters the public domain when the copyright expires. Because the copyright term has been extended by Congress many times, determining when a work enters the public domain is not easy. Work produced since 1978 is protected in the U.S. for 70 years after the death of the author. All work published before 1923 is in the public domain, and work published between 1923 and 1963 is in the public domain if copyright was not renewed. If a work was published between 1923 and 1963, and copyright was renewed within 28 years, the copyright runs for 95 years after the publication date. For work published with the proper copyright notice between 1964 and 1977, copyright extends from

Copyrights of works first published in US

Year of first publication (Note: publication is not creation)	Copyright duration
* before 1923 * during 1923–63: without notice, or with notice but not renewed within 28 years of first publication * during 1964–77: without notice * from 1978 to March 1, 1989: without notice and without registration within 5 years of first publication	Work has entered US public domain
* during 1923–63: with notice and renewed * during 1964–77: with notice	Copyrighted for 95 years after first publication
* from 1978 to March 1, 1989: pre-1978 creation with notice, or without notice but registered within 5 years of first publication * from March 2, 1989 to 2002: pre-1978 creation	If author is known, copyrighted until the later of either 70 years pma or Dec 31, 2047. If author is unknown or corporate authorship, the earlier of 95 years after first publication or 120 years after creation, but not earlier than Dec 31, 2047.
* from 1978 to March 1, 1989: post-1977 creation with notice, or without notice but registered within 5 years of first publication * from March 2, 1989 to 2002: post-1977 creation * unpublished before 2003 (i.e. first published after 2002)	If author is known, copyrighted for 70 years pma. If author is unknown or corporate authorship, the earlier of 95 years after first publication, or 120 years after creation.

Glossary:
*pma: post mortem auctoris, or "after the author's death"

> **Example:** The copyright to the film "It's a Wonderful Life" expired in 1975, which meant that the film could be broadcast without paying royalties. However, the movie was based on the story "The Greatest Gift," which still is protected by copyright. The musical score for the movie is also copyright protected.

95 years after the date of publication. Note that the copyright in part of a work may expire. Other elements may remain protected.

Fair Use

There is no part of copyright law that is more misunderstood than fair use. Indeed, the Supreme Court described it as "the most troublesome in the whole law of copyright." Everyone, it seems, "knows" what the rule is, and "knows" how it works. The internet is full of free advice on fair use, and what it is supposed to mean. But the boundaries of fair use are ambiguous and you only really know whether a use qualifies as fair use after the issue is litigated in an infringement lawsuit.

Fair use is a defense to a claim of copyright infringement. Much of the confusion surrounding it probably comes from the fact that it is not defined in copyright law. The vagueness was intentional: when Congress rewrote the copyright laws in 1976, it was decided to let fair use evolve, and adapt to new uses and new technologies that were not foreseen at the time.

COPYING SOLELY FOR ELECTRONIC SEARCHING IS FAIR USE

Authors Guild v. Google, Inc.
(Copyright Holders) v. (Search Engine)
804 F.3d 202 (2d Cir. 2015)

INSTANT FACTS:
Google (D) scanned copies of library books so they could be searched electronically, and claimed its copying was fair use.

BLACK LETTER RULE:
Making a digital copy of books for a search function is transformative, and is fair use of the copyrighted books.

FACTS:
In 2004, Google (D) started its library project. The project involved scanning books that were supplied by participating libraries, extracting a machine-readable text, and creating an index of the text of each book. Google (D) kept the original scan of each book, in part to improve accuracy as image-to-text conversion technologies improve. Some of the books include were protected by copyright, but Google (D) did not obtain the permission of the copyright holders (P) before scanning books. The search results display information about the book, as well as a limited amount of the text.

The Authors Guild (P) claimed that Google (D) was infringing copyrights. Google (D) claimed that the library project was fair use. The district court agreed.

ISSUE:
Was Google's (D) copying fair use?

DECISION AND RATIONALE:
(Leval, J.) Yes. Making a digital copy of books for a search function is transformative, and is fair use of the copyrighted books.

When a claim of fair use is made, the court considers all of the fair use factors: the purpose and nature of the copying, the nature of the copied work, the relative amount taken, and the effect on the market or potential market for the copied work. As applied to the copying in this case, the four factors work as follows:

- The purpose of the copying was creating a copy of electronic searching. This is a transformative use, and transformative uses are more likely to be considered fair use.

- The nature of the use is to provide information about the copied work, instead of just duplicating it. This factor favors fair use.

- Entire works are copied, but the whole works are not displayed to the users of the search function. This factor also favors fair use.

- The potential market for the copied books is not affected, because the search does not give users an effective substitute for the original. On average, no more than 16% of the copied book is displayed.

Considering all four factors leads to the conclusion that Google's (D) copying is fair use. Affirmed.

ANALYSIS:
When there is a claim of fair use, all four factors must be considered. In theory, no one factor is more important than any other. In practice, courts put a great deal of emphasis on looking for a transformative use, and on the harm to the potential market.

> **Example:** A rap group did a cover version of a well-known "golden oldie." Their cover added some lyrics that changed the tone of the song from a romantic ballad to a more cynical view of relationships. The Supreme Court held that the cover version created a new work that commented on the old, and could therefore be fair use. *Campbell v. Acuff-Rose Music,* 510 U.S. 569 (1994).

The Copyright Act says that the fair use of a copyrighted work is not infringement. Although fair use is not defined, its purpose is to promote free expression by permitting some use of copyrighted work in some circumstances. The copyright law identifies certain types of uses that may qualify as fair use, including criticism, comment, news reporting, teaching, scholarship, and research.

The courts decide whether a particular use of someone else's work is fair use on a case-by-case basis. There is no one thing that will lead a court to find fair use. Instead, courts balance a variety of factors, including:

1. The purpose and character of the use. This factor considers whether the use was for commercial or other reasons. A noncommercial use for teaching is more likely to be fair use than copying articles to distribute in a business. Courts will also consider whether a use is "transformative:" if a use adds some new expression, meaning, or message, and isn't a substitute for the original work, it is more likely to be fair use.

2. The nature of the copyrighted work. This factor analyzes the nature of the copyright in the infringed work. Highly creative works, such as novels, movies, and symphonies, are less likely to support fair use claims than a factual work, where only the exact expression of the underlying facts is protected. Therefore, it is easier to make fair use of the factual content of a news article or history book, than parts of a movie's musical score.

3. The relative amount taken. Contrary to what you may have heard, there is no ratio, no fraction, and no maximum number of words that will guarantee that a particular use is still fair. Instead, the test is whether the amount taken was reasonable in relation to the purpose of the copying. In other words, you may not use more of another work than is strictly necessary.

> A good rule of thumb for fair use is to put yourself in the shoes of the other author, and take no more than you would be comfortable with someone taking from your work. But there is no formula or quantity of the work that will guarantee fair use. Fair use is assessed on a case-by-case basis.

4. The effect on the potential market for the original. Copying is less likely to be fair use if it harms, or could harm, the market for the original. This factor considers the

PLAINTIFF MUST SHOW MORE THAN SIMILARITIES AND A POSSIBILITY THAT DEFENDANTS HAD ACCESS TO COPYRIGHTED MUSIC TO CLAIM INFRINGEMENT

Batiste v. Lewis
(Jazz Musician) v. (Hip-hop Duo)
976 F.3d 493 (5th Cir. 2020)

Ben Haggerty, better known as "Macklemore," and Ryan Lewis form the world-famous hip-hop duo Macklemore & Ryan Lewis. Macklemore and Lewis's rise to fame drew the attention of Paul Batiste, a self-proclaimed "legendary" jazz musician in New Orleans. Batiste sued Macklemore and Lewis for copyright infringement, claiming that the duo copied eleven of his songs. His allegations focus on the practice of "digital sampling," which involves copying sounds from an existing recording and incorporating them, with or without alteration, into a new one. Batiste contends that the defendants sampled brief snippets of his copyrighted sound recordings in five of their songs: "Thrift Shop," "Can't Hold Us," "Same Love," "Neon Cathedral," and "Need to Know." [. . .] The [trial] court held that Batiste presented insufficient evidence to create a genuine dispute as to whether the defendants actually copied his music. We agree.

Batiste's copyright ownership isn't challenged, at least not adequately, so we focus on copying.

[. . .] In this context, copying has two components: "factual" copying and "actionable" copying. The plaintiff must first establish factual copying, which requires proof that the defendant "actually used the copyrighted material to create his own work." Absent direct evidence of copying, which is hard to come by, a plaintiff can raise an inference of factual copying from "(1) proof that the defendant had access to the copyrighted work prior to creation of the infringing work and (2) probative similarity." A plaintiff can show probative similarity by pointing to "any similarities between the two works," [. . .] "that, in the normal course of events, would not be expected to arise independently."

A strong showing of probative similarity can make up for a lesser showing of access. In fact, a plaintiff may raise an inference of factual copying without any proof of access if the works are "strikingly similar." But the reverse is not true. Even with "overwhelming proof of access," a plaintiff can't establish factual copying "without some showing of probative similarity."

If factual copying is proven, the plaintiff must then establish that the copying is legally actionable by showing "that the allegedly infringing work is substantially similar to protectable elements of the infringed work." This usually requires a "side-by-side comparison" of the works' protectable elements "to determine whether a layman would view the two works as 'substantially similar.'"

To prove access, a plaintiff must show that "the person who created the allegedly infringing work had a reasonable opportunity to view [or hear] the copyrighted work." A "bare possibility" of access isn't enough, nor is a theory of access "based on speculation and conjecture." To withstand summary judgment, then, the plaintiff must present evidence that is "*significantly probative* of a *reasonable opportunity* for access."

Batiste tries to prove access through "widespread dissemination" of his music and a "chain of events" linking his music to the defendants. [W]e have found a work's widespread dissemination in a relevant market in which the defendant took part sufficient to show a "reasonable opportunity for access." [. . .] The evidence required to show widespread dissemination will vary, but courts typically consider "the degree of a work's commercial success and . . . its distribution through radio, television, and other relevant mediums." Simply put, the plaintiff must show that the work has enjoyed considerable success or publicity.

Although Batiste claims that his music was sold nationwide, the record shows meager sales in only a handful of local stores. And he admits that his downloads and streams—which didn't begin until 2013, after the defendants had released all but one of the allegedly infringing songs—have been "sparse." All in all, dissemination of Batiste's music was quite limited.

Batiste's chain-of-events theory fares no better. He claims that Macklemore and Lewis once performed in New Orleans at Siberia Bar, which is "not too far" from a record store that sold his music. Evidence that the defendants were near a store that sold Batiste's records creates only a "bare possibility" of access. [. . .] Macklemore and Lewis might have spent a night in New Orleans in 2011, but they testified that they didn't visit any record stores in town.

On the record before us, no reasonable jury could find more than a bare possibility that the defendants had an opportunity to hear and copy Batiste's music. Thus, Batiste failed to create a genuine dispute on access.

Without proof of access, Batiste's must show "striking similarity" between the defendants' songs and his. To meet that burden, he must point to " 'similarities . . . that can only be explained by copying, rather than by coincidence, independent creation, or prior common source.' " [. . .] Striking similarity isn't "merely a function of the number of identical notes" in two songs. To be "striking," the similarities must "appear in a sufficiently unique or complex context." Evidence of complexity or uniqueness is crucial in cases involving popular music, because most songs "are relatively short and tend to build on or repeat a basic theme."

Batiste doesn't even try to meet the striking-similarity standard. He argues instead that, considering his "overwhelming evidence of access," the district court erred by requiring him to show striking similarity. Given Batiste's refusal to offer any argument on striking similarity, either below or on appeal, this issue is forfeited. Even if Batiste had preserved this issue, though, he offered no admissible evidence of similarities aside from audio recordings of the songs themselves. After carefully listening to each of Batiste's songs and the defendants' song that allegedly infringes it, we conclude that the songs "are in no way similar enough" for a reasonable jury to find striking similarity. Because Batiste can't show access or striking similarity, he can't prove factual copying.

AFFIRMED.

Example: A fan of the Harry Potter books published an "unofficial lexicon" of the fictional facts in the series. J.K. Rowling, the author of the books, had planned to do her own similar lexicon (a derivative work), but she dropped the idea because the unauthorized lexicon would hurt the sales of the one she had planned. The unofficial lexicon was infringement and not fair use. *Warner Bros. Entertainment, Inc. v. RDR Books,* 575 F. Supp. 2d 513 (S.D.N.Y. 2008).

harm to the market for derivative works. The court will want to determine whether the copier's use would replace or preempt the demand for the original.

II. Trademark

Businesspeople often confuse trademark and copyright protection. We have just learned that copyright protects creative expression in a work. **Trademark** law, protect the distinctive identification of goods that indicates the goods come from a particular source. Although we will use the term trademark, the law protects other kinds of distinctive marks. **Service marks**, identify and distinguish the services of a provider

TRADEMARK: Something that is used to identify the source or origin of goods. Some of the things that may be a trademark include words, sounds, symbols, devices, logos, or phrases.

(Google search engine services). **Collective marks** are used by an association to identify products or services or membership in the association (Girl Scout cookies). **Certification marks** are used on goods or services to indicate place of origin, quality, or some other characteristic (Good Housekeeping seal of approval). For purposes of this discussion, "trademark" will imply other kinds of distinctive marks.

Trademark protection can arise from state common law or state statutes. This discussion will focus on federal law. The Lanham Act, also known as the Trademark Act) defines trademarks as any word, name, symbol, or device, or any combination that is:

- used by a merchant or manufacturer,
- to identify and distinguish their goods from those manufactured or sold by others, and
- indicate the source of the goods.

From this definition, it is evident that trademark protects a valuable business interest a company has in the marks related to its goods. But also, it functions as a signal to consumers about the quality of the goods.

Think about the value of trademarks to companies in terms of brands. A company's brand is related to the reputation of its products and services. The trademark is the legal protection of those interests. All trademarks are also brands (but not all brands are trademarks. Trademarked brands are worth billions to companies like Amazon, Apple, and McDonalds.

Trademarks are also important to consumers. When you a choosing a soft drink, the you are likely to have an opion about whether you prefer a Coca Cola to a Pepsi. The trademark has signaled to you something about the quality and taste of the product. The distinctive mark protects you from confusion. This is the standard used when protecting a trademark from infringement. Infringement occurs when a competing product creates in the mind of the consuming public a "likelihood of confusion" regarding the source or origin of goods or services.

The standard is "likelihood of confusion." Actual confusion is not required to show infringement, but infringement will not be found if there is only a vague, theoretical possibility of confusion. Courts will consider many factors, but the overall idea is to determine if a reasonable consumer is likely to be confused.

> Trade name v. Trademarks. A trade name identifies a company. A trademark is connected to a brand: it is an adjective that modifies the generic name for goods or services. "Rolex watch" is a trademark. "Rolex," the name of the company, is a trade name.

In the U.S., almost anything that functions as a trademark can serve as a trademark. Examples can include words, like Apple computers. Strings of words or slogans may also serve as trademarks. When you hear "I'm loving it," it is probably you are thinking of McDonald's restaurant services for which the slogan is a registered mark. Colors, sounds, the shape of a product, and smells can all function as trademarks, as long as the color, sound, shape, or smell is not a part of what makes the product function. So, the distinctive blue of a jewelry package from Tiffany & Co. can be trademarked. Likewise, Twentieth Centry Fox has an official Homer Simpson "D'oh!" trademark for entertainment services. The shape of a Coca Cola bottle functions as a trademark for the company's soft-drink. In 2018, Habro registered the smell its Play-Doh modeling compound.

In order to be legally protected, including nationwide registration with the U.S. Patent and Trademark Office (PTO), the trademark must be distinctive. The more distinctive the trademark, the strong it is and the more likely it can be registered. While some marks may be distinctive when applied to any product, others will only be distinctive in some situations. The different levels of distinctiveness are:

1. **Fanciful.** A fanciful mark is a something the owner of the product or services made up soley for marking purposes. These made up words create inherently distinctive trademarks and get the highest level of protection. Some examples include Google for Internet search engine or Lexus for a luxury automobile. These are fanciful, because the made-up word had no meaning in the English language prior to the trademark attached to the product.

2. **Arbitrary.** Arbitrary marks are also strong and inherently distinctive. These trademarks are real words that are attached to a product or service that is unrelated. Famous arbitrary marks include Amazon for online marketplace, Apple for computer products, and Coach for luxury handbags.

3. **Suggestive.** A suggestive mark calls to mind some aspect or quality of the product, but do not directly describe the quality, requiring customers to use their imagination. These marks are also considered distinctive. Examples include Coppertone which suggests skin color from this sun tanning lotion or Jaguar suggesting a fast automobile.

4. **Descriptive.** A descriptive mark says something directly about the product, or about the function of a product. The trademark, in this case, actually describes the product or service. They are not inherently distinctive because they may not help consumers differentiate among goods from more than one source. Merely descriptive trademarks cannot be immediately registered. A descriptive mark is not regarded as distinctive, unless there is proof of a **secondary meaning**. Secondary meaning requires the trademark holder to prove that in the minds of the consuming public, the product attached to its descriptive mark comes from a unique supplier. Secondary meaning can include market research, media coverage, and customer

SECONDARY MEANING:
A special meaning that attaches to a descriptive mark through use and advertising.

GENERIC MARKS NOT PROTECTED
Abercrombie & Fitch Co. v. Hunting World, Inc.
(Clothing Retailer) v. (Competitor)
537 F.2d 4 (2d Cir. 1999)

INSTANT FACTS:
Abercrombie & Fitch (P) claimed that Hunting World (D) infringed its trademark "Safari."

BLACK LETTER RULE:
In ascending order of the degree of protection given to a mark, the categories of trademarks are generic, descriptive, suggestive, and arbitrary or fanciful.

FACTS:
Abercrombie & Fitch's (A&F) (P) advertised and promoted products identified with its mark "Safari." The mark was used on clothing, hats, and shoes. Hunting World (D) operated a competing store near A&F's (P) main store. Hunting World (D) sold sporting apparel, including hats and shoes. Some of this apparel was identified by the use of the term "Safari" alone, or by expressions such as "Minisafari" and "Safariland."

A&F (P) sued Hunting World for trademark infringement. Hunting World (D) claimed that "safari" is an ordinary, common, descriptive, geographic, and generic word and was not eligible for protection as a trademark. Hunting World (D) asked the court to cancel all of A&F's (P) registrations that used the word "Safari" on the ground that A&F (P) had fraudulently failed to disclose the true nature of the term to the PTO. The district court entered judgment for Hunting World (D), saying that the term "Safari" was merely descriptive. The court also cancelled the registrations of all of A&F's (P) marks that used the word "Safari."

ISSUE:
Was the "Safari" mark merely descriptive?

DECISION AND RATIONALE:
(Friendly, J.) No. In ascending order of the degree of protection given to a mark, the categories of trademarks are generic, descriptive, suggestive, and arbitrary or fanciful. The distinctions between these categories are not always clear. A term that is in one category for a particular product may be in a different one for another. A term may shift categories through different usage through time, because a term may have one meaning to one group of users and a different one to others, or because the same term might be put to different uses for a single product.

A generic term is one that refers, or is understood to refer, to the genus of which the particular product is a species. A generic mark is not entitled to trademark protection. Applied to specific types of clothing, "Safari" has become a generic term. "Minisafari" may be used for a smaller brim hat. "Safari" has not become a generic term for boots or shoes. It is either "suggestive" or "merely descriptive." It is a valid trademark even if "merely descriptive" since it has become incontestable under the trademark laws. The trial court's cancellation of the "Safari" marks for some clothing is upheld. The remainder of the court's judgment is reversed.

ANALYSIS:
This case, which dates from the years A&F (P) was primarily a retailer of high-end outdoors equipment. It is the leading case that sets out the hierarchy of trademarks: generic, descriptive, suggestive, arbitrary, and fanciful. That hierarchy is commonly referred to as the "Abercrombie & Fitch hierarchy."

feedback. There are many descriptive marks, all needed substantial marketing to establish secondary meaning. Examples of distinctive marks with secondary meaning include: Cran-Apple for cranberry apple juice from Ocean Spray or "I'm lovin' it" for McDonald's restaurant services.

5. **Generic.** A generic term cannot be registered or used as a trademark. It is the actual noun that describes a product or category of products. Since trademarks are distinctive adjectives that describe goods, generics can never be trademarked.

> A generic mark may have started out as a distinctive trademark, but became generic. A mark becomes generic when it comes to stand for the category of the product itself in the minds of consumers. Yo-yo and zipper were trademarks for toys and fasteners, but through misuse of the trademarks as nouns, they became generic. Companies must police their marks to ensure their trademarks don't become generic.

Other Distinctive Marks

Other distinctive marks that indicate source sponsorship or affiliation may also be protected under trademark law.

A trademark is a signal a manufacturer or merchant uses to identify the source or origin of goods. If a business is a seller or supplier of services, it would use a **service mark**. A service mark is a mark that identifies the source or origin of services.

Service marks are subject to the same rules for registration and distinctiveness as trademarks.

Other distinctive marks can also be valuable business assets that have a consumer function, as well. **Certification marks** are used to show compliance with a set of standards, that the goods come from a region known for quality (Idaho potatoes) or meet certain quality standards (Good Housekeeping Seal of Approval for products passing rigorous testing standards). It may also indicate the product was produced under certain conditions (Fair Trade coffee, or Certified Organic products). Typically certification marks are owned by trade associations or

CERTIFICATION MARK:
A type of trademark whereby a third party certifies some characteristic of a product, such as the place of origin, method of manufacture, quality, or material.

COLLECTIVE MARK:
A type of trademark that shows membership in a group, or that identifies the goods or services offered by the members of the group.

INCONTESTABLE:
A trademark that is immune from legal challenge to its validity.

> *Example:* Sovann runs a catering business. Although it is merely descriptive, "Cuisine by Sovann," could be registered as a service mark if it acquires secondary meaning for catering services. He capitalizes on the popularity of his business by selling a line of cookware, "Cuisine by Sovann." As used for the cookware, the name could also be registered as a trademark.

centralized commercial groups. They can be a valuable signal to customers about the quality of the goods.

Collective marks are another kind of trademark that are owned by members of an association, union, or other collective. For example, the letters AAA inside an oval indicate membership in the American Automobile Association. "Girl Scouts" is also a collective trademark that can only be used by members of that group.

> When reading or discussing trademark law, the term "trademark" can almost always be understood to mean "trademark or service mark."

Trade Dress

Trade dress is a broad category of trademarks. Rather than being a sign or symbol related to the product, trade dress is product design, trade dress applies to things that are to words or images. Sounds, colors, smells, and the look and feel of the product are trade dress if it indicates the source of the goods. Trade dress can include the design or configuration of a product (like Pepperidge Farm's crackers in the shape of a goldfish with a smile and eye); color (Tiffany & Co.'s distinctive blue box); product packaging (shape of the Coca-Cola bottle), or distinctive décor (Dunkin' Donuts, orange and pink interior design).

A product's trade dress may be registered, just as a trademark is registered. In order to be registered, trade dress must be distinctive. Except for product packaging, most trade dress is not inherently distinctive. This is true even though the design is very unusual, as a cocktail shaker shaped like a penguin. In order to be protected, the applicant for registration will have to show that the dress has a secondary meaning associating it with a product. Consumers must be able to identify a product by the trade dress.

Functional aspects of a product design may not be registered because the functional aspects are not distinctive. In this context, functional means that a feature is essential to the use or purpose of the product, or if it affects the cost or quality of the article. The elements claimed to make up trade dress must be purely ornamental and used to identify the product and its source.

> Functional parts of a product could be protected by utility patents.

Although trade dress may be registered with the PTO, and acquire the same protection as a trademark, registration is not necessary for legal protection of a design. A suit may be brought against a person who copies a design

Example: A bakery claimed that its design of a small apple pie was trade dress. The court held that a single piece of dough folded around fruit filling was functional, and not trade dress. *Sweet Street Desserts, Inc., v. Chudleigh's Ltd.*, 119 U.S.P.Q. 2d 1641 (3d Cir. 2016).

or packaging. The suit would be brought on the grounds that the copying is likely to cause confusion among consumers.

Trademark Use and Registration

The U.S. has a complex web of state and federal trademark laws. In some states, the common law will protect your mark. Others have statewide registration systems, in addition to the common law.

Trademarks can be either federal or state matters. Every state has its own trademark law. Most of these laws are similar to the federal trademark law, but as with trade secrets, any action to enforce a state-granted trademark

---

FIRST AMENDMENT MAY DEFEAT TRADEMARK CLAIMS
Mattel, Inc. v. Walking Mountain Productions
(Toy Company) v. (Artist)
353 F.3d 792 (9th Cir. 2003)

INSTANT FACTS:
Walking Mountain (D) sold photographs of a toy made by Mattel (P) in unusual situations, and Mattel (P) claimed trademark infringement.

BLACK LETTER RULE:
First Amendment concerns trump a trademark owner's right to control public discourse a mark has a meaning beyond its source-identifying function.

FACTS:
Walking Mountain (D) developed a series of 78 photographs that depicted Barbie dolls manufactured by Mattel (P) in various absurd and often sexualized positions. The word "Barbie" was used in some of the titles of the works. The photographs generally showed one or more nude Barbie dolls juxtaposed with vintage kitchen appliances. Walking Mountain (D) said that the photographs were an attempt to "critique [ ] the objectification of women associated with [Barbie], and [ ][to] lambast [ ] the conventional beauty myth and the societal acceptance of women as objects because this is what Barbie embodies." Mattel (P) claimed trademark infringement. The district court entered judgment for Walking Mountain (D).

ISSUE:
Was the use of the Barbie dolls in the photographs trademark infringement?

DECISION AND RATIONALE:
(Pregerson, J.) No. First Amendment concerns trump a trademark owner's right to control public discourse a mark has a meaning beyond its source-identifying function. The purpose of trademark protection is to avoid confusion in marketplace, so consumers are not duped into buying a product they mistakenly believe is sponsored by a trademark owner. Walking Mountain's (D) use Mattel's (D) mark was relevant to Walking Mountain's (D) artistic work, and Walking Mountain (D) did not explicitly mislead as to Mattel's (P) sponsorship of the work. The public interest in free and artistic expression greatly outweighed Mattel's (P) concerns about potential consumer confusion.

Walking Mountain's (D) use of Mattel's (P) trade dress in parody photographs was noninfringing, nominative fair use. The trade dress was a necessary point of reference for Walking Mountain's (D) work, and only so much of the trade dress as was reasonably necessary was use. There was nothing to suggest Mattel's (P) sponsorship of the work. Affirmed.

ANALYSIS:
The irony of this case is that Mattel (P) may have been too successful with its mark. "Barbie" or "Barbie doll" has become such a common term that a reminder of its original product-identifying function is necessary.

must be brought in state court. The authority to enforce orders or judgment in a state court trademark infringement action stops at the state's borders.

A trademark registered with the PTO receives nationwide protection. Actions to enforce or protect a federal trademark are brought in federal court. Although federal registration of a trademark is often more complex than state registration, it may be worth the trouble to get nationwide protection for a trademark.

In order to receive nation-wide protection under federal law, registration is required. Since trademark law identifies the source of goods or services, all of these laws require that the mark be used in commerce before it receives legal protection.

The Lanham Act governs trademark protection at the national level. Before the mark can be registered, the business must use it on the goods or services in interstate commerce, an application for registration, it is necessary that the goods or services.

Before registering, or even using, a trademark it is a good idea to conduct a search. The search will tell you if anyone else is using the same, or similar, mark. This is a necessary first step for both legal and business reasons. From the legal standpoint, the U.S. Patent and Trademark Office will not register your mark if it is already being used on a similar product or if it is too similar to another mark. Businesses typically hire law firms or trademark search services to help them to make sure the trademark isn't already taken at the state or national level. If the same or a confusingly similar mark is already in use, not only is your mark not registrable, but you could be liable for infringement. From a business standpoint, it only makes sense that you would want to avoid using a mark that is too similar to one used by someone else.

If you are satisfied that the mark you want to use is not in use, the next step is to start using the mark. Make note of the date the mark was first used in commerce. At this point, it is a good idea to use "TM" or "SM" after the mark to indicate use of the name as a trademark or service mark. The mark should be attached to the goods being provided. If you are registering a service mark, the mark should appear in any promotional or advertising materials.

> An "intent to use" registration (ITU) is an exception to the requirement that the mark must be used in commerce prior to registration. Businesses spend a great deal of time and money developing effective brands. The ITU registration allows the business to "hold" a trademark for a specific category of product if you have a *bona fide* intent to use it in the next three to four years.

The next step is to submit your application to the PTO, along with the filing fee. The application must include a drawing of the mark and a specimen of how the mark is being used. For example, Nike would have submitted a drawing of its swoosh design as well as a photograph of the swoosh on athletic shoes or clothing. The specimen is not just a drawing or diagram. For services, the specimen would show the mark in advertisements or promotional materials.

> The filing fee is not refunded if registration is denied.

Once the application is submitted, it is first reviewed to make sure all of the requirements for an application are met (that is, all of the spaces on the application are filled in and the filing fee has been paid). If the minimum filing requirements are met, the application is assigned a serial number and forwarded to an examiner. The examiner reviews the application to decide if the mark meets the substantive legal standards for registering a trademark. The review may take several months to complete. If the examiner decides that the mark should not be registered, the PTO issues an **office action** explaining the reasons for refusal. The office action gives the applicant a chance to respond, and possibly fix any deficiencies. The person applying for the trademark must respond to the office action within six months. If she does not, the application is declared abandoned.

If the refusal is based on technical requirements in the application, the PTO may informally advise the applicant of what she needs to do in order to bring the application up to the proper standards. An application may, however, be denied on substantive grounds. Substantive grounds for denying registration include:

- Likelihood of confusion. The examiner does a search of existing trademarks and applications for registration to decide whether the marks are similar, and to related goods or services. The similarity could be visual, or it could be that the words in a mark sound alike. A mark does not have to be identical to another one for the registration to be refused.

- Merely descriptive. A mark that is merely descriptive just tells about some aspect of the product. A descriptive mark could still be registered if the applicant proves that a secondary meaning has been attached to the mark. This would require submitting marketing and other data to indicate that in the minds of the consuming public, the descriptive mark means goods from the applicant.

- Deceptively misdescriptive. This is a descriptive mark that is false. The quality or characteristic it describes is not associated with the product. For example, selling costume jewelery under the name "Real Gems" is deceptively misdescriptive because it falsely states a quality the goods do not have.

- Geographically descriptive or geographically deceptively misdescriptive. A geographically descriptive mark has no significance as anything other than a geographic location. It is like a merely descriptive mark in that it is accurate. For example, "California Cheese" for cheese that comes from California, cannot be registered (unless it has acquired secondary meaning). A geographi-

OFFICE ACTION:
An examiner's communication with the applicant for a patent, usually giving reasons why the application is denied.

cally deceptively misdescriptive mark would falsely indicate the product's geographic origin. For example, "California Cheese" produced in Iowa would be deceptive. There are many exceptions to these rules, particularly in areas know for certain products. It is best to consult with a lawyer before using a geographic trademark.

- Surname. Typically, a family name cannot be registered as a trademark without proof of a secondary meaning that the public associates the name with the product. This has allowed names like McDonald's and Ford to be registered.

- Ornamentation. Decoration on a product that does not serve to identify the product does not qualify as a trademark.

If the examiner does not object to the application, or if the objections are corrected, the mark is approved for publication in the "Official Gazette," a weekly publication of the PTO. After publication, anyone who believes he may be damaged by the registration of the mark may file an opposition. An opposition will result in a hearing before the Trademark Trial and Appeal Board.

If there is no opposition filed, or the opposition is unsuccessful, the mark is registered, the applicant receives a certificate of registration and can use the ® in connection with their registered trademark. The registration is for ten years, and may be renewed for an unlimited number of additional ten-year periods as long as the mark continues to be used and does not become generic. In theory, a properly registered and renewed trademark could last forever, if the holder wanted to continue to use it commercially.

> Trademarks do not come from the same constitutional authority as copyrights and patents, so there is no requirement that they have a limited term.

Dilution

In the late 19th century, amateur photography was a newly-popular hobby. The hobby was dominated by the Eastman Kodak Company's products. Kodak sold almost all of the film and cameras on the market, so in all likelihood, a family photograph was taken with a Kodak camera, using Kodak film.

Kodak built goodwill and customer loyalty through its branded products. In 1897, an enterprising bicycle manufacturer decided to take advantage of that goodwill. He started making and selling "Kodak Bicycles." Since Eastman Kodak was not in the bicycle business, it was thought that this would not infringe on their trademark because there was no likelihood consumers would be confused that Eastman Kodak was the source of the bicycles. The use did not infringe, but diluted the distinctiveness of Eastman Kodak's trademarks. The court issued an injunction against making or selling Kodak Bicycles.

Trademark dilution is not infringement. The Lanham Act provides federal protection for famous marks from dilution. Trademark infringement and dilution are different. Infringement

> **Example:** A seafood wholesaler's use of the slogan "The Other Red Meat" to describe its salmon was held likely to dilute the slogan "The Other White Meat," used to describe pork. *National Pork Board v. Supreme Lobster & Seafood Co.*, 96 U.S.P.Q. 2d 1479 (T.T.A.B. 2010).

occurs when someone's use of a mark on similar goods is likely to cause consumer confusion. Dilution occurs as in the Eastman Kodak example, when someone uses the mark on noncompeting goods which can decrease the association between the goods or services and the famous mark.

> A "famous" mark is one that is widely recognized by the consuming public.

There are two kinds of dilution.

- Dilution that blurs or weakens the connection made in consumer's mind between the famous mark and the products or services it identifies. Blurring occurs because the use by another party will erode the selling power of the original mark.

- Dilution by tarnishment occurs when the famous mark is used in connection with inferior products, or by using it in an unwholesome or unsavory manner, such as in connection with sex or illegal drugs. Tarnishment hurts the owner's reputation.

A mark may dilute another even if it is not identical or substantially similar to the famous mark. The two marks must only be sufficiently similar that consumers "conjure up" the famous mark when they see the second mark.

Injunctions are typically the only relief granted in dilution cases.

Protecting Trademarks

Once a trademark is issued, it is up to the owner of the mark to protect it. The PTO is not an enforcement agency, so it is up to the trademark owner to enforce her rights in the mark. Trademark protection is an ongoing job. It must be done continuously and consistently.

> **Example:** "Band-Aid" is a registered trademark. The advertising and promotional material for the product always refers to "Band-Aid Brand Adhesive Bandages."

> **Example:** Many companies advertise to remind consumers and competitors not to misuse their trademarks. Xerox Corporation did this effectively, including an advertisement featuring a zipper. At one time, Zipper was a powerful trademark for a clothing fastener that became generic through misuse.

SAYING THE NAME OF A TRADEMARK IS NOT INFRINGEMENT

New Kids on the Block v. News America Publishing, Inc.
(Boy Band) v. (Newspaper Publisher)
971 F.2d 302 (9th Cir. 1992)

INSTANT FACTS:
New Kids on the Block (NKB) (P) alleged that a newspaper's poll on the popularity of NKB (P) violated their trademark.

BLACK LETTER RULE:
Trademark fair use prevents a trademark owner from taking a descriptive term for exclusive use and preventing others from accurately describing the characteristics of the owner's product.

FACTS:
The New Kids on the Block (NKB) (P) were a popular musical group in the early 1990s. News America (D), the proprietor of two newspapers of national circulation, conducted separate polls of their readers. The polls sought an answer to a pressing question: Which one of the New Kids (P) was the most popular? NKB (P) claimed that the newspaper poll infringed on their trademark. The district court entered judgment for News America (D).

ISSUE:
Did the newspaper poll infringe on NKB's (P) trademark?

DECISION AND RATIONALE:
(Kozinski, J.) No. Trademark fair use prevents a trademark owner from taking a descriptive term for exclusive use and preventing others from accurately describing the characteristics of the owner's product. When someone other than the owner uses a trademark to describe the product of the owner, rather than the user's, the user is entitled to nominative fair use defense. In order for the defense to apply, the product or service in question must be one that is not really identifiable without the use of trademark, and only so much of the mark as is reasonably necessary to identify the product is used. There can be nothing to suggest sponsorship or endorsement by trademark holder.

There was nothing false or misleading about News America's (D) use of NKB's (P) mark. News America (D) referred to the trademark only as needed to identify the NKB (P) as the subject of the polls. Nothing suggested joint sponsorship or endorsement by the NKB (P). News America (D) was entitled to the nominative fair use defense to the infringement action. Affirmed.

ANALYSIS:
It is difficult to speak of popular entertainers without using their trademarks. In this case, the court noted that NKB's (P) trademark was on more than 500 products or services. The court referred to the situation as a "multi-media publicity blitzkrieg."

The first step in protecting a trademark is to use it, and use it properly. A trademark registration will be cancelled if the mark does not continue to be used in commerce. Proper use includes spelling it properly, if it is a word, and always using the racol (®) next to the mark if it is registered. A trademark is an identifier, so it should always be used as an adjective modifying a generic noun. The mark describes the thing. It is not the thing itself. Therefore, "Rollerblade® inline skates" is a proper trademark use, whereas "Rollerblade" is not.

Trademark owners must police their marks for misuse by third parties. When inline skates were first introduced to the market, the company that owned the Rollerblade trademark carefully policed its mark by sending cease and desist letters to anyone misusing their brand as a noun. If they had not done so, "Rollerblade" could have become a generic. A trademark may be lost if third parties are allowed to use it improperly, so continuous monitoring is essential.

It can become necessary to sue those infringing your trademark. A lawsuit to protect a trademark may be brought against a defendant who is acting in a way that is "likely to cause confusion, or to cause mistake, regarding the source, affiliation, connection, or sponsorship" of goods or services. This rule is generally expressed by the shorter term "likelihood of confusion."

Fair Use

Fair use is a defense to a trademark infringement action. Trademark fair use lets a person use someone else's mark in some circumstances without liability. Trademark fair use works differently than fair use in a copyright infringement action, largely because trademarks and copyrights protect different interests.

> Most writing on the subject uses the full term "trademark fair use," to distinguish it from the more familiar type of fair use in copyright cases.

There are two types of trademark fair use. The first is "classic," or descriptive, fair use. Classic fair use is found when a descriptive trademark is used to describe the goods or services of another. The use must be done in good faith. Classic fair use protects the use of common meanings of ordinary words.

The other type of trademark fair use is "nominative" fair use. Nominative fair use is when a trademark is used to refer to the goods or services of the trademark owner. The Pepsi Challenge, a famous marketing campaign of the 1970s, is a prime example of nominative fair use. In that campaign, Pepsi set up blind taste tests between Pepsi and Coke around the country. This kind of comparative advertising is nominative fair use. Nominative fair use cannot imply any endorsement or sponsorship by the trademark holder. The use must be accurate, and not misleading. There must be no easier way to refer to the owner of the products. No more of the trademark than is necessary to identify the owner may be used (for example, a name may be used, but probably not a logo). The use must not create a likelihood of confusion.

Example: The defendant in a trademark infringement case used the phrase "all in ONE" on a catalog. The plaintiff company had separately registered "ALL-IN-ONE" as a trademark. The court held that there was no infringement because the phrase was used for its descriptive, everyday meaning, and not to identify the source or origin of goods. *Marketquest Group, Inc. v. Bic Corp.*, 2015 WL 1757766 (S.D. Cal. 2015).

Example: Toni operates an auto repair shop. On her webpage, she includes the statement that "We specialize in servicing late-model Volkswagens." There is no Volkswagen logo on the page, and Toni does not say that she is an "official" Volkswagen repair shop. Toni's use of the mark "Volkswagen" is nominative fair use.

III. Patents

Patents have a long and important history in the United States. The same clause in the Constitution that granted Congress the power to protect authors with copyright also gave Congress the power to protect inventors by establishing patents. Patents are one way to protect inventions. Only the federal government may issue patents.

A patent is a government-granted form of intellectual property that give the patent holder powerful exclusive rights to prevent anyone from making, using, selling, or importing a product that infringes that patent. In exchange for those monopoly like rights, the inventor discloses the invention, and how it works, to the public.

> U.S. Patent number 1 was issued in 1790 to Samuel Hopkins of Philadelphia. His invention was a process for making potash, an ingredient of fertilizer.

There are three kinds of patents: utility patents, design patents, and plant patents.

Utility Patents

A utility patent is the most common type of patent. According to the PTO, 90% of all patent applications are applications for a utility patent.

Utility patents probably are what most people think of when they hear the word "patent."

Utility patents are issued for new inventions. The patent grants the holder the sole right to manufacture and sell the invention. The invention may be for a:

- New machine or manufactured device,
- Non-obvious improvement of an existing invention,
- Composition of matter, such as a new medication,
- Synthetic genetic sequence, or
- Methods.

> Amazon.com's "1 Click" ordering system is a good example of a patented business method.

Utility patents apply to the use or function of an invention. The appearance or decoration would be covered by a design patent.

> U.S. Patent 5443036A, now expired, was granted for the use of laser pointers to exercise cats.

Example: Cayden receives a patent for a new type of juice extractor that has three speeds: high, medium, and low. Liam buys an extractor, and modifies it so that it has four speeds: high, medium high, medium low, and low. Liam cannot get a patent on his modified extractor because it is an obvious modification.

ABSTRACT IDEAS MAY NOT BE PATENTED

O'Reilly v. Morse
(Inventor) v. (Inventor of the Telegraph)
56 U.S. 62, 15 How. 62, 14 L. Ed. 601 (1854)

INSTANT FACTS:
Morse (P) received patents for his invention of the telegraph, and also received a patent on any method of transmitting messages electronically.

BLACK LETTER RULE:
Abstract ideas are not eligible for patent protection.

FACTS:
Morse (P) received patents for his invention of the telegraph. One of his claims was not limited to "specific machinery or parts of machinery." Instead, the claim was for "[t]he use of the motive power of the electric or galvanic current, which I call electro-magnetism, however developed for marking or printing intelligible characters, signs, or letters, at any distances." O'Reilly (D) claimed that this claim was too broad. The trial court agreed.

ISSUE:
Was Morse's (P) claim too broad?

DECISION AND RATIONALE:
(Taney, C.J.) Yes. Abstract ideas are not eligible for patent protection. Morse (P) did not discover that the electric or galvanic current will always print at a distance, no matter what may be the form of the machinery or mechanical contrivances through which it passes. Other persons may discover and disclose to the public other ways to use electromagnetic force to transmit messages. These other ways may be cheaper or work better. In effect, Morse (P) claims an exclusive right to use a manner and process which he has not described and that he has not invented. His claim is too broad, and not warranted by law. Affirmed.

ANALYSIS:
A patent is granted only for an invention that implements an idea. The general idea furthered by an invention, no matter how novel, does not receive protection. It should be noted that there were several other inventors who claimed to have invented telegraphy at around the same time, but the courts upheld Morse's (P) claim to be first.

Patent protection is not automatic. An application must be approved after it is examined. The application will be extensively examined at the PTO to ensure the invention meets the legal qualifications for a patent. If it does, the patent will be granted. Once the patent it granted, a third party can challenge the grant in a trial like procedure at the PTO. The term of a utility patent is generally twenty years from the date the patent is filed. Once the term expires, the invention enters the public domain, and public is free to use the invention without the permission of the inventor.

Not everything is patentable. The PTO will not grant patents in laws of nature or scientific principles, physical phenomena, or abstract ideas. The 2011 update of U.S. patent law, the America Invents Act (AIA), also specifically excluded the patenting of human organisms, although that had never been allowed in practice.

Federal law requires all patents to be novel, useful, and provide a non-obvious improvement over previous inventions.

Novelty means that the invention has not been patented anywhere in the world, described in a

> **Example:** Rob invents a hat that is equipped with small propellers that spin when the wearer blinks. His invention is useful, for patent application purposes. His friend Teresa designs a perpetual motion machine that is supposed to power respirators. Her "invention" is not useful, because it cannot work.

printed publication, in public use, on sale, available to the public, or described in another patent application. This means that prior to applying for the patent, the inventor must treat the invention as a trade secret, or will be refused the patent.

Useful is another way of saying that the invention will actually function, and is not just a hypothetical idea. The technical term for this is utility, meaning that the invention is "susceptible to industrial application." The bar for an invention being "useful" is a low one. "Useful" is just a requirement that the must produce some identifiable benefit, and be capable of use.

Non-Obvious means that the claimed invention would not have been obvious to a person with ordinary skill in the general field of the invention. Trivial or obvious modifications to prior inventions will not be enough for a patent grant.

Design Patents

Design patents are granted for novel, original, and purely ornamental elements of a manufactured article, not the article itself. A design patent protects how the invention looks. It grants the patent holder the exclusive right to exclude others from making, using, or selling that design for a term of fourteen or fifteen years, depending on whether the application was filed before or after May 13, 2015.

The design must be purely ornamental. If the design is somehow essential to how the product works or operates, it is functional and cannot be protected by a design patent. This means that the design cannot be dictated by the function of the article. The design of a chair, for example, may be patented, but only if the design does not add a new function.

Plant Patents

A plant patent is granted to a person who has invented or discovered and asexually reproduced a new variety of plant. The new plant cannot be a tuber (such as a potato), or a plant that can be found in an uncultivated state. If the plant were "discovered," it must have been discovered in a cultivated area.

The term "plant" for purposes of patent law is given its ordinary meaning. There are limitations on what plants are eligible for a plant patent:

- A patent may be grated for a living plant organism that has a single, genetic makeup or genotype, and which can only be duplicated through asexual reproduction.

> **Example:** Until a 2013 Supreme Court decision, portions of naturally occurring DNA could be patented. Myriad Genetics developed a process for identifying breast cancer genes based on isolated DNA material. The Court focused on the fact that the DNA occurred naturally, and held that just isolating a portion of DNA does not make that portion patentable. As a result of this decision, synthetic DNA is still patentable, but human DNA is not. *Association for Molecular Pathology v. Myriad Genetics, Inc.*, 569 U.S. 576 (2013).

- Sports (a part of a plant, such as a bud or branch, that has a different form or structure from the rest of the plant), mutants, or hybrids are eligible.

- Algae and large (macro) fungi are patentable as plants, but bacteria are not.

> Asexual plant reproduction is reproduction without fertilization, such as by cuttings. The new plant is genetically identical to the original patented plant.

The purpose of asexual reproduction is to show that uniformity and stability of the plant, and that it retains the distinguishing characteristics of the original invented or discovered plant. The plant patent allows its holder to prevent others from asexually reproducing, selling, offering for sale, or importing the plant into the U.S. for a period of twenty years.

A plant patent will only be granted if the invented or discovered plant meets the basis requirement that the plant be novel, non-obvious, and useful (that is, it must actually exist). Seeds, genes, and other newly invented elements of plant life may be patented, but the patent applied for would be a utility patent.

PATENT EXHAUSTION DOES NOT ALLOW COPYING
Bowman v. Monsanto Co.
(Farmer) v. (Seed Maker)
569 U.S. 278, 133 S. Ct. 1761, 185 L. Ed. 2d 931 (2013)

INSTANT FACTS: Bowman (D) planted the progeny of soybeans grown from Monsanto's (P) patented seeds without permission.

BLACK LETTER RULE: The doctrine of patent exhaustion says that the purchaser of a patented article is entitled to use or resell that article, but not to make copies of it.

FACTS: Monsanto (P) invented and patented soybean seeds that were genetically altered to allow them to survive exposure to a certain herbicide. The seeds were sold subject to a licensing agreement that permitted farmers to plant the seed in one, and only one, growing season. Farmers may not save any of the harvested soybeans for replanting. Bowman (D) purchased soybeans intended for consumption from a grain elevator, planted them and treated them plants with herbicide. The plants without Monsanto's (P) genetic alteration died. Bowman (D) harvested the resulting soybeans that contained the alteration and saved some of these harvested seeds to use in the next season. Monsanto (P) sued Bowman (D) for patent infringement. Bowman raised the defense of patent exhaustion. The court entered judgment for Monsanto (P).

ISSUE:
Was Bowman's (D) planting of the soybeans protected by patent exhaustion?

DECISION AND RATIONALE:
(Kagan, J.) No. The doctrine of patent exhaustion says that the purchaser of a patented article is entitled to use or resell that article, but not to make copies of it. The doctrine restricts a patent holder's rights only as to the particular article" It does not affect the patent holder's ability to prevent a buyer from making new copies of the patented item. If the purchaser of that article could make and sell endless copies, the patent would effectively protect the invention for just a single sale. The exhaustion doctrine does not enable Bowman (D) to make additional patented soybeans without Monsanto's (P) permission, either express or implied. Affirmed.

ANALYSIS:
The Court was careful to note that its opinion applied only to the particular situation before it. Justice Kagan noted that self-replicating products "are becoming ever more prevalent, complex, and diverse." How patent exhaustion would apply to such an invention is not addressed in this opinion.

Securing a Patent

A patent is issued after an application is submitted by the inventor or someone to whom the invention has been assigned. The application must then be approved by the Patent and Trademark Office. The application process can be both complicated and time consuming.

The first step in applying for a patent is to do a patent search. Remember that patents are granted only for new inventions. A search is done to make sure that an invention is in fact novel. If an invention has already been disclosed to the public, it is not considered. A patent search should include foreign patents and technical literature, as well as existing patents and applications. A search done before an application is submitted will not be conclusive, because the PTO does its own search. It should, however, give the inventor a better idea as to whether someone else has come up with the same invention.

> While it is possible for an inventor to do her own patent search, the PTO recommends using an attorney or agent to do the search.

Once the search is completed, the application for a patent is submitted. The application consists of three parts: the written application, the claim, and the fee. The written application contains three parts:

1. The specification. A specification is a written description of the invention, and of the manner and process for manufacturing it. The specification has to be clear enough that a person with ordinary skill in the field that the invention is to work in could make and use it.

2. A drawing. The drawing must be clear enough to show how the invention will work.

3. The oath or declaration. The oath states that the inventor swears that he "believes himself to be the original and first inventor of the process, machine, manufacture, or composition of matter, or improvement thereof, for which he solicits a patent; and shall state of what country he is a citizen."

The claim is the inventor's statement of what is new or original about the invention. It sets the boundaries for what the patent does, and does not, cover. If a patent is issued, the patent protection will extend only to what is set out in the claim. A utility patent application may contain multiple claims, but plant and design patents usually contain only one.

The fee for filing a patent is in addition to the fee for the search and examination done by the PTO.

After a complete application is submitted, it is referred to a PTO examiner. The examiner reviews the application to see if the invention meets the requirements for being patented. If the examiner decides that the invention does not meet the requirements for a patentable invention, she will explain her reasons. The inventor may either correct the application, or try to convince the examiner to change her mind. If the examiner does not change her mind, or corrections to the application are not made, the application is rejected. The inventor has the right to appeal.

If the application is granted, a patent is issued. The AIA added a new procedure called Post Grant Review. This is a trial like proceeding in the PTO where third parties can challenge patent within nine months of the grant. A utility patent or plant patent is good for 20 years after the date the application was filed (not the date the patent was issued). The inventor or owner of the patent must pay maintenance fees. A fee is paid 3 ½ years, 7 ½ years, and 11 ½ years after issuance. If the fee is not paid, the patent is abandoned and no longer exists for the invention. Many patents are abandoned because the maintenance fee costs more than the value of the invention.

IV. Trade Secrets

Trade secrets are another form of intellectual property. They differ from copyrights, patents, and trademarks in that their value come from the fact that the information is secret. Trade secrets can be extremely valuable. For example, Coca-Cola made the choice to protect its recipe as a trade secret, rather than patent, since the latter would require them to disclose their ingredients and how to make their product. While patents only last for twenty years, trade secret protection will last as long as they can be kept secret. Google's search algorithm and the New York Time's definition of "best seller" are other examples of valuable trade secrets.

Trade secret protection developed in the United States as a common law tort, from a first case decided in the early 1830s. This meant that the level of protection for secret commercial information varied from state to state. In an effort to achieve nationwide uniformity in trade secret laws, a group called the Uniform Law Commission proposed model legislation, the Uniform Trade Secret Act (UTSA). Its purpose was to help the national business environment by creating standards for protecting commercially valuable information. Today, forty-eight states and the District of Columbia have adopted a version of the UTSA. New York and North Carolina have not adopted the UTSA. Protecting trade secrets had to be done on a state-by-state basis. That changed in May of 2016 when the Defend Trade Secrets Act (DTSA) was signed into law. The DSTA articulated three goals:

- To provide a federal civil remedy for trade secret owners, so that they could enforce their rights in federal courts in the same way that copyright, patent, and trademark owners could;

- To promote uniformity in trade secret law with a national standard with clear rules and predictability; and

- To better address concerns of "a globalized and national economy," since trade secret could be easily taken out of a state jurisdiction.

The DTSA was extremely popular legislation. It passed unanimously in the Senate and only two representatives voted against it in the House. This is a testament to the perceived importance of trade secrets to our nation's economy.

There are three requirements to receiving protection under either the DTSA or the UTSA. Trade secrets are:

- Information. A wide range of information can receive protection, including formulas, patterns, compilations, programs devices, techniques, processes. The DTSA goes on to explain that "all forms and types pf financial, business, scientific, technical, economic or technical information" is protected, regardless of the form of the information.

- Independently valuable. The information must have **independent economic value**, that is **actual** or **potential** because it is not generally known or not easy to figure out through proper means.

- A secret. The owner must take **reasonable measures** to keep the information secret.

The value of a trade secret is the actual or potential competitive advantage that comes from knowing the information. If it is not known to

> *Example:* The marketing department of a car company takes several weeks to prepare a report on highway miles driven by residents of each state. The report will be used to target advertising and marketing of cars, and will also be used to design new vehicles. The report is just a list of facts, so it cannot be copyrighted. It cannot be trademarked, because it is not being used to identify the source or origin of goods or services. It cannot be patented, because it is not an invention. But if it is kept secret at the company, and the report contains more than publicly available information, then the report could be a trade secret that provides a competitive advantage.

> **CAREERS IN LAW**
>
> Intellectual property is big business. It accounts for over 70% of business assets in the United States. As a result, intellectual property is a great place to look for career options. Intellectual property analysts determine ways to maximize profit from a given patent, copyright, or trademark. They may find new markets for an idea, or discover new ways to use, sell, or license intellectual property. Intellectual property managers help maintain and enforce existing assets. They ensure that intellectual property ownership is clear and help stop infringement and piracy. Intellectual property paralegals and legal assistants are highly specialized paraprofessionals who work exclusively with patent law firms or attorneys specializing in intellectual property. These individuals work directly with attorneys who are filing, enforcing, and litigating intellectual property issues.

others, then they obviously cannot use it. If a competitor would have to pay money to find or develop the information, it has economic value.

There is no limit on how long a trade secret can last. It may be a secret permanently. It may be revealed to the public at some time, such as when a patent for the invention is filed. When a trade secret is revealed to the public, of course, it stops being a trade secret.

Protecting Trade Secrets

For information to be a legally protected trade secret, it is not enough that it not be generally known. The information must also be subject to reasonable efforts to maintain the secrecy. What constitutes reasonable efforts is not always clear, but in general, the more valuable the trade secret, the more robust secrecy measure must be. Some industries have security standards. Complying with those standards will be reasonable efforts. These efforts can include non-disclosure agreements or strictly limiting the people who have access to the information.

> In 2011, the only acknowledged copy of the recipe for Coca Cola was moved to a secure vault at the company's headquarters in Atlanta.

Nondisclosure or confidentiality agreements with employees and licensees are a common means of protecting trade secrets. Because employees have a legal duty to keep confidential information secret, even after their employment ends, it may be sufficient to inform employees that they are not to disclose anything that goes on in the workplace.

However, confidentiality agreements with employees provide additional assurances that an employee understands their obligations and have notice of their responsibilities. It is especially important that these agreements set out clearly which information, or what types of information, will be considered secret. There are other ways to protect trade secrets. Other actions might be considered as reasonable, including placing "Proprietary and Confidential" on documents or presentations, keeping secrets in locked files or encrypted on-line files, restricting access to secret information to only those with a need to know, or restricting access to areas in which the trade secrets are

> *Example:* A restaurant has a signature cocktail that it advertises heavily as its own special creation. Whenever the restaurant hires a new bartender, she is told that one of the conditions of her employment is that she never reveal the recipe for the cocktail. Whether this is a reasonable effort to maintain the secret is a question of fact for the court to decide.

used. Confidentiality agreements should also be obtained from non-employees who may be exposed to confidential information.

Improper use of a trade secret is called **misappropriation**. If a trade secret is improperly revealed, litigation may be necessary. Generally, the goal of trade secret litigation is to prevent or minimize further disclosure of the secret.

V. International Protection

Intellectual property is vital to the wealth of many nations. Since the late nineteenth century, countries have worked to create minimum levels of protection for intellectual property.

International coordination of intellectual property is governed by a series of treaties, or **conventions**. These conventions offer certain advantages to the owners of intellectual property in member nations. In order to allow the owners to get these advantages, the intellectual property laws of member nations must meet certain requirements. There are three principal conventions that relate to intellectual property:

- The Berne Convention for the Protection of Literary and Artistic Works, which governs copyright,
- The Paris Convention for the Protection of Industrial Property, which governs trademarks and patents, and
- The Agreement on Trade-Related Aspects of Intellectual Property Rights (TRIPS), which provides minimum standards for copyright, patent, trademarks, and trade secrets and provides a mechanism to ensure countries enforce intellectual property rights within their borders.

The United States is a contracting party to each of these three conventions. Contracting or member states must conform their national laws to the terms provided in each of the conventions.

The Berne Convention, which originated in 1886, requires the copyright laws of member states to conform to certain requirements.

> The requirement to incorporate moral rights into law kept the United States out of the Berne Convention until March 1, 1989, when the Berne Convention Implementation Act of 1988 was enacted. Although moral rights are now part of U.S. law, many contracts require authors to assign or waive their moral rights.

CONVENTION:
In international law, an agreement among several nations.

The most important provisions of the Berne Convention are:

- Equal treatment of works from other member states. For instance, a Canadian work distributed in the United States is automatically entitled to the full protection of U.S. copyright law.

- No formalities may be required for protection. Registration may not be required in order for a work to be copyright protected.

- Copyright must last for a minimum of the life of the author plus 50 years. It may last longer, but life plus 50 years is the minimum.

- Certain **moral rights** must be recognized. Moral rights are rights that an author has in addition to the economic rights discussed earlier in the chapter. The Berne Convention requires two: the right to claim authorship and the right to object to the mutilation, modification, or derogatory actions related to the work that would be prejudicial to the author's honor or reputation.

The Paris Convention of 1883 also sets out requirements that the laws of member states must follow. Those requirements include:

- Independence of patents. If one member state grants a patent, other members are not required to grant a patent. Refusal by one member to grant a patent does not obligate another member to refuse a patent for the same invention.

- Trademark registration. With some exceptions, a trademark registered in one member state must be accepted for registration in other member states.

- Protection against unfair competition. Laws must provide for protection against unfair competition, or the false indication of the source of goods.

Both the Berne and Paris Conventions are administered by the World Intellectual Property Organization (WIPO), headquartered in Geneva, Switzerland. WIPO also administers other more recent intellectual property conventions.

The TRIPS agreement, which came into effect on January 1, 1995, is the most comprehensive multilateral agreement on intellectual property. Its purpose is to reduce impediments to global trade by promoting adequate and effective protection of intellectual property rights. Part of what makes this such an important agreement is that each of the 159 members of the World Trade Organization is required to transpose the TRIPS requirements into national law and each is required to enforce those laws. When it was first introduced, this

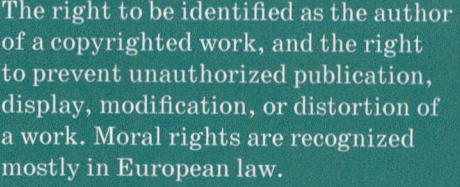

MORAL RIGHTS: The right to be identified as the author of a copyrighted work, and the right to prevent unauthorized publication, display, modification, or distortion of a work. Moral rights are recognized mostly in European law.

meant that many countries had to substantially modify their laws to ensure compliance with this important agreement.

The TRIPS agreement covers all the main areas of intellectual property, including copyrights (and related rights), trademarks (including service marks and geographical indications), patents, and trade secrets. In each of these main areas, TRIPS sets out the minimum standards of protection each WTO member must provide under its law, including the minimum duration of protection. Member states are allowed to provide more protection, and many do.

TRIPS incorporates the most recent versions of the Paris Convention and the Berne Convention, with the exception that countries are not required to adopt moral rights. The TRIPS agreement added requirements not included in the Paris and Berne conventions, particularly in providing protection for software and databases. Because of these additions, TRIPS is often described a Paris and Berne plus agreement.

A second aspect of TRIPS that makes it so important is that it requires each WTO nation to include national procedures and remedies for individuals to enforce their intellectual property rights. If any member nation fails in its obligations to incorporate minimum standards or to enforce them, other member states can bring an action against that country at the WTO. In other words, if a country fails in it obligations, trade sanctions may be imposed.

Note that none of these international agreements create international causes of action for holders of intellectual property rights. Rather, they require individual countries to change their laws so that individuals receive adequate protection in those countries.

VI. Enforcing Intellectual Property Rights

The federal government can bring criminal charges against individuals who infringe copyrights, patents, and trademarks or steal trade secrets. U.S. businesses lose billions of dollars a year to illegal use or theft of intellectual property. Rights holders are quick to point out that Americans can lose jobs because of of piracy. Piracy can also pose serious health and safety risks for consumers, whether it be counterfeit drugs or fake N95 masks. FBI and the U.S. Attorneys General have made investigating and preventing intellectual property piracy a top priority.

This section will consider civil actions for infringement.

Civil Infringement or Misappropriation

Since each type of intellectual property protects something different, the standards for a finding that the owner's rights have been violated, or infringed, are different.

Copyright Infringement: Copyright infringement is using someone's copyright protected creative work without permission. There are many kinds of copyright infringement that get individuals and business into trouble. Copying a work is only one form of infringement. Performing a work in public without permission is infringing as is creating another work from the original copyrighted piece. Some examples of copyright infringement include, playing copyrighted songs at the neighborhood coffee shop without paying a licensing fee or using someone's photograph on your website without permission. What many people forget is that most of what they see on the internet is copyright protected and cannot be used without permission.

> Most photocopying machines that are available for public use have a notice posted nearby advising users of the penalties for copyright infringement.

To prove copyright infringement, the owner must show:

- They own a valid copyright, and
- The defendant copied original elements of the work.

Copying may be proved by direct or indirect evidence. There may be direct evidence of unauthorized copying, such as performing a song at a public event without getting permission first. Often, however, the proof of copying is indirect. Indirect proof (or circumstantial evidence) of copying is done by showing access to the copyrighted work, and a "substantial similarity" between the original work and the allegedly infringing work.

Access means that the alleged infringer had a reasonable opportunity to see or hear the original work. It does not mean a bare possibility that the infringer could have seen the work, or that it was theoretically possible. Access can be proven by showing that the original work was so widely distributed that it was likely the infringer knew about it. It can also be proven by showing that a third party connected with both the infringer and the author of the original had access. For example, access has been found when a composer's assistant sent copies of sheet music to a publisher who also published the work of the infringing songwriter. Finally, access will be inferred if the allegedly infringing work is so similar to the original that it is highly likely that the works were not created independently.

The definition of "substantial similarity" can be hard to nail down. If there has been verbatim copying, such as using a lengthy clip from a movie in another work, there is a substantial similarity if the clip was a "significant" clip from the earlier work. There is no clear definition for what a "significant" amount would be.

Example: Grokster offered a peer-to-peer file sharing platform. The courts found that the primary use of Grokster (90%, by some estimates) was the unauthorized sharing and distribution of music and other files. Although Grokster did not do any of the copying itself, by offering the platform and not policing it for unlawful sharing, Grokster was indirectly infringing. *MGM Studios, Inc. v. Grokster, Ltd.*, 545 U.S. 913 (2005).

If the copying were not verbatim, a substantial similarity may also be found if the overall look and feel of the first work were copied. Courts have developed several different tests for finding copying.

There are defenses to copyright infringement. A defendant may rebut the allegation of copying if they can show that their work was interdependently created. Fair use is also a defense to infringement that will release an infringer from liability. The defendant may also prove that the parts of the work used were not protected by copyright, either because they were unprotected facts or because the work was in the public domain.

If an owner is successful in proving infringement, several remedies are available. The court may award either the actual damages the owner suffered and any profit of the infringer that can be attributed to the infringement. Because these damages can be hard to prove, the copyright owner may elect statutory damages at a rate of between $750 and $30,000 per infringement "as the court considers just." The infringer may also be ordered to pay statutory damages for willful infringement. The copyright owner is also entitled to an injunction, to stop the infringement. The court may also order that the infringing items be impounded and disposed of.

Trademark Infringement: Trademark infringement is the unauthorized use of a trademark or service mark in connection with goods or services. The test for trademark infringement is whether a defendant's actions are "likely to cause confusion, or to cause mistake, regarding the source, affiliation, connection, or sponsorship" of goods or services. This rule is generally expressed by the shorter term, "likelihood of confusion." Actual confusion is not required, but if there is in fact evidence of confusion, that will be used to show the likelihood. Courts have adopted various tests to determine whether there is a likelihood of confusion. Typical factors that are considered include:

- **Strength of senior user's mark.** Because trademark protection is acquired by use, it is the first, or senior user, who brings the lawsuit. The more distinctive the mark, the more likely a court will find confusion. So, there is more likely to be confusion if the mark is arbitrary or fanciful than if it is descriptive with secondary meaning.

- **Similarity of the marks.** The more similar the marks, the more likely the court will find likelihood of confusion. They look at all aspects of the mark, including its design, typeface, and even how the marks sound.

- **Similarity of the products or services.** The closer the goods and services are in the marketplace, the more likelihood of confusion. If the products or services are dissimilar, then confusion is less likely. For instance, "Delta" attached to faucets is not likely to confuse consumers that the faucets come from Delta Airlines.

- Likelihood that the senior user will **bridge the gap.** It is probable that the first user of the trademark will expand its business into the junior user's product area, the more likely it is that there will be confusion.

- The junior user's **intent** in adopting the mark. If a court finds the junior user chose the trademark to freeride on the good will of the original mark, a finding of confusion is more likely.

- **Evidence of actual confusion** is not required, but if the senior user can present evidence that consumers have actually been confused, that is strong evidence to support infringement.

- **Sophistication of the consumers** is also a factor. The less sophisticated the consumer, the more likely they will be confused.

Note that identical marks are not necessarily infringing. The PTO shows 30 live trademarks using of the word "Catalina," registered to numerous different users, for products including bathing suits, snack mix, and building materials.

Remedies for trademark infringement include money damages, including the infringer's profits, the plaintiff's losses and, in some cases, the cost of the lawsuit and plaintiff's attorney fees. The court can order an injunction preventing the defendant from using the infringing mark and can order the destruction of the infringing articles.

> **FIRST SALE:**
> A defense to an action for copyright, trademark, or patent infringement. A person who lawfully acquires a copyright, trademark, or patent protected item may resell that item without infringing the copyright, trademark, or patent.

Patent Infringement: A person infringes a patent when they make, use, offer to sell, sell, or import something that contains the patent's claims. The patent owner must prove its invention was used without permission. A patent infringement action involves two steps: claim construction and comparison.

Claim construction is the central part of a patent infringement lawsuit. It looks at what claims of the original patent are alleged to be infringed. The court tries to decide what the claim says that the invention is supposed to be. The plain language of the claim is considered. If that is unclear, the court may look at other evidence, such as scientific and technical literature, or expert opinion. Claims must be given their broadest reasonable interpretation.

The second step is comparison. The claims of the two inventions are compared. An invention infringes on the patent of another even if it copies only one claim. The copying may be literal, meaning that every element of the claim is copied. Each and every element of the claim must be found in the infringing device. Copying may also be equivalent, meaning that the differences between the two would be regarded as insubstantial by a person skilled in the field. The equivalence is between elements in individual claims, not the invention as a whole.

There are defenses to patent infringement. Typically, an alleged infringer will assert that the patent is not valid, that it did not originally meet the requirements for novelty or non-obviousness. If the patent is not valid, there can be no infringement.

Remedies for patent infringement include money damages which might be actual damages, a reasonable royalty, or both and sometimes costs and lawyer fees. The court may also order an injunction to stop the infringing behavior.

Trade Secret Misappropriation: Trade secrets are not infringed, they are misappropriated. A plaintiff in a trade secret action has to prove:

- The subject matter was a trade secret,
- The owner took reasonable precautions to keep it secret, and
- The trade secret was **misappropriated**, or wrongly taken.

Misappropriation of a trade secret includes doing either of the following without permission of the owner of the secret:

- Acquiring a trade secret that was knowingly obtained through improper means, or
- Disclosing or using a trade secret without express or implied consent by a person who used **improper means** to acquire the trade secret or had reason to know it was acquired by improper means, including from someone who had a duty to keep it secret.

The term "improper means" includes theft, bribery, misrepresentation, breach of a contractual or fiduciary duty, inducing a violation of a duty to maintain secrecy, or commercial espionage. The term does not include reverse engineering or independent derivation if the person lawfully obtained the product reverse engineered. A "whistleblower" who relevels trade secret to a government agency to report a violation of the law is immune from liability under the DTSA.

Remedies for trade secret misappropriation include damages for the actual loss to the owner as well as unjust enrichment. Exemplary or putative damages are available for willful or malicious misappropriation. The court may also award attorney's fees. Courts may issue protective orders to keep the information secret and injunctions to stop the use of the trade secret.

Unfortunately, while damages can help compensate a company for its losses, once the trade secret is out in the public, it loses its status as a trade secret. The DTSA added a new remedy allowing for an ex parte seizure of property to prevent the dissemination of the trade secret. Ex parte means that the court may issue the order based on an application from the trade secret owner without the opportunity for the alleged defendant to be heard. Such orders are only issued in "extraordinary circumstances."

VII. Licenses and Assignments

Licenses and assignments are grants by the intellectual property owner to someone the right to use some or all of their exclusive rights. A **license** is a grant of some of the rights and an **assignment** is a grant of all rights, title, and interests in the property. Licensing and assignments are matters of contract between the parties. The legal requirements for a valid license are generally the same as those for any other contract, although licenses and assignments must be in writing and signed by the owner or holder of those rights. The specific terms of the licensing agreement are worked out by those involved in the agreement. Often, an employer will require employees to assign the intellectual property invented in the scope of their employment to the company.

Pros and Cons

There are definite advantages and disadvantages to licensing intellectual property. Whether the good outweighs the bad depends on the people involved in the agreement, and the type of property being licensed.

Pros: The author of copyrighted material, or the inventor of a patented or trade secret protected invention, is often interested in making money from the creation or invention. It is often the case that the author or inventor can't find a way to do that on her own. She may not have the resources, or she may not know how to do it. By licensing or assigning her rights to someone who can exploit the property, the author or inventor can share in the profits.

The advantage to the person who receives the license or assignment is getting access to new work or inventions without having to develop it on his own.

Licensing intellectual property may also expand the use of a work or invention into a new market. It may also give a new form to the licensed work, such as putting illustrations from a children's book on dishes or clothing. Licensing can expand the geographic reach of goods or services beyond their original territory.

Cons: Licensing intellectual property calls for a close examination, both of the property involved and the person who will receive the license or assignment. The person who receives the license wants to be sure that the property is worth her trouble to license. The person who is granting the license needs to make sure that the license will use his property to its best advantage.

Licensing also means giving up a certain amount of control over the use of the property. Assignments means giving up all control over the intellectual property. While a well-crafted licensing agreement will provide for adequate quality control, there is always the chance that mistakes will be made. These mistakes can damage the reputation of the property covered by the license, or may cause the owner to lose control of the property entirely.

Example: Willie is an amateur motorcycle mechanic. He gets a patent for a new, very efficient hand brake. Willie cannot manufacture enough of his new brakes to be profitable, and he cannot get the financing to set himself up for manufacturing. He also has no idea how to bring his invention to market. The Yoash Company, a large manufacturer of motorcycle components, licenses the patent from Willie, and manufactures and sells the new brake.

> *Example:* Peter opens a restaurant in Philadelphia called "Mother's," and gives it a theme reminiscent of a nightclub in a *film noir* movie. Peter registers a trademark in the name and trade dress of the restaurant. Edie, a patron visiting Philadelphia from Houston, enjoys the restaurant and wants to open one just like it in Houston. Peter can license the trademark and trade dress to Edie.

> *Example:* In the example above, Edie is careless about hygiene standards at the Houston restaurant. There is an outbreak of salmonella among patrons who have eaten there. News of the outbreak reaches Philadelphia, and the business at Peter's restaurant drops off noticeably.

Contractual Safeguards

Every licensing agreement is different and key terms will vary based on the kind of property being licensed as well as industry standards. The needs and interests of the parties are going to differ in each agreement, and it is important to make sure that the agreement meets those needs and interests. An "off the shelf" agreement will seldom be good enough.

While there are no standardized requirements for a licensing agreement, there are some contract provisions that should at least be considered.

Description of the Property: The exact property to be licensed should be described clearly enough to eliminate any uncertainty about what the license covers. A clear description is especially important if the property being licensed is from a catalog or collection (for example, a set of stock photos offered for license on a website). If the licensed property is a patent, giving the number of the patent is sufficient.

The Grant: The owner of intellectual property will most likely want to limit how it is used. This description of allowed uses is called the "grant." An owner may want to grant licenses for different uses to different parties. He may want to make sure that the property is not used in a way that would hurt his reputation, or that would make it appear that he is endorsing ideas or behavior he does not approve of.

If the original owner of the property to be licensed wants to limit how the property will be used, the limits need to be set out in the licensing agreement. Some typical considerations in the grant are whether it is an exclusive license and whether the licensee can sublicense its rights to someone else. To prevent sublicensing, clearly say so in the agreement.

Payment: Payment is the reason for most licensing agreements. Payment could be a lump sum, royalties, or a combination of both. The agreement should be very clear about how and when payment is made to the person granting the license. If payment is to be made by royalties, clear descriptions of whether they are based on a percentage of gross or net earnings and how they will be calculated. The contract should also specify when and how payment will be made.

Accounting: If payment is to take the form of royalties, there should be some provision for an accounting. This responsibility allows the person granting the license to make sure she is receiving the proper amount of royalties. If there is a possibility of renewing the license, it can also help her decide if she will renew the license with that same party, or if she will find someone else.

Dispute Resolution: Disputes can arise under even the best-crafted agreement. Planning for those disputes by putting in a mechanism for resolving them (such as mediation or arbitration) can help those disputes be resolved efficiently, without undue expense.

VIII. Intellectual Property and Technology

Before the 24-hour news cycle became a feature of modern life, getting news from around the world was a challenge. The regular media outlets relied upon by most people were selective in their reporting. A person who wanted to hear from another source had limited options. Today, of course, the situation has changed. The internet and cable television let us have instant, convenient, and inexpensive access to information from virtually everywhere in the world. It is no longer remarkable to have conversations with a friend halfway around the world, or to be able to follow a sports league in a foreign country.

Technological changes present new challenges for intellectual property law. Copyright law has had to adapt to digital content and the universal availability of devices that will copy other work. Trademark law has adapted to the single, global marketplace brought about by the internet. Patent law has adapted to new developments in biotechnology, software, and medicine.

In recent years, intellectual property law has managed to accommodate the new technologies. While it is tempting to try and predict what the future will bring, the past has shown us that any kind of prediction is apt to miss the mark.

Increased Enforcement Challenges

There are two essential features of the internet that have made intellectual property enforcement challenging. The first is the ease of infringement. The second is the possibility of anonymity.

The ease of use means that copying other work is easier than ever before. Digital content can be downloaded from the web, and uploaded to another site in a matter of seconds. The ease of use, and the ready availability of material, can lead to a lax attitude about respecting the property of others. For example, while most people would not take the time to photocopy all the pages of a 300-page book, many would download an online version of that book for free, without giving it much thought.

The potential for anonymity makes it hard to know whom to pursue for intellectual property violations. It can also be hard to know where to

> **Example:** A cartoonist has developed a popular cartoon character. That character has been adopted, without the cartoonist's permission, as the symbol of a political ideology he opposes. Since he does not know who is responsible for the unpermitted use of his work, the cartoonist likewise does not know whom he would sue for infringement.

look for them. Without having an identifiable person to pursue for infringement, it is virtually impossible to enforce intellectual property rights.

Protection of Technical Intellectual Property

Protection of new types of technology has often followed the popular perception of that technology. In 1972, the U.S. Supreme Court ruled that a software program was just a mathematical algorithm, and that algorithm could not be patented. Nearly ten years later, the Court backtracked somewhat, holding that, while the algorithm could not be patented, the use made of it could be a patentable invention. It was not until the mid-1990s, when computers had become commonplace, that software was recognized as a patentable invention as long as it embodied an invention or method and was more than an abstract idea. The rules for these inventions are complex and constantly changing.

New technology receives legal protection if it is able to fit into the existing categories of intellectual property. Thus, some software can be protected by a patent because it meets evolving criteria as an invention. The essential scope of patent law did not change. Instead, what changed was the perception of the nature of software. Inventions and works of authorship will receive protection, and it is vital that any new technology be understood as an invention or work of authorship.

CHAPTER SUMMARY

Intellectual property law can protect creations, inventions, and distinctive identifiers on goods and services. A person who invents something may be eligible to receive trade secret or patent protection. A person who creates other types of work—a book, a song, a picture—receives copyright protection if the work meets the requirements of copyright law. The creation of a mark to identify the unique source of commercial goods or services is a trademark.

Each type of intellectual property protects a different interest and serves a different policy goal. The main principle is that property is entitled to protection even if it is intangible, and not physical property. The act of creation and invention is encouraged by granting and recognizing this protection.

Review Questions

Review question 1.
What is a copyright? How does a copyright happen? Is registration required? How is a copyright shown on a work?

Review question 2.
What is a derivative work? What effect does a derivative work have on an original copyright? Who may create a derivative work? How is a derivative work different from an idea in terms of copyright protection?

Review question 3.
What is a work for hire? How does an author know if a work is a work for hire? How does the work for hire change ordinary copyright interests?

Review question 4.
What is the legal definition of trademark infringement? If a trademark is infringed, how can the trademark holder seek compensation? Are there circumstances under which the use of a trademark or trade name by another is not an infringement?

Review question 5.
What is a service mark? How are service marks protected? May they be infringed? How would you show that a service mark is registered with the government?

Review question 6.
What types of trademarks have the most legal strength? What types are weaker? How does a trademark become generic? Why would a trademark holder want to avoid that?

Review question 7.
What is a trade secret? In what circumstances might a company choose to protect its intellectual property this way rather than another means? What are the advantages of a trade secret? How are they protected? How long do they last?

Review question 8.
How long does a patent last? May it be renewed? Is it possible to make a change to a patent and refile it as a new patent? If so, what changes would be adequate?

Review question 9.

What are the different types of patents? What do they protect? Where would a company register a patent?

Review question 10.

What is patent infringement? Does the product need to be the same as the original product incorporating the patent? How does a patent holder enforce patent rights?

Review question 11.

Why would a company decide to use a trade secret model rather than pursue a patent? What are the advantages and disadvantages of each model for business?

Review question 12.

What treaties apply to intellectual property? How do they change the rights of intellectual property owners?

Discussion Questions

Question 1:

Kano and Dave have come up with a new machine for cleaning and smoothing cymbals. They call their new system the Toph 2022, and start to sell it under that name. To help promote the product, they enlist their friend Miriam, a drummer, to make a short video showing how she uses the Toph 2022. Kano starts working on some new promotional material. He shows it to Dave, and both agree that they will not reveal any of the new promotional material until next year.

> Can anything in this situation may be protected by a patent? If so, what?
>
> Is there anything that may be protected by copyright? If so, what?
>
> Is the new promotional material a trade secret? Why, or why not?
>
> Explain how Kano and Dave could get trademark protection for the name "Toph 2022."

Question 2:

Jamal owns a childcare center. The center does not advertise outside of Jamal's neighborhood, and there is only one location. He calls his center "Jamal's Jym." One day, he receives a letter from an attorney representing "Jamal's Gym," an upscale fitness center. The letter says that Jamal is infringing on the trademark of the fitness center. Jamal's Gym does not advertise or do business in Jamal's area.

> Is Jamal infringing on the fitness center's trademark? Why or why not?

> How would you recommend Jamal and the gym resolve the issue?

Question 3:

Carlos and Betty own a coffee shop. Last Saturday, they staged the "World's Worst Karaoke" contest. Contestants were encouraged to sing along with recorded music, and sing as badly as they can. The recordings are not licensed for commercial use.

> Is this copyright infringement? Why or why not?

> Suppose Carlos and Betty claim that their event was fair use, as a commentary on the recorded songs. Would this defense succeed? Why or why not?

Question 4:

Hannah devises a simple machine that lets her roll large quantities of meatballs.

> How would she get patent protection for her invention? What if she wanted patent protection in another country?

> How could Hannah grant a right to produce the machine to a manufacturer while retaining her patent?

Question 5:

Olaf is an ice sculptor. His works have been featured in many bridal magazines, and his work is popular at conferences and restaurant openings. Olaf sees a photograph of one of his sculptures on the website of one of his competitors, Sven. The photograph was taken at a wedding reception by one of the guests, and Sven downloaded the picture from the guest's Facebook page. Sven is using the photo to advertise that he can create the same sculpture. Olaf angrily calls Sven, but Sven says, "An ice sculpture isn't exactly fixed in a permanent form, so you don't have a copyright!"

Who has a copyright in the sculpture in the photograph? Who has a copyright to the photograph?

What potential copyright disputes are raised by this set of facts? Are there any defenses to those claims?

Question 6:

Jan makes a protoype for a tool to remove the top of strawberries. The tool makes strawberry preparation much faster, but it is not unique enough to be patentable. Jan wants to make sure the tool has a very marketable name to give it a competitive advantage.

If Jan wants to trademark the name, what should he keep in mind?

What do you think would be a good name for this tool?

Is it necessary to trademark the name of the tool? Is a good product name for marketing purposes necessarily a good name for trademarking?

Question 7:

Chazza Inc. wants to copy the formula for a popular face cream produced by a competitor.

If the formula is patented, where would Chazza find the formula? What are the issues with using a patented formula?

If the formula is not patented, what other type of intellectual property might it be?

Is there a legal means for Chazza to discover the cream's formula? Under what circumstances?

Question 8:

The Susan & Susan Company produces wine under the label "Professor's Friend." The company advertises mainly online with a series of funny videos and related social media commentary. The videos are made by an independent production company hired by Susan & Susan. The social media posts are made by an employee of the company. The wine is produced using a freezing stage to bring out the sweetness of the grapes. The specific freezing process was developed at the company, and involves particular temperatures and a rate of cooling that only a few people at Susan & Susan know.

> What types of intellectual property exist at Susan & Susan?

> Are there any issues with ownership of the intellectual property? What issues should Susan & Susan guard against?

Question 9:

Erum writes a screenplay about talking rats in New York City. The rats comment on the strange things people do. The screenplay is rejected by several production companies. Two years later, though, one of the companies puts out an animated series about mice living on a farm. The mice comment on the strange things the farmer and her family do.

> Does Erum have a possible claim for infringement against the production company? Why or why not?

Question 10:

Some old trademarks have been reactivated in recent years for new products. One example is Shinola, which was originally a trademark for shoe polish in the first half of the 20th century. The new owner of the Shinola trademark produces watches and vintage-look lifestyle goods.

> What is the value of buying and using an existing trademark? What do you think Shinola intended to achieve?

> The Shinola trademark cost the new company one million dollars. Do you think it was worth that price? Why or why not?

10 AGENCY

KEY OBJECTIVES:
- Explain how the law of agency applies.
- Describe the concept of vicarious liability.
- Define the limits of "scope of authority."

CHAPTER OVERVIEW

This chapter covers the law of agency. Agency is a relationship that allows one person (the **agent**) to act on behalf of another person (the **principal**). Agency law governs the obligations and responsibilities involved when one person acts through another.

In this chapter, we will look at the law of agency. We will look at how and when agency occurs, the relationship's legal limits, and how that relationship comes to an end. We will also consider one of the most important agency issues for businesses, the principal's liability for an agent's actions.

INTRODUCTION

Agency is a very common legal relationship. Think about how often people act on another person's behalf: lawyers, real estate brokers, and insurance agents are just a few examples.

AGENT:
A person who is authorized to act for another person.

PRINCIPAL:
A person who authorizes another to act on her behalf.

These representatives are serving as agents, even if they do not think of the relationship in that way. Agency can also involve corporations. In fact, corporations and LLCs are required to have an agent to accept legal documents on behalf of the company. Agency law governs the day-to-day issues raised by one entity or person acting through another.

In an agency relationship, the principal generally authorizes action by the agent. Because the agent takes action as if he were the principal and on his behalf, the principal may face liability for the agent's acts. For instance, if an agent signs a contract for a principal within the scope of their agency relationship, the principal cannot legally refuse to honor the contract. The contract is just as valid as one signed by the principal.

However, it would be wrong to assume that the principal is responsible for everything his agent does. Agency law sets many limits for the relationship between a principal and agent. The principal is limited in what she can ask of an agent, and there are circumstances in which an agent is no longer considered to be acting for the principal.

This chapter covers agency relationships through the following concepts: agency creation, duties and liabilities, scope, apparent and actual authority, and termination.

I. Creating an Agency Relationship

Agency is a contractual relationship. Without agreement, there is no agency relationship. Both the principal and the agent agree to the relationship. The agreement may be as explicit as a written agreement, or it may be inferred from the parties' actions. Much of the focus of agency law is on agent interactions with third parties. The most basic inquiry, however, is identifying whether there is an agreement creating a principal/agent relationship.

An agency agreement may be written or oral. An unwritten agency agreement can be shown by statements, or by conduct.

Whatever form an agency agreement takes, there must be an intention to create an agency relationship. The principal must intend that the agent will act for her, and the agent must intend to act on behalf of the principal. Both parties must also intend that the agent's actions be subject to the control of the principal.

Agency is an important part of day-to-day business. For almost all organizations, some work will need to be delegated to employees. While not all agents are employees, employees are most often considered to be agents. (An employee is

> *Example:* Nick is helping his friend Tom fix his fence. Tom asks Nick to drive to the hardware store to buy nails and paint for the project. Nick is Tom's agent while he runs the errand. The relationship is shown by Tom's spoken request and Nick's actions.

> *Example:* Jasmine just received a job offer in a new city. She contacts Phil, a real estate agent in that city, and asks for help to find a new place to live. Phil sends over his standard agency agreement. Under the agreement, Phil will act as an exclusive agent for Jasmine for her real estate search. If Jasmine finds a property on her own or with a different agent while Phil is still Jasmine's exclusive agent, Jasmine will still owe Phil a commission, even though Phil did not help with that transaction.

> *Example:* Chris incorporates a teeshirt printing business. The venture is a success, and Chris cannot keep up with all the work. Acting as the head of the business, Chris hires Amal to handle shipping and Bea to take care of bookkeeping. Amal and Bea are employees and agents for the business, which could not operate with Chris alone.

not always an agent, but those circumstances are beyond this discussion.) Employees take care of various parts of the business's operations. No one individual could handle all of the tasks for most organizations. The business delegates some work to be handled by employees, who act on behalf of the business as agents.

Many agents are not employees. Real estate agents are an excellent example of an agent who is not an employee of the principal. Suppose a real estate agent is helping a prospective buyer purchase a home. That agent acts on behalf of her principal (the buyer) to find a property, negotiate a purchase price, complete all necessary paperwork, and close the sale. The principal (buyer) ultimately chooses the property to buy arranges financing or payment, and takes all the necessary steps presented by the agent to purchase the home. The agent acts under the principal's direction to find the right neighborhood and type of home.

Another common type of non-employee agency agreement is the **power of attorney.** A power of attorney is an explicit grant of authority to act on behalf of another.

> An agent who has a power of attorney is called the "attorney in fact." No legal training or licensure is implied by that title. Instead, this use of "attorney" simply refers to a person acting on behalf of another person.

The power of attorney may give the agent broad authority to make virtually any type of financial or business decision. The power may also be a special power of attorney. A special power means that the agent's authority is limited to certain designated functions. For example, a person may grant a power of attorney to someone only for the purpose of selling a certain piece of property.

As with most agency and contractual relationships, a person must be of "sound mind" before he can give power of attorney to another. Generally, the power is revoked if that situation changes. For example, if a person who grants a power of attorney is in an accident and is unconscious for an extended period, the power will be revoked.

The "sound mind" rule has two exceptions:

1. Health Care Decisions: Many states recognize a document known as a **health care power of attorney**. A health care power of attorney grants the authority to make decisions regarding another person's health care if that person cannot do so.

POWER OF ATTORNEY:
A document by which a principal gives an agent authority to perform specified acts on behalf of the principal.

HEALTH CARE POWER OF ATTORNEY:
A power of attorney that allows another to make health care decisions when the principal is unable to make those choices.

LIVING WILL:
A document that shows a person's choices for end-of-life care when he is unable to indicate those preferences.

Unlike a living will, a health care power of attorney does not apply only to end-of-life decision making. The health care power of attorney comes into effect if a person is temporarily unable to communicate his wishes.

2. Durable Power of Attorney: A durable power of attorney is one that states that it will remain in effect even if the person granting it becomes incapacitated. It is in full effect when the person granting it is of sound mind, but it does not end if that status changes. A durable power of attorney may cover the same power as any other power of attorney. It may relate to business and financial matters, to health care decisions, or to both.

Neither the health care power of attorney nor the durable power of attorney change the requirement that the person granting the power be of sound mind when signing the power of attorney document.

A springing power of attorney is a type of durable power of attorney. A springing power of attorney only goes into effect when the person granting it becomes incapacitated. It has no effect when the person granting it is capable of conducting his affairs.

Agency agreements are not always made in advance. An agency agreement may still exist if the principal ratifies the actions of another person. Ratification is when the deed is done, and the principal approves and accepts the benefits of it.

Some state laws also create an agency relationship even without an agreement between the parties. For example, in many states, a person who drives a car with the permission of the owner is the agent of the owner while driving the car.

> **DURABLE POWER OF ATTORNEY:**
> A power of attorney that remains effective even if the principal becomes incapacitated.
>
> **SPRINGING POWER OF ATTORNEY:**
> A power of attorney that becomes effective when the principal becomes incapacitated (it "springs" into effect).
>
> **RATIFY:**
> Accepting or confirming a prior act.

Example: Min is in the reception area of Constanza's office, waiting for an appointment with Constanza. A man comes in and says he had called earlier about buying a computer from Constanza. The man gives Min a check for what he says was the purchase price, and takes the computer. When Constanza comes out, she sees that the computer is gone and that there is a check for the price she wanted. Constanza takes the check and thanks Min for taking care of the sale. Constanza has ratified Min's actions.

> *Example:* Patrice is a talent agent representing The Amazing Paulo, a magician. Patrice goes to a venue to try to book a show for Paulo. Another magician is setting up for a show, and says he will hire her as an assistant for his act if she takes Paulo's booking elsewhere. Even though Patrice has always wanted to be a magician's assistant, she cannot take the offer. Her responsibility is to act for the best interests of The Amazing Paulo.

II. Duties and Liabilities

When a person agrees to act as the agent of another person, she agrees to take on certain duties. Likewise, the principal has certain duties and obligations to his agent. These responsibilities are governed primarily by the agreement between the principal and the agent. There are, however, also duties that are implied by law, even if they are not explicitly stated. In other words, each party may have obligations to one another that are legally required, even though neither party may have known that these additional duties existed.

The most important implied legal duty in agency flows from the agent to his principal. Agents owe a **fiduciary duty** to their principals. This essential duty includes a series of other responsibilities the agent owes to the principal. All of the duties in the following list are part of the overall fiduciary duty.

FIDUCIARY/FIDUCIARY DUTY:
A fiduciary is a person required to act for the benefit of another person. A fiduciary owes the other person the duties of good faith, trust, confidence, and candor.

INSURANCE COMPANY THAT PROVIDED COVERAGE ON POLICIES SOLD BY INSURANCE AGENT DID NOT OWE THE AGENT A FIDUCIARY DUTY

MDM Group Associates, Inc. v. CX Reinsurance Company Ltd.
(Insurance Broker) v. (Insurance Company)
165 P.3d 882 (Colo. Ct. App. 2007)

This action involves claims for breach of fiduciary duty asserted by an insurance broker against several insurance companies. Defendants, CX Reinsurance Company Ltd., appeal the judgment entered upon a jury verdict awarding $6,750,783 to plaintiff, MDM Group Associates, Inc. We affirm in part, reverse in part, and remand.

MDM is an insurance broker. Joseph McNasby, its president, developed an insurance program for insuring ski resorts against the risk that the number of "paid skier days" during a ski season would fall below a specified minimum. CX and others agreed to write insurance policies covering the risk for a year, starting with the 1997–1998 ski season, and issued such policies to a number of ski resorts in exchange for premium payments.

During that initial year, the policies generated premiums of about $550,000 [on which MGM made a large commission]. The ski resorts and the underwriters renewed the policies for a second year, and the program had similar results during the 1998–1999 ski season.

Before the 1999–2000 ski season, several underwriters declined to renew their involvement. However, CX issued policies for that year, which, because more ski resorts purchased the coverage, generated total premiums of approximately $3 million. MDM received commissions totaling approximately $378,000.

The 1999–2000 ski season was not a good one for the insured resorts. There was little snowfall in the United States until well after the Christmas and New Year's ski holidays, and vacation travel was reduced because of concerns related to the millennium change. All insured resorts, including Vail, Mammoth, and Booth Creek, submitted claims. CX negotiated, mediated, and litigated the claims, ultimately paying in excess of $23 million to completely settle them. CX declined to renew the insurance policies after their one-year term expired in May 2000.

MDM initiated this action against CX asserting liability [for a number of claims]. In addition, MDM asserted a breach of fiduciary duty claim, contending that CX, as the principal in an agency relationship with MDM, owed it a fiduciary duty, and breached its duty by improperly handling the ski resorts' claims.

CX contends that MDM's breach of fiduciary duty claim must fail because a principal cannot owe a fiduciary duty to an agent as a matter of law. Alternatively, CX contends that it did not owe MDM any fiduciary duty here. We agree that CX did not owe MDM any fiduciary duty under these circumstances.

The existence of a fiduciary relationship is a prerequisite to the finding of a breach of a fiduciary duty. . . . A fiduciary duty arises among parties through a relationship of trust, confidence, and reliance. Certain types of relationships give rise to general fiduciary duties as a matter of law, such as attorney-client, principal-agent, and trustee-beneficiary. However, fiduciary duties are owed by only one of the parties in these relationships. "The very nature of these relationships encompasses an extensive line of duties that are performed for the total benefit of *only one of the parties* to the relationship."

In the principal-agent context, it is the *agent* who owes a fiduciary duty to the principal as a matter of law. "An agent has a fiduciary duty to act loyally for the principal's benefit in all matters connected with the agency relationship." Restatement (Third) of Agency § 8.01 (2006).

A principal does owe *some* duties to an agent. See Restatement (Third) of Agency, §§ 8.138.15. However, the "obligations that a principal owes an agent . . . *are not fiduciary*." Restatement (Third) of Agency, § 1.01 cmt. e (emphasis supplied).

Here, the jury was instructed, over CX's objection, as follows:

> A fiduciary relationship exists whenever one person is entrusted to act for the benefit of or in the interest of another and has the legal authority to do so. If you find that the underwriters were acting as a principal of MDM, and MDM was acting as agent with respect to MDM's insurance program, then you are instructed that the underwriters were acting as fiduciaries for MDM in its insurance program.

Thus, the jury was wrongly instructed that there was a fiduciary duty as a matter of law if it found that an agency relationship existed. As a matter of law, a principal is not a fiduciary of an agent. The principal is not "entrusted to act for the benefit of or in the interest of another." It is the principal who entrusts business to the agent to act for the principal's benefit. Any duties owed by a principal to an agent are not fiduciary. *See* Restatement (Third) of Agency, § 1.01 cmt. e.

Further, even if a principal could owe an agent a fiduciary duty under some circumstances, no such circumstances were demonstrated here. MDM did not show that it relaxed its care or vigilance because of its relationship with CX. MDM did not entrust anything to CX. MDM was an independent insurance broker looking out for its own interests. And as previously noted, MDM was not marketing "its own" insurance policies, even though the concept of the "lost paid skier days" coverage originated with MDM.

Accordingly, the judgment in favor of MDM on this claim cannot stand.

> **Example:** Charles asks Ben to file a deed with the property office. Ben drives to the office, parks at a meter, pays for a half-hour of parking, and goes into the office. After 30 minutes, Ben is still in line, and is told that if he leaves, he will lose his place. Ben is five minutes late back to the car, and he has a parking ticket. Because Ben was acting as an agent for Charles, Charles should pay the parking ticket.

- Duty of Loyalty—the agent must act for the benefit of the principal, above his own self-interest. For instance, the agent must avoid conflicts of interest with the principal, and may not take advantage of her position as agent to gain a personal benefit.

- Duty of Obedience—the agent must obey the principal's lawful instructions.

- Duty to Provide an Accounting—the agent must keep an account of any property or money that the agent handles for the principal, and provide those records to the principal if requested.

- Duty of Due Care—the agent has a duty to use reasonable skill and diligence in pursuit of the principal's goals.

- Duty of Notification—the agent must keep the principal informed of all developments in the matters the agent is handling on the principal's behalf.

The agent's fiduciary duty is the most important responsibility in the agency relationship. The many requirements of a fiduciary duty help the principal feel confident that the agent will act appropriately when handling the principal's concerns. There are also some implied legal duties from the principal to the agent. Principals owe the following duties to their agents:

- Duty of Compensation—the principal must pay the agent for his services in a timely manner.

- Duty of Reimbursement—the principal must reimburse the agent for necessary costs reasonably spent in carrying out the agency relationship.

- Duty of Indemnification—the principal must compensate the agent for liabilities the agent incurs while the agent is lawfully taking care of authorized business for the principal.

- Duty of Cooperation—the principal must cooperate with and assist the agent so that she can perform her role.

- Duty to Provide Safe Working Conditions—if the principal provides workspace or equipment, it is the principal's responsibility to make sure it is safe. The principal must also notify the agent if there are any safety issues.

When an agent acts on behalf of a principal, the agent is "subject to the principal's control." The control is not necessarily minute-by-minute

> **Example:** Lucy is a fashion designer. She makes an agreement with Otis that Otis will receive half of the proceeds obtained from his efforts to market clothes designed by Lucy. Although the agreement does not say so explicitly, Otis has an obligation to act in good faith and to attempt to market Lucy's designs. *Wood v. Lucy, Lady Duff-Gordon,* 222 N.Y. 88, 118 N.E. 214 (1917).

> An agent is under no obligation to follow unlawful instructions. If a principal tells an agent to commit a crime, the agent should not do so. The agent's fiduciary and good faith duties do not include committing crimes for the principal.

> The duty of good faith and fair dealing also requires the principal not to interfere with the agent's performance of her duties.

control, although a particular agency agreement could include that level of supervision. "Subject to the principal's control" normally means just that the agent must follow the principal's lawful instructions. The general contractual duty for the parties to act in good faith requires that the agent make at least a reasonable effort to follow the principal's instructions.

The agent's duty to act also includes a responsibility to use the reasonable care and skill necessary in order to do the job. The level of care and skill necessary is the ordinary degree of care and skill that would be considered the reasonable standard for the job. In other words, an agent is not required to be the best in the field; he just needs to be reasonably competent.

An agent acts according to the principal's lawful instructions. The **scope of authority** refers to the range of power delegated to an

> **SCOPE OF AUTHORITY:** The amount of power granted to an agent under a specific agency agreement.

> **Example:** Nick is helping Tom fix his fence. Tom asks Nick to buy nails and paint for the project. Nick returns with the requested items, which he bought himself. Tom must reimburse Nick.

> **Example:** Sandra asks Leigh to eliminate a virus on her laptop. While Leigh works on the virus, she also reorganizes all Sandra's files. Even though the reorganization makes the files easier to find, Leigh acted beyond the scope of her authority.

agent. Anything an agent does must be within the scope of his authority, or the principal will not be responsible for it.

The principal also takes on certain duties when making an agency agreement. There is the duty to act in good faith, and to follow the terms of the agency contract. If compensation is part of the agency agreement, the principal must pay as agreed. The principal is also responsible to reimburse the agent for the agent's expenses and payments made in the course of the agency.

The principal also must **indemnify** and defend the agent against claims or liabilities that arise in the course of the agent's performance.

If an agent breaches an agency agreement, that violation will often release the principal from further contractual obligations to the agent. The breach of the agreement must be material enough to show that the agent repudiates the agreement.

Vicarious Liability

Agents can legally act for principals, but that also means that principals are responsible for their agents' actions. **Vicarious liability** means that a principal must answer for his agent's actions. The principal bears liability for the agent's activities while acting for the principal.

A principal is vicariously liable for her agent's wrongful acts. Vicarious liability for these acts attaches to actions done by the agent within the scope of his authority as agent. If a principal would face consequences for having a car accident while driving to a business meeting, the principal also bears responsibility if an agent is in that position instead. If a principal sends an agent to a meeting, and the agent has a car accident on the way, the principal is

> **INDEMNIFY:**
> To insure or secure another party against a future loss or liability.
>
> **VICARIOUS LIABILITY:**
> A principal's legal responsibility for the action or inaction of its agent while the agent was working on behalf of the principal.

> Vicarious liability is summed up by the Latin words *respondeat superior*, or "let the master respond."

Example: Super Grocery Corp. hires Luis to find sales leads in a new market. As part of this work, Luis drives to various grocery stores and restaurants to talk to potential customers. One day before starting his rounds, Luis goes to a doctor's appointment. When leaving the doctor's office, he runs into another car in the parking lot. Super Grocery is not responsible for the damage in the parking lot because Luis was not working as an agent in attending a medical appointment. This result does not change even if Luis claims that he had to go to the doctor because of stress caused by his work for Super Grocery.

EMPLOYER'S LIABILITY FOR DISCRIMINATION DEPENDS ON REASONABLENESS OF EMPLOYER'S CONDUCT

Faragher v. City of Boca Raton
(Former Lifeguard) v. (Employer)
524 U.S. 775, 118 S. Ct. 2275, 141 L. Ed. 2d 662 (1998)

INSTANT FACTS:
Faragher (P) argues that Boca Raton (D) should be liable for sexual harassment by two of her immediate supervisors.

BLACK LETTER RULE:
An employer may be vicariously liable for sexual harassment by a supervisory employee.

FACTS:
Faragher (P) was a lifeguard for the City of Boca Raton (D). After she quit her job, she brought suit against Boca Raton (D) and Terry (D) and Silverman (D), her supervisors. She claimed that Terry (D) and Silverman (D) had created a "sexually hostile atmosphere" at work. Faragher (P) said that they had repeatedly subjected female lifeguards to offensive touching and lewd remarks. She also said that they talked about women in offensive ways.

The district court held that Boca Raton (D) could be held liable for the harassment by Terry (D) and Silverman (D). The court found that the harassment was pervasive enough to support an inference that Boca Raton (D) had knowledge or constructive knowledge of it. The court also found that Terry (D) and Silverman (D) were acting as Boca Raton's (D) agents when they harassed, and a third supervisor knew of the harassment but failed to report it. The Court of Appeals reversed. It held that Terry (D) and Silverman (D) were not acting within the scope of their employment, that their agency relationship with Boca Raton (D) did not facilitate the harassment. Boca Raton (D) could not be considered to have known about the harassment because of its pervasiveness or because the other supervisor knew about it.

ISSUE:
Could Boca Raton (D) be vicariously liable for the harassment by Terry (D) and Silverman (D)?

DECISION AND RATIONALE:
(Souter, J.) Yes. An employer may be vicariously liable for sexual harassment by a supervisory employee. The employment relationship makes it possible for supervisory employees to abuse their authority and subject the employees they supervise to sexual harassment. The victim may be reluctant to accept the risks of blowing the whistle on a superior. When a supervisor discriminates against employees, his actions necessarily draw upon his superior position. An employee generally cannot deal with a supervisor's abusive conduct the same way she might deal with abuse from a co-worker.

Vicarious liability for harassment is not automatic. If the victim could have avoided harm, an employer who took reasonable care to prevent the harm will not be liable. If damages could have been mitigated, there can be no award for what a victim's own efforts could have avoided. Reversed.

DISSENT:
(Thomas, J.) An employer should be held vicariously liable for hostile environment sexual harassment only if the employee suffers some adverse employment consequence.

ANALYSIS:
The holding in this case was limited 15 years later by the case of *Vance v. Ball State Univ.*, 133 S. Ct. 2434 (2013). In that case, the Court refined the definition of "supervisor." For purposes of vicarious liability for harassment, a supervisor is defined as a person who can take "tangible actions" against employees, such as hiring or firing.

vicariously liable for the accident. This outcome reflects the fact that the agent is standing in for the principal.

Vicarious liability does not apply to criminal acts committed by the agent, even if they are intended to benefit the principal. If an agent commits a crime in the course of his agency, it is the agent, rather than the principal, who is liable. If the principal participates in the crime, she may be liable as a co-conspirator or an accomplice.

Employer Liability for Negligence

Negligence is the failure to exercise the degree of care that a reasonably prudent person would have exercised in a given situation. Negligent acts include everything from traffic accidents to professional malpractice. They are generally considered to be unintentional acts.

Principals are liable for the negligent acts of agents committed within the scope of the agent's authority. When a case involves a negligent act, the principal's liability is clearer than in cases involving an intentional act of the agent. A principal can make a strong claim that an agent's intentional wrongdoing was not authorized, but a lawful, authorized action may be done in a negligent way and cause injury.

Principal Liability for Agent Malfeasance

"Malfeasance" is an unlawful or wrongful act. The term typically refers to an intentional or deliberate act, such as fraud, misrepresentation, or embezzlement. Malfeasance is distinct from negligent or unintentional acts.

Principals seldom, if ever, authorize agents to engage in intentional wrongdoing. A principal will still be liable for an agent's wrongdoing if it was committed within the scope of the agency. There are different tests for determining what is within the scope of employment. Most courts look at the agent's motivation. If the agent was motivated by a desire to further the employer's interests, the malfeasance will have been committed within the scope of the agency relationship. The principal will therefore be liable.

> *Example:* Abie is driving a delivery truck for Rose's Irish Bakery. When he looks down for the address for his next delivery, he misses seeing a pedestrian crossing the street. Abie hits the pedestrian, injuring her severely. Rose's Irish Bakery is vicariously liable for the pedestrian's injuries.

> *Example:* Inez is a salesperson at Rory's art gallery. To sell a painting, she tells a customer that the painting was created by a locally famous artist. Inez knows that the painting was actually done by an amateur painter who learned to copy the famous artist's style. Rory is liable for Inez's misrepresentation.

"SCOPE OF EMPLOYMENT" MUST BE DECIDED ON A CASE-BY-CASE BASIS DEPENDING ON THE FACTS

Edgewater Motels, Inc. v. Gatzke
(Fire-Damaged Motel) v. (Fire-Starting Motel Guest)
277 N.W.2d 11 (Minn. 1979)

INSTANT FACTS:
Gatzke (D) negligently started a fire in his hotel room after smoking a cigarette while he filled out his expense account during a business trip.

BLACK LETTER RULE:
The smoking of a cigarette, if done while engaged in the business of the employer, is within the employee's scope of employment because it is a minor deviation from the employee's work-related activities, and thus merely an act done incidental to general employment.

FACTS:
Gatzke (D), a district manager for Walgreen's (D), stayed in the Edgewater Motel (P) while he was in Minnesota supervising the opening of a Walgreen-owned restaurant. Gatzke (D) lived at the Edgewater (P) at the company's expense. He was allowed to call home at company expense, and his laundry, living expenses, and entertainment were all items of reimbursement. There were no constraints as to where he would perform his duties or at what time of day they would be performed.

Near midnight one night, Gatzke (D) left work with others on the job. Gatzke (D) and Hubbard went to a restaurant to have a drink. Over the course of an hour, Gatzke (D) consumed a total of four brandy Manhattans, three of which were "doubles." Gatzke (D) and Hubbard spent part of the time discussing the operation of the newly opened restaurant. Gatzke (D) also spoke to the bartender about the mixing and pricing of drinks, as he was interested in learning the bar business because the new Walgreen's (D) restaurant served liquor. Around 1:30 a.m., Gatzke (D) and Hubbard walked back to the Edgewater Motel (P). Gatzke (D) apparently looked and acted sober at that time.

Gatzke (D) went straight to his room, and then "probably" sat down at a desk to fill out his expense account, as was his habit. While Gatzke (D) completed the expense account he "probably" smoked a cigarette. The record indicates Gatzke (D) smoked about two packs of cigarettes per day. A maid testified that the ash trays in Gatzke's (D) room would generally be full when she cleaned the room. She also noticed that at times the plastic wastebasket next to the desk contained cigarette butts. After filling out the expense form, Gatzke (D) went to bed. A fire broke out soon thereafter. Gatzke (D) escaped the burning room, but the fire spread rapidly and caused $330,360 in damages to the motel.

Dr. Anderson, a fire reconstruction specialist, testified that the fire started in, or next to, the plastic wastebasket located to the side of the desk in Gatzke's (D) room. He also stated that the fire was caused by a burning cigarette or match. After the fire, the plastic wastebasket was a melted to a "blob." Dr. Anderson stated that x-ray examination of the remains of the basket disclosed the presence of cigarette filters and paper matches. The jury found Gatzke (D) to be guilty of 60% of the negligence and the motel guilty of the remainder. It also found Walgreen (D) liable for Gatzke (D). The trial judge concluded, however, that Gatzke (D) was not within the scope of his employment.

ISSUE:
Can an employee's smoking of a cigarette constitute conduct within his scope of employment?

DECISION AND RATIONALE:
(Scott, J.) Yes. After careful consideration of the issue we are persuaded by the reasoning of the courts that hold that smoking can be an act within an employee's scope of employment. It seems only logical to conclude that an employee does not abandon his employment as a matter of law while temporarily acting for his personal comfort when such activities involve only slight deviations from work that are reasonable under the circumstances, such as eating, drinking, or smoking. We hereby hold that an employer can be held vicariously liable for his employee's negligent smoking of a cigarette if he was otherwise acting in the scope of his employment at the time of the negligent act.

The record contains a reasonable basis from which a jury could find that Gatzke (D) was involved in serving his employer's interests while he was at the bar. More importantly, even assuming that Gatzke (D) was outside the scope of his employment while he was at the bar, there is evidence from which a jury could reasonably find that Gatzke (D) resumed his employment activities after he returned to his motel room and filled out his expense account form. The filling out of the expense form can be viewed as serving a dual purpose; that of furthering Gatzke's (D) personal interests and that of promoting his employer's business purposes. Accordingly, it is reasonable for the jury to find that the completion of the expense account is an act done in furtherance of the employer's business purposes.

Additionally, the record indicates that Gatzke (D) was an executive who had no set working hours. It was therefore reasonable for the jury to determine that the filling out of his expense account was done within authorized time and space limits of his employment.

In light of the above, we hold that it was reasonable for the jury to find that Gatzke (D) was acting within the scope of his employment when he completed his expense account. Accordingly, we set aside the trial court's grant of judgment for Walgreens and reinstate the jury's determination that Gatzke (D) was working within the scope of his employment at the time of his negligent act.

ANALYSIS:
To support a finding that an employee's negligent act occurred within his scope of employment, it must be shown that his conduct was, to some degree, in furtherance of the interests of his employer. Other factors to be considered in the scope-of-employment determination are whether the conduct is of the kind that the employee is authorized to perform and whether the act occurs substantially within authorized time and space restrictions. No hard and fast rule can be applied to resolve the inquiry. Each case must be decided on its own individual facts.

The initial question raised by this factual situation is whether an employee's smoking of a cigarette can constitute conduct within his scope of employment. A number of courts have ruled that the act of smoking, even when done simultaneously with work-related activity, is not within the employee's scope of employment because it is a matter personal to the employee that is not done in furtherance of the employer's interest. Other courts have reasoned that the smoking of a cigarette, if done while engaged in the business of the employer, is within an employee's scope of employment because it is a minor deviation from the employee's work-related activities, and thus merely an act done incidental to general employment. The "incidental to employment" position was the view this court adopted.

CASE VOCABULARY:

ISSUE OF FIRST IMPRESSION:
Refers to the first time a question of law is considered for determination by a court.

JUDGMENT N.O.V.:
Literally: notwithstanding the verdict. A judgment which reverses the determination of the jury, and is granted when a judge determines that the jury verdict had no reasonable support in fact or was contrary to law.

NEGLIGENCE:
Failure to exercise that degree of care which a reasonable person would exercise under the same circumstances.

REASONABLE PERSON:
A hypothetical person who exercises those qualities of attention, knowledge, intelligence and judgment which society requires of its members for the protection of their own interest and the interests of others.

SCOPE OF EMPLOYMENT:
An act of a servant done with the intention to perform it as a part of or incident to a service on account of which he is employed.

Negligent Hiring and Retention

Vicarious liability depends on a finding that the agent was acting within the scope of his authority. If the agent was not within the scope of his authority, the principal is not vicariously liable. She still could be directly liable on the theory that she was negligent in hiring the agent, or negligent in keeping him on. This type of liability differs from vicarious liability. The principal is being held liable for her own negligence, not for the acts of her agent.

A claim for negligent hiring is based on the idea that an employer should not hire a person who has a background that would show that the person is untrustworthy or dangerous. The negligence lies in hiring such a person when the employer knew or should have known about the employee's background. If a person is being hired for a position that involves a lot of public contact, or that brings them into unsupervised contact with the property of others, the employer should look into the person's background.

> Many states have laws requiring criminal background checks when a person is hired for a certain type of position, such as a job involving working with children. Volunteer programs may also be required to perform checks on their volunteer staff.

Any negligence claim, including a negligent hiring claim, requires evidence that the employer's negligence caused the victim's injury. If the employer's negligence did not cause the harm, there is no liability. Causation may be shown by evidence that the employer put the employee in contact with the victim, and that the harm done by the employee was caused by the same type of conduct that would have been revealed in an investigation.

Negligent hiring claims depend on information about an employee's background that the employer knew or should have known. There are practical and legal limits to what can be learned from even a thorough background check. If the employer could not reasonably have found out

Example: Matias has served two separate prison sentences for financial fraud. Hassan does not do a background check, but hires Matias to work as a personal banker. Matias uses his access to customer bank accounts to steal money from customers. Hassan could be liable for the negligent hiring of Matias.

Example: Assume that in the prior example, Matias had convictions for assault instead of fraud. Hassan's negligence in not checking Matias's background did not cause the loss to customers. Hassan might be vicariously liable for Matias's actions in a civil lawsuit for "conversion," a non-criminal taking of property.

> *Example:* When Claude was sixteen, he worked in a jewelry shop. He was arrested and convicted for stealing jewelry and watches left with his employer for repair. Because he was a juvenile, his record was sealed, and is not accessible to the public. Two years later, he goes to work for Jack, a jeweler in another city. Jack does a background check on Claude, but the records of his earlier thefts are not found. Claude once again steals property left by customers. Jack is not liable for negligent hiring, because he did not know, and could not have known, that there was a risk that Claude would steal.

> *Example:* Roger hires Nancy after a background check reveals nothing negative in her record. After Nancy has worked for Roger for a few months, Nancy is arrested for assault on three separate occasions. Roger learns of the arrests, but does not terminate Nancy. After her second arrest, Nancy gets in an argument with a person delivering furniture to the office, and she assaults the delivery person. Roger may be liable for negligent retention of Nancy.

about something in the employee's background, it is not negligent to hire that employee.

Negligent retention relates to situations in which the employer learned of an employee's dangerous tendencies after he was hired. Despite learning of these tendencies, if the employer still does not terminate the employee, it may be considered negligence if the employee later injures someone. As with a negligent hiring claim, negligent retention looks at both the employer's knowledge, and whether the failure to act caused the victim's harm.

III. Scope of Authority

When discussing a principal's vicarious liability, it is always necessary to know what the scope of an agent's authority is. The **scope of authority** can be understood as a limitation on both the agent and the principal. The agent's actions on behalf of the principal are limited by her scope of authority, and the principal is not responsible for anything done by the agent outside the scope of authority.

A principal may grant an agent explicit permission to do certain actions, or to accom-

> *Example:* Jodi is hired by Leo to open a branch of Leo's financial planning office in another city. Jodi rents an office, obtains office equipment, and purchases office supplies. Jodi has the implied authority for all of those transactions.

> **Example:** Linh is a salesperson employed by Tatu, Inc. Linh has several sales calls to make during the day, but this afternoon, she has some unexpected extra time between calls. She decides to drive to a department store ten miles away to buy a gift for her sister. While on the way back from the store, she accidentally hits and injures a pedestrian. Linh was on a frolic, so the company would not be liable. But assume that instead of going shopping, Linh decides to kill time by stopping for coffee at a place across the street from her next call. While walking across the street, she accidentally bumps into another pedestrian, spilling hot coffee on the pedestrian, who is burned. Linh probably would not be considered to be engaged in a frolic, and Tatu would be vicariously liable.

plish certain tasks. This is known as **express authority**. The scope of the express authority is defined by the agency agreement.

The grant of express authority will not always list every step the agent must take, or every individual thing the agent must do. This may be intentional, as it would be difficult to draft an agency agreement that could cover every conceivable situation that might arise. In appropriate situations, the agent will have the implied authority to act. **Implied authority** is the authority to do whatever is reasonably necessary to accomplish the task set out in the grant of express authority.

Implied authority also includes the authority to act in an emergency. This authority extends to protecting and preserving the property of the principal. It may include the authority to do things that would normally be outside the scope of the agent's authority.

The scope of the agent's authority is limited to those actions done to further the principal's interests. If the agent makes a major physical departure from performing his duties, he may be engaged in a **frolic**. The principal is not liable for the acts of the agent done during a frolic.

> **EXPRESS AUTHORITY:**
> Actions and tasks that the principal specifically assigns to an agent.
>
> **IMPLIED AUTHORITY:**
> The agent's power to do whatever is necessary to accomplish specific responsibilities assigned by the principal.
>
> **FROLIC:**
> An agent's significant deviation from the principal's business for personal reasons.
>
> **DETOUR:**
> An agent's minor deviation from the principal's business for personal reasons.

> A **detour** is a lesser departure. A principal could still be liable for an agent's actions during a detour.

To decide if an agent is engaged in a frolic, courts will look at several factors, such as:

- How much time does the departure take?

- Was this foreseeable? Has it happened in the past, or does it happen with other agents?

- Did this happen somewhere the agent would not be expected to be?

- Was the agent's motive to help the employer, or was it solely for her own benefit?

IV. Actual and Apparent Authority

Agency relationships may have consequences outside of the parties' agreement. If a third party believes someone to be acting as an agent, they may make decisions about doing business with the agent that they otherwise would not. For instance, if a theater owner wants to book a certain comedian, the owner might contract with a person that the owner believes to be the comedian's agent rather than with the comedian himself.

Powers a principal grants to an agent are the agent's *actual authority*. Of course, few outsiders are going to know the extent of the actual authority granted by a particular agency relationship. Those third parties will determine whether there is a real agency relationship based on how the principal allows the agent to act. A third party's reasonable conclusions about whether an agent has the power to act for a principal is an agent's *apparent authority*.

Apparent authority may be assumed from the principal's actions. When the principal acts in a way that makes her unable to deny the existence of agency, then other people are allowed to rely on the apparent authority of the "agent." The principal's actions must make it seem to others that a specific person is the agent of that principal. A person cannot simply claim to be an agent.

In order for apparent authority to exist, the principal's actions must be of a kind that would lead a reasonable person to conclude that there is an agency relationship. The reasonable person is one who is familiar with typical business practices and customs. If such a person would be justified in believing that an agency relationship exists, apparent authority will be found. The consequence of apparent authority is that the principal is responsible for the actions of the "agent" who reasonably seems to have authority.

Remember that it is the actions of the principal that create apparent authority. Actions of the agent alone are not sufficient. Also, a single, isolated act by the "principal" will seldom be sufficient to justify apparent authority. Instead, the principal must demonstrate a pattern of behavior that justifies others drawing a reasonable conclusion that the "agent" has authority.

ACTUAL AUTHORITY:
The powers actually granted to an agent by the principal.

APPARENT AUTHORITY:
The reasonable assumption that an agent is allowed to act for a principal under given circumstances.

Example: Ahmet lets his brother Caleb use his office for his own business. Caleb uses Ahmet's telephone and e-mail address for his business communication. Ahmet also lets Caleb order business supplies using Ahmet's business account. Caleb regularly orders supplies from one particular supplier. Shortly after Caleb places a large order, he leaves on an extended vacation. The supplier looks to Ahmet for payment. Ahmet has allowed the creation of apparent authority, so he will be treated as if Caleb was acting as his agent. Ahmet must pay the supplier's bill.

Example: Assume the same facts as in the prior example, except Ahmet does not know Caleb uses his office for business. He has never given Caleb permission to do so. Caleb does not have apparent authority, because Ahmet has not acted in a way that would lead others to believe that Caleb is his agent.

INJURED HOTEL GUEST'S WIFE HAD APPARENT AUTHORITY TO SIGN LEGAL RELEASE

Rogers v. Mashantucket Pequot Gaming Enterprise
(Hotel Guest) v. (Hotel Operator)
6 Mash. Rep. 374 (Mashantucket Pequot Tribal Court 2016)

The plaintiff, John Rogers, brought a negligence suit against the defendant, the Mashantucket Pequot Gaming Enterprise ("Gaming Enterprise"), for injuries stemming from a slip and fall incident in a hotel bathroom at the MGM Grand Hotel at Foxwoods Resort and Casino, which is operated by the Gaming Enterprise.

The plaintiff and his wife, Bernadette Rogers, stayed at the MGM Grand Hotel for their honeymoon from July 6, 2013 to July 8, 2013. The bathroom shower door was missing trim or had a defective seal on the bottom of the door, which allowed water to escape from the shower onto the tile floor. The plaintiff claims that he slipped on the wet tile floor of the bathroom on July 6, 2013 resulting in injury to his lower back and right leg.

After the slip and fall, the plaintiff's wife . . . explained to [the hotel] her husband's slip and fall, the persistent water leaks, and the failure to address their complaints were contributing to a very unsatisfactory honeymoon stay at the hotel. In response, the Gaming Enterprise offered to "comp" the plaintiff and his wife's three night hotel stay and provide a $120 restaurant voucher. Ms. Toscano informed Mrs. Rogers that she would visit their hotel room to obtain a signature for a release agreement to implement the comp.

The plaintiff did not sign the release, but instead his wife did. The key terms of the release were summarized in the heading of the document, which provided:

RELEASE OF ALL CLAIMS AND AGREEMENT TO INDEMNIFY
FOR AND IN CONSIDERATION OF THE ISSUANCE OF A COMP
3 NIGHT'S STAY AT MGM GRAND at
FOXWOODS (7/6–8/2013) & $120.00 DINNER
Redeemable to: John Rogers

Before addressing liability and damages associated with the slip and fall, the Court must address the threshold issue of whether the "release of all claims" signed by the plaintiff's wife validly released any claim the plaintiff may have against the Gaming Enterprise for the injury resulting from the slip and fall.

Having heard and reviewed the parties' trial testimony, arguments, and evidence, the Court finds that the plaintiff's wife, Bernadette Rogers, acted with apparent authority to bind the plaintiff to the terms of the release agreement.

The validity of an agreement signed by a third party implicates actual and apparent authority, a subset of agency law. . . . [A] brief overview of basic principles of agency law is instructive. "An agency relationship is created when, by express or implied contract or by law, one party (the agent) may act on behalf of another party (the principal) and bind that other party by words or actions. The three elements required to show the existence of an agency relationship include: (1) manifestation by the principal that the agent will act for him; (2) acceptance by the agent of the undertaking; and (3) an understanding between the parties that the principal will be in control of the undertaking." The Gaming Enterprise has failed to present sufficient evidence to show that an agency relationship existed between the plaintiff and his wife.

The Court must also address the related, but different issue of whether an agreement signed by a non-agent is nevertheless binding on the parties under the doctrine of apparent authority. . . . It is not necessary to find that an agency relationship existed between the plaintiff and his wife in order to find that her signature bound the plaintiff to the terms of the release. A principal can be bound by the actions of another—whether or not an agent—if apparent authority exists. "Apparent authority is the power held by an agent *or other actor* to affect a principal's legal relations with third parties when a third party reasonably believes *the actor* has authority to act on behalf of the principal and that belief is traceable to the principal's manifestations." Restatement (Third) of Agency § 2.03 (2006) (emphasis added). "A party can be held liable to a third party if its actions caused a third party to believe that there was a principal and agent relationship between it and another."

In other words, "[a]pparent authority is derived not from the acts of the agent but from the deliberate or inadvertent acts of the principal. Apparent authority has two elements. First, it must appear from the acts of the principal that the principal held the agent out as possessing sufficient authority to embrace that act in question, or knowingly permitted him to act as having such authority. . . . Second, the party seeking to bind the principal must have acted in good faith reliance on that appearance of authority."

"A person manifests assent or intention through written or spoken words or other conduct." Restatement (Third) of Agency § 1.03. "A manifestation is conduct by a person, observable by others, that expresses meaning. It is a broader concept than communication. The relevant state of mind is that of the person who observes or otherwise learns of the manifestation. . . . Silence may constitute a manifestation when, in light of all the circumstances, a reasonable person would express dissent to the inference that other persons will draw from silence. Failure then to express dissent will be taken as a manifestation of affirmance." *Id.* § 1.03(b). "A principal's inaction creates apparent authority when it provides a basis for a third party reasonably to believe the principal intentionally acquiesces in the agent's representations or actions." *Id.* § 3.03(b).

[T]he Gaming Enterprise carries the burden of proof to show by a preponderance of the evidence that Mrs. Rogers had the authority to sign and bind the plaintiff to the terms of the release agreement. . . . Here, the relevant inquiry is whether it was reasonable under the circumstances for the Gaming Enterprise's representative to believe, based on the manifested actions or inactions of the plaintiff, that the plaintiff's wife had the authority to sign and legally bind the plaintiff to the terms of the release agreement. Additionally, Ms. Toscano must have acted in good faith reliance on the wife's appearance of authority.

The plaintiff testified that he did not verbally authorize his wife to sign on his behalf to release any personal injury claim resulting from the slip and fall. The Court does not doubt the veracity of this testimony. However, this testimony is irrelevant to an analysis of apparent authority. As stated above, any manifestations the plaintiff made to his wife would bear on the formation of an agency relationship and the grant of actual authority. In determining the existence of apparent authority, the relevant focus is on the manifestations from the principal (plaintiff) to the third party[.]

[T]he critical moment occurred during the brief time that Ms. Toscano entered the plaintiff's hotel room and obtained the signature from the wife. This was the only opportunity for Ms. Toscano to observe any manifestations made by Mr. Rogers.

According to the plaintiff, after entering the room and exchanging pleasantries, Ms. Toscano proceeded to discuss the release with Mrs. Rogers only. The plaintiff claims that he was able to hear his wife and Ms. Toscano talk, but that he was unable to hear the actual words of their conversation.

Ms. Toscano had a much different recollection: After entering the room and exchanging pleasantries, she proceeded to explain the terms of the release, speaking in a "back and forth" manner to both the plaintiff lying in bed and Mrs. Rogers sitting in the desk chair. Ms. Toscano testified that the conversation was directed toward the plaintiff and that she explained the general form of compensation to him, which included using the word "release." Ms. Toscano indicated to the plaintiff that she needed a signature. [W]hen she presented the release to the plaintiff for signature, he indicated with a "little shrug" to give the release to his wife. Ms. Toscano then gave the release to Mrs. Rogers for signature.

The testimony presents conflicting stories. The Court finds that apparent authority exists under either scenario.

Under Ms. Toscano's version of events, apparent authority would clearly be established. She testified that when she offered the release to the plaintiff for signature, the plaintiff indicated with a "little shrug" to give the release to his wife, which she then did. It is reasonable to interpret this nonverbal cue as a manifestation from the plaintiff to her that his wife had the authority to sign on his behalf. Additionally, the fact that it was the plaintiff's wife, opposed to someone else, who had previously been communicating with [the hotel] and was the one to sign the release is important. While the plaintiff's marital status does not in itself establish an agency relationship or actual or apparent authority, it does contribute to the reasonable belief that the plaintiff's wife would have the authority to sign on his behalf.

Even under the plaintiff's version of events, apparent authority exists. The plaintiff and his wife contend that hotel room conversation was brief, that all communication was directed to the wife, and that Ms. Toscano did not explain to the plaintiff or his wife that the document was a release. Even if this is true, the plaintiff's silence and inaction in the presence of Ms. Toscano at that time of signature reasonably supports a finding of apparent authority. The plaintiff testified that he knew someone from [the hotel] was coming to his hotel room to discuss some type of compensation for his injuries. The plaintiff further testified that he saw his wife sign the release and that his wife did not commonly make financial decisions on his behalf. If the plaintiff did not intend for his wife to act on his behalf, a reasonable person would expect him to express some form of dissent when his wife undertakes to sign a document pertaining to his injuries. Despite knowing the purpose of the visit and viewing his wife sign the release, the plaintiff remained silent at that critical moment[.] In the face of circumstances that fairly cried out for an objection on the part of the plaintiff, it was reasonable to interpret the plaintiff's silence and inaction as an affirmation that Mrs. Rogers had the authority to act on the plaintiff's behalf in signing the release.

Additionally, there is nothing to indicate that Ms. Toscano acted in bad faith. She reasonably relied on the plaintiff's action or inaction. The Gaming Enterprise has met its burden in showing by a preponderance of the evidence that Mrs. Rogers had apparent authority to sign and bind the plaintiff to the terms of the release agreement.

[T]he Court finds that the defendant has met its burden of proof. Judgment shall enter for the Gaming Enterprise.

V. Termination

Termination of agency means that the former agent no longer has the authority to act for the principal. Whenever an agency relationship ends, it is the principal's responsibility to make sure that others know that the relationship is over. In some instances, the principal must just avoid any actions that could create apparent authority. In other cases, such as in a business where the agent had ongoing relationships with customers, it is wise for the principal to inform those customers of the change directly. In rare circumstances, principals may publish a legal notice saying the agency relationship has terminated.

An agency relationship may be terminated in three ways: by lapse of time, act of the parties, or operation of law.

Lapse of Time

A principal and agent may agree that an agency relationship will last for a definite period of time. When that period of time expires, the agency terminates automatically. If no time for the expiration of the agreement is stated, the agency relationship could continue indefinitely.

Act of the Parties

Agency is based on an agreement. As with all agreements, the parties are allowed to end the agreement by mutual consent. The parties may agree to end their relationship at any time, even

Example: A well-known actor decides to change agents. The actor hears that the former agent still has the actor's photo in his office, suggesting that he is still representing the actor. The actor may decide to contact major studios to inform them that he has a new agent.

Example: Alex is an independent consultant with no employees. His consulting practice is very busy, and he occasionally travels to client offices out of state. A client asks that he spend three weeks at a facility overseas. Alex asks his sister Maria to manage the office, take calls, and make bank deposits during his absence. When Alex returns from his business trip, Maria is no longer his agent.

if the agreement said that the agency was to last for a certain period of time.

Either the principal or agent may terminate the relationship without the consent of the other party. If the agent terminates the agreement, it is called **renunciation**. If the principal ends the agreement, it is **revocation**.

If a party revokes or renounces the agency agreement, it is still possible that the party who acts to terminate the agreement may be in breach of contract. Whether there is a breach of contract will depend on the terms of the agreement. For example, many employment agreements may be terminated by either party at any time. On the other hand, an employer may not terminate the relationship for reasons that would constitute employment discrimination.

Operation of Law

Certain events may cause the termination of an agency agreement by "operation of law." Parties may agree in advance on what events can cause the agreement to end. If or when that event happens, the relationship is terminated. An agency relationship also may be limited to a specific purpose. In those cases, the relationship will end when that purpose has been accomplished.

The bankruptcy of one party may terminate agency. A corporate debtor in a Chapter 11 bankruptcy (a reorganization) may reject an ongoing agency agreement. Rejection could lead to renegotiation of the agreement, or just its termination.

CAREERS IN THE LAW

Agents bear special legal duties to their clients. Many specific types of agency therefore require training and licensing to protect those clients. Real estate agents are a perfect example. People buying or selling real estate rely on the expertise and candor of their representatives in navigating the complex legal rules involved in property transactions.

Real estate agents must seek special training and may be required to work initially with an existing agent or broker. Agents must pass a licensing exam for the states where they will operate; brokers may need to take additional training and pass further exams. In addition to state requirements, real estate agents can choose to join the National Association of REALTORS®, a trade association that provides further ethics rules and advanced training and tools for its members.

Real estate agents provide a trusted and essential service to buyers and sellers. They also enjoy the freedom to handle as many or as few listings as they would like. For this reason, it is possible to become a part-time real estate agent to see if the work is something that you would like to pursue full time.

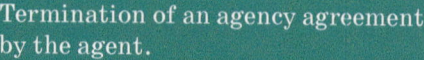

RENUNCIATION:
Termination of an agency agreement by the agent.

REVOCATION:
Termination of an agency agreement by the principal.

An agency agreement is a type of contract. Any of the events that would terminate a contract will also make an agency agreement end. Events that make performance impossible, such as the goal of a contract becoming impossible or one of the parties dying, will bring the agency agreement to an end.

CHAPTER SUMMARY

Agency is how one person acts through another person. Some "persons," such as corporations, can act only through their agents. The rule of "respondeat superior" sums up agency law. When an agent acts for another person, or principal, the principal may be responsible for those actions. Acts done on behalf of the principal are the principal's responsibility.

Review Questions

Review question 1.
Why is agency so important to business operations?

Review question 2.
When is the term "respondeat superior" relevant? What does it mean, and why does it matter?

Review question 3.
How do parties create an agency relationship? Are there specific formalities? Do agency agreements need to be in writing? Why or why not?

Review question 4.
What is negligent hiring? What are some of the circumstances in which a principal would be considered not to be negligent in hiring, even though the person had a history of bad acts?

Review question 5.
What is negligent retention? What are a principal-employer's responsibilities when he discovers that an agent-employee is untrustworthy or dangerous?

Review question 6.
When is a principal vicariously liable for the non-criminal wrongful acts of an agent? What is negligence? When is someone considered to be negligent?

Review question 7.

Is a principal responsible for criminal activity by an agent? What if that activity was in furtherance of the principal's interests?

Review question 8.

Describe what a "fiduciary duty" is. What fiduciary duties does an agent owe to his principal?

Review question 9.

What duties does a principal owe to an agent? Are those duties fiduciary or non-fiduciary? Do the different duties between the parties seem appropriate? Why or why not?

Review question 10.

What is a frolic? A detour? How do these concepts affect the scope of a principal's liability for an agent's actions?

Review question 11.

What is the difference between actual and apparent authority? Why is the difference important? Who is the difference important to?

Review question 12.

What does a "power of attorney" do? What are some of the different types of powers of attorney? Why would a person want to have one? What does a person need to have to be able to make a valid power of attorney appointment?

Review question 13.

What is an example of a common agency model other than a power of attorney? Why is agency so common? What are its benefits? What are its drawbacks?

Review question 14.

How is an agency relationship terminated? Does the termination always need to be included in the agency agreement? What circumstances might cause an agency relationship to end without an agreement?

Discussion Questions

Question 1:

Charles is a talent agent. He represents a former professional wrestler, Big Bad Ben. He books Big Bad Ben for corporate events and conventions. Big Bad Ben decides that his spouse is going to manage his career from now on, so he fires Charles. Charles has a friend who is a Big Bad Ben impersonator, and he is pretty convincing. Charles was making a lot of money from Ben's appearances and most people know him as Ben's agent, so he starts booking his friend instead of Ben. On one occasion, the friend does not show up, and the client calls Big Bad Ben and threatens to sue for the appearance fee. Big Bad Ben had no idea that Charles was continuing to book appearances with an impersonator.

> What authority did Charles have in this situation? What authority did the clients think he had?
>
> Has Charles violated any fiduciary duties to Big Bad Ben?
>
> Does Big Bad Ben have to pay the disappointed client? Why or why not?
>
> How could Big Bad Ben have avoided this situation?

Question 2:

Nelson is a bouncer at a bar. One night, he forces Bob to leave the bar by picking him up by the back of his shirt collar, and tossing him out on the sidewalk. Bob lands face-first on the sidewalk, and loses three teeth.

> Bob is being ejected because he is very loud and unruly, trying to start fights with other patrons. Is the bar owner liable for Bob's injuries? Why or why not?
>
> Bob is being ejected because he and Nelson got into a heated, but non-disruptive and non-violent, political argument. Is the bar owner liable for Bob's injuries?

Question 3:

Emin plans to take a six-week vacation from the clothing store he operates. He leaves his assistant Lamar in charge, telling him to keep the store running the usual hours, and in the usual way. A week after Emin leaves, a shipment of sweaters arrives. Lamar accepts the shipment, and signs for the delivery. A few days after that, one of the salespeople quits, and Lamar hires Henry to replace him. Two weeks before Emin is to return, a hurricane bears down on the city where the store is located. The state governor orders everyone to evacuate. Lamar boards up the windows, closes the store, and leaves town with the employees.

> What is the scope of Lamar's express authority here?

> Did Lamar have the authority to accept the shipment of sweaters? Why or why not?

> Did he have the authority to hire Henry? Why or why not?

> Did Lamar have the authority to close the store? Why or why not?

Question 4:

Shiny Shoes hires an agent to find a new location for the company's offices.

> What types of things should the business know about the agent? What types of background research would be advisable?

> Do you think it is important for an agent to be aligned with the business's culture and values? Why or why not?

Question 5:

Givens Gifts employs John and Felicia. John works in IT and Felicia works in sales. John and Felicia become romantically involved and move in together. The relationship starts to sour, and John and Felicia argue, but never at work. During one fight at home, John punches Felicia, knocking her unconscious. He is convicted of assault and goes to prison. Felicia finds another job while John is in prison.

When John is released, he applies to be rehired by Givens Gifts. Two managers disagree about whether hiring John is a good idea. One manager says that John has a history of assaulting co-workers, so the hire would be negligent. The other says that John did not assault a co-worker but was involved in a domestic violence crime, and has paid his debt to society. This manager also argues that the proposed IT job keeps John out of contact with most of the remaining workforce. He also admits that he told John he could have his job back after prison.

>Which side do you agree with? Why?

>Is this a case of potential negligent hiring? Negligent retention?

>Do you think the manager was authorized to make promises to John about re-hire?

>Do any of your answers change if John was never officially terminated by Givens Gifts?

Question 6:

Nancy arranges to interview Khalid for a job. When he arrives, she brings him to her office and asks him to wait a minute. While she is gone, a delivery driver arrives with an envelope for Nancy. He asks if Khalid will sign for the envelope, which Khalid does. Nancy returns and Khalid informs her of the delivery.

>Did Khalid become Nancy's agent? Why or why not?

>How can Nancy ratify Khalid's action?

>Suppose that Nancy was avoiding the delivery because it contained summons for a lawsuit against her. She tells Khalid he should not have accepted the envelope. Is Khalid responsible to Nancy for accepting the unwanted package?

Question 7:

Juno is living overseas. She grants her brother Drew a power of attorney to sell her house. Drew places the property with a real estate agent and keeps it tidy, but the house doesn't sell. On the advice of the real estate agent, Drew pays an exterminator to remove bats in the attic and a painter to freshen up the interior walls. The house still doesn't sell. Drew then pays a contractor to finish the basement. He also tells his neighbor that if the neighbor doesn't buy Juno's house, he will report the neighbor's son to the police for dealing drugs. The son is not a drug dealer. Juno is unaware of any of these actions beyond the house listing.

> Which of Drew's actions are within the scope of his authority under the power of attorney? For which items did he have apparent authority?
>
> Is Juno vicariously liable for the debts to the contractor, painter, and exterminator? Why or why not?
>
> Is Juno responsible to Drew's neighbor? Why or why not?

Question 8:

Jingyi asks her business manager Paul to go to a bank meeting in a town 25 miles away. As Paul is driving to the meeting, he receives a call from his aunt, who says that Paul's favorite uncle is in the hospital. The hospital is 10 miles out of Paul's way.

> Suppose Paul decides to change course and go to the hospital. About a mile after he turned off of the highway to the bank, Paul is in a car accident. The police say the accident was Paul's fault, and the people in the other car want to be compensated. Is Jingyi liable to the people in the other car? Why or why not?
>
> Suppose Paul decides to go to the meeting and see his uncle later. After he arrives in town, he decides to drive two blocks out of his way to order "get well" balloons for his uncle. As he is pulling in to park in front of the shop, he hits a person on a bicycle, who is injured. Is Jingyi liable to the injured bicyclist? Is the outcome the same as the result in the last scenario? Why or why not?

11 EMPLOYMENT

KEY OBJECTIVES:
- ▶ Define the employment relationship and its roles.
- ▶ Explain the major federal laws intended to protect employees from discrimination and injury.
- ▶ Describe the role of unions in the workplace.

CHAPTER OVERVIEW

This chapter examines the laws governing the employment relationship in the United States. Most businesses, regardless of industry, hire workers on a temporary or ongoing basis. As a result, an understanding of the laws governing workers and employers is critical to everyone involved in business.

This chapter first looks at the employment relationship and employer and employee responsibilities. It then covers some of the major anti-discrimination and health and safety laws designed to protect workers. Finally, the chapter examines the role of unions and collective bargaining in the workplace.

INTRODUCTION

The employee relationship is fundamental to business. Commercial entities need workers in order to successfully run their operations. Employment is equally important for the workers, who need to work to provide compensation and other benefits for themselves and their families. Employment has a significant impact on an individual's standard of living and quality of life, issues of health and safety, and access to health care. As such, it is fair to say that employment and employment-related issues touch on nearly all aspects of life. Therefore, the law attempts to strike a balance between the rights of employers and those of employees.

Not all workers are treated the same under the law. Indeed, there is an important distinction between employees and non-employees. Once an employment relationship is established, the employer takes on a number of responsibilities with respect to its employees. Employees are entitled to benefits and protections not available to non-employee workers. Employers must meet wage standards and provide a safe workplace. They are also bound by anti-discrimination laws. In a unionized workplace, employers must take care to follow the terms of their agreement with labor. These issues and related concerns are examined in this chapter.

I. Employment Relationship

When a person is hired for a wage, salary, or payment to perform work for an employer under a contract of employment, that person is generally—but not always—an **employee**. An employee provides services on a regular basis in exchange for compensation. An employee enters into the relationship as an individual, rather than as an independent business contracting with another company. Employees usually work for continuous periods with no specified end date. An employee works under the instructions and training provided by the employer. The employer provides the tools or equipment needed to perform the job.

A key characteristic of an employment relationship is that the employer has substantial control over the manner in which the work is completed. The employer controls employees' hours, where they work, and what tasks are to be completed.

Being an employee gives a worker certain rights. The alternative is working as an independent contractor. Independent contractors do not have as many rights as employees, but they are subject to more freedom in how and where they perform the work. These distinctions will be discussed further in this section.

At-Will Employment

Today, most employees are **at-will employees**. At-will employment means that either the employer or employee may end the relationship at any time. Under at-will employment, an employer may fire the employee without cause. In other words, the employer does not need a reason to fire the employee.

> **EMPLOYEE:**
> A person working for another person or a business firm for pay.
>
> **AT-WILL EMPLOYMENT:**
> An employment relationship under which the employer or employee may end the relationship at any time.

Employee documents often indicate that an employee is hired at-will. For instance, the job application, employment offer, and employee handbook may state that the employee is entering an at-will employment relationship.

> The following is a sample at-will employment statement you might find in an employee handbook: "As an employee of the Company, you are employed at will. You may terminate your employment at any time, for any reason, with or without cause. Similarly, the Company may end the employment relationship with you at any time, for any reason, with or without cause."

These documents might also state that the employee can be "fired for any reason." A statement of that type establishes an at-will relationship. Generally, unless some documentation or action by the employer shows the employment is not at-will, the law assumes all employment relationships are at-will.

Some employees have a contract stating that the employee may only be fired for certain reasons. For instance, the employment contract might state the employee may only be fired for illegal or unethical behavior. In that situation, the employee is not an at-will employee. If an employer fires a non-at-will employee and does not do so for a reason stated in the agreement, the employee may sue the employer.

Even in at-will employment, however, the employer may not discriminate against employees on the basis of certain personal characteristics. The anti-discrimination laws

EMPLOYEE MANUAL MAY CREATE A CONTRACTUAL RELATIONSHIP

Pine River State Bank v. Mettille
(Bank) v. (Terminated Loan Officer)
333 N.W.2d 622 (Minn. 1983)

INSTANT FACTS:
Plaintiff employee claimed the employer was required to follow procedures identified in employee handbook in order to terminate his employment.

BLACK LETTER RULE:
An employee handbook may create a contract between the employee and employer.

FACTS:
The plaintiff was a loan officer at a bank. His employment was terminated due to poor performance. The employee sued, claiming that the bank did not comply with the terms of the employee handbook given to bank employees. The manual included provisions that required two reprimands before an employee could be suspended or discharged. Under the terms of the handbook, the employer could terminate employment only after a factual review performed according to certain procedures. Employees were to be given a chance to improve after a reprimand. The bank did not follow the procedures in the handbook before terminating the plaintiff's employment.

ISSUE:
Does an employee handbook create a contract between the employee and employer?

DECISION AND RATIONALE:
Yes. The Minnesota Supreme Court held that the employment handbook constituted a binding agreement. The bank's failure to follow the disciplinary provision of the handbook could be considered a breach of contract. The Court stated that the employer issued an offer of employment when it disseminated the handbook. By continuing to work for the employer after the handbook came out, the employee accepted the terms. The employer was then contractually obligated to follow the procedures specified in the handbook.

ANALYSIS:
This decision provided employees with significant rights. Prior to this ruling, Minnesota employers could terminate at-will employees as they pleased. Many employers now skirt this and similar holdings in other states by including a disclaimer in the employee handbook. For instance, the handbook may include a statement that it is subject to change and is not binding on the employer, or specifically provide that the handbook is not a contract.

---

applicable to employers are discussed later in this chapter.

INDEPENDENT CONTRACTORS:
Workers with a high level of independence who are in business for themselves.

Employers take on a range of responsibilities for employees. With respect to employees, employers must withhold and pay Social Security and Medicare taxes. Employers also pay unemployment tax on wages paid to an employee. Half of the estimated state and federal income tax owed by an employee is withheld by the employer. Employers are also bound by minimum wage standards and other protections.

Independent Contractor

Independent contractors are workers with a high level of independence who are in business for themselves. Freelancers, contract or "gig" workers, and temporary workers are generally considered independent contractors.

If the parties intend to enter an independent contractor relationship, the employer and worker typically sign an agreement stating that the worker is an independent contractor. Payment is then made on invoices submitted by the contractor rather than as regular wages. However, an agreement between the employer and worker does not definitively decide independent contractor status. To determine if a worker is an employee or an independent contractor, the law looks at all of the circumstances. No single issue is enough to decide the matter one way or the other.

Several factors are examined to determine if a person is working as an employee or an independent contractor, but no single element is enough on its own. All the factors must be considered in balance. The factors include:

- Does the worker or employer supply the equipment, materials and tools?
- Does the worker or employer control the hours of employment?
- Is the work temporary or permanent?
- Does the worker or employer control the tasks that are performed?
- Does the employer provide training?
- Does the worker complete tasks for more than one company?
- Is the worker's presence required at certain events?

> Since the late 2000s, businesses based on a model utilizing independent contractors for short-term projects and tasks have boomed. These businesses use technology to match individuals who are willing to perform a requested task with persons looking for assistance with a specific task. For example, DoorDash connects people who want restaurant food brought to their homes with individuals who are willing to pick up and deliver their orders. The work is done on a task-by-task basis.
>
> Proponents of the gig economy argue that this model brings more wage-earning opportunities to more people. Critics argue that this business model eliminates traditional, secure jobs and replaces them with part-time, low-paid work without employee benefits. Others note that the number of independent contractor workers was increasing well before the gig economy took hold.
>
> The use of this model by businesses raises important questions. Are the individuals accepting the company's gigs independent contractors or employees? Because independent contractors do not have taxes withheld or receive benefits, gig companies have far lower costs. But some workers have sued to be treated as employees, with some success.

Many companies try to save money by hiring independent contractors. Companies do not have to pay benefits or taxes on those workers,

TECHNOLOGIST WHO WORKED FOR SAME COMPANY FOR THREE YEARS MAY HAVE BEEN MISCLASSIFIED AS AN INDEPENDENT CONTRACTOR

Weiss v. Loomis, Sayles & Company, Inc.
(Technology Worker) v. (Employer)
97 Mass. App. Ct. 1 (2020)

In 2010, a recruiter at Eliassen Group, LLC, a large information technology staffing firm, contacted Weiss about certain project-based work at Loomis, a financial services company. On August 4, 2010, Loomis entered into a "professional services vendor agreement" with Eliassen for "Joel Weiss for technology services." The only JoSol employee authorized to provide services to Loomis was Weiss. On February 1, 2013, Loomis and Eliassen entered into a second "professional services vendor agreement" for "Joel Weiss for Technology Services." That contract [stated] that Weiss was "free to accept engagements from others during the term of this Agreement, so long as such actions [did] not impair [his] ability to perform his . . . services to Loomis Sayles."

In September 2010, Weiss commenced work in Loomis's technology group. Weiss worked on at least fifteen Loomis projects. Weiss reported to [Loomis employee] McGuire, among others. During their daily interactions, McGuire "would give [Weiss] direction" and Weiss would bring issues to McGuire. Weiss worked directly with the Loomis employees who used the applications, assisting with specific issues and upgrades.

Loomis assigned Weiss to a cubicle directly across from McGuire's office and provided Weiss with a desk, computer, office supplies, a badge allowing building access, a Loomis picture identification card, a Loomis telephone number, and a Loomis e-mail address. Although Weiss had no set work hours, "the conventional wisdom" was that he should be in the office during business hours.

[T]he Eliassen recruiter informed Weiss that his contract was "open ended" and that he had "never had a consultant finish [at Loomis]." [Loomis terminated Weiss after he took a project for another employer that did not interfere with his Loomis work hours.]

Misclassification claim. "Under [state statute], an individual who performs services shall be considered to be an employee . . . unless the employer satisfies its burden of proving by a preponderance of the evidence that '(1) the individual is free from control and direction in connection with the performance of the service, both under his contract for the performance of service and in fact; and (2) the service is performed outside the usual course of the business of the employer; and (3) the individual is customarily engaged in an independently established trade, occupation, profession or business of the same nature as that involved in the service performed.' " Thus a putative employer like Loomis may rebut the statutory presumption of employment by establishing by a preponderance of the evidence the three prongs of an independent contractor relationship. If Loomis failed to satisfy even one statutory prong, Weiss was Loomis's employee.

Here, the evidence demonstrated that Loomis contracted with Eliassen not for the services of JoSol, but for "Joel Weiss for technology services." In fact, Weiss was the only JoSol employee authorized by Loomis to perform the services in issue. Weiss provided his personal services to Loomis for three years, working forty to sixty hours per week. Due to time constraints and the contractual restriction that Loomis imposed on Weiss's work for others, a jury could find that the services of Weiss, the alleged independent contractor, were not "actually available to entities beyond [Loomis], even if they [were] purport[ed] to be so." Although other factors could support a finding of a legitimate business-to-business relationship exempt from liability under [state law], the factual issue should have been submitted to the jury.

i. Freedom from control and direction. Based on the evidence presented, the jury could have reasonably found that Weiss was subject to Loomis control and direction, both under his contract for the performance of the services, and in fact. The issue turns on whether Loomis had the right to supervise, direct, and control the details of Weiss's performance, or whether Weiss was free from supervision "not only as to the result to be accomplished but also as to the means and methods that are to be utilized in the performance of the work[.]"

Here, JoSol's contract with Eliassen restricted Weiss's ability to perform services for others that might have interfered with his work at Loomis. Before agreeing to the engagement, Loomis supervisors interviewed Weiss. McGuire gave Weiss assignments and directions, and actively supervised the performance of Weiss's services from McGuire's office directly across from Weiss's cubicle. Weiss brought McGuire his "issues" and attended meetings where progress was discussed. E-mail messages established that Weiss and McGuire frequently communicated and discussed the technical details of projects. As part of his daily job, Weiss performed required tasks for other Loomis managers. Loomis also provided Weiss with a work station and the supplies and equipment he needed to perform the services. In order to get paid, Weiss was required to submit his hours weekly to his supervisor at Loomis for approval. Loomis paid Weiss by the hour, not by the project, and had the authority to grant raises. Loomis monitored and limited Weiss's hours, and terminated Weiss at will without reason. This evidence was sufficient to support a finding of control[.]

ii. Usual course of business. In assessing whether services are performed outside the usual course of business of the company, one relevant factor is whether the services are necessary or merely incidental to the business. The Supreme Judicial Court has illustrated the concept of services provided within the employer's usual course of business with three examples: an art instructor providing services on a "regular or continuous basis" within an art museum; musicians performing as a "usual and customary activity" of a beer bar; and an organist playing music as a "usual part of" a funeral home's business (citations omitted). We conclude that the jury applying these principles could have found that Weiss performed services within the usual course of Loomis's business.

Loomis is in the business of managing and investing money for its clients. The jury could have found that Loomis maintained a large technology group as part of its normal operations; and that Loomis staffed it on a regular and continuous basis with a significant number of independent contractors. Indeed, according to one Eliassen recruiter, the contractors never finished at Loomis. The contractors provided the technology services needed by Loomis's investment professionals, working full time for years on assignments from their Loomis managers. There was intermingling within the technology group to the point that neither Loomis employees nor contractors knew whether they were interfacing with fellow employees or independent contractors.

iii. Independently established business. [T]he question is whether at the time the services were provided, the individual was "wearing the hat" of the putative employer or the "hat of his own independent enterprise." The determination whether this statutory prong is satisfied "must be based upon a comprehensive analysis of the totality of relevant facts and circumstances of the working relationship. No one factor is outcome-determinative." We need not repeat the evidence that would establish that Loomis did not, as a matter of law, necessarily meet its evidentiary burden with respect to this prong. Suffice it to say that a jury could have found that in reality, Weiss was not free to provide services to anyone of his choice; and that the hat he wore for three years through fifteen different projects had a Loomis label on it. Of particular significance was the restriction inserted by Loomis in the contract that Weiss was only free to work for others "so long as such actions [did] not impair [his] ability to perform his . . . services to Loomis Sayles."

In sum, in order to prevail, Weiss had to prevail on only one of the statutory prongs, and there was evidence from which the jury could have found in favor of Weiss on each of the statutory prongs. At the time the trial judge granted the motion for a directed verdict on the misclassification claim, Loomis had not proved that Weiss was an independent contractor as a matter of law. The verdict was directed in error. A new trial on the misclassification claim will be required.

providing substantial savings. But it is important for employers to classify workers correctly as employees or independent contractors. The classification of a worker as an employee or contractor has consequences for the employer and the worker. The classification also affects the employer's responsibilities to withhold and pay certain taxes. Employment status may also provide certain employment benefits offered by the employer. Independent contractors do not receive the benefits afforded to employees.

> **Example:** Erin works for Marmco. Erin sits in a four-desk pod with three other workers. The other workers are all full time employees and do the exact same work as Erin. Marmco supplies a computer, a phone extension, and an email address. Erin is required to work 8:00 a.m. to 4:30 p.m. Monday through Friday. Under these facts, Erin is likely to be considered an employee.
>
> Assume instead that Erin is paid $1,200 per week to provide graphic design services for Marmco. Marmco provides a small desk for her use, but Erin is not required to work on-site. Erin provides her own computer and phone. Erin often works at home, from 6:00 a.m. to 3:00 p.m. Sometimes, she chooses to work from 8:00 a.m. to 4:30 p.m. instead. Based on these facts, Erin is likely to be considered an independent contractor.

Because there is no clear test to determine if a party is an employee or independent contractor, an employer may incorrectly classify a worker. It is usually cheaper for an employer if a worker is classified as an independent contractor. This creates an incentive for employers to classify workers as independent contractors. When discussing the **misclassification** of workers, then, the issue is whether an independent contractor should have been treated as an employee. Employers are subject to penalties for the misclassification of workers.

> In recent years, the government has engaged in a concerted effort to fight worker misclassification. The U.S. Department of Labor awarded millions of dollars in grants to a number of states to combat employee misclassification. Recent federal budget requests similarly sought funding to provide further grants. Numerous states have worked together to create inter-agency task forces to study the misclassification problem and coordinate enforcement efforts.

II. Employer Responsibilities

Employee status comes with several significant benefits for the employee. An employee works for the employer for compensation. The employer and employee agree to the wage to be paid to the employee. The parties typically have great discretion to determine the amount of pay. However, minimum wage and overtime pay rules do impose some restrictions on the wage.

Employers must provide a few benefits to employees by law. Employers may voluntarily offer additional benefits. **Employee benefits** refers to non-cash compensation and services provided to employees, including insurance

MISCLASSIFICATION: When an employer incorrectly classifies an employee as an independent contractor.

programs, paid absences, pensions, stock ownership plans, or other services.

Minimum Wage

Most employers are subject to **minimum wage** laws. Minimum wage laws require employers to pay a minimum hourly wage to its workers. The Fair Labor Standards Act, a federal law, applies to businesses that produce goods for interstate commerce and engage in interstate commerce. Many states also have minimum wage laws. Certain groups of employees are exempt from the minimum wage laws. Salaried employees, including executive, administrative, and professional employees, some seasonal workers, and casual babysitters and companions to the elderly are all exempt from the minimum wage laws.

> As of this writing, the federal minimum wage was $7.25/hour. That minimum was set in 2009.

EMPLOYEE BENEFITS: Non-cash compensation and services provided to employees by employers.

MINIMUM WAGE: The lowest wage permitted by law to be paid to workers.

OVERTIME PAY: Additional compensation paid to workers for hours worked in excess of forty hours per week.

Overtime Pay

A regular workweek is considered 40 hours of work in a week. Employees are entitled to **overtime pay** for hours worked over 40 hours in one week. Employers must pay 1.5 times the worker's normal hourly wage for each hour worked over 40 hours in one week. The employees exempt from the minimum wage requirements and several other groups of employees are exempt from overtime rules.

Mandated Benefits

Employers often provide a number of benefits to their employees. For example, employers might offer paid vacation time, tuition reimbursement, and retirement savings plans. These employee benefits are not legally required and are only voluntarily provided by employers.

A few other benefits are required by law. Employers must withhold Social Security, Medicare, and Federal Insurance Contributions Act (FICA) payments. Employers must also provide unemployment insurance and workers' compensation insurance. Under the Affordable Care Act, large employers must offer minimal essential health coverage to at least 95 percent of its full-time employees and their dependents. In addition, employees who leave a company that provided health insurance have the right to continue their health insurance coverage by assuming the premium payments. This continuation is often referred to as COBRA coverage, after the Consolidated Omnibus Budget Reconciliation Act of 1985 that established the right. Beyond health care coverage and other benefits, many employees are entitled to family and medical leave.

Family and Medical Leave

Under the Family and Medical Leave Act, employees may take up to 12 weeks of unpaid leave during a 12-amonth period for family and medical reasons. The Act applies to companies with 50 or more employees.

A qualifying employee of such a business cannot be fired for taking **family and medical leave**. To qualify, the employee must work 1,250 hours for the employer in the twelve months prior to the leave. An employee may take family and medical leave after the birth or adoption of a child, to care for a family member (spouse, son, daughter, or parent) with a serious health condition. The leave may also be available if the employee is unable to perform her job because of a serious health condition. The amount of leave rises to 26 weeks in a year if the family member for whom leave is sought is a member of the armed services and became ill or injured while on active duty.

Other Leaves

Paternity/Maternity Leave: **Maternity leave** is a period of absence from work for an employee for the purpose of giving birth and taking care of the infant child. **Paternity leave** is an absence from work provided to fathers upon the birth or adoption of a child. The Family and Medical Leave Act provides 12 weeks of unpaid leave after an employee has had or adopted a child. Many states also require employers to provide maternity or paternity leave. Some employers voluntarily provide paid maternity and paternity leave for their employees. Employers may also provide more than 12 weeks of unpaid maternity or paternity leave as an employee benefit—12 weeks is only the legal threshold for larger employers.

> **FAMILY AND MEDICAL LEAVE:**
> An unpaid leave from work taken by an employee for family and medical reasons.
>
> **MATERNITY LEAVE:**
> A period of absence from work for an employee for the purpose of giving birth and taking care of an infant child.
>
> **PATERNITY LEAVE:**
> An absence from work provided to fathers upon the birth of a child.
>
> **SICK LEAVE:**
> An absence from work when an employee is sick.

> In the past, companies would often provide separate amounts of time off for personal days, sick leave, and vacation time. Currently, many companies offer employees a certain number of hours of Paid Time Off, or PTO. Typical PTO policies combine sick leave, vacation leave, and floating holidays into a single amount of PTO. Employees may use PTO time as they wish, for vacation, sick time, appointments, or other reasons. Under many PTO policies, the employee accrues a specific number of PTO hours during each pay period.

Military Service Leave: The Uniform Services Employment and Reemployment Rights Act requires all employers to provide unpaid leave for military service. The employee must give the employer notice of the intention to take military leave. The law covers all employers, regardless of size. The leave covers National Guard and Reserve service, as well as joining the regular armed services.

Sick Leave: Employers are not required to provide paid sick leave for employees. Sick leave is time off of work when an employee is sick. However, many employers choose to offer a certain amount of paid sick leave for their employees.

Vacation Leave and Holidays: Employers are not required to provide paid vacation time to their employees. Many employers voluntarily offer some amount of vacation leave to employees. Many companies also provide a number of paid days off on certain holidays each year.

Types of Leave	
Type of Leave	*Description*
Family and Medical Leave	• Unpaid leave, for up to 12 weeks during a 12-month period, for family and medical reasons • Required under federal law for employers with 50 or more employees
Paternity/Maternity Leave	• A period of absence from work for an employee for the purpose of birth or adoption and/or taking care of an infant child • Paid leave is not required by federal law
Military Service Leave	• Unpaid leave to serve in the military with advance notice to employer • Required by federal law with no minimum employer size
Sick Leave	• Time off during illness • Not required by law in most jurisdictions
Vacation Leave	• Time off for vacation • Not required by law
Jury Leave	• Employees must be allowed to serve on a jury • In many states, employer has the right to deduct juror's payment from the employee's paycheck

Jury Leave: Employees may be required to serve on a jury. When that happens, the employer cannot penalize the employee for serving on a jury. A few states do not allow employers to deduct pay for employee time spent on jury duty. Although not required, many employers choose to provide paid leave for jury duty.

III. Termination of Employment

When an employer chooses to end the employment relationship, the employer **terminates** the employee. Under at-will employment, an employer does not need to provide a specific notice period before terminating an employee. An employer must pay the employee for all time worked until termination. In most states, state laws require the employer to provide the employee's final paycheck within a specified amount of time.

Severance Pay

Sometimes, the employer and employee enter a **severance agreement** following termination. Under such an agreement, the employer agrees to give the employee a severance package. In exchange, the employee agrees not to sue the employer for wrongful termination. As part of the severance package, the employee typically receives a cash payment. The employer may also agree to pay for continued health insurance, training opportunities, or assistance in finding other employment.

IV. Employee Protection Laws

Many employment laws protect workers from unfair actions by their employers. These laws include anti-discrimination provisions, employee safety rules, and worker's compensation programs.

Anti-Discrimination Laws

The law recognizes the importance of fairness in employment relationships. Federal and state laws prohibit employers from discriminating against employees based on race or skin color, national origin, genetic information (such as family medical history), gender or pregnancy, religion, disability, and age. These personal characteristics are referred to as **protected classes**. Some state anti-discrimination laws may prohibit discrimination on additional grounds, such as marital status, political affiliation, and sexual orientation. Employers are legally responsible for discrimination by managers, supervisors, or other employees.

TERMINATION:
When an employee is fired from his or her job.

SEVERANCE AGREEMENT:
A contract between an employer and employee detailing the rights and responsibilities of both parties after job termination.

PROTECTED CLASS:
A personal characteristic that cannot be targeted for discrimination.

Title VII

Title VII of the Civil Rights Act of 1964 is the main source of anti-discrimination law. Title VII applies to most businesses with 15 or more employees. It is illegal for employers to discriminate based upon race or skin color, national origin, genetic information (such as family medical history), gender or pregnancy, and religion in hiring, compensation, training, promotion, termination or any other terms or condition of employment.

Title VII does have a narrow exception. An employer may discriminate on the basis of religion, sex, or national origin if that characteristic is a **bona fide occupational qualification**. A bona fide occupational qualification (often shortened to BFOQ) is a job qualification that is reasonably necessary to the normal operation of the business. For instance, it might be a bona fide occupational qualification for the president of a religious college to be a member of that religion. It is less likely that the groundskeeper at the college would need to share that faith. The courts view this exception very critically, so the organization must have a compelling case for the discrimination if it is challenged.

> BFOQ discrimination is not allowed for race under Title VII or any other law. It is allowed for age under the federal Age Discrimination in Employment Act.

A Title VII violation may result from intentional conduct or conduct that appears to have been based on a discriminatory motive if it cannot be explained otherwise. **Disparate treatment** refers to employer actions that appear to be based directly on a discriminatory motivation.

Disparate treatment refers to any adverse employment action—failure to hire, failure to promote, demotions, unfavorable assignments, and so forth. Once an initial case is shown that there may have been disparate treatment, the burden shifts to the employer to show that there was a legitimate and non-discriminatory reason for that treatment.

The other side may be able to show that the given reason is actually a pretext, and discrimination was the real motive. An employer may not use a job requirement as a pretext for discrimination based on a protected characteristic. Discrimination may occur when an employee is

---

TITLE VII:
A section of the Civil Rights Act of 1964 prohibiting employment discrimination on the basis of sex, race, color, national origin, and religion.

BONA FIDE OCCUPATIONAL QUALIFICATION:
An employment qualification, related to an essential job duty, that employers may consider in making decisions about hiring and retention of employees.

DISPARATE TREATMENT:
Intentional, unequal treatment of an employee on the basis of a protected class by an employer.

TITLE VII CLAIM THAT SEXUAL HARASSMENT CREATED A HOSTILE WORK ENVIRONMENT IS NOT BARRED BECAUSE THE ALLEGED HARASSERS ARE THE SAME SEX AS PLAINTIFF

Oncale v. Sundowner Offshore Services, Inc.
(Employee) v. (Employer)
523 U.S. 75, 118 S. Ct. 998, 140 L. Ed. 2d 201 (1998)

INSTANT FACTS:
A male drilling-rig employee sued his employer and individual supervisors and coworkers for sexual harassment because of verbal abuse and physical assault from male coworkers.

BLACK LETTER RULE:
A Title VII claim of sex discrimination based on a hostile working environment is not barred because the plaintiff and the alleged harasser(s) are of the same sex.

PROCEDURAL BASIS:
Certiorari granted to review a Fifth Circuit decision affirming a District Court grant of summary judgment in favor of employer holding that same-sex harassment could not be a Title VII violation.

FACTS:
Sundowner Offshore Services, Inc. ("Sundowner") (D) employed Joseph Oncale ("Oncale") (P) as a roustabout on an oil platform in the Gulf of Mexico. Oncale (P) alleged that three members of the eight-man crew, including two supervisors ("Lyons" (D) and "Pippen" (D)), subjected him to sex-related humiliation in front of the others. He also alleged that the two supervisors physically assaulted him in a sexual manner, and that Lyons (D) threatened to rape him. Oncale (P) also alleged that Sundowner (D) took no action when he complained. Oncale (D) quit Sundowner (D) saying that he feared that if he had stayed on, he would have been raped.

Oncale (D) filed a complaint in federal court. The Eastern District of Louisiana granted summary judgment for Sundowner (D), citing the Fifth Circuit's holding in Garcia that Title VII did not support an action for same sex harassment. The Fifth Circuit affirmed. Oncale (P) sought review and we granted certiorari.

ISSUE:
Can workplace harassment of an individual by someone of the same sex be a sexual discrimination violation under Title VII?

DECISION AND RATIONALE:
(Justice Scalia) Yes. Oncale's (P) claim of sex discrimination under Title VII is not barred because Oncale (P) and the individuals alleged to have sexually harassed him were all males. Title VII of the Civil Rights Act of 1964 made it unlawful for employers to "discriminate against any individual with respect to his compensation, terms, conditions, or privileges of employment because of such individual's . . . sex." Elsewhere, we held that sex discrimination covers more than differential compensation or promotion and may be the result of sexual harassment sufficiently pervasive and severe to create an abusive work environment.

Courts have generally recognized the possibility of same sex discrimination in differential compensation or promotion cases, but have not uniformly extended that reasoning to cases in which discrimination is alleged to arise from an abusive work environment. Some circuits have ruled that Title VII recognizes no same-sex harassment, while other circuits allow such claims with proof that the harasser is homosexual. Finally, some circuits have held that Title VII supports harassment claims "regardless of the harasser's sex, sexual orientation, or motivations." It is not relevant that eliminating same-sex harassment was not Congress' primary motive in adopting Title VII. The statute covers any type of harassment "that meets the statutory requirements."

Sundowner (D) argues that recognition of same-sex harassment will expand Title VII into "a general civility code." Title VII, however, does not ban all types of harassment in the workplace, but only that constituting discrimination because of sex. Juries may have an easier time construing the facts of male-female harassment as sex discrimination, because the conduct may involve explicit propositions that the trier may assume would not be directed at workers of the harasser's sex. Juries might make the same assumptions in same-sex harassment cases involving a homosexual harasser. Title VII does not, however, require that the harasser be motivated by sexual desire. What matters under Title VII is that the harassment is sex-specific and rises to the level of discrimination.

Innocuous interactions and ordinary socializing (including some horseplay or flirtation) are not violations of Title VII, only "conduct . . . severe or pervasive enough to create an objectively hostile or abusive work environment" rises to that level. Moreover, same-sex harassment must be evaluated considering the totality of the circumstances. Considering the context of the employment (e.g., ball field versus office building) will also guide juries in distinguishing between those behaviors reasonable persons would consider harassment and those they would consider benign. This case is reversed and remanded.

ANALYSIS:

Through the early history of its judicial interpretation, the term "sex" as used in Title VII covered discrimination based on gender differences, where the purpose of the discriminatory behavior was to elicit sexual favors. A new wrinkle was added when the courts found that behavior that created an abusive work environment was also sex discrimination under Title VII. In Oncale, the plaintiff alleged hostile work environment discrimination, but in this case both the victim and the alleged harasser were males. This defied the stereotypical idea of discrimination based on mistreatment or disrespect for an individual or group identifiably different from others in the workplace.

Further complicating the facts is the all-male work environment of the drilling platform. Oncale (P) thus could not show that he was treated differently than females at his workplace. The Court's opinion identified one further reason that courts had been reluctant to find same sex discrimination: our natural association of sexual discrimination with sexual desire. This also explains why courts were willing to find discrimination in same-sex situations where the party accused of harassment was homosexual.

Importantly, the Court points out that the motivation for the discrimination is irrelevant to finding that conduct has been sufficiently pervasive or severe to create a hostile work environment. Thus, the fact that the alleged harasser is of the same sex as the victim is irrelevant to establishing discrimination under Title VII.

Example: Xeta Corporation is a large multinational corporation. The Global Accounts Business Group consists of 45 employees. The manager of the Global Accounts Group, who is also Caucasian, has hired five Caucasian employees in the past two years. Emily is a Black applicant for a position at Xeta. She is fully qualified for the position, and the interview goes well. After the interview, the manager sends her a letter that Xeta is not proceeding with her application. Emily notices that the job continues to be advertised with the same requirements. Emily later hears that the job has been filled by an acquaintance who is white. Based on these facts, it appears that Xeta's failure to hire Emily may have been disparate treatment.

DISCRIMINATION CAN BE SHOWN BY CIRCUMSTANTIAL EVIDENCE

Desert Palace, Inc. v. Costa
(Casino Development) v. (Equipment Operator)
539 U.S. 90, 123 S. Ct. 2148, 156 L. Ed. 2d 84 (2003)

INSTANT FACTS:
Female employee sued employer for sex discrimination based on circumstantial evidence of discrimination.

BLACK LETTER RULE:
Circumstantial evidence is sufficient to prove mixed motive discrimination.

FACTS:
A female employee who worked as a heavy equipment operator at Desert Palace Casino was terminated. She brought a sex discrimination lawsuit, claiming that she experienced sex discrimination as an employee. The employee presented evidence that she had been stalked by a supervisor, received harsher discipline than male employees for the same conduct, received less favorable treatment than men regarding overtime, and was subjected to sex-based slurs by her supervisors. At trial, the jury instructions stated that jurors were to rule for the employee if they determined that sex was a motivating factor in the firing. The jurors were to do so even if other legal factors were also present. The jury ruled in favor of the employee. Desert Palace appealed, arguing that the instructions incorrectly shifted the burden of proof to the defendant. A full panel of Eleventh Circuit judges upheld the jury verdict.

ISSUE:
Is a plaintiff required to show direct evidence of discrimination in order to prove mixed motive discrimination?

DECISION AND RATIONALE:
No. Circumstantial evidence of discrimination is sufficient to prove a claim for mixed motive discrimination. The Supreme Court found that a reasonable jury could conclude that the plaintiff's sex was a motivating factor in the employer's decision, based on the circumstantial evidence presented by the plaintiff. The Court upheld the jury verdict.

ANALYSIS:
Under the mixed-motive theory of discrimination, the plaintiff must show that both legitimate and illegitimate reasons motivated the employer's decision. Prior to this decision, the courts held that direct evidence of discrimination was necessary to prove mixed-motive discrimination. The direct evidence standard was considered a heightened standard of proof. This decision lowered the standard of proof for plaintiffs trying to prove discrimination claims.

Example: A lumber company requires applicants to lift and carry 125 pounds up three flights of stairs. The policy has a negative impact on female applicants. Lumber company employees need to lift heavy weight. The company did not intentionally mean to discriminate against female employees. The company would have to show that lifting that amount of weight for that distance is necessary and job-related. If the lumber company always uses cranes for loads over 50 pounds, then the requirement is too broad, and any disparate impact is discriminatory.

not promoted or provided other advancement or opportunities, is not hired, or is terminated because of the characteristic. State anti-discrimination laws may prohibit discrimination on additional grounds.

An employer may also violate Title VII through conduct that tends to disfavor a particular groups. A neutral employment policy may violate Title VII if the policy has a **disparate impact** on members of a protected class. A disparate impact policy is illegal if the employer cannot justify the policy as a job-related business necessity.

If an employee believes they have been discriminated against, they must file a Charge of Discrimination with the Equal Employment Opportunity Commission (EEOC). The EEOC will investigate the complaint. After the investigation, the EEOC may issue a Notice of Right to Sue. That notice gives the employee permission to file a lawsuit in a court of law.

Age Discrimination

The Age Discrimination in Employment Act (ADEA) forbids employment discrimination against anyone 40 years of age or older. The ADEA prohibits discrimination in hiring, promotion, compensation, or termination of employment and layoffs. In a slight difference from Title VII, the ADEA applies to employers with 20 or more employees.

Employers may not indicate an age preference or limit in job notices or advertisements.

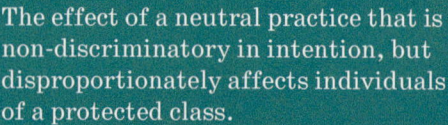

DISPARATE IMPACT:
The effect of a neutral practice that is non-discriminatory in intention, but disproportionately affects individuals of a protected class.

STUDENT WHO WAS OFFERED REASONABLE ACCOMMODATION FOR DISABILITY DID NOT HAVE A LEGAL CLAIM AGAINST UNIVERSITY

Mallon v. Frostburg State University
(Student) v. (University)
2021 WL 4215331 (D. Md. 2021)

In 2017, plaintiff enrolled as a student at defendant Frostburg State University ("FSU"). [P]laintiff's student account was put on hold because he had not complied with FSU's immunization policy. FSU's immunization policy "requires all students to be immunized or show proof of immunity for measles, mumps, rubella, diphtheria, and tetanus, and have documentation of such immunity [.]" Plaintiff reported to FSU that he had been diagnosed with a medical condition, rheumatoid arthritis, that he takes immunosuppressive medications to treat this condition, and that he therefore cannot receive vaccinations.

Defendants advised plaintiff that he could comply with the immunization policy by (1) obtaining his childhood vaccination records; (2) taking a measles, mumps, and rubella ("MMR") antibody titer blood test "to see if his childhood vaccines still provided him with immunity;" or (3) signing a religious exemption waiver[.] Plaintiff advised that he was previously vaccinated [but] had no way to obtain his vaccination records. Plaintiff also declined to take an MMR antibody titer test.

Additionally, plaintiff declined to sign the religious exemption waiver. FSU also offered plaintiff the option of signing a newly created waiver "for reasons of conscience," but plaintiff declined. Therefore, FSU would not lift the hold on plaintiff's account to allow him to register.

Pursuant to Title II of the ADA, "no qualified individual with a disability shall, by reason of such disability, be excluded from participation in or be denied the benefits of the services, programs, or activities of a public entity, or be subject to discrimination by any such entity." [P]laintiff must first demonstrate a prima facie case: (1) that he has a disability; (2) that he is otherwise qualified to receive the benefit of a service, program, or activity of a public entity; and (3) that he was excluded from such a benefit, or was otherwise discriminated against, on the basis of his disability. Next, if plaintiff successfully establishes this prima facie case, a burden-shifting approach is applied. Defendants must offer a non-discriminatory explanation for their actions, and then plaintiff must rebut defendants' explanation as pretextual for discrimination.

Regarding the first element of his prima facie case, plaintiff can demonstrate he has a disability if he: "(1) has a physical or mental impairment that substantially limits one or more of [plaintiff's] major life activities; (2) has a record of such an impairment; or (3) is regarded as having such an impairment." Plaintiff provided no evidence of his disability during the discovery process. In plaintiff's Motion, he attaches a page from what appears to be a Social Security disability opinion regarding his disability, and states that it was on file with defendant FSU. "[U]nsworn reports are inadmissible on summary judgment unless accompanied by affidavits or depositions swearing to their contents and conclusions." This unauthenticated, unsworn, single page . . . does not adequately support that plaintiff has a disability.

[E]ven if plaintiff argued that defendants were aware of plaintiff's rheumatoid arthritis diagnosis or plaintiff's adverse reactions to vaccinations, mere awareness does not generate a factual issue as to whether defendants regarded plaintiff as disabled. Accordingly, plaintiff has failed to generate a factual dispute as to whether he has a disability. While plaintiff may have a disability, plaintiff has not adduced admissible evidence to support that he has a disability.

As for the second element, plaintiff must show that he is otherwise qualified to receive the benefit of a service, program, or activity of a public entity. "To determine whether a plaintiff has satisfied this burden, a court must decide whether he has presented sufficient evidence to show (1) that he could satisfy the essential eligibility requirements of the program, . . . and (2) if not, whether any reasonable accommodation by the [defendants] would enable the plaintiff to meet these requirements."

In this case, defendants argue that their immunization policy is an essential eligibility requirement because of the public health necessity to prevent the spread of serious communicable diseases such as measles, mumps, and rubella, and to ensure protection against severe infections such as tetanus and diphtheria. Approximately "1 in 5 unvaccinated people in the U.S. who get measles [are] hospitalized." For tetanus, "1 to 2 in 10 cases are fatal." Regarding unvaccinated individuals who get diphtheria, "[w]ithout treatment, up to half of patients can die," and "with treatment, about 1 in 10 patients . . . die." [Defendants accordingly require vaccinations or proof of vaccinations.]

Defendants maintain that plaintiff has failed to meet his burden to generate a factual dispute as to whether he could satisfy this requirement because he did not provide documentation that he was unable to obtain a Tdap vaccination, he did not provide admissible evidence regarding his MMR or Tdap vaccination records, and he refused to take an MMR antibody titer test. [P]laintiff admitted he had a Tdap vaccination in 2011 but refused to provide any [information on those records]. Accordingly, plaintiff has not offered evidence sufficient to create a factual dispute.

The question then becomes whether plaintiff has offered sufficient evidence to show that a "reasonable accommodation by the [defendants] would enable the plaintiff to meet these requirements." Plaintiff has failed to do so. Here, defendants offered multiple reasonable accommodations—they indicated that plaintiff could obtain MMR antibody titer test instead of providing proof of vaccination for measles, mumps, and rubella. Defendants also offered plaintiff the option to sign a religious exemption waiver or a conscientious exemption waiver for all the required vaccinations.

Plaintiff refused to accept any of these reasonable accommodations, because they were "invasive" and compromised his principles. Plaintiff argues that defendants should have allowed him to take online classes as a reasonable accommodation. Defendants are not required, however, to provide "the best" accommodation, or plaintiff's preferred accommodation. The only evidence of record is that defendants provided plaintiff with several reasonable accommodations that would enable him to meet the immunization requirement. Plaintiff declined to accept those reasonable accommodations. Plaintiff has failed to generate any material factual disputes to indicate that defendants' reasonable accommodations would not have enabled plaintiff to meet the essential eligibility requirements. Consequently, plaintiff has failed to meet his burden to establish the second element of a prima facie case.

Even if plaintiff had met the first two requirements of a prima facie case, he has failed to establish the third element, that he was excluded from the benefit of a service, program, or activity of a public entity, or was otherwise discriminated against, on the basis of his disability. [P]laintiff has failed to generate a factual dispute that defendants excluded him from FSU on the basis of his disability.

[P]laintiff has failed to demonstrate that defendants' multiple accommodations were unreasonable in this case. Accordingly, plaintiff has failed to generate factual disputes as to any of the elements of his prima facie case. Therefore, summary judgment for defendants is appropriate on all counts.

Example: In 2016, McDonald's Corporation settled a disability discrimination suit by the U.S. Equal Employment Opportunity Commission (EEOC). The EEOC alleged that McDonald's refused to interview a deaf job applicant once it learned of his disability. The applicant was unable to hear or speak, but had previously worked at a McDonald's in another state. The suit claimed that the restaurant manager canceled his job interview upon learning that he needed an interpreter. The applicant's sister offered to serve as an interpreter. The restaurant interviewed and hired new workers after the applicant tried to reschedule an interview. McDonalds agreed to pay $56,500 and provide training to its managers regarding ADA requirements.

Example: A salon manager refused an accommodation requested by a stylist employee. The employee suffered from claustrophobia and asked for an end station. The employee was originally given an end station, but the salon manager then moved the employee to a different station between two other stylists. The employee had a panic attack. The salon corporation agreed to pay $60,000 in damages and to provide ADA training to its managers at several salon locations in that state.

Employers also may not deny benefits to older employees. In a few exceptions, the employer may specify an age limit if age is a bona fide occupational qualification necessary to the job. For instance, age limits are appropriate for obvious situations (a young actor is necessary to play a young character in a movie). There is also a public safety exception. Thus, police and fire departments may use maximum hiring and mandatory retirement ages. An employer may favor an older employee over a younger one, even if the younger employee is 40 or more years old.

Many employers used to impose a mandatory retirement age that required workers to retire once they reached a certain age. Generally speaking, the ADEA does not allow the use of a mandatory retirement age policy. There is an exception for certain individuals. Employers may enforce a mandatory retirement age of 65 for executive "high policymakers" who will receive an annual retirement payment of at least $44,000.

Disability Discrimination

The law prohibits discrimination in employment based on an employee's disability. The Americans with Disabilities Act (ADA) forbids discrimination in the hiring, promotion, compensation, training, and firing of disabled workers. The ADA requires employers to make a **reasonable accommodation** for a disabled worker unless the accommodation would cause "undue hardship" for the business. A reasonable accommodation is a modification or adjustment to enable people with disabilities to perform job duties. Accommodations vary depending upon the individual employee. Depending on the circumstances, some examples of a reasonable accommodation by an employer might include:

- Modify facilities to make them accessible and usable by persons with disabilities.
- Restructure a position.
- Allow a modified work schedule.
- Obtain new equipment or devices.
- Provide readers or interpreters.

An undue hardship exists where the accommodation would require significant difficulty or expense for the employer. Whether an accommodation creates an undue hardship depends on several factors, including the employer's size, financial resources, and the nature of its operation. An employer is not required to lower its quality standards to make an accommodation. Also, an employer does not need to provide personal items, such as glasses or hearing aids. Employers must ensure that employees understand ADA requirements and the need to provide reasonable accommodations.

Employee Safety

Employers must provide a safe workplace for their employees. The Occupational and Safety Health Act governs an employer's responsibili-

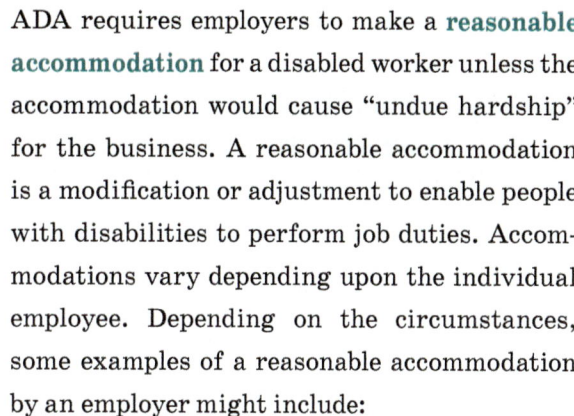

REASONABLE ACCOMMODATION: A modification or adjustment to enable people with disabilities to perform job duties.

ties for a safe workplace. The goal of the act is to protect employees from toxic chemicals, excessive noise, mechanical dangers, and unsanitary working conditions. The Occupational and Safety Health Administration administers the workplace safety laws. All employers are subject to **OSHA** requirements. Employers who violate OSHA standards are subject to fines.

> A Dollar General store was cited for several safety violations, including blocking of an emergency exit door, blocked electrical panels, and failure to keep a clear path to an emergency exit door. OSHA proposed $215,578 in fines.

To comply with OSHA requirements, employers must:

- Allow employees to access their medical records maintained by the employer.
- Provide well-maintained tools and equipment.
- Provide employees with personal protective equipment to protect against hazards, such as helmets, eye protection, hearing protection, and hard-toed shoes.

OSHA:
The Occupational Safety and Health Administration, which implements and enforces workplace safety rules. Also refers to the federal Occupational Safety and Health Act.

- Train employers on how to handle hazardous materials.
- Report accidents to OSHA within eight hours of the accident.
- Keep records of work-related accidents, injuries, and illnesses.

Employees have the right to file an OSHA complaint without retaliation from the employer. Employees also have the right to participate in OSHA workplace inspections. Employees also have some responsibilities. Employees must review employer-provided OSHA standards and requirements and attend safety training provided by employers.

> According to OSHA, the top 10 safety violations in 2020 were:
> 1. Lack of fall protection.
> 2. Hazard communication.
> 3. Lack of respiratory protection.
> 4. Scaffolds.
> 5. Ladders.
> 6. Lockout/tagout (failure to disable machinery during repair or maintenance).
> 7. Powered industrial trucks.
> 8. Fall protection training.
> 9. Lack of eye/face protection.
> 10. Machine guarding.

OSHA is a federal law. Before OSHA became law, a number of states already had workplace safety laws in place. At the time OSHA passed, each state had the option to submit an occupational safety and health plan to the Secretary of Labor. In states where the Secretary adopted the state plan, employers follow the state plan instead of the federal law.

> There are 22 state and territories known as "state plan" jurisdictions: Alaska, Arizona, California, Hawaii, Indiana, Iowa, Kentucky, Maryland, Michigan, Minnesota, Nevada, New Mexico, North Carolina, Oregon, Puerto Rico, South Carolina, Tennessee, Utah, Vermont, Virginia, Washington, and Wyoming. Another six states and territories have plans applying to government employees: Connecticut, Illinois, Maine, New Jersey, New York, and the U.S. Virgin Islands.

Many state plans have standards identical to OSHA. State plans may address hazards that are not included in the federal OSHA rules. States may also impose fines and penalties that are stricter than those under federal law.

Workers' Compensation

Workers' compensation is a type of insurance providing benefits to employees who are injured on the job. State laws require most employers, depending on the number of employees, to have workers' compensation for their employees. Workers' compensation benefits are generally available without any finding of negligence or fault on the employer.

WORKERS' COMPENSATION: A type of insurance providing benefits to employees who are injured on the job.

Example: Arne works for Atlantic-Pacific Power Company. As part of their expansion efforts, the company is building a new cooling tower. Scaffolding was built for the construction workers working on the new tower. The scaffolding was built quickly and not up to code in order to allow the workers to achieve construction goals ahead of schedule. The platform of the scaffolding gave way and collapsed inward with Arne and 17 workers on it. Arne and the other workers suffered severe injuries. The workers would be entitled to workers' compensation for their injuries.

Assume that Arne was managing the crew of workers on the platform. He knew that company policy was to limit the number of workers on the platform to only 15 employees, but he made the decision to allow three additional workers on the platform. Arne's violation of company policy might bar his recovery of benefits.

Each state has its own workers' compensation statute. To receive benefits, the employee's injury must occur in the course of employment. This means that the injury must take place while the employee is engaged in work duties. An employee may not receive benefits if the injury were self-inflicted, if the injury happened while committing a crime, or if the employee violated company policy.

The purpose of workers' compensation is to compensate workers for job-related injuries without the expense of litigation. Generally, the employee may recover compensation for loss of income and for medical expenses. Benefits are available for both temporary and permanent injuries. If a worker were to die from his injuries, workers' compensation would provide payment to the family. Employees agree to give up their right to sue the employer when they accept workers' compensation.

> It is illegal for an employer to fire, retaliate, or discriminate against an employee who files a worker's compensation claim.

Disability Insurance

Disability insurance is a program of the Social Security Administration. **Disability insurance** provides income protection to individuals who become disabled and cannot work for a long period of time. Social Security disability income insurance is available to employees who have made Federal Insurance Contributions Act (FICA) contributions. FICA requires employees to contribute part of their earnings to the program.

The purpose of disability insurance is to help disabled workers maintain their standard of living and pay their expenses during a period of disability. Disability insurance replaces only a portion of income; it does not provide full replacement income during the disability. Unlike workers' compensation, disability insurance coverage is provided even if the disability is not job-related.

Generally, a doctor's report is required to establish the disability. To qualify for the insurance, the employee must be unable to engage in any substantial activity because of a physical or mental impairment. The impairment must either be expected to last for at least 12 months or result in death. The amount of the disability payment is determined through a formula using the worker's earnings before he became disabled.

The Social Security Administration will consider the following five factors to determine if an individual is eligible for disability benefits.

- To be eligible for disability benefits, the individual generally cannot be working, or cannot make more than the base amount set by Social Security.

DISABILITY INSURANCE: A type of insurance providing income protection to individuals who become disabled and cannot work for a long period of time.

> *Example:* Donna has worked for Albright Industries for the past 29 years. She is in charge of accounts payable for the company. Donna recently suffered a stroke, during which her brain lacked oxygen for several minutes. The stroke left Donna partially paralyzed and unable to concentrate for more than a few minutes at a time. She cannot perform her job duties. In light of her age and the severity of the condition, doctors do not expect her to recover her mental abilities. Donna is likely to be eligible for disability benefits.

- The condition must significantly interfere with basic work activities.

- The disability must be on the Social Security Administration list of conditions, or of equal severity.

- The disability must interfere with the individual's ability to perform work they did previously.

- The worker must be unable to perform a different job that is less demanding, based on the individual's condition, age, and experience.

Some employers also offer private disability insurance options to employees. These insurance policies are not run by the Social Security Administration and may provide benefits under different circumstances.

Affirmative Action

Affirmative action refers to hiring and employment programs designed to remedy prior societal discrimination. Affirmative action programs take measures to increase minority and female representation in hiring. These programs are premised on the idea that past discrimination has left minorities at a disadvantage. Thus, affirmative action programs actively seek out minority and female candidates.

The government has adopted affirmative action program requirements. At the federal level, businesses that contract with the federal government must implement a written affirmative action policy to recruit and promote qualified minorities, women, persons with disabilities, and covered veterans. The affirmative actions might include training programs and outreach. Many states also require some sort of affirmative action for public employers or businesses working with the government. In recent years, however, a number of states have passed laws that prohibit government employers from giving preferential treatment based on race, national origin, or gender in employment.

Unless contracting with the government, private employers are not required to have an affirmative action program. Anti-discrimination laws still apply; employers cannot discriminate against workers based on race, gender, or other protected characteristics. Many private employers choose to have a diversity program. Although not required to do so, employers find that such policies benefit the business. These policies often focus on outreach to minorities and promoting inclusion in the workplace.

> ### UNIVERSITIES MAY CONSIDER RACE IN ADMISSIONS DECISIONS
> *Fisher v. University of Texas*
> *(College Applicant) v. (University)*
> *579 U.S. 365, 136 S. Ct. 2198, 195 L. Ed. 2d 511 (2016)*
>
> **INSTANT FACTS:**
> White university applicant challenged University's admission policy that considered race as one factor in the admissions process.
>
> **BLACK LETTER RULE:**
> University admissions policy may consider race as one factor in determining admission eligibility.
>
> **FACTS:**
> The University of Texas utilizes a two-part admissions policy. Under the first part, all students who graduated in the top ten percent of their high school class are admitted to the university. Under the second part of the policy, the University selects applicants to fill the remaining spots by considering a number of factors. Race is considered indirectly as part of an applicant's Personal Achievement Score, including race. A Caucasian applicant to the University, whose application was rejected, challenged the policy. The applicant claimed the second part of the policy violates the Equal Protection Clause. The trial court and Court of Appeals found in favor of the university.
>
> **ISSUE:**
> Can a university consider race in its admission policy?
>
> **DECISION AND RATIONALE:**
> Yes. A university may implement a race-conscious admissions policy to achieve the educational benefits of student diversity. The policy may not use specific numbers or goals. The university showed a compelling interest in achieving a diverse student body. None of the alternatives suggested by the plaintiff was feasible to achieve the university's interest.
>
> **ANALYSIS:**
> The decision affirmed the importance of diversity in society, but it does not open the door to all affirmative action policies. To be upheld, a policy must be based on concrete diversity goals. It must also further a university's compelling interest. The decision was not unanimous. Justice Alito issued a long dissent, joined by two other Justices. The dissent stated that the university did not demonstrate the need for a race-based policy. Affirmative action proponents consider the decision a significant development for diversity efforts.

Employers must take care to ensure that race or gender is only one of many factors considered in an employment decision.

Protection for Terminated Workers

The law provides certain rights to employees who have lost their jobs.

Health Insurance Continuation: Terminated employees have the right to continuing health insurance coverage. Under federal law, employers with 20 or more employees must allow terminated employees to continue participation in the employer's health insurance plan. The employer does not pay for the health insur-

> **UNEMPLOYMENT COMPENSATION:**
> Insurance benefits paid by the government to individuals who are out of work.

ance. It is the employee's responsibility to pay the insurance premiums.

Unemployment Compensation: In some circumstances, terminated employees may qualify for **unemployment compensation**. Unemployment payments provide temporary financial assistance for workers who have lost a job. When qualified, an unemployed worker may receive unemployment compensation while searching for a new job. Unemployment compensation provides a percentage of the employee's regular pay for up to 26 weeks.

WARN Act: The WARN Act requires employers to provide 60 days' notice before a plant closing or mass layoff. It applies to employers with 100 or more employees. With respect to plant closings, notice is required if the shutdown will result in loss of employment for 50 or more employees in a 30-day period. Notice is required for a mass layoff resulting in employment loss for 500 or more employees, or 50–499 employees if they make up at least 33% of the employer's active workforce.

V. Immigration and Employment

In today's world, employers often look outside the United States to find workers with the skills and experience they require. However, United States immigration law imposes restrictions on the ability of foreign workers to take employment positions in the U.S. Generally, anyone who wishes to enter the United States must obtain a visa from the U.S. government. Non-immigrant visas allow foreign visitors a temporary stay. A worker visa is required for those visitors who want to come to the United States for employment. All foreign workers must have authorization to work in the United States. Only an immigrant visa allows for permanent residence.

Employees must provide proof that they are legally able to work in the United States. Before hiring a new employee, all U.S. employers must request proof of immigration status or right to work through an Employment Authorization Document. Employers may be sanctioned for violating this rule.

Employers must use an I-9 form when hiring an employee, regardless of the employee's immigration status. The I-9 form requires the employee to produce documentation to show that he may work legally in the United States. Employers must make a reasonable effort to ensure that the documents provided are genuine.

Permanent Resident Status

Employers often wish to hire foreign citizens to fill certain positions in their company. This need may arise because specialized knowledge or experience is necessary for the position, or because there is a shortage of workers in the United States. Employers may sponsor employees for permanent resident status. The employer must complete and file an application with U.S. Citizenship and Immigration Services. By filing the petition, the employer is indicating its intent to hire the employee if the petition is approved.

To obtain permanent status, foreign workers must show that they have unique skills, or will not negatively affect U.S. workers. Generally,

Employment Eligibility Verification
Department of Homeland Security
U.S. Citizenship and Immigration Services

USCIS
Form I-9
OMB No. 1615-0047
Expires 10/31/2022

▶ **START HERE:** Read instructions carefully before completing this form. The instructions must be available, either in paper or electronically, during completion of this form. Employers are liable for errors in the completion of this form.

ANTI-DISCRIMINATION NOTICE: It is illegal to discriminate against work-authorized individuals. Employers **CANNOT** specify which document(s) an employee may present to establish employment authorization and identity. The refusal to hire or continue to employ an individual because the documentation presented has a future expiration date may also constitute illegal discrimination.

Section 1. Employee Information and Attestation *(Employees must complete and sign Section 1 of Form I-9 no later than the first day of employment, but not before accepting a job offer.)*

Last Name *(Family Name)*	First Name *(Given Name)*	Middle Initial	Other Last Names Used *(if any)*

Address *(Street Number and Name)*	Apt. Number	City or Town	State	ZIP Code

Date of Birth *(mm/dd/yyyy)*	U.S. Social Security Number	Employee's E-mail Address	Employee's Telephone Number

I am aware that federal law provides for imprisonment and/or fines for false statements or use of false documents in connection with the completion of this form.

I attest, under penalty of perjury, that I am (check one of the following boxes):

☐ 1. A citizen of the United States

☐ 2. A noncitizen national of the United States *(See instructions)*

☐ 3. A lawful permanent resident   (Alien Registration Number/USCIS Number): _____

☐ 4. An alien authorized to work   until (expiration date, if applicable, mm/dd/yyyy): _____
Some aliens may write "N/A" in the expiration date field. *(See instructions)*

Aliens authorized to work must provide only one of the following document numbers to complete Form I-9:
An Alien Registration Number/USCIS Number OR Form I-94 Admission Number OR Foreign Passport Number.

1. Alien Registration Number/USCIS Number: _____
   OR
2. Form I-94 Admission Number: _____
   OR
3. Foreign Passport Number: _____
   Country of Issuance: _____

QR Code - Section 1
Do Not Write In This Space

Signature of Employee	Today's Date *(mm/dd/yyyy)*

Preparer and/or Translator Certification (check one):

☐ I did not use a preparer or translator.   ☐ A preparer(s) and/or translator(s) assisted the employee in completing Section 1.
(Fields below must be completed and signed when preparers and/or translators assist an employee in completing Section 1.)

I attest, under penalty of perjury, that I have assisted in the completion of Section 1 of this form and that to the best of my knowledge the information is true and correct.

Signature of Preparer or Translator	Today's Date *(mm/dd/yyyy)*

Last Name *(Family Name)*	First Name *(Given Name)*

Address *(Street Number and Name)*	City or Town	State	ZIP Code

🛑 *Employer Completes Next Page* 🛑

Form I-9 10/21/2019

Employment Eligibility Verification
Department of Homeland Security
U.S. Citizenship and Immigration Services

USCIS Form I-9
OMB No. 1615-0047
Expires 10/31/2022

Section 2. Employer or Authorized Representative Review and Verification
(Employers or their authorized representative must complete and sign Section 2 within 3 business days of the employee's first day of employment. You must physically examine one document from List A OR a combination of one document from List B and one document from List C as listed on the "Lists of Acceptable Documents.")

Employee Info from Section 1	Last Name *(Family Name)*	First Name *(Given Name)*	M.I.	Citizenship/Immigration Status

List A Identity and Employment Authorization	OR	List B Identity	AND	List C Employment Authorization
Document Title		Document Title		Document Title
Issuing Authority		Issuing Authority		Issuing Authority
Document Number		Document Number		Document Number
Expiration Date *(if any) (mm/dd/yyyy)*		Expiration Date *(if any) (mm/dd/yyyy)*		Expiration Date *(if any) (mm/dd/yyyy)*
Document Title				
Issuing Authority		Additional Information		QR Code - Sections 2 & 3 Do Not Write In This Space
Document Number				
Expiration Date *(if any) (mm/dd/yyyy)*				
Document Title				
Issuing Authority				
Document Number				
Expiration Date *(if any) (mm/dd/yyyy)*				

Certification: I attest, under penalty of perjury, that (1) I have examined the document(s) presented by the above-named employee, (2) the above-listed document(s) appear to be genuine and to relate to the employee named, and (3) to the best of my knowledge the employee is authorized to work in the United States.

The employee's first day of employment *(mm/dd/yyyy)*: _____ *(See instructions for exemptions)*

Signature of Employer or Authorized Representative	Today's Date *(mm/dd/yyyy)*	Title of Employer or Authorized Representative
Last Name of Employer or Authorized Representative	First Name of Employer or Authorized Representative	Employer's Business or Organization Name

Employer's Business or Organization Address *(Street Number and Name)*	City or Town	State	ZIP Code

Section 3. Reverification and Rehires *(To be completed and signed by employer or authorized representative.)*

A. New Name *(if applicable)*			B. Date of Rehire *(if applicable)*
Last Name *(Family Name)*	First Name *(Given Name)*	Middle Initial	Date *(mm/dd/yyyy)*

C. If the employee's previous grant of employment authorization has expired, provide the information for the document or receipt that establishes continuing employment authorization in the space provided below.

Document Title	Document Number	Expiration Date *(if any) (mm/dd/yyyy)*

I attest, under penalty of perjury, that to the best of my knowledge, this employee is authorized to work in the United States, and if the employee presented document(s), the document(s) I have examined appear to be genuine and to relate to the individual.

Signature of Employer or Authorized Representative	Today's Date *(mm/dd/yyyy)*	Name of Employer or Authorized Representative

Form I-9 10/21/2019

LISTS OF ACCEPTABLE DOCUMENTS
All documents must be UNEXPIRED

Employees may present one selection from List A or a combination of one selection from List B and one selection from List C.

LIST A Documents that Establish Both Identity and Employment Authorization	LIST B Documents that Establish Identity	LIST C Documents that Establish Employment Authorization

1. U.S. Passport or U.S. Passport Card
 	
2. Permanent Resident Card or Alien Registration Receipt Card (Form I-551)
 	
3. Foreign passport that contains a temporary I-551 stamp or temporary I-551 printed notation on a machine-readable immigrant visa
 	
4. Employment Authorization Document that contains a photograph (Form I-766)
 	
5. For a nonimmigrant alien authorized to work for a specific employer because of his or her status:
  a. Foreign passport; and
  b. Form I-94 or Form I-94A that has the following:
    (1) The same name as the passport; and
    (2) An endorsement of the alien's nonimmigrant status as long as that period of endorsement has not yet expired and the proposed employment is not in conflict with any restrictions or limitations identified on the form.
 	
6. Passport from the Federated States of Micronesia (FSM) or the Republic of the Marshall Islands (RMI) with Form I-94 or Form I-94A indicating nonimmigrant admission under the Compact of Free Association Between the United States and the FSM or RMI
	1. Driver's license or ID card issued by a State or outlying possession of the United States provided it contains a photograph or information such as name, date of birth, gender, height, eye color, and address
	
	2. ID card issued by federal, state or local government agencies or entities, provided it contains a photograph or information such as name, date of birth, gender, height, eye color, and address
	
	3. School ID card with a photograph
	
	4. Voter's registration card
	
	5. U.S. Military card or draft record
	
	6. Military dependent's ID card
	
	7. U.S. Coast Guard Merchant Mariner Card
	
	8. Native American tribal document
	
	9. Driver's license issued by a Canadian government authority
	
	For persons under age 18 who are unable to present a document listed above:
	
	10. School record or report card
	11. Clinic, doctor, or hospital record
	12. Day-care or nursery school record
		1. A Social Security Account Number card, unless the card includes one of the following restrictions:
		  (1) NOT VALID FOR EMPLOYMENT
		  (2) VALID FOR WORK ONLY WITH INS AUTHORIZATION
		  (3) VALID FOR WORK ONLY WITH DHS AUTHORIZATION
		
		2. Certification of report of birth issued by the Department of State (Forms DS-1350, FS-545, FS-240)
		
		3. Original or certified copy of birth certificate issued by a State, county, municipal authority, or territory of the United States bearing an official seal
		
		4. Native American tribal document
		
		5. U.S. Citizen ID Card (Form I-197)
		
		6. Identification Card for Use of Resident Citizen in the United States (Form I-179)
		
		7. Employment authorization document issued by the Department of Homeland Security

Examples of many of these documents appear in the Handbook for Employers (M-274).

Refer to the instructions for more information about acceptable receipts.

Form I-9 10/21/2019

Types of Permanent Worker Visas

EB-1—Priority Workers	Extraordinary professors and researchers, multinational executives and managers
EB-2—Professionals With Advanced Degrees or Persons With Exceptional Ability	Exceptional ability in the sciences, arts, or business; will substantially benefit the economy or interests of the U.S.
EB-3—Professional or Skilled Workers	Professionals with a college degree; capable of performing skilled or unskilled labor for which qualified workers are not available in the United States

Common Temporary Worker Visa Categories

H-1B: Person in Specialty Occupation	To work in a specialty occupation; requires a higher education degree
H-2A: Temporary Agricultural Worker	Temporary or seasonal agricultural work
H-2B: Temporary Non-agricultural Worker	Temporary or seasonal non-agricultural work
H-3: Trainee or Special Education visitor	To receive training not available in the home country
L: Intracompany Transferee	To work at a branch, parent, affiliate, or subsidiary of the current employer; managerial or executive capacity, or with specialized knowledge
O: Individual with Extraordinary Ability or Achievement	Extraordinary ability in the sciences, arts, education, business, or athletics

the employer needs to obtain a permanent **labor certification** from the Department of Labor before filing a petition to USCIS. The Department of Labor certifies that there are insufficient U.S. workers who are qualified and available to perform the job. The certification also indicates that employment of the foreign worker will not negatively affect U.S. workers. In order to obtain the certification, the employer must conduct a recruiting and hiring process to make sure no U.S. workers are qualified and willing to take the job.

Temporary Work Visas

Temporary work visas are available to foreign workers who wish to enter the United States for temporary employment. Before an employee seeks a visa, the employer must file a petition with the U.S. Citizenship and Immigration Services. Some temporary worker categories have a limited number of petitions available each year. The employee must have an employment offer before a visa may be granted. There are different types of temporary work visas for various kinds of work.

Work Permits

Many foreign nationals live in the U.S. under various types of non-work visas. For instance, asylees, spouses of various visa holders, people with Temporary Protected Status, and students experiencing economic hardship are all examples of foreign nationals living in the U.S. under non-work visas. If individuals under a non-work visa wish to work in the United States, they must apply for a **work permit** from U.S. Citizenship and Immigration Services. If granted, USCIS will issue a photo identity card, called an Employment Authorization Document, to the worker. The Employment Authorization Document is similar to a driver's license and provides proof of the individual's right to work in the U.S.

VI. Labor Organization

A **labor union** is an organized association of workers in the same trade that is formed for the purpose of representing the members' interests regarding wages, benefits, and working conditions. Unions permit workers to act together to achieve more favorable terms of employment. All workers in the United States have the right

LABOR CERTIFICATION: A statement from the Department of Labor indicating that there are insufficient U.S. workers who are qualified and available to perform a particular job, and that employment of a foreign worker for the job will not negatively affect U.S. workers.

WORK PERMIT: Authorization from U.S. Citizenship and Immigration Services allowing individuals living in the United States under non-work visas to work in the U.S.

LABOR UNION: An organized association of workers in the same trade that is formed for the purpose of representing the members' interests regarding wages, benefits, and working conditions.

to join a union. Employees also have the right to form unions in the workplace.

Employers may not interfere with union activities, discriminate against union employees, or retaliate against union organizing. Specifically, employers may not do any of the following:

- Threaten to shut the business down if workers form a union.

- Question workers about union matters, meetings, or supporters.

- Ask workers whether they belong to a union.

- Fire or punish workers for engaging in union activity.

- Retaliate through firing, reassignment, or layoffs against workers because of union activity.

The National Labor Relations Board (NLRB) provides a process for forming a union at a workplace. If 30 percent of the employees show interest in forming a union, the employees can petition the NLRB to hold a representative election. No managers or supervisors may vote for unionization. The NLRB will then hold an election. If a majority of the employees vote for unionization, a union is established.

Collective Bargaining

Collective bargaining is the process through which unions negotiate terms of employment with employers on behalf of the employees. These terms of employment may include pay, health care, pensions, hours, health and safety policies, and other benefits. The union employees select a representative who negotiates on their behalf. The union members then vote to approve or reject the proposed contract terms. The agreed-upon contract is called a **collective bargaining agreement**.

Employees and employers must engage in good faith bargaining. The employer has a duty to provide some information to the union during the collective bargaining process. The union

> **COLLECTIVE BARGAINING:**
> The process through which unions negotiate terms of employment with employers on behalf of the employees.
>
> **COLLECTIVE BARGAINING AGREEMENT:**
> The agreed-upon contract between union employees and the employer.

Example: Aida Company manufactures electronic components. Its employees belong to a union. The employees requested a pay increase. Aida Company claims that it is financially unable to provide the increase. The union requested Aida Company's financial information to verify its argument. Aida Company will likely have to provide its financial information to the union.

must show that the information is relevant to the employer/employee relationship. Generally, the employer must provide information about wages and benefits. Sometimes, the employer must produce additional information.

In some circumstances, the employer may withhold confidential information, such as highly personal information or trade secret information. The union must also produce relevant information requested by the employer.

If the union and cannot agree on contract terms, the union members may decide to **strike**. A strike occurs when all of the union workers refuse to come to work. The purpose of the strike is to disrupt the employer's business. Workers use a strike to persuade the employer to keep negotiating or to agree to their terms. Strikes are typically used as a last resort measure. The workers do not receive pay during the strike. The employer may hire replacement workers during the strike.

In September 2016, Long Island University locked out all of its faculty members a few days before classes started. The faculty members were barred from campus and their email accounts. The faculty members were part of a union, and their contract with the University had recently expired. In a vote, the union members rejected the University's proposed contract terms. Negotiations between the University and the faculty union ended with a faculty strike, so the University conducted a lockout to avoid another strike. The lockout ended after 12 days when the faculty union and University reached an agreement.

The National Labor Relations Act gives union employees the right to strike. However, the law also imposes restrictions on the right to strike. To be lawful, a strike must take place for a lawful purpose. Both economic strikers and unfair labor strikers are lawful. **Economic strikers** strike to obtain an economic benefit such as a higher wage or shorter hours. Economic strikers maintain their status as employees, but they can be permanently replaced by the employer. **Unfair labor practice strikers** protest an unfair labor practice by the employer. Unfair labor practice strikers cannot be discharged or permanently replaced. A strike may be considered unlawful if the workers strike to support an unfair union labor practice, the strike violates a no-strike provision of a contract, or the strikers engage in misconduct.

STRIKE:
A collective effort of union employees to refuse to work in order to persuade the employer to negotiate or accept contract terms.

ECONOMIC STRIKERS:
Striking union workers seeking to obtain an economic benefit for the workers.

UNFAIR LABOR PRACTICE STRIKERS:
Union workers who are striking to protest an unfair labor practice by the employer.

LOCKOUT:
A temporary work stoppage implemented by the employer.

In contrast to a strike, a **lockout** is a temporary work stoppage started by the employer. In a lockout, the employer typically refuses to allow employees on the premises. The purpose of the lockout is to persuade employees to accept the terms offered by the employer. During the lockout, the employer may hire temporary replacement workers. The employer must rehire the union employees after the lockout.

Right to Work Laws

Right to work laws hold that workers cannot be required or forced to join to a union. These laws prohibit union security agreements between employers and labor unions. Union security agreements may require employee membership in a union or the payment of union dues. The right to work laws allow non-union workers to work at unionized workplaces without having to join the union or pay union dues or fees. Currently 28 states have right to work statutes in place.

Right to work laws have been the subject of disagreement. Those in favor of the laws argue that forcing parties to join unions is unfair and violates the employees' right to freedom of association. Opponents of the laws argue that the laws undermine the union system by allowing workers a "free ride" to enjoy the benefits of union-negotiated terms of employment without contributing to the union.

CHAPTER SUMMARY

Regardless of the path chosen, nearly every individual and organization involved in business deals with employment issues. From the entry-level employee at a retail store to the CEO of a large corporation, employment law affects all workers. As a worker, one's status as an employee brings about certain benefits and protections not available to independent contractors. For employers, employment law imposes obligations that may affect business and organizational decisions beyond the basic working conditions and terms of employment. Whether as the employee or employer, the rules of employment will likely affect every businessperson's career or business operation.

> **CAREERS IN THE LAW**
>
> Human resources professionals work with the law every day. They must stay up-to-date on documentation requirements, anti-discrimination laws, contract issues, tax concerns, and other legal matters. For these reasons, HR often works closely with legal and compliance departments in an organization. HR is a crucial part of modern organizations, and a great career path.

> **RIGHT TO WORK LAWS:**
> Laws prohibiting agreements between employers and unions that require workers to join the union or pay union dues or fees.

Review Questions

Review question 1.
What is at-will employment? What are the limits on at-will employment? What are some of the employees and groups who are not at-will?

Review question 2.
What role could an employee handbook or manual play in whether or not employees are considered to be at-will? How can employers address this issue?

Review question 3.
What are the differences between employees and independent contractors? What is the most important distinction to determine? What are the pros and cons of hiring an employee or an independent contractor? What are the pros and cons of being an employee or an independent contractor?

Review question 4.
What is the minimum wage? Who does it apply to? What is the difference between federal and state minimum wages?

Review question 5.
What benefits are employees entitled to? What bearing does the number of employees have on available benefits? What amount of time off is required for at-will employees?

Review question 6.
What types of family and medical leave are available to employees? For family leave, what are some of the qualifying relationships for which leave may be taken? For medical leave, what types of medical conditions support the right to take leave?

Review question 7.
What additional types of leave may an employee take? What are the conditions for those leaves? What laws apply?

Review question 8.
What groups are protected by Title VII? What other anti-discrimination laws offer protection to employees at the federal level? What employers are subject to the various anti-discrimination laws? How may state laws differ?

Review question 9.

If an employee believes that she has been discriminated against at work, what will she need to prove? How may an employer rebut the employee's case?

Review question 10.

What must an employer do to provide a safe workplace? Which agency oversees safety in the workplace? What is worker's compensation? Who is eligible for disability benefits?

Review question 11.

When can foreign citizens work in the United States? What are the employer's responsibilities when hiring a foreign citizen?

Review question 12.

What is collective bargaining? What is "right to work" and how does it impact union votes? How does a strike differ from a lockout?

Discussion Questions

Question 1:

Amy is a software programmer. Amy works for a company called Amazing Apps, Inc. She is paid for each app when she notifies the company that it is complete. Amazing Apps creates mobile phone apps. Customers submit an app idea to Amazing Apps, which then assigns the programming job to one of its programmers. Once an app project is assigned to Amy, she can work on it during whatever hours she chooses, as long as she works at least eight hours per day. She may work from home most days, but she is required to come to the office to work at least one day per week. She may work in the office every day, if she likes. Amazing Apps' workplace is set up with temporary desks for everyone. People may claim whichever workspace they want once they get to the office, and they must remove all of their materials from the workspace at the end of the day. Lockers are available for workers to keep their materials. Amazing Apps provided Amy with a cell phone and computer. Once the app is completed, Amy must demo the app to the customer. This is sometimes done in person, sometimes with internet technology, such as Skype. During these demos, the programmers are required to wear a shirt with the Amazing Apps logo provided by Amazing Apps.

Is Amy an employee of Amazing Apps or independent contractor?

If Amy is an employee, what are the effects of employee status for Amy and Amazing Apps?

Assume Amazing Apps, Inc. classifies her as an independent contractor, but the EEOC later determines Amy was an employee. What consequences might Amazing Apps face?

Question 2:

Lois is a Black female employee of Energy Enterprises. Energy Enterprises has 267 employees. Lois is 48 years old, and has worked at the company for 25 years. Lois has received good work performance evaluations and has received several promotions over the years. She is currently a project manager. Last year, the company reorganized and restructured its business operations. As a result, Lois now has a new supervisor, Barry. Barry is a white male who is 55 years old. Lois overheard Barry telling another employee that "Lois is very attractive if you like that sort of thing," that "she is thinner than you'd expect" and a "cougar." Several months ago, Lois told Barry that she is suffering from migraines, which the doctors think may be caused by the new computer screens installed at the office. Barry told her there was nothing he could do about the screens because upper management really likes the new screens. Last week, Barry promoted one white male and one white female employee to Senior Project Managers. The male employee is 41 years old and has worked at the company for 10 years. The female employee is 35 years old and has worked at the company for eight years. The new Senior Project Managers received the same performance evaluation rating as Lois.

Does Lois have a claim for discrimination against the employer? If so, on what grounds?

Assume Lois has a claim for sex discrimination. Is it based on disparate treatment or disparate impact?

Are there any reasonable accommodations that the employer might offer to Lois?

Question 3:
Chris is a human resources manager for Bigg & Large Corp., a multinational corporation headquartered in Memphis. Bigg & Large manufacturers, distributes, and sells a variety of food products worldwide. The company employs 6,000 workers across the world, 5,000 of which work in Memphis. Tennessee is a right to work state. The workers are currently undergoing a unionization campaign. The head of the research division, Alberto Ienstien, would like to hire a worker from Italy to assist in research and development of some new Italian food products at the lab in Memphis. He has recruited an employee who is an Italian citizen and has a Ph.D. in food science. How should Chris respond to these questions from Alberto?

> What must Bigg & Large do to be able to hire the recruit to work in the United States?

> The recruit has indicated an interest in voting in the unionization election, and has asked Alberto a lot of questions about it. If the vote takes place while the recruit is working there, is there anything that Alberto cannot say to him about unionization?

> If the unionization campaign is successful, is the recruit required to join the union?

Question 4:
Maher works at 4Q Manufacturing in assembly. When he started work, he received an employee handbook. The handbook contained a section about discipline. The section said that if an employee broke a rule, then he or she would receive an oral warning. If the employee broke a second rule, then he or she would receive a written warning. If the employee broke a third rule, then he or she would be terminated.

What are your thoughts on the following scenarios?

> On his first day of work, Maher made a mistake when assembling a component. His supervisor said, "That's strike one, Maher!" A year later, Maher forgot to lock the storeroom door at the end of a shift, and he was written up. Ten years later, Maher had to leave early because of a family emergency, and failed to clock out. 4Q terminated him because he had broken a third rule.

Maher works for three years at the company without a problem, and then is caught on CCTV stealing office supplies. His supervisor says that Maher is fired, but Maher says that he should keep his job and just receive an oral warning.

Maher has a great record at 4Q. He works alongside Jill, who is the supervisor's niece. Jill is often late and ignores instructions, but is never given any warnings. Maher has a bad week where he is late twice and forgets to check safety gear once. Maher is terminated.

Question 5:

Title VII prohibits discrimination on the basis of race, color, national origin, sex, or religion. Some state human rights laws add further protections, such as sexual orientation, gender identity, or "creed" (a subset of religion usually referring to how an individual legally pursues his or her religion). Do the following examples describe discrimination? What would you recommend in each case?

James works for a restaurant. James recently converted to Sikhism and started wearing a turban. His manager fires him because he cannot wear the hat and hairnet that comes with his uniform when wearing the turban, which James will not remove.

Denise is married to Val. Val is originally from Russia, but is a legal resident of the United States and is applying for citizenship. Denise works at a treatment center for alcohol and drug dependency. Denise's boss finds out that Val is Russian and starts checking Denise's work more thoroughly. When Denise asks if there is a problem, her boss says, "Well, you live with a Russian, and vodka is their national drink, so I have concerns about your commitment to the cause."

Assume the same facts as above, only Val does not have legal residence status and Denise and Val are only engaged.

Bertha was brought up Catholic, but does not attend mass any more. Her family is still Catholic. Bertha starts working as a teacher's assistant in a Christian grade school. Bertha is assigned to a teacher who immediately asks, "Are you Christian?" Bertha replies, "Well, I was brought up Catholic, but I'm not very religious now." The teacher does not reply, but later asks to have Bertha assigned elsewhere because "Catholics are not really Christians."

Question 6:

Jen is a member of the National Guard. She is 42 years old. Jen works for a small florist that employs only two full-time employees other than the owner. Jen informs her boss that she will need to take a week off for annual training with the Guard. Her boss does not respond. A few days later, Jen's boss terminates her, saying, "I just need to be sure that my employees are reliable, and I just don't know if I can count on you. I mean, you need glasses now to even see the work up close!"

> Is this termination legal? Why or why not? What laws might apply?
>
> What facts could be changed to give different answers to the prior set of questions?

Question 7:

An airline hires only conventionally attractive, physically fit women for flight attendant positions. The job are well-paid and offer great flexibility. A man applies for a flight attendant job, and is refused. He brings a lawsuit against the airline, claiming sex discrimination. The airline defends itself by saying that gender is a bone fide occupational qualification. The airline primarily serves mid-week business travelers, the majority of whom are men, and those customers indicate a strong preference for good-looking female flight attendants. If the airline were to change its policy, it would lose a competitive edge.

> How will this argument fare in court? Is this a legitimate bone fide occupational qualification?
>
> What if instead of an airline, the employer had been a fashion retailer whose retail employees also model the company's clothes while at work?
>
> What if the employees of the retailer also monitor the dressing rooms?

(Wilson v. Southwest Airlines 517 F. Supp. 292 (N.D. Tex. 1981))

Question 8:

Acme Manufacturing runs multiple production facilities. One of Acme's products is a component in car CD players, and demand has dropped off dramatically as fewer and fewer cars feature CD players. Acme will need to close the facility that makes that part. It will not be able to absorb all of the employees in other roles at other locations.

What requirements does Acme need to consider before terminating employees?

What does the HR director need to check before proceeding with the reduction in force?

What other concerns and risks might the HR director and senior management need to consider before terminating these employees?

12 Business Topics

KEY OBJECTIVES:
- Describe the laws concerning investor relations.
- Explain how antitrust rules affect business operation.
- Outline some of the legal concerns raised by international business.

CHAPTER OVERVIEW

This chapter covers special topics related to businesses. These topics involve regulation of businesses in their relations to their investors and to one another. This area of law generally focuses on large businesses that are traded on public exchanges, such as the New York Stock Exchange. Because of their power and reach, the behavior of these businesses can change the fortunes of citizens. The government works to ensure that these businesses influence the people and the economy in positive ways.

In this chapter, we will look at some of the laws that have the greatest impact on these issues. This chapter will consider investor relations and how rules applying to businesses protect individual and commercial investors. The chapter will also look at laws relating to transactions between businesses. Businesses must avoid cooperation with other companies that could hurt consumers or the economy. Finally, this chapter will look at some of the issues involved in international transactions between businesses.

INTRODUCTION

Most of the areas of the law covered in this textbook apply to businesses and individuals alike. For example, contract law, which is arguably the foundation of all business transactions, uses much the same rules for individuals and business entities. In most situations, there is not one law for business and another for individuals.

There are, however, laws that are unique to businesses. They deal with the operations of a business. While most legal rules (such as contracts and torts) will apply to these operations, some types of operations involve legal rules that are unique to the business world. Most of these rules are meant to ensure fair dealing. Examples of these rules are those involving investor relations, or the laws on antitrust. Others are geared more towards the mechanics of a business operation. These rules include those that relate to shipment of goods and payment of import tariffs.

I. Investor Relations

Why does a corporation exist? With some exceptions and qualifications, the answer is, "to make money." Make money for whom? The answer to that question is even simpler. Corporations are often said to exist to make money for their owners, the shareholders. Maximizing shareholder value is an important goal of corporate directors and officers.

> While turning a profit is central to running a business, that does not mean that companies cannot have other goals. Directors' decisions are protected by the "business judgment rule"—a presumption that the directors acted in the best interests of the company. Those interests often go beyond generating revenue. Many businesses make substantial positive changes in their communities by donating to charities or sponsoring events. Companies may commit to being more environmentally friendly than the law requires, even if that commitment means that shareholders receive a lower return.

Maximizing value is not the end of the responsibilities directors and officers owe to shareholders. Directors in particular owe the duties of loyalty and care to the business and its shareholders. The duty of loyalty means that the director focuses his efforts on the company and does not take opportunities from the business. For instance, a director for a consulting company who hears of a consulting contract should refer that information to the company. She should not take the contract for herself personally or for her family. In short, a director should not personally take advantage of the company or leverage his position for personal gain. The company's interests should be ahead of the director's own.

Directors also owe a duty of care. The duty of care simply means that directors will act for the company in good faith, and will behave as a reasonably prudent person would in the circumstances. The duty of care means that directors may not act on a whim or take unreasonable risks for the company.

In publicly-traded corporations, there is an added duty of transparency. This transparency extends to both shareholders and potential shareholders. It is generally included within the broader category of investor relations. "Investor relations" refers to communication between a corporation and the investment community. These communications let investors make informed decisions about the value of a company's stock, and whether it is worth their while to invest in it. In many companies, investor relations are part of the duties of the public relations department.

Investor relations is a very active area of law. The **Sarbanes-Oxley Act** gave increased importance to investor relations in publicly-traded companies. The Act places an increased emphasis on the accuracy of the information that is disclosed to the public. Sarbanes-Oxley also gave a new emphasis on internal controls for publicly-traded companies. The internal controls are ways a company ensures compliance and prevent violations of laws or rules. The effectiveness of these controls is also something that is disclosed to the investing public.

Important and effective federal laws already regulated securities prior to Sarbanes-Oxley. The Securities Laws, made up of acts from 1933 and 1934, established reporting requirements.

SARBANES-OXLEY ACT:
A federal law that protects investors from fraudulent accounting practices.

The goal of the Securities Laws was to provide investors with the information needed to make sound investments. The 1933 Act focused on the initial release of securities to the public from the issuer. The Act established the securities registration and prospectus publication requirements that public companies still follow. A prospectus lists the securities to be offered for sale and described how the securities issuer (the company offering the stock, for instance) is managed. In addition, the prospectus provides independently certified financial statements.

The 1934 Securities Exchange Act created the Securities and Exchange Commission to enforce the federal law. While the 1933 Act covered issuance of new securities, this Act focused on regulation of the secondary market—how securities are traded and sold among investors, brokers, and others after the initial issuance. It contains substantial anti-fraud measures.

One of the most notable anti-fraud tools is SEC Rule 10b–5, which originated with the 1934 Act. Rule 10b–5 bars the use of "any manipulative or deceptive device or contrivance in contravention of such rules and regulations as the Commission may prescribe as necessary or appropriate in the public interest or for the protection of investors." In practice, the SEC uses Rule 10b–5 to pursue insider trading, price fixing, and fraudulent techniques to boost the price of specific securities. It can also be used to penalize failures to disclose pertinent information to would-be investors.

The Securities Laws provided a sound basis for the market, and the laws proved equal to many challenges over the years. At the end of the last century, however, the market faced new regulatory issues. In the mid-1990s, the stock market surged. Stock prices rose to record high levels. New entrants in the market, especially those doing business through the then-new internet ("dot com" companies), drove much of this surge. The surge ended abruptly in 2000, and stock prices collapsed.

> Established companies brought down by turn-of-the-century scandals included Enron, WorldCom, and Tyco International. Arthur Andersen, a venerable accounting firm that was convicted of obstructing justice for trying to hide its role in Enron's false reporting also failed in the early 2000s. Note, though, that Enron and others were sanctioned under existing securities law, and not by Sarbanes-Oxley. Sarbanes-Oxley was a reaction to the crisis.

Investigations showed that the surging market was accompanied by fraud and misdealing. The boom in stock prices made many corporate executives focus on short-term profits that would drive stock prices, rather than on strategies that would keep a company in business over the long-term. Several publicly-traded companies had disclosed false information in their required reports—an unlawful act under federal law. Some financial reports were also adjusted to show that goals for earnings were being met.

Investors who relied on the accuracy of the false reports lost billions of dollars. By some estimates, more individual investors lost money in the 2000 downturn than in the 1929 Wall Street crash, because more individual investors had money invested. Many companies, including established companies and new start-ups, collapsed. The collapse of these companies also made many investors lose faith in the integrity of U.S. securities markets.

In response, the Sarbanes-Oxley Act was enacted in 2002. Sarbanes-Oxley, also known as the "Public Company Accounting Reform and Investor Protection Act," was the Congressional response to the scandals of the early 2000s. Commonly referred to as "SOX," its goal is to protect investors and the public by improving the financial reporting landscape for publicly-held companies. Accountability standards for corporate insiders were tightened, and the oversight of accountants and auditors was strengthened. SOX includes both civil and criminal provisions, meaning that violators could be subject to both lawsuits and to criminal prosecution.

> SOX passed with nearly unanimous votes in both houses of Congress.

Accountants and Auditors

The first sections of SOX relate to accountants and auditors. Sarbanes-Oxley created a federal regulatory agency, the Public Company Accounting Oversight Board. All public accounting companies must register with the Board. When they register, firms must provide:

- A list of their clients,
- The fees paid from each client,
- A complete financial disclosure,
- A statement of quality control, and
- A list of the accountants working for the firm.

The firm must also disclose all legal actions in which the firm is involved.

Reports of firm activity are submitted to the Board annually. Accounting firms that provide services to 100 or more publicly-traded companies are subject to annual inspection by the Board. Firms that provide services to fewer than 100 companies are subject to inspection every three years. Inspection reports are available to the public.

Accounting firms also must develop a set of internal quality control standards. These standards must promote compliance with all securities laws and regulations of the Board. If the Board finds that these quality control standards are insufficient, it may send in advisors to assist and monitor the firm as it develops adequate standards.

The Board may investigate any firm at its discretion. It may require any accountant at a firm, or at the client of the firm, to testify. A violation of accounting standards could subject an individual to a fine of up to $750,000 for each individual violation. Violators could also face permanent suspension of their accounting licenses.

In addition to accounting practices, SOX addresses auditing practices and the independence of auditors. Many of the dishonest accounting practices committed in the 1990s were undertaken by auditors who had close relationships with the management of the companies they were supposed to be auditing. Painting a favorable picture of a company's financial state was beneficial for the business of the accounting firm.

To help ensure independence of auditors, a public accounting firm may not provide audit services for a client for more than five years in a row. This limitation removes an incentive for collaboration between the corporate board and the accountants.

Another requirement of Sarbanes-Oxley is that every public company must have an audit committee that is directly responsible for the appointment, compensation, and oversight of the work of an accounting firm. All services to be provided by an accounting firm must be pre-approved by the audit committee. Audit committee members are usually members of the board of directors.

The audit committee must also establish quality controls to ensure that audit reporting is accurate and complete. Audit committees are responsible for monitoring and receiving complaints from employees about questionable accounting practices or about ethics issues.

SOX sets forth nine prohibited activities that public accounting firms may not provide when they are performing auditing services. The list of prohibited services helps prevent conflicts of interests by preventing accounting firms from auditing their own work. These prohibited services include:

1. Corporate management functions,
2. Legal or expert services,
3. Bookkeeping or services related to financial statements,
4. Appraisals or valuations,
5. Actuarial services,
6. Internal audit outsourcing,
7. Financial information systems design,
8. Broker-dealer, or investment banking services, and
9. Any other service prohibited by the Board.

> No corporate officer or director, or any other person acting under their direction, may do anything that would fraudulently influence, coerce, manipulate, or mislead an accountant performing an audit of the financial statements of the company for the purpose of making those financial statements materially misleading.

Financial Reporting

Some of the most significant provisions of Sarbanes-Oxley relate to responsibility for financial reports. Reports filed with the Securities and Exchange Commission (SEC) are public information. The required disclosures made to the SEC must be certified as accurate by the officers of the corporation who sign those disclosures. The disclosure and certification requirements recognize that disclosure is meaningless unless the information that is being disclosed is accurate.

The certification must state that:

- The signing officer has reviewed the disclosure.

- To the best of the officer's knowledge, the disclosure does not contain any false statement of fact, or an omission of a fact.

- Based on the officer's knowledge, the financial information in the disclosure is a fair representation of the financial condition of the company.

The CEO and CFO of a publicly traded corporation must also disclose the company's "disclosure controls and procedures." Disclosure controls and procedures are the mechanisms that a corporation has in place to make sure that disclosures are made in a timely manner. Under Sarbanes-Oxley, this process includes certifying that these controls and procedures are working, and that their effectiveness has been evaluated. The officers must also certify that auditors have been informed of any deficiencies in the corporation's procedures for providing information to auditors. Any significant changes in internal controls, or any related factors that could have an impact on internal controls, must be reported.

Certification is not the only Sarbanes-Oxley requirement for financial statements. Certifications only cover items that the signing officer personally knows. In addition to the certification, the financial statements must actually be accurate. A certification that an officer knows some of the details is not an excuse for inaccurate statements. Accurate information may go beyond what the signing officer knows herself. All material information must be included, whether or not the signing officer knows about it.

There are a number of items that a signing officer may not know personally, but that are accurate about the company's finances. As one example, the financial disclosure cannot leave out "off-balance sheet" items. Off-balance sheet items are those that are not reported on a company's balance sheet.

The SEC may file a civil action against officers who violate the disclosure requirements. Private civil lawsuits may also be brought by aggrieved investors.

Internal Controls

Section 404 of the Sarbanes-Oxley Act requires all annual financial reports to include an internal control report. This report affirms that

> *Example:* A certain model airliner has a useful life of 25 years. TravelsOn Airlines leases one for five years. The rental payments for the plane are not included on TravelsOn's balance sheet as rental payments. Instead, they are deducted from the airline's profits as operating expenses. The lease payments are an off-balance sheet item. They must be disclosed on TravelsOn's financial reports.

management is responsible for having adequate internal control structures in place. "Adequate internal controls" provide reasonable assurance that:

- The financial reporting is reliable, and
- Financial statements have been prepared according to generally accepted accounting principles.

Management must assess the effectiveness of the control structure. Any shortcomings in the control structures must be reported. In addition, registered external auditors must verify the accuracy of management's report on the company's internal controls.

Criminal Penalties

SOX imposes criminal penalties for violations of some of its provisions. Criminal prosecutions under SOX are brought by the Department of Justice, rather than the SEC. A person who certifies a financial statement knowing that the periodic report that goes with the statement does not meet SOX's requirements may be fined not more than $1 million, sentenced to prison for not more than 10 years, or receive both a fine and a prison sentence. If the false certification is willful, the penalty is a fine of not more than $5 million, imprisonment for up to 20 years, or both a fine and a prison term.

> SOX does not define the distinction between "knowing" and "willful" certification. In other contexts, federal courts have concluded that "willful" could mean deliberately ignoring facts.

A person who alters, destroys, mutilates, conceals, or falsifies records, documents, or tangible objects with the intent to obstruct, impede, or influence a legal investigation may be fined a maximum of $5 million or sentenced to up to 20 years in prison.

> A fisherman threw undersized fish back into the ocean in order to avoid a fine for violating size limits for commercial fishing. Federal prosecutors argued that throwing undersized fish back was a way of concealing information to tamper with an investigation. According to the prosecutors, the fish were "tangible objects" under SOX. The U.S. Supreme Court later held that the "tangible objects" provision is meant to apply only to financial records and not to fish. *Yates v. U.S.*, 574 U.S. 528 (2015).

SOX also places criminal penalties for retaliating against employees who report their employers' Sarbanes-Oxley violations. Any person who acts to hurt the livelihood of a whistleblower may be fined not more than $1 million, sentenced to prison for not more than 10 years, or receive both a fine and a prison sentence.

The requirements of the Sarbanes-Oxley Act have increased the expense and complexity of investor relations. At the same time, the knowledge that there are individuals who are personally accountable for the accuracy of financial information has benefitted the market by raising investor confidence.

II. Antitrust Laws

While most people start businesses focused on serving customers, a significant part of daily operation involves interacting with other businesses. Every company needs to deal with other businesses as suppliers, vendors, and competitors.

Most businesspeople may think of other businesses only as competition. Even though competition in a given market, or a given industry, may be keen, there is much cooperation and joint effort among competitors. Even though businesses may be competitors, they still have many common interests that lead them to work together for a common end. Cooperation between competitors is not unlawful. That cooperation, however, may be taken too far.

Antitrust law deals with businesses who take their cooperation too far, and who have substituted cooperation for competition. It is generally held that the benefits of competition to consumers outweigh the negative effects competition may have on individual businesses. Antitrust laws do not bar a business from growing if it does so by operating a better business. Instead, it prohibits the use of unfair tactics to take over or divide up a market.

> Outside the U.S., antitrust laws are referred to as "competition laws."

There are two principal federal antitrust laws: the Sherman Antitrust Act and the Clayton Act.

Sherman Act: The Sherman Antitrust Act was passed in 1890, and has been amended several times since then. It was the first federal legislation against monopolies or cartels. The law was a reaction to popular sentiment against the growing economic power of big business.

There are two essential provisions of the Sherman Act. The foundational provisions contained in Section 1 of the Act declare that every "contract, combination in the form of trust or otherwise, or conspiracy, in restraint of trade or commerce among the several States, or with foreign nations" is illegal.

> Somewhat unexpectedly, the Sherman Act does not define "trust."

CARTEL: A combination of sellers or producers of a product who join together to control production or price.

Example: A small town has enough business to support only two gas stations. Neither station will sell gas at a higher price than the other station, but selling gas too cheaply would undercut a station's profit. Without agreeing to do so, both stations end up charging the same price for gas. There is no violation of the Sherman Act.

ANTITRUST PLAINTIFF MUST ALLEGE ALL ELEMENTS OF CITED ANTITRUST LAW TO CONTINUE WITH PRIVATE LAWSUIT

Coronavirus Reporter v. Apple Inc.
(App Developer) v. (Phone Manufacturer)
2021 WL 5936910 (N.D. Cal. 2021)

Plaintiffs bring this action against Apple, Inc. to challenge Apple's allegedly monopolist operation of its "App Store" through "curation" and "censor[ship]" of smartphone apps.

Apple launched the iPhone and its proprietary iOS ecosystem in 2007. Apple introduced the App Store the following year. App developers wishing to distribute apps on the App Store must enter into two agreements with Apple: the Developer Agreement and the Developer Program License Agreement ("DPLA"). Developers must also abide by the App Store Review Guidelines (the "Guidelines"). The Developer Agreement governs the relationship between a developer and Apple, while the DPLA governs the distribution of apps created using Apple's proprietary tools and software. By signing the DPLA, developers "understand and agree" that Apple may reject apps in its "sole discretion." The Guidelines set out the standards Apple applies when exercising that discretion to review and approve apps for distribution on the App Store, a process known as "App Review."

Plaintiffs allege they are developers of "a diverse group" of apps. Two of these apps, Coronavirus Reporter and Bitcoin Lottery, were never approved for distribution on the App Store. The Coronavirus Reporter app was rejected by Apple on March 6, 2020, under Apple's policy requiring that any apps related to COVID-19 be submitted by a recognized health entity such as a government organization or medical institution. Similarly, Apple allegedly rejected Bitcoin Lottery, a "blockchain app" developed by Plaintiff Primary Productions, under its alleged policy "generally block[ing] blockchain apps." [Other apps were alleged to be] subject to ranking suppression[.] Through "ranking suppression," Plaintiff allege that Apple rendered the app "invisible on App Store searches" by end users.

The core of Plaintiffs antitrust claims are challenges to Apple's alleged exercise of market power in reviewing proposed apps and to Apple's unilateral authority to approve or deny which apps are allowed on the App Store. Plaintiffs challenge Apple's unilateral control over the ability of developers to access and provide apps to iOS users, including Apple's alleged practice of suppressing the visibility of apps which compete with Apple's own apps or apps of Apple's "cronies."

Plaintiffs' antitrust theory allegedly "flow[s] logically" from the key fact that "the only marketplace, the only seller of apps to end-users, is Apple itself" and thus Apple monopolizes an "institutional smartphone application software marketplace" in which Apple "purchase[s]" apps from developers—by approving or rejecting them through the App Review process—and then resells them to consumers on its own terms.

Plaintiffs allege [violations of sections 1 and 2 of the Sherman Act related to restraint of trade, among other claims]. Plaintiffs seek damages of an estimated $200 billion and a permanent injunction restraining Apple from "denying developers access to the smartphone enhance Internet userbase."

Apple argues that all of Plaintiffs' antitrust claims should be dismissed because Plaintiffs fail to allege facts sufficient to meet two threshold conditions to proceed on any antitrust theory: (1) Plaintiffs fail to allege a plausible relevant market for their claims, and (2) Plaintiffs fail to allege antitrust injury. As explained below, the Court dismisses all of the antitrust claims for Plaintiffs' failure to satisfy these threshold conditions.

1. Relevant Market for Antitrust Claims

"A threshold step in any antitrust case is to accurately define the relevant market, which refers to 'the area of effective competition.'" Typically, the relevant market is the "arena within which significant substitution in consumption or production occurs." Where a complaint fails to adequately allege a relevant market underlying its antitrust claims, those claims must be dismissed.

First, Apple correctly observes that the [complaint] lacks clarity as to the relevant product markets for Plaintiffs' antitrust claims. The [complaint] articulates and references at least fifteen different markets and does not always define the boundaries of or differences between those markets. For example, Plaintiffs mention the "the App Market" twice in the complaint but do not define it. . . . [T]he [complaint] does not provide sufficient clarity for the Court to assess the threshold question of whether there is a relevant market for Plaintiffs antitrust claims. One cannot discern what is included and what is not, and thus analysis of cross-elasticity of demand is not possible. Nor do the newly asserted markets appear to correspond to the markets and allegations pleaded.

2. Antitrust Injury

Apple also argues that Plaintiffs fail to plead antitrust injury.

To plausibly state antitrust claims in this market for transactions of apps, Plaintiffs must allege injury to "competition in the market as a whole"—such as marketwide reduction in output or increase in prices—"not merely injury to itself as a competitor" in the market. This alleged harm also must be " 'attributable to an anticompetitive aspect of the practice under scrutiny' "; "harm that could have occurred under the normal circumstances of free competition" does not suffice.

Apple argues that Plaintiffs' theory of injury is that *their* apps were rejected from the App Store or subjected to alleged ranking suppression. Yet, Apple contends, Plaintiffs make no allegation that Apple's conduct excluded Apple competitors, suppressed output of the market, increased app prices, or otherwise harmed competition *in the market* beyond Plaintiffs' conclusory allegations of "damage to an entire market," or unadorned references to "restricted output, quality, and innovation."

Additionally, Apple argues that Plaintiffs ignore the nature of the App Store platform such that for every app that is allegedly "suppressed" in search rankings, another app's visibility is lifted. The effect of "suppression" in search rankings affects the relative positions among products in the market; but there is no showing of harm to competition across the market. Effects on *Plaintiffs'* apps alone, which may raise equitable issues as *between* app developers, do not establish *antitrust* injury. As the Court noted [. . .], "[t]he antitrust laws . . . were enacted for the protection of competition not competitors."

Finally, Apple argues that Plaintiffs cannot merely declare that every app rejection injures competition by decreasing output and constricting consumer choice, because "if that were the rule, the Sherman Act would inhibit competition by requiring all platforms to increase the number of available apps—no matter if they contained malware, were offensive, sought to scam users, or were inferior copycats that could confuse consumers." Apple contends that consumers instead "should be able to choose between the type of ecosystems and antitrust law should not artificially eliminate them." The App Store's curation—which differentiates it from other platforms—helps "maintain[ ] a healthy ecosystem that ultimately benefits" users and developers. Thus, Apple concludes, Plaintiffs offer no plausible theory that Apple's policies reduce the net quality of transactions in a relevant market, their allegations amount only to individual harm.

Plaintiffs' allege various types of antitrust injury, all of which are insufficient[.] [The complaint's assertions] amount to conclusory and "threadbare recitals" of the elements of antitrust injury that are insufficient to state a claim.

[T]he allegation [asserting that Apple's App Review process necessarily injures competition by excluding a number of developers from launching apps on Apple's App Store] on its own is not sufficient to plead to antitrust injury for two reasons. First, Plaintiffs ignore the App Store serves a two-sided transaction market. [I]n a two-sided transaction market, there must be consideration of the "effects on both sides of the market." Plaintiffs' theory of antitrust injury alleges injury on only one side of the transaction—developers—but fails to grapple with the second side of the transaction market, consumers.

Second, even if it is assumed that Apple exercised monopsonist market power in the apps transaction market, its decisions as to which apps are allowed to sell through the App Store is not an act that in itself causes harm the antitrust laws were designed to protect. Plaintiffs failed to make any allegation the Apple benefits from its rejection of apps or from suppression of apps in the search function. There is no showing that Apple is reaping the fruits of anti-competitive conduct. The deficiency of Plaintiffs' claim in asserting an antitrust injury is demonstrated by the following analogy. Query: if the only newspaper in town decides which advertisements may properly be posted or which advertisements to accept, does a rejected advertiser suffer an anti-trust injury?

No. That is not the kind of injury antitrust laws are intended to protect. As noted above, antitrust law protections competition, not competitors. In contrast, if the newspaper attempted to squelch competition by telling advertisers if they dare advertise in an up-and-coming competing newspaper or radio station, they will be barred from its newspaper, that could suffice to show anti-trust injury. Plaintiffs do not allege facts any such antitrust injury.

For the foregoing reasons, the Court GRANTS Apple's motion to dismiss all of Plaintiffs' claims against Apple.

Example: Ace Construction Co. and Expert Contracting, Ltd., agree with each other on a schedule of prices for certain common construction jobs. Each company agrees to charge no less than the price on the schedule for these jobs. Ace and Expert have committed a *per se* violation.

The prohibition is against agreements to restrain trade. If competition is limited through market forces, there is no violation.

Although the Sherman Act is clear that every contract or combination is unlawful, the Supreme Court has held that Section 1 prohibits only "unreasonable" restraints of trade. An unreasonable restraint is one that involves a blatant attempt to restrain trade. These blatant attempts are called *per se* violations. If a *per se* violation is proven, there is no defense or legal justification for the combination. The motive or intent of the parties to the agreement are not considered. *Per se* violations are always regarded as harmful to commerce.

Most alleged violations of Section 1 are not clearly blatant. In those more common cases, the courts use what is called the "rule of reason" to determine if a contract or combination is unreasonable, and therefore unlawful. The rule of reason approach looks at the totality of the circumstances before deciding if a practice is unlawful. A court will look at the reasons for taking an action before making a judgment. The motives and intent of the actors is relevant. The court will also consider the economic benefits and costs of the action, to determine whether that action causes bad economic effects.

Section 2 of the Sherman Act prohibits monopolies. To prove a violation of Section 2 in court, it must be shown that the defendant:

- Has **monopoly** power in the relevant market, and
- That power was acquired or maintained willfully.

> An agreement between competitors to fix prices or otherwise restrict trade is known as a "horizontal restraint."

MONOPOLY:
Control over a market by one company or individual.

> **Example:** Suppose the manufacturers of laptop computers agreed that their portable products will use common specifications for power cables. This agreement restrains trade, in that it limits the type of power supplies that can be produced. On the other hand, it allows standardization, so that consumers can use any power supply on any laptop. The agreement is reasonable, and not a violation of the Act.

Section 2 does not prohibit all monopolies. A monopoly is unlawful if competition is driven out or kept away by deliberate action, such as coercion or pricing decisions. If a business has a monopoly either through no deliberate action of its own, or by offering a superior product, there is no violation of Section 2.

Monopolies are unlawful if they come about through misconduct, such as an agreement to bar competition.

> A monopoly is generally found when one business has between 70–90% of the market.

A violation of either provision of the Sherman Act is a felony. The maximum penalty is a fine of $100 million for a corporation and $1 million for an individual. An individual could also be sentenced to up to 10 years in prison. The maximum fine may be increased to twice the

> **Example:** Two daily newspapers, the Journal and the Gazette, were published in the same city. The Journal hired a new editor who expanded the coverage of the paper's internet site, and who started running new features sections. The Gazette did not change how it did business. The changes from the new publisher proved very popular, and the Journal started adding subscribers and advertisers. The Gazette lost too much income to continue, and went out of business. The Journal has a monopoly, but it did not attain that monopoly through unlawful means. There is no violation of Section 2.

> **Example:** Instead of going out of business, the Gazette fights back. It reaches a secret agreement with prominent local merchants that they will advertise only in the Gazette. The loss of advertising revenue means that the Journal cannot pay for its expensive new improvements, so the paper closes. The Gazette attained its monopoly through unlawful means, and there is a Section 2 violation.

VERTICAL INTEGRATION VIOLATES THE SHERMAN ACT

U.S. v. Paramount Pictures
(Government) v. (Motion Picture Company)
334 U.S. 131, 68 S. Ct. 915, 92 L. Ed. 1260 (1948)

INSTANT FACTS:
The U.S. Government (P) claimed that the methods Paramount (D) and other companies used for distributing movies violated antitrust laws.

BLACK LETTER RULE:
A vertically integrated enterprise is a monopoly, which violates the Sherman Anti-Trust Act.

FACTS:
The U.S. Government (P) brought an antitrust action against Paramount (D) and other motion picture distributors. The U.S. (P) alleged that the distributors violated antitrust laws by implementing five practices for distributing movies:

- Scheduling movies so that they would be shown only at certain theaters, to avoid competing with another theater's showing ("clearances and runs"),
- The joint ownership of theaters by two competing movie studios ("Pooling"),
- Allocating profits among theaters that showed a particular film,
- Requiring theaters to take an entire group of films for showing ("Block booking"), which Paramount (D) and the other defendants argued was a legitimate exercise of their copyrights in their movies, and
- Discriminating against smaller theaters in favor of larger chains.

The District Court found that clearances and runs had a legitimate purpose, and were not a restraint of trade. The District Court found that the remaining practices were unlawful restraints, and issued an injunction ordering the practices stopped. The court also concluded that it did not have the authority to continue an arbitration mechanism set up in a previous case involving the same parties.

ISSUE:
Did the movie distribution practices constitute an unlawful restraint of trade?

DECISION AND RATIONALE:
(Douglas, J.) Yes. A vertically integrated enterprise is a monopoly, which violates the Sherman Anti-Trust Act. The enterprise is unlawful if there is a power to exclude competition, and a purpose or intent to do so. The evidence that the distribution practices are unlawful restraints of trade is incontestable.

The pooling agreements and joint ownership were just to substitute monopoly for competition. Block booking was an unlawful enlargement of the producer's copyright. The evidence supported the conclusion that smaller theaters were discriminated against. However, the District Court did have the authority to continue the arbitration mechanism. Affirmed in part, reversed in part.

DISSENT:
(Frankfurter, J.) The Supreme Court should have deferred to the District Court's determination that it did not have the power to continue the arbitration program.

ANALYSIS:
This case is often cited as bringing an end to the "golden age" of Hollywood. Motion picture studios were required to divest themselves of theaters, and new, independent film distributors were able to enter the market. The Court's decision in this case, coupled with other factors like the rise of television, put the film industry into a slump from which it did not recover until the early 1970s.

Note that acquisitions leading to a monopoly are not the only way to create an anti-competitive enterprise. Companies may also grow without acquiring other enterprises, and eventually occupy a market to the extent that regulators become involved.

amount gained from the illegal acts or twice the money lost by the victims of the crime, if either of those amounts is over $100 million.

Clayton Act: The Clayton Act was passed in 1914. The purpose of the Act was to address anti-competitive practices that became popular after the Sherman Act was passed. For example, the Sherman Act prohibited cartels and combinations, but did not prevent companies merging to dominate markets. The Sherman Act was also used in ways that the sponsors of the law did not intend, such as breaking up unions.

The Clayton Act is enforced primarily through civil lawsuits. These lawsuits are brought either by private parties or the U.S. government.

> Approximately 90% of all Clayton Act lawsuits are brought by private parties.

MERGER:
The combining or uniting of two companies.

ACQUISITION:
Gaining of possession or control over a company.

A successful suit under the Clayton Act may result in a damage award that is three times the actual damages proven.

The Clayton Act makes certain enumerated types of activities unlawful. The four types of unlawful activities are:

- Price discrimination between different purchasers that substantially lessens competition or tends to create a monopoly,

- Sales conditioned on the buyer not dealing with competitors of the seller, or on the buyer also purchasing another different product if those requirements substantially lessen competition,

- **Mergers** and **acquisitions** that may substantially lessen competition, and

- Any person acting as a director of two or more competing corporations, if a merger of those corporations would violate the anti-trust laws by merging.

The prohibition against price discrimination prevents sellers from selling the same goods to different purchasers at different prices other than in specific contexts. To violate the prohibition, the goods must have been of a "like grade or quality." The sales to different customers must also have been made in the same general

Example: A salt wholesaler advertised a quantity discount, but made the discount available only to five national grocery chains. The five chains were the only ones that bought sufficient quantities to qualify for the discount. The salt wholesaler was engaged in unlawful price discrimination. *Federal Trade Commission v. Morton Salt,* 334 U.S. 37 (1948).

> **Example:** A manufacturer of printers tells customers that the warranty will be voided if the customer does not buy toner cartridges and paper from the manufacturer. The toner cartridges are manufactured to detailed specifications relating to their function, but the paper sold by the manufacturer is no different than the paper sold by any other company. The toner cartridge requirement may not be unlawful, but the paper requirement probably is.

time period. Unlawful price discrimination includes practices such as:

- Below-cost sales in certain locations,
- Price differences that cannot be explained by cost savings, or the need to compete on price in one area, or
- Promotional allowances, such as special introductory prices.

Making sales conditioned on buying another product made by the seller tends to create a monopoly for the seller. There may be a justification for the condition, to ensure compliance with product standards. A violation is usually found when the products have no relation to one another, or when there is no technical reason why products from a different seller could not be used.

The most significant provisions of the Clayton Act relate to mergers. While some mergers can benefit competition and consumers by allowing greater efficiencies, other mergers damage the market by eliminating competition. This could result in higher prices and lower quality for consumers.

The Clayton Act prohibits mergers and acquisitions whose effect could be "substantially to lessen competition, or to tend to create a monopoly." Three kinds of mergers may have this effect:

1. horizontal mergers, which involve two competitors;
2. vertical mergers, which involve firms in a buyer-seller relationship; and
3. potential competition mergers.

In a potential competition merger, one company is likely to enter the market and become a potential competitor of the other.

Horizontal mergers eliminate competitors. They may change the competitive environment so the remaining firms could coordinate on competitive practices, such as pricing. The surviving firm could also raise prices on its own without facing any competitive pressures.

Vertical mergers are between firms in a buyer-seller relationship. The manufacturer of a product might merge with a distributor, or with a company that sells a component of the product. Vertical mergers can lead to significant cost savings. They can also improve market efficiency, by improving the coordination between different companies in the supply chain. A vertical merger could also pose problems for competition. A competitor might be unable to gain access to an important component or to a channel of distribution.

A potential competition merger is where one competitor buying a company that is planning to enter its market to compete. That type of merger could prevent the increased competition that would result from a new entry into the market. It could also eliminate the effect that potential competitor could have. Companies already in the market would not be inclined to take competitive steps that might make it less attractive for a newcomer to enter the market.

The rules against anti-competitive mergers are applied before a merger occurs. The Federal Trade Commission and U.S. Department of Justice must be notified before certain large mergers may take place. The federal agencies are then given an opportunity to review the effect the proposed merger may have on competition. The merger may not take place if it is determined that the merger would have an adverse effect on U.S. commerce.

> The FTC approved the merger of OfficeMax and Office Depot in 2013, but rejected a merger between Office Depot and Staples in 2015.

III. International Business Transactions

Many businesses center on producing tangible goods—that is, they make physical products rather than provide services. Transactions in goods leads inevitably to questions about the practicalities buying or selling them. It also leads to questions about getting them from the seller to the buyer.

> Inland waterways include navigable rivers, canal systems, and ship passages. The St. Lawrence Seaway System is a good example. Ocean vessels are able to navigate from the Atlantic Ocean through St. Lawrence System locks into the Great Lakes. Such ships can go as far inland as Duluth, Minnesota—over 1,600 miles by road.

CAREERS IN THE LAW

As businesses grow internationally, they need more specialized assistance to stay on track. International trade relies on customs brokers to categorize goods and to file the necessary forms to have imports released from customs. Customs brokers typically work for brokerage houses or transportation companies, but many businesses hire customs brokers as employees. In-house customs brokers work solely on their employer's shipments.

There are a variety of training programs for customs brokers, but specific training is not required to become a broker. Many people choose to work for a broker as an entry agent to learn the basics, and then take the Customs Broker License Exam (CBLE). The CBLE is given by U.S. Customs and Border Protection. Applicants must be U.S. citizens and must report on their activity as a broker to the agency each year.

Customs brokers work directly with federal regulations to make sure their clients pay the correct amount of import tax. They also work with companies to develop strategies to make imports more effective. Customs brokerage is an excellent and well-compensated way to be involved in international business and the law.

Transporting goods costs money. Domestically, transport may be by truck, train, or air. Internationally, many shipments are also made via ocean or inland waterway.

Whatever way the goods are moved, the buyer and seller must agree who will pay for transport. There are also ways that buyers and sellers can split those costs. These options are more complicated the longer it takes for the goods to arrive at their destination. International transactions with shipment are among these longer transits.

The fees charged for shipping are not the only potential cost involved. There is also the risk that the goods being shipped will be destroyed or damaged, or will otherwise not make it to their destination. If the goods are lost, the financial loss depends on which party was considered to have had responsibility or ownership for the goods at the time.

Transportation Risk and Costs

Most consumer sales transactions are simple. We go into a store, make a selection, pay the price, and take our purchase with us. We own the item as soon as we pay for it. Our understanding of a sale as an exchange of money for goods is built around this model. When this model is altered by not making the change of possession immediate, or by requiring delivery

> Deciding who has the risk of loss will also affect a party's obligation or need to purchase insurance coverage. If a seller is responsible for insurance but does not purchase a policy, the seller may be financially responsible for the loss directly.

to a different location, a new concern is raised. That concern is the "risk of loss."

The risk of loss deals with the question of who is responsible for goods that are damaged, lost, or destroyed. At some point in every sales transaction, that risk passes from the seller to the buyer. The parties may have agreed who bears the risk of loss, and that agreement will control. If one party breaches the shipping agreement, that party bears the risk of loss, even when the breach does not relate to the loss.

If there is no contract breach, Article 2 of the Uniform Commercial Code sets out rules for determining who has the risk of loss in a given situation. Article 2 is commonly used in domestic transactions in the United States, but may also be used by international trading partners. When the seller does not handle the delivery, but transfers goods to a common carrier for transport, the risk depends on the terms of the shipping contract. If the contract does not require the seller to deliver the goods

> **Example:** Allied Widget purchases three lathes from D & C Equipment Sales. The sales contract states that the lathes are to be delivered no later than November 16. Due to administrative errors at D & C, the lathes are do not arrive at Allied until November 18. Two of the lathes are damaged when they are delivered. D & C has the risk of loss, and is responsible for the damage.

\multicolumn{4}{c}{*Comparison of Selected Trade Terms*}
UCC Trade Term	*Meaning*	*Incoterm 2020*	*Meaning*
CIF (destination)	"Cost, Insurance, and Freight" • Buyer's cost for goods includes Seller's expense for shipment and for shipping insurance. • Seller must arrange shipping and insurance and provide documentation to Buyer. • Risk of loss passes to Buyer once the goods are loaded, but the insurance covers Buyer in case of loss. • Applies to any type of shipment.	CIF (destination port)	"Cost, Insurance, and Freight" • Buyer's cost for goods includes Seller's expense for shipment and for shipping insurance. • Seller must arrange shipping and insurance and provide documentation to Buyer. • Risk of loss passes to Buyer once goods are on board, but the insurance covers Buyer in case of loss. • Only applies to ocean and inland seaway shipments.
FOB (shipment location)	"Free on Board" • Seller places goods in the possession of shipper and supplies documentation to Buyer. • Seller pays expenses until the goods are provided to shipper; all remaining costs pass to Buyer. • Risk of loss passes to Buyer once the goods are put in shipper's possession. • Applies to any type of shipment.	FOB (shipment port)	"Free on Board" • Seller delivers goods to shipper at named port of shipment and provides documentation to Buyer; all remaining costs pass to Buyer. • Risk of loss passes when goods are on board; all remaining costs pass to Buyer. • Only applies to ocean and inland waterway shipments.

	Comparison of Selected Trade Terms		
UCC Trade Term	**Meaning**	**Incoterm 2020**	**Meaning**
FOB (destination)	"Free on Board" • Seller must arrange and pay for transport of the goods to destination; all remaining costs pass to Buyer. • Risk of loss passes to Buyer once goods are delivered. • Applies to any type of shipment.	DDP (destination)	"Delivered Duty Paid" • Seller must arrange and pay for transport of goods to Buyer; Buyer's only cost is unloading. • Seller must arrange for import clearance formalities and payment of import fees and duties. • Risk of loss passes to Buyer when the goods are at Buyer's location. • Applies to any type of shipment.
Ex Ship (destination port, terminal, or airport)	"Ex[terior] of Ship" • Seller must arrange and pay for transport of the goods to destination transportation facility; all remaining costs pass to Buyer. • Risk of loss passes to Buyer once goods unloaded. • Applies to any type of shipment.	DAP (named destination)	"Delivered at Place" • Seller must arrange and pay for transport of the goods to destination; all remaining costs pass to Buyer. • Risk of loss passes to Buyer when goods are at the destination facility. • Applies to any type of shipment.

to a particular address, but says that the seller will deliver the goods to a carrier for shipment (a shipment contract), the risk passes to the buyer on delivery to the carrier.

A "destination" contract, which requires delivery of the goods, keeps the risk of loss with the seller until the buyer receives the goods. The

> **Example:** Damon orders sound recording equipment from Euthyphro Acoustics. The contract says that Euthyphro will ship the equipment via common carrier. Euthyphro delivers the equipment to the North Western Railway for shipment. The risk of loss passes to Damon when equipment is delivered to the railway.

seller is also obligated to pay the costs of shipping the goods to the destination.

A "shipment" contract puts the risk of loss on the buyer. The buyer is responsible for the costs of delivering the goods to the carrier for shipment, but has no obligation for further delivery costs. Shipment contracts are presumed, unless there is language that makes an agreement a destination contract.

To make shipping easier, trade terms provide a short-hand for common transport practices. These short codes define buyer and seller responsibilities in a few letters. For domestic shipments or for international shipments using Article 2, businesses use the Uniform Commercial Code trade terms. The International Chamber of Commerce "Incoterms" are commonly used for international shipments.

Since the terms vary, it is important to choose the correct one. The parties must also define where shipment or delivery takes place. That location is listed after the trade term in parentheses. The table shows just a few of the common terms from each system, and how they differ.

Harmonized Tariff Schedule

Many businesses import products or components, or export goods to buyers in other countries. In these cases, costs are different than they would be for a domestic sale. Aside from shipment and documentation costs, customs duties may also be imposed. Sometimes, there are further customs fees covering services such as short-term warehousing or inspections.

Customs duties are taxes applied to goods entering a country. Duties are used to control imports to achieve policy goals. For instance, a high duty rate on cigarettes discourages smoking by restricting the supply of imported cigarettes and by making the consumer cost higher. Duties may be lower for goods from friendly countries, and much higher for the same

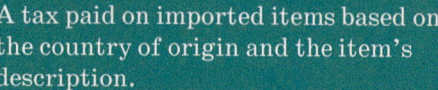

CUSTOMS DUTY:
A tax paid on imported items based on the country of origin and the item's description.

> A customs duty is the tax paid on an import. It is based on the product's value or quantity, or a combination of value and quantity. A tariff is a list (or "schedule") of the customs duties. Despite the difference, businesspeople often refer to customs duties as "tariffs."

products from disfavored nations. Governments can also use customs duties to shield domestic producers from competition.

In order to make customs duties easy to understand, the United States developed the Harmonized Tariff Schedule (HTS). The HTS became effective in 1989. The schedule consists of numbered categories of possible imports that allow customs officials to identify an import accurately. Each numbered description is followed by applicable duty rates.

The customs duty on an import may vary depending on its country of origin. Most countries' imports will receive a standard duty rate. If a country is in a negotiated trade relationship with the United States, however, imports from that country may receive a lower rate. If there are trade sanctions on a country, imports will receive a high duty rate.

The graphic shows a page from the HTS. Heading 6911 covers plates; this is the first page for that heading. The excerpt shows the HTS's precision and the range of duties. Under Rates of Duty

Example: In 1930, Congress passed the Smoot-Hawley Tariff Act. The Act raised customs duties on thousands of items commonly imported into the United States. The Act's goal was to discourage imports of goods that U.S. companies produced at home. Congress believed that Smoot-Hawley would improve the economy. Instead, other countries retaliated by raising duties on American products, which reduced the markets for U.S. goods. Congress intended that the Act would improve the Great Depression, but the economy continued to decline. It is difficult to determine the extent of Smoot-Hawley's economic impact, but most economists agree that the Act at least contributed to the Depression.

AGREED SHIPPING TERM CONTROLS THE RISK OF LOSS
St. Paul Guardian Insurance Company v. Neuromed Medical Systems & Support
(Insurance Company) v. (Equipment Seller)
2002 WL 465312 (S.D.N.Y. 2002)

Plaintiffs St. Paul Guardian Insurance Company and Travelers Property Casualty Insurance Company have brought this action to recover $285,000 they paid to Shared Imaging for damage to a mobile magnetic resonance imaging system ("MRI") purchased by Shared Imaging from defendant Neuromed Medical Systems & Support GmbH ("Neuromed"). Neuromed has moved to dismiss the complaint.

The crux of Neuromed's argument is that it had no further obligations regarding the risk of loss once it delivered the MRI to the vessel at the port of shipment due to a "CIF" clause included in the underlying contract. Plaintiffs respond that (1) the generally understood definition of the "CIF" term as defined by the International Chamber of Commerce's publication, *Incoterms 1990*, is inapplicable here and (2) the "CIF" term was effectively superceded by other contract terms such that the risk of loss remained on Neuromed.

Shared Imaging, an American corporation, and Neuromed, a German corporation, entered into a contract of sale for a Siemens Harmony 1.0 Tesla mobile MRI. Thereafter, both parties engaged various entities to transport, insure and provide customs entry service for the MRI. According to the complaint, the MRI was loaded aboard the vessel "Atlantic Carrier" undamaged and in good working order. When it reached its destination of Calmut City, Illinois, it had been damaged and was in need of extensive repair, which led plaintiffs to conclude that the MRI had been damaged in transit.

The one page contract of sale [. . .] provides, "CIF New York Seaport, the buyer will arrange and pay for customs clearance as well as transport to Calmut City." [U]nder "Disclaimer" it states, "system including all accessories and options remain the property of Neuromed till complete payment has been received."

Neuromed contends that because the delivery terms were "CIF New York Seaport," its contractual obligation, with regard to risk of loss or damage, ended when it delivered the MRI to the vessel at the port of shipment and therefore the action must be dismissed because plaintiffs have failed to state a claim for which relief can be granted. Plaintiffs respond that the generally accepted definition of the "CIF" term as defined in *Incoterms 1990*, is inapplicable. Moreover, plaintiffs suggest that other provisions of the contract are inconsistent with the "CIF" term because Neuromed, pursuant to the contract, retained title subsequent to delivery to the vessel at the port of shipment and thus, Neuromed manifestly retained the risk of loss.

The parties concede that the U.N. Convention on Contracts for the International Sale of Goods ("CISG") governs this transaction because (1) both the U.S. and Germany are Contracting States to that Convention, and (2) neither party chose, by express provision in the contract, to opt out of the application of the CISG. The CISG aims to bring uniformity to international business transactions, using simple, non-nation specific language. To that end, it is comprised of rules applicable to the conclusion of contracts of sale of international goods.

"CIF," which stands for "cost, insurance and freight," is a commercial trade term that is defined in *Incoterms 1990*, published by the International Chamber of Commerce ("ICC"). The aim of INCOTERMS, which stands for international commercial terms, is "to provide a set of international rules for the interpretation of the most commonly used trade terms in foreign trade." These "trade terms are used to allocate the costs of freight and insurance" in addition to designating the point in time when the risk of loss passes to the purchaser. INCOTERMS are incorporated into the CISG.

At the time the contract was entered into, *Incoterms 1990* was applicable. INCOTERMS define "CIF" (named port of destination) to mean the seller delivers when the goods pass "the ship's rail in the port of shipment." The seller is responsible for paying the cost, freight and insurance coverage necessary to bring the goods to the named port of destination, but the risk of loss or damage to the goods passes from seller to buyer upon delivery to the port of shipment. Further, "CIF" requires the seller to obtain insurance only on minimum cover.

Plaintiffs argue that Neuromed's explicit retention of title in the contract to the MRI machine modified the "CIF" term, such that Neuromed retained title and assumed the risk of loss. INCOTERMS, however, only address passage of risk, not transfer of title. Under the CISG, the passage of risk is likewise independent of the transfer of title.

Pursuant to the CISG, "[t]he risk passes without taking into account who owns the goods. The passing of ownership is not regulated by the CISG[.]" Moreover . . . the passage of risk and transfer of title need not occur at the same time, as the seller's retention of "documents controlling the disposition of the goods does not affect the passage of risk." Neuromed's retention of title did not thereby implicate retention of the risk of loss or damage.

For the foregoing reasons, Neuromed's motion to dismiss for failure to state a claim is granted and the complaint is dismissed.

Harmonized Tariff Schedule of the United States (2016) Supplement-1
Annotated for Statistical Reporting Purposes

XIII
69-8

Heading/ Subheading	Stat. Suffix	Article Description	Unit of Quantity	Rates of Duty		
				1		2
				General	Special	
6911		Tableware, kitchenware, other household articles and toilet articles, of porcelain or china:				
6911.10		Tableware and kitchenware:				
6911.10.10	00	Hotel or restaurant ware and other ware not household ware..	doz.pcs......	25%	Free (A+, AU, BH, CA, CL, CO, D, E, IL, JO, MA, MX, P, PA, PE, SG) 5% (OM) 12.5% (KR)	75%
		Other: Of bone chinaware:				
6911.10.15	00	Valued not over $31.50 per dozen pieces......	doz.pcs......	8%	Free (A, AU, BH, CA, CL, CO, D, E, IL, JO, KR, MA, MX, OM, P, PA, PE, SG)	75%
6911.10.25	00	Other..	doz.pcs......	6%	Free (A, AU, BH, CA, CL, CO, D, E, IL, JO, KR, MA, MX, OM, P, PA, PE, SG)	75%
		Other: Available in specified sets:				
6911.10.35		In any pattern for which the aggregate value of the articles listed in additional U.S. note 6(b) of this chapter is not over $56....	....	26%	Free (A, AU, BH, CA, CL, CO, D, E, IL, JO, MA, MX, OM, P, PA, PE, SG) 13% (KR)	75%
	10	Plates not over 27.9 cm in maximum dimension; teacups and saucers; mugs; soups, fruits and cereals, the foregoing not over 22.9 cm in maximum dimension...........................	doz. pcs.			
	50	Other..	doz. pcs.			

on the right, the "General" column shows the standard rate (6 to 26 percent, depending on the product). The "Special" column shows the rates for specific trade agreements (free to 13 percent). The trade agreements are shown by short abbreviations. Column 2 shows rates applied to countries under sanction (75 percent). This is only the first page of four covering plates. The entire HTS is a very large document.

Buyers and sellers must pay close attention to HTS categories. If imports are not correctly categorized, there may be substantial fines and back duties to pay. U.S. Customs and Border Protection may conduct audits of import records to determine the extent of underpayment. And deliberate use of an inaccurate tariff category to avoid customs duties is a federal crime. U.S. Customs can help importers categorize products before they ship.

SUMMARY JUDGMENT NOT APPROPRIATE IN DISPUTE OVER CLASSIFICATION OF ACTION FIGURES

Toy Biz, Inc. v. U.S.
(Toy Importer) v. (Customs Authority)
24 C.I.T. 1351 (2000)

INSTANT FACTS:
The U.S. Customs Service (D) classified action figures as "dolls," rather than "toys."

BLACK LETTER RULE:
Summary judgment is inappropriate when there is a genuine issue as to any material fact.

FACTS:
Toy Biz (P) imported X-Men and other action figures from China. The U.S. Customs Service (D) classified the figures as "dolls," subject to an import duty of 12%. The Harmonized Tariff Schedules stated that "dolls" represented "only human beings and parts and accessories thereof." The Customs Service (D) argued that lexicographic authorities and case law defined "doll" broadly. Courts have recognized that dolls do not have to include all the anatomical elements of a real person, and may include additional characters or things. Toy Biz (P) argued that the figures were "toys," subject to a duty of 6.8%. Toy Biz (P) noted that the figures had non-human features, robotic limbs, tentacles, wings, or silver metallic skin. Toy Biz (P) said that Customs (D) used the wrong test to classify the action figures at issue, and argued that figures possessing both human and non-human characteristics are classified as "toys," even when the figures have predominantly human characteristics. Both parties moved for summary judgment.

ISSUE:
Was there an issue of fact as to whether the figures were "toys" or "dolls?"

DECISION AND RATIONALE:
(Ridgway, J.) Yes. Summary judgment is inappropriate when there is a genuine issue as to any material fact. Summary proceedings are not intended to substitute for trial when it is indeed necessary to find material facts.

The dispositive issue here is the obviousness of any non-human features. If a figure has any feature which is both clearly non-human and readily apparent to a casual observer, the figure represents some non-human creature, rather than a human being. Customs (D) cannot reasonably be required to closely scrutinize every detail of every figure in a search for non-human features, in order to classify the figure as a doll or a toy. In addition, it would not be reasonable to require Customs (D) to speculate on the human-ness of a particular feature or characteristic. Because genuine issues of material fact are embedded in the application of the "casual observer" standard to the action figures here, and because the parties do not agree on those material facts, summary judgment is not appropriate. Motions denied.

> **ANALYSIS:**
> After trial, the court agreed with Toy Biz (P). The action figures were "toys," not "dolls." The Harmonized Tariff Schedule has since been amended, and there is no difference in the tariffs for "dolls" and "toys."
>
> **CASE VOCABULARY:**
> **SUMMARY JUDGMENT:**
> Judgment for a party rendered without a trial, granted when there is no genuine issue of material fact.

Trading Areas

The Harmonized Tariff Schedule shows how trading relationships between countries can result in lower duty rates for businesses. There are many types of trade relationships that countries can create. Each relationship has its own unique benefits and responsibilities, supported by agreement between the countries. Trade agreements are primarily about economic issues, but often include clauses about other issues of concern. Including these conditions is one way that the United States builds alliances with other countries.

Many trade relationships are bilateral, meaning that they only involve two countries. The United States has several bilateral agreements of varying complexity. One example is the Peru Trade Promotion Agreement. That agreement eliminated the majority of duties on U.S. agricultural exports to Peru, and reduced or eliminated U.S. duties on imports of Peruvian products. The agreement also includes terms dealing with environmental and labor protections.

Sometimes, a bilateral agreement may grow to involve more countries. An agreement between the United States and Canada later became the basis for the North American Free Trade Agreement (NAFTA). The Canada-United States Free Trade Agreement dates to 1987. The negotiation of a three-party North American agreement among Mexico, Canada, and the United States followed. NAFTA was signed by the parties in 1992. NAFTA was replaced by the United States Mexico Canada Agreement (USMCA), which maintains the free trade relationship among the parties.

Trade relationships take several forms. The most common types are:

- Free trade areas.
- Customs unions.
- Common markets.

Free trade areas include countries that have signed a free trade agreement. The members of a free trade area reduce or eliminate duties and other limitations on each other's products in order to promote trade among the area's countries. NAFTA (now USMCA) established a free

> **FREE TRADE AREA:**
> Countries that negotiate a free trade agreement to reduce or eliminate customs duties and other trade barriers between themselves.

trade area for the three member countries. The countries do not need to share a border to be considered a free trade area.

Customs unions are free trade areas with another level of economic coordination. In addition to reducing or eliminating duties on each other's products, customs union members also agree to use a consistent tariff schedule and customs duty rates for non-members. These rates are likely higher than the rates within the area, but they are still attractive rates. This "common external tariff" makes the customs union attractive to businesses outside the area.

> Trading areas allow businesses to access a larger potential market than they would find in any individual country. These areas generally make import and export rules clearer and easier for businesses to follow. But businesses seeking international sales should remember that they are still subject to local law when trading overseas. Businesses cannot export goods that do not meet legal requirements at the destination, for instance. These requirements could include labeling laws, materials disclosures, or other country-specific rules.

Businesses can export to any member and receive the same rates. With the rates inside the area at low levels or eliminated entirely, businesses have more flexibility for transportation and market development in a customs union.

Common markets use the customs union concept but with far more internal interaction and coordination among members. A common market involves a geographic area that eliminates duties and trade restrictions among the member countries. In addition, a common market strives to achieve free movement of capital and labor among members.

> The East African Community (EAC) is a customs union that originally formed in 1967. The member countries include Burundi, Kenya, Rwanda, South Sudan, Tanzania, and Uganda. The EAC has an interesting history. It grew from an innovative earlier agreement in the 1940s, and was still ahead of its time in 1967. The union disbanded in the late 1970s, but reformed in 2000. The EAC is working to deepen its agreement while coordinating productively with other African trade blocs.

The European Union is one of the most complex trade areas. The European Union's founding documents define four freedoms as necessary to a common market:

- Free movement of capital.
- Free movement of goods.
- Free movement of services.
- Free movement of people.

CUSTOMS UNION: A free trade area that also adopts a common external tariff.

COMMON MARKET: A geographic group of countries that seek to eliminate trade barriers among themselves and promote free movement of capital and labor within the member countries.

CHAPTER SUMMARY

Businesses interact with the rest of the world on many levels, and not just with customers. Misleading a company's investors is prohibited by the Sarbanes-Oxley Act. Antitrust laws prohibited agreeing with other businesses to limit competition, or restrain trade. Rules on the risk of loss when goods are transported provide certainty about who is responsible when goods are damaged in shipment. Tariffs and trading areas regulate the ways business is transacted across national borders.

> The free movement of capital can only be fully achieved by a shared currency. A common currency (such as the Euro) eliminates the trade issue posed by fluctuating exchange rates and related fees. Some European Union members chose not to participate in the common currency when it was introduced. One of those countries, Great Britain, has since left the European Union, commonly known as "Brexit."

As businesses grow and become more complex, they are subject to increasing levels of regulation. These regulations are designed to prevent overreach by large businesses and to maintain accountability. But the law is also designed to promote healthy businesses for the good of the economy. Successful businesses should not shy away from regulatory requirements.

In a fully evolved common market, there would be unrestrained trade and movement among member countries, much as there is unrestrained trade and movement among states in the United States.

Review Questions

Review question 1.
What are the "Securities Laws" from the 1930s? What was their goal? What agency was established? What is its role?

Review question 2.
What is SEC Rule 10b–5? How does the SEC use the rule? What types of wrongdoing are subject to the rule?

Review question 3.

What is the Sarbanes-Oxley Act? How does it impact financial reporting? Are there businesses that do not need to adhere to the Act? Why or why not?

Review question 4.

Who is responsible for the accuracy of financial statements of publicly-traded corporations? What type of financial information must be disclosed?

Review question 5.

What impact does Sarbanes-Oxley have on accountants and auditors? What is the reasoning behind these requirements?

Review question 6.

What is a "horizontal" merger? What is a "vertical" merger? How does the law treat each type of merger? What law requires government approval of large corporate mergers? Does federal law prohibit monopolies?

Review question 7.

What is the Sherman Act? What does it require? What is its purpose? Who enforces it?

Review question 8.

What is the Clayton Act? How is it enforced? What is the role of private parties in the law? What is the aim of the law?

Review question 9.

What are the four freedoms and how do they work within a common market? What are the differences between a common market and a customs union? Between a customs union and a free trade area?

Review question 10.

Define "F.O.B." How does F.O.B. differ under the UCC and Incoterms? What is the purpose of trade terms? What other information should be included with F.O.B. or other trade terms?

Discussion Questions

Question 1:

Delish, O-So-Yummy, and Jim Norton are competing companies that operate chains of donut shops. They agree to form an association, the National Donut Association, to discuss and address common interests. At the Association's first meeting, discussions revolve around land use restrictions, environmental marketing, and food labeling requirements.

> Is the Association an antitrust violation? Why or why not?

> In many cities, the competing donut shops are very close to each other. Delish instructs shop managers to send employees every day to O-So-Yummy and Jim Norton to learn what prices are being charged and what promotions are being offered. Managers are directed to match prices, and run similar promotions. Is this an antitrust violation? Why or why not?

Question 2:

Acme Inc. is a publicly traded company. It is recruiting Chris to be its new CEO. Chris is concerned about legal responsibilities as the CEO of a large corporation.

> What does Chris need to be concerned about? How would the role differ from serving as CEO of a private company?

Question 3:

A shoe manufacturer in Levelland, Texas ordered a shaping machine from a dealer in Cleveland, Ohio. When the machine arrives on June 23, it is damaged beyond repair. Explain which party bears the risk of loss in each of these situations.

> The sales contract contained the term "F.O.B. Cleveland."

> The sales contract contained the term "F.O.B. Levelland."

> The sales contract was silent on risk of loss.

> The sales contract was silent on risk of loss, but stated that the machine was to be delivered no later than June 19.

Question 4:

Refer back to the prior question.

> What would change if the parties were in different countries?
>
> How would the meaning of the term change?
>
> How would risk of loss change, if at all?

Question 5:

Super Corporation is the biggest widget producer and seller in the nation. Super has 65 percent of the widget market. Its nearest competitor, Terrific Company, also makes widgets, and has 25 percent of the market. The quality and use of the widgets are comparable across the two companies. Super would like to reduce the competitive pressure from Terrific or acquire Terrific.

> What activities should Super avoid?
>
> What problems might Super face if a merger or acquisition is pursued?

Question 6:

The United States is a member of several bilateral trade agreements. It is also the member of the three-party United States Mexico Canada Agreement.

> Does the membership of USMCA change the country's responsibilities under its various bilateral trade agreements?
>
> What if another USMCA country started trade sanctions against one of the United States' bilateral trade partners? What impact would that have on the agreement? On USMCA relationships?

Question 7:

Pravesh Industries, a Belgian company, makes wooden toys with natural finishes. The toys have been very popular domestically. The CEO attends a trade show, and a buyer for a U.S. retailer shows interest. Pravesh Industries has never exported its products.

> What does the CEO need to know about international transportation? About product classification? About customs duties?

13 REGULATORY PROGRAMS

KEY OBJECTIVES:
- Explain the basic principles of administrative law.
- Describe examples of major business regulations.
- Define the goals of large-scale regulatory programs.

CHAPTER OVERVIEW

This chapter covers regulatory procedures and major areas of federal regulation. The term "regulations" refers to the body of law created by government administrative agencies. Agencies make rules and regulations by using authority delegated to them by the legislature in statutes. Agencies exist at both the state and federal levels, with authority granted to them by state and federal legislation.

A few major federal regulatory regimes have the greatest impact on business. Those regulations establish standards for advertising and marketing, including deceptive trade practices and consumer protection laws. Publicly traded businesses are regulated by the Securities and Exhange Commision and other agencies to maintain a fair stock market. Environmental rules control hazardous materials and air and water pollution by businesses. While the focus is on federal regulations here, remember that there is an additional layer of regulation in each state.

INTRODUCTION

Business operations must comply with legislation, but they must also follow rules and regulations set forth by administrative agencies. These agencies act with authority granted to them by the legislature. Although legislation is important, much of the day-to-day "street level" regulation of business is done by government agencies. These bodies make rules and regulations that have the same force as if they were passed by the legislative branch and approved by the executive.

The idea of unelected regulatory regimes may seem undemocratic. But Congress delegates authority to regulatory agencies to create these regulations. This authority is strictly limited. Further, regulatory agencies often deal with highly specialized or technical matters. The agencies and their staff have developed the expertise to address these issues in a knowledgeable way.

ADMINISTRATIVE PROCEDURE ACT:
The federal law that establishes the procedure for rulemaking and adjudication by federal administrative agencies.

I. Administrative Procedure Act

The process of making administrative rules requires many clearly defined steps. Federal agencies make their rules according to the **Administrative Procedure Act** (APA). The APA sets standards for federal regulatory activity.

> Many states have laws about the adoption of administrative regulations patterned after the APA.

The purposes of the APA include:

- Requiring agencies to keep the public informed of their organization, procedures and rules,

- Providing for public participation in the rulemaking process,

- Establishing uniform standards for the conduct of formal rulemaking and **adjudication**, and

- Defining the scope of **judicial review**.

Federal agencies act according to authority granted by Congress. When an agency identifies a need for a regulation that is within its authority, or when Congress mandates the adoption of a rule, the agency develops the specifics of the rule. When drafting a rule, agencies are required to take into account the benefits and costs to all parties. Once a proposed rule is ready, the agency will publish it in the **Federal**

> Public comments may come from interested industry representatives, lobby groups, individual businesses, and non-profits. But the "public" is also well-represented by individual comments. Public comment periods bring in all sorts of commentary, from hand-written postcards to carefully argued memoranda.
>
> In 2019, the U.S. Department of Education published proposed regulations to require new processes for colleges and universities dealing with sexual misconduct allegations against students. Around 100,000 public comments were made. Some were nothing more than insults directed to the department head. Others were detailed discussions of the drawbacks of the department's plans. Some interest groups provided details on how to comment, while others handed out blank notecards or gave instructions on how to comment via websites. After this large volume of comments, however, the proposed regulations were put into effect without major changes.

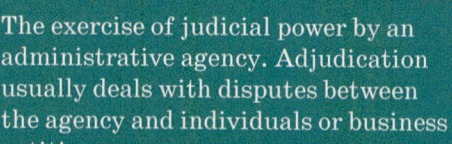

ADJUDICATION:
The exercise of judicial power by an administrative agency. Adjudication usually deals with disputes between the agency and individuals or business entities.

JUDICIAL REVIEW:
A court's review of an administrative agency's factual or legal findings.

FEDERAL REGISTER:
A daily publication containing documents and orders issued by Executive Branch agencies.

Register. The notice will solicit comments from the public on the proposed rule, and tell the public when comments must be received. After the agency considers any public feedback and makes any appropriate changes, it then publishes a final rule in the Federal Register. In issuing a final rule, the agency must describe and respond to the public comments that were received. Agencies are not required to revise the rule to take into account such comments, but they often do.

The publication of a new rule will include the date when it becomes effective and therefore enforceable. Major rules take effect 60 days after their final publication date.

> "Major rules" are defined as rules likely to have an annual effect on the national economy of $100 million or more; that will increase costs and prices for certain constituencies such as consumers or state and local governments; or that will have some other adverse effect on the economy.

Other rules go into effect 30 days after the final publication. The delay period allows Congress to review the rule and, if necessary, act to invalidate the regulation. If Congress disapproves of a new regulation, it may pass a joint resolution of disapproval. The joint resolution must be signed by the president. If signed, the rule will not take effect.

ADMINISTRATIVE AGENCIES HELP THE LEGISLATIVE, EXECUTIVE, AND JUDICIAL BRANCHES OF BOTH FEDERAL AND STATE GOVERNMENTS TO REGULATE CERTAIN INDUSTRIES AND ACTIVITIES

Fund for Animals, Inc. v. Rice
(Environmental Conservation Group) v. (Army Corps of Engineers Official)
85 F.3d 535 (11th Cir. 1996)

INSTANT FACTS:
An environmental group filed suit against the Army Corps of Engineers, the Fish and Wildlife Service, and the Environmental Protection Agency when those agencies approved the building of a landfill in an area that would allegedly harm two endangered species.

BLACK LETTER RULE:
Administrative agencies act on behalf of the three branches of government in making rules for the regulation of certain activities, enforcing those rules, and then adjudicating certain disputes that arise with respect to those rules.

PROCEDURAL BASIS:
Appeal to the Eleventh Circuit Court of Appeals of a federal district court decision approving of the actions of three administrative agencies with regard to the building of a landfill.

FACTS:
On November 22, 1989, Sarasota County, Florida, filed an application with the Army Corps of Engineers (the Corps) (D) for a permit to build a landfill on a 6,150 acre site in the county. The County was required to seek a permit from the Corps (D) because the proposed landfill affected some wetlands. Under federal law, the Corps (D) had to approve of any discharge of dredged or fill materials into the waters of the United States.

The plan received some opposition and had to be altered in various ways over the next few years. The original plan, which affected 120 acres of wetlands, was later modified so that only 74 acres would be affected. This modification was the result of Clean Water Act concerns expressed by the Environmental Protection Agency (EPA) (D). Concern was also expressed that the landfill would adversely affect two endangered species—the Florida panther and the Eastern Indigo Snake—though the Fish and Wildlife Service (FWS) (D) ultimately determined in two separate opinions that those species would not be injured by the plan.

Finally, on April 13, 1995, a permit for the building of the proposed landfill was given. Based on its view that the FWS (D) and the Corps (D) were incorrect in determining that the panther and the snake would not be adversely affected by the landfill, Fund For Animals, Inc. (P), an environmental group, filed suit in federal court against the Corps (D), the FWS (D), and the EPA (D), among others.

ISSUE:
Did the district court err in affirming the decisions of the Corps (D) and the FWS (D) with respect to the landfill and the endangered species?

DECISION AND RATIONALE:
(Dubina, J.) No. The judgment of the district court is affirmed.

ANALYSIS:
Fund for Animals is a good example of how our nation's administrative agency system works in a real-life situation.

Three separate administrative agencies play a role in the decision here. The first is the Army Corps of Engineers. As the opinion states, the Corps is charged with granting permits for the discharge of dredged or fill material into the "waters of the United States"—federal law prohibits any such discharge without permission from the Corps. Congress created the Corps, in part, to assist it and the executive branch in protecting our nation's waterways.

The second administrative agency involved in this case is the Environmental Protection Agency. The EPA is charged with, among other things, reviewing "proposed permit issuances for consistency with" certain environmental guidelines that it has promulgated. In this sense, the EPA acts for Congress, the executive branch, and the judiciary in a number of ways. First, it has created guidelines for the issuance of permits by the Corps. In that sense, it engaged in (and continues to engage in) legislative activity—it is making rules that all citizens must follow. In reviewing proposed permit issuances for consistency, the EPA is adjudicating. It is determining which permits will be allowed to stand and which will not, much like a criminal or civil court determines whether a person's activities are or have been in conformance with the law. And finally, in enforcing its promulgated regulations, the EPA is performing executive activities. Congress, the president and the judiciary do not have the time or expertise to create detailed rules for the discharge of materials into waterways and to then enforce those rules as necessary. To assist them in doing so, the EPA was created.

The third administrative agency involved in this case is the Fish and Wildlife Service. As the opinion demonstrates, the FWS is charged with administering the Endangered Species Act. In doing so it issues opinions regarding the way in which individual endangered species will be affected by certain proposed activities. In performing these duties, it is assisting all three branches of government in carrying out their activities.

Final regulations may also be challenged by court actions. These actions are brought by affected parties. A new rule will not be overturned by the court under the Administrative Procedure Act unless the court finds that it was "arbitrary and capricious, an abuse of discretion, or otherwise not in accordance with the law." Because it is difficult to prove that a regulation is "arbitrary and capricious," regulations typically remain in force when challenged in this way.

II. Advertising and Marketing

Advertising is an important part of American business. It is also closely regulated. One reason for this regulation is to protect consumers, but it also serves to protect the integrity of business dealings.

Any kind of government regulation of communication raises First Amendment concerns over free speech. For many years, the courts held that commercial or business advertising ("commercial speech") was not entitled to any protections under the First Amendment. The law now states that commercial speech is subject to protection from unwarranted governmental regulation.

Suppose an industry challenged a regulation limiting advertising. If the industry's advertising relates to lawful activity and is not misleading the courts would look at whether there was an undue constraint on commercial speech. To do so, the court would review the government's purpose in regulating the advertising. The governmental interest served by the regulation must be substantial. Even so, the regulation will be considered lawful only if it directly advances that governmental interest. It must also be no more extensive than necessary to serve that interest.

Using that test, courts have allowed many advertising regulations to remain in force. Some examples include bans on ads that are deceptive or fraudulent. Other examples of advertising prohibitions upheld by the courts include ads that:

- Further criminal schemes (for instance, ads promoting a **pyramid scheme**),

- Invade personal privacy (for example, ads that use someone's likeness without their permission),

- Infringe on the rights of others (such as ads that violate a trademark), and

- Publicize illegal goods or services.

There are two federal agencies that regulate advertising. The Food and Drug Administration (FDA), which is part of the Department of Health and Human Services, regulates certain aspects of the advertising for medications. The other agency, the Federal Trade Commission

> **PYRAMID SCHEME:**
> Business model based on making payments to members for enrolling new members, instead of providing a return on investment or products and services.

> *Example:* Lynn runs a travel company that specializes in trips to Las Vegas. She runs an ad for an "all-inclusive gambling junket" in a state that does not allow any type of gambling. The state may not restrict her advertisement. Lynn is advertising gambling that will take place in a state where it is legal. It is not illegal to travel to Las Vegas, so the ad does not advertise illegal goods or services, or further a criminal scheme.

FOOD MAKER CANNOT CLAIM SPECIFIC HEALTH BENEFITS WITHOUT ADEQUATE SCIENTIFIC STUDIES

POM Wonderful, LLC v. Federal Trade Commission
(Beverage Maker) v. (FTC)
777 F.3d 478 (D.C. Cir. 2015)

POM Wonderful, LLC produces, markets, and sells a number of pomegranate-based products. In a series of advertisements from 2003 to 2010, POM touted medical studies ostensibly showing that daily consumption of its products could treat, prevent, or reduce the risk of various ailments, including heart disease, prostate cancer, and erectile dysfunction. Many of those ads mischaracterized the scientific evidence concerning the health benefits of POM's products with regard to those diseases.

In 2010, the Federal Trade Commission filed an administrative complaint charging that POM and related parties had made false, misleading, and unsubstantiated representations in violation of the Federal Trade Commission Act. After extensive administrative proceedings, the full Commission voted to hold POM and the associated parties liable for violating the FTC Act and ordered them to cease and desist from making misleading and inadequately supported claims about the health benefits of POM products. The Commission's order also bars POM and the related parties from running future ads asserting that their products treat or prevent any disease unless armed with at least two randomized, controlled, human clinical trials demonstrating statistically significant results. [. . .] POM and the related parties argued that they should not have been held liable at all[.]

In determining whether an advertisement is deceptive in violation of section 5 of the FTC Act, the Commission engages in a three-step inquiry, considering: (i) what claims are conveyed in the ad, (ii) whether those claims are false, misleading, or unsubstantiated, and (iii) whether the claims are material to prospective consumers. At the first step, the Commission "will deem an advertisement to convey a claim if consumers acting reasonably under the circumstances would interpret the advertisement to contain that message." The Commission "examines the overall net impression" left by an ad, and considers whether "at least a significant minority of reasonable consumers" would "likely" interpret the ad to assert the claim[.]

In identifying the claims made by an ad, the Commission distinguishes between "efficacy claims" and "establishment claims." An efficacy claim suggests that a product successfully performs the advertised function or yields the advertised benefit, but includes no suggestion of scientific proof of the product's effectiveness. An establishment claim, by contrast, suggests that a product's effectiveness or superiority has been scientifically established.

The distinction between efficacy claims and establishment claims gains salience at the second step of the Commission's inquiry, which calls for determining whether the advertiser's claim is false, misleading, or unsubstantiated. If an ad conveys an efficacy claim, the advertiser must possess a "reasonable basis" for the claim.

For establishment claims [. . .] the amount of substantiation needed for an establishment claim depends on whether the claim is "specific" or "non-specific." If an establishment claim "states a specific type of substantiation," the "advertiser must possess the specific substantiation claimed." If an ad instead conveys a non-specific establishment claim—e.g., an ad stating that a product's efficacy is "medically proven" or making use of "visual aids" that "clearly suggest that the claim is based upon a foundation of scientific evidence"—the advertiser "must possess evidence sufficient to satisfy the relevant scientific community of the claim's truth." The Commission therefore "determines what evidence would in fact establish such a claim in the relevant scientific community" and "then compares the advertisers' substantiation evidence to that required by the scientific community."

[T]he Commission determined that thirty-six of petitioners' advertisements and promotional materials conveyed efficacy claims asserting that POM products treat, prevent, or reduce the risk of heart disease, prostate cancer, or erectile dysfunction. The Commission further concluded that thirty-four of those ads also conveyed establishment claims representing that clinical studies substantiate the efficacy of POM products in treating, preventing, or reducing the risk of the same ailments.

For both petitioners' efficacy claims and their non-specific establishment claims, the Commission found that "experts in the relevant fields" would require one or more "properly randomized and controlled human clinical trials"—"RCTs"—in order to "establish a causal relationship between a food and the treatment, prevention, or reduction of risk" of heart disease, prostate cancer, or erectile dysfunction. Without at least one such RCT, the Commission concluded, POM's efficacy claims and its non-specific establishment claims were inadequately substantiated.

The Commission examined each of the studies invoked by petitioners in their ads, concluding that the referenced studies fail to qualify as RCTs of the kind that could afford adequate substantiation. Petitioners' claims therefore were deceptive. Moreover, in light of petitioners' selective touting of ostensibly favorable study results and nondisclosure of contrary indications from the same or a later study, the Commission found that there were "many omissions of material facts in [the] ads that consumers cannot verify independently." Petitioners, the Commission observed, "made numerous deceptive representations and were aware that they were making such representations despite the inconsistency between the results of some of their later studies and the results of earlier studies to which [they] refer in their ads."

The Commission drew on expert testimony to explain why the attributes of well-designed RCTs are necessary to substantiate petitioners' claims. A control group, for example, " 'allows investigators to distinguish between real effects from the intervention, and other changes, including those due to the mere act of being treated ('placebo effect') [and] the passage of time.' " Random assignment of a study's subjects to treatment and control groups "increases the likelihood that the treatment and control groups are similar in relevant characteristics, so that any difference in the outcome between the two groups can be attributed to the treatment." And when a study is "double-blinded" (i.e., when neither the study participants nor the investigators know which patients are in the treatment group and which patients are in the control group), it is less likely that participants or investigators will consciously or unconsciously take actions potentially biasing the results.

We acknowledge that RCTs may be costly, although we note that the petitioners nonetheless have been able to sponsor dozens of studies, including several RCTs. Yet if the cost of an RCT proves prohibitive, petitioners can choose to specify a lower level of substantiation for their claims. As the Commission observed, "the need for RCTs is driven by the claims [petitioners] have chosen to make." An advertiser who makes "express representations about the level of support for a particular claim" must "possess the level of proof claimed in the ad" and must convey that information to consumers in a non-misleading way. An advertiser thus still may assert a health-related claim backed by medical evidence falling short of an RCT if it includes an effective disclaimer disclosing the limitations of the supporting research. Petitioners did not do so.

[T]he Commission's order will require petitioners to possess at least one RCT before making disease claims covered by that provision[.]

So ordered.

(FTC), is an independent agency that has been delegated the power to regulate most of the other types of advertising that we see.

> An "independent agency" is one that is not a part of a cabinet-level department.

Deceptive Trade Practices

The Federal Trade Commision has the power to enforce the federal laws against "unfair or deceptive acts in commerce." Because the FTC has nationwide jurisdiction, its rules are especially important.

The FTC issues general guidelines that define whether a practice will be deemed deceptive. A practice will be called deceptive if a party makes a material representation, omits important information, or otherwise acts in a way that is likely to mislead a consumer.

If there is express or intentional deception by the advertiser, the FTC will presume it was material. Implied claims about health, safety, durability, or performance are also presumed to be material.

> According to the FTC, a representation is "material" if it is likely to affect a consumer's conduct or decision with regard to a product or service.

An act may be deemed deceptive even if there is no proof of actual deception. The question is whether it is *likely* to mislead. Any factual claims in advertising must be supported by evidence. "Qualifying" (limiting) information that changes the meaning of the claims may not be omitted.

A demonstration or mock-up of how a product works is deceptive if the ad implies that it was actual proof of performance.

Endorsements of products or services are deceptive if they do not reflect the honest opinions or beliefs of the endorsing party. "Endorsements"

> Trident Gum used a claim that "Four out of five dentists surveyed recommended sugarless gum for their patients who chew gum." Rather than four out of five (80 percent) of *all* dentists, it covers those dentists who took a survey on the issue. Those dentist are not recommending gum in general, but sugarless gum, and only for those patients who choose to chew gum. The claim sounds impressive, but the qualifying information tones it down slightly.

Example: A company sold a set of 40 games. The company advertised that training on these games for 10 to 15 minutes three or four times a week could help users achieve their "full potential in every aspect of life." The games were advertised as improving performance on everyday tasks, delaying age-related cognitive decline, and reducing cognitive impairment associated with health conditions. The company also advertised that scientific studies proved these benefits. In fact, there was no reliable scientific evidence supporting these claims. The advertisement was deceptive. *In the Matter of Lumos Lab, Inc.*, F.T.C. File No. 132 3212 (2016).

are defined as a message that consumers are likely to believe comes from someone other than the advertiser.

Endorsements cannot make representations that would be deceptive if it was made directly by the sponsor. There must also be reason to believe that the endorser continues as an actual user of the product for as long as the advertisement is run.

> *Example:* A car company manufactures a hybrid gasoline/electric vehicle. The company claims in its ads that the car goes 150 miles on a single gallon of gasoline. The car did achieve that gas mileage on one occasion when driven by a professional driver on a closed track under ideal conditions. Actual mileage for the car is much lower, particularly when the temperature is below freezing. The advertising claim does not have a reasonable factual basis. It also omitted qualifying information, such as "your mileage may vary" depending on driving conditions and how the car is driven.

> *Example:* A bakery advertised its "Dieter's Friend" bread as having "33% fewer calories per slice than our regular bread." The advertisements omit the fact that Dieter's Friend bread is the same as the bakery's regular bread, sliced 33% thinner. The ad is deceptive.

> *Example:* A tire company runs an advertisement that shows a picture of a small child in a toy car with the caption "The Best Tires for Today's Cars." There is no endorsement, as a consumer is not likely to believe that the opinion comes from the child pictured. The same caption runs under a picture of a well-known racing driver. There is an endorsement, even if the caption is not labeled as a quotation from the driver.

> *Example:* An advertisement for Parolacxas Beer includes the line "The flavor, mmm! It's quite okay!" That is a statement of opinion, and not deceptive. Another ad for the same beer says "98% of all beer drinkers agree: Parolacxas Beer is quite okay!" If the 98% figure does not represent the results of a real survey, the ad is deceptive.

Note that the definitions and examples of deceptive practices all relate to factual claims, as distinct from opinions. Factual claims can be proven or disproven, and will require substantiation. On the other hand, there is no way an opinion can be proven or disproven. As long as the opinion statement does not represent a false endorsement, it will not be considered deceptive.

The FTC has issued guidance for advertisers in different industries, or for advertisers who want to make certain types of claims about their products. This guidance is not an official regulation, but is advice from the FTC on what it considers appropriate.

An example of advertiser guidance is the "Green Guide." The Green Guide was first issued in 1992, and has been supplemented and updated three times since. It is guidance for advertisers who wish to make environmental claims about their products or services. The Guide does not create any new rules. Instead, existing rules are placed in context. Advertisers who use terms such as "biodegradable," "recyclable," or "ozone safe" are told how the terms can and should be used in advertising. Advertisers are also cautioned not to use overly broad terms ("Environmentally friendly" or "eco-friendly") that cannot be substantiated.

State Deceptive Practices Law

Most states also have laws regarding deceptive practices. These laws usually have a list of specific practices that will be regarded as deceptive. Although the list of prohibited practices will vary from state-to-state, the prohibited practices typically fall into one of three general categories:

- Misrepresentations,
- False sponsorship, and
- Disparagement.

> Disparagement in this context means a false statement that the advertiser's product or service performs better than a competitor's product or service.

Common examples of deceptive trade practices prohibited by state regulations include:

- Falsely representing the source, sponsorship, approval, certification, accessories, characteristics, benefits, or quantities of a product or service,

- Representing goods as original or new when they are in fact reconditioned or used,

- Falsely stating that replacements or repairs are needed,

- Advertising goods or services not intending to sell them as advertised, or not having enough in stock to meet reasonably expected demand,

- Passing off goods or services as those of another (for example, mislabeling goods), or

- Representing goods or services as having a sponsorship, approval, or certification that they do not have.

> *Example:* Maggie designs and markets a new type of pillow. She is allowed to give a presentation about her pillow to the National Insomnia Institute, an organization of sleep researchers. Maggie's advertising claims that the pillow is the "Official Pillow of the National Insomnia Institute," but the Institute has done nothing beyond allowing her to promote her pillow at its meeting. Maggie has committed a deceptive trade practice.

State deceptive trade practices laws are usually enforced by the state attorney general, who brings an action on behalf of all consumers in that state. However, it is possible that private lawsuits by individuals harmed by such practices can also be brought against a company.

III. Labelling and Packaging

Product labels and packaging are an important factor in influencing consumer buying choices. The package that contains a product, or the label on that package, can be just as deceptive as a false advertisement. To ensure that consumer packaging does not deceive or mislead consumers, Congress enacted the Fair Packaging and Labeling Act (FPLA) in 1967.

The FPLA authorizes the FTC and the FDA to issue regulations for sellers and manufacturers to follow when putting **consumer products** on the market. These regulations must require all consumer commodities to be labeled to disclose:

- The net quantity of the contents of the package, in both metric and U.S. customary (inch/pound) units,
- The identity of the item or material inside the package, and
- The name and place of business of the product's manufacturer, packer, or distributor.

The agencies that administer the FPLA may also make additional regulations if necessary to prevent consumer deception (or to make it easier to compare value). These additional regulations may cover descriptions of ingredients, packaging requirements, or the characterization of package sizes (such as "economy size" or similar denominiations).

Some types of goods are exempt from the FPLA. The labelling and packaging of these products may be regulated by another federal law. For example, alcoholic beverages are not covered by the FPLA, but alcohol packaging is heavily regulated by other programs.

Manufacturers or sellers may request an FPLA exemption for a particular type of product. If granted, the exemption will often have different

> **CONSUMER PRODUCT:** For purposes of the Fair Packaging and Labeling Act, a product customarily produced or distributed for sale through retail sales for consumption by individuals, or use by individuals for personal care or household services.

requirements that still allow consumers to know how much of a product they are purchasing.

The FPLA is not the only federal law dealing with packaging and labelling. Other laws deal with packaging of specific commodities (for example, the Federal Meat Inspection Act). Packaging and labelling are also subject to the requirements that they not be deceptive or misleading.

Many states also have laws that regulate the packaging and labelling of consumer goods. If there is a conflict between the state laws and the FPLA or regulations that implement the FPLA, federal law will control if the state laws are less stringent or require information different from FPLA requirements.

> When the federal government regulates an area more stringently than state governments, the federal rules are said to **preempt** the state regulation. This is known as the **preemption** doctrine.

The packaging and labelling of a commodity that is exempt from the FPLA may still be regulated by a state's weights and measures law.

IV. Consumer Protection Laws

Consumer protection laws are an attempt to level the playing field in the marketplace. Although traditional free-market economics would make all business transactions matters freely negotiated between the parties, consumer protection laws recognize that there is a disparity between consumers and the companies that sell them products. The laws are an effort to equalize the bargaining power of consumers against the companies that sell goods and services to them.

PREEMPTION: The principle that federal law can supersede state law or regulation.

Example: An FTC regulation provides that Christmas tree ornaments are exempt from the net quantity labelling rules. The package containing the ornaments must express the quantity "in terms of numerical count of the ornaments." The ornaments must also be packaged so that the ornaments are clearly visible to the purchaser at the time of purchase. 16 C.F.R. § 501.2.

Example: The FPLA requires accurate labelling of the quantity of goods in a package. State law in California has a similar requirement. The regulations implementing the FPLA say that packages containing flour may lawfully vary from the weight on the label, to allow for variations in weight caused by loss of moisture. California law has no such allowance. Federal law supersedes the state law. *Jones v. Rath Packing Co.*, 430 U.S. 519 (1977).

A "consumer sale" is a sale of goods to a buyer who plans to use the goods for personal or household (non-business) purposes. The sale of the goods takes place in the normal course of the seller's business. A sale of business goods or a casual sale by a non-business seller are not consumer sales.

Most consumer protection laws regulate the way the sale is made. Companies must make specific disclosures to consumers about their products and services. Disclosure laws aim to give consumers enough information to make an informed decision about what they are buying.

The laws relating to advertising emphasize accuracy and truthfulness, packaging and labelling laws require accurate information for meaningful comparisons between different products. Although there probably can never be complete equality of bargaining power in a consumer transaction, consumer protection laws reduce the imbalance.

Consumer Sales

State and federal laws regarding deceptive or unfair trade practices provide consumers basic protection when they buy goods. Accuracy in labelling and honesty in product descriptions are the overall goals.

While the consumer protection laws discussed so far address factual claims and information about products, some state and federal laws regulate how a sales transaction is made. These laws usually apply to specific types of transactions or products. These laws focus on the potential for abuse that exists when selling to consumers.

Telemarketing: Telemarketing is an enduring topic of legislative concern. The federal Telephone Consumer Protection Act (TCPA) regulates telephone solicitations. The law authorizes the FTC and Federal Communications Commission (FCC) to make rules that require telemarketers to disclose that they are making a sales call. The rules say that telemarketers are also required to provide:

- The telemarketer's name,
- The name of the entity for whom the call is made, and
- A telephone number or address at which this entity can be contacted.

Intentional misrepresentations are prohibited. Telemarketers must give a clear statement of the total cost of any goods or services offered. They must also set out the terms of the sale. Financial services must be paid for only after they have been performed or delivered.

"Cooling Off" Periods: Buyers usually cannot cancel a contract. Once a buyer agrees to purchase a computer, a hair dryer, or a pair of jeans, the deal is final. In some cases, retailers may provide generous return policies that allow buyers to return goods. Such policies are purely voluntary. Retailers generally have no obligation to allow returns after the sale is complete.

But state and federal law make exceptions for cancellation of some types of sales, or for sales made under certain circumstances. Under FTC rules, a person who buys something worth $25 or more in a door-to-door consumer sales transaction has three business days to cancel the sale.

> **Example:** An appliance store rents space for three days at a home remodeling show. Any sales of appliances it makes at the sale are subject to the buyer's right to cancel. If a customer agrees to purchase an appliance, but completes the transaction at the seller's regular store, the right to cancel does not apply.

> Under FTC rules, a "business day" includes Saturday, but does not include Sunday or federal holidays.

> State cooling-off laws are similar, but apply only to specific goods or services, such as gym memberships, timeshares, or dating services.

Likewise, a person who purchases goods for $130 or more at a sale at a location away from the seller's usual place of business has three business days to cancel the transaction. The seller must tell the buyer about the right to cancel at the time of the sale, and give the buyer two copies of a cancellation form.

A buyer may generally cancel such a sale for any reason. To cancel such a sale, the buyer must mail a copy of the cancellation form to the seller. If the buyer does not have a cancellation form, the buyer can write a cancellation letter. The letter or form must be post-marked before midnight of the third business day after the date of the sales contract. The seller then has 10 days to refund the money paid by the buyer. If goods have already been delivered, the seller must either pick up the items within 20 days or reimburse the buyer for mailing expenses to send back the items. The buyer must make any goods received available to the seller in the same condition as when they were received.

The federal rule does not apply to sales made at art or craft fairs. It also does not apply to motor vehicle sales if the dealer has at least one permanent place of business.

Plain Language: A persistent complaint of many consumers is that they cannot understand what a contract says. The information that is in the contract might be accurate, but that doesn't help the consumer who is unable to understand it.

To address this problem, many states have enacted "plain English" or "readability" laws. These laws seek to make consumer contracts to understand. Although some states have general requirements that contracts be clearly written and use ordinary words, some states have a more detailed list of requirements. For example, the Pennsylvania statute lists nine "language guidelines" and three "visual guidelines" that are looked at when deciding if a document meets readability requirements.

Note that violating the readability statutes will not make a contract void or unenforceable in most states. Some state statutes do, however, provide for a consumer's right to sue for violations of the law.

Unconscionability: Consumer sales contracts are subject to the rules on unconscionability. In this case, an unconscionable contract is one that is markedly unfair or oppressive to the buyer. Such a contract typically suggests that the seller abused its position to take advantage of the buyer. An unconscionable contract or clause is not be enforceable.

Consumer Health and Safety

Dangerous products make it into the marketplace. The traditional remedy for a consumer who is injured by a dangerous product is to bring a products liability suit for damages. This approach is unsatisfactory for several reasons. First, it is inefficient. A lawsuit for a defective or dangerous product can take years to resolve. Second, it is expensive. Manufacturers and sellers may have to pay large verdicts and settlements, and the lawsuits themselves are expensive to bring and to defend. Third, and perhaps most important, the whole system depends on a person or people being injured or killed before improvements are made.

Although it is impossible to ensure that no one is ever injured by a product, federal law does attempt to minimize that possibility. The Consumer Product Safety Act created the Consumer Product Safety Commission (CPSC), an independent agency with the mission to promote consumer safety.

The CPSC has a broad grant of authority. It is authorized to ban or recall dangerous consumer products. It also has power to research and establish product safety requirements. These standards are often developed in cooperation with industry groups. The CPSC also regulates consumer products when it identifies a consumer product hazard that is not already addressed by a voluntary standard, or when Congress orders rulemaking. These rules may set manufacturing requirements or effectively ban certain products.

> The CPSC does not deal with safety issues for motor vehicles. Those are within the jurisdiction of the National Highway Traffic Safety Administration.

The CPSC can order product recalls. Manufacturers must notify the CPSC if it finds that a product:

- Fails to comply with an applicable consumer product safety rule or with a voluntary consumer product safety standard,

- Fails to comply with any other rule, regulation, standard, or ban under a law enforced by the CPSC,

- Contains a defect which could create a substantial product hazard, or

- Creates an unreasonable risk of serious injury or death.

The CPSC evaluates such reports to determine the hazard posed by the product. An immediate recall will be ordered when the risk of death or grievous injury or illness is likely or very likely, or serious injury or illness is very likely. Lesser hazards are evaluated to decide what corrective action would be warranted.

Warranties: A warranty is a promise that a product will perform in a certain manner.

> *Example:* In 2007, toys imported from China were found to contain lead-based paint. Lead in paint has been linked to serious health problems for children, including behavioral problems, learning disorders, and even death. U.S. manufacturers recalled over 10 million toys and other children's items, because of excessive amounts of lead.

Article 2 of the Uniform Commercial Code (UCC) relates to express and implied warranties for goods. Although Article 2 sets out general requirements for the creation and disclaimer of warranties, the requirements for informing buyers about warranty terms is unclear. Instead, the federal Magnuson-Moss Warranty Act, sets out detailed requirements for the terms of a warranty.

The Magnuson-Moss Warranty Act's purpose is to make consumer product warranties more understandable and enforceable. The Act applies to consumers and consumer products, and gives the FTC further consumer protection authority. There is no requirement in the law that a product come with a warranty. If a warranty is given, however, it must comply with the Act. Failure to comply is an unfair trade practice.

The Magnuson-Moss Warranty Act provides that a written warranty, if given, must disclose the terms and conditions of the warranty. The FTC sets the specific disclosure requirements. The disclosure must be complete and conspicuous. It must be written in simple, readily understood language. A warranty must also state whether it is a **full warranty** or a **limited warranty**.

V. Investor Protection

The U.S. economy depends on the integrity of financial markets. The federal government began regulating the markets for **securities** in the 1930s. The passage of the laws regulating securities trading was a reaction to predatory trading practices that contributed to the stock market crash of 1929 and the Great Depression that followed.

Federal securities laws created the Securities and Exchange Commission (SEC). The SEC's mission is to:

- Protect investors,
- Maintain fair, orderly, and efficient markets, and
- Make it possible for companies to raise capital from investors.

The SEC enforces the laws that require **publicly-traded companies** to prepare annual reports that describe the company's operations in the preceding year. These reports allow investors to make informed decisions when they buy and sell securities. The SEC also enforces laws against **insider trading** and other fraudulent practices.

The SEC does not give an opinion on the safety or profitability of any security. Investors make their own decisions, based on the information available to the public. The SEC also does not guarantee or insure against investors' losses.

> The SEC is governed by a board of five commissioners. No more than three commissioners may be of the same political party.

Federal Securities Regulation

Federal securities regulation is based on eight principal laws. Each law has different objectives.

Securities Act of 1933: Many people call this Act the "truth in securities" law. It has two main goals:

- Requiring that investors receive significant information about securities offered to the public, and

- Prohibiting deceit, misrepresentations, and other fraud in the sale of securities.

The 1933 Act requires the disclosure of important financial information when securities are offered for sale. These disclosures help investors make better judgments about a company's securities. The information must be accurate, but the SEC does not guarantee it.

In general, all securities sold in the U.S. must be registered with the SEC unless they are of an exempt type or part of an exempt transaction. All registration forms become public information after they are filed. The registration forms call for:

- A description of the company's business,

- A description of the security to be offered for sale,

- Information about the management of the company, and

- Certified financial statements prepared by independent accountants.

FULL WARRANTY:
Under the Magnuson-Moss Warranty Act, a warranty that obliges the seller of a product to remedy a defective product within a reasonable time. If the defect cannot be remedied after a reasonable number of attempts, the seller must replace it, or refund the price paid.

LIMITED WARRANTY:
Under the Magnuson-Moss Warranty Act, a warranty that does not meet the requirements of a full warranty. Limited warranties must be clearly labelled as "limited."

SECURITY:
An instrument that evidences an ownership right in a company, such as stock, or that is evidence of a debt or obligation (bonds, debentures, or notes).

PUBLICLY-TRADED COMPANIES:
A company whose stock is freely traded among members of the general public.

INSIDER TRADING:
A corporate insider's use of nonpublic information to trade the shares of a company.

Securities Exchange Act of 1934: This law established the Securities and Exchange Commission. The Act gives the SEC broad authority over virtually every aspect of the securities industry, and prohibits fraudulent activity. The 1934 Act covers not only initial sale of securities, but also subsequent sales. The Act empowers the SEC to require periodic reporting of information by companies with publicly traded securities. Companies with more than $10 million in assets and whose securities are held by more than 500 owners must make these reports to the SEC. The SEC then makes the reports available to the public.

The 1934 Act authorized the SEC to create rules to regulate the markets. One of the SEC's resulting regulations is Rule 10b–5. The broad rule bars fraud or deceit when buying or selling securities.

Trust Indenture Act: This Act applies to debt securities such as bonds, debentures, and notes offered for public sale.

CAREERS IN THE LAW

Regulatory programs provide a range of legal career options for non-lawyers. On the regulatory side, state and federal agencies require staff to develop, implement, enforce, and adjudicate legally binding regulations. If you have a strong interest in environmental issues, you might look at working with the state environmental agency or the federal Environmental Protection Agency. People who work for regulators typically enjoy great advancement potential, superior benefits, and interesting assignments.

On the other side, organizations employ compliance professionals to improve their ethical and regulatory profiles. Many former regulators later work in the private sector, bringing their strategic knowledge and skills to corporations. Others start and remain on the organizational side. Corporate compliance is a growing field with strong opportunities for advancement. While compliance work is based in the law, most compliance roles (even at the top level) do not require a law degree.

AFFIRMATIVE FRAUD IS NOT REQUIRED TO ESTABLISH A RULE 10b–5 VIOLATION

Affiliated Ute Citizens v. United States
(Citizens' Group) v. (Federal Government)
406 U.S. 128, 92 S. Ct. 1456, 31 L. Ed. 741 (1972)

INSTANT FACTS:
The defendants withheld material facts reasonably likely to influence stockholders' financial decisions.

BLACK LETTER RULE:
Facts are considered material if a reasonable investor might have considered them important in the making of an investment decision.

PROCEDURAL BASIS:
Certiorari to review an undisclosed appellate decision.

FACTS:
Gale and Haslem worked for a bank representing members of a Native American tribe to assist with the sale of shares in a corporation (UDC) that had been formed to hold tribal assets. While representing their interests, Gale and Haslem induced mixed-blood stockholders to sell their shares, without informing them that their stock could sell at a higher price on the real estate market. By so doing, Gale and Haslem reaped financial benefits. The federal court of appeals held that no 10b–5 violation occurred, because there was no evidence of reliance on a material factual misrepresentation made by Gale and Haslem.

ISSUE:
Can the causation requirement under Rule 10b–5 be established by a failure to disclose a material fact?

DECISION AND RATIONALE:
(Blackmun, J.) Yes. The second subparagraph of Rule 10b–5 plainly specifies as securities violations the making of an untrue statement of material fact and the failure to state material facts. The defendants cannot withhold material facts from the stockholders and thereafter claim the stockholders did not rely upon their statements. "Under the circumstances of this case, involving primarily a failure to disclose, positive proof of reliance is not a prerequisite of recovery. All that is necessary is that the facts withheld be material in the sense that a reasonable investor might have considered them important in the making of this decision."

ANALYSIS:
In American Ute Citizens, Justice Blackmun indicated that facts are material if a reasonable investor "might" rely upon them. Whether semantic or not, the Supreme Court clarified this position in TSC Industries, Inc. v. Northway, Inc., 426 U.S. 438 (1976), where it stated that American Ute Citizens did not "articulate a precise definition of materiality, but only [gave] a 'sense' of the notion." The Court thereafter established that "[a]n omitted fact is material if there is a substantial likelihood that a reasonable shareholder would consider it important in deciding how to vote," explaining that if a reasonable investor would consider an omitted fact to alter the information available, the omitted fact is material.

CASE VOCABULARY:

CAUSATION:
The causing or producing of an effect.

CONCEALMENT:
The act of refraining from disclosure, especially an act by which one prevents or hinders the discovery of something.

MISREPRESENTATION:
The act of making a false or misleading statement about something, usually with the intent to deceive.

RELIANCE:
Dependence or trust by a person, especially when combined with action based on that dependence or trust.

Investment Company Act: The Investment Company Act regulates companies, such as mutual funds, that engage primarily in investing and trading in securities, if their own securities are offered for sale to the public. The goal of this Act is to minimize the conflicts of interest that may arise in this type of operation.

Investment Advisers Act: This law requires some individuals or entities who advise others about securities investments to register with the SEC.

Sarbanes-Oxley Act: The Sarbanes-Oxley Act of 2002 (often referred to as "SOX") put in place a number of reforms. SOX followed quickly after the collapse of Enron, an energy company that defrauded its investors. The Act's reforms are designed to enhance corporate responsibility, improve financial disclosures, and fight corporate and accounting fraud.

Under the law, principal financial and executive officers of publicly-traded companies are required to personally certify the accuracy of financial reporting. This change improved the accountability of executives for financial disclosures. The Act also created the "Public Company Accounting Oversight Board" to oversee corporate auditing.

Sarbanes-Oxley placed new emphasis on corporate ethics. Publicly-traded companies are required to disclose to the public whether they have a code of ethics. SOX illustrates a trend in corporate regulation toward encouraging ideal behavior instead of only punishing poor behavior.

Dodd-Frank Wall Street Reform and Consumer Protection Act:

The Dodd-Frank Act attempts to reshape the U.S. financial regulatory system. Enacted in the wake of the 2007–08 global financial crisis, Dodd-Frank addresses consumer protection, trading restrictions, credit ratings, financial products, corporate governance, and transparency.

Commentators called Dodd-Frank the most comprehensive financial regulatory reform since the Great Depression. But not everyone approves of the law. Under President Trump, several provisions were adjusted, reducing the regulatory burden on banks. The main thrust of Dodd-Frank remains intact, despite these changes.

Jumpstart Our Business Startups Act (the "JOBS Act"):

The JOBS Act minimizes SEC regulatory requirements for many companies. The goal is to make it easier for businesses to raise funds in public capital markets. The JOBS Act calls on the SEC to make rules to address **crowdfunding** investment solicitations, and to make them exempt from many of the more burdensome requirements of securities registration.

Consumer Financial Protection Bureau

The global financial crisis shook the banking and finance industry. The crisis revealed some of the fundamental weaknesses of the consumer finance industry, and highlighted the failings of the existing regulatory system. There was

---

BOND: A written promise to pay money. In securities law, long-term, interest bearing debt instruments, backed by the assets of the issuer.

DEBENTURE: A bond backed only by the general credit and financial reputation of the company issuing the bond.

NOTE: An unconditional written promise to pay money.

CROWDFUNDING: Funding a project or venture by soliciting money from a large number of people, usually via internet solicitation.

CHAPTER 13: *Regulatory Programs*

> Political disputes about the structure of the Board meant that the first Director of the Board was not confirmed by the Senate until July 2013.

no single agency responsible or accountable for the protection of consumers in the financial industry.

The Dodd-Frank Act established the Consumer Financial Protection Bureau (CFPB), to oversee consumer finance.

The CFPB regulates:

- traditional financial institutions, such as banks and credit unions, and
- payday lenders, foreclosure relief services, debt collectors, and mortgage servicers.

The CFPB prioritizes oversight of credit cards, mortgages, and student loans.

The CFPB enforces its rules through administrative proceedings and court actions. Enforcement actions are brought against companies that violate rules or defraud or discriminate against consumers. The CFPB pursues companies that take action against companies who take action against **whistleblowers** who report a company's violations. Successful enforcement actions usually result in some combination of a **civil penalty**, **restitution** for affected consumers, and an agreement to comply with CFPB regulations.

In addition to its enforcement activities, the CFPB conducts research about consumer financial markets and consumer behavior. This research helps identify potential problems and possible responses to those problems. The Bureau also has an extensive program of

WHISTLEBLOWER:
An employee who reports her employer's wrongdoing to the government or to law enforcement.

CIVIL PENALTY:
A fine assessed for a violation of a statute or regulation. A civil penalty is not considered to be punishment for a crime.

RESTITUTION:
Payment to a victim in compensation for a loss. Restitution is usually ordered as a part of a civil or criminal penalty.

Example: A financial company that operated as an indirect auto lender allowed dealers who arranged financing through the company for car sales to charge a higher interest rate to African American, Hispanic, and Asian consumers. The CFPB ordered the company to pay $80 million in restitution to affected consumers. The company was also ordered to pay a civil penalty to the CFPB of $18 million, and to monitor the interest rates charged by dealers, to prevent discrimination. *In the Matter of Ally Financial Inc.*, 2013-CFPB-0010 (Dec. 20, 2013).

public outreach, including to students, service members, and older Americans.

State Securities Law

Securities are regulated at the state level, as well as at the federal level. State securities laws are referred to as "Blue Sky Laws." The origin of the term is uncertain, but it may come from the first such law, passed in Kansas in 1911. The state's Banking Commissioner, arguing for passage of the law, argued against "blue sky merchants," who sold fraudulent investments backed by nothing but "the blue sky of Kansas."

Every state has a Blue Sky Law. These state laws vary, but do have several features in common:

- Registration of securities offered for sale in the state,
- Registration of broker-dealers, and
- Registration of securities firms.

Unless exempt, securities must be registered in every state in which they will be sold. The registration must be completed before offering securities for sale.

> Securities sold on national exchanges, such as NYSE or the NASDAQ/National Market, are exempt.

States have limited authority to regulate the sale of securities. Most regulation is done by the Securities and Exchange Commission. States do have the authority to conduct investigations and bring lawsuits for securities fraud.

Each state's authority to enforce its Blue Sky Laws is limited to securities sold within its borders. Before federal securities laws were passed, many traders openly advocated getting around Blue Sky Laws by selling securities through the mail. The gaps in the ability to enforce securities laws were a strong motive for the passage of the federal legislation.

VI. Environmental Protection

Until the 1960s, environmental regulation in the United States was largely a matter for private lawsuits. There were very few environmental laws, so most complaints about air or water pollution were dealt with by tort litigation against an alleged polluter. Actions for torts such as **nuisance** or **trespass** were brought to seek either damages or injunctive relief against polluters.

Relying on tort litigation for clean air and water has its limitations. By nature, litigation is a piecemeal way to proceed, addressing problems only when and where a lawsuit is brought. In addition, litigation is remedial, not preventative. It does nothing to prevent new problems from arising in the future with different parties.

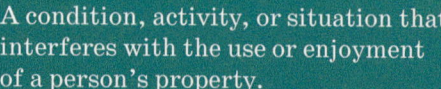

NUISANCE:
A condition, activity, or situation that interferes with the use or enjoyment of a person's property.

TRESPASS:
An unlawful act against the person or property of another. The term is usually used to mean entry onto another person's property without the permission of the owner.

> **Example:** Bacon is affordable in the United States because of large-scale domestic hog farms. The problem is that an adult hog produces over 10 pounds of solid waste a day. To deal with that level of production, the waste may be kept in open "lagoons" that produce ammonia and methane gases. In recent years, dozens of federal lawsuits have been brought against hog farms in North Carolina, Missouri, and other states by people living and working near these operations. These lawsuits allege that the smell was a legal nuisance. The plaintiffs claim the smell and gases make their homes unlivable, and cause health problems. Several claims have already been successful, leading to efforts to limit damages in similar nuisance actions.

Comprehensive environmental laws and regulations limit hazards before they become a problem. No harm must be shown before an environmental violation can be stopped. A system of statutes and regulations also provides certainty. Litigation is often unpredictable. The parties concerned can better predict outcomes if a rule is in place.

COOPERATIVE FEDERALISM: The collective cooperative interaction of state, local, and federal governments to solve common problems.

Federal and State Environmental Laws

State and federal legislatures both enact environmental laws. Many cities and counties also have environmental ordinances. The laws are usually justified as protecting the health and safety of the people. The power to regulate nuisances is another justification. Sometimes, environmental laws are justified under a theory of public trust: natural resources are regarded as being held in trust for the benefit of all people, and protecting that trust is a legitimate exercise of governmental authority. In some states, a clean environment is regarded as a human rights issue.

> **Example:** All persons are born free and have certain inalienable rights. They include the right to a clean and healthful environment and the rights of pursuing life's basic necessities, enjoying and defending their lives and liberties, acquiring, possessing and protecting property, and seeking their safety, health and happiness in all lawful ways. In enjoying these rights, all persons recognize corresponding responsibilities. *Mont. Const. Art. 2, § 3.*

State and federal environmental laws are often similar, or even identical. Unlike other areas in which federal and state laws overlap, there is little tension between the different layers of regulation. Enforcement of environmental laws is often done jointly, with federal and state regulators working together. This **cooperative federalism** is regarded by those who enforce environmental laws as "fundamental to the structure and effectiveness of environmental laws."

Air Quality Rules

The Clean Air Act requires the Environmental Protection Agency (EPA) to set rules for air pollutants. EPA rules relate to two major types of air pollution representing air quality concerns.

First, the EPA sets National Ambient Air Quality Standards (NAAQS). These standards set the amount of known pollutants that may be in the air. There are two types of ambient air quality standards, labeled primary and secondary. Primary standards are for the protection of public health. This includes the protection of the health of sensitive populations, such as people with asthma, children, and the elderly. Secondary standards are limits that are set to protect the public welfare. The "public welfare" includes protection against decreased visibility, and damage to animals, crops, vegetation, and buildings.

The second type of air pollution regulated by the EPA is hazardous air pollutants, also known as "air toxics." Hazardous air pollutants are pollutants that are known or suspected to cause serious health effects or adverse environmental effects. The EPA has identified nearly 200 toxic air pollutants. Hazardous pollutant regulations are intended to reduce the air emissions of these pollutants to the environment.

EPA regulations address hazardous air pollutants from major sources, area sources, and mobile sources. "Major sources" are large industrial facilities. The Clean Air Act requires the EPA to regulate hazardous air pollutants from major sources in two phases. The first phase is "technology-based," with standards based on emissions levels that are already being achieved in an industry. In the second phase, the EPA assesses the remaining health risks from each source category to determine whether the

> Individual area sources, such as gas stations and dry cleaners, usually have much lower emissions than major sources. These sources can, however, be numerous and widespread. They may also be located in heavily populated urban areas. The area source program includes a community support component. This recognizes that communities with disproportionate risks from hazardous air pollutants may be able to reduce some toxic sources more quickly and effectively through local initiatives. Mobile source regulations involve setting emissions standards for engines used for transportation.

COOPERATIVE FEDERALISM: The collective cooperative interaction of state, local, and federal governments to solve common problems.

CHAPTER 13: *Regulatory Programs* 439

> **NAVIGABLE WATERS:**
> A body of water used, or capable of being used, for commerce. The term includes the tributaries of such bodies of water.

Water Quality Rules

The EPA's water quality regulation is based on the Clean Water Act. The purpose of the Clean Water Act is to restore and maintain the quality of the country's **navigable waters**. The Act is designed to achieve acceptable water quality standards. The Act also places restrictions on the discharge of pollutants.

standards protect public health with an ample margin of safety, and also protect against adverse environmental effects.

"Area sources" are smaller sources. "Mobile sources" are motor vehicles, locomotives, and commercial marine vessels.

> The first federal environmental law was the Rivers and Harbors Act of 1899, which prohibited discharging refuse into navigable waters without a permit.

"WETLANDS" ARE NOT "NAVIGABLE WATERS"
Rapanos v. United States
(Shopping Mall Developer/Wetlands Owner) v. (Prosecuting Government)
547 U.S. 715, 126 S. Ct. 2208, 165 L. Ed. 2d 159 (2006)

INSTANT FACTS: The plaintiffs discharged fill material into wetlands properties they owned in order to build a shopping mall and condominiums, and the government brought legal action against them because they did not obtain a permit before beginning development.

BLACK LETTER RULE: The phrase "the waters of the United States," as used in the Clean Water Act, includes only those relatively permanent or continuously flowing bodies of water forming geographic features such as streams, oceans, rivers, and lakes, and does not include channels through which water intermittently flows or channels that provide periodic drainage for rainfall.

PROCEDURAL BASIS: Supreme Court review of a federal circuit court decision affirming the district court's judgment in favor of the defendant.

FACTS: The Clean Water Act makes it unlawful to discharge fill material into "navigable waters" without a permit, and it defines "navigable waters" to include "the waters of the United States." The Army Corps of Engineers, which issues permits for the discharge of fill material into navigable waters, interpreted "the waters of the United States" expansively to include not only traditional navigable waters, but also tributaries of such waters and wetlands "adjacent" to such waters and tributaries. The cases before the Court involved four Michigan wetlands lying near ditches or man-made drains that eventually emptied into traditional navigable waters. The United States brought civil enforcement proceedings against the petitioners, who had backfilled certain of these areas without a permit. The district court found federal jurisdiction over the wetlands because they were adjacent to "waters of the United States" or adjacent to "navigable waters." The Sixth Circuit affirmed.

ISSUE:
Did the courts below err in concluding that the wetlands in these cases constitute "navigable waters," such that the petitioners were required to obtain a permit under the Clean Water Act before discharging fill material into them?

DECISION AND RATIONALE:
(Scalia, J.) Yes. The phrase "the waters of the United States," as used in the Clean Water Act, includes only those relatively permanent or continuously flowing bodies of water forming geographic features such as streams, oceans, rivers, and lakes, and does not include channels through which water intermittently flows or channels that provide periodic drainage for rainfall.

We first addressed the meaning of "the waters of the United States," as used in the Clean Water Act, in U.S. v. Riverside Bayview Homes, Inc., 474 U.S. 121 (1985), in which we upheld the Corps' interpretation of this statutory phrase to include wetlands that abut traditional navigable waters. The petitioners contend here, however, that the waters must actually be navigable, or capable of navigation, to fall into the statutory category. Although the meaning of "navigable waters" as used in the Act is broader than the traditional dictionary definition, the Clean Water Act authorizes federal jurisdiction only over "waters," which connotes relatively permanent bodies of water, as opposed to ordinarily dry channels through which water occasionally flows. The Act's use of the phrase "navigable waters" also suggests that it confers jurisdiction only over relatively permanent bodies of water. Moreover, the Clean Water Act itself categorizes the channels that carry intermittent flows of water separately from "navigable waters."

Riverside Bayview rested on an ambiguity in defining where "water" ends and its abutting ("adjacent") wetlands begin, which allowed the Corps to rely in that case on ecological considerations to resolve the ambiguity in favor of treating all abutting wetlands as waters. But isolated ponds are not "waters of the United States" and present no boundary-drawing problem justifying reliance on ecological factors. Thus, we conclude that only those wetlands with a continuous surface connection to bodies that are "waters of the United States" in their own right, such that there is no clear demarcation between the two, are "adjacent" to such waters and covered by the Act. Because the Sixth Circuit applied an incorrect standard to determine whether the wetlands at issue are covered "waters," and because of the paucity of the record, the cases are remanded for further proceedings.

ANALYSIS:
In one of the cases before the Court here, Rapanos had filled 54 acres of wetlands with sand in preparation for the construction of a shopping mall, without filing for a permit. In another case, Carabell had actually proactively sought a permit to build condominiums on 19 acres of wetlands, but the request was denied. Neither of these parties prevailed in the lower courts.

The Act leaves much of the responsibility for clean water with the states. A state or local government may adopt or enforce its own standards or limitations regarding water pollution, except that these standards may not be less stringent than the federal regulations.

The Clean Water Act requires the EPA to develop or revise criteria for water quality. These criteria are developed after consultation with state and other federal agencies, and with input from other interested persons. They must reflect the latest scientific knowledge on the effects of pollutants on health and welfare, the concentration and dispersal of pollutants and their byproducts, and the effects of pollutants on biological community diversity, productivity, and stability.

States must adopt and review standards for water quality every three years. These standards are subject to EPA approval. Whenever a state revises or adopts a water quality standard, the standard must be submitted to the EPA for approval. Any new or revised state standard must be accompanied by a supporting analysis.

> **Example:** In September 2016, the Washington State developed a rule that updates the state's water quality standards for certain toxic chemicals. The state rule sets standards for 97 chemicals, as opposed to 85 covered by federal rules. The Washington rule also sets standards for pollutants that were not regulated before.

Waste Management

Governmental efforts to combat air and water pollution do not address solid waste disposal on land. State and local governments have long regulated waste disposal by restricting landfills or junkyards, prohibiting households from burning trash, or making littering an offense. Federal regulators tended to regard solid waste as a local matter.

The federal government took on solid waste in 1976 with the passage of the Resource Conservation and Recovery Act (RCRA). RCRA governs the treatment, storage, and disposal of solid and hazardous waste. RCRA puts in place a national framework for solid waste control.

> In conversation, "RCRA" is pronounced "wreck-rah."

RCRA explicitly recognizes that the collection and disposal of solid waste is primarily a matter of state, local, or regional control. In this way, the law gives states the principal role in managing nonhazardous solid waste disposal programs. The EPA regulations set out the general criteria for these programs. Solid waste must be used for resource recovery, or it must be disposed of in a sanitary manner.

> "Resource recovery" is extracting materials from solid waste for a specific next use. It can include recycling, energy generation, or composting.

Open dumping of waste is not allowed. Municipal and industrial waste disposal facilities must meet the EPA criteria for design, location restrictions, and assurances of financial viability. Facilities must also have a plan for corrective action or cleanup of improperly handled waste, and there must be a plan for the eventual closure of the facility. A state may impose requirements that are more stringent than the federal requirements, but if a state does not develop a plan, the EPA rules will apply.

RCRA also authorizes the EPA to make regulations regarding hazardous waste. EPA regulations are intended to ensure the safe management of solid waste from the time it is generated until its final disposal ("cradle-to-grave" management). "Hazardous waste" is defined as solid waste which may:

- Cause, or significantly contribute to an increase in mortality or an increase in serious irreversible, or incapacitating reversible illness; or

- Pose a substantial present or potential hazard to human health or the environment when improperly treated, stored, transported, or disposed of, or otherwise managed.

Hazardous waste regulation is also left primarily to the states. If a state does not have a hazardous waste program, the EPA will implement a program. EPA regulations set the criteria for hazardous waste generators, transporters, and for treatment, storage and disposal facilities. The EPA criteria include permitting requirements, enforcement, and corrective action or cleanup.

The cleanup of hazardous waste sites is regulated by the Comprehensive Environmental Response, Compensation, and Liability Act (CERCLA). CERCLA, also known as the "Superfund" law, provides for the prompt cleanup of hazardous waste site. The costs of that cleanup are imposed on anyone who is determined to be potentially responsible for the contamination. This determination can include past owners of the property who are no longer involved, as well as the current owners who may have damaged the property. These costs are imposed even if the activity that generated the waste took place before CERCLA was enacted in 1980.

> In conversation, the acronym "CERCLA" is pronounced "sir-klah."

CERCLA authorizes the EPA to respond to threatened or actual releases of hazardous substances.

Toxic Substances

Not all hazardous substances are "waste." Industry often uses hazardous or toxic substances as a regular part of business. The Toxic Substances Control Act (TSCA) puts these substances under EPA regulation. EPA regulations mandate reporting, record-keeping and testing requirements, and restrictions on chemical substances or mixtures.

The list of toxic substances includes more than 83,000 chemicals. Manufacturers, processors, and distributors of chemical substances must inform the EPA if the substance presents a substantial risk of injury to health or the envi-

> The TSCA does not cover food, drugs, cosmetics, or pesticides.

Example: From 1965 to 1974, a metal plating business disposed of some chemicals used in its business by dumping them in an unpaved lot behind the business's building. Only small amounts were disposed of at any given time, and no one responsible thought this posed any danger. The metal plating business moved to a new location in 1974, and other owners occupied the property. In 2010, a developer bought the property to develop it for housing. Tests showed that the soil was contaminated by hazardous waste. The metal plating business is responsible for some of the costs of cleanup.

ronment. If a new chemical will be manufactured, the maker must inform the EPA.

EPA rules on toxic substances preempt state or local rules, unless the state or local rule bans the use of the toxic substance, or if the rule was adopted under the authority of a federal law (such as the Clean Air Act). State and local authorities may apply for permission to adopt more stringent requirements.

Pesticides: The EPA regulates pesticides through the Federal Insecticide, Fungicide, and Rodenticide Act (FIFRA). FIFRA defines pesticides as any substance or mixture of substances intended for preventing, destroying, repelling, or mitigating any pest. That law prohibits the sale of unregistered pesticides. An application for registration must include a statement as to whether the pesticide is intended for general use, for use by anyone, or restricted use, meaning use only by certified applicators.

CHAPTER SUMMARY

Not all law is made by the legislative branch and signed by the executive. A significant body of law is made by governmental agencies. This law consists of administrative regulations that are usually related to specialized areas. These regulations are meant to implement or interpret laws passed by the legislative branch. Regulations can only be created if the administrative agency has authority delegated to it by the legislature through enabling laws.

Examples of these regulations include rules on advertising, consumer protection, and unfair or deceptive trade practices. An extensive set of regulations deal with environmental subjects. Investor relations and publicly traded securities are also regulated by administrative law. Administrative regulations cover the fine details of complex topics, and compliance with these rules is critical to a successful business.

Review Questions

Review question 1.
What is administrative law? What bodies create it? What is it called?

Review question 2.
What authority does an administrative agency need to create a regulation or rule? Does this process happen only at the federal level or also at the state level?

Review question 3.
What is the name of the federal law that sets out how administrative regulations are made? Describe the process for rule-making set out under that law. How does legislation interact with administrative regulations?

Review question 4.
What are "Blue Sky" laws? How do they interact with other types of securities laws? Where are these laws enacted?

Review question 5.
If a state and the federal government both regulate an issue, how does a business know which regulation applies? How can businesses and the public become involved in state and federal rule-making?

Review question 6.
What federal agencies regulate advertising? Does it matter what product is advertised? How do standards differ for various products?

Review question 7.
According to the FTC, when is a representation "material?"

Review question 8.
What crisis prompted the passage of the Sarbanes Oxley Act? The Dodd Frank Act? What do those laws authorize agencies to do? Which agencies?

Review question 9.
How are agencies created? What law created the Securities and Exchange Commission? What is the difference between a cabinet agency and an independent agency?

Review question 10.
Describe SEC 10b–5 and its importance. How does Sarbanes-Oxley differ from rules like 10b–5? That is, how does legislation differ from regulation? Why entrust a government agency with these decisions?

Review question 11.
How is advertising regulated? Product packaging? Which federal agency enforces rules in these areas? Are there also state regulations or laws?

Review question 12.
How do regulations protect consumers against predatory sales? What is a cooling off period and when does it apply? What rules cover telemarketing?

Review question 13.
What does the Magnuson-Moss Warranty Act address? What agency enforces rules under that statute?

Review question 14.
What is the difference between the Securities Acts of 1933 and 1934? What are the goals of securities regulations? What federal agency oversees this area?

Review question 15.
What is a "Superfund" site? Which federal law deals with these sites? Which agency regulates how they are treated?

Discussion Questions

Question 1:
Bill opens a business selling bicycles. His inventory consists of bicycles he builds from parts of other bicycles. He advertises these as "New Handmade Bikes by Bill."

Is Bill committing a deceptive trade practice? Why or why not?

Is Bill's advertisement deceptive under FTC rules? Why or why not?

A customer calls Bill on the phone and asks if Bill will fix a bike he sells if something goes wrong with it. Bill says, "Sure, I guess so." Under Magnuson-Moss, has Bill given a warranty? Why or why not?

Question 2:

Acrylic acid is on the official list of toxic substances. Clarinda has obtained a quantity of acrylic acid. She operates a business that makes industrial adhesives, and she intends to use the acrylic acid to manufacture a specialty glue. Clarinda is concerned that the chemical is illegal for her to use. She lobbies the city council for help, and the city council passes an ordinance that allows the use of acrylic acid if the user obtains a city permit. The only criterion for a permit is paying a small fee.

> Is the city ordinance the only rule Clarinda needs to follow to use acrylic acid? Why or why not?

> Does the fact that acrylic acid is on the list of toxic substances mean Clarinda may not use it? Why or why not?

> If the acrylic acid is found to have leaked into the ground, is Clarinda liable for the cleanup costs? Why or why not?

Question 3:

Shadi has come up with a recipe for a new beverage made from fruit and vegetable extracts. He starts to sell the beverage, advertising it as "Delicately Delicious." Unfortunately, the usual reaction of anyone who tries the drink is to spit it out because of its acrid taste. Shadi then decides to repurpose the drink. He starts to sell the drink as a nutritious weight loss supplement. Shadi has no reason to believe the drink helps lose weight, beyond his reasoning that dieters are advised to eat lots of fruit and vegetables. Shadi gives a supply of his drink to ten university professors with Ph.Ds in fields such as sociology and economics. Seven of them report losing weight after drinking the drink for several weeks, so Shadi notes in an advertisement that "a majority of the doctors surveyed report that their tests show" that the drink is effective for weight loss.

> Is calling the drink "Delicately Delicious" deceptive advertising? Why or why not?

> Is advertising the drink as a weight loss supplement deceptive advertising? Why or why not?

> Is the claim about the survey of doctors deceptive advertising? Why or why not?

Question 4:

Sunrise Dawn Farms is a small organic farm operation. The CEO does not use any mass-produced pesticides, but developed his own completely organic solution by soaking fresh garlic and coffee grounds in diluted orange juice. It does not eliminate all the insects that attack crops, but it does kill some and discourages others. The CEO starts the making the recipe on a larger scale and selling it in spray bottles as "Sunset for Bugs."

> Does Sunrise Dawn Farms need to comply with any regulations when producing and selling Sunset for Bugs?
>
> Is there a difference if Sunrise Dawn does not sell the product, but just requires employees to apply it?
>
> Does it matter that the product is completely organic? That it does not kill all the insects it is applied to?

Question 5:

In which of the following cases would the consumer be granted a cooling off period? Are there situations where a cooling off period would make sense, even though the law does not allow for one?

> Purchasing groceries at the local store.
>
> Ordering a custom tailored suit.
>
> Buying a vacation package on the phone.
>
> Purchasing a vacuum cleaner from a door-to-door salesperson.
>
> Buying kitchen gadgets at a home presentation hosted by a friend.
>
> Buying furniture on a rent-to-own basis that results in paying more than the furniture is worth over time.

Question 6:

Congress creates a new agency through legislation. The agency has the power to regulate private trips to Earth orbit. The agency creates a licensing program for near-Earth trips. A billionaire applies for a license for such a trip, but the agency turns him down. When asked why, the agency head will not respond, but does mention in an interview that the billionaire "is not friendly to the licensing model" and "doesn't show the agency enough respect."

>Are these valid grounds? Why or why not?

>How could the billionaire challenge the agency decision? What authority could he use? What standard would he need to meet?

Question 7:

Jeananne seeks investors for her business. She claims that she is building affordable housing in the areas of most need using easily replicated building plans, meaning that the time from building permission to profitability is shortened. She promises quick returns. To satisfy her initial investors, Jeananne pays distributions using investment funds from later investors. All of the investors are making money so far, and there have been no complaints.

>What type of investment model is this? Why does it have that name?

>Is this model allowed under federal regulations? Why or why not?

>What agency would be involved if there were a problem with this model?

Question 8:

Acme manufactures consumer beauty products in Canada for import to the U.S. The packaging shows what is in the package and the quantity of each product in metric. The packaging also includes the name of the importer and the import's address.

>What other information should be on the packaging?

>What law is relevant to this scenario?

Question 9:

Zed starts a new company. To get off the ground, Zed seeks investment through a crowdfunding site. He raises all the money he needs in one month.

>Is this type of fundraising allowed?

>What federal law covers this type of fundraising? What is the goal of that law?

Question 10:

Both federal and state regulations cover a scenic waterway in State A.

> Which level of regulation will prevail in a dispute, if either?
>
> How do state and federal rules correspond to each other in the environmental area?

14 CRIMINAL LAW

KEY OBJECTIVES:
- Understand the basic principles of criminal law.
- List the elements of business-related crimes.
- Explain when a business may be held criminally liable.

CHAPTER OVERVIEW

This chapter covers criminal law, and particularly business-related crimes. Criminal law deals with wrongs done to the general public, or against the public order. While the primary victim of a given crime is typically an individual or a small group, the community as a whole is also a victim in a larger sense. For this reason, criminal cases are brought by the government (usually, the government of the state where the crime took place) against the accused person or organization. Government prosecutors represent the people against the criminal defendant.

In this chapter, we will explore the aspects of criminal law that occur in the business world. We will explain the basic principles of criminal law in general. We will look at specific crimes that arise in the business context, and consider the circumstances in which directors, officers, and employees, or even a corporation itself, may be convicted of a crime.

INTRODUCTION

Criminal law is enduringly fascinating. Crime, criminals, victims, the circumstances in which crimes arise, trials, and punishment have been staples of popular culture for centuries. It also provides fodder for endless political and social debates.

Television dramas and popular fiction focus on violent crimes. In recent years, however, there has been increasing interest in business, or white collar crimes (named to reflect the white-collared shirts that the individuals who commit the crimes supposedly wear). Business crimes are offenses that are related to the business's activities. They typically include such crimes as fraud, embezzlement, and insider trading.

These crimes have an enormous impact. According to the U.S. Department of Justice, white-collar crime cost the U.S. economy over $426 billion a year. This figure includes the costs of prosecuting and punishing business criminals. It also encompasses the less immediate costs to the economy of failed businesses, lost jobs, and higher consumer prices. Corporate crimes cause substantial damage to the larger community, and prosecutors and courts take these offenses very seriously.

I. Basic Principles of Criminal Law

There are crimes that are easy for us to understand. Even if we don't know the precise legal terminology or elements, we have some idea of what is meant by crimes such as assault or burglary. There are other crimes that are harder to conceptualize, such as insider trading.

However simple or complex a crime may be, though, every crime is made up of at least two parts: **mens rea**, or guilty state of mind, and **actus reus**, the criminal act or acts. In order to obtain a conviction for a crime, the government prosecuting the crime must prove mens rea and actus reus **beyond a reasonable doubt.**

Mens Rea

Deciding the criminality of a person's actions depends the state of her mind when she completed the actions that made up a crime. A lawful act may be criminal if it is done in a certain mental state (*mens rea*). The person's state of mind may also determine the degree of criminality with which the act was conducted. The critical issue is that intent, and whether that intent was deliberately unlawful.

> "State of mind" is not the same as the "motive." A prosecutor does not have to prove motive to obtain a conviction. Looking for individuals with a motive is often a useful technique for investigators, though, and can make the prosecutor's case more compelling to a jury.

For most crimes, the *mens rea* will be either general intent or specific intent. The type of intent required to prove a particular crime depends on the legislation defining the crime.

MENS REA:
Latin for "guilty mind." The mental state of a person committing the criminal act (actus reus).

ACTUS REUS:
Latin for "guilty act." Actions that constitute a crime when done with the appropriate state of mind (actus reus).

BEYOND A REASONABLE DOUBT:
Standard of proof for a criminal conviction. "Reasonable doubt" is when jurors are not convinced of the defendant's guilt, or when they believe there is a reasonable possibility that the defendant is not guilty.

STRICT LIABILITY:
A crime that does not require proof of a guilty state of mind.

General Intent Mens Rea: General intent refers to the intent to do the physical actions that constitute a crime. The term refers only to a voluntary intentional act done by the person accused of breaking the law (defendant). General intent does not mean that the defendant intended to commit a crime, or to cause any harm, only that she voluntarily intentionally did the act that led to the harm that made up the crime. The intent to cause harm is inferred from the fact that the defendant acted voluntarily and intentionally.

General intent means that a defendant's actions were deliberate, conscious, or purposeful. They were not done through accident, mistake, carelessness, or absent-mindedness. In most cases, showing that the defendant did the act which

> *Example:* Daryl is upset that his partner Jesse refuses to clean up their house. One day as they are leaving the house, Daryl throws a lit cigarette on a stack of magazines. Daryl believes that this will do nothing more than create some smoke, which will scare Jesse into cleaning up. Unfortunately, the cigarette starts a fire, which destroys the house. Daryl had the general intent to throw a lit cigarette onto the magazines. Therefore, Daryl has intentionally destroyed their house by fire.

constitutes the crime is enough to show general intent of the mens rea to commit the crime.

A defendant will not be guilty of a general intent crime if she can prove that her actions were not voluntary (not done willingly). It is a defense to most crimes to prove that the criminal actions were done under **duress**, or out of **necessity**.

The duress and necessity defenses depend on either the actions of other parties (in the case of duress), or on circumstances outside of the defendant's control (necessity). Actions voluntarily taken by a defendant cannot negate her own general intent. For the defense of duress or necessity to apply, someone other than the defendant must have forced the defendant to take an action that resulted in a crime.

> Duress and necessity are not defenses to any type of **homicide**.

It is not a defense to a general intent crime to show that the injury caused was not the injury intended, or that the defendant intended to harm another victim. The doctrine of **transferred intent** will "shift" the intent so that the defendant is considered to have intended the harm that did result in the specific manner in which the injury occurred.

Specific Intent Mens Rea: Specific intent is the intent to bring about a particular criminal result. In order to convict a person of a specific intent crime, the prosecutor must prove that the defendant took the specific action intending to cause harm. The crucial point is that a defendant has the subjective intention to cause harm

DURESS:
Threats of harm or other pressure that force a person to commit a criminal act against his will.

NECESSITY:
A defense to a criminal charge that says that the defendant acted in an emergency situation not of her own creation to prevent a harm greater than the harm caused by her actions.

HOMICIDE:
The taking of another person's life.

TRANSFERRED INTENT:
Shifting intent from the crime the defendant originally intended to commit to the crime that actually was committed.

> **Example:** Lisa spends an evening at a bar drinking heavily. After she is asked to leave, she picks up a rock from the street and throws it through the front window of the bar. Lisa argues that she was too drunk to intend to throw the rock. She will still be held responsible. Her voluntary intoxication may not be used to attempt to prove that she did not have general intent to destroy the window, because no other person forced Lisa to drink. If Lisa were involuntarily intoxicated (for instance, if someone added alcohol or drugs to a drink without her knowledge), then there is a different result. In that case, if the intoxication against her will meant she was unable to understand that what she was doing was wrong, Lisa could successfully use duress as a defense.

> **Example:** Assume the same facts as in the prior example, except that Lisa argues that she did not throw the rock at the window, but at Kate, a former friend who was passing by. Kate ducked at the right moment, and the rock hit the window instead. Lisa still had the general intent to throw the rock at the window even though she was aiming at Kate. Lisa's intent to hit Kate is transferred to the window that she broke.

regardless of the specific type of harm that results from his intention.

A crime is a specific intent crime if the description of the criminal act in the statute requires an intent to do some further act, or cause an additional consequence. For instance, in many states, burglary is defined as entering or remaining unlawfully in a building with the intent to commit a crime in the building. Burglary is a specific intent crime, because the crime requires intent to do something besides the original voluntary act of entering or remaining in a building. It also requires a further act to commit a crime while in the building.

It is a defense to show that the defendant did not, or could not, have the specific intent required to meet the *mens rea* element of a particular crime. The lack of specific intent may be due to the

> **Example:** Charla hides at a library, intending to steal a valuable book after hours. While she waits, she starts reading a mystery, and becomes so involved in the story that she keeps reading through the night until the library opens the next morning. When she sees that the library is open, Charla goes home, leaving behind the book. Charla committed burglary because she stayed in the building with the specific intent to steal something, even though she did not go through with stealing the book.

> **Example:** After a night of heavy drinking, Bela tries to walk home. He is too drunk to recognize that the house he enters belongs to his next-door neighbors. Bela falls asleep on the living room couch. Since Bela did not intend to commit a crime in his neighbors' house, he is not guilty of burglary. Bela made a mistake that negates the guilty mind element required to prove a crime.

defendant's own actions, including a mistake of fact (an honest and reasonable mistake) that negates the *mens rea* element of a crime.

There are also some crimes that result from **strict liability**, which means that the person committing the crime is guilty with no intent required. Strict liability crimes do not require proof of a mental state. No *mens rea* needs to be proven by the prosecution. Strict liability is criminal responsibility without fault. It applies to actions that, regardless of the care taken, are specifically not allowed by statute. Selling alcohol to a minor is a good example of a strict liability crime.

To obtain a conviction for a strict liability crime, it is enough to show that the defendant did certain prohibited acts. It does not matter that she did not know that the acts were criminal, because *mens rea* is not required. As such, she is strictly liable for her acts, and the harm that results.

Strict liability and general intent crimes are not the same, even though both types of crimes require proof of certain actions occurring. A strict liability crime requires proof of the defendant actually doing the prohibited criminal act. It is not necessary to prove that the defendant did not intend or did not know the act was legally prohibited. The defendant is still liable. Ignorance of the law or of facts is not a defense. Except in rare cases, there is no defense to a strict liability crime.

Actus Reus

The *actus reus*, or guilty act, is a physical action that is criminal when done with the required *mens rea* intent. A person cannot be convicted of a crime merely for having criminal thoughts. Some action besides thinking is required. A person's status (who they are, or a medical condition that the person possesses, for instance) cannot be a crime. Laws making it a crime merely to be a drug addict have been held to be unconstitutional, but the acts of selling or possessing illegal drugs are crimes, regardless of whether the seller or possessor is an addict.

> **Example:** In most of the United States, it is legal to sell alcoholic beverages. It is, however, generally a crime to sell alcohol to a person under 21. A person who sells alcohol to a minor will be guilty even if she didn't know that the person was under 21.

> **Example:** Lars is watching a friend cutting down a tree. He sees his ex-wife's new husband Evan walking nearby. He realizes that his friend cannot see Evan, and that Evan doesn't realize the tree is about to fall, or that it will probably fall on him. Lars thinks that outcome would be poetic justice, so he says nothing and gives no warning. The tree falls on Evan, killing him. Lars' voluntary failure to warn Evan or to stop his friend is *actus reus*.

> **Example:** Emil suffered a seizure while driving. He struck and killed a group of children. Prior to the accident, Emil had a long history of seizures. He noticed his hand jerking before losing control of his car, but he did not stop driving. Emil was guilty of criminal negligence. *People v. Decina*, 2 N.Y.2d 133, 138 N.E.2d 799 (1956).

An omission or failure to act may also be an *actus reus*. The reasoning is that there was a voluntary choice not to perform an act when action was required to be taken. The absence of an action is thus considered a voluntary "action."

A physical act will not be an *actus reus* if it was done involuntarily (accidentally). A reflex or convulsion, or a movement done while a person is asleep or unconscious, will not be an *actus reus*. But if a person knows that she is prone to an involuntary action (such as seizures) but acts despite knowing of the risk of her involuntary seizures, then she is liable for any harm resulting from her involuntary action.

> Showing that a person had no control over her actions while sleepwalking, for instance, is a defense in many states.

Elements

Mens rea and *actus rea* make up elements of specific crimes. An "element" is a necessary part of any legal action, civil or criminal. In criminal law, each and every defined element must be proven beyond a reasonable doubt to secure a conviction. If even a single element is not proven, the defendant will be acquitted of that crime.

The elements encompass *mens rea* and *actus rea*, but these requirements are defined for each crime. For example, the elements of federal wire fraud include:

1. The defendant knowingly participated in a scheme or plan to defraud, or a scheme or plan for obtaining money or property by means of false or fraudulent pretenses, representations, or promises;

2. The statements made as part of the scheme were material; that is, they had a natural

> **Elements of a Crime in Jury Instructions**
>
> In 2011, the United States prosecuted Lindsey Manufacturing Company as a corporation for violations of the Foreign Corrupt Practices Act. The following text is an excerpt from the jury instructions in that criminal trial. The jury for the case found that the prosecution proved all of the elements shown here beyond a reasonable doubt and convicted the corporation; however, the conviction was dismissed later in the year based on a showing of misconduct by the prosecutors.
>
> ---
>
> Lindsey Manufacturing Company is a corporation. A corporation may be found guilty of an offense. A corporation acts only through its agents and employees, that is, those officers, agents, employees, or other persons authorized or employed to act for it.
>
> To sustain the charge of conspiracy to violate the Foreign Corrupt Practices Act ("FCPA") or violation of the FCPA against Lindsey Manufacturing Company, the government must prove the following propositions:
>
> - First, the offense charged was committed by one or more agents or employees of Lindsey Manufacturing Company;
> - Second, in committing the offense, the agent or employee intended, at least in part, to benefit Lindsey Manufacturing Company; and
> - Third, the acts by the agent or employee were committed within the authority or scope of his employment.
>
> For an act to be within the authority of an agent or the scope of the employment of an employee, it must deal with a matter whose performance is generally entrusted to the agent or employee by Lindsey Manufacturing Company.
>
> It is not necessary that the particular act was itself authorized or directed by Lindsey Manufacturing Company.
>
> If an agent or an employee was acting within the authority or scope of his employment, Lindsey Manufacturing Company is not relieved of its responsibility because the act was illegal.

tendency to influence, or were capable of influencing, a person to part with money or property;

3. The defendant acted with the intent to defraud, that is, the intent to deceive and cheat; and

4. The defendant used an interstate wire communication to carry out or attempt to carry out an essential part of the scheme.

This list of elements includes the *mens rea* specific to the crime: knowing participation and acting with intent to defraud. The list also includes the *actus rea*: material statements and use of an interstate wire communication (typically communication by telephone) to obtain money or property. Unless each element is proven, the defendant will not be guilty of the crime.

Most crimes are defined and prosecuted at the state level. The elements set forth for each crime may vary between states. "First degree murder" means different things in different states, for instance. In New York, murder in the first degree must involve an aggravating factor, which may be killing a witness or court official or killing someone while committing another felony. In Illinois, the identity of the victim is not considered; the perpetrator must have intended to kill or cause great bodily harm to the victim. In both states, there are some alternatives that will also lead to convictions.

In order to make sure that convictions are based on the elements established in the law, courts use jury instructions. Jury instructions explain to the jury how they should carry out their responsibilities. The jury instructions also provide a list of the elements for each crime for which the defendant stands accused. The jury must discuss each element and determine if it is proved beyond a reasonable doubt. Only after every element is separately considered and found to be proven may the jury agree to convict for that crime.

Search and Seizure

The law of search and seizure gives rise to more confusion and misunderstanding than just about any other legal topic. Search and seizure does not deal with acts that make up a crime. Instead, it deals with the investigation and prosecution of crime. It is a procedural legal issue (the process of how a search was conducted), rather than a substantive legal issue (the application of individual rights to the person being searched).

The law of search and seizure is founded on the Fourth Amendment to the U.S. Constitution. The Amendment has two separate, but related provisions:

1. Protection against "unreasonable" searches and seizures; and

2. Rules limiting the issuance of search or arrest **warrants**.

The Fourth Amendment reads as follows:

> The right of the people to be secure in their persons, houses, papers, and effects, against unreasonable searches and seizures, shall not be violated, and no Warrants shall issue, but upon probable cause, supported by Oath or affirmation, and particularly describing the place to be searched, and the persons or things to be seized.

Most state constitutions contain provisions that echo the Fourth Amendment to the U.S. Constitution.

WARRANT: Written authority to conduct a search or to seize property or arrest a person.

Example: A warrant to search any building in Boston for smuggled goods would be a general warrant. It grants too much power to the warrant holder.

> **Example:** A police officer suspects that a man is using and selling drugs from his home. On garbage collection day in the man's neighborhood, the officer lifts full trash bags from the curb in front of the man's house. The bags are opaque and sealed, but the officer finds evidence of drug sales in the bags' content. While the man may complain that the police officer's rummage through his garbage bags required a warrant, the Supreme Court has ruled that there is no reasonable expectation of privacy in trash put out for collection. Bags put on the curb are "readily accessible to animals, children, scavengers, [and] snoops" as well as police officers. *California v. Greenwood*, 486 U.S. 35 (1988).

Search and seizure may conjure images of the police looking for drugs, weapons, or criminals themselves. Searches are just as common in white-collar cases, though. Police may look for evidence, including financial records and digital files, or seek individuals involved in corporate fraud. Search warrants may cover homes, offices, storage facilities, and other locations, and police can confiscate computers and cell phones to preserve evidence.

The first question for deciding Fourth Amendment issues is to ask if a search or a seizure occurred. The definition of "search" is not limited to a physical inspection or intrusion. The Fourth Amendment protects people, not places. The test for whether a search or a seizure has taken place looks at whether there was an intrusion on a person's reasonable expectation of privacy. Activities that violate the privacy upon which a person justifiably relied constitute a "search and seizure" under the Fourth Amendment. However, if no intrusion occurred, there was no search and no violation of the Fourth Amendment.

This definition leads to some interesting outcomes. For example, listening in on a conversation can be a search, even without a physical entry into a building. Likewise, attaching a location tracker to a person's car is considered a search, because the owner of the car has a reasonable expectation of privacy in the location of the car. On the other hand, flying a helicopter 400 feet over a person's house to conduct surveillance is not a search, because the homeowner could not have any reasonable expectation of privacy in what could be seen from that altitude.

The Fourth Amendment prohibits only "unreasonable" searches and seizures. While there is no definition established for "reasonable" searches, there has long been a judicial preference for searches and seizures to be performed under warrant. A search or seizure without a warrant is not always unreasonable, but it is presumed that a legitimate warrant makes the search or seizure reasonable.

When the Constitution and the Bill of Rights were drafted, the Framers were mindful of the abuses of power by British authorities in the Colonies. One of these abuses was the "general warrant." A general warrant was an order that granted an official broad discretion to search unnamed premises, or arrest unnamed persons.

The Fourth Amendment bars general warrants, by requiring that the warrant specifically describe the place to be searched, or the persons or things to be seized. If the warrant says that the police may search "211 Pine Street, apartment 1" for illegal weapons, they may not also search apartment 2. They also may not search for drugs in apartment 1.

In addition, a warrant will be issued only "upon probable cause." **Probable cause** means that there are facts that support an objective belief that a person has committed a crime, or that there is evidence of a crime in the place to be searched. Facts are essential to probable cause; opinions or conclusions are inadequate to support a warrant. These facts are put into an **affidavit**, and presented to an official who is asked to issue a warrant. Probable cause does not require a mathematically measurable probability of a crime, but it must rely on more than a simple hunch or suspicion.

An additional requirement for warrants not found in the U.S. Constitution is that the warrant be issued by a neutral and detached official. Repeated court decisions over many years

> If drugs are seen during the warranted search for weapons, the police may seize them. They may not conduct a search to look for drugs if they don't see them. Just being in a property does not grant the police the right to expand the scope of the warrant.

> Probable cause is not the same as proof beyond a reasonable doubt. Probable cause is a lower bar that applies to issuance of warrants. "Beyond a reasonable doubt" is a standard that juries apply when determining whether a criminal defendant is guilty. The higher bar applies when a person's liberty is at stake.

PROBABLE CAUSE:
An objective and fact-based belief that a person has committed a crime or that there is evidence of a crime in a specific place.

AFFIDAVIT:
A written statement of facts given under oath.

Example: Juanita, a narcotics officer, lives across the street from a house she believes is used for drug trafficking. Cars often drive up to the house, stay for a few minutes, and leave. Juanita has never spoken to the occupants of the house, and has never seen the inside of the house. Her neighbors tell her that they don't know what goes on in the house. Based only on these facts, Juanita does not have probable cause for a warrant.

> **Example:** A judge issues a warrant based on information furnished by law enforcement. Acting in reliance on the warrant, the police raid a house and seize a quantity of drugs. At a later hearing, a different judge concludes that there was no probable cause because the information used to apply for the warrant was stale. The U.S. Supreme Court held that, since the police relied in good faith on the validity of the warrant, a search pursuant to the warrant was lawful. *U.S. v. Leon,* 468 U.S. 897 (1984).

made this requirement a part of basic search and seizure law. The purpose of this part of search and seizure law is to include an objective party in the decision. Review of a warrant application by someone with no stake in the outcome of the case prevents corruption and abuse of power.

The official reviewing the warrant application must be someone connected with the court system, and is usually a judge. The official must be capable of deciding whether probable cause exists. If an official issues the warrant without adequate probable cause, the resulting search is lawful as long as the law enforcement officers who executed it acted under a good faith belief that the warrant was valid.

Searches performed without a warrant are presumed to be unreasonable. There are many exceptions to this rule, including but not limited to the following:

- **Consent.** A search is not unreasonable if the person gives his permission.

- **Lawful arrest.** If a person is lawfully arrested, either through an arrest warrant or on other probable cause, she may be searched at the time of arrest.

- **Exigent circumstances.** If there is evidence or contraband that is in danger of being destroyed, a warrant is not required for a search and seizure.

- **Plain view.** Evidence that is in the plain sight of law enforcement officers where the officers have a right to be may be seized without a warrant.

> **Example:** A police officer pulls over a red Camaro for running a traffic light. The car has a personalized license plate that reads "YUMM13." After going to the driver's window to issue a ticket, the officer receives a transmission that a bank was just robbed a few blocks away, and that the getaway car was a red sports car with a plate starting with a Y. Because there is probable cause to believe that the car was involved in the crime, the officer would be entitled to search any area of the car where the proceeds of a bank robbery could be stashed. (The officer would probably be justified in calling for back-up first.)

> **Example:** A neighborhood watch member sneaks into a neighbor's house and looks in the kitchen drawer, where he sees stolen jewelry. This unlawful search would not exclude the evidence, because the search was performed by a private citizen.
>
> If a police officer looked in the drawer rather than a neighborhood watch member, the search would be illegal, and the jewelry could not be used as evidence. If another police officer arrived at the front door with a warrant to search for the jewelry while the first officer was looking at another area in the kitchen, though, the jewelry might be used as evidence. Even though the first officer's search was illegal, the discovery of the jewelry was inevitable by the second officer. The evidence may be admitted.

- **Cars.** There are many circumstances that allow the warrantless search of a car. If there is probable cause to believe that a car contains evidence of criminal activity, for instance, an officer may lawfully search any area of the vehicle in which the evidence might be found.

If a search is unlawful, the evidence found as a result of the search usually may not be introduced into evidence in the criminal trial. This principle is known as the **exclusionary rule**. The purpose of the exclusionary rule is to deter misconduct by law enforcement. In cases where an unlawful search was done by a private party (for example, a security guard), the rule will not apply to the private party. The evidence may be introduced in court. The rule also does not apply if the evidence would have been found anyway (inevitable discovery).

EXCLUSIONARY RULE: A rule that prohibits illegally obtained evidence from being used in court.

Sentencing

A sentence is the consequence of a criminal conviction. It is ordered by the judge following the conviction of a defendant. The rationale behind criminal sentencing can vary. Many regard sentencing as an opportunity for vengeance or retribution, to be exacted by society. Others look at criminal sentences as a way of deterring other potential criminals. Some also believe that a criminal sentence should be used as an opportunity to rehabilitate a wrongdoer, or just a means to take him off the streets.

Criminal sentencing is limited by the Eighth Amendment to the U.S. Constitution. The Eighth Amendment prohibits imposing excessive fines or inflicting "cruel and unusual punishments." Courts have interpreted this limitation to mean that a criminal sentence must not be grossly disproportionate to the crime. Imposing a death sentence in a case that does not involve a homicide would generally be considered grossly disproportionate. In cases not involving murder, prison sentences

POLICE USE OF CELL PHONE LOCATION DATA WITHOUT WARRANT WAS REASONABLE TO FIND MURDER SUSPECT

Commonwealth v. Almonor
(State Government) v. (Criminal Defendant)
482 Mass. 35, 120 N.E.3d 1183 (2019)

This appeal raises an issue of first impression in Massachusetts: whether police action causing an individual's cell phone to reveal its real-time location constitutes a search in the constitutional sense[.]

At approximately 5:19 P.M. on August 10, 2012, a Brockton police officer responded to a reported shooting. When he arrived at the scene [. . .] [h]e found the victim inside the car, unconscious, with a gunshot wound to the chest. The victim [. . .] was pronounced dead approximately one hour later.

An eyewitness was interviewed by police at approximately 8:15 P.M. [. . .] The eyewitness later identified the defendant from a photographic array. By 9:10 P.M., two officers interviewed the man who had been in the car with the defendant [who] provided police with the defendant's cell phone number. He also informed the officers [. . .] that the defendant still had the shotgun. By 11 P.M., the police had conducted numerous witness interviews and performed multiple identifications of the defendant [as well as learning of the defendant's ex-girlfriend's address].

On the basis of the information they received, [an] officer provided the defendant's cell phone number and requested several pieces of information [from the service provider], including the "precise location . . . (GPS location)" of the defendant's cell phone. As grounds for the request, the officer wrote, "outstanding murder suspect, shot and killed victim with shotgun. Suspect still has shotgun." [GPS data placed the defendant at or near his ex-girlfriend's house.]

The homeowner, the former girlfriend's father [. . .] indicated that he knew the defendant but did not believe that the defendant was at the house. He said that his daughter should be upstairs in her room, and he gave police permission to go upstairs and speak with her.

[Police arrested the defendant and] secured the scene while one officer requested a warrant to search the house. After receiving the warrant, police searched the house and seized, among other items, the shotgun and vest.

An individual has a reasonable expectation of privacy if (i) the individual has "manifested a subjective expectation of privacy in the object of the search," and (ii) if "society is willing to recognize that expectation as reasonable"[.]

The intrusive nature of police action that causes an individual's cell phone to transmit its real-time location raises distinct privacy concerns. When the police ping a cell phone, as they did in this case, they compel it to emit a signal, and create a transmission identifying its real-time location information. This action and transmission is initiated and effectively controlled by the police, and is done without any express or implied authorization or other involvement by the individual cell phone user. Without police direction, such data would also not otherwise be collected and retained by the service provider.

Manipulating our phones for the purpose of identifying and tracking our personal location presents an even greater intrusion. [. . .] Indeed, prior to the advent of cell phones, law enforcement officials were generally required, by necessity, to patrol streets, stake out homes, interview individuals, or knock on doors to locate persons of interest. For this reason, society's expectation has been that law enforcement could not secretly and instantly identify a person's real-time physical location at will.

To allow such conduct without judicial oversight would undoubtedly "shrink the realm of guaranteed privacy" [. . .] and leave legitimate privacy rights at the "mercy of advancing technology." Accordingly, we conclude that by causing the defendant's cell phone to reveal its real-time location, the Commonwealth conducted a search in the constitutional sense.

Where police conduct a search without a warrant, the search is presumptively unreasonable. Because the "ultimate touchstone" of art. 14 is reasonableness, however, "the warrant requirement is subject to certain carefully delineated exceptions."

> Specifically, we consider whether police had "reasonable grounds to believe that obtaining a warrant would be impracticable under the circumstances because the delay in doing so would pose a significant risk that (1) the suspect may flee, (2) evidence may be destroyed, or (3) the safety of the police or others may be endangered."
>
> As to the risk of flight in this case, there were reasonable grounds to believe that the defendant would have been aware that police would be looking for him. [The crime happened in daytime with at least two witnesses.]
>
> As to the risk of destruction of evidence, the record reflects that police learned that the defendant still possessed the sawed-off shotgun at the time he fled the scene of the shooting. Because a sawed-off shotgun is per se illegal, it requires ongoing concealment from authorities. This fact, when coupled with the fact that the suspect likely knew he could be identified and would have reason to fear capture, gave police reasonable grounds to believe that there was a risk that the suspect would attempt to conceal or destroy the shotgun before he was located by police.
>
> Finally, police also had reasonable grounds to believe that the defendant posed an immediate risk to the safety of police and others. [T]he officers had reasonable grounds to believe that if the suspect shot one person, when unprovoked and seemingly undeterred by fear of discovery or reprisal, other individuals were in danger as well.
>
> With these considerations in mind, we conclude that under the circumstances at the time the defendant's cell phone was pinged, the police had reasonable grounds to believe that obtaining a warrant would be impracticable because taking the time to do so would have posed a significant risk that the suspect may flee, evidence may be destroyed, or the safety of the police or others may be endangered.
>
> Motion to suppress reversed.

are rarely found to be disproportionate. When considering if a sentence is disproportionate, courts consider several factors, including:

- The seriousness of the crime.
- The harm done to the victim.
- The defendant's involvement in the crime.
- The intent and motive in behind the crime.
- Sentences imposed on other defendants for the same or similar crime.

The statutes that define or create a crime will often set out the maximum possible sentence for that crime. The sentence may be incarceration, a monetary fine, or both. In many cases, a sentencing judge is authorized to sentence a defendant to **probation**, or to impose a **suspended sentence**.

Federal and state laws include a system of guidelines for felony sentencing. These guidelines were adopted to make sentences equivalent for similar defendants. Every defendant convicted for a certain crime would ideally receive a similar sentence, regardless of race, gender, or socio-economic status. The sentencing guidelines group offenses together according to

PROBATION:
A criminal sentence in which the defendant is not imprisoned, but is allowed to remain free, subject to certain conditions.

SUSPENDED SENTENCE:
A criminal sentence that the defendant is not required to serve immediately.

> **Example:** Henry and Kenneth have been convicted of burglary. The law of their state imposes a maximum sentence of 10 years in prison for the level of burglary for which they were convicted. Henry has no prior criminal record, so the state's sentencing guidelines call for him to be placed on probation, and a **stayed sentence** of a year and a day. Kenneth has four prior felony convictions, so the guidelines call for him to receive a sentence of 24 months in prison.

severity, and then set the penalty as a function of the severity of the crime and the defendant's criminal history. Sentencing judges are allowed to consider certain aggravating or mitigating factors to increase or decrease a sentence, but they are usually required to give the reasons for these variations.

> As a rule, a **felony** is a crime punishable by more than one year in prison, while a **misdemeanor** has a maximum penalty of one year or less. The focus is on the possibility of a year or more of punishment; a person convicted of a felony may serve less than a year in prison, but that does not change the felony conviction to a misdemeanor.

II. Inchoate Crimes

"Inchoate" is another way of saying incomplete. Inchoate crimes are crimes that a person failed to complete. The act of taking steps towards the crime is deemed criminal even though no harm was done. Inchoate crimes include:

- Attempts to commit a crime.
- Soliciting another person to commit a crime.
- Conspiring to commit a crime.
- Being an accessory or accomplice to a crime.

The underlying crime that was attempted, solicited, or conspired about is not always committed.

Inchoate crimes are punished for two main reasons. One reason is to prevent another crime. If a person is seen attempting a burglary, it is better to catch him before the burglary is complete. The second reason is deterrence. Punishing a person for attempting to commit

FELONY:
A crime punishable by a sentence of more than one year, or by death.

MISDEMEANOR:
A crime punishable by a fine or imprisonment of no more than one year.

STAYED SENTENCE:
A sentence that the court imposes, but delays the requirement that the defendant comply with it immediately. For example, a stayed prison sentence will allow the defendant to remain free as long as he remains law abiding and complies with the conditions of probation.

> **Example:** Mazen and Greg work for the same company. Greg thinks of a way to create false invoices to put in for payment. He asks Mazen, who works in the accounting department, to process the invoices. Mazen refuses. Greg sends in the invoices himself, but they are determined to be fakes and are not paid. Greg is guilty of the inchoate crimes of soliciting another person to commit a crime, and of the attempt to commit embezzlement himself.

a crime will discourage her from trying again and eventually completing the crime.

Inchoate crimes are "specific intent" crimes because there is an intent to commit the crime that was not completed.

Attempt

The crime of attempt involves more than planning or thinking about committing a crime. Attempt requires a substantial step towards the commission of a crime. The substantial step must be done with the intent or motive of committing a crime. The attempt is not necessarily an unlawful act on its own—the intent causes the unlawfulness. Once the act is done, the crime of attempt is complete.

Preparation is not the same as attempt. For an attempt, the defendant must come close to completing the crime, and there can be no reasonable doubt about the defendant's motive to commit that crime. In some states, a defendant will not be convicted of attempt unless he has completed all but the last step in committing the crime.

> If a crime is actually committed, the defendant may not be convicted of both attempt and the crime that was committed.

Abandonment is a defense to attempt only if the defendant shows a complete withdrawal from the crime. Postponing or delaying the crime is not abandonment. In addition, the attempt must have been abandoned out of a change of heart, or remorse. It is not abandonment if the attempt is stopped because the crime became more difficult, or if the defendant decided it were more likely she would be caught.

> **Example:** Albert has made a plan to burn down a vacant building that he owns in order to collect the insurance money. He goes to a gas station and buys a can of gas and some matches, then goes home and hides them in his garage. Albert is not guilty of attempted arson. Two nights later, he drives to the building and pries the door open, while carrying the gas and matches. A passer-by thinks Albert is a burglar, and grabs him before he can go into the building. Albert is guilty of attempted arson.

In some jurisdictions, legal impossibility is a defense to attempt. Legal impossibility is when the defendant believes that what he is about to do is illegal when it in fact is legal.

There is a distinction between factual and legal impossibility. Factual impossibility means that an attempted crime cannot be completed because the facts are different than what the defendant thought they were. Factual impossibility is not a defense to an attempt charge.

Solicitation

Solicitation is the crime of asking or urging someone to commit a crime. It does not matter that the person solicited does not commit, attempt, or even agree to commit the crime.

> If the person being solicited does not receive the communication, there is no solicitation.

The crime of solicitation is complete when the request is made to, and received by, the person being solicited.

A conviction for solicitation requires proof that the defendant intended to promote or facilitate the commission of a crime. There must be evidence that strongly corroborates the defendant's specific intent to have a crime committed. Corroborating evidence includes evidence of the circumstances surrounding a defendant's conversations about the crime, as well as evidence of a defendant's discussions with other people. The evidence must show that the defendant was serious, and not just venting or complaining.

Conspiracy

A conspiracy is an agreement between two or more people to commit an unlawful act. In some states, a conspiracy may also be an agreement to commit a lawful act by unlawful means. The conspiracy is a crime distinct from the agreed-

Example: Nestor plans to break into a store by smashing the front window. He gets a large hammer and swings at the window. The window is not glass; it is made out of an unbreakable plastic. The hammer bounces off, and the window does not break. Nestor is guilty of attempt, even though it is factually impossible for him to complete the crime as he planned.

Example: Dion knows that if his building burns down, he would be a suspect. In order to create an alibi, he asks Dwayne to set a fire in the building while Dion is out of town on vacation. Dwayne hears Dion's request, but does not respond to it. Dion is guilty of solicitation.

upon crime, and it may be punished separately, or in addition to that crime.

In most jurisdictions, the crime of conspiracy is not complete unless there is an overt act performed in furtherance of the conspiracy. In other words, the agreement alone is not enough. The overt act is apart from, and in addition to, the act of making an agreement to commit a crime. The act does not have to be unlawful, but it must be done to further the conspiracy. It may be something other than the crime that is agreed to be committed.

A person who is a part of a conspiracy is responsible for all acts done to further the conspiracy. This includes responsibility for all of the criminal actions agreed to, and also those outcomes that were not part of the agreement, but which were foreseeable as natural and probable consequences of the conspiracy. Co-conspirators are guilty even if they were not physically present at the time a criminal act was done, and even if they did not know about the participation of the conspirator who did the criminal act.

> At common law, conspiracy required an agreement to commit a felony, but that rule has been changed by statute.

Conspiracy is different from solicitation. Solicitation does not require an agreement. Conspiracy also differs from attempt, in that the conspirators are guilty even though they did not take a substantial step towards commission of the crime. In jurisdictions that require an overt act to prove a conspiracy, any overt act separate from making the agreement will suffice. It does not have to be a substantial step as long as the act (no matter how small) furthers the commission of the crime.

Example: Theo and Davi agree to rob a local bank. They plan the robbery down to the smallest detail. In jurisdictions that require an overt act, they are not guilty of conspiracy—planning itself is not an overt act in furtherance of the crime. If Theo goes to a car dealer and rents a car to use as the getaway car, however, that is an overt act. Upon the car rental, the crime of conspiracy is complete.

Example: Anya and Viktor devise a plan to smuggle valuable artwork into the United States from Mexico. Anya travels to Mexico alone to pick up the art. While she is there, Viktor bribes a customs officer back in the United States to let Viktor know if there are suspicions about his and Anya's activities. Anya and Viktor are both guilty of bribery.

III. "White-Collar" Crimes

There are certain crimes that have special relevance in the business world. These crimes relate to the integrity of business relationships and transactions. Handling or misappropriating money is not required for all of these crimes, but each of the crimes will have a financial impact.

Fraud

The term "fraud" is used broadly by many people. It is often used to describe any type of deceit or dishonesty. In the law, though, fraud is a misrepresentation of a fact that induces another person to act.

Fraud may be either civil or criminal. In most jurisdictions, there is no single crime of fraud. Instead, acts done in certain contexts or with regard to certain transactions are crimes if they are done fraudulently. While every jurisdiction defines fraud or fraudulent acts differently, the usual elements of fraud are:

- A knowing and purposeful misrepresentation of a material fact.
- The intent to defraud (fool) the victim.
- Reasonable reliance by the victim on the misrepresentation.
- In many states, some damage to the victim due to the misrepresentation is required; however, federal law does not require any actual monetary damage to the victim.

> A "material fact" is one that is essential to the transaction; in other words, a deal breaker.

Fraud requires a misrepresentation of fact, not a statement of opinion. The defendant must also know that the factual statement was false when she made it. The misrepresented fact must tend to influence the person making a decision.

A misrepresentation is not fraudulent unless the person hearing it relied upon it. That reliance must be justifiable or reasonable. Reliance is not justifiable or reasonable if a person with intelligence, education, or experience similar to the victim's would not have relied on the misrepresentation.

There are many different types of fraud crime. Fraudulent acts are made criminal in several different contexts. Two of the most common

Example: Nobusuke admires an antique sword that Roberta is selling. Roberta tells him that the sword was carried by a cavalry officer in the Civil War. In fact, Roberta knows that the sword was made recently by a local metalworking shop. Roberta says that she believes the sword would impress guests to Nobusuke's home. Roberta's claim that the sword was carried in the Civil War is fraudulent. Her remarks about the impression the sword would make are only opinion, so they are not fraudulent.

Example: Bruce, a college graduate who works in a bank, is visiting his cousin Phyllis. Phyllis never finished high school, and does not read the news or follow business matters. While Bruce is visiting, Doug, an acquaintance of Phyllis's boss, stops by to tell them about an "exciting" new business opportunity that is "guaranteed" to double their investments in one month. The opportunity is a supposed resort development out-of-state. Doug knows that the plans for this development have already fallen through, but he is trying to raise money to pay off earlier investors (a classic **Ponzi scheme**). If Bruce were to invest, his reliance probably would be neither justified nor reasonable, since his education and experience should lead him to decline to rely on Doug's representations. Phyllis's reliance would probably be considered justifiable, since she is inexperienced and probably not knowledgeable about common business schemes.

fraud crimes are mail fraud and wire fraud. Mail fraud is the use of the U.S. Postal Service for fraudulent communications. Wire fraud uses the telephone or electronic communications for fraud. Both types of crimes cross state borders, which make the crimes interstate activities that trigger federal laws.

PONZI SCHEME: A fraudulent investment scheme in which money contributed by investors is used to pay people who made a prior investment. Usually, money is not invested in any revenue-producing enterprise, or if it is, the enterprise does not generate expected revenue.

Example: Gabriel sends a letter to Hailey through the mail, identifying himself as a physician working in an impoverished country. The letter says that Gabriel is soliciting funds to help build an urgently needed clinic. In fact, Gabriel lives in the United States, and has no involvement with any charitable or medical group. Gabriel has committed mail fraud.

Hailey sends Gabriel a monetary contribution. After he receives the contribution, Gabriel decides to go a little further. He calls Hailey on the telephone to thank her for her donation. He then asks if she can contribute more money to help train a nurse for the clinic. Hailey declines to send any further money. Gabriel is guilty of wire fraud because he used the telephone (an interstate activity) to contact Hailey. It is irrelevant that Hailey does not send money in response to the telephone call.

Federal criminal law requires an intent to defraud. It does not require that the victim have sustained any actual monetary loss as a result of the fraud. Therefore, use of the mail or of telephones or electronic communication in furtherance of a fraudulent plan is a crime, even if no one falls for the message.

UNPAID TAXES ARE "PROPERTY" FOR PURPOSES OF FRAUD LAWS

Fountain v. U.S.
(Person Convicted of Mail and Wire Fraud) v. (Prosecuting Government)
357 F.3d 250 (2d Cir. 2004)

INSTANT FACTS:
Fountain (P) was convicted of mail and wire fraud arising out of a scheme to circumvent Canadian tobacco taxes.

BLACK LETTER RULE:
The elements of mail or wire fraud violation are (1) a scheme to defraud, (2) money or property as the object of the scheme, and (3) use of the mails or wires to further the scheme.

FACTS:
Fountain (P) pled guilty to mail and wire fraud. The charges were based on his participation in a scheme to circumvent high Canadian taxes on tobacco products. The scheme involved using cashier's checks and wire transfers, and exchanging Canadian for U.S. currency. The currency was then used to transport cigarettes from Canada into the St. Regis Mohawk Reservation in New York, then back to Canada, to be sold on the black market.

Fountain (P) pled guilty to the charges, and was sentenced to 60 months in prison. He later brought a petition for *habeas corpus* relief. Fountain (P) claimed that his guilty plea was based on his participation in a scheme to defraud the Canadian government out of taxes. He argued that unpaid taxes are not "property" in the possession of a fraud victim, so the scheme could not constitute mail or wire fraud. Fountain (P) also argued that the "revenue rule," a common-law rule that says U.S. courts should not recognize foreign tax judgments. The District Court denied his petition.

ISSUE:
Was Fountain (P) guilty of mail and wire fraud?

DECISION AND RATIONALE:
(Katzmann, J.) Yes. The elements of mail or wire fraud violation are (1) a scheme to defraud, (2) money or property as the object of the scheme, and (3) use of the mails or wires to further the scheme. For purposes of the mail and wire fraud statutes, the thing obtained must be property in the hands of the victim. Taxes owed to the government are property in the hands of the government even if they have not yet been collected. Unless the law clearly states otherwise, the question of who properly has the right of use of the money owed the government for the period it is owed is answered in favor of the government. Because a government has a property right in tax revenues when they accrue, the tax revenues that would have been owed to Canadian governments are "property" for purposes of the mail and wire fraud statutes.

The common law revenue rule does not apply to this case. The mail and wire fraud statute do not preclude the prosecution of a defendant for participating in a scheme to defraud a foreign government of tax revenue. Affirmed.

ANALYSIS:
The revenue rule is a rule of international law that says courts should not hear suits to collect foreign taxes. The prosecution of Fountain (P) was not a suit to collect taxes, but a criminal prosecution for schemes to avoid those taxes. The result of the suit was incarceration upon a conviction, not an order to pay taxes.

CASE VOCABULARY:
HABEAS CORPUS:
A proceeding brought to challenge the legality of a person's confinement.

Embezzlement

"Embezzlement" conjures visions of some elaborate scheme to divert corporate funds to a secret offshore bank account. While that series of events probably would constitute embezzlement, the crime is typically much simpler.

Embezzlement is defined as the fraudulent taking of another person's property by one who is lawfully in possession of that property. The property is then used or applied to purposes other than the purpose for which it was originally held. The distinction between embezzlement and other types of theft is that the person who takes the other person's property is originally lawfully in possession of the property. The property is not taken from the owner. Instead, the embezzler has come into possession of the property lawfully, with the owner's express or implied consent. The intent to take the property may develop after the person comes into possession of it. If a person gains possession of property in good faith, but later changes his mind and acts in bad faith, he has committed embez-

> *Example:* Terry is a secretary and is in charge of the office's supply of petty cash. One day, she is short of lunch money, so she helps herself to $20 from the cash drawer, without getting permission. Technically, Terry may be guilty of embezzlement, even though she may have intended to repay petty cash.

> *Example:* Terry takes the $20 from petty cash, but plans to stop at an ATM after work in order to replace the $20 the next morning. In states that require proof of an intent to deprive the owner of property permanently, Terry may not be guilty of embezzlement.

> *Example:* Hank owns a cattle feed lot. He is hired by Ben to feed and care for several head of cattle for a week before they are sent to auction. Towards the end of the week, Hank learns that Ben has filed for bankruptcy and will be going out of business. Hank calls Nicole, his accountant, to ask what he should do. She tells him that he may dispose of the cattle and keep the proceeds. Hank does so. Unfortunately, Nicole has misunderstood the situation. The cattle are actually to be turned over to the bankruptcy trustee. If Hank lives in a state that requires knowledge that conduct was unlawful, Hank may not be guilty of embezzlement. Depending on the state where he lives, though, Hank may be guilty of misappropriation, larceny, or theft, because the proceeds did not rightfully belong to Hank.

zlement, regardless of whether the property is later returned.

In some states, embezzlement requires an intent to deprive the owner of the property permanently. In other states, the crime of embezzlement is complete when the property is taken or appropriated.

In some jurisdictions, a defendant will be guilty of embezzlement only if he acted knowingly, being aware that his act was unlawful. In other jurisdictions, there is no requirement that the defendant know the conduct is illegal.

Insider Trading

The buying and selling of securities depends on the free flow of accurate information. Investors rely on this information to make informed decisions about their investments. Fairness demands that all investors have equal access to the same information, so that no one investor or group of investors is given an advantage. Securities laws therefore require that publicly-traded corporations make public any material (important) information that has the likelihood of affecting an investor's decision to invest in a company. While all important information must be presented to the public, there is an advantage to those who learn about it first. The first inves-

Example: Malik is an engineer with the National Transportation Safety Board. He is in charge of a safety investigation that may result in the recall of thousands of cars sold by Charon Motors. In his investigation, he works with Paolo, the chief safety engineer for Charon, and Liu, an attorney with an outside law firm representing Charon. Paolo makes regular reports on the progress of the investigation to Frank, the chief operating officer of Charon. Frank's secretary Ivan makes copies of Paolo's reports, and skims them before handing them to Frank. When the investigation is nearly complete, Malik comes home and tells his partner Logan that the NTSB is going to order a recall of virtually all cars manufactured by Charon for the past three years. Malik, Paolo, Liu, Frank, Ivan, and Logan are all insiders.

Example: In the example above, Malik tells Logan that the recall of Charon Motors cars will be made in one week, on September 15. Logan calls his stock broker on September 13, and places an order to sell 5,000 shares of Charon stock immediately before the recall is announced. Liu owns 2,500 shares of Charon stock that she bought before her firm started representing the company. She sells her stock on September 16, the day after the recall is announced. Logan is guilty of insider trading; Liu is not.

> **Example:** Continuing with the facts from the prior example, Malik's recently-deceased mother owned 1,000 shares of Charon stock, as well as stock in several other companies. She left all of her stock to Malik. In order to settle a dispute with his siblings over their mother's estate, Malik agrees to sell the stock as soon as he receives permission from the probate court, and divide the proceeds with his siblings. The court grants its permission on September 12, and Malik sells all of the stock that day. Malik is not guilty of insider trading.

tors to learn something important about their investments will be able to take advantage of it by buying or selling their stock before that information has a chance to make an impact on the market. By contrast, diligent investors who monitor news carefully and act quickly have an advantage, but it is a fair advantage. Any investor could take the same action if she took the time and effort.

There are, however, investors who will learn important news before it is made available to the public. These are insiders. They become aware of important information because of their positions within a company, performing work on behalf of the company, or information they obtained from someone within the company. Insiders include corporate officers, employees, directors, and outside professionals who have access to confidential information, government employees who have access to sensitive information, or people who receive this information from other insiders.

> In addition to criminal liability, a person engaged in insider trading may be held liable in a civil lawsuit brought by the Securities and Exchange Commission, which regulates the securities trade.

Insiders are allowed to buy and sell stock in their corporation, the same as any investor. Insider trading is criminal only when the insider makes a trade on information not available to the public.

The Securities and Exchange Commission (SEC), the federal agency responsible for regulating securities markets, takes the position that insider trading is not unlawful if a person is not aware of the non-public information. Insider trading is also not unlawful if the non-public information was not a factor in the decision to trade in the stock. Examples of trades where non-public information include trades made pursuant to a pre-existing plan or an agreement to trade that was made in good faith regardless of the non-public information.

Federal Criminal Statutes

While any crime can be a corporate crime, several federal statutes have a business focus. These laws can result in white-collar prosecutions of individuals and possibly their employers. Corporations should be aware of these laws and make sure to guard against them through training, audits, and executive oversight.

Antitrust Laws: Antitrust laws are designed to maintain fair competition among businesses to benefit consumers through competitive pricing and continuous improvement to earn their business. Several federal laws work together to prevent companies from engaging in anti-competitive activities. Typical violations include price fixing, dividing markets, bid rigging, and other collusion with competing businesses. The government reserves criminal prosecutions for the most collusive behavior between businesses.

> In the late 1990s, the U.S. pursued several vitamin companies for creating secret cartels. The cartels divided the market and set pricing. The companies paid hundreds of millions of dollars in fines.

Immigration Control and Reform Act (ICRA): In the United States, non-citizens can only hold jobs if they have government permission to do so. The ICRA outlaws employment of undocumented aliens. Immigration and Customs Enforcement (ICE) can investigate companies for violations of the ICRA, including immigration "raids." Business owners, managers, and other employees involved in hiring unauthorized workers can face prosecution, as can the company itself.

Racketeer Influenced and Corrupt Organizations Act (RICO): RICO bans criminal organizations. The law was intended to target criminal syndicates such as crime families or gangs that order people to commit crimes, but it has also been used to investigate and prosecute "legitimate" businesses that engage in criminal activity. In the late 1980s, for example, investment bank Drexel Burnham Lambert entered into a plea deal after it was investigated for criminal insider trading, including RICO violations. An executive, Michael Milken, received a prison sentence. Drexel Burnham Lambert declared bankruptcy in 1990, even though it was one of the largest American investment banks.

Foreign Corrupt Practices Act (FCPA): The FCPA bans U.S. companies or people representing them from bribing government officials in other countries to gain a business advantage. Employees or agents of a company that engage in payments may cause the company itself to be investigated or prosecuted. Settlements of FCPA charges are among the most expensive fines levied on corporations worldwide. In 2020, Goldman Sachs agreed to pay $2.3 billion to settle alleged violations of the FCPA in Malaysia and in the United Arab Emirates. The government claimed that the company used a third party to pay high-level officials; however, Goldman Sachs pled guilty to only one count of conspiracy to commit an FCPA violation as part of its settlement.

> The FCPA still applies to U.S. organizations and the people who represent them, even though their activities may take place outside the U.S. This type of law is said to have "extra-territorial" scope.

Example: The Apophis Corporation operates a warehouse in a state where the crime of homicide includes negligently causing the death of another person. State law does not exclude a corporation from the definition of person. Max, the manager of the warehouse, decides he can increase the capacity of the warehouse, and thus increase revenue for Apophis, by moving temporary shelving units in front of an emergency exit. The next day, a fire breaks out, and three employees die because they are not able to reach an exit. Both Max and Apophis could be guilty of criminal homicide.

Example: Curtis is the president of Curtis Fine Art Galleries, Inc. He hires Wolfgang, an accomplished but little-known painter, to make copies of paintings. An employee, Gladys, is put in charge of selling the paintings. She puts offers to sell them on the gallery's website, claiming that they are original paintings by named famous painters. Wolfgang has a brochure printed that repeats the claim made by Gladys, and sends a brochure through the U.S. mail. Curtis Fine Art Galleries could be guilty of wire fraud and mail fraud.

Other Crimes

A corporation may be found guilty of almost any crime. While corporate crime is often thought of as encompassing only financial crimes, crimes of violence against a person may also be committed by a corporation. Criminal statutes refer to acts done by a "person," and the statutes are generally written so that "person" can include a corporation. As long as the test for determining whether a criminal act was done to benefit the corporation is met, the corporation may be held criminally liable.

A corporation may be criminally liable as long as all of the elements of the crime are committed by its directors, officers, agents, or employees. All of the actions constituting the crime do not have to be done by the same person.

IV. Corporate Criminal Liability

For many purposes, corporations are regarded as "persons." One aspect of that personhood is that a corporation may be convicted of a crime. Corporate criminal liability is based on the action or inaction of a company's directors, officers, employees, or agents that perform work on behalf of the company.

> As a general rule, an employee or agent is not subject to personal criminal liability for work undertaken for a business that is not criminal in itself. For instance, an employee who is instructed to transfer money, unaware that the transfer is money laundering, is not criminally liable. Instead, the corporation is held liable, and higher-level officials might also be held personally liable.

> **Example:** Charon Motors' vice president in charge of manufacturing calculates that if the company reduces the quality of the material used to filter exhaust fumes by 20 percent, the cars will still pass initial government emissions tests. However, the exhaust filtration's effectiveness will deteriorate below environmental standards after three years on the road. At that point, it will not properly filter exhaust fumes. The vice president orders the change to save the company money. Charon Motors is criminally responsible for this officer's actions, because the decision to use the less effective filters was within the scope of the vice president's authority, and the decision benefited the company.

Federal law makes a corporation guilty of a crime, if the crime was:

- Committed by the corporation's directors, officers, employees, or agents,

- Taken within the scope of authority of their employment,

- Done at least in part for the benefit of the corporation, and

- The act was imputed (attributed) to the corporation.

An activity falls within a person's scope of authority if that person takes the action on the corporation's behalf, and in performance of her general line of work. If this standard is met, the corporation will be liable even though it explicitly told the person not to commit the offense.

Many state criminal laws limit corporate criminal liability to misconduct by upper-level management officials (senior management such as directors and officers). The corporation will not be liable unless conduct was authorized by an officer or director. The motive to benefit the corporation must still be present. Additionally, under the responsible corporate officer doctrine, a court may assess criminal liability on a corporate executive or officer who did not engage in, direct, or know about a specific criminal violation. This liability is found when the corporate executive or officer is responsible for ensuring the company's compliance with the law, but fails to do so.

A CORPORATION CAN BE CRIMINALLY LIABLE FOR THE ACTS OF ITS EMPLOYEES

New York Central & Hudson River Railroad Co. v. United States
(Railroad Company) v. (Federal Government)
212 U.S. 481, 29 S. Ct. 304, 53 L. Ed. 613 (1909)

INSTANT FACTS:
An employee of a railroad company made a deal with a sugar refining company to pay the sugar company rebates in return for use of the railroad company lines, in violation of a federal statute.

BLACK LETTER RULE:
A corporation can be criminally liable for the acts of its employees.

PROCEDURAL BASIS:
Appeal of a federal circuit court decision finding the railroad company guilty of violating a federal statute against rebates.

FACTS:
An employee of the New York Central and Hudson River Railroad Company ("railroad company") (D) made a deal to pay rebates to the American Sugar Refining Company if they used the railroad company's (D) lines to ship its sugar. Under this [sweet deal], the railroad company (D) would ship the sugar between New York and Detroit at a rate of $0.18 per 100 lbs. instead of the published rate of $0.23—$0.21 per 100 lbs. Such rebates were illegal under federal law. The railroad company (D) and its assistant traffic manager were convicted under the statute for the payment of rebates to the sugar company and others. The railroad company (D) appealed the conviction arguing that the statute was unconstitutional because a corporation cannot be held criminally liable for the actions of its employees.

ISSUE:
Can a corporation be held criminally liable for the acts of its employees?

DECISION AND RATIONALE:
(Day, J.) Yes. The railroad company (D) argues that it is unconstitutional to hold a corporation liable to criminal prosecution because any punishment imposed would actually punish innocent stockholders and deprive them of their property in violation of due process. While earlier common law held that corporations were excluded from criminal liability, the modern rule accepts the capacity of corporations to commit crime.

It is an established rule that a corporation can be held responsible in tort for the damages caused by acts of one of its agents acting in the scope of his employment. Since a corporation acts by its officers and agents, their individual "purposes, motives, and intent" are part of the corporation. If a corporation can engage in conduct, it can intend to do such conduct. The officer or agent is acting to benefit the principal, which is, in this case, a corporation. If the conduct is criminal, the corporation must be held accountable for the acts.

The payment of rebates by its agents and officers benefited the corporation, and if only the agents and officers may be held liable, the statute against rebates could not be effectively enforced. There is "no valid objection in law, and every reason in public policy" why a corporation cannot be held liable for the actions and intent of its agents to whom the corporation has vested its authority in and whose actions and purposes are otherwise attributable to the corporation for whom they work. In modem times, a great majority of business transactions are conducted through corporations. To afford corporations immunity from all criminal punishment "would virtually take away the only means of effectually controlling the subject matter and correcting the abuses aimed at." Judgment affirmed.

ANALYSIS:
The underlying theory for imposing liability on a corporation is analogous to the doctrine of respondeat superior. Under respondeat superior, an employer can be held liable for torts committed by an employee during the scope of employment. Courts hold the employer or the corporation liable because they assume that the agent, when acting in the scope of her employment, is committing the wrongdoing for the benefit of the employer or corporation. Thus, it seems logical to hold the superior actor liable for the actions of subordinates to whom the superior delegates authority.

Of course, a corporation cannot be held liable for crimes that cannot be committed by corporations in a practical sense. For example, an employee of the corporation may burglarize a competitor's home, but the act of breaking and entering can only be committed by an individual, not the corporation.

CASE VOCABULARY:

AMENDATORY:
Supplemental, additional.

WRIT OF ERROR:
An order by an appellate court directing the trial court to produce the record of the case it is reviewing.

FRATERNITY THAT ACCIDENTALLY CAUSED DEATH OF A PLEDGE DURING HAZING RITUAL IS CRIMINALLY RESPONSIBLE

Commonwealth v. Pi Delta Psi, Inc.
(State) v. (Fraternity)
211 A.3d 875 (Pa. Super. Ct. 2019)

Near the close of the 2013 fall semester, student members of Pi Delta Psi, Inc. . . . rented a house [in Pennsylvania] to perform the final rites and rituals of their new-member program[.] This time, something went horribly wrong. A ritual known as "The Crossing," a gauntlet where members tackle and body-slam associate members, killed a freshman. The Commonwealth filed charges against the student members; certain national officers; and Pi Delta Psi, Inc., itself. A jury convicted the corporation of hazing, involuntary manslaughter, aggravated assault, conspiracy to commit aggravated assault, hindering apprehension, and conspiracy to hinder apprehension. The corporation now appeals[.]

The corporation, by and through its national president, directly participated in at least one new-member event of the [Baruch College chapter], although no national officers attended the Crossing. The national president helped the student members and officers conceal the cause of death and the corporation's connection to it from investigators. He instructed the student members and officers to lie to police and to hide the fraternity's letters, heraldry, and regalia before officers searched the rented house.

Facing criminal homicide charges, members decided to cooperate with prosecutors and began to implicate the corporation. The Commonwealth eventually charged the corporation with a host of crimes, the most severe of which was murder of the third degree. The jury acquitted the corporation of murder and voluntary manslaughter but convicted it on charges of involuntary manslaughter and many lesser offenses. The corporation timely appealed.

The corporation raises ten appellate issues [including]: Did the trial court deprive the corporation of its constitutional rights to present its defense by excluding exhibits as irrelevant?

[T]he corporation claims the trial court deprived it of a fair trial by excluding certain expert testimony. The trial court prohibited David L. Westol, an expert on collegiate fraternities, from testifying that the corporation met the national standard of care by promulgating and enforcing an anti-hazing policy. The corporation argues that decision was incorrect.

Such an argument disregards our deferential standard of review for a trial court's evidentiary rulings. When reviewing a decision to admit or to exclude expert opinion testimony, we use an abuse-of-discretion standard. Abuse of discretion only "occurs if the trial court renders a judgment that is manifestly unreasonable, arbitrary or capricious; that fails to apply the law; or that is motivated by partiality, prejudice, bias or ill-will." In other words, a reasonable judgment by the trial court is not an abuse of discretion, even if this Court disagrees with that judgment.

The trial court's opinion rejecting Mr. Westol's opinion testimony on the national standard of care is firmly rooted in the Rules of Evidence, the criminal law, and our appellate precedents. The court's analysis is quite reasonable and does not misapply or override the law.

Because the prosecution's theory as to this corporation's guilt rested entirely upon its vicarious liability for its agents' misconduct, we cannot say that the trial court abused its discretion in excluding the expert's opinion on the standard of care. "Corporations are criminally accountable for the actions of a 'high managerial agent' who commits a wrongdoing in the scope of his office. This corporate accountability is based upon a simple principal/agency relationship and not upon a corporation affirming the officer's act."

Thus, the instant corporation would be vicariously liable for everything that the [chapter]'s officers and the national president did in furtherance of the new-member-education program and its initiations rituals, regardless of whether the corporation met the national standard of care by disavowing hazing. To the extent that the local and national officers committed any crimes in causing the death of this associate member, so did the corporation, i.e., the principle whose interests all of the agents/officers were pursuing when they physically assaulted the freshman and tried to hide their crimes.

> Even if the corporation's anti-hazing policy and training met the national standard of care for all Greek-lettered organizations, meeting industry standards will not excuse involuntary manslaughter, hazing, and the other crimes for which the jury convicted this corporation, when 'high managerial agents' committed those crimes specifically as part of the rites and rituals for imitation into the corporation's membership. Moreover, if the officers of the Baruch [chapter] and the national president met the national standard of care and this associate member died anyway, then Greek Life certainly needs to raise its national standards. If, on the other hand, their conduct did not meet the national standard of care by their conduct, then the corporation, vicariously speaking, did not meet it, as well. Either way, the opinion testimony that the corporation met the national standard of care was of no relevance to the ultimate issue of the corporation's criminal culpability.
>
> Thus, the trial court was well within its sphere of discretion in deeming Mr. Westol's opinion on the corporation's conformity to the national standard of care irrelevant in a criminal trial. Accordingly, we dismiss [this] appellate issue as meritless.
>
> [Judgment affirmed in part and reversed in part; remanded for re-sentencing. Three fraternity members received prison sentences; fourteen others received probation. The corporation received a large fine. Baruch College permanently barred the fraternity from operating on campus. The student's family separately sued the fraternity and several individuals including the organization's founder for wrongful death and other torts.]

Sentencing

Conviction of a crime leads to punishment. A corporation cannot be put in jail (although directors, officers, employees, and agents who committed the crime can be imprisoned). The range of punishments that may be given to a business are different from those that would apply to a human being. The sentence against a company may include fines, restitution, probation, confiscation of property, or involuntary dissolution of the organization.

Fines: Criminal statutes often provide for monetary fines as punishment. These laws include a maximum amount for that fine. The judge sentencing the corporation may be given a great deal of discretion in determining the exact amount that the company will be required to pay.

The Federal Sentencing Guidelines for Organizations (FSGO) set standards for corporate criminal fines. The fine imposed is based on the severity of the offense. The fined organization pays the fine amount to the government entity that brought charges against the corporation.

> Many government agencies may bring enforcement actions against corporations. The Environmental Protection Agency pursues polluting companies, for example, and the Securities and Exchange Commission goes after companies that commit securities fraud.

Restitution: Monetary restitution (compensation) is ordered to pay the victims of a crime for the losses they have sustained. Unlike a fine, restitution is to go directly to the victims, rather than to the government. When it is imposed, restitution may be in addition to any fine or other penalty.

RESTITUTION:
Money paid by a defendant to repay a victim's loss.

Probation: Probation may be imposed instead of, or in addition to, a fine or other penalty. Probation is designed to ensure that the corporation complies with all court orders and conditions of the sentence. Some of these conditions may include instituting a corporate compliance program, publicizing the conviction, undergoing regular audits, or engaging in community service. A term of probation may also include a prohibition against conducting certain types of business, or against contracting with the government.

> A corporation may mitigate its sentence by having a compliance and ethics program in place prior to any investigations.

Confiscation of Property: Forfeiture statutes allow the government to take any property used in the commission of a crime. The proceeds of a crime are also subject to forfeiture.

Involuntary Dissolution: Involuntary dissolution can force a company to close its doors. Companies are established at the state level. Dissolution occurs when a state's secretary of state believes sufficient reason exists to terminate a company's business operations. If the secretary of state believes that a company's directors have abused their power, the state can force the company to close.

For federal crimes involving business entities, courts look to the Federal Sentencing Guidelines for Organizations. The guidelines (abbreviated as "FSGO") are maintained by the U.S. Sentencing Commission, a government agency.

When a company is convicted or admits to a federal crime, sentencing will involve FSGO standards. Companies receive more favorable sentencing treatment if they can show that they observe the best practices recommended by the FSGO. Two fundamental standards are having an effective compliance program and an ethical corporate culture. The FSGO set forth seven "pillars" of an effective compliance program. Having these items in place prior to a criminal accusation—and cooperating with authorities—can greatly reduce the consequences for a company facing federal charges.

CHAPTER SUMMARY

As an old radio program said, "The weed of crime bears bitter fruit." Criminal law is the government's way of protecting us from bad actors and punishing those who harm others.

Example: TravelsOn Airways uses one of its aircraft to smuggle drugs into the U.S. The company is convicted of conspiracy and smuggling, and ordered to pay a fine. TravelsOn is also ordered to forfeit its airplane, and to forfeit all of the profits earned from smuggling drugs into the U.S.

Criminal law is about more than violent crime. More and more, criminal law is about misconduct by businesses. A corporation that commits a crime is subject to punishment, even though that punishment may not take the same form as that given to an individual.

The power to protect is not absolute. Constitutional limitations restrict what the government may do when investigating or punishing criminal activity. Criminal law thus protects us not just from criminals, but from those who would go too far in pursuing them.

CAREERS IN THE LAW

If you are interested in preventing crime, many career options await you. The most obvious example is a career in law enforcement. Police are the front line in preventing and investigating crime at every level. The education required can vary depending on the department, with many asking for an associate's or bachelor's degree before police training. Another law enforcement option is to seek a job at the federal level. A Special Agent for the Federal Bureau of Investigation must have a bachelor's degree and complete rigorous physical training. For this role and other FBI options, visit fbijobs.gov. Because many state and federal government agencies enforce legal rules, you might be interested in a job auditing, investigating, or analyzing wrongdoing. An informational interview with an agency employee can provide insight. At the state level, search for your state's name and "jobs" to see the variety of options open to enthusiastic and qualified workers.

Review Questions

Review question 1.

What is *mens rea*? What are the two types of intent and how do they differ? What types of crimes are related to each type of intent? Under what circumstances is intent irrelevant to criminal responsibility?

Review question 2.

How does *mens rea* differ from *actus reus*? How are both important to establishing criminal liability?

Review question 3.

How do legal definitions of crime express the *mens rea* and *actus rea* requirements? How are those requirements used in jury instructions? What is the jury's responsibility with regard to the elements of a crime? What standard must the prosecution reach on a crime's elements to achieve a conviction?

Review question 4.
What is the difference between a felony and a misdemeanor? How do sentences for each differ? Are most crimes defined at the state or federal level? Why?

Review question 5.
How does the Constitution protect us against overreach in search and seizure? What is a warrant, and when is it required? What are some of the exceptions to the warrant requirement? How do search rules apply to digital information?

Review question 6.
What is an inchoate crime? Is there a difference between an inchoate crime and an attempted crime? What is necessary for a conspiracy to become a crime? Why do we punish "incomplete" crimes?

Review question 7.
What are the differences between sentences for corporations and organizations and those for individuals? What are the Federal Sentencing Guidelines for Organizations? What tips do those Guidelines offer for reducing potential sentences? What federal criminal law leads to particularly high fines against companies? Why do judges have discretion in determining sentences for those convicted of crimes?

Review question 8.
When can a corporation be held criminally responsible? If only one person is responsible for a company's criminal act, did that person also act criminally? Are there limits to the types of crimes that a corporation can be prosecuted for?

Review question 9.
What is embezzlement? How does it differ from other types of theft? Is it still embezzlement if the person taking the funds just "borrows" the money with the intent to replace it?

Review question 10.
When is insider trading unlawful? Who is an "insider"? When may an insider act despite having special knowledge about a company or transaction? Why does the law bar insider trading? At what point is information no longer considered "inside"?

Review question 11.

What is antitrust law? How does it benefit people? What are some examples of antitrust violations?

Review question 12.

Who may be held responsible for employing undocumented workers? What enforcement body investigates potential violations of the Immigration Reform and Control Act?

Review question 13.

What type of organizations were targeted by the Racketeer Influenced and Corrupt Organizations Act? Is RICO limited in the type of organizations that can be pursued under the law?

Review question 14.

What does the Foreign Corrupt Practices Act prohibit? Can the FCPA be enforced for actions outside the U.S.? What is notable about the penalties for companies under the FCPA?

Review question 15.

What individuals and roles are critical to holding an entire organization criminally liable for actions? What is necessary to show that criminal activity was on behalf of the organization?

Discussion Questions

Question 1:

Betty works as a bookkeeper for a corporation. One day, she tells her boss, Carlos, that she is short of money. Carlos says, "Just do what I used to do. Every now and then, cut yourself a company check. No one will care, as long as you don't make the checks too big." Betty starts writing herself a check for $25 each week.

> Is Betty guilty of embezzlement? Why or why not?

> Is there a conspiracy between Betty and Carlos? Why or why not?

> Suppose Betty makes out the first check, but takes it home with her overnight because her bank is not open. Is Betty guilty of an attempted crime? Why or why not?
>
> What if Betty takes home the first check, then has second thoughts and tears it up?

Question 2:

Sheriff Omar believes that Edgar is using or trafficking in marijuana, but has been unable to find any proof, beyond smelling marijuana smoke whenever Edgar is nearby. Omar asks two of Edgar's neighbors if they know anything about his marijuana use. The neighbors say that they have seen marijuana plants growing in Edgar's basement, and that they bought marijuana from him. In reality, neither neighbor has ever been in Edgar's house, and they are just trying to get even with him for a property dispute. Omar puts the information from the neighbors in a search warrant application that he presents to Leigh, the county judge. Leigh approves the warrant. Omar then orders a team of his deputies to execute the warrant. The deputies go to Edgar's house and search it. They find a small amount of marijuana. One of the deputies sees two handguns on a coffee table. The deputy seizes those guns, and later learns that they were stolen from a gun shop.

> Is the search warrant valid? Why or why not?
>
> Will the exclusionary rule prevent using the marijuana as evidence at trial? Why or why not?
>
> Will the exclusionary rule prevent using the handguns as evidence at trial? Why or why not?

Question 3:

Gil is a paralegal working for a publicly-traded corporation, and his girlfriend, Bertha, is a computer technician for the same company. Gil learns that the corporation they work for could be a target of a takeover attempt by a hedge fund. He and Bertha discuss the matter, and come to the conclusion that the value of the stock in their employer would increase dramatically if a takeover bid were made. They decide to buy stock in the company. In order to stay anonymous, Gil enlists his roommate Pete to make the purchases with money supplied by Gil and Bertha. Gil and Bertha do not tell him why they are buying the stock now. Pete puts the money in his bank account, planning to open an online brokerage account to make the purchase. After making the deposit, but before opening the account, Pete suffers a heart attack while sitting at his desk. He is taken to the hospital and does not make the purchases.

> Were Gil and Bertha insiders? Why or why not?
>
> Was Pete an insider? Why or why not?
>
> Was there a conspiracy? Why or why not? If this took place in a jurisdiction that requires an overt act for a conspiracy, identify the overt act.
>
> Assume Gil and Bertha are insiders. Are they guilty of attempted insider trading? Why or why not?

Question 4:

David does the accounting for his employer, Avaricia, Inc. Sheila, the CEO of Avaricia, tells him that the company needs to get a loan, but the bank does not feel that Avaricia has enough revenue coming in to make the payments. Sheila asks David to prepare a series of false invoices and receipts to present to the bank. David agrees, and prepares the false documents. Sheila then puts them in the mail to the bank, and also sends copies via fax. The bank approves the loan.

> Identify the crimes that may have been committed in this scenario. Explain why you believe those crimes could have been committed.
>
> Could Avaricia be held criminally liable in this situation? Why or why not?

Question 5:

Carla is browsing in a clothing store. The only other person there is Emma, a sales clerk. Emma has a large stack of clothes that she is putting on the rack. She decides she likes one of the blouses she is hanging up, and puts in under her arm to take it home. Emma sees Carla watching her, and says "I have it coming. They treat me like dirt here. In fact, I quit! Help yourself to whatever you like," and walks out of the store with the blouse. Carla takes a few seconds to process what happened. She picks up a blouse from the rack and runs out the door with it, but drops it on her way out of the building.

Is Emma guilty of embezzlement? Why or why not?

Is Carla guilty of an attempted crime? Is she guilty of attempted embezzlement? Why or why not?

Unbeknownst to Carla, the owner of the store was giving away all of the inventory because she was about to close the business down. Is Carla guilty of an attempted theft? Why or why not?

Question 6:

Sure-enough Co. wants to expand its operations to include a manufacturing facility in the country of Desmia. It believes it will benefit from access to natural materials and lower wage costs. Desmia is also a good retail market for the company's products. Sure-enough sends its president to Desmia, where she meets a translator who will help her with the necessary transactions. The first thing that Sure-enough needs is a business license in Desmia. At the government office for the license, the translator suggests an extra payment to the official to ensure the license is approved. The president does not understand this conversation, but pays the amount of money the translator relays to her.

Is the payment a violation of the Foreign Corrupt Practices Act? Why or why not?

Does it matter that the president could not understand the conversation?

Can the translator be considered an agent of Sure-enough? Does that matter for the FCPA?

Question 7:

A scooter manufacturer is based in a state where there is a crime of "reckless involuntary manslaughter." The crime's elements are that the defendant is aware of the risk of death to another person from an action, but the defendant acts anyway. The manufacturer is making a limited edition scooter with specialized features. Three different prototypes swerve and catch fire during testing. The company's CEO decides to release the edition anyway because "these are just for publicity."

Suppose someone riding one of the scooters dies after the scooter swerves into traffic. Who, if anyone, can be prosecuted for the death?

Is there any difference in the outcome if the chief engineer knew of the problem but hid that information?

What other potential lawsuits might arise?

Question 8:

You are on a jury in a criminal fraud trial. One of the elements of the crime is that the defendant's purpose in misrepresenting the facts was to convince people to give him money or property. The defendant testifies that he just wanted people to like him, so he made up stories. Some people did give the defendant money and property, but none of them convinced you that the lies and those gifts were connected. None of the evidence proved to you that the defendant asked for money or property.

Without this element, can the jury convict the defendant? Why or why not?

Suppose you think that the defendant might have intended to convince people to give him property and money. What standard should be applied to deciding whether or not that was his intention?

Suppose instead that the defendant says that he asked for help with his rent once, but he was not thinking clearly because his dog knocked him over and he hit his head. The dog is pretty big, so it seems possible, but unlikely. How do you draw the line on "doubt" when considering a criminal act?

APPENDICES

1. Constitution of the United States

CONSTITUTION OF THE UNITED STATES

Preamble

We the People of the United States, in Order to form a more perfect Union, establish Justice, insure domestic Tranquility, provide for the common defense, promote the general Welfare, and secure the Blessings of Liberty to ourselves and our Posterity, do ordain and establish this Constitution for the United States of America.

Article I

SECTION 1. All legislative Powers herein granted shall be vested in a Congress of the United States, which shall consist of a Senate and House of Representatives.

SECTION 2. The House of Representatives shall be composed of Members chosen every second Year by the People of the several States, and the Electors in each State shall have the Qualifications requisite for Electors of the most numerous Branch of the State Legislature.

No Person shall be a Representative who shall not have attained to the Age of twenty five Years, and been seven Years a Citizen of the United States, and who shall not, when elected, be an Inhabitant of that State in which he shall be chosen.

Representatives and direct Taxes shall be apportioned among the several States which may be included within this Union, according to their respective Numbers, which shall be determined by adding to the whole Number of free Persons, including those bound to Service for a Term of Years, and excluding Indians not taxed, three fifths of all other Persons. The actual Enumeration shall be made within three Years after the first Meeting of the Congress of the United States, and within every subsequent Term of ten Years, in such Manner as they shall by Law direct. The Number of Representatives shall not exceed one for every thirty Thousand, but each State shall have at Least one Representative; and until such enumeration shall be made, the State of New Hampshire shall be entitled to chuse three, Massachusetts eight, Rhode-Island and Providence Plantations one, Connecticut five, New-York six, New Jersey four, Pennsylvania eight, Delaware one, Maryland six, Virginia ten, North Carolina five, South Carolina five, and Georgia three.

When vacancies happen in the Representation from any State, the Executive Authority thereof shall issue Writs of Election to fill such Vacancies.

The House of Representatives shall chuse their Speaker and other Officers; and shall have the sole Power of Impeachment.

SECTION 3. The Senate of the United States shall be composed of two Senators from each State, chosen by the Legislature thereof, for six Years; and each Senator shall have one Vote.

Immediately after they shall be assembled in Consequence of the first Election, they shall be divided as equally as may be into three Classes. The Seats of the Senators of the first Class shall be vacated at the Expiration of the second Year, of the second Class at the Expiration of the fourth Year, and of the third Class at the Expiration of the sixth Year, so that one third may be chosen every second Year; and if Vacancies happen by Resignation, or otherwise, during the Recess of the Legislature of any State, the Executive thereof may make temporary Appointments until the next Meeting of the Legislature, which shall then fill such Vacancies.

No Person shall be a Senator who shall not have attained to the Age of thirty Years, and been nine Years a Citizen of the United States, and who shall not, when elected, be an Inhabitant of that State for which he shall be chosen.

The Vice President of the United States shall be President of the Senate, but shall have no Vote, unless they be equally divided.

The Senate shall chuse their other Officers, and also a President pro tempore, in the Absence of the Vice President, or when he shall exercise the Office of President of the United States.

The Senate shall have the sole Power to try all Impeachments. When sitting for that Purpose, they shall be on Oath or Affirmation. When the President of the United States is tried, the Chief Justice shall preside: And no Person shall be convicted without the Concurrence of two thirds of the Members present.

Judgment in Cases of Impeachment shall not extend further than to removal from Office, and disqualification to hold and enjoy any Office of honor, Trust or Profit under the United States: but the Party convicted shall nevertheless be liable and subject to Indictment, Trial, Judgment and Punishment, according to Law.

SECTION 4. The Times, Places and Manner of holding Elections for Senators and Representatives, shall be prescribed in each State by the Legislature thereof; but the Congress may at any time by Law make or alter such Regulations, except as to the Places of chusing Senators.

The Congress shall assemble at least once in every Year, and such Meeting shall *be on the first Monday in December*, unless they shall by Law appoint a different Day.

SECTION 5. Each House shall be the Judge of the Elections, Returns and Qualifications of its own Members, and a Majority of each shall constitute a Quorum to do Business; but a smaller Number may adjourn from day to day, and may be authorized to compel the Attendance of absent Members, in such Manner, and under such Penalties as each House may provide.

Each House may determine the Rules of its Proceedings, punish its Members for disorderly Behaviour, and, with the Concurrence of two thirds, expel a Member.

Each House shall keep a Journal of its Proceedings, and from time to time publish the same, excepting such Parts as may in their Judgment require Secrecy; and the Yeas and Nays of the Members of either House on any question shall, at the Desire of one fifth of those Present, be entered on the Journal.

Neither House, during the Session of Congress, shall, without the Consent of the other, adjourn for more than three days, nor to any other

Place than that in which the two Houses shall be sitting.

SECTION 6. The Senators and Representatives shall receive a Compensation for their Services, to be ascertained by Law, and paid out of the Treasury of the United States. They shall in all Cases, except Treason, Felony and Breach of the Peace, be privileged from Arrest during their Attendance at the Session of their respective Houses, and in going to and returning from the same; and for any Speech or Debate in either House, they shall not be questioned in any other Place.

No Senator or Representative shall, during the Time for which he was elected, be appointed to any civil Office under the Authority of the United States, which shall have been created, or the Emoluments whereof shall have been encreased during such time; and no Person holding any Office under the United States, shall be a Member of either House during his Continuance in Office.

SECTION 7. All Bills for raising Revenue shall originate in the House of Representatives; but the Senate may propose or concur with Amendments as on other Bills.

Every Bill which shall have passed the House of Representatives and the Senate, shall, before it become a Law, be presented to the President of the United States: If he approve he shall sign it, but if not he shall return it, with his Objections to that House in which it shall have originated, who shall enter the Objections at large on their Journal, and proceed to reconsider it. If after such Reconsideration two thirds of that House shall agree to pass the Bill, it shall be sent, together with the Objections, to the other House, by which it shall likewise be reconsidered, and if approved by two thirds of that House, it shall become a Law. But in all such Cases the Votes of both Houses shall be determined by Yeas and Nays, and the Names of the Persons voting for and against the Bill shall be entered on the Journal of each House respectively. If any Bill shall not be returned by the President within ten Days (Sundays excepted) after it shall have been presented to him, the Same shall be a Law, in like Manner as if he had signed it, unless the Congress by their Adjournment prevent its Return, in which Case it shall not be a Law.

Every Order, Resolution, or Vote to which the Concurrence of the Senate and House of Representatives may be necessary (except on a question of Adjournment) shall be presented to the President of the United States; and before the Same shall take Effect, shall be approved by him, or being disapproved by him, shall be repassed by two thirds of the Senate and House of Representatives, according to the Rules and Limitations prescribed in the Case of a Bill.

SECTION 8. The Congress shall have Power To lay and collect Taxes, Duties, Imposts and Excises, to pay the Debts and provide for the common Defence and general Welfare of the United States; but all Duties, Imposts and Excises shall be uniform throughout the United States;

To borrow Money on the credit of the United States;

To regulate Commerce with foreign Nations, and among the several States, and with the Indian Tribes;

To establish an uniform Rule of Naturalization, and uniform Laws on the subject of Bankruptcies throughout the United States;

To coin Money, regulate the Value thereof, and of foreign Coin, and fix the Standard of Weights and Measures;

To provide for the Punishment of counterfeiting the Securities and current Coin of the United States;

To establish Post Offices and post Roads;

To promote the Progress of Science and useful Arts, by securing for limited Times to Authors and Inventors the exclusive Right to their respective Writings and Discoveries;

To constitute Tribunals inferior to the supreme Court;

To define and punish Piracies and Felonies committed on the high Seas, and Offences against the Law of Nations;

To declare War, grant Letters of Marque and Reprisal, and make Rules concerning Captures on Land and Water;

To raise and support Armies, but no Appropriation of Money to that Use shall be for a longer Term than two Years;

To provide and maintain a Navy;

To make Rules for the Government and Regulation of the land and naval Forces;

To provide for calling forth the Militia to execute the Laws of the Union, suppress Insurrections and repel Invasions;

To provide for organizing, arming, and disciplining, the Militia, and for governing such Part of them as may be employed in the Service of the United States, reserving to the States respectively, the Appointment of the Officers, and the Authority of training the Militia according to the discipline prescribed by Congress;

To exercise exclusive Legislation in all Cases whatsoever, over such District (not exceeding ten Miles square) as may, by Cession of particular States, and the Acceptance of Congress, become the Seat of the Government of the United States, and to exercise like Authority over all Places purchased by the Consent of the Legislature of the State in which the Same shall be, for the Erection of Forts, Magazines, Arsenals, dock-Yards, and other needful Buildings;—And

To make all Laws which shall be necessary and proper for carrying into Execution the foregoing Powers, and all other Powers vested by this Constitution in the Government of the United States, or in any Department or Officer thereof.

SECTION 9. The Migration or Importation of such Persons as any of the States now existing shall think proper to admit, shall not be prohibited by the Congress prior to the Year one thousand eight hundred and eight, but a Tax or duty may be imposed on such Importation, not exceeding ten dollars for each Person.

The Privilege of the Writ of Habeas Corpus shall not be suspended, unless when in Cases of Rebellion or Invasion the public Safety may require it.

No Bill of Attainder or ex post facto Law shall be passed.

No Capitation, or other direct, Tax shall be laid, unless in Proportion to the Census or enumeration herein before directed to be taken.

No Tax or Duty shall be laid on Articles exported from any State.

No Preference shall be given by any Regulation of Commerce or Revenue to the Ports of one State over those of another; nor shall Vessels bound to, or from, one State, be obliged to enter, clear, or pay Duties in another.

No Money shall be drawn from the Treasury, but in Consequence of Appropriations made by Law; and a regular Statement and Account of the Receipts and Expenditures of all public Money shall be published from time to time.

No Title of Nobility shall be granted by the United States: And no Person holding any Office of Profit or Trust under them, shall, without the Consent of the Congress, accept of any present, Emolument, Office, or Title, of any kind whatever, from any King, Prince, or foreign State.

SECTION 10. No State shall enter into any Treaty, Alliance, or Confederation; grant Letters of Marque and Reprisal; coin Money; emit Bills of Credit; make any Thing but gold and silver Coin a Tender in Payment of Debts; pass any Bill of Attainder, ex post facto Law, or Law impairing the Obligation of Contracts, or grant any Title of Nobility.

No State shall, without the Consent of the Congress, lay any Imposts or Duties on Imports or Exports, except what may be absolutely necessary for executing its inspection Laws: and the net Produce of all Duties and Imposts, laid by any State on Imports or Exports, shall be for the Use of the Treasury of the United States; and all such Laws shall be subject to the Revision and Control of the Congress.

No State shall, without the Consent of Congress, lay any Duty of Tonnage, keep Troops, or Ships of War in time of Peace, enter into any Agreement or Compact with another State, or with a foreign Power, or engage in War, unless actually invaded, or in such imminent Danger as will not admit of delay.

Article II

SECTION 1. The executive Power shall be vested in a President of the United States of America. He shall hold his Office during the Term of four Years, and, together with the Vice President, chosen for the same Term, be elected, as follows:

Each State shall appoint, in such Manner as the Legislature thereof may direct, a Number of Electors, equal to the whole Number of Senators and Representatives to which the State may be entitled in the Congress: but no Senator or Representative, or Person holding an Office of Trust or Profit under the United States, shall be appointed an Elector.

The Electors shall meet in their respective States, and vote by Ballot for two Persons, of whom one at least shall not be an Inhabitant of the same State with themselves. And they shall make a List of all the Persons voted for, and of the Number of Votes for each; which List they shall sign and certify, and transmit sealed to the Seat of the Government of the United States, directed to the President of the Senate. The President of the Senate shall, in the Presence of the Senate and House of Representatives, open all the Certificates, and the Votes shall then be counted. The Person having the greatest Number of Votes shall be the President, if such Number be a Majority of the whole Number of Electors appointed; and if there be more than one who have such Majority, and have an equal Number of Votes, then the House of Representatives shall immediately chuse by Ballot one of them for President; and if no Person have a Majority, then from the five highest on the List the said House shall in like Manner chuse the President. But in chusing the President, the Votes shall be taken by States, the Representatives from each State having one Vote; a quorum for this Purpose shall consist of a Member or Members from two thirds of the States, and a Majority of all the States shall be necessary to a Choice. In every Case, after the Choice of the President, the Person having the greatest Number of Votes of the Electors shall be the Vice President. But if there should remain two or more who have equal Votes, the Senate shall chuse from them by Ballot the Vice-President.

The Congress may determine the Time of chusing the Electors, and the Day on which they shall give their Votes; which Day shall be the same throughout the United States.

No Person except a natural born Citizen, or a Citizen of the United States, at the time of the Adoption of this Constitution, shall be eligible to the Office of President; neither shall any person be eligible to that Office who shall not have attained to the Age of thirty five Years, and been fourteen Years a Resident within the United States.

In Case of the Removal of the President from Office, or of his Death, Resignation, or Inability to discharge the Powers and Duties of the said Office, the Same shall devolve on the Vice President, and the Congress may by Law provide for the Case of Removal, Death, Resignation or Inability, both of the President and Vice President, declaring what Officer shall then act as President, and such Officer shall act accordingly, until the Disability be removed, or a President shall be elected.

The President shall, at stated Times, receive for his Services, a Compensation, which shall neither be encreased nor diminished during the Period for which he shall have been elected, and he shall not receive within that Period any other Emolument from the United States, or any of them.

Before he enter on the Execution of his Office, he shall take the following Oath or Affirmation:—"I do solemnly swear (or affirm) that I will faithfully execute the Office of President of the United States, and will to the best of my Ability, preserve, protect and defend the Constitution of the United States."

SECTION 2. The President shall be Commander in Chief of the Army and Navy of the United States, and of the Militia of the several States, when called into the actual Service of the United States; he may require the Opinion, in writing, of the principal Officer in each of the executive Departments, upon any Subject relating to the Duties of their respective Offices, and he shall have Power to Grant Reprieves and Pardons for Offences against the United States, except in Cases of Impeachment.

He shall have Power, by and with the Advice and Consent of the Senate, to make Treaties, provided two thirds of the Senators present concur; and he shall nominate, and by and with the Advice and Consent of the Senate, shall appoint Ambassadors, other public Ministers and Consuls, Judges of the supreme Court, and all other Officers of the United States, whose Appointments are not herein otherwise provided for, and which shall be established by Law: but the Congress may by Law vest the Appointment of such inferior Officers, as they think proper, in the President alone, in the Courts of Law, or in the Heads of Departments.

The President shall have Power to fill up all Vacancies that may happen during the Recess of the Senate, by granting Commissions which shall expire at the End of their next Session.

SECTION 3. He shall from time to time give to the Congress Information on the State of the Union, and recommend to their Consideration such Measures as he shall judge necessary and expedient; he may, on extraordinary Occasions, convene both Houses, or either of them, and in Case of Disagreement between them, with Respect to the Time of Adjournment, he may adjourn them to such Time as he shall think proper; he shall receive Ambassadors and other public Ministers; he shall take Care that the Laws be faithfully executed, and shall Commission all the Officers of the United States.

SECTION 4. The President, Vice President and all Civil Officers of the United States, shall be removed from Office on Impeachment for, and Conviction of, Treason, Bribery, or other high Crimes and Misdemeanors.

Article III

SECTION 1. The judicial Power of the United States, shall be vested in one supreme Court, and in such inferior Courts as the Congress may from time to time ordain and establish. The Judges, both of the supreme and inferior Courts, shall hold their Offices during good Behaviour, and shall, at stated Times, receive for their Services, a Compensation, which shall not be diminished during their Continuance in Office.

SECTION 2. The judicial Power shall extend to all Cases, in Law and Equity, arising under this Constitution, the Laws of the United States, and Treaties made, or which shall be made, under their Authority;—to all Cases affecting Ambassadors, other public ministers and Consuls;—to all Cases of admiralty and maritime Jurisdiction;—to Controversies to which the United States shall be a Party;—to Controversies between two or more States;—between a State and Citizens of another State;—between Citizens of different States;—between Citizens of the same State claiming Lands under Grants of different States, and between a State, or the Citizens thereof, and foreign States, Citizens or Subjects.

In all Cases affecting Ambassadors, other public Ministers and Consuls, and those in which a State shall be Party, the supreme Court shall have original Jurisdiction. In all the other Cases before mentioned, the supreme Court shall have appellate Jurisdiction, both as to Law and Fact, with such Exceptions, and under such Regulations as the Congress shall make.

The Trial of all Crimes, except in Cases of Impeachment, shall be by Jury; and such Trial shall be held in the State where the said Crimes shall have been committed; but when not committed within any State, the Trial shall be at such Place or Places as the Congress may by Law have directed.

SECTION 3. Treason against the United States, shall consist only in levying War against them, or in adhering to their Enemies, giving them Aid and Comfort. No Person shall be convicted of Treason unless on the Testimony of two Witnesses to the same overt Act, or on Confession in open Court.

The Congress shall have Power to declare the Punishment of Treason, but no Attainder of Treason shall work Corruption of Blood, or Forfeiture except during the Life of the Person attainted.

Article IV

SECTION 1. Full Faith and Credit shall be given in each State to the public Acts, Records, and judicial Proceedings of every other State. And the Congress may by general Laws prescribe the Manner in which such Acts, Records and Proceedings shall be proved, and the Effect thereof.

SECTION 2. The Citizens of each State shall be entitled to all Privileges and Immunities of Citizens in the several States.

A Person charged in any State with Treason, Felony, or other Crime, who shall flee from Justice, and be found in another State, shall on Demand of the executive Authority of the State from which he fled, be delivered up, to be removed to the State having Jurisdiction of the Crime.

No Person held to Service or Labour in one State, under the Laws thereof, escaping into another, shall, in Consequence of any Law or Regulation therein, be discharged from such Service or Labour, but shall be delivered up on Claim of the Party to whom such Service or Labour may be due.

SECTION 3. New States may be admitted by the Congress into this Union; but no new State shall be formed or erected within the Jurisdiction of any other State; nor any State be formed by the Junction of two or more States, or Parts of States, without the Consent of the Legislatures of the States concerned as well as of the Congress.

The Congress shall have Power to dispose of and make all needful Rules and Regulations respecting the Territory or other Property belonging to the United States; and nothing in this Constitution shall be so construed as to Prejudice any Claims of the United States, or of any particular State.

SECTION 4. The United States shall guarantee to every State in this Union a Republican Form of Government, and shall protect each of them against Invasion; and on Application of the Legislature, or of the Executive (when the Legislature cannot be convened) against domestic Violence.

Article V

The Congress, whenever two thirds of both Houses shall deem it necessary, shall propose Amendments to this Constitution, or, on the Application of the Legislatures of two thirds of the several States, shall call a Convention for proposing Amendments, which, in either Case, shall be valid to all Intents and Purposes, as Part of this Constitution, when ratified by the Legislatures of three fourths of the several States, or by Conventions in three fourths thereof, as the one or the other Mode of Ratification may be proposed by the Congress; Provided that no Amendment which may be made prior to the Year One thousand eight hundred and eight shall in any Manner affect the first and fourth Clauses in the Ninth Section of the first Article; and that no State, without its Consent, shall be deprived of its equal Suffrage in the Senate.

Article VI

All Debts contracted and Engagements entered into, before the Adoption of this Constitution, shall be as valid against the United States under this Constitution, as under the Confederation.

This Constitution, and the Laws of the United States which shall be made in Pursuance thereof; and all Treaties made, or which shall be made, under the Authority of the United States, shall be the supreme Law of the Land; and the Judges in every State shall be bound thereby, any Thing in the Constitution or Laws of any state to the Contrary notwithstanding.

The Senators and Representatives before mentioned, and the Members of the several State Legislatures, and all executive and judicial Officers, both of the United States and of the several States, shall be bound by Oath or Affirmation, to support this Constitution; but no religious Test shall ever be required as a Qualification to any Office or public Trust under the United States.

Article VII

The Ratification of the Conventions of nine States, shall be sufficient for the Establishment of this Constitution between the States so ratifying the Same.

2. **Amendments to the Constitution**

AMENDMENTS

Amendment I (1791)

Congress shall make no law respecting an establishment of religion, or prohibiting the free exercise thereof; or abridging the freedom of speech, or of the press; or the right of the people peaceably to assemble, and to petition the Government for a redress of grievances.

Amendment II (1791)

A well regulated Militia, being necessary to the security of a free State, the right of the people to keep and bear Arms, shall not be infringed.

Amendment III (1791)

No Soldier shall, in time of peace be quartered in any house, without the consent of the Owner, nor in time of war, but in a manner to be prescribed by law.

Amendment IV (1791)

The right of the people to be secure in their persons, houses, papers, and effects, against unreasonable searches and seizures, shall not be violated, and no Warrants shall issue, but upon probable cause, supported by Oath or affirmation, and particularly describing the place to be searched, and the persons or things to be seized.

Amendment V (1791)

No person shall be held to answer for a capital, or otherwise infamous crime, unless on a presentment or indictment of a Grand Jury, except in cases arising in the land or naval forces, or in the Militia, when in actual service in time of War or public danger; nor shall any person be subject for the same offence to be twice put in jeopardy of life or limb; nor shall be compelled in any criminal case to be a witness against himself, nor be deprived of life, liberty, or property, without due process of law; nor shall private property be taken for public use, without just compensation.

Amendment VI (1791)

In all criminal prosecutions, the accused shall enjoy the right to a speedy and public trial, by an impartial jury of the State and district wherein the crime shall have been committed, which district shall have been previously ascertained by law, and to be informed of the nature and cause of the accusation; to be confronted with the witnesses against him; to have compulsory process for obtaining witnesses in his favor, and to have the Assistance of Counsel for his defence.

Amendment VII (1791)

In Suits at common law, where the value in controversy shall exceed twenty dollars, the right of trial by jury shall be preserved, and no fact tried by a jury, shall be otherwise re-examined in any Court of the United States, than according to the rules of the common law.

Amendment VIII (1791)

Excessive bail shall not be required, nor excessive fines imposed, nor cruel and unusual punishments inflicted.

Amendment IX (1791)

The enumeration in the Constitution, of certain rights, shall not be construed to deny or disparage others retained by the people.

Amendment X (1791)

The powers not delegated to the United States by the Constitution, nor prohibited by it to the States, are reserved to the States respectively, or to the people.

Amendment XI (1795/1798)

The Judicial power of the United States shall not be construed to extend to any suit in law or equity, commenced or prosecuted against one of the United States by Citizens of another State, or by Citizens or Subjects of any Foreign State.

Amendment XII (1804)

The Electors shall meet in their respective states and vote by ballot for President and Vice-President, one of whom, at least, shall not be an inhabitant of the same state with themselves; they shall name in their ballots the person voted for as President, and in distinct ballots the person voted for as Vice-President, and they shall make distinct lists of all persons voted for as President, and of all persons voted for as Vice-President, and of the number of votes for each, which lists they shall sign and certify, and transmit sealed to the seat of the government of the United States, directed to the President of the Senate;—The President of the Senate shall, in the presence of the Senate and House of Representatives, open all the certificates and the votes shall then be counted;—The person having the greatest Number of votes for President, shall be the President, if such number be a majority of the whole number of Electors appointed; and if no person have such majority, then from the persons having the highest numbers not exceeding three on the list of those voted for as President, the House of Representatives shall choose immediately, by ballot, the President. But in choosing the President, the votes shall be taken by states, the representation from each state having one vote; a quorum for this purpose shall consist of a member or members from two-thirds of the states, and a majority of all the states shall be necessary to a choice. And if the House of Representatives shall not choose a President whenever the right of choice shall devolve upon them, before the fourth day of March next following, then the Vice-President shall act as President, as in the case of the death or other constitutional disability of the President—The person having the greatest number of votes as Vice-President, shall be the Vice-President, if such number be a majority of the whole number of Electors appointed, and if no person have a majority, then from the two highest numbers on the list, the Senate shall choose the Vice-President; a quorum for the purpose shall consist of two-thirds of the whole number of Senators, and a majority of the whole number shall be necessary to a choice. But no person constitutionally ineligible to the office of President shall be eligible to that of Vice-President of the United States.

Amendment XIII (1865)

Section 1. Neither slavery nor involuntary servitude, except as a punishment for crime whereof the party shall have been duly convicted, shall exist within the United States, or any place subject to their jurisdiction.

Section 2. Congress shall have power to enforce this article by appropriate legislation.

Amendment XIV (1868)

SECTION 1. All persons born or naturalized in the United States and subject to the jurisdiction thereof, are citizens of the United States and of the State wherein they reside. No State shall make or enforce any law which shall abridge the privileges or immunities of citizens of the United States; nor shall any State deprive any person of life, liberty, or property, without due process of law; nor deny to any person within its jurisdiction the equal protection of the laws.

SECTION 2. Representatives shall be apportioned among the several States according to their respective numbers, counting the whole number of persons in each State, excluding Indians not taxed. But when the right to vote at any election for the choice of electors for President and Vice President of the United States, Representatives in Congress, the Executive and Judicial officers of a State, or the members of the Legislature thereof, is denied to any of the male inhabitants of such State, being twenty-one years of age, and citizens of the United States, or in any way abridged, except for participation in rebellion, or other crime, the basis of representation therein shall be reduced in the proportion which the number of such male citizens shall bear to the whole number of male citizens twenty-one years of age in such State.

SECTION 3. No person shall be a Senator or Representative in Congress, or elector of President and Vice President, or hold any office, civil or military, under the United States, or under any State, who, having previously taken an oath, as a member of Congress, or as an officer of the United States, or as a member of any State legislature, or as an executive or judicial officer of any State, to support the Constitution of the United States, shall have engaged in insurrection or rebellion against the same, or given aid or comfort to the enemies thereof. But Congress may by a vote of two-thirds of each House, remove such disability.

SECTION 4. The validity of the public debt of the United States, authorized by law, including debts incurred for payment of pensions and bounties for services in suppressing insurrection or rebellion, shall not be questioned. But neither the United States nor any State shall assume or pay any debt or obligation incurred in aid of insurrection or rebellion against the United States, or any claim for the loss or emancipation of any slave; but all such debts, obligations and claims shall be held illegal and void.

SECTION 5. The Congress shall have power to enforce, by appropriate legislation, the provisions of this article.

Amendment XV (1870)

SECTION 1. The right of citizens of the United States to vote shall not be denied or abridged by the United States or by any State on account of race, color, or previous condition of servitude.

SECTION 2. The Congress shall have power to enforce this article by appropriate legislation.

Amendment XVI (1913)

The Congress shall have power to lay and collect taxes on incomes, from whatever source derived, without apportionment among the several States, and without regard to any census or enumeration.

Amendment XVII (1913)

The Senate of the United States shall be composed of two Senators from each State, elected by the people thereof, for six years; and each Senator shall have one vote. The electors in each State shall have the qualifications requisite for electors of the most numerous branch of the State legislatures.

When vacancies happen in the representation of any State in the Senate, the executive authority of such State shall issue writs of election to fill such vacancies: Provided, That the legislature of any State may empower the executive thereof to make temporary appointments until the people fill the vacancies by election as the legislature may direct.

This amendment shall not be so construed as to affect the election or term of any Senator chosen before it becomes valid as part of the Constitution.

Amendment XVIII (1919)

SECTION 1. After one year from the ratification of this article the manufacture, sale, or transportation of intoxicating liquors within, the importation thereof into, or the exportation thereof from the United States and all territory subject to the jurisdiction thereof for beverage purposes is hereby prohibited.

SECTION 2. The Congress and the several States shall have concurrent power to enforce this article by appropriate legislation.

SECTION 3. This article shall be inoperative unless it shall have been ratified as an amendment to the Constitution by the legislatures of the several States, as provided in the Constitution, within seven years from the date of the submission hereof to the States by the Congress.

Amendment XIX (1920)

The right of citizens of the United States to vote shall not be denied or abridged by the United States or by any State on account of sex.

Congress shall have power to enforce this article by appropriate legislation.

Amendment XX (1933)

SECTION 1. The terms of the President and Vice President shall end at noon on the 20th day of January, and the terms of Senators and Representatives at noon on the 3d day of January, of the years in which such terms would have ended if this article had not been ratified; and the terms of their successors shall then begin.

SECTION 2. The Congress shall assemble at least once in every year, and such meeting shall begin at noon on the 3d day of January, unless they shall by law appoint a different day.

SECTION 3. If, at the time fixed for the beginning of the term of the President, the President elect shall have died, the Vice President elect shall become President. If a President shall not have been chosen before the time fixed for the beginning of his term, or if the President elect shall have failed to qualify, then the Vice President elect shall act as President until a President shall have qualified; and the Congress may by law provide for the case wherein neither a President elect nor a Vice President elect shall have qualified, declaring who shall then act as President, or the manner in which one who is to act shall be selected, and such person shall act accordingly until a President or Vice President shall have qualified.

SECTION 4. The Congress may by law provide for the case of the death of any of the persons from whom the House of Representatives may choose a President whenever the right of choice shall have devolved upon them, and for the case of the death of any of the persons from whom the Senate may choose a Vice President whenever the right of choice shall have devolved upon them.

SECTION 5. Sections 1 and 2 shall take effect on the 15th day of October following the ratification of this article.

SECTION 6. This article shall be inoperative unless it shall have been ratified as an amendment to the Constitution by the legislatures of three-fourths of the several States within seven years from the date of its submission.

Amendment XXI (1933)

SECTION 1. The eighteenth article of amendment to the Constitution of the United States is hereby repealed.

SECTION 2. The transportation or importation into any State, Territory, or possession of the United States for delivery or use therein of intoxicating liquors, in violation of the laws thereof, is hereby prohibited.

SECTION 3. This article shall be inoperative unless it shall have been ratified as an amendment to the Constitution by conventions in the several States, as provided in the Constitution, within seven years from the date of the submission hereof to the States by the Congress.

Amendment XXII (1951)

SECTION 1. No person shall be elected to the office of the President more than twice, and no person who has held the office of President, or acted as President, for more than two years of a term to which some other person was elected President shall be elected to the office of the

President more than once. But this Article shall not apply to any person holding the office of President, when this Article was proposed by the Congress, and shall not prevent any person who may be holding the office of President, or acting as President, during the term within which this Article becomes operative from holding the office of President or acting as President during the remainder of such term.

SECTION 2. This article shall be inoperative unless it shall have been ratified as an amendment to the Constitution by the legislatures of three-fourths of the several States within seven years from the date of its submission to the States by the Congress.

Amendment XXIII (1961)

SECTION 1. The District constituting the seat of Government of the United States shall appoint in such manner as the Congress may direct:

A number of electors of President and Vice President equal to the whole number of Senators and Representatives in Congress to which the District would be entitled if it were a State, but in no event more than the least populous State; they shall be in addition to those appointed by the States, but they shall be considered, for the purposes of the election of President and Vice President, to be electors appointed by a State; and they shall meet in the District and perform such duties as provided by the twelfth article of amendment.

SECTION 2. The Congress shall have power to enforce this article by appropriate legislation.

Amendment XXIV (1964)

SECTION 1. The right of citizens of the United States to vote in any primary or other election for President or Vice President for electors for President or Vice President, or for Senator or Representative in Congress, shall not be denied or abridged by the United States or any State by reason of failure to pay any poll tax or other tax.

SECTION 2. The Congress shall have power to enforce this article by appropriate legislation.

Amendment XXV (1967)

SECTION 1. In case of the removal of the President from office or of his death or resignation, the Vice President shall become President.

SECTION 2. Whenever there is a vacancy in the office of the Vice President, the President shall nominate a Vice President who shall take office upon confirmation by a majority vote of both Houses of Congress.

SECTION 3. Whenever the President transmits to the President pro tempore of the Senate and the Speaker of the House of Representatives his written declaration that he is unable to discharge the powers and duties of his office, and until he transmits to them a written declaration to the contrary, such powers and duties shall be discharged by the Vice President as Acting President.

SECTION 4. Whenever the Vice President and a majority of either the principal officers of the executive departments or of such other body as Congress may by law provide, transmit to the President pro tempore of the Senate and the Speaker of the House of Representatives their written declaration that the President is unable to discharge the powers and duties of his office, the Vice President shall immediately assume the powers and duties of the office as Acting President.

Thereafter, when the President transmits to the President pro tempore of the Senate and the Speaker of the House of Representatives his written declaration that no inability exists, he shall resume the powers and duties of his office unless the Vice President and a majority of either the principal officers of the executive department or of such other body as Congress may by law provide, transmit within four days to the President pro tempore of the Senate and the Speaker of the House of Representatives their written declaration that the President is unable to discharge the powers and duties of his office. Thereupon Congress shall decide the issue, assembling within forty-eight hours for that purpose if not in session. If the Congress, within twenty-one days after receipt of the latter written declaration, or, if Congress is not in session, within twenty-one days after Congress is required to assemble, determines by two-thirds vote of both Houses that the President is unable to discharge the powers and duties of his office, the Vice President shall continue to discharge the same as Acting President; otherwise, the President shall resume the powers and duties of his office.

Amendment XXVI (1971)

SECTION 1. The right of citizens of the United States, who are eighteen years of age or older, to vote shall not be denied or abridged by the United States or by any State on account of age.

SECTION 2. The Congress shall have power to enforce this article by appropriate legislation.

Amendment XXVII (1992)

No law varying the compensation for the services of the Senators and Representatives shall take effect, until an election of Representatives shall have intervened.

3. Sarbanes-Oxley Act of 2002 (Selected Provisions)

SARBANES-OXLEY ACT OF 2002

[PUBLIC COMPANY ACCOUNTING REFORM AND INVESTOR PROTECTION ACT]
(Selected Provisions)

15 U.S.C. § 7201—Definitions

Except as otherwise specifically provided in this Act, in this Act, the following definitions shall apply:

(1) Appropriate State regulatory authority. The term "appropriate State regulatory authority" means the State agency or other authority responsible for the licensure or other regulation of the practice of accounting in the State or States having jurisdiction over a registered public accounting firm or associated person thereof, with respect to the matter in question.

(2) Audit. The term "audit" means an examination of the financial statements of any issuer by an independent public accounting firm in accordance with the rules of the Board or the Commission (or, for the period preceding the adoption of applicable rules of the Board under section 7213 of this title, in accordance with then-applicable generally accepted auditing and related standards for such purposes), for the purpose of expressing an opinion on such statements.

(3) Audit committee. The term "audit committee" means—

(A) a committee (or equivalent body) established by and amongst the board of directors of an issuer for the purpose of overseeing the accounting and financial reporting processes of the issuer and audits of the financial statements of the issuer; and

(B) if no such committee exists with respect to an issuer, the entire board of directors of the issuer.

(4) Audit report. The term "audit report" means a document or other record—

(A) prepared following an audit performed for purposes of compliance by an issuer with the requirements of the securities laws; and

(B) in which a public accounting firm either—

(i) sets forth the opinion of that firm regarding a financial statement, report, or other document; or

(ii) asserts that no such opinion can be expressed.

(5) Board. The term "Board" means the Public Company Accounting Oversight Board established under section 7211 of this title.

(6) Commission. The term "Commission" means the Securities and Exchange Commission.

(7) Issuer. The term "issuer" means an issuer (as defined in section 78c of this title), the securities of which are registered under section 78*l* of this title, or that is required to file reports under section 78*o*(d) of this title, or that files or has filed a registration statement that has not yet become effective under the Securities Act of 1933 (15 U.S.C. 77a et seq.), and that it has not withdrawn.

(8) Non-audit services. The term "non-audit services" means any professional services provided to an issuer by a registered public accounting firm, other than those provided to an issuer in connection with an audit or a review of the financial statements of an issuer.

(9) Person associated with a public accounting firm

(A) In general. The terms "person associated with a public accounting firm" (or with a "registered public accounting firm") and "associated person of a public accounting firm" (or of a "registered public accounting firm") mean any individual proprietor, partner, shareholder, principal, accountant, or other professional employee of a public accounting firm, or any other independent contractor or entity that, in connection with the preparation or issuance of any audit report—

(i) shares in the profits of, or receives compensation in any other form from, that firm; or

(ii) participates as agent or otherwise on behalf of such accounting firm in any activity of that firm.

(B) Exemption authority. The Board may, by rule, exempt persons engaged only in ministerial tasks from the definition in subparagraph (A), to the extent that the Board determines that any such exemption is consistent with the purposes of this Act, the public interest, or the protection of investors.

(C) Investigative and enforcement authority. For purposes of sections 7202(c), 7211(c), 7215, and 7217(c) of this title and the rules of the Board and Commission issued thereunder, except to the extent specifically excepted by such rules, the terms defined in subparagraph (A) shall include any person associated, seeking to become associated, or formerly associated with a public accounting firm, except that—

(i) the authority to conduct an investigation of such person under section 7215(b) of this title shall apply only with respect to any act or practice, or omission to act, by the person while such person was associated or seeking to become associated with a registered public accounting firm; and

(ii) the authority to commence a disciplinary proceeding under section 7215(c)(1) of this title, or impose sanctions under section 7215(c)(4) of this title, against such person shall apply only with respect to—

(I) conduct occurring while such person was associated or seeking to become associated with a registered public accounting firm; or

(II) non-cooperation, as described in section 7215(b)(3) of this title, with respect to a demand in a Board investigation for testimony, documents, or other information relating to a period when such person was associated or seeking to become associated with a registered public accounting firm.

(10) Professional standards. The term "professional standards" means—

(A) accounting principles that are—

(i) established by the standard setting body described in section 19(b) of the Securities Act of 1933 [15 U.S.C. 77s(b)], or prescribed by the Commission under section 19(a) of that Act [15 U.S.C. 77s(a)] or section 78m(b) of this title; and

(ii) relevant to audit reports for particular issuers, or dealt with in the quality control system of a particular registered public accounting firm; and

(B) auditing standards, standards for attestation engagements, quality control policies and procedures, ethical and competency standards, and independence standards (including rules implementing title II) that the Board or the Commission determines—

(i) relate to the preparation or issuance of audit reports for issuers; and

(ii) are established or adopted by the Board under section 7213(a) of this title, or are promulgated as rules of the Commission.

(11) Public accounting firm. The term "public accounting firm" means—

(A) a proprietorship, partnership, incorporated association, corporation, limited liability company, limited liability partnership, or other legal entity that is engaged in the practice of public accounting or preparing or issuing audit reports; and

(B) to the extent so designated by the rules of the Board, any associated person of any entity described in subparagraph (A).

(12) Registered public accounting firm. The term "registered public accounting firm" means a public accounting firm registered with the Board in accordance with this Act.

(13) Rules of the Board. The term "rules of the Board" means the bylaws and rules of the Board (as submitted to, and approved, modified, or amended by the Commission, in accordance with section 7217 of this title), and those stated policies, practices, and interpretations of the Board that the Commission, by rule, may deem to be rules of the Board, as necessary or appropriate in the public interest or for the protection of investors.

(14) Security. The term "security" has the same meaning as in section 78c(a) of this title.

(15) Securities laws. The term "securities laws" means the provisions of law referred to in section 78c(a)(47) of this title and includes the rules, regulations, and orders issued by the Commission thereunder.

(16) State. The term "State" means any State of the United States, the District of Columbia, Puerto Rico, the Virgin Islands, or any other territory or possession of the United States.

(17) Foreign auditor oversight authority. The term "foreign auditor oversight authority" means any governmental body or other entity empowered by a foreign government to conduct inspections of public accounting firms or otherwise to administer or enforce laws related to the regulation of public accounting firms.

15 U.S.C. § 7241 [Section 302]—Corporate Responsibility for Financial Reports

(a) Regulations required. The Commission shall, by rule, require, for each company filing periodic reports under section 78m(a) or 78o(d) of this title, that the principal executive officer or officers and the principal financial officer or officers, or persons performing similar functions, certify in each annual or quarterly report filed or submitted under either such section of this title that—

(1) the signing officer has reviewed the report;

(2) based on the officer's knowledge, the report does not contain any untrue statement of a material fact or omit to state a material fact necessary in order to make the statements made, in light of the circumstances under which such statements were made, not misleading;

(3) based on such officer's knowledge, the financial statements, and other financial information included in the report, fairly present in all material respects the financial condition and results of operations of the issuer as of, and for, the periods presented in the report;

(4) the signing officers—

(A) are responsible for establishing and maintaining internal controls;

(B) have designed such internal controls to ensure that material information relating to the issuer and its consolidated subsidiaries is made known to such officers by others within those entities, particularly during the period in which the periodic reports are being prepared;

(C) have evaluated the effectiveness of the issuer's internal controls as of a date within 90 days prior to the report; and

(D) have presented in the report their conclusions about the effectiveness of their internal controls based on their evaluation as of that date;

(5) the signing officers have disclosed to the issuer's auditors and the audit committee of the board of directors (or persons fulfilling the equivalent function)—

(A) all significant deficiencies in the design or operation of internal controls which could adversely affect the issuer's ability to record, process, summarize, and report financial data and have identified for the issuer's auditors any material weaknesses in internal controls; and

(B) any fraud, whether or not material, that involves management or other employees who have a significant role in the issuer's internal controls; and

(6) the signing officers have indicated in the report whether or not there were significant changes in internal controls or in other factors that could significantly affect internal controls subsequent to the date of their evaluation, including any corrective actions with regard to significant deficiencies and material weaknesses.

(b) Foreign reincorporations have no effect. Nothing in this section shall be interpreted or applied in any way to allow any issuer to lessen the legal force of the statement required under this section, by an issuer having reincorporated or having engaged in any other transaction that resulted in the transfer of the corporate domicile or offices of the issuer from inside the United States to outside of the United States.

(c) Deadline. The rules required by subsection (a) shall be effective not later than 30 days after July 30, 2002.

15 U.S.C. § 7242 [Section 303]—Improper Influence on Conduct of Audits

(a) Rules to prohibit. It shall be unlawful, in contravention of such rules or regulations as the Commission shall prescribe as necessary and appropriate in the public interest or for the protection of investors, for any officer or director of an issuer, or any other person acting under the direction thereof, to take any action to fraudulently influence, coerce, manipulate, or mislead any independent public or certified accountant engaged in the performance of an audit of the financial statements of that issuer for the purpose of rendering such financial statements materially misleading.

(b) Enforcement. In any civil proceeding, the Commission shall have exclusive authority to enforce this section and any rule or regulation issued under this section.

(c) No preemption of other law. The provisions of subsection (a) shall be in addition to, and shall not supersede or preempt, any other provision of law or any rule or regulation issued thereunder.

(d) Deadline for rulemaking. The Commission shall—

(1) propose the rules or regulations required by this section, not later than 90 days after July 30, 2002; and

(2) issue final rules or regulations required by this section, not later than 270 days after July 30, 2002.

15 U.S.C. § 7261 [Section 401]—Disclosure in Periodic Reports

(a) Omitted

(b) Commission rules on pro forma figures. Not later than 180 days after July 30, 2002, the Commission shall issue final rules providing that pro forma financial information included in any periodic or other report filed with the Commission pursuant to the securities laws, or in any public disclosure or press or other release, shall be presented in a manner that—

(1) does not contain an untrue statement of a material fact or omit to state a material fact necessary in order to make the pro forma financial information, in light of the circumstances under which it is presented, not misleading; and

(2) reconciles it with the financial condition and results of operations of the issuer under generally accepted accounting principles.

(c) Study and report on special purpose entities

(1) Study required. The Commission shall, not later than 1 year after the effective date of adoption of off-balance sheet disclosure rules required by section 78m(j) of this title, complete a study of filings by issuers and their disclosures to determine—

(A) the extent of off-balance sheet transactions, including assets, liabilities, leases, losses, and the use of special purpose entities; and

(B) whether generally accepted accounting rules result in financial statements of issuers reflecting the economics of such off-balance sheet transactions to investors in a transparent fashion.

(2) Report and recommendations. Not later than 6 months after the date of completion of the study required by paragraph (1), the Commission shall submit a report to the President, the Committee on Banking, Housing, and Urban Affairs of the Senate, and the Committee on Financial Services of the House of Representatives, setting forth—

(A) the amount or an estimate of the amount of off-balance sheet transactions, including assets, liabilities, leases, and losses of, and the use of special purpose entities by, issuers filing periodic reports pursuant to section 78m or 78o of this title;

(B) the extent to which special purpose entities are used to facilitate off-balance sheet transactions;

(C) whether generally accepted accounting principles or the rules of the Commission result in financial statements of issuers reflecting the economics of such transactions to investors in a transparent fashion;

(D) whether generally accepted accounting principles specifically result in the consolidation of special purpose entities sponsored by an issuer in cases in which the issuer has the majority of the risks and rewards of the special purpose entity; and

(E) any recommendations of the Commission for improving the transparency and quality of reporting off-balance sheet transactions in the financial statements and disclosures required to be filed by an issuer with the Commission.

15 U.S.C. § 7262 [Section 404]—Management Assessment of Internal Controls

(a) Rules required. The Commission shall prescribe rules requiring each annual report required by section 78m(a) or 78o(d) of this title to contain an internal control report, which shall—

(1) state the responsibility of management for establishing and maintaining an adequate internal control structure and procedures for financial reporting; and

(2) contain an assessment, as of the end of the most recent fiscal year of the issuer, of the effectiveness of the internal control structure and procedures of the issuer for financial reporting.

(b) Internal control evaluation and reporting. With respect to the internal control assessment required by subsection (a), each registered public accounting firm that prepares or issues the audit report for the issuer, other than an issuer that is an emerging growth company (as defined in section 78c of this title), shall attest to, and report on, the assessment made by the management of the issuer. An attestation made under this subsection shall be made in accordance with standards for attestation engagements issued or adopted by the Board. Any such attestation shall not be the subject of a separate engagement.

(c) **Exemption for smaller issuers.** Subsection (b) shall not apply with respect to any audit report prepared for an issuer that is neither a "large accelerated filer" nor an "accelerated filer" as those terms are defined in Rule 12b–2 of the Commission (17 C.F.R. 240.12b–2).

18 U.S.C. § 1519 [Section 802]—Destruction, Alteration, or Falsification of Records in Federal Investigations and Bankruptcy

Whoever knowingly alters, destroys, mutilates, conceals, covers up, falsifies, or makes a false entry in any record, document, or tangible object with the intent to impede, obstruct, or influence the investigation or proper administration of any matter within the jurisdiction of any department or agency of the United States or any case filed under title 11, or in relation to or contemplation of any such matter or case, shall be fined under this title, imprisoned not more than 20 years, or both.

18 U.S.C. § 1350 [Section 906]—Corporate Responsibility for Financial Reports

(a) **Certification of Periodic Financial Reports.** Each periodic report containing financial statements filed by an issuer with the Securities Exchange Commission pursuant to section 13(a) or 15(d) of the Securities Exchange Act of 1934 (15 U.S.C. 78m(a) or 78*o*(d)) shall be accompanied by a written statement by the chief executive officer and chief financial officer (or equivalent thereof) of the issuer.

(b) **Content.** The statement required under subsection (a) shall certify that the periodic report containing the financial statements fully complies with the requirements of section 13(a) or 15(d) of the Securities Exchange Act pf [sic] 1934 (15 U.S.C. 78m or 78*o*(d)) and that information contained in the periodic report fairly presents, in all material respects, the financial condition and results of operations of the issuer.

(c) **Criminal Penalties.** Whoever—

(1) certifies any statement as set forth in subsections (a) and (b) of this section knowing that the periodic report accompanying the statement does not comport with all the requirements set forth in this section shall be fined not more than $1,000,000 or imprisoned not more than 10 years, or both; or

(2) willfully certifies any statement as set forth in subsections (a) and (b) of this section knowing that the periodic report accompanying the statement does not comport with all the requirements set forth in this section shall be fined not more than $5,000,000, or imprisoned not more than 20 years, or both.

18 U.S.C. § 1513 [Section 1107]—Retaliating Against a Witness, Victim, or an Informant

(a)

(1) Whoever kills or attempts to kill another person with intent to retaliate against any person for—

(A) the attendance of a witness or party at an official proceeding, or any testimony given or any record, document, or other object produced by a witness in an official proceeding; or

(B) providing to a law enforcement officer any information relating to the commission or possible commission of a Federal offense or a violation of conditions of probation, supervised release, parole, or release pending judicial proceedings, shall be punished as provided in paragraph (2).

(2) The punishment for an offense under this subsection is—

(A) in the case of a killing, the punishment provided in sections 1111 and 1112; and

(B) in the case of an attempt, imprisonment for not more than 30 years.

(b) Whoever knowingly engages in any conduct and thereby causes bodily injury to another person or damages the tangible property of another person, or threatens to do so, with intent to retaliate against any person for—

(1) the attendance of a witness or party at an official proceeding, or any testimony given or any record, document, or other object produced by a witness in an official proceeding; or

(2) any information relating to the commission or possible commission of a Federal offense or a violation of conditions of probation, supervised release, parole, or release pending judicial proceedings given by a person to a law enforcement officer; or attempts to do so, shall be fined under this title or imprisoned not more than 20 years, or both.

(c) If the retaliation occurred because of attendance at or testimony in a criminal case, the maximum term of imprisonment which may be imposed for the offense under this section shall be the higher of that otherwise provided by law or the maximum term that could have been imposed for any offense charged in such case.

(d) There is extraterritorial Federal jurisdiction over an offense under this section.

(e) Whoever knowingly, with the intent to retaliate, takes any action harmful to any person, including interference with the lawful employment or livelihood of any person, for providing to a law enforcement officer any truthful information relating to the commission or possible commission of any Federal offense, shall be fined under this title or imprisoned not more than 10 years, or both.

(f) Whoever conspires to commit any offense under this section shall be subject to the same penalties as those prescribed for the offense the commission of which was the object of the conspiracy.

(g) A prosecution under this section may be brought in the district in which the official proceeding (whether pending, about to be instituted, or completed) was intended to be affected, or in which the conduct constituting the alleged offense occurred.

4. **Delaware General Corporate Law (Selected Provisions)**

DELAWARE GENERAL CORPORATION LAW

(Selected Provisions)

§ 101 Incorporators; how corporation formed; purposes.

(a) Any person, partnership, association or corporation, singly or jointly with others, and without regard to such person's or entity's residence, domicile or state of incorporation, may incorporate or organize a corporation under this chapter by filing with the Division of Corporations in the Department of State a certificate of incorporation which shall be executed, acknowledged and filed in accordance with § 103 of this title.

(b) A corporation may be incorporated or organized under this chapter to conduct or promote any lawful business or purposes, except as may otherwise be provided by the Constitution or other law of this State.

(c) Corporations for constructing, maintaining and operating public utilities, whether in or outside of this State, may be organized under this chapter, but corporations for constructing, maintaining and operating public utilities within this State shall be subject to, in addition to this chapter, the special provisions and requirements of Title 26 applicable to such corporations.

§ 102 Contents of certificate of incorporation.

(a) The certificate of incorporation shall set forth:

(1) The name of the corporation, which (i) shall contain 1 of the words "association," "company," "corporation," "club," "foundation," "fund," "incorporated," "institute," "society," "union," "syndicate," or "limited," (or abbreviations thereof, with or without punctuation), or words (or abbreviations thereof, with or without punctuation) of like import of foreign countries or jurisdictions (provided they are written in roman characters or letters); provided, however, that the Division of Corporations in the Department of State may waive such requirement (unless it determines that such name is, or might otherwise appear to be, that of a natural person) if such corporation executes, acknowledges and files with the Secretary of State in accordance with § 103 of this title a certificate stating that its total assets, as defined in § 503(i) of this title, are not less than $10,000,000, or, in the sole discretion of the Division of Corporations in the Department of State, if the corporation is both a nonprofit nonstock corporation and an association of professionals, (ii) shall be such as to distinguish

it upon the records in the office of the Division of Corporations in the Department of State from the names that are reserved on such records and from the names on such records of each other corporation, partnership, limited partnership, limited liability company or statutory trust organized or registered as a domestic or foreign corporation, partnership, limited partnership, limited liability company or statutory trust under the laws of this State, except with the written consent of the person who has reserved such name or such other foreign corporation or domestic or foreign partnership, limited partnership, limited liability company or statutory trust, executed, acknowledged and filed with the Secretary of State in accordance with § 103 of this title, or except that, without prejudicing any rights of the person who has reserved such name or such other foreign corporation or domestic or foreign partnership, limited partnership, limited liability company or statutory trust, the Division of Corporations in the Department of State may waive such requirement if the corporation demonstrates to the satisfaction of the Secretary of State that the corporation or a predecessor entity previously has made substantial use of such name or a substantially similar name, that the corporation has made reasonable efforts to secure such written consent, and that such waiver is in the interest of the State, (iii) except as permitted by § 395 of this title, shall not contain the word "trust," and (iv) shall not contain the word "bank," or any variation thereof, except for the name of a bank reporting to and under the supervision of the State Bank Commissioner of this State or a subsidiary of a bank or savings association (as those terms are defined in the Federal Deposit Insurance Act, as amended, at 12 U.S.C. § 1813), or a corporation regulated under the Bank Holding Company Act of 1956, as amended, 12 U.S.C. § 1841 et seq., or the Home Owners' Loan Act, as amended, 12 U.S.C. § 1461 et seq.; provided, however, that this section shall not be construed to prevent the use of the word "bank," or any variation thereof, in a context clearly not purporting to refer to a banking business or otherwise likely to mislead the public about the nature of the business of the corporation or to lead to a pattern and practice of abuse that might cause harm to the interests of the public or the State as determined by the Division of Corporations in the Department of State;

(2) The address (which shall be stated in accordance with § 131(c) of this title) of the corporation's registered office in this State, and the name of its registered agent at such address;

(3) The nature of the business or purposes to be conducted or promoted. It shall be sufficient to state, either alone or with other businesses or purposes, that the purpose of the corporation is to engage in any lawful act or activity for which corporations may be organized under the General Corporation Law of Delaware, and by such statement all lawful acts and

activities shall be within the purposes of the corporation, except for express limitations, if any;

(4) If the corporation is to be authorized to issue only 1 class of stock, the total number of shares of stock which the corporation shall have authority to issue and the par value of each of such shares, or a statement that all such shares are to be without par value. If the corporation is to be authorized to issue more than 1 class of stock, the certificate of incorporation shall set forth the total number of shares of all classes of stock which the corporation shall have authority to issue and the number of shares of each class and shall specify each class the shares of which are to be without par value and each class the shares of which are to have par value and the par value of the shares of each such class. The certificate of incorporation shall also set forth a statement of the designations and the powers, preferences and rights, and the qualifications, limitations or restrictions thereof, which are permitted by § 151 of this title in respect of any class or classes of stock or any series of any class of stock of the corporation and the fixing of which by the certificate of incorporation is desired, and an express grant of such authority as it may then be desired to grant to the board of directors to fix by resolution or resolutions any thereof that may be desired but which shall not be fixed by the certificate of incorporation. The foregoing provisions of this paragraph shall not apply to nonstock corporations. In the case of nonstock corporations, the fact that they are not authorized to issue capital stock shall be stated in the certificate of incorporation. The conditions of membership, or other criteria for identifying members, of nonstock corporations shall likewise be stated in the certificate of incorporation or the bylaws. Nonstock corporations shall have members, but failure to have members shall not affect otherwise valid corporate acts or work a forfeiture or dissolution of the corporation. Nonstock corporations may provide for classes or groups of members having relative rights, powers and duties, and may make provision for the future creation of additional classes or groups of members having such relative rights, powers and duties as may from time to time be established, including rights, powers and duties senior to existing classes and groups of members. Except as otherwise provided in this chapter, nonstock corporations may also provide that any member or class or group of members shall have full, limited, or no voting rights or powers, including that any member or class or group of members shall have the right to vote on a specified transaction even if that member or class or group of members does not have the right to vote for the election of the members of the governing body of the corporation. Voting by members of a nonstock corporation may be on a per capita, number, financial interest, class, group, or any other basis set forth. The provisions referred to in the 3 preceding

sentences may be set forth in the certificate of incorporation or the bylaws. If neither the certificate of incorporation nor the bylaws of a nonstock corporation state the conditions of membership, or other criteria for identifying members, the members of the corporation shall be deemed to be those entitled to vote for the election of the members of the governing body pursuant to the certificate of incorporation or bylaws of such corporation or otherwise until thereafter otherwise provided by the certificate of incorporation or the bylaws;

(5) The name and mailing address of the incorporator or incorporators;

(6) If the powers of the incorporator or incorporators are to terminate upon the filing of the certificate of incorporation, the names and mailing addresses of the persons who are to serve as directors until the first annual meeting of stockholders or until their successors are elected and qualify.

(b) In addition to the matters required to be set forth in the certificate of incorporation by subsection (a) of this section, the certificate of incorporation may also contain any or all of the following matters:

(1) Any provision for the management of the business and for the conduct of the affairs of the corporation, and any provision creating, defining, limiting and regulating the powers of the corporation, the directors, and the stockholders, or any class of the stockholders, or the governing body, members, or any class or group of members of a nonstock corporation; if such provisions are not contrary to the laws of this State. Any provision which is required or permitted by any section of this chapter to be stated in the bylaws may instead be stated in the certificate of incorporation;

(2) The following provisions, in haec verba, (i), for a corporation other than a nonstock corporation, viz:

"Whenever a compromise or arrangement is proposed between this corporation and its creditors or any class of them and/or between this corporation and its stockholders or any class of them, any court of equitable jurisdiction within the State of Delaware may, on the application in a summary way of this corporation or of any creditor or stockholder thereof or on the application of any receiver or receivers appointed for this corporation under § 291 of Title 8 of the Delaware Code or on the application of trustees in dissolution or of any receiver or receivers appointed for this corporation under § 279 of Title 8 of the Delaware Code order a meeting of the creditors or class of creditors, and/or of the stockholders or class of stockholders of this corporation, as the case may be, to be summoned in such manner as the said court directs. If a majority in number representing three fourths in value of the creditors or class of creditors, and/or of the stockholders or class of stockholders of this corporation, as the case may be, agree to any compromise or arrangement and to any reorganization of this corporation as consequence of such compromise or arrangement, the said compromise or arrangement and the said reorganization shall, if sanctioned by the court to which the said application has been made, be binding on all the creditors or class of creditors, and/or on all the stockholders or class of stockholders, of this corporation, as the case may be, and also on this corporation"; or

(ii), for a nonstock corporation, viz:

"Whenever a compromise or arrangement is proposed between this corporation and its creditors or any class of them and/or between this corporation and its members or any class of them, any court of equitable jurisdiction within the State of Delaware may, on the application in a summary way of this corporation or of any creditor or member thereof or on the application of any receiver or receivers appointed for this corporation under § 291 of Title 8 of the Delaware Code or on the application of trustees in dissolution or of any receiver or receivers appointed for this corporation under § 279 of Title 8 of the Delaware Code order a meeting of the creditors or class of creditors, and/or of the members or class of members of this corporation, as the case may be, to be summoned in such manner as the said court directs. If a majority in number representing three fourths in value of the creditors or class of creditors, and/or of the members or class of members of this corporation, as the case may be, agree to any compromise or arrangement and to any reorganization of this corporation as consequence of such compromise or arrangement, the said compromise or arrangement and the said reorganization shall, if sanctioned by the court to which the said application has been made, be binding on all the creditors or class of creditors, and/or on all the members or class of members, of this corporation, as the case may be, and also on this corporation";

(3) Such provisions as may be desired granting to the holders of the stock of the corporation, or the holders of any class or series of a class thereof, the preemptive right to subscribe to any or all additional issues of stock of the corporation of any or all classes or series thereof, or to any securities of the corporation convertible into such stock. No stockholder shall have any preemptive right to subscribe to an additional issue of stock or to any security convertible into such stock unless, and except to the extent that, such right is expressly granted to such stockholder in the certificate of incorporation. All such rights in existence on July 3, 1967, shall remain in existence unaffected by this paragraph unless and until changed or terminated by appropriate action which expressly provides for the change or termination;

(4) Provisions requiring for any corpo-

rate action, the vote of a larger portion of the stock or of any class or series thereof, or of any other securities having voting power, or a larger number of the directors, than is required by this chapter;

(5) A provision limiting the duration of the corporation's existence to a specified date; otherwise, the corporation shall have perpetual existence;

(6) A provision imposing personal liability for the debts of the corporation on its stockholders to a specified extent and upon specified conditions; otherwise, the stockholders of a corporation shall not be personally liable for the payment of the corporation's debts except as they may be liable by reason of their own conduct or acts;

(7) A provision eliminating or limiting the personal liability of a director to the corporation or its stockholders for monetary damages for breach of fiduciary duty as a director, provided that such provision shall not eliminate or limit the liability of a director: (i) For any breach of the director's duty of loyalty to the corporation or its stockholders; (ii) for acts or omissions not in good faith or which involve intentional misconduct or a knowing violation of law; (iii) under § 174 of this title; or (iv) for any transaction from which the director derived an improper personal benefit. No such provision shall eliminate or limit the liability of a director for any act or omission occurring prior to the date when such provision becomes effective. All references in this paragraph to a director shall also be deemed to refer to such other person or persons, if any, who, pursuant to a provision of the certificate of incorporation in accordance with § 141(a) of this title, exercise or perform any of the powers or duties otherwise conferred or imposed upon the board of directors by this title.

(c) It shall not be necessary to set forth in the certificate of incorporation any of the powers conferred on corporations by this chapter.

(d) Except for provisions included pursuant to paragraphs (a)(1), (a)(2), (a)(5), (a)(6), (b)(2), (b)(5), (b)(7) of this section, and provisions included pursuant to paragraph (a)(4) of this section specifying the classes, number of shares, and par value of shares a corporation other than a nonstock corporation is authorized to issue, any provision of the certificate of incorporation may be made dependent upon facts ascertainable outside such instrument, provided that the manner in which such facts shall operate upon the provision is clearly and explicitly set forth therein. The term "facts," as used in this subsection, includes, but is not limited to, the occurrence of any event, including a determination or action by any person or body, including the corporation.

(e) The exclusive right to the use of a name that is available for use by a domestic or foreign corporation may be reserved by or on behalf of:

(1) Any person intending to incorporate

or organize a corporation with that name under this chapter or contemplating such incorporation or organization;

(2) Any domestic corporation or any foreign corporation qualified to do business in the State of Delaware, in either case, intending to change its name or contemplating such a change;

(3) Any foreign corporation intending to qualify to do business in the State of Delaware and adopt that name or contemplating such qualification and adoption; and

(4) Any person intending to organize a foreign corporation and have it qualify to do business in the State of Delaware and adopt that name or contemplating such organization, qualification and adoption.

The reservation of a specified name may be made by filing with the Secretary of State an application, executed by the applicant, certifying that the reservation is made by or on behalf of a domestic corporation, foreign corporation or other person described in paragraphs (e)(1)–(4) of this section above, and specifying the name to be reserved and the name and address of the applicant. If the Secretary of State finds that the name is available for use by a domestic or foreign corporation, the Secretary shall reserve the name for the use of the applicant for a period of 120 days. The same applicant may renew for successive 120-day periods a reservation of a specified name by filing with the Secretary of State, prior to the expiration of such reservation (or renewal thereof), an application for renewal of such reservation, executed by the applicant, certifying that the reservation is renewed by or on behalf of a domestic corporation, foreign corporation or other person described in paragraphs (e)(1)–(4) of this section above and specifying the name reservation to be renewed and the name and address of the applicant. The right to the exclusive use of a reserved name may be transferred to any other person by filing in the office of the Secretary of State a notice of the transfer, executed by the applicant for whom the name was reserved, specifying the name reservation to be transferred and the name and address of the transferee. The reservation of a specified name may be cancelled by filing with the Secretary of State a notice of cancellation, executed by the applicant or transferee, specifying the name reservation to be cancelled and the name and address of the applicant or transferee. Unless the Secretary of State finds that any application, application for renewal, notice of transfer, or notice of cancellation filed with the Secretary of State as required by this subsection does not conform to law, upon receipt of all filing fees required by law the Secretary of State shall prepare and return to the person who filed such instrument a copy of the filed instrument with a notation thereon of the action taken by the Secretary of State. A fee as set forth in § 391 of this title shall be paid at the time of the reservation of any name, at the time of the renewal of any such reservation and at the time of the filing of a notice of the transfer or cancellation of any such reservation.

(f) The certificate of incorporation may not contain any provision that would impose liability on a stockholder for the attorneys' fees or expenses of the corporation or any other party in connection with an internal corporate claim, as defined in § 115 of this title.

§ 106 Commencement of corporate existence.

Upon the filing with the Secretary of State of the certificate of incorporation, executed and acknowledged in accordance with § 103 of this title, the incorporator or incorporators who signed the certificate, and such incorporator's or incorporators' successors and assigns, shall, from the date of such filing, be and constitute a body corporate, by the name set forth in the certificate, subject to § 103(d) of this title and subject to dissolution or other termination of its existence as provided in this chapter.

§ 107 Powers of incorporators.

If the persons who are to serve as directors until the first annual meeting of stockholders have not been named in the certificate of incorporation, the incorporator or incorporators, until the directors are elected, shall manage the affairs of the corporation and may do whatever is necessary and proper to perfect the organization of the corporation, including the adoption of the original bylaws of the corporation and the election of directors.

§ 108 Organization meeting of incorporators or directors named in certificate of incorporation.

(a) After the filing of the certificate of incorporation an organization meeting of the incorporator or incorporators, or of the board of directors if the initial directors were named in the certificate of incorporation, shall be held, either within or without this State, at the call of a majority of the incorporators or directors, as the case may be, for the purposes of adopting bylaws, electing directors (if the meeting is of the incorporators) to serve or hold office until the first annual meeting of stockholders or until their successors are elected and qualify, electing officers if the meeting is of the directors, doing any other or further acts to perfect the organization of the corporation, and transacting such other business as may come before the meeting.

(b) The persons calling the meeting shall give to each other incorporator or director, as the case may be, at least 2 days' written notice thereof by any usual means of communication, which notice shall state the time, place and purposes of the meeting as fixed by the persons calling it. Notice of the meeting need not be given to anyone who attends the meeting or who signs a waiver of notice either before or after the meeting.

(c) Any action permitted to be taken at the organization meeting of the incorporators or directors, as the case may be, may be taken without a meeting if each incorporator or director, where there is more than 1, or the sole incorporator or director where there is only 1, signs an instrument which states the action so taken.

(d) If any incorporator is not available to act, then any person for whom or on whose behalf the incorporator was acting directly or indirectly as employee or agent, may take any action that such incorporator would have been authorized to take under this section or § 107 of this title; provided that any instrument signed by such other person, or any record of the proceedings of a meeting in which such person participated, shall state that such incorporator is not available and the reason therefor, that such incorporator was acting directly or indirectly as employee or agent for or on behalf of such person, and that such person's signature on such instrument or participation in such meeting is otherwise authorized and not wrongful.

§ 109 Bylaws.

(a) The original or other bylaws of a corporation may be adopted, amended or repealed by the incorporators, by the initial directors of a corporation other than a nonstock corporation or initial members of the governing body of a nonstock corporation if they were named in the certificate of incorporation, or, before a corporation other than a nonstock corporation has received any payment for any of its stock, by its board of directors. After a corporation other than a nonstock corporation has received any payment for any of its stock, the power to adopt, amend or repeal bylaws shall be in the stockholders entitled to vote. In the case of a nonstock corporation, the power to adopt, amend or repeal bylaws shall be in its members entitled to vote. Notwithstanding the foregoing, any corporation may, in its certificate of incorporation, confer the power to adopt, amend or repeal bylaws upon the directors or, in the case of a nonstock corporation, upon its governing body. The fact that such power has been so conferred upon the directors or governing body, as the case may be, shall not divest the stockholders or members of the power, nor limit their power to adopt, amend or repeal bylaws.

(b) The bylaws may contain any provision, not inconsistent with law or with the certificate of incorporation, relating to the business of the corporation, the conduct of its affairs, and its rights or powers or the rights or powers of its stockholders, directors, officers or employees. The bylaws may not contain any provision that would impose liability on a stockholder for the attorneys' fees or expenses of the corporation or any other party in connection with an internal corporate claim, as defined in § 115 of this title.

§ 121 General powers.

(a) In addition to the powers enumerated in § 122 of this title, every corporation, its officers, directors and stockholders shall possess and may exercise all the powers and privileges granted by this chapter or by any other law or by its certificate of incorporation, together with any powers incidental thereto, so far as such powers and privileges are necessary or convenient to the conduct, promotion or attainment of the business or purposes set forth in its certificate of incorporation.

(b) Every corporation shall be governed by the provisions and be subject to the restrictions and liabilities contained in this chapter.

§ 122 Specific powers.

Every corporation created under this chapter shall have power to:

(1) Have perpetual succession by its corporate name, unless a limited period of duration is stated in its certificate of incorporation;

(2) Sue and be sued in all courts and participate, as a party or otherwise, in any judicial, administrative, arbitrative or other proceeding, in its corporate name;

(3) Have a corporate seal, which may be altered at pleasure, and use the same by causing it or a facsimile thereof, to be impressed or affixed or in any other manner reproduced;

(4) Purchase, receive, take by grant, gift, devise, bequest or otherwise, lease, or otherwise acquire, own, hold, improve, employ, use and otherwise deal in and with real or personal property, or any interest therein, wherever situated, and to sell, convey, lease, exchange, transfer or otherwise dispose of, or mortgage or pledge, all or any of its property and assets, or any interest therein, wherever situated;

(5) Appoint such officers and agents as the business of the corporation requires and to pay or otherwise provide for them suitable compensation;

(6) Adopt, amend and repeal bylaws;

(7) Wind up and dissolve itself in the manner provided in this chapter;

(8) Conduct its business, carry on its operations and have offices and exercise its powers within or without this State;

(9) Make donations for the public welfare or for charitable, scientific or educational purposes, and in time of war or other national emergency in aid thereof;

(10) Be an incorporator, promoter or manager of other corporations of any type or kind;

(11) Participate with others in any corporation, partnership, limited partnership, joint venture or other association of any kind, or in any transaction, undertaking or arrangement which the participating corporation would have power to conduct by itself, whether or not such participation involves sharing or delegation of control with or to others;

(12) Transact any lawful business which the corporation's board of directors shall find to be in aid of governmental authority;

(13) Make contracts, including contracts of guaranty and suretyship, incur liabilities, borrow money at such rates of interest as the corporation may deter-

mine, issue its notes, bonds and other obligations, and secure any of its obligations by mortgage, pledge or other encumbrance of all or any of its property, franchises and income, and make contracts of guaranty and suretyship which are necessary or convenient to the conduct, promotion or attainment of the business of (a) a corporation all of the outstanding stock of which is owned, directly or indirectly, by the contracting corporation, or (b) a corporation which owns, directly or indirectly, all of the outstanding stock of the contracting corporation, or (c) a corporation all of the outstanding stock of which is owned, directly or indirectly, by a corporation which owns, directly or indirectly, all of the outstanding stock of the contracting corporation, which contracts of guaranty and suretyship shall be deemed to be necessary or convenient to the conduct, promotion or attainment of the business of the contracting corporation, and make other contracts of guaranty and suretyship which are necessary or convenient to the conduct, promotion or attainment of the business of the contracting corporation;

(14) Lend money for its corporate purposes, invest and reinvest its funds, and take, hold and deal with real and personal property as security for the payment of funds so loaned or invested;

(15) Pay pensions and establish and carry out pension, profit sharing, stock option, stock purchase, stock bonus, retirement, benefit, incentive and compensation plans, trusts and provisions for any or all of its directors, officers and employees, and for any or all of the directors, officers and employees of its subsidiaries;

(16) Provide insurance for its benefit on the life of any of its directors, officers or employees, or on the life of any stockholder for the purpose of acquiring at such stockholder's death shares of its stock owned by such stockholder.

(17) Renounce, in its certificate of incorporation or by action of its board of directors, any interest or expectancy of the corporation in, or in being offered an opportunity to participate in, specified business opportunities or specified classes or categories of business opportunities that are presented to the corporation or 1 or more of its officers, directors or stockholders.

§ 124 **Effect of lack of corporate capacity or power; ultra vires.**

No act of a corporation and no conveyance or transfer of real or personal property to or by a corporation shall be invalid by reason of the fact that the corporation was without capacity or power to do such act or to make or receive such conveyance or transfer, but such lack of capacity or power may be asserted:

(1) In a proceeding by a stockholder against the corporation to enjoin the doing of any act or acts or the transfer of real or personal property by or to the corporation. If the unauthorized acts or transfer

sought to be enjoined are being, or are to be, performed or made pursuant to any contract to which the corporation is a party, the court may, if all of the parties to the contract are parties to the proceeding and if it deems the same to be equitable, set aside and enjoin the performance of such contract, and in so doing may allow to the corporation or to the other parties to the contract, as the case may be, such compensation as may be equitable for the loss or damage sustained by any of them which may result from the action of the court in setting aside and enjoining the performance of such contract, but anticipated profits to be derived from the performance of the contract shall not be awarded by the court as a loss or damage sustained;

(2) In a proceeding by the corporation, whether acting directly or through a receiver, trustee or other legal representative, or through stockholders in a representative suit, against an incumbent or former officer or director of the corporation, for loss or damage due to such incumbent or former officer's or director's unauthorized act;

(3) In a proceeding by the Attorney General to dissolve the corporation, or to enjoin the corporation from the transaction of unauthorized business.

§ 141 Board of directors; powers; number, qualifications, terms and quorum; committees; classes of directors; nonstock corporations; reliance upon books; action without meeting; removal.

(a) The business and affairs of every corporation organized under this chapter shall be managed by or under the direction of a board of directors, except as may be otherwise provided in this chapter or in its certificate of incorporation. If any such provision is made in the certificate of incorporation, the powers and duties conferred or imposed upon the board of directors by this chapter shall be exercised or performed to such extent and by such person or persons as shall be provided in the certificate of incorporation.

(b) The board of directors of a corporation shall consist of 1 or more members, each of whom shall be a natural person. The number of directors shall be fixed by, or in the manner provided in, the bylaws, unless the certificate of incorporation fixes the number of directors, in which case a change in the number of directors shall be made only by amendment of the certificate. Directors need not be stockholders unless so required by the certificate of incorporation or the bylaws. The certificate of incorporation or bylaws may prescribe other qualifications for directors. Each director shall hold office until such director's successor is elected and qualified or until such director's earlier resignation or removal. Any director may resign at any time upon notice given in writing or by electronic transmission to the corporation. A resignation is effective when the resignation is delivered unless the resignation specifies a later effective date or an effective date determined upon the happening of an event or events. A resignation which is conditioned upon the director failing to receive a specified vote for reelection as a director may provide that it is irrevocable. A majority of the total number of directors shall constitute a quorum for the transaction of business unless the certificate of incorporation or the bylaws require a greater number. Unless the certificate of incorporation provides otherwise, the bylaws may provide that a number less than a majority shall constitute a quorum which in no case shall be less than 1/3 of the total number of directors. The vote of the majority of the directors present at a meeting at which a quorum is present shall be the act of the board of directors unless the certificate of incorporation or the bylaws shall require a vote of a greater number.

(c)(1) All corporations incorporated prior to July 1, 1996, shall be governed by this paragraph (c)(1) of this section, provided that any such corporation may by a resolution adopted by a majority of the whole board elect to be governed by paragraph (c)(2) of this section, in which case this paragraph (c)(1) of this section shall not apply to such corporation. All corporations incorporated on or after July 1, 1996, shall be governed by paragraph (c)(2) of this section. The board of directors may, by resolution passed by a majority of the whole board, designate 1 or more committees, each committee to consist of 1 or more of the directors of the corporation. The board may designate 1 or more directors as alternate members of any committee, who may replace any absent or disqualified member at any meeting of the committee. The bylaws may provide that in the absence or disqualification of a member of a committee, the member or members present at any meeting and not disqualified from voting, whether or not the member or members present constitute a quorum, may unanimously appoint another member of the board of directors to act at the meeting in the place of any such absent or disqualified member. Any such committee, to the extent provided in the resolution of the board of directors, or in the bylaws of the corporation, shall have and may exercise all the powers and authority of the board of directors in the management of the business and affairs of the corporation, and may authorize the seal of the corporation to be affixed to all papers which may require it; but no such committee shall have the power or authority in reference to amending the certificate of incorporation (except that a committee may, to the extent authorized in the resolution or resolutions providing for the issuance of shares of stock adopted by the board of directors as provided in § 151(a) of this title, fix the designations and any of the preferences or rights of such shares relating to dividends, redemption, dissolution, any distribution of assets of the corporation or the conversion into, or the exchange of such shares for, shares of any other class or classes or any other series of the same or any other class or classes of stock of the corporation or fix the number of shares of any series of stock or authorize the increase or decrease of the shares of any series), adopting an agreement of merger or consolidation under § 251, § 252, § 254, § 255, § 256, § 257, § 258, § 263 or § 264 of this title, recommending to the stockholders the sale, lease or exchange of all or substantially all of the corporation's property and assets, recommending to the stockholders a dissolution of the corporation or a revocation of a dissolution, or amending the bylaws of the corporation; and, unless the resolution, bylaws or certificate of incorporation expressly so provides, no such committee shall have the power or authority to declare a dividend, to authorize the issuance of stock or to adopt a certificate of ownership and merger pursuant to § 253 of this title.

(2) The board of directors may designate 1 or more committees, each committee to consist of 1 or more of the directors of the corporation. The board may designate 1 or more directors as alternate members of any committee, who may replace any absent or disqualified member at any meeting of the committee. The bylaws may provide that in the absence or disqualification of a member of a committee, the member or members present at any meeting and not disqualified from voting, whether or not such member or members constitute a quorum, may unanimously appoint another member of the board of directors to act at the meeting in the place of any such absent or disqualified member. Any such committee, to the extent provided in the resolution of the board of directors, or in the bylaws of the corporation, shall have and may exercise all the powers and authority of the board of directors in the management of the business and affairs of the corporation, and may authorize the seal of the corporation to be affixed to all papers which may require it; but no such committee shall have the power or authority in reference to the following matter: (i) approving or adopting, or recommending to the stockholders, any action or matter (other than the election or removal of directors) expressly required by this chapter to be submitted to stockholders for approval or (ii) adopting, amending or repealing any bylaw of the corporation.

(3) Unless otherwise provided in the certificate of incorporation, the bylaws or the resolution of the board of directors designating the committee, a committee may create 1 or more subcommittees, each subcommittee to consist of 1 or more members of the committee, and delegate to a subcommittee any or all of the powers and authority of the committee. Except for references to committees and members of committees in subsection (c) of this section, every reference in this chapter to a committee of the board of directors or a member of a committee shall be deemed to include a reference to a subcommittee or member of a subcommittee.

(4) A majority of the directors then serving on a committee of the board

of directors or on a subcommittee of a committee shall constitute a quorum for the transaction of business by the committee or subcommittee, unless the certificate of incorporation, the bylaws, a resolution of the board of directors or a resolution of a committee that created the subcommittee requires a greater or lesser number, provided that in no case shall a quorum be less than 1/3 of the directors then serving on the committee or subcommittee. The vote of the majority of the members of a committee or subcommittee present at a meeting at which a quorum is present shall be the act of the committee or subcommittee, unless the certificate of incorporation, the bylaws, a resolution of the board of directors or a resolution of a committee that created the subcommittee requires a greater number.

(d) The directors of any corporation organized under this chapter may, by the certificate of incorporation or by an initial bylaw, or by a bylaw adopted by a vote of the stockholders, be divided into 1, 2 or 3 classes; the term of office of those of the first class to expire at the first annual meeting held after such classification becomes effective; of the second class 1 year thereafter; of the third class 2 years thereafter; and at each annual election held after such classification becomes effective, directors shall be chosen for a full term, as the case may be, to succeed those whose terms expire. The certificate of incorporation or bylaw provision dividing the directors into classes may authorize the board of directors to assign members of the board already in office to such classes at the time such classification becomes effective. The certificate of incorporation may confer upon holders of any class or series of stock the right to elect 1 or more directors who shall serve for such term, and have such voting powers as shall be stated in the certificate of incorporation. The terms of office and voting powers of the directors elected separately by the holders of any class or series of stock may be greater than or less than those of any other director or class of directors. In addition, the certificate of incorporation may confer upon 1 or more directors, whether or not elected separately by the holders of any class or series of stock, voting powers greater than or less than those of other directors. Any such provision conferring greater or lesser voting power shall apply to voting in any committee, unless otherwise provided in the certificate of incorporation or bylaws. If the certificate of incorporation provides that 1 or more directors shall have more or less than 1 vote per director on any matter, every reference in this chapter to a majority or other proportion of the directors shall refer to a majority or other proportion of the votes of the directors.

(e) A member of the board of directors, or a member of any committee designated by the board of directors, shall, in the performance of such member's duties, be fully protected in relying in good faith upon the records of the corporation and upon such information, opinions, reports or statements presented to the corporation by any of the corporation's officers or employees, or committees of the board of directors, or by any other person as to matters the member reasonably believes are within such other person's professional or expert competence and who has been selected with reasonable care by or on behalf of the corporation.

(f) Unless otherwise restricted by the certificate of incorporation or bylaws, any action required or permitted to be taken at any meeting of the board of directors or of any committee thereof may be taken without a meeting if all members of the board or committee, as the case may be, consent thereto in writing, or by electronic transmission and the writing or writings or electronic transmission or transmissions are filed with the minutes of proceedings of the board, or committee. Such filing shall be in paper form if the minutes are maintained in paper form and shall be in electronic form if the minutes are maintained in electronic form. Any person (whether or not then a director) may provide, whether through instruction to an agent or otherwise, that a consent to action will be effective at a future time (including a time determined upon the happening of an event), no later than 60 days after such instruction is given or such provision is made and such consent shall be deemed to have been given for purposes of this subsection at such effective time so long as such person is then a director and did not revoke the consent prior to such time. Any such consent shall be revocable prior to its becoming effective.

(g) Unless otherwise restricted by the certificate of incorporation or bylaws, the board of directors of any corporation organized under this chapter may hold its meetings, and have an office or offices, outside of this State.

(h) Unless otherwise restricted by the certificate of incorporation or bylaws, the board of directors shall have the authority to fix the compensation of directors.

(i) Unless otherwise restricted by the certificate of incorporation or bylaws, members of the board of directors of any corporation, or any committee designated by the board, may participate in a meeting of such board, or committee by means of conference telephone or other communications equipment by means of which all persons participating in the meeting can hear each other, and participation in a meeting pursuant to this subsection shall constitute presence in person at the meeting.

(j) The certificate of incorporation of any nonstock corporation may provide that less than 1/3 of the members of the governing body may constitute a quorum thereof and may otherwise provide that the business and affairs of the corporation shall be managed in a manner different from that provided in this section. Except as may be otherwise provided by the certificate of incorporation, this section shall apply to such a corporation, and when so applied, all references to the board of directors, to members thereof, and to stockholders shall be deemed to refer to the governing body of the corporation, the members thereof and the members of the corporation, respectively; and all references to stock, capital stock, or shares thereof shall be deemed to refer to memberships of a nonprofit nonstock corporation and to membership interests of any other nonstock corporation.

(k) Any director or the entire board of directors may be removed, with or without cause, by the holders of a majority of the shares then entitled to vote at an election of directors, except as follows:

> (1) Unless the certificate of incorporation otherwise provides, in the case of a corporation whose board is classified as provided in subsection (d) of this section, stockholders may effect such removal only for cause; or

> (2) In the case of a corporation having cumulative voting, if less than the entire board is to be removed, no director may be removed without cause if the votes cast against such director's removal would be sufficient to elect such director if then cumulatively voted at an election of the entire board of directors, or, if there be classes of directors, at an election of the class of directors of which such director is a part.

Whenever the holders of any class or series are entitled to elect 1 or more directors by the certificate of incorporation, this subsection shall apply, in respect to the removal without cause of a director or directors so elected, to the vote of the holders of the outstanding shares of that class or series and not to the vote of the outstanding shares as a whole.

§ 142 Officers; titles, duties, selection, term; failure to elect; vacancies.

(a) Every corporation organized under this chapter shall have such officers with such titles and duties as shall be stated in the bylaws or in a resolution of the board of directors which is not inconsistent with the bylaws and as may be necessary to enable it to sign instruments and stock certificates which comply with §§ 103(a)(2) and 158 of this title. One of the officers shall have the duty to record the proceedings of the meetings of the stockholders and directors in a book to be kept for that purpose. Any number of offices may be held by the same person unless the certificate of incorporation or bylaws otherwise provide.

(b) Officers shall be chosen in such manner and shall hold their offices for such terms as are prescribed by the bylaws or determined by the board of directors or other governing body. Each officer shall hold office until such officer's successor is elected and qualified or until such officer's earlier resignation or removal. Any officer may resign at any time upon written notice to the corporation.

(c) The corporation may secure the fidelity of any or all of its officers or agents by bond or otherwise.

(d) A failure to elect officers shall not dissolve or otherwise affect the corporation.

(e) Any vacancy occurring in any office of the corporation by death, resignation, removal or otherwise, shall be filled as the bylaws provide. In the absence of such provision, the vacancy shall be filled by the board of directors or other governing body.

§ 152 Issuance of stock; lawful consideration; fully paid stock.

The consideration, as determined pursuant to § 153(a) and (b) of this title, for subscriptions to, or the purchase of, the capital stock to be issued by a corporation shall be paid in such form and in such manner as the board of directors shall determine. The board of directors may authorize capital stock to be issued for consideration consisting of cash, any tangible or intangible property or any benefit to the corporation, or any combination thereof. The resolution authorizing the issuance of capital stock may provide that any stock to be issued pursuant to such resolution may be issued in 1 or more transactions in such numbers and at such times as are set forth in or determined by or in the manner set forth in the resolution, which may include a determination or action by any person or body, including the corporation, provided the resolution fixes a maximum number of shares that may be issued pursuant to such resolution, a time period during which such shares may be issued and a minimum amount of consideration for which such shares may be issued. The board of directors may determine the amount of consideration for which shares may be issued by setting a minimum amount of consideration or approving a formula by which the amount or minimum amount of consideration is determined. The formula may include or be made dependent upon facts ascertainable outside the formula, provided the manner in which such facts shall operate upon the formula is clearly and expressly set forth in the formula or in the resolution approving the formula. In the absence of actual fraud in the transaction, the judgment of the directors as to the value of such consideration shall be conclusive. The capital stock so issued shall be deemed to be fully paid and nonassessable stock upon receipt by the corporation of such consideration; provided, however, nothing contained herein shall prevent the board of directors from issuing partly paid shares under § 156 of this title.

§ 211 Meetings of stockholders.

(a)(1) Meetings of stockholders may be held at such place, either within or without this State as may be designated by or in the manner provided in the certificate of incorporation or bylaws, or if not so designated, as determined by the board of directors. If, pursuant to this paragraph or the certificate of incorporation or the bylaws of the corporation, the board of directors is authorized to determine the place of a meeting of stockholders, the board of directors may, in its sole discretion, determine that the meeting shall not be held at any place, but may instead be held solely by means of remote communication as authorized by paragraph (a)(2) of this section.

(2) If authorized by the board of directors in its sole discretion, and subject to such

guidelines and procedures as the board of directors may adopt, stockholders and proxyholders not physically present at a meeting of stockholders may, by means of remote communication:

a. Participate in a meeting of stockholders; and

b. Be deemed present in person and vote at a meeting of stockholders, whether such meeting is to be held at a designated place or solely by means of remote communication, provided that (i) the corporation shall implement reasonable measures to verify that each person deemed present and permitted to vote at the meeting by means of remote communication is a stockholder or proxyholder, (ii) the corporation shall implement reasonable measures to provide such stockholders and proxyholders a reasonable opportunity to participate in the meeting and to vote on matters submitted to the stockholders, including an opportunity to read or hear the proceedings of the meeting substantially concurrently with such proceedings, and (iii) if any stockholder or proxyholder votes or takes other action at the meeting by means of remote communication, a record of such vote or other action shall be maintained by the corporation.

(b) Unless directors are elected by written consent in lieu of an annual meeting as permitted by this subsection, an annual meeting of stockholders shall be held for the election of directors on a date and at a time designated by or in the manner provided in the bylaws. Stockholders may, unless the certificate of incorporation otherwise provides, act by written consent to elect directors; provided, however, that, if such consent is less than unanimous, such action by written consent may be in lieu of holding an annual meeting only if all of the directorships to which directors could be elected at an annual meeting held at the effective time of such action are vacant and are filled by such action. Any other proper business may be transacted at the annual meeting.

(c) A failure to hold the annual meeting at the designated time or to elect a sufficient number of directors to conduct the business of the corporation shall not affect otherwise valid corporate acts or work a forfeiture or dissolution of the corporation except as may be otherwise specifically provided in this chapter. If the annual meeting for election of directors is not held on the date designated therefor or action by written consent to elect directors in lieu of an annual meeting has not been taken, the directors shall cause the meeting to be held as soon as is convenient. If there be a failure to hold the annual meeting or to take action by written consent to elect directors in lieu of an annual meeting for a period of 30 days after the date designated for the annual meeting, or if no date has been designated, for a period of 13 months after the latest to occur of the organization of the corporation, its last annual meeting or the last action by written consent to elect directors in lieu of an annual meeting, the

Court of Chancery may summarily order a meeting to be held upon the application of any stockholder or director. The shares of stock represented at such meeting, either in person or by proxy, and entitled to vote thereat, shall constitute a quorum for the purpose of such meeting, notwithstanding any provision of the certificate of incorporation or bylaws to the contrary. The Court of Chancery may issue such orders as may be appropriate, including, without limitation, orders designating the time and place of such meeting, the record date or dates for determination of stockholders entitled to notice of the meeting and to vote thereat, and the form of notice of such meeting.

(d) Special meetings of the stockholders may be called by the board of directors or by such person or persons as may be authorized by the certificate of incorporation or by the bylaws.

(e) All elections of directors shall be by written ballot unless otherwise provided in the certificate of incorporation; if authorized by the board of directors, such requirement of a written ballot shall be satisfied by a ballot submitted by electronic transmission, provided that any such electronic transmission must either set forth or be submitted with information from which it can be determined that the electronic transmission was authorized by the stockholder or proxy holder.

§ 212 Voting rights of stockholders; proxies; limitations.

(a) Unless otherwise provided in the certificate of incorporation and subject to § 213 of this title, each stockholder shall be entitled to 1 vote for each share of capital stock held by such stockholder. If the certificate of incorporation provides for more or less than 1 vote for any share, on any matter, every reference in this chapter to a majority or other proportion of stock, voting stock or shares shall refer to such majority or other proportion of the votes of such stock, voting stock or shares.

(b) Each stockholder entitled to vote at a meeting of stockholders or to express consent or dissent to corporate action in writing without a meeting may authorize another person or persons to act for such stockholder by proxy, but no such proxy shall be voted or acted upon after 3 years from its date, unless the proxy provides for a longer period.

(c) Without limiting the manner in which a stockholder may authorize another person or persons to act for such stockholder as proxy pursuant to subsection (b) of this section, the following shall constitute a valid means by which a stockholder may grant such authority:

(1) A stockholder may execute a writing authorizing another person or persons to act for such stockholder as proxy. Execution may be accomplished by the stockholder or such stockholder's authorized officer, director, employee or agent signing such writing or causing such person's signature to be affixed to such writing by any reasonable means including, but not

limited to, by facsimile signature.

(2) A stockholder may authorize another person or persons to act for such stockholder as proxy by transmitting or authorizing the transmission of a telegram, cablegram, or other means of electronic transmission to the person who will be the holder of the proxy or to a proxy solicitation firm, proxy support service organization or like agent duly authorized by the person who will be the holder of the proxy to receive such transmission, provided that any such telegram, cablegram or other means of electronic transmission must either set forth or be submitted with information from which it can be determined that the telegram, cablegram or other electronic transmission was authorized by the stockholder. If it is determined that such telegrams, cablegrams or other electronic transmissions are valid, the inspectors or, if there are no inspectors, such other persons making that determination shall specify the information upon which they relied.

(d) Any copy, facsimile telecommunication or other reliable reproduction of the writing or transmission created pursuant to subsection (c) of this section may be substituted or used in lieu of the original writing or transmission for any and all purposes for which the original writing or transmission could be used, provided that such copy, facsimile telecommunication or other reproduction shall be a complete reproduction of the entire original writing or transmission.

(e) A duly executed proxy shall be irrevocable if it states that it is irrevocable and if, and only as long as, it is coupled with an interest sufficient in law to support an irrevocable power. A proxy may be made irrevocable regardless of whether the interest with which it is coupled is an interest in the stock itself or an interest in the corporation generally.

§ 275 Dissolution generally; procedure.

(a) If it should be deemed advisable in the judgment of the board of directors of any corporation that it should be dissolved, the board, after the adoption of a resolution to that effect by a majority of the whole board at any meeting called for that purpose, shall cause notice of the adoption of the resolution and of a meeting of stockholders to take action upon the resolution to be mailed to each stockholder entitled to vote thereon as of the record date for determining the stockholders entitled to notice of the meeting.

(b) At the meeting a vote shall be taken upon the proposed dissolution. If a majority of the outstanding stock of the corporation entitled to vote thereon shall vote for the proposed dissolution, a certification of dissolution shall be filed with the Secretary of State pursuant to subsection (d) of this section.

(c) Dissolution of a corporation may also be authorized without action of the directors if all the stockholders entitled to vote thereon shall consent in writing and a certificate of dissolution shall be filed with the Secretary of State pursuant to subsection (d) of this section.

(d) If dissolution is authorized in accordance with this section, a certificate of dissolution shall be executed, acknowledged and filed, and shall become effective, in accordance with § 103 of this title. Such certificate of dissolution shall set forth:

(1) The name of the corporation;

(2) The date dissolution was authorized;

(3) That the dissolution has been authorized by the board of directors and stockholders of the corporation, in accordance with subsections (a) and (b) of this section, or that the dissolution has been authorized by all of the stockholders of the corporation entitled to vote on a dissolution, in accordance with subsection (c) of this section;

(4) The names and addresses of the directors and officers of the corporation; and

(5) The date of filing of the corporation's original certificate of incorporation with the Secretary of State.

(e) The resolution authorizing a proposed dissolution may provide that notwithstanding authorization or consent to the proposed dissolution by the stockholders, or the members of a nonstock corporation pursuant to § 276 of this title, the board of directors or governing body may abandon such proposed dissolution without further action by the stockholders or members.

(f) Upon a certificate of dissolution becoming effective in accordance with § 103 of this title, the corporation shall be dissolved.

§ 342 Close corporation defined; contents of certificate of incorporation.

(a) A close corporation is a corporation organized under this chapter whose certificate of incorporation contains the provisions required by § 102 of this title and, in addition, provides that:

(1) All of the corporation's issued stock of all classes, exclusive of treasury shares, shall be represented by certificates and shall be held of record by not more than a specified number of persons, not exceeding 30; and

(2) All of the issued stock of all classes shall be subject to 1 or more of the restrictions on transfer permitted by § 202 of this title; and

(3) The corporation shall make no offering of any of its stock of any class which would constitute a "public offering" within the meaning of the United States Securities Act of 1933 [15 U.S.C. § 77a et seq.] as it may be amended from time to time.

(b) The certificate of incorporation of a close corporation may set forth the qualifications of stockholders, either by specifying classes of persons who shall be entitled to be holders of record of stock of any class, or by specifying classes of persons who shall not be entitled to be holders of stock of any class or both.

(c) For purposes of determining the number of holders of record of the stock of a close corporation, stock which is held in joint or common tenancy or by the entireties shall be treated as held by 1 stockholder.

§ 343 Formation of a close corporation.

A close corporation shall be formed in accordance with §§ 101, 102 and 103 of this title, except that:

(1) Its certificate of incorporation shall contain a heading stating the name of the corporation and that it is a close corporation; and

(2) Its certificate of incorporation shall contain the provisions required by § 342 of this title.

§ 351 Management by stockholders.

The certificate of incorporation of a close corporation may provide that the business of the corporation shall be managed by the stockholders of the corporation rather than by a board of directors. So long as this provision continues in effect:

(1) No meeting of stockholders need be called to elect directors;

(2) Unless the context clearly requires otherwise, the stockholders of the corporation shall be deemed to be directors for purposes of applying provisions of this chapter; and

(3) The stockholders of the corporation shall be subject to all liabilities of directors.

Such a provision may be inserted in the certificate of incorporation by amendment if all incorporators and subscribers or all holders of record of all of the outstanding stock, whether or not having voting power, authorize such a provision. An amendment to the certificate of incorporation to delete such a provision shall be adopted by a vote of the holders of a majority of all outstanding stock of the corporation, whether or not otherwise entitled to vote. If the certificate of incorporation contains a provision authorized by this section, the existence of such provision shall be noted conspicuously on the face or back of every stock certificate issued by such corporation.

§ 355 Stockholders' option to dissolve corporation.

(a) The certificate of incorporation of any close corporation may include a provision granting to any stockholder, or to the holders of any specified number or percentage of shares of any class of stock, an option to have the corporation dissolved at will or upon the occurrence of any specified event or contingency. Whenever any such option to dissolve is exercised, the stockholders exercising such option shall give written notice thereof to all other stockholders. After the expiration of 30 days following the sending of such notice, the dissolution of the corporation shall proceed as if the required number of stockholders having voting power had consented in writing to dissolution of the corporation as provided by § 228 of this title.

(b) If the certificate of incorporation as originally filed does not contain a provision authorized by subsection (a) of this section, the certificate may be amended to include such provision if adopted by the affirmative vote of the holders of all the outstanding stock, whether or not entitled to vote, unless the certificate of incorporation specifically authorizes such an amendment by a vote which shall be not less than 2/3 of all the outstanding stock whether or not entitled to vote.

(c) Each stock certificate in any corporation whose certificate of incorporation authorizes dissolution as permitted by this section shall conspicuously note on the face thereof the existence of the provision. Unless noted conspicuously on the face of the stock certificate, the provision is ineffective.

§ 362 Public benefit corporation defined; contents of certificate of incorporation.

(a) A "public benefit corporation" is a for-profit corporation organized under and subject to the requirements of this chapter that is intended to produce a public benefit or public benefits and to operate in a responsible and sustainable manner. To that end, a public benefit corporation shall be managed in a manner that balances the stockholders' pecuniary interests, the best interests of those materially affected by the corporation's conduct, and the public benefit or public benefits identified in its certificate of incorporation. In the certificate of incorporation, a public benefit corporation shall:

(1) Identify within its statement of business or purpose pursuant to § 102(a)(3) of this title 1 or more specific public benefits to be promoted by the corporation; and

(2) State within its heading that it is a public benefit corporation.

(b) "Public benefit" means a positive effect (or reduction of negative effects) on 1 or more categories of persons, entities, communities or interests (other than stockholders in their capacities as stockholders) including, but not limited to, effects of an artistic, charitable, cultural, economic, educational, environmental, literary, medical, religious, scientific or technological nature. "Public benefit provisions" means the provisions of a certificate of incorporation contemplated by this subchapter.

(c) The name of the public benefit corporation may contain the words "public benefit corporation," or the abbreviation "P.B.C.," or the designation "PBC," which shall be deemed to satisfy the requirements of § 102(a)(*l*)(i) of this title. If the name does not contain such language, the corporation shall, prior to issuing unissued shares of stock or disposing of treasury shares, provide notice to any person to whom such stock is issued or who acquires such treasury shares that it is a public benefit corporation; provided that such notice need not be provided if the issuance or disposal is pursuant to an offering registered under the Securities Act of 1933 [15 U.S.C. § 77r et seq.] or if, at the time of issuance or disposal, the corporation has a class of securities that is registered under the Securities Exchange Act of 1934 [15 U.S.C. § 78a et seq.].

§ 365 Duties of directors.

(a) The board of directors shall manage or direct the business and affairs of the public benefit corporation in a manner that balances the pecuniary interests of the stockholders, the best interests of those materially affected by the corporation's conduct, and the specific public benefit or public benefits identified in its certificate of incorporation.

(b) A director of a public benefit corporation shall not, by virtue of the public benefit provisions or § 362(a) of this title, have any duty to any person on account of any interest of such person in the public benefit or public benefits identified in the certificate of incorporation or on account of any interest materially affected by the corporation's conduct and, with respect to a decision implicating the balance requirement in subsection (a) of this section, will be deemed to satisfy such director's fiduciary duties to stockholders and the corporation if such director's decision is both informed and disinterested and not such that no person of ordinary, sound judgment would approve.

(c) The certificate of incorporation of a public benefit corporation may include a provision that any disinterested failure to satisfy this section shall not, for the purposes of § 102(b)(7) or § 145 of this title, constitute an act or omission not in good faith, or a breach of the duty of loyalty.

§ 366 Periodic statements and third-party certification.

(a) A public benefit corporation shall include in every notice of a meeting of stockholders a statement to the effect that it is a public benefit corporation formed pursuant to this subchapter.

(b) A public benefit corporation shall no less than biennially provide its stockholders with a statement as to the corporation's promotion of the public benefit or public benefits identified in the certificate of incorporation and of the best interests of those materially affected by the corporation's conduct. The statement shall include:

(1) The objectives the board of directors has established to promote such public benefit or public benefits and interests;

(2) The standards the board of directors has adopted to measure the corporation's progress in promoting such public benefit or public benefits and interests;

(3) Objective factual information based on those standards regarding the corporation's success in meeting the objectives for promoting such public benefit or public benefits and interests; and

(4) An assessment of the corporation's success in meeting the objectives and promoting such public benefit or public benefits and interests.

(c) The certificate of incorporation or bylaws of a public benefit corporation may require that the corporation:

(1) Provide the statement described in subsection (b) of this section more frequently than biennially;

(2) Make the statement described in subsection (b) of this section available to the public; and/or

(3) Use a third-party standard in connection with and/or attain a periodic third-party certification addressing the corporation's promotion of the public benefit or public benefits identified in the certificate of incorporation and/or the best interests of those materially affected by the corporation's conduct.

5. JAMS Comprehensive Arbitration Rules & Procedures

JAMS COMPREHENSIVE ARBITRATION RULES & PROCEDURES (EFFECTIVE JULY 1, 2014)

(Reproduced by permission)

Rule 1. Scope of Rules

(a) The JAMS Comprehensive Arbitration Rules and Procedures ("Rules") govern binding Arbitrations of disputes or claims that are administered by JAMS and in which the Parties agree to use these Rules or, in the absence of such agreement, any disputed claim or counterclaim that exceeds $250,000, not including interest or attorneys' fees, unless other Rules are prescribed.

(b) The Parties shall be deemed to have made these Rules a part of their Arbitration agreement ("Agreement") whenever they have provided for Arbitration by JAMS under its Comprehensive Rules or for Arbitration by JAMS without specifying any particular JAMS Rules and the disputes or claims meet the criteria of the first paragraph of this Rule.

(c) The authority and duties of JAMS as prescribed in the Agreement of the Parties and in these Rules shall be carried out by the JAMS National Arbitration Committee ("NAC") or the office of JAMS General Counsel or their designees.

(d) JAMS may, in its discretion, assign the administration of an Arbitration to any of its Resolution Centers.

(e) The term "Party" as used in these Rules includes Parties to the Arbitration and their counsel or representatives.

(f) "Electronic filing" (e-file) means the electronic transmission of documents to and from JAMS and other Parties for the purpose of filing via the Internet. "Electronic service" (e-service) means the electronic transmission of documents via JAMS Electronic Filing System to a Party, attorney or representative under these Rules.

Rule 2. Party Self-Determination and Emergency Relief Procedures

(a) The Parties may agree on any procedures not specified herein or in lieu of these Rules that are consistent with the applicable law and JAMS policies (including, without limitation, Rules 15(i), 30 and 31). The Parties shall promptly notify JAMS of any such Party-agreed procedures and shall confirm such procedures in writing. The Party-agreed procedures shall be enforceable as if contained in these Rules.

(b) When an Arbitration Agreement provides that the Arbitration will be non-administered or administered by an entity other than JAMS and/or conducted in accordance with rules other than JAMS Rules, the Parties may subsequently agree to modify that Agreement to provide that the Arbitration will be administered by JAMS and/or conducted in accordance with JAMS Rules.

(c) Emergency Relief Procedures. These Emergency Relief Procedures are available in Arbitrations filed and served after July 1, 2014, and where not otherwise prohibited by law. Parties may agree to opt out of these Procedures in their Arbitration Agreement or by subsequent written agreement.

(i) A Party in need of emergency relief prior to the appointment of an Arbitrator may notify JAMS and all other Parties in writing of the relief sought and the basis for an Award of such relief. This Notice shall include an explanation of why such relief is needed on an expedited basis. Such Notice shall be given by facsimile, email or personal delivery. The Notice must include a statement certifying that all other Parties have been notified. If all other Parties have not been notified, the Notice shall include an explanation of the efforts made to notify such Parties.

(ii) JAMS shall promptly appoint an Emergency Arbitrator to rule on the emergency request. In most cases the appointment of an Emergency Arbitrator will be done within 24 hours of receipt of the request. The Emergency Arbitrator shall promptly disclose any circumstance likely, on the basis disclosed in the application, to affect the Arbitrator's ability to be impartial or independent. Any challenge to the appointment of the Emergency Arbitrator shall be made within 24 hours of the disclosures by the Emergency Arbitrator. JAMS will promptly review and decide any such challenge. JAMS' decision will be final.

(iii) Within two business days, or as soon as practicable thereafter, the Emergency Arbitrator shall establish a schedule for the consideration of the request for emergency relief. The schedule shall provide a reasonable opportunity for all Parties to be heard taking into account the nature of the relief sought. The Emergency Arbitrator has the authority to rule on his or her own jurisdiction and shall resolve any disputes with respect to the request for emergency relief.

(iv) The Emergency Arbitrator shall determine whether the Party seeking emergency relief has shown that immediate and irreparable loss or damage will result in the absence of emergency relief and whether the requesting Party is entitled to such relief. The Emergency Arbitrator shall enter an order or Award granting or denying the relief, as the case may be, and stating the reasons therefor.

(v) Any request to modify the Emergency Arbitrator's order or Award must be based on changed circumstances and may be made to the Emergency Arbitrator until such time as an Arbitrator or Arbitrators are appointed in accordance with the Parties' Agreement and JAMS' usual procedures. Thereafter, any request related to the relief granted or denied by the Emergency Arbitrator shall be determined by the Arbitrator(s) appointed in accordance with the Parties' Agreement and JAMS' usual procedures.

(vi) At the Emergency Arbitrator's discretion, any interim Award of emergency relief may be conditioned on the provision of adequate security by the Party seeking such relief.

Rule 3. Amendment of Rules

JAMS may amend these Rules without notice. The Rules in effect on the date of the commencement of an Arbitration (as defined in Rule 5) shall apply to that Arbitration, unless the Parties have agreed upon another version of the Rules.

Rule 4. Conflict with Law

If any of these Rules, or modification of these Rules agreed to by the Parties, is determined to be in conflict with a provision of applicable law, the provision of law will govern over the Rule in conflict, and no other Rule will be affected.

Rule 5. Commencing an Arbitration

(a) The Arbitration is deemed commenced when JAMS issues a Commencement Letter based upon the existence of one of the following:

(i) A post-dispute Arbitration Agreement fully executed by all Parties specifying JAMS administration or use of any JAMS Rules; or

(ii) A pre-dispute written contractual provision requiring the Parties to arbitrate the dispute or claim and specifying JAMS administration or use of any JAMS Rules or that the Parties agree shall be administered by JAMS; or

(iii) A written confirmation of an oral agreement of all Parties to participate in an Arbitration administered by JAMS or conducted pursuant to any JAMS Rules; or

(iv) The Respondent's failure to timely object to JAMS administration; or

(v) A copy of a court order compelling Arbitration at JAMS.

(b) The issuance of the Commencement Letter confirms that requirements for commencement have been met, that JAMS has received all payments required under the applicable fee schedule and that the Claimant has provided JAMS with contact information for all Parties along with evidence that the Demand for Arbitration has been served on all Parties.

(c) If a Party that is obligated to arbitrate in accordance with subparagraph (a) of this Rule fails to agree to participate in the Arbitration process, JAMS shall confirm in writing that Party's failure to respond or participate, and, pursuant to Rule 22(j), the Arbitrator, once appointed, shall schedule, and provide appropriate notice of, a Hearing or other opportunity for the Party demanding the Arbitration to demonstrate its entitlement to relief.

(d) The date of commencement of the Arbitration is the date of the Commencement Letter but is not intended to be applicable to any legal requirements such as the statute of limitations, any contractual limitations period or claims notice requirements. The term "commencement," as used in this Rule, is intended only to pertain to the operation of this and other Rules (such as Rules 3, 13(a), 17(a) and 31(a)).

Rule 6. Preliminary and Administrative Matters

(a) JAMS may convene, or the Parties may request, administrative conferences to discuss any procedural matter relating to the administration of the Arbitration.

(b) If no Arbitrator has yet been appointed, at the request of a Party and in the absence of Party agreement, JAMS may determine the location of the Hearing, subject to Arbitrator review. In determining the location of the Hearing, such factors as the subject matter of the dispute, the convenience of the Parties and witnesses, and the relative resources of the Parties shall be considered.

(c) If, at any time, any Party has failed to pay fees or expenses in full, JAMS may order the suspension or termination of the proceedings. JAMS may so inform the Parties in order that one of them may advance the required payment. If one Party advances the payment owed by a non-paying Party, the Arbitration shall proceed, and the Arbitrator may allocate the non-paying Party's share of such costs, in accordance with Rules 24(f) and 31(c). An administrative suspension shall toll any other time limits contained in these Rules or the Parties' Agreement.

(d) JAMS does not maintain an official record of documents filed in the Arbitration. If the Parties wish to have any documents returned to them, they must advise JAMS in writing within thirty (30) calendar days of the conclusion of the Arbitration. If special arrangements are required regarding file maintenance or document retention, they must be agreed to in writing, and JAMS reserves the right to impose an additional fee for such special arrangements. Documents that are submitted for e-filing are retained for thirty (30) calendar days following the conclusion of the Arbitration.

(e) Unless the Parties' Agreement or applicable law provides otherwise, JAMS, if it determines that the Arbitrations so filed have common issues of fact or law, may consolidate Arbitrations in the following instances:

(i) If a Party files more than one Arbitration with JAMS, JAMS may consolidate the Arbitrations into a single Arbitration.

(ii) Where a Demand or Demands for Arbitration is or are submitted naming Parties already involved in another Arbitration or Arbitrations pending under these Rules, JAMS may decide that the new case or cases shall be consolidated into one or more of the pending proceedings and referred to one of the Arbitrators or panels of Arbitrators already appointed.

(iii) Where a Demand or Demands for Arbitration is or are submitted naming Parties that are not identical to the Parties in the existing Arbitration or Arbitrations, JAMS may decide that the new case or cases shall be consolidated into one or more of the pending proceedings and referred to one of the Arbitrators or panels of Arbitrators already appointed.

When rendering its decision, JAMS will take into account all circumstances, including the links between the cases and the progress already made in the existing Arbitrations.

Unless applicable law provides otherwise, where JAMS decides to consolidate a proceeding into a pending Arbitration, the Parties to the consolidated case or cases will be deemed to have waived their right to designate an Arbitrator as well as any contractual provision with respect to the site of the Arbitration.

(f) Where a third party seeks to participate in an Arbitration already pending under these Rules or where a Party to an Arbitration under these Rules seeks to compel a third party to participate in a pending Arbitration, the Arbitrator shall determine such request, taking into account all circumstances he or she deems relevant and applicable.

Rule 7. Number and Neutrality of Arbitrators; Appointment and Authority of Chairperson

(a) The Arbitration shall be conducted by one neutral Arbitrator, unless all Parties agree otherwise. In these Rules, the term "Arbitrator" shall mean, as the context requires, the Arbitrator or the panel of Arbitrators in a tripartite Arbitration.

(b) In cases involving more than one Arbitrator, the Parties shall agree on, or, in the absence of agreement, JAMS shall designate, the Chairperson of the Arbitration Panel. If the Parties and the Arbitrators agree, a single member of the Arbitration Panel may, acting alone, decide discovery and procedural matters, including the conduct of hearings to receive documents and testimony from third parties who have been subpoenaed to produce documents.

(c) Where the Parties have agreed that each Party is to name one Arbitrator, the Arbitrators so named shall be neutral and independent of the appointing Party, unless the Parties have agreed that they shall be non-neutral.

Rule 8. Service

(a) The Arbitrator may at any time require electronic filing and service of documents in an Arbitration. If an Arbitrator requires electronic filing, the Parties shall maintain and regularly monitor a valid, usable and live email address for the receipt of all documents filed through JAMS Electronic Filing System. Any document filed electronically shall be considered as filed with JAMS when the transmission to JAMS Electronic Filing System is complete. Any document e-filed by 11:59 p.m. (of the sender's time zone) shall be deemed filed on that date. Upon completion of filing, JAMS Electronic Filing System shall issue a confirmation receipt that includes the date and time of receipt. The confirmation receipt shall serve as proof of filing.

(b) Every document filed with JAMS Electronic Filing System shall be deemed to have been signed by the Arbitrator, Case Manager, attorney or declarant who submits the document to JAMS Electronic Filing System, and shall bear the typed name, address and telephone number of a signing attorney. Documents containing signatures of third parties (i.e., unopposed motions, affidavits, stipulations, etc.) may also be filed electronically by indicating that the original signatures are maintained by the filing Party in paper format.

(c) Delivery of e-service documents through JAMS Electronic Filing System to other registered users shall be considered as valid and effective service and shall have the same legal effect as an original paper document. Recipients of e-service documents shall access their documents through JAMS Electronic Filing System. E-service shall be deemed complete when the Party initiating e-service completes the transmission of the electronic document(s) to JAMS Electronic Filing System for e-filing and/or e-service. Upon actual or constructive receipt of the electronic document(s) by the Party to be served, a Certificate of Electronic Service shall be issued by JAMS Electronic Filing System to the Party initiating e-service, and that Certificate shall serve as proof of service. Any Party who ignores or attempts to refuse e-service shall be deemed to have received the electronic document(s) 72 hours following the transmission of the electronic document(s) to JAMS Electronic Filing System.

(d) If an electronic filing or service does not occur because of (1) an error in the transmission of the document to JAMS Electronic Filing System or served Party that was unknown to the sending Party; (2) a failure to process the electronic document when received by JAMS Electronic Filing System; (3) the Party being erroneously excluded from the service list; or (4) other technical problems experienced by the filer, the Arbitrator or JAMS may, for good cause shown, permit the document to be filed *nunc pro tunc* to the date it was first attempted to be sent electronically. Or, in the case of service, the Party shall, absent extraordinary circumstances, be entitled to an order extending the date for any response or the period within which any right, duty or other act must be performed.

(e) For documents that are not filed electronically, service by a Party under these Rules is effected by providing one signed copy of the document to each Party and two copies in the case of a sole Arbitrator and four copies in the case of a tripartite panel to JAMS. Service may be made by hand-delivery, overnight delivery service or U.S. mail. Service by any of these means is considered effective upon the date of deposit of the document.

(f) In computing any period of time prescribed or allowed by these Rules for a Party to do some act within a prescribed period after the service of a notice or other paper on the Party and the notice or paper is served on the Party only by U.S. mail, three (3) calendar days shall be added to the prescribed period.

Rule 9. Notice of Claims

(a) Each Party shall afford all other Parties reasonable and timely notice of its claims, affirmative defenses or counterclaims. Any such notice shall include a short statement of its factual basis. No claim, remedy, counterclaim or affirmative defense will be considered by the Arbitrator in the absence of such prior notice to the other Parties, unless the Arbitrator determines that no Party has been unfairly prejudiced by such lack of formal notice or all Parties agree that such consideration is appropriate notwithstanding the lack of prior notice.

(b) Claimant's notice of claims is the Demand for Arbitration referenced in Rule 5. It shall include a statement of the remedies sought. The Demand for Arbitration may attach and incorporate a copy of a Complaint previously filed with a court. In the latter case, Claimant may accompany the Complaint with a copy of any Answer to that Complaint filed by any Respondent.

(c) Within fourteen (14) calendar days of service of the notice of claim, a Respondent may submit to JAMS and serve on other Parties a response and a statement of any affirmative defenses, including jurisdictional challenges, or counterclaims it may have.

(d) Within fourteen (14) calendar days of service of a counterclaim, a Claimant may submit to JAMS and serve on other Parties a response to such counterclaim and any affirmative defenses, including jurisdictional challenges, it may have.

(e) Any claim or counterclaim to which no response has been served will be deemed denied.

(f) Jurisdictional challenges under Rule 11 shall be deemed waived, unless asserted in a response to a Demand or counterclaim or promptly thereafter, when circumstances first suggest an issue of arbitrability.

Rule 10. Changes of Claims

After the filing of a claim and before the Arbitrator is appointed, any Party may make a new or different claim against a Party or any third party that is subject to Arbitration in the proceeding. Such claim shall be made in writing, filed with JAMS and served on the other Parties. Any response to the new claim shall be made within fourteen (14) calendar days after service of such claim. After the Arbitrator is appointed, no new or different claim may be submitted, except with the Arbitrator's approval. A Party may request a hearing on this issue. Each Party has the right to respond to any new or amended claim in accordance with Rule 9(c) or (d).

Rule 11. Interpretation of Rules and Jurisdictional Challenges

(a) Once appointed, the Arbitrator shall resolve disputes about the interpretation and applicability of these Rules and conduct of the Arbitration Hearing. The resolution of the issue by the Arbitrator shall be final.

(b) Jurisdictional and arbitrability disputes, including disputes over the formation, existence, validity, interpretation or scope of the agreement under which Arbitration is sought, and who are proper Parties to the Arbitration, shall be submitted to and ruled on by the Arbitrator. The Arbitrator has the authority to determine jurisdiction and arbitrability issues as a preliminary matter.

(c) Disputes concerning the appointment of the Arbitrator shall be resolved by JAMS.

(d) The Arbitrator may, upon a showing of good cause or *sua sponte*, when necessary to facilitate the Arbitration, extend any deadlines established in these Rules, provided that the time for rendering the Award may be altered only in accordance with Rules 22(i) or 24.

Rule 12. Representation

(a) The Parties, whether natural persons or legal entities such as corporations, LLCs or partnerships, may be represented by counsel or any other person of the Party's choice. Each Party shall give prompt written notice to the Case Manager and the other Parties of the name, address, telephone and fax numbers and email address of its representative. The representative of a Party may act on the Party's behalf in complying with these Rules.

(b) Changes in Representation. A Party shall give prompt written notice to the Case Manager and the other Parties of any change in its representation, including the name, address, telephone and fax numbers and email address of the new representative. Such notice shall state that the written consent of the former representative, if any, and of the new representative, has been obtained and shall state the effective date of the new representation.

Rule 13. Withdrawal from Arbitration

(a) No Party may terminate or withdraw from an Arbitration after the issuance of the Commencement Letter (see Rule 5), except by written agreement of all Parties to the Arbitration.

(b) A Party that asserts a claim or counterclaim may unilaterally withdraw that claim or counterclaim without prejudice by serving written notice on the other Parties and the Arbitrator. However, the opposing Parties may, within seven (7) calendar days of service of such notice, request that the Arbitrator condition the withdrawal upon such terms as he or she may direct.

Rule 14. Ex Parte Communications

(a) No Party may have any *ex parte* communication with a neutral Arbitrator, except as provided in section (b) of this Rule. The Arbitrator(s) may authorize any Party to communicate directly with the Arbitrator(s) by email or other written means as long as copies are simultaneously forwarded to the JAMS Case Manager and the other Parties.

(b) A Party may have *ex parte* communication with its appointed neutral or non-neutral Arbitrator as necessary to secure the Arbitrator's services and to assure the absence of conflicts, as well as in connection with the selection of the Chairperson of the arbitral panel.

(c) The Parties may agree to permit more extensive *ex parte* communication between a Party and a non-neutral Arbitrator. More extensive communication with a non-neutral Arbitrator may also be permitted by applicable law and rules of ethics.

Rule 15. Arbitrator Selection, Disclosures and Replacement

(a) Unless the Arbitrator has been previously selected by agreement of the Parties, JAMS may attempt to facilitate agreement among the Parties regarding selection of the Arbitrator.

(b) If the Parties do not agree on an Arbitrator, JAMS shall send the Parties a list of at least five (5) Arbitrator candidates in the case of a sole Arbitrator and ten (10) Arbitrator candidates in the case of a tripartite panel. JAMS shall also provide each Party with a brief description of the background and experience of each Arbitrator candidate. JAMS may replace any or all names on the list of Arbitrator candidates for reasonable cause at any time before the Parties have submitted their choice pursuant to subparagraph (c) below.

(c) Within seven (7) calendar days of service upon the Parties of the list of names, each Party may strike two (2) names in the case of a sole Arbitrator and three (3) names in the case of a tripartite panel, and shall rank the remaining Arbitrator candidates in order of preference. The remaining Arbitrator candidate with the highest composite ranking shall be appointed the Arbitrator. JAMS may grant a reasonable extension of the time to strike and rank the Arbitrator candidates to any Party without the consent of the other Parties.

(d) If this process does not yield an Arbitrator or a complete panel, JAMS shall designate the sole Arbitrator or as many members of the tripartite panel as are necessary to complete the panel.

(e) If a Party fails to respond to a list of Arbitrator candidates within seven (7) calendar days after its service, or fails to respond according to the instructions provided by JAMS, JAMS shall deem that Party to have accepted all of the Arbitrator candidates.

(f) Entities whose interests are not adverse with respect to the issues in dispute shall be treated as a single Party for purposes of the Arbitrator selection process. JAMS shall determine whether the interests between entities are adverse for purposes of Arbitrator selection, considering such factors as whether the entities are represented by the same attorney and whether the entities are presenting joint or separate positions at the Arbitration.

(g) If, for any reason, the Arbitrator who is selected is unable to fulfill the Arbitrator's duties, a successor Arbitrator shall be chosen in accordance with this Rule. If a member of a panel of Arbitrators becomes unable to fulfill his or her duties after the beginning of a Hearing but before the issuance of an Award, a new Arbitrator will be chosen in accordance with this Rule, unless, in the case of a tripartite panel, the Parties agree to proceed with the remaining two Arbitrators. JAMS will make the final determination as to whether an Arbitrator is unable to fulfill his or her duties, and that decision shall be final.

(h) Any disclosures regarding the selected Arbitrator shall be made as required by law or within ten (10) calendar days from the date of appointment. Such disclosures may be provided in electronic format, provided that JAMS will produce a hard copy to any Party that requests it. The Parties and their representatives shall disclose to JAMS any circumstance likely to give rise to justifiable doubt as to the Arbitrator's impartiality or independence, including any bias or any financial or personal interest in the result of the Arbitration or any past or present relationship with the Parties or their representatives. The obligation of the Arbitrator, the Parties and their representatives to make all required disclosures continues throughout the Arbitration process.

(i) At any time during the Arbitration process, a Party may challenge the continued service of an Arbitrator for cause. The challenge must be based upon information that was not available to the Parties at the time the Arbitrator was selected. A challenge for cause must be in writing and exchanged with opposing Parties, who may respond within seven (7) calendar days of service of the challenge. JAMS shall make the final determination as to such challenge. Such determination shall take into account the materiality of the facts and any prejudice to the Parties. That decision will be final.

(j) Where the Parties have agreed that a Party-appointed Arbitrator is to be non-neutral, that Party-appointed Arbitrator is not obliged to withdraw if requested to do so only by the Party who did not appoint that Arbitrator.

Rule 16. Preliminary Conference

At the request of any Party or at the direction of the Arbitrator, a Preliminary Conference shall be conducted with the Parties or their counsel or representatives. The Preliminary Conference may address any or all of the following subjects:

(a) The exchange of information in accordance with Rule 17 or otherwise;

(b) The schedule for discovery as permitted by the Rules, as agreed by the Parties or as required or authorized by applicable law;

(c) The pleadings of the Parties and any agreement to clarify or narrow the issues or structure the Arbitration Hearing;

(d) The scheduling of the Hearing and any pre-Hearing exchanges of information, exhibits, motions or briefs;

(e) The attendance of witnesses as contemplated by Rule 21;

(f) The scheduling of any dispositive motion pursuant to Rule 18;

(g) The premarking of exhibits, the preparation of joint exhibit lists and the resolution of the admissibility of exhibits;

(h) The form of the Award; and

(i) Such other matters as may be suggested by the Parties or the Arbitrator.

The Preliminary Conference may be conducted telephonically and may be resumed from time to time as warranted.

Rule 16.1. Application of Expedited Procedures

(a) If these Expedited Procedures are referenced in the Parties' agreement to arbitrate or are later agreed to by all Parties, they shall be applied by the Arbitrator.

(b) The Claimant or Respondent may opt into the Expedited Procedures. The Claimant may do so by indicating the election in the Demand for Arbitration. The Respondent may opt into the Expedited Procedures by so indicating in writing to JAMS with a copy to the Claimant served within fourteen (14) days of receipt of the Demand for Arbitration. If a Party opts into the Expedited

Procedures, the other side shall indicate within seven (7) calendar days of notice thereof whether it agrees to the Expedited Procedures.

(c) If one Party elects the Expedited Procedures and any other Party declines to agree to the Expedited Procedures, each Party shall have a client or client representative present at the first Preliminary Conference (which should, if feasible, be an in-person conference), unless excused by the Arbitrator for good cause.

Rule 16.2. Where Expedited Procedures Are Applicable

(a) The Arbitrator shall require compliance with Rule 17(a) prior to conducting the first Preliminary Conference. Each Party shall confirm in writing to the Arbitrator that it has so complied or shall indicate any limitations on full compliance and the reasons therefor.

(b) Document requests shall (1) be limited to documents that are directly relevant to the matters in dispute or to its outcome; (2) be reasonably restricted in terms of time frame, subject matter and persons or entities to which the requests pertain; and (3) not include broad phraseology such as "all documents directly or indirectly related to." The Requests shall not be encumbered with extensive "definitions" or "instructions." The Arbitrator may edit or limit the number of requests.

(c) E-Discovery shall be limited as follows:

(i) There shall be production of electronic documents only from sources used in the ordinary course of business. Absent a showing of compelling need, no such documents are required to be produced from backup servers, tapes or other media.

(ii) Absent a showing of compelling need, the production of electronic documents shall normally be made on the basis of generally available technology in a searchable format that is usable by the requesting Party and convenient and economical for the producing Party. Absent a showing of compelling need, the Parties need not produce metadata, with the exception of header fields for email correspondence.

(iii) The description of custodians from whom electronic documents may be collected should be narrowly tailored to include only those individuals whose electronic documents may reasonably be expected to contain evidence that is material to the dispute.

(iv) Where the costs and burdens of e-discovery are disproportionate to the nature of the dispute or to the amount in controversy, or to the relevance of the materials requested, the Arbitrator may either deny such requests or order disclosure on the condition that the requesting Party advance the reasonable cost of production to the other side, subject to the allocation of costs in the final Award.

(v) The Arbitrator may vary these Rules after discussion with the Parties at the Preliminary Conference.

(d) Depositions of percipient witnesses shall be limited as follows:

(i) The limitation of one discovery deposition per side (Rule 17(b)) shall be applied by the Arbitrator, unless it is determined, based on all relevant circumstances, that more depositions are warranted. The Arbitrator shall consider the amount in controversy, the complexity of the factual issues, the number of Parties and the diversity of their interests and whether any or all of the claims appear, on the basis of the pleadings, to have sufficient merit to justify the time and expense associated with the requested discovery.

(ii) The Arbitrator shall also consider the additional factors listed in the JAMS Recommended Arbitration Discovery Protocols for Domestic Commercial Cases.

(e) Expert depositions, if any, shall be limited as follows: Where written expert reports are produced to the other side in advance of the Hearing (Rule 17(a)), expert depositions may be conducted only by agreement of the Parties or by order of the Arbitrator for good cause shown.

(f) Discovery disputes shall be resolved on an expedited basis.

(i) Where there is a panel of three Arbitrators, the Parties are encouraged to agree, by rule or otherwise, that the Chair or another member of the panel is authorized to resolve discovery issues, acting alone.

(ii) Lengthy briefs on discovery matters should be avoided. In most cases, the submission of brief letters will sufficiently inform the Arbitrator with regard to the issues to be decided.

(iii) The Parties should meet and confer in good faith prior to presenting any issues for the Arbitrator's decision.

(iv) If disputes exist with respect to some issues, that should not delay the Parties' discovery on remaining issues.

(g) The Arbitrator shall set a discovery cutoff not to exceed seventy-five (75) calendar days after the Preliminary Conference for percipient discovery and not to exceed one hundred five (105) calendar days for expert discovery (if any). These dates may be extended by the Arbitrator for good cause shown.

(h) Dispositive motions (Rule 18) shall not be permitted, except as set forth in the JAMS Recommended Arbitration Discovery Protocols for Domestic Commercial Cases or unless the Parties agree to that procedure.

(i) The Hearing shall commence within sixty (60) calendar days after the cutoff for percipient discovery. Consecutive Hearing days shall be established unless otherwise agreed by the Parties or ordered by the Arbitrator. These dates may be extended by the Arbitrator for good cause shown.

(j) The Arbitrator may alter any of these Procedures for good cause.

Rule 17. Exchange of Information

(a) The Parties shall cooperate in good faith in the voluntary and informal exchange of all non-privileged documents and other information (including electronically stored information ("ESI")) relevant to the dispute or claim immediately after commencement of the Arbitration. They shall complete an initial exchange of all relevant, non-privileged documents, including, without limitation, copies of all documents in their possession or control on which they rely in support of their positions, and names of individuals whom they may call as witnesses at the Arbitration Hearing, within twenty-one (21) calendar days after all pleadings or notice of claims have been received. The Arbitrator may modify these obligations at the Preliminary Conference.

(b) Each Party may take one deposition of an opposing Party or of one individual under the control of the opposing Party. The Parties shall attempt to agree on the time, location and duration of the deposition. If the Parties do not agree, these issues shall be determined by the Arbitrator. The necessity of additional depositions shall be determined by the Arbitrator based upon the reasonable need for the requested information, the availability of other discovery options and the burdensomeness of the request on the opposing Parties and the witness.

(c) As they become aware of new documents or information, including experts who may be called upon to testify, all Parties continue to be obligated to provide relevant, non-privileged documents to supplement their identification of witnesses and experts and to honor any informal agreements or understandings between the Parties regarding documents or information to be exchanged. Documents that were not previously exchanged, or witnesses and experts that were not previously identified, may not be considered by the Arbitrator at the Hearing, unless agreed by the Parties or upon a showing of good cause.

(d) The Parties shall promptly notify JAMS when a dispute exists regarding discovery issues. A conference shall be arranged with the Arbitrator, either by telephone or in person, and the Arbitrator shall decide the dispute. With the written consent of all Parties, and in accordance with an agreed written procedure, the Arbitrator may appoint a special master to assist in resolving a discovery dispute.

Rule 18. Summary Disposition of a Claim or Issue

The Arbitrator may permit any Party to file a Motion for Summary Disposition of a particular claim or issue, either by agreement of all interested Parties or at the request of one Party, provided other interested Parties have reasonable notice to respond to the request.

Rule 19. Scheduling and Location of Hearing

(a) The Arbitrator, after consulting with the Parties that have appeared, shall determine the date, time and location of the Hearing. The Arbitrator and the Parties shall attempt to schedule consecutive Hearing days if more than one day is necessary.

(b) If a Party has failed to participate in the Arbitration process, the Arbitrator may set the Hearing without consulting with that Party. The non-participating Party shall be served with a Notice of Hearing at least thirty (30) calendar days prior to the scheduled date, unless the law of the relevant jurisdiction allows for, or the Parties have agreed to, shorter notice.

(c) The Arbitrator, in order to hear a third-party witness, or for the convenience of the Parties or the witnesses, may conduct the Hearing at any location. Any JAMS Resolution Center may be designated a Hearing location for purposes of the issuance of a subpoena or subpoena *duces tecum* to a third-party witness.

Rule 20. Pre-Hearing Submissions

(a) Except as set forth in any scheduling order that may be adopted, at least fourteen (14) calendar days before the Arbitration Hearing, the Parties shall file with JAMS and serve and exchange (1) a list of the witnesses they intend to call, including any experts; (2) a short description of the anticipated testimony of each such witness and an estimate of the length of the witness' direct testimony; (3) any written expert reports that may be introduced at the Arbitration Hearing; and (4) a list of all exhibits intended to be used at the Hearing. The Parties should exchange with each other copies of any such exhibits to the extent that they have not been previously exchanged. The Parties should pre-mark exhibits and shall attempt to resolve any disputes regarding the admissibility of exhibits prior to the Hearing.

(b) The Arbitrator may require that each Party submit a concise written statement of position, including summaries of the facts and evidence a Party intends to present, discussion of the applicable law and the basis for the requested Award or denial of relief sought. The statements, which may be in the form of a letter, shall be filed with JAMS and served upon the other Parties at least seven (7) calendar days before the Hearing date. Rebuttal statements or other pre-Hearing written submissions may be permitted or required at the discretion of the Arbitrator.

Rule 21. Securing Witnesses and Documents for the Arbitration Hearing

At the written request of a Party, all other Parties shall produce for the Arbitration Hearing all specified witnesses in their employ or under their control without need of subpoena. The Arbitrator may issue subpoenas for the attendance of witnesses or the production of documents either prior to or at the Hearing pursuant to this Rule or Rule 19(c). The subpoena or subpoena *duces tecum* shall be issued in accordance with the applicable law. Pre-issued subpoenas may be used in jurisdictions that permit them. In the event a Party or a subpoenaed person objects to the production of a witness or other evidence, the Party or subpoenaed person may file an objection with the Arbitrator, who shall promptly rule on the objection, weighing both the burden on the producing Party and witness and the need of the proponent for the witness or other evidence.

Rule 22. The Arbitration Hearing

(a) The Arbitrator will ordinarily conduct the Arbitration Hearing in the manner set forth in these Rules. The Arbitrator may vary these procedures if it is determined to be reasonable and appropriate to do so.

(b) The Arbitrator shall determine the order of proof, which will generally be similar to that of a court trial.

(c) The Arbitrator shall require witnesses to testify under oath if requested by any Party, or otherwise at the discretion of the Arbitrator.

(d) Strict conformity to the rules of evidence is not required, except that the Arbitrator shall apply applicable law relating to privileges and work product. The Arbitrator shall consider evidence that he or she finds relevant and material to the dispute, giving the evidence such weight as is appropriate. The Arbitrator may be guided in that determination by principles contained in the Federal Rules of Evidence or any other applicable rules of evidence. The Arbitrator may limit testimony to exclude evidence that would be immaterial or unduly repetitive, provided that all Parties are afforded the opportunity to present material and relevant evidence.

(e) The Arbitrator shall receive and consider relevant deposition testimony recorded by transcript or videotape, provided that the other Parties have had the opportunity to attend and cross-examine. The Arbitrator may in his or her discretion consider witness affidavits or other recorded testimony even if the other Parties have not had the opportunity to cross-examine, but will give that evidence only such weight as he or she deems appropriate.

(f) The Parties will not offer as evidence, and the Arbitrator shall neither admit into the record nor consider, prior settlement offers by the Parties or statements or recommendations made by a mediator or other person in connection with efforts to resolve the dispute being arbitrated, except to the extent that applicable law permits the admission of such evidence.

(g) The Hearing, or any portion thereof, may be conducted telephonically or videographically with the agreement of the Parties or at the discretion of the Arbitrator.

(h) When the Arbitrator determines that all relevant and material evidence and arguments have been presented, and any interim or partial Awards have been issued, the Arbitrator shall declare the Hearing closed. The Arbitrator may defer the closing of the Hearing until a date determined by the Arbitrator in order to permit the Parties to submit post-Hearing briefs, which may be in the form of a letter, and/or to make closing arguments. If post-Hearing briefs are to be submitted or closing arguments are to be made, the Hearing shall be deemed closed upon receipt by the Arbitrator of such briefs or at the conclusion of such closing arguments, whichever is later.

(i) At any time before the Award is rendered, the Arbitrator may, *sua sponte* or on application of a Party for good cause shown, reopen the Hearing. If the Hearing is reopened, the time to render the Award shall be calculated from the date the reopened Hearing is declared closed by the Arbitrator.

(j) The Arbitrator may proceed with the Hearing in the absence of a Party that, after receiving notice of the Hearing pursuant to Rule 19, fails to attend. The Arbitrator may not render an Award solely on the basis of the default or absence of the Party, but shall require any Party seeking relief to submit such evidence as the Arbitrator may require for the rendering of an Award. If the Arbitrator reasonably believes that a Party will not attend the Hearing, the Arbitrator may schedule the Hearing as a telephonic Hearing and may receive the evidence necessary to render an Award by affidavit. The notice of Hearing shall specify if it will be in person or telephonic.

(k) Any Party may arrange for a stenographic or other record to be made of the Hearing and shall inform the other Parties in advance of the Hearing.

(i) The requesting Party shall bear the cost of such stenographic record. If all other Parties agree to share the cost of the stenographic record, it shall be made available to the Arbitrator and may be used in the proceeding.

(ii) If there is no agreement to share the cost of the stenographic record, it may not be provided to the Arbitrator and may not be used in the proceeding, unless the Party arranging for the stenographic record agrees to provide access to the stenographic record either at no charge or on terms that are acceptable to the Parties and the reporting service.

(iii) If the Parties agree to the Optional Arbitration Appeal Procedure (Rule 34), they shall, if possible, ensure that a stenographic or other record is made of the Hearing and shall share the cost of that record.

(iv) The Parties may agree that the cost of the stenographic record shall or shall not be allocated by the Arbitrator in the Award.

Rule 23. Waiver of Hearing

The Parties may agree to waive the oral Hearing and submit the dispute to the Arbitrator for an Award based on written submissions and other evidence as the Parties may agree.

Rule 24. Awards

(a) The Arbitrator shall render a Final Award or a Partial Final Award within thirty (30) calendar days after the date of the close of the Hearing, as defined in Rule 22(h) or (i), or, if a Hearing has been waived, within thirty (30) calendar days after the receipt by the Arbitrator of all materials specified by the Parties, except (1) by the agreement of the Parties; (2) upon good cause for an extension of time to render the Award; or (3) as provided in Rule 22(i). The Arbitrator shall provide the Final Award or the Partial Final Award to JAMS for issuance in accordance with this Rule.

(b) Where a panel of Arbitrators has heard the dispute, the decision and Award of a majority of the panel shall constitute the Arbitration Award.

(c) In determining the merits of the dispute, the Arbitrator shall be guided by the rules of law agreed upon by the Parties. In the absence of such agreement, the Arbitrator shall be guided by the rules of law and equity that he or she deems to be most appropriate. The Arbitrator may grant any remedy or relief that is just and equitable and within the scope of the Parties' agreement, including, but not limited to, specific performance of a contract or any other equitable or legal remedy.

(d) In addition to a Final Award or Partial Final Award, the Arbitrator may make other decisions, including interim or partial rulings, orders and Awards.

(e) Interim Measures. The Arbitrator may grant whatever interim measures are deemed necessary, including injunctive relief and measures for the protection or conservation of property and disposition of disposable goods. Such interim measures may take the form of an interim or Partial Final Award, and the Arbitrator may require security for the costs of such measures. Any recourse by a Party to a court for interim or provisional relief shall not be deemed incompatible with the agreement to arbitrate or a waiver of the right to arbitrate.

(f) The Award of the Arbitrator may allocate Arbitration fees and Arbitrator compensation and expenses, unless such an allocation is expressly prohibited by the Parties' Agreement. (Such a prohibition may not limit the power of the Arbitrator to allocate Arbitration fees and Arbitrator compensation and expenses pursuant to Rule 31(c).)

(g) The Award of the Arbitrator may allocate attorneys' fees and expenses and interest (at such rate and from such date as the Arbitrator may deem appropriate) if provided by the Parties' Agreement or allowed by applicable law. When the Arbitrator is authorized to award attorneys' fees and must determine the reasonable amount of such fees, he or she may consider whether the failure of a Party to cooperate reasonably in the discovery process and/or comply with the Arbitrator's discovery orders caused delay to the proceeding or additional costs to the other Parties.

(h) The Award shall consist of a written statement signed by the Arbitrator regarding the disposition of each claim and the relief, if any, as to each claim. Unless all Parties agree otherwise, the Award shall also contain a concise written statement of the reasons for the Award.

(i) After the Award has been rendered, and provided the Parties have complied with Rule 31, the Award shall be issued by serving copies on the Parties. Service may be made by U.S. mail. It need not be sent certified or registered.

(j) Within seven (7) calendar days after service of a Partial Final Award or Final Award by JAMS, any Party may serve upon the other Parties and on JAMS a request that the Arbitrator correct any computational, typographical or other similar error in an Award (including the reallocation of fees pursuant to Rule 31(c) or on account of the effect of an offer to allow judgment), or the Arbitrator may *sua sponte* propose to correct such errors in an Award. A Party opposing such correction shall have seven (7) calendar days thereafter in which to file any objection. The Arbitrator may make any necessary and appropriate corrections to the Award within twenty-one (21) calendar days of receiving a request or fourteen (14) calendar days after his or her proposal to do so. The Arbitrator may extend the time within which to make corrections upon good cause. The corrected Award shall be served upon the Parties in the same manner as the Award.

(k) The Award is considered final, for purposes of either the Optional Arbitration Appeal Procedure pursuant to Rule 34 or a judicial proceeding to enforce, modify or vacate the Award pursuant to Rule 25, fourteen (14) calendar days after service is deemed effective if no request for a correction is made, or as of the effective date of service of a corrected Award.

Rule 25. Enforcement of the Award

Proceedings to enforce, confirm, modify or vacate an Award will be controlled by and conducted in conformity with the Federal Arbitration Act, 9 U.S.C. Sec 1, *et seq.*, or applicable state law. The Parties to an Arbitration under these Rules shall be deemed to have consented that judgment upon the Award may be entered in any court having jurisdiction thereof.

Rule 26. Confidentiality and Privacy

(a) JAMS and the Arbitrator shall maintain the confidential nature of the Arbitration proceeding and the Award, including the Hearing, except as necessary in connection with a judicial challenge to or enforcement of an Award, or unless otherwise required by law or judicial decision.

(b) The Arbitrator may issue orders to protect the confidentiality of proprietary information, trade secrets or other sensitive information.

(c) Subject to the discretion of the Arbitrator or agreement of the Parties, any person having a direct interest in the Arbitration may attend the Arbitration Hearing. The Arbitrator may exclude any non-Party from any part of a Hearing.

Rule 27. Waiver

(a) If a Party becomes aware of a violation of or failure to comply with these Rules and fails promptly to object in writing, the objection will be deemed waived, unless the Arbitrator determines that waiver will cause substantial injustice or hardship.

(b) If any Party becomes aware of information that could be the basis of a challenge for cause to the continued service of the Arbitrator, such challenge must be made promptly, in writing, to the Arbitrator or JAMS. Failure to do so shall constitute a waiver of any objection to continued service by the Arbitrator.

Rule 28. Settlement and Consent Award

(a) The Parties may agree, at any stage of the Arbitration process, to submit the case to JAMS for mediation. The JAMS mediator assigned to the case may not be the Arbitrator or a member of the Appeal Panel, unless the Parties so agree, pursuant to Rule 28(b).

(b) The Parties may agree to seek the assistance of the Arbitrator in reaching settlement. By their written agreement to submit the matter to the Arbitrator for settlement assistance, the Parties will be deemed to have agreed that the assistance of the Arbitrator in such settlement efforts will not disqualify the Arbitrator from continuing to serve as Arbitrator if settlement is not reached; nor shall such assistance be argued to a reviewing court as the basis for vacating or modifying an Award.

(c) If, at any stage of the Arbitration process, all Parties agree upon a settlement of the issues in dispute and request the Arbitrator to embody the agreement in a Consent Award, the Arbitrator shall comply with such request, unless the Arbitrator believes the terms of the agreement are illegal or undermine the integrity of the Arbitration process. If the Arbitrator is concerned about the possible consequences of the proposed Consent Award, he or she shall inform the Parties of that concern and may request additional specific information from the Parties regarding the proposed Consent Award. The Arbitrator may refuse to enter the proposed Consent Award and may withdraw from the case.

Rule 29. Sanctions

The Arbitrator may order appropriate sanctions for failure of a Party to comply with its obligations under any of these Rules or with an order of the Arbitrator. These sanctions may include, but are not limited to, assessment of Arbitration fees and Arbitrator compensation and expenses; assessment of any other costs occasioned by the actionable conduct, including reasonable attorneys' fees; exclusion of certain evidence; drawing adverse inferences; or, in extreme cases, determining an issue or issues submitted to Arbitration adversely to the Party that has failed to comply.

Rule 30. Disqualification of the Arbitrator as a Witness or Party and Exclusion of Liability

(a) The Parties may not call the Arbitrator, the Case Manager or any other JAMS employee or agent as a witness or as an expert in any pending or subsequent litigation or other proceeding involving the Parties and relating to the dispute that is the subject of the Arbitration. The Arbitrator, Case Manager and other JAMS employees and agents are also incompetent to testify as witnesses or experts in any such proceeding.

(b) The Parties shall defend and/or pay the cost (including any attorneys' fees) of defending the Arbitrator, Case Manager and/or JAMS from any subpoenas from outside parties arising from the Arbitration.

(c) The Parties agree that neither the Arbitrator, nor the Case Manager, nor JAMS is a necessary Party in any litigation or other proceeding relating to the Arbitration or the subject matter of the Arbitration, and neither the Arbitrator, nor the Case Manager, nor JAMS, including its employees or agents, shall be liable to any Party for any act or omission in connection with any Arbitration conducted under these Rules, including, but not limited to, any disqualification of or recusal by the Arbitrator.

Rule 31. Fees

(a) Each Party shall pay its *pro rata* share of JAMS fees and expenses as set forth in the JAMS fee schedule in effect at the time of the commencement of the Arbitration, unless the Parties agree on a different allocation of fees and expenses. JAMS› agreement to render services is jointly with the Party and the attorney or other representative of the Party in the Arbitration. The non-payment of fees may result in an administrative suspension of the case in accordance with Rule 6(c).

(b) JAMS requires that the Parties deposit the fees and expenses for the Arbitration from time to time during the course of the proceedings and prior to the Hearing. The Arbitrator may preclude a Party that has failed to deposit its *pro rata* or agreed-upon share of the fees and expenses from offering evidence of any affirmative claim at the Hearing.

(c) The Parties are jointly and severally liable for the payment of JAMS Arbitration fees and Arbitrator compensation and expenses. In the event that one Party has paid more than its share of such fees, compensation and expenses, the Arbitrator may award against any other Party any such fees, compensation and expenses that such Party owes with respect to the Arbitration.

(d) Entities whose interests are not adverse with respect to the issues in dispute shall be treated as a single Party for purposes of JAMS' assessment of fees. JAMS shall determine whether the interests between entities are adverse for purpose of fees, considering such factors as whether the entities are represented by the same attorney and whether the entities are presenting joint or separate positions at the Arbitration.

Rule 32. Bracketed (or High-Low) Arbitration Option

(a) At any time before the issuance of the Arbitration Award, the Parties may agree, in writing, on minimum and maximum amounts of damages that may be awarded on each claim or on all claims in the aggregate. The Parties shall promptly notify JAMS and provide to JAMS a copy of their written agreement setting forth the agreed-upon minimum and maximum amounts.

(b) JAMS shall not inform the Arbitrator of the agreement to proceed with this option or of the agreed-upon minimum and maximum levels without the consent of the Parties.

(c) The Arbitrator shall render the Award in accordance with Rule 24.

(d) In the event that the Award of the Arbitrator is between the agreed-upon minimum and maximum amounts, the Award shall become final as is. In the event that the Award is below the agreed-upon minimum amount, the final Award issued shall be corrected to reflect the agreed-upon minimum amount. In the event that the Award is above the agreed-upon maximum amount, the final Award issued shall be corrected to reflect the agreed-upon maximum amount.

Rule 33. Final Offer (or Baseball) Arbitration Option

(a) Upon agreement of the Parties to use the option set forth in this Rule, at least seven (7) calendar days before the Arbitration Hearing, the Parties shall exchange and provide to JAMS written proposals for the amount of money damages they would offer or demand, as applicable, and that they believe to be appropriate based on the standard set forth in Rule 24(c). JAMS shall promptly provide copies of the Parties' proposals to the Arbitrator, unless the Parties agree that they should not be provided to the Arbitrator. At any time prior to the close of the Arbitration Hearing, the Parties may exchange revised written proposals or demands, which shall supersede all prior proposals. The revised written proposals shall be provided to JAMS, which shall promptly provide them to the Arbitrator, unless the Parties agree otherwise.

(b) If the Arbitrator has been informed of the written proposals, in rendering the Award, the Arbitrator shall choose between the Parties' last proposals, selecting the proposal that the Arbitrator finds most reasonable and appropriate in light of the standard set forth in Rule 24(c). This provision modifies Rule 24(h) in that no written statement of reasons shall accompany the Award.

(c) If the Arbitrator has not been informed of the written proposals, the Arbitrator shall render the Award as if pursuant to Rule 24, except that the Award shall thereafter be corrected to conform to the closest of the last proposals and the closest of the last proposals will become the Award.

(d) Other than as provided herein, the provisions of Rule 24 shall be applicable.

Rule 34. Optional Arbitration Appeal Procedure

The Parties may agree at any time to the JAMS Optional Arbitration Appeal Procedure. All Parties must agree in writing for such procedure to be effective. Once a Party has agreed to the Optional Arbitration Appeal Procedure, it cannot unilaterally withdraw from it, unless it withdraws, pursuant to Rule 13, from the Arbitration.

6. Sample Corporate Bylaws (eBay, Inc.)

SAMPLE CORPORATE BYLAWS AMENDED AND RESTATED BYLAWS OF EBAY INC.

(a Delaware corporation)

eBay Inc. (the "*Corporation*"), pursuant to the provisions of Section 109 of the Delaware General Corporation Law, hereby adopts these Amended and Restated Bylaws, which restate, amend and supersede the bylaws of the Corporation, as previously amended and restated, in their entirety as described below:

ARTICLE I.

STOCKHOLDERS

SECTION 1.1: Place of Meetings. Meetings of the stockholders of the Corporation may be held at such place, either within or without the State of Delaware, as may be designated from time to time by the Board of Directors. The Board of Directors may, in its sole discretion, determine that the meeting shall not be held at any place, but may instead be held solely by means of remote communication as provided under the Delaware General Corporation Law.

SECTION 1.2: Annual Meetings. If required by applicable law, an annual meeting of stockholders shall be held for the election of directors at such date and time, as the Board of Directors shall each year fix. Any other proper business may be transacted at the annual meeting.

SECTION 1.3: Special Meetings.

(a) General. Special meetings of the stockholders, for any purpose or purposes described in the notice of the meeting, may be called by (i) the Board of Directors pursuant to a resolution adopted by a majority of the total number of authorized directors (whether or not there exist any vacancies in previously authorized directorships at the time any such resolution is presented to the Board of Directors for adoption), (ii) the Chairman of the Board or (iii) the Chief Executive Officer of the Corporation, and shall be held at such place, if any, on such date, and at such time as they shall fix. Subject to the provisions of Section 1.3(b) and other applicable provisions of these bylaws, a special meeting of stockholders shall be called by the Secretary of the Corporation upon the written request (a "*Stockholder Requested Special Meeting*") of one or more stockholders of record of the Corporation that together have continuously held, for their own account or on behalf of others, beneficial ownership of at least a twenty-five percent (25%) aggregate "net long position" of the outstanding common stock of the Corporation (the "*Requisite Percent*") for at least thirty (30) days as of the date such request is delivered to the Corporation. For purposes of determining the Requisite Percent, "net long position" shall be determined with respect to each requesting holder in accordance with the definition thereof set forth in Rule 14e–4 under the Securities Exchange Act of 1934, as amended, and the rules and regulations thereunder (as so amended and inclusive of such rules and regulations, the "*Exchange Act*"); *provided* that (x) for purposes of such definition, (A) "the date that a tender offer is first publicly announced or otherwise made known by the bidder to the holders of the security to be acquired" shall be the date of the relevant Special Meeting Request, (B) the "highest tender offer price or stated amount of the consideration offered for the subject security" shall refer to the closing sales price of the Corporation's common stock on the NASDAQ Global Select Market (or any successor thereto) on such date (or, if such date is not a trading day, the next succeeding trading day), (C) the "person whose securities are the subject of the offer" shall refer to the Corporation, and (D) a "subject security" shall refer to the outstanding common stock of the Corporation; and (y) the net long position of such holder shall be reduced by the number of shares of common stock of the Corporation as to which such holder does not, or will not, have the right to vote or direct the vote at the special meeting or as to which such holder has entered into any derivative or other agreement, arrangement or understanding that hedges or transfers, in whole or in part, directly or indirectly, any of the economic consequences of ownership of such shares. Whether the requesting holders have complied with the requirements of this Article I and related provisions of the Bylaws shall be determined in good faith by the Board of Directors, which determination shall be conclusive and binding on the Corporation and the stockholders.

(b) Stockholder Requested Special Meetings. In order for a Stockholder Requested Special Meeting to be called, one or more requests for a special meeting (each, a "*Special Meeting Request*," and collectively, the "*Special Meeting Requests*") must be signed by the Requisite Percent of stockholders submitting such request and by each of the beneficial owners, if any, on whose behalf the Special Meeting Request is being made and must be delivered to the Secretary of the Corporation. The Special Meeting Request(s) shall be delivered to the Secretary of the Corporation at the principal executive offices of the Corporation by overnight express courier or registered mail, return receipt requested. Each Special Meeting Request shall (i) set forth a statement of the specific purpose(s) of the meeting and the matters proposed to be acted on at it, (ii) bear the date of signature of each such stockholder signing the Special Meeting Request, (iii) set forth (A) the name and address, as they appear in the Corporation's books, of each stockholder signing such request and the beneficial owners, if any, on whose behalf such request is made, and (B) the class, if applicable, and the number of shares of common stock of the Corporation that are owned of record and beneficially (within the meaning of Rule 13d–3 under the Exchange Act) by each such stockholder and the beneficial owners, if any, on whose behalf such request is made, (iv) include documentary evidence that the stockholders requesting the special meeting own the Requisite Percent as of the date on which the Special Meeting Request is delivered to the Secretary of the Corporation; *provided, however,* that if the stockholders are not the beneficial owners of the shares constituting all or part of the Requisite Percent, then to be valid, the Special Meeting Request must also include documentary evidence (or, if not simultaneously provided with the Special Meeting Request, such documentary evidence must be delivered to the Secretary of the Corporation within ten (10) days after the date on which the Special Meeting Request is delivered to the Secretary of the Corporation) that the beneficial owners on whose behalf the Special Meeting Request is made beneficially own such shares as of the date on which such Special Meeting Request is delivered to the Secretary of the Corporation, (v) an agreement by each of the stockholders requesting the special meeting and each beneficial owner, if any, on whose behalf the Special Meeting Request is being made to notify the Corporation promptly in the event of any decrease in the net long position held by such stockholder or beneficial owner following the delivery of such Special Meeting Request and prior to the special meeting and an acknowledgement that any such decrease shall be deemed to be a revocation of such Special Meeting Request by such stockholder or beneficial owner to the extent of such reduction, and (vi) contain the information required by Section 1.14 and Section 1.15, as applicable, provided that all references to "Proposing Person" in Section 1.14 and all references to "Nominating Person" in Section 1.15 shall, for purposes of this Section 1.3(b), mean (i) the stockholders of record making the Special Meeting Request, (ii) any beneficial owner or beneficial owners, if different, on whose behalf the Special Meeting Request is being made, and (iii) any affiliate or associate (each within the meaning of Rule 12b–2 under the Exchange Act for purposes of these Bylaws) of such stockholder or beneficial owner. Each stockholder making a Special Meeting Request and each beneficial owner, if any, on whose behalf the Special Meeting Request is being made is required to update the notice delivered pursuant to this Section 1.3(b) in accordance with Section 1.14(d) or Section 1.15(d), as applicable. Any requesting stockholder may revoke his, her or its Special Meeting Request at any time prior to the special meeting by written revocation delivered to the Secretary of the Corporation at the principal executive offices of the Corporation. If at any time after sixty (60) days following the earliest dated Special Meeting Request, the unrevoked (whether by specific written revocation by the stockholder or pursuant to clause (b)(v) of this Section 1.3) valid Special Meeting Requests represent in the aggregate less than the Requisite Percent, then the requesting stockholder(s) or beneficial owner(s) shall be deemed to have withdrawn such request (in connection with which the Board may cancel the meeting).

In determining whether a special meeting of stockholders has been requested by stockholders holding in the aggregate at least the Requisite Percent, multiple Special Meeting Requests delivered to the Secretary of the Corporation will be considered together only if (i) each Special Meeting Request identifies substantially the same purpose or purposes of the special meeting and substantially the same matters proposed to be acted on at the special meeting (in each case as determined in good faith by the Board of Directors), and (ii) such Special Meeting Requests have been delivered to the Secretary of the Corporation within sixty (60) days of the earliest dated Special Meeting Request.

(c) Calling of a Special Meeting. Except as provided in the next sentence, a special meeting requested by stockholders shall be held at such date, time and place within or without the State of Delaware as may be fixed by the Board of Directors; *provided, however*, that the date of any such special meeting shall be not more than ninety (90) days after the date on which valid Special Meeting Request(s) constituting the Requisite Percent are delivered to the Secretary of the Corporation (such date of delivery being the "*Delivery Date*"). Notwithstanding the foregoing, the Secretary of the Corporation shall not be required to call a special meeting of stockholders if (i) the Board of Directors calls an annual meeting of stockholders, or a special meeting of stockholders at which a Similar Item (as defined in this Section 1.3(c)) is to be presented pursuant to the notice of such meeting, in either case to be held not later than sixty (60) days after the Delivery Date; (ii) the Delivery Date is during the period commencing ninety (90) days prior to the first anniversary of the date of the immediately preceding annual meeting and ending on the earlier of (A) the date of the next annual meeting and (B) thirty (30) days after the first anniversary of the date of the immediately preceding annual meeting; or (iii) the Special Meeting Request(s) (A) contain an identical or substantially similar item (as determined in good faith by the Board of Directors, a "*Similar Item*") to an item that was presented at any meeting of stockholders held not more than one hundred and twenty (120) days before the Delivery Date (and, for purposes of this clause (iii) the election of directors shall be deemed a "Similar Item" with respect to all items of business involving the election or removal of directors); (B) relate to an item of business that is not a proper subject for action by the stockholders under applicable law; (C) were made in a manner that involved a violation of Regulation 14A under the Exchange Act or other applicable law; or (D) do not comply with the provisions of this Section 1.3.

(d) Business Transacted at a Special Meeting. Business transacted at any Stockholder Requested Special Meeting shall be limited to the purpose or purposes stated in the Special Meeting Request(s) for such special meeting; *provided, however*, that nothing herein shall prohibit the Board of Directors from submitting additional matters to stockholders at any such special meeting pursuant to the Corporation's notice of meeting. If none of the stockholders who submitted a Special Meeting Request appears at or sends a duly authorized representative to the Stockholder Requested Special Meeting to present the matters to be presented for consideration that were specified in the Special Meeting Request, the corporation need not present such matters for a vote at such meeting.

SECTION 1.4: Notice of Meetings. Notice of all meetings of stockholders shall be given that shall state the place, if any, date and time of the meeting, the means of remote communications, if any, by which stockholders and proxy holders may be deemed to be present in person and vote at such meeting and, in the case of a special meeting, the purpose or purposes for which the meeting is called. Unless otherwise required by applicable law or the Certificate of Incorporation of the Corporation as currently in effect (the "*Certificate of Incorporation*"), such notice shall be given not less than ten (10) nor more than sixty (60) days before the date of the meeting to each stockholder entitled to vote at such meeting.

SECTION 1.5: Manner of Giving Notice; Affidavit of Notice.

(a) Notice of any meeting of stockholders, if mailed, is given when deposited in the United States mail, postage prepaid, directed to the stockholder at his, her or its address as it appears on the records of the Corporation.

(b) Except as otherwise prohibited by the Delaware General Corporation Law and without limiting the foregoing, any notice to stockholders given by the Corporation under any provision of the Delaware General Corporation Law, the Certificate of Incorporation or these Bylaws shall be effective if given by a form of electronic transmission consented to (and not properly revoked by written notice to the Corporation) by the stockholder to whom the notice is given, to the extent such consent is required by the Delaware General Corporation Law. Any such consent shall be revocable by the stockholder by written notice to the Corporation. Any such consent shall be deemed revoked if (i) the Corporation is unable to deliver by electronic transmission two (2) consecutive notices given by the Corporation in accordance with such consent and (ii) such inability becomes known to the Secretary or an Assistant Secretary of the Corporation or to the transfer agent of the Corporation, or other person responsible for the giving of notice; *provided, however*, the inadvertent failure to treat such inability as a revocation shall not invalidate any meeting or other action. Any such notice shall be deemed given (i) if by facsimile telecommunication, when directed to a number at which the stockholder has consented to receive notice; (ii) if by electronic mail, when directed to an electronic mail address at which the stockholder has consented to receive notice; (iii) if by a posting on an electronic network together with separate notice to the stockholder of such specific posting, upon the later of (A) such posting and (B) the giving of such separate notice; and (iv) if by any other form of electronic transmission, when directed to the stockholder.

(c) For the purposes of these Bylaws, an "*electronic transmission*" means any form of communication, not directly involving the physical transmission of paper, that creates a record that may be retained, retrieved and reviewed by a recipient thereof, and that may be directly reproduced in paper form by such a recipient through an automated process.

(d) Except as otherwise prohibited under the Delaware General Corporation Law and without limiting the manner by which notice otherwise may be given to stockholders, any notice to stockholders given by the Corporation under any provision of the Delaware General Corporation Law, the Certificate of Incorporation or these Bylaws may be given by a single written notice to stockholders who share an address if consented to by the stockholders at that address to whom such notice is given. Such consent shall have been deemed to have been given if a stockholder fails to object in writing to the Corporation within sixty (60) days of having been given written notice by the Corporation of its intention to send the single notice in accordance with this Section 1.5(d). Any such consent shall be revocable by the stockholders by written notice to the Corporation.

(e) An affidavit of the Secretary or an Assistant Secretary of the Corporation or of the transfer agent or other agent of the Corporation that the notice has been given shall, in the absence of fraud, be *prima facie* evidence of the facts stated therein.

SECTION 1.6: Adjournments. Any meeting of stockholders may adjourn from time to time to reconvene at the same or another place, if any, or by means of remote communications, if any, by which stockholders and proxy holders may be deemed to be present in person and vote at such meeting, and notice need not be given of any such adjourned meeting if the place, if any, time and date thereof, and the means of remote communications, if any, by which stockholders and proxy holders may be deemed to be present in person and vote at such adjourned meeting are announced at the meeting at which the adjournment is taken; *provided, however*, that if the adjournment is for more than thirty (30) days, or if after the adjournment a new record date is fixed for the adjourned meeting, then a notice of the adjourned meeting shall be given to each stockholder of record entitled to vote at the meeting. At the adjourned meeting the Corporation may transact any business that might have been transacted at the original meeting.

SECTION 1.7: Quorum. At each meeting of stockholders the holders of a majority of the shares of stock entitled to vote at the meeting, present in person or represented by proxy, shall constitute a quorum for the transaction of business, except if otherwise required by applicable law. Where a separate vote by a class or classes or series is required, a majority of the shares of such class or classes or series then outstanding and entitled to vote present in person or by proxy shall constitute a quorum entitled to take action with respect to that vote on that matter. If a quorum shall fail to attend any meeting, the chairman of the meeting or the holders of a majority of the shares entitled to vote who are present, in person or by proxy, at the meeting may adjourn the meeting. Shares of the Corporation's stock belonging to the Corporation (or to another corporation, if a majority of the shares entitled to vote in the election of directors of such other corporation are held, directly or indirectly, by the Corporation), shall neither be entitled to vote nor be counted for quorum purposes; *provided, however,* that the foregoing shall not limit the right of the Corporation or any other corporation to vote any shares of the Corporation's stock held by it in a fiduciary capacity.

SECTION 1.8: Conduct of Business. Meetings of stockholders shall be presided over by such person as the Board of Directors may designate as chairman of the meeting, or, in the absence of such a person, the Chairman of the Board, or, in the absence of such person, the President of the Corporation, or, in the absence of such person, such person as may be chosen by the holders of a majority of the shares entitled to vote who are present, in person or by proxy, at the meeting. The Secretary of the Corporation shall act as secretary of the meeting, but in his or her absence the chairman of the meeting may appoint any person to act as secretary of the meeting. The Board of Directors shall be entitled to make such rules or regulations for the conduct of meetings of stockholders as it shall deem necessary, appropriate or convenient. Subject to such rules and regulations of the Board of Directors, if any, the chairman of the meeting shall have the right and authority to prescribe such rules, regulations and procedures and to do all such acts as, in the judgment of such chairman, are necessary, appropriate or convenient for the proper conduct of the meeting, including, without limitation, adjourning the meeting if the chairman determines in his or her sole discretion that an adjournment is advisable, establishing an agenda or order of business for the meeting, rules and procedures for maintaining order at the meeting and the safety of those present, limitations on participation in the meeting to stockholders of record of the Corporation, their duly authorized and constituted proxies and such other persons as the chairman shall permit, restrictions on entry to the meeting after the time fixed for the commencement thereof, limitations on the time allotted to questions or comments by participants and regulation of the opening and closing of the polls for balloting and matters which are to be voted on by ballot.

SECTION 1.9: Voting; Proxies. Unless otherwise provided by law or the Certificate of Incorporation, each stockholder shall be entitled to one (1) vote for each share of stock held by such stockholder of record according to the records of the Corporation. The stockholders entitled to vote at any meeting of stockholders shall be determined in accordance with the provisions of Section 1.11 of these Bylaws, subject to Section 217 (relating to voting rights of fiduciaries, pledgors and joint owners of stock) and Section 218 (relating to voting trusts and other voting agreements) of the Delaware General Corporation Law. Each stockholder entitled to vote at a meeting of stockholders may authorize another person or persons to act for such stockholder by proxy. Such a proxy may be prepared, transmitted and delivered in any manner permitted by applicable law. Unless otherwise provided in the Certificate of Incorporation or a Certificate of Designation relating to a series of Preferred Stock, directors shall be elected as provided in Section 2.2 of these Bylaws. Unless otherwise provided by applicable law, the rules or regulations of any stock exchange applicable to the Corporation, the Certificate of Incorporation or these Bylaws, every matter other than the election of directors shall be decided by the affirmative vote of the holders of a majority in voting power of the shares of stock entitled to vote thereon that are present in person or represented by proxy at the meeting.

SECTION 1.10: [Intentionally Omitted.]

SECTION 1.11: Fixing Date for Determination of Stockholders of Record. In order that the Corporation may determine the stockholders entitled to notice of or to vote at any meeting of stockholders or any adjournment thereof or entitled to receive payment of any dividend or other distribution or allotment of any rights, or entitled to exercise any rights in respect of any change, conversion or exchange of stock or for the purpose of any other lawful action, the Board of Directors may fix, in advance, a record date, which (i) in the case of determination of stockholders entitled to vote at any meeting of stockholders or adjournment thereof, shall, unless otherwise required by law, not be more than sixty (60) nor less than ten (10) days before the date of such meeting, and (ii) in the case of any other action, shall not be more than sixty (60) days prior to any such other action. If no record date is fixed by the Board of Directors, then the record date shall be as provided by applicable law. A determination of stockholders of record entitled to notice of or to vote at a meeting of stockholders shall apply to any adjournment of the meeting; *provided, however*, that the Board of Directors may fix a new record date for the adjourned meeting.

SECTION 1.12: List of Stockholders Entitled to Vote. A complete list of stockholders entitled to vote at any meeting of stockholders, arranged in alphabetical order and showing the address of each stockholder and the number of shares registered in the name of each stockholder, shall be open to the examination of any stockholder, for any purpose germane to the meeting, for a period of at least ten (10) days prior to the meeting, (i) on a reasonably accessible electronic network, provided that the information required to gain access to such list is provided with the notice of the meeting, or (ii) during ordinary business hours, at the principal place of business of the Corporation. In the event that the Corporation determines to make the list available on an electronic network, the Corporation may take reasonable steps to ensure that such information is available only to the stockholders of the Corporation. If the meeting is to be held at a place, then the list shall be produced and kept at the time and place of the meeting during the whole time thereof and may be inspected by any stockholder who is present. If the meeting is to be held solely by means of remote communication, then the list shall also be open to the examination of any stockholder during the whole time of the meeting on a reasonably accessible electronic network, and the information required to access such list shall be provided with the notice of the meeting. Except as otherwise provided by law, such list shall be the only evidence as to who are the stockholders entitled to examine the list of stockholders required by this Section 1.12 or to vote in person or by proxy at any meeting of the stockholders. The Corporation shall not be required to include electronic mail addresses or other electronic contact information on such list.

SECTION 1.13: Inspectors of Elections.

(a) Applicability. Unless otherwise provided in the Corporation's Certificate of Incorporation or required by the Delaware General Corporation Law, the following provisions of this Section 1.13 shall apply only if and when the Corporation has a class of voting stock that is:

(i) listed on a national securities exchange;

(ii) authorized for quotation on an interdealer quotation system of a registered national securities association; or

(iii) held of record by more than 2,000 stockholders; in all other cases, observance of the provisions of this Section 1.13 shall be optional, and at the discretion of the Corporation.

(b) Appointment. The Corporation shall, in advance of any meeting of stockholders, appoint one or more inspectors of election to act at the meeting and make a written report thereof. The Corporation may designate one or more persons as alternate inspectors to replace any inspector who fails to act. If no inspector or alternate is able to act at a meeting of stockholders, the person presiding at the meeting shall appoint one or more inspectors to act at the meeting.

(c) Inspector's Oath. Each inspector of election, before entering upon the discharge of his or her duties, shall take and sign an oath faithfully to execute the duties of inspector with strict impartiality and according to the best of his or her ability.

(d) Duties of Inspectors. At a meeting of stockholders, the inspectors of election shall

(i) ascertain the number of shares outstanding and the voting power of each share;

(ii) determine the shares represented at a meeting and the validity of proxies and ballots;

(iii) count all votes and ballots;

(iv) determine and retain for a reasonable period of time a record of the disposition of any challenges made to any determination by the inspectors; and

(v) certify their determination of the number of shares represented at the meeting, and their count of all votes and ballots. The inspectors may appoint or retain other persons or entities to assist the inspectors in the performance of the duties of the inspectors.

(e) Opening and Closing of Polls. The date and time of the opening and the closing of the polls for each matter upon which the stockholders will vote at a meeting shall be announced by the inspectors at the meeting. No ballot, proxies or votes, nor any revocations thereof or changes thereto, shall be accepted by the inspectors after the closing of the polls unless the Court of Chancery upon application by a stockholder shall determine otherwise.

(f) Determinations. In determining the validity and counting of proxies and ballots, the inspectors shall be limited to an examination of the proxies, any envelopes submitted with those proxies, any information provided in connection with proxies in accordance with Section 211(e) or Section 212(c)(2) of the Delaware General Corporation Law, or any information provided pursuant to Section 211(a)(2)(B)(i) or (iii) of the Delaware General Corporation Law, ballots and the regular books and records of the Corporation, except that the inspectors may consider other reliable information for the limited purpose of reconciling proxies and ballots submitted by or on behalf of banks, brokers, their nominees or similar persons which represent more votes than the holder of a proxy is authorized by the record owner to cast or more votes than the stockholder holds of record. If the inspectors consider other reliable information for the limited purpose permitted herein, the inspectors at the time they make their certification of their determinations pursuant to this Section 1.13 shall specify the precise information considered by them, including the person or persons from whom they obtained the information, when the information was obtained, the means by which the information was obtained and the basis for the inspectors' belief that such information is accurate and reliable.

SECTION 1.14: Notice of Stockholder Business to be Brought Before an Annual or Special Meeting.

(a) Business Properly Brought Before an Annual or Special Meeting. At an annual meeting of the stockholders, only such business shall be conducted as shall have been properly brought before the meeting. To be properly brought before an annual meeting, business must be

(i) brought before the meeting by the Corporation and specified in the notice of meeting given by or at the direction of the Board of Directors, (ii) brought before the meeting by or at the direction of the Board of Directors, or (iii) otherwise properly brought before the meeting by a stockholder who (A) was a stockholder of record (and, with respect to any beneficial owner, if different, on whose behalf such business is proposed, only if such beneficial owner was the beneficial owner of shares of the Corporation) both at the time of giving the notice provided for in this Section 1.14 and at the time of the meeting, (B) is entitled to vote at the meeting, and (C) has complied with this Section 1.14 as to such business. Except for proposals properly made in accordance with Rule 14a–8 under the Exchange Act, and included in the notice of meeting given by or at the direction of the Board of Directors, the foregoing clause (iii) shall be the exclusive means for a stockholder to propose business to be brought before an annual meeting of the stockholders. Stockholders shall not be permitted to propose business to be brought before a special meeting of the stockholders (other than pursuant to a Special Meeting Request in accordance with the requirements set forth in Section 1.3), and the only matters that may be brought before a special meeting are the matters specified in the Corporation's notice of meeting. Stockholders seeking to nominate persons for election to the Board must comply with Section 1.15 of these Bylaws, and this Section 1.14 shall not be applicable to nominations except as expressly provided in Section 1.15 of these Bylaws.

(b) Requirement of Timely Notice of Stockholder Business. Without qualification, for business to be properly brought before an annual meeting by a stockholder, the stockholder must (i) provide Timely Notice (as defined below) thereof in writing and in proper form to the Secretary of the Corporation and (ii) provide any updates or supplements to such notice at the times and in the forms required by this Section 1.14. To be timely, a stockholder's notice with respect to an annual meeting of stockholders must be delivered by overnight express courier or registered mail, return receipt requested, and received at, the principal executive offices of the Corporation not less than ninety (90) days nor more than one hundred twenty (120) days prior to the one year anniversary of the preceding year's annual meeting; *provided, however,* that if the date of the annual meeting is more than thirty (30) days before or more than sixty (60) days after such anniversary date, notice by the stockholder to be timely must be so delivered, or mailed and received, not earlier than the one hundred twentieth (120th) day prior to such annual meeting and not later than the ninetieth (90th) day prior to such annual meeting or, if later, the tenth (10th) day following the day on which public disclosure of the date of such annual meeting was first made (such notice within such time periods, *"Timely Notice"*). In no event shall any adjournment or postponement of an annual meeting or the announcement thereof commence a new time period for the giving of Timely Notice as described above.

(c) Requirements for Proper Form of Stockholder Notice of Proposed Business. To be in proper form for purposes of this Section 1.14, a stockholder's notice to the Secretary shall set forth:

(i) Stockholder Information. As to each Proposing Person (as defined below), (A) the name and address of such Proposing Person (including, if applicable, the name and address that appear on the Corporation's books and records), (B) the class or series and number of shares of the Corporation that are, directly or indirectly, owned of record or beneficially owned (within the meaning of Rule 13d–3 under the Exchange Act) by such Proposing Person, except that such Proposing Person shall in all events be deemed to beneficially own any shares of any class or series of the Corporation as to which such Proposing Person has a right to acquire beneficial ownership at any time in the future and (C) representation whether such Proposing Person intends or is part of a group that intends (x) to deliver a proxy statement and/or form of proxy to holders of at least the percentage of the Corporation's outstanding stock required to approve or adopt the proposal or (y) otherwise to solicit proxies from stockholders in support of such proposal;

(ii) Information Regarding Disclosable Interests. As to each Proposing Person, (A) any derivative, swap or other transaction or series of transactions engaged in, directly or indirectly, by such Proposing Person, the purpose or effect of which is to give such Proposing Person economic risk similar to ownership of shares of any class or series of the Corporation, including due to the fact that the value of such derivative, swap or other transactions are determined by reference to the price, value or volatility of any shares of any class or series of the Corporation, or which derivative, swap or other transactions provide, directly or indirectly, the opportunity to profit from any increase in the price or value of shares of any class or series of the Corporation ("*Synthetic Equity Interests*"), which such Synthetic Equity Interests shall be disclosed without regard to whether (x) such derivative, swap or other transactions convey any voting rights in such shares to such Proposing Person, (y) the derivative, swap or other transactions are required to be, or are capable of being, settled through delivery of such shares or (z) such Proposing Person may have entered into other transactions that hedge or mitigate the economic effect of such derivative, swap or other transactions, (B) any proxy (other than a revocable proxy or consent given in response to a solicitation made pursuant to, and in accordance with, Section 14(a) of the Exchange Act by way of a solicitation statement filed on Schedule 14A), agreement, arrangement, understanding or relationship pursuant to which such Proposing Person has or shares a right to vote any shares of any class or series of the Corporation, (C) any agreement, arrangement, understanding or relationship, including any repurchase or similar so-called "stock borrowing" agreement or arrangement, engaged in, directly or indirectly, by such Proposing Person, the purpose or effect of which is to mitigate loss to, reduce the economic risk (of ownership or otherwise) of shares of any class or series of the Corporation by, manage the risk of share price changes for, or increase or decrease the voting power of, such Proposing Person with respect to the shares of any class or series of the Corporation, or which provides, directly or indirectly, the opportunity to profit from any decrease in the price or value of the shares of any class or series of the Corporation ("*Short Interests*"), (D) any rights to dividends on the shares of any class or series of the Corporation owned beneficially by such Proposing Person that are separated or separable from the underlying shares of the Corporation,

(E) any performance related fees (other than an asset based fee) that such Proposing Person is entitled to based on any increase or decrease in the price or value of shares of any class or series of the Corporation, or any Synthetic Equity Interests or Short Interests, if any, and (F) any other information relating to such Proposing Person that would be required to be disclosed in a proxy statement or other filing required to be made in connection with solicitations of proxies or consents by such Proposing Person in support of the business proposed to be brought before the meeting pursuant to Section 14(a) of the Exchange Act (the disclosures to be made pursuant to the foregoing clauses (A) through (F) are referred to as "*Disclosable Interests*"); *provided, however*, that Disclosable Interests shall not include any such disclosures with respect to the ordinary course business activities of any broker, dealer, commercial bank, trust company or other nominee who is a Proposing Person solely as a result of being the stockholder directed to prepare and submit the notice required by these Bylaws on behalf of a beneficial owner; and

(iii) Description of Proposed Business. As to each item of business the stockholder proposes to bring before the annual or special meeting, (A) a reasonably brief description of the business desired to be brought before the annual or special meeting, the reasons for conducting such business at the annual or special meeting and any material interest in such business of each Proposing Person, (B) the text of the proposal or business (including the text of any resolutions proposed for consideration), and (C) a reasonably detailed description of all agreements, arrangements and understandings (x) between or among any of the Proposing Persons or (y) between or among any Proposing Person and any other person or entity (including their names) in connection with the proposal of such business by such stockholder.

(iv) Definition of Proposing Person. For purposes of this Section 1.14, the term "*Proposing Person*" shall mean (i) the stockholder providing the notice of business proposed to be brought before an annual or special meeting, (ii) the beneficial owner or beneficial owners, if different, on whose behalf the notice of the business proposed to be brought before the annual or special meeting is made, and (iii) any affiliate or associate of such stockholder or beneficial owner.

(d) Update and Supplement of Stockholder Notice of Proposed Business. A stockholder providing notice of business proposed to be brought before an annual or special meeting shall further update and supplement such notice, if necessary, so that the information provided or required to be provided in such notice pursuant to this Section 1.14 or in any Special Meeting Request delivered pursuant to Section 1.3(b) shall be true and correct as of the record date for the meeting and as of the date that is ten (10) business days prior to the meeting or any adjournment or postponement thereof, and such update and supplement shall be delivered to, or mailed and received by, the Secretary at the principal executive offices of the Corporation not later than five (5) business days after the record date for the meeting (in the case of the update and supplement required to be made as of the record date), and not later than eight (8) business days prior to the date of the meeting, or in the case of any adjournment or postponement thereof, eight (8) business days prior to the date of such adjournment or postponement.

(e) Business Not Properly Brought Before a Meeting. Notwithstanding anything in these Bylaws to the contrary, no business shall be conducted at an annual or special meeting except in accordance with this Section 1.14. The presiding officer of the meeting shall, if the facts warrant, determine that the business was not properly brought before the meeting in accordance with this Section 1.14, and if he or she should so determine, he or she shall so declare to the meeting and any such business not properly brought before the meeting shall not be transacted.

(f) Exchange Act Compliance. This Section 1.14 is expressly intended to apply to any business proposed to be brought before an annual or special meeting of stockholders other than any proposal made pursuant to Rule 14a–8 under the Exchange Act. In addition to the requirements of this Section 1.14 with respect to any business proposed to be brought before an annual or special meeting, each Proposing Person shall comply with all applicable requirements of the Exchange Act with respect to any such business. Nothing in this Section 1.14 shall be deemed to affect the rights of stockholders to request inclusion of proposals in the Corporation's proxy statement pursuant to Rule 14a–8 under the Exchange Act.

(g) Definition of Public Disclosure. For purposes of these Bylaws, *"public disclosure"* shall mean disclosure in a press release reported by a national news service or in a document publicly filed by the Corporation with the Securities and Exchange Commission pursuant to Sections 13, 14 or 15(d) of the Exchange Act.

SECTION 1.15: Nominations.

(a) Who May Make Nominations. Nominations of any person for election to the Board of Directors at an annual meeting or at a special meeting (but only if the election of directors is a matter specified in the notice of meeting given by or at the direction of the person calling such special meeting) may be made at such meeting only (i) by or at the direction of the Board of Directors, including by any committee or persons appointed by the Board of Directors, or (ii) by a stockholder who (A) was a stockholder of record (and, with respect to any beneficial owner, if different, on whose behalf such nomination is proposed to be made, only if such beneficial owner was the beneficial owner of shares of the Corporation) both at the time of giving the notice provided for in this Section 1.15 and at the time of the meeting, (B) is entitled to vote at the meeting, and (C) has complied with this Section 1.15 as to such nomination. The foregoing clause (ii) shall be the exclusive means for a stockholder to make any nomination of a person or persons for election to the Board of Directors at an annual meeting or special meeting (other than pursuant to a Special Meeting Request in accordance with the requirements set forth in Section 1.3).

(b) Requirement of Timely Notice of Stockholder Nominations. Without qualification, for a stockholder to make any nomination of a person or persons for election to the Board of Directors at an annual meeting, the stockholder must (i) provide Timely Notice (as defined in Section 1.14 of these Bylaws) thereof in writing and in proper form to the Secretary of the Corporation and (ii) provide any updates or supplements to such notice at the times and in the forms required by this Section 1.15. Without qualification, if the election of directors is a matter specified in the notice of meeting given by or at the direction of the person calling such special meeting, then for a stockholder to make any nomination of a person or persons for election to the Board of Directors at a special meeting, the stockholder must (i) provide timely notice thereof in writing and in proper form to the Secretary of the Corporation at the principal executive offices of the Corporation, and (ii) provide any updates or supplements to such notice at the times and in the forms required by this Section 1.15. To be timely, a stockholder's notice for nominations to be made at a special meeting (other than pursuant to a Special Meeting Request in accordance with the requirements set forth in Section 1.3) must be delivered to, or mailed and received at, the principal executive offices of the Corporation not earlier than the one hundred twentieth (120th) day prior to such special meeting and not later than the ninetieth (90th) day prior to such special meeting or, if later, the tenth (10th) day following the day on which public disclosure (as defined in Section 1.14 of these Bylaws) of the date of such special meeting was first made. In no event shall any adjournment or postponement of an annual meeting or special meeting or the announcement thereof commence a new time period for the giving of a stockholder's notice as described above.

(c) Requirements for Proper Form of Notice of Stockholder Nominations. To be in proper form for purposes of this Section 1.15, a stockholder's notice to the Secretary shall set forth:

(i) Stockholder Information. As to each Nominating Person (as defined below), (A) the name and address of such Nominating Person (including, if applicable, the name and address that appear on the Corporation's books and records), (B) the class or series and number of shares of the Corporation that are, directly or indirectly, owned of record or beneficially owned (within the meaning of Rule 13d–3 under the Exchange Act) by such Nominating Person, except that such Nominating Person shall in all events be deemed to beneficially own any shares of any class or series of the Corporation as to which such Nominating Person has a right to acquire beneficial ownership at any time in the future and (C) a representation whether such Nominating Person intends or is part of a group that intends (x) to deliver a proxy statement and/or form of proxy to holders of at least the percentage of the Corporation's outstanding stock reasonably believed by the Nominating Person to be sufficient to elect the nominee or nominees proposed to be nominated by the Nominating Person;

(ii) Information Regarding Disclosable Interests. As to each Nominating Person, any Disclosable Interests (as defined in Section 1.14(c)(ii), except that for purposes of this Section 1.15 the term "Nominating Person" shall be substituted for the term "Proposing Person" in all places it appears in Section 1.14(c)(ii)), and the disclosure in clause (F) of Section 1.14(c)(ii) shall be made with respect to the election of directors at the meeting;

(iii) Information Regarding Proposed Nominees. As to each person whom a Nominating Person proposes to nominate for election as a director, (A) all information with respect to such proposed nominee that would be required to be set forth in a stockholder's notice pursuant to this Section 1.15 if such proposed nominee were a Nominating Person, (B) all information relating to such proposed nominee that is required to be disclosed in a proxy statement or other filings required to be made in connection with solicitations of proxies for election of directors in a contested election pursuant to Section 14(a) under the Exchange Act (including such proposed nominee's written consent to being named in the proxy statement as a nominee and to serving as a director if elected), (C) a description of all direct and indirect compensation and other material monetary agreements, arrangements and understandings during the past three years, and any other material relationships, between or among any Nominating Person, on the one hand, and each proposed nominee, his or her respective affiliates and associates, on the other hand, including, without limitation, all information that would be required to be disclosed pursuant to Item 404 under Regulation S-K if such Nominating Person were the "registrant" for purposes of such rule and the proposed nominee were a director or executive officer of such registrant, and (D) a statement as to whether the proposed nominee, if elected, intends to tender, promptly following such person's election or re-election, an irrevocable resignation effective upon the occurrence of both (1) such person's failure to receive the required vote for re-election at the next meeting at which such person would face re-election and (2) acceptance of such resignation in accordance with Section 2.2 of these Bylaws and the Corporation's Governance Guidelines for the Board of Directors; and

(iv) Other Information to be Furnished by Proposed Nominees. The Corporation may require any proposed nominee to furnish such other information (A) as may reasonably be required by the Corporation to determine the eligibility of such proposed nominee to serve as an independent director of the Corporation in accordance with the Corporation's Governance Guidelines or (B) that could be material to a reasonable stockholder's understanding of the independence or lack of independence of such proposed nominee.

(v) Definition of Nominating Person. For purposes of this Section 1.15, the term "Nominating Person" shall mean (i) the stockholder providing the notice of the nomination proposed to be made at the meeting, (ii) the beneficial owner or beneficial owners, if different, on whose behalf the notice of the nomination proposed to be made at the meeting is made, and (iii) any affiliate or associate of such stockholder or beneficial owner.

(d) Update and Supplement of Stockholder Notice of Nominations. A stockholder providing notice of any nomination proposed to be made at a meeting shall further update and supplement such notice, if necessary, so that the information provided or required to be provided in such notice pursuant to this Section 1.15 or in any Special Meeting Request delivered pursuant to Section 1.3(b) shall be true and correct as of the record date for the meeting and as of the date that is ten (10) business days prior to the meeting or any adjournment or postponement thereof, and such update and supplement shall be delivered to, or mailed and received by, the Secretary at the principal executive offices of the Corporation not later than five (5) business days after the record date for the meeting (in the case of the update and supplement required to be made as of the record date), and not later than eight (8) business days prior to the date of the meeting, or in the case of any adjournment or postponement thereof, eight (8) business days prior to the date of such adjournment or postponement.

(e) Defective Nominations. Notwithstanding anything in these Bylaws to the contrary, no person shall be eligible for election as a director of the Corporation unless nominated in accordance with this Section 1.15. The presiding officer at the meeting shall, if the facts warrant, determine that a nomination was not properly made in accordance with this Section 1.15, and if he or she should so determine, he or she shall so declare such determination to the meeting and the defective nomination shall be disregarded.

(f) Compliance with Exchange Act. In addition to the requirements of this Section 1.15 with respect to any nomination proposed to be made at a meeting, each Nominating Person shall comply with all applicable requirements of the Exchange Act with respect to any such nominations.

ARTICLE II.

BOARD OF DIRECTORS

SECTION 2.1: Number; Qualifications. The Board of Directors shall consist of one or more members. The initial number of directors shall be five (5), and thereafter shall be fixed from time to time by resolution of the Board of Directors. No decrease in the authorized number of directors constituting the Board of Directors shall shorten the term of any incumbent director. Directors need not be stockholders of the Corporation.

SECTION 2.2: Election.

(a) The directors shall be elected as provided in the Certificate of Incorporation.

(b) Each director to be elected by the stockholders of the Corporation shall be elected by the affirmative vote of a majority of the votes cast with respect to such director by the shares represented and entitled to vote therefor at a meeting of the stockholders for the election of directors at which a quorum is present (an "*Election Meeting*"); *provided, however*, that if the Board of Directors determines that the number of nominees exceeds the number of directors to be elected at such meeting (a "*Contested Election*"), and the Board of Directors has not rescinded such determination by the date that is twenty (20) days prior to the date of the Election Meeting as initially announced, each of the directors to be elected at the Election Meeting shall be elected by the affirmative vote of a plurality of the votes cast by the shares represented and entitled to vote at such meeting with respect to the election of such director. For purposes of this Section 2.2, a "*majority of the votes cast*" means that the number of votes cast "for" a candidate for director exceeds the number of votes cast "against" that director. In an election other than a Contested Election, stockholders will be given the choice to cast votes "for" or "against" the election of directors or to "abstain" from such vote and shall not have the ability to cast any other vote with respect to such election of directors. In a Contested Election, stockholders will be given the choice to cast "for" or "withhold" votes for the election of directors and shall not have the ability to cast any other vote with respect to such election of directors. In the event an Election Meeting involves the election of directors by separate votes by class or classes or series, the determination as to whether an election constitutes a Contested Election shall be made on a class by class or series by series basis, as applicable.

(c) In the event one or more incumbent directors (each, a "*Subject Director*") fails to receive the affirmative vote of a majority of the votes cast at an Election Meeting at which there was no Contested Election, either (i) the Corporate Governance and Nominating Committee or (ii) if one or more of the members of the Corporate Governance and Nominating Committee is a Subject Director or the Board of Directors determines that any decision to be made with respect to a Subject Director should be made by a committee other than the Corporate Governance and Nominating Committee, a committee consisting solely of independent directors (as determined in accordance with any stock exchange rules and regulations applicable to the Corporation and any additional criteria set forth in the Corporation's Governance Guidelines for the Board of Directors or Corporate Governance and Nominating Committee Charter, as applicable) who are not Subject Directors (the committee described in clause (i) or (ii) of this sentence, the "*Committee*") will make a determination as to whether to accept or reject any previously tendered Resignations (as defined below), or whether other action should be taken (including whether to request that a Subject Director resign from the Board of Directors if no Resignation had been tendered prior to the relevant Election Meeting). The Committee will act with respect to any Subject Directors within ninety (90) days from the date of the certification of the election results and shall notify the Subject Directors of its decision. The Committee may consider all factors it considers relevant, including any stated reasons for "against" votes, whether the underlying cause or causes of the "against" votes are curable, the relationship between such causes and the actions of such Subject Director, the factors, if any, set forth in the Corporation's Governance Guidelines for the Board of Directors or other policies that are to be considered by the Corporate Governance and Nominating Committee in evaluating potential candidates for the Board of Directors as such criteria relate to such Subject Director, the length of service of such Subject Director, the size and holding period of such Subject Director's stock ownership in the Corporation, and such Subject Director's contributions to the Corporation. Subject Directors shall not participate in the deliberation or decision(s) of the Committee. The Corporation shall publicly disclose the decision(s) of the Committee in a Current Report on Form 8-K filed with the Securities and Exchange Commission. Notwithstanding the foregoing, if the result of accepting all tendered Resignations then pending and requesting resignations from incumbent directors who did not submit a Resignation prior to the relevant Election Meeting, would be that the Corporation would have fewer than three (3) directors who were in office before the election of directors, the Committee may determine to extend such ninety (90)-day period by an additional ninety (90) days if it determines that such an extension is in the best interests of the Corporation and its stockholders. For purposes of this Section 2.2, a "*Resignation*" is an irrevocable resignation submitted by an incumbent director nominated for re-election prior to the relevant Election Meeting that will become effective upon the occurrence of both (i) the failure to receive the affirmative vote of a majority of the votes cast at an Election Meeting at which there was no Contested Election and (ii) acceptance of such resignation by the Committee.

(d) If a Subject Director's tendered Resignation is not accepted by the Committee or such Subject Director does not otherwise submit his or her resignation to the Board of Directors, such director shall continue to serve until his or her successor is duly elected, or his or her earlier resignation or removal pursuant to Section 2.3. If a Subject Director's Resignation is accepted by the Committee pursuant to this Section 2.2, or if a nominee for director is not elected and the nominee is not an incumbent director, then the Board of Directors, in its sole discretion, may fill any resulting vacancy pursuant to the provisions of Section 2.3 or decrease the size of the Board of Directors pursuant to the provisions of Section 2.1 of these Bylaws.

SECTION 2.3: Resignation; Removal; Vacancies. Subject to the provisions of the Certificate of Incorporation, each director shall serve until his or her successor is duly elected and qualified, or until his or her earlier death, resignation, retirement or removal from service as a director. Any director may resign at any time upon notice given in writing or by electronic transmission to the Corporation. Subject to the rights of any holders of Preferred Stock then outstanding and the Certificate of Incorporation:

(i) (A) prior to the third annual meeting of stockholders following the effectiveness of the Amended and Restated Certificate of Incorporation that declassifies the Board of Directors (the *"Declassification Amendment"*), any director or the entire Board of Directors may be removed, only for cause, by the holders of a majority of the shares then entitled to vote at an election of directors and (B) after the third annual meeting of stockholders following the effectiveness of the Declassification Amendment, the holders of a majority of the shares entitled to vote in an election of directors may remove any director or the entire Board of Directors with or without cause, and

(ii) any vacancy occurring in the Board of Directors for any reason, and any newly created directorship resulting from any increase in the authorized number of directors to be elected by all stockholders having the right to vote as a single class, shall be filled only by a majority of the directors then in office, although less than a quorum, or by a sole remaining director.

SECTION 2.4: Regular Meetings. Regular meetings of the Board of Directors may be held at such places, within or without the State of Delaware, and at such times as the Board of Directors may from time to time determine. Notice of regular meetings need not be given if the date, times and places thereof are fixed by resolution of the Board of Directors.

SECTION 2.5: Special Meetings. Special meetings of the Board of Directors may be called by the Chairman of the Board, the Chief Executive Officer or a majority of the members of the Board of Directors then in office and may be held at any time, date or place, within or without the State of Delaware, as the person or persons calling the meeting shall fix. Notice of the time, date and place of such meeting shall be given, orally or in writing, by the person or persons calling the meeting to all directors at least four (4) days before the meeting if the notice is mailed, or at least twenty-four (24) hours before the meeting if such notice is given by telephone, hand delivery, overnight express courier, facsimile, electronic mail or other electronic transmission. Unless otherwise indicated in the notice, any and all business may be transacted at a special meeting. The notice shall be deemed given

(i) in the case of hand delivery or notice by telephone, when received by the director to whom notice is to be given or by any person accepting such notice on behalf of such director,

(ii) in the case of delivery by mail, upon deposit in the United States mail, postage prepaid, directed to the director to whom notice is being given at such director's address as it appears on the records of the Corporation,

(iii) in the case of delivery by overnight express courier, on the first business day after such notice is dispatched, and

(iv) in the case of delivery via facsimile, electronic mail or other electronic transmission, when sent to the director to whom notice is to be given or by any person accepting such notice on behalf of such director at such director's facsimile number or electronic mail address, as the case may be, as it appears on the Corporation's records.

SECTION 2.6: Telephonic Meetings Permitted. Members of the Board of Directors, or any committee of the Board of Directors, may participate in a meeting of the Board of Directors or such committee by means of conference telephone or similar communications equipment by means of which all persons participating in the meeting can hear each other, and participation in a meeting pursuant to conference telephone or similar communications equipment shall constitute presence in person at such meeting.

SECTION 2.7: Quorum; Vote Required for Action. At all meetings of the Board of Directors a majority of the total number of authorized directors shall constitute a quorum for the transaction of business. Except as otherwise provided herein or in the Certificate of Incorporation, or required by law, the vote of a majority of the directors present at a meeting at which a quorum is present shall be the act of the Board of Directors. If a quorum is not present at any meeting of the Board of Directors, then the directors present thereat may adjourn the meeting from time to time, without notice other than announcement at the meeting, until a quorum is present.

SECTION 2.8: Chairman of the Board. The Board of Directors shall have the power to elect the Chairman of the Board from among the members of the Board of Directors. The Chairman of the Board shall have the power to preside at all meetings of the Board of Directors and shall have such other powers and duties as provided in these Bylaws and as the Board of Directors may from time to time prescribe.

SECTION 2.9: Organization. Meetings of the Board of Directors shall be presided over by the Chairman of the Board, or in his or her absence by the Chief Executive Officer, or in his or her absence by a chairman chosen at the meeting. The Secretary shall act as secretary of the meeting, but in his or her absence the chairman of the meeting may appoint any person to act as secretary of the meeting.

SECTION 2.10: Written Action by Directors. Any action required or permitted to be taken at any meeting of the Board of Directors, or of any committee thereof, may be taken without a meeting if all members of the Board or such committee, as the case may be, consent thereto in writing, or by electronic transmission and the writing or writings or electronic transmission or transmissions are filed with the minutes of proceedings of the Board or committee, respectively. Such filing shall be in paper form if the minutes are maintained in paper form and shall be in electronic form if the minutes are maintained in electronic form.

SECTION 2.11: Powers. The Board of Directors may, except as otherwise required by law or the Certificate of Incorporation, exercise all such powers and do all such acts and things as may be exercised or done by the Corporation.

SECTION 2.12: Compensation of Directors. Directors, as such, may receive, pursuant to a resolution of the Board of Directors, fees and other compensation for their services as directors, including without limitation their services as members of committees of the Board of Directors.

ARTICLE III.

COMMITTEES

SECTION 3.1: Committees. The Board of Directors may, by resolution passed by a majority of the authorized number of directors, designate one or more committees, each committee to consist of one or more of the directors of the Corporation. The Board may designate one or more directors as alternate members of any committee, who may replace any absent or disqualified member at any meeting of the committee. In the absence or disqualification of a member of the committee, the member or members thereof present at any meeting of such committee who are not disqualified from voting, whether or not he, she or they constitute a quorum, may unanimously appoint another member of the Board of Directors to act at the meeting in place of any such absent or disqualified member. Any such committee, to the extent provided in a resolution of the Board of Directors, shall have and may exercise all the powers and authority of the Board of Directors in the management of the business and affairs of the Corporation and may authorize the seal of the Corporation to be affixed to all papers that may require it; but no such committee shall have power or authority in reference to the following matters: (i) approving or adopting, or recommending to the stockholders, any action or matter (other than the election or removal of directors) expressly required by the Delaware General Corporation Law to be submitted to stockholders for approval, or (ii) adopting, amending or repealing any Bylaw of the Corporation.

SECTION 3.2: Committee Rules. Unless the Board of Directors otherwise provides, each committee designated by the Board of Directors may make, alter and repeal rules for the conduct of its business. In the absence of such rules each committee shall conduct its business in the same manner as the Board of Directors conducts its business pursuant to Article II of these Bylaws.

ARTICLE IV.

OFFICERS

SECTION 4.1: Generally. The officers of the Corporation shall consist of a Chief Executive Officer and/or a President, one or more Vice Presidents, a Secretary, a Treasurer and such other officers, including a Chief Financial Officer, as may from time to time be appointed by the Board of Directors. All officers shall be elected by the Board of Directors; *provided, however*, that the Board of Directors may empower the Chief Executive Officer of the Corporation to appoint officers other than the Chief Executive Officer, the President, the Chief Financial Officer or the Treasurer. Each officer shall hold office until his or her successor is elected and qualified or until his or her earlier resignation or removal. Any number of offices may be held by the same person. Any officer may resign at any time upon written notice to the Corporation. Any vacancy occurring in any office of the Corporation by death, resignation, removal or otherwise may be filled by the Board of Directors.

SECTION 4.2: Chief Executive Officer. Subject to the control of the Board of Directors and such supervisory powers, if any, as may be given by the Board of Directors, the powers and duties of the Chief Executive Officer of the Corporation are:

> (a) To act as the general manager and, subject to the control of the Board of Directors, to have general supervision, direction and control of the business and affairs of the Corporation;
>
> (b) To preside at all meetings of the stockholders;
>
> (c) To call meetings of the stockholders to be held at such times and, subject to the limitations prescribed by law or by these Bylaws, at such places as he or she shall deem proper; and
>
> (d) To affix the signature of the Corporation to all deeds, conveyances, mortgages, guar-

antees, leases, obligations, bonds, certificates and other papers and instruments in writing which have been authorized by the Board of Directors or which, in the judgment of the Chief Executive Officer, should be executed on behalf of the Corporation; to sign certificates for shares of stock of the Corporation; and, subject to the direction of the Board of Directors, to have general charge of the property of the Corporation and to supervise and control all officers, agents and employees of the Corporation.

The President shall be the Chief Executive Officer of the Corporation unless the Board of Directors shall designate another officer to be the Chief Executive Officer. If there is no President, and the Board of Directors has not designated any other officer to be the Chief Executive Officer, then the Chairman of the Board shall be the Chief Executive Officer.

SECTION 4.3: President. The President shall be the Chief Executive Officer of the Corporation unless the Board of Directors shall have designated another officer as the Chief Executive Officer of the Corporation. Subject to the provisions of these Bylaws and to the direction of the Board of Directors, and subject to the supervisory powers of the Chief Executive Officer (if the Chief Executive Officer is an officer other than the President), and subject to such supervisory powers and authority as may be given by the Board of Directors to the Chairman of the Board, and/or to any other officer, the President shall have the responsibility for the general management and the control of the business and affairs of the Corporation and the general supervision and direction of all of the officers, employees and agents of the Corporation (other than the Chief Executive Officer, if the Chief Executive Officer is an officer other than the President) and shall perform all duties and have all powers that are commonly incident to the office of President or that are delegated to the President by the Board of Directors.

SECTION 4.4: Vice President. Each Vice President shall have all such powers and duties as are commonly incident to the office of Vice President, or that are delegated to him or her by the Board of Directors or the Chief Executive Officer. A Vice President may be designated by the Board to perform the duties and exercise the powers of the Chief Executive Officer in the event of the Chief Executive Officer's absence or disability.

SECTION 4.5: Chief Financial Officer. Subject to the direction of the Board of Directors and the President, the Chief Financial Officer shall perform all duties and have all powers that are commonly incident to the office of chief financial officer.

SECTION 4.6: Treasurer. The Treasurer shall have custody of all monies and securities of the Corporation. The Treasurer shall make such disbursements of the funds of the Corporation as are authorized and shall render from time to time an account of all such transactions. The Treasurer shall also perform such other duties and have such other powers as are commonly incident to the office of Treasurer, or as the Board of Directors or the President may from time to time prescribe.

SECTION 4.7: Secretary. The Secretary shall issue or cause to be issued all authorized notices for, and shall keep, or cause to be kept, minutes of all meetings of the stockholders and the Board of Directors. The Secretary shall have charge of the corporate minute books and similar records and shall perform such other duties and have such other powers as are commonly incident to the office of Secretary, or as the Board of Directors or the President may from time to time prescribe.

SECTION 4.8: Delegation of Authority. The Board of Directors may from time to time delegate the powers or duties of any officer to any other officers or agents, notwithstanding any provision hereof.

SECTION 4.9: Removal. Any officer of the Corporation shall serve at the pleasure of the Board of Directors and may be removed at any time, with or without cause, by the Board of Directors. Such removal shall be without prejudice to the contractual rights of such officer, if any, with the Corporation.

ARTICLE V.

STOCK

SECTION 5.1: Certificates. The shares of the Corporation shall be represented by certificates, provided that the Board of Directors may provide by resolution or resolutions that some or all of any or all classes or series of the Corporation's stock shall be uncertificated shares. Any such resolution shall not apply to shares represented by a certificate until such certificate is surrendered to the Corporation. Every holder of stock represented by certificates shall be entitled to have a certificate signed by or in the name of the Corporation by the Chairman or Vice-Chairman of the Board of Directors, or the President or a Vice President, and by the Treasurer or an Assistant Treasurer, or the Secretary or an Assistant Secretary, of the Corporation, representing the number of shares registered in certificate form. Any or all of the signatures on the certificate may be a facsimile.

SECTION 5.2: Lost, Stolen or Destroyed Stock Certificates; Issuance of New Certificates or Uncertificated Shares. The Corporation may issue a new certificate of stock or uncertificated shares in the place of any certificate previously issued by it, alleged to have been lost, stolen or destroyed, and the Corporation may require the owner of the lost, stolen or destroyed certificate, or such owner's legal representative, to agree to indemnify the Corporation and/or to give the Corporation a bond sufficient to indemnify it, against any claim that may be made against it on account of the alleged loss, theft or destruction of any such certificate or the issuance of such new certificate or uncertificated shares.

SECTION 5.3: Other Regulations. The issue, transfer, conversion and registration of stock certificates or uncertificated shares shall be governed by such other regulations as the Board of Directors may establish.

ARTICLE VI.

INDEMNIFICATION

SECTION 6.1: Indemnification of Officers and Directors. Each person who was or is made a party to, or is threatened to be made a party to, or is involved in any action, suit or proceeding, whether civil, criminal, administrative or investigative (a "*proceeding*"), by reason of the fact that he or she (or a person of whom he or she is the legal representative), is or was a director or officer of the Corporation or a Reincorporated Predecessor (as defined below) or is or was serving at the request of the Corporation or a Reincorporated Predecessor (as defined below) as a director, officer or employee of another corporation, or of a partnership, joint venture, trust or other enterprise, including service with respect to employee benefit plans (each such director, officer or employee, a "*Covered Person*"), shall be indemnified and held harmless by the Corporation to the fullest extent permitted by the Delaware General Corporation Law, against all expenses, liability and loss (including attorneys' fees, judgments, fines, ERISA excise taxes and penalties and amounts paid or to be paid in settlement) reasonably incurred or suffered by such person in connection therewith; *provided, however*, that the Corporation shall indemnify any such Covered Person seeking indemnity in connection with a proceeding (or part thereof) initiated by such Covered Person only if such proceeding (or part thereof) was authorized by the Board of Directors of the Corporation. As used herein, the term "*Reincorporated Predecessor*" means a corporation that is merged with and into the Corporation in a statutory merger where (a) the Corporation is the surviving corporation of such merger; (b) the primary purpose of such merger is to change the corporate domicile of the Reincorporated Predecessor to Delaware.

SECTION 6.2: Advance of Expenses. The Corporation shall pay all expenses (including attorneys' fees) incurred by a Covered Person in defending any such proceeding as they are incurred in advance of its final disposition; *provided, however*, that if the Delaware General Corporation Law then so requires, the payment of such expenses incurred by a Covered Person in advance of the final disposition of such proceeding shall be made only upon delivery to the Corporation of an undertaking, by or on behalf of such Covered Person, to repay all amounts so advanced if it should be determined ultimately that such Covered Person is not entitled to be indemnified under this Article VI or otherwise; and provided, further, that the Corporation shall not be required to advance any expenses to a Covered Person against whom the Corporation directly brings a claim, in a proceeding, alleging that such person has breached his or her duty of loyalty to the Corporation, committed an act or omission not in good faith or that involves intentional misconduct or a knowing violation of law, or derived an improper personal benefit from a transaction.

SECTION 6.3: Non-Exclusivity of Rights. The rights conferred on any person in this Article VI shall not be exclusive of any other right that such person may have or hereafter acquire under any statute, provision of the Certificate of Incorporation, Bylaw, agreement, vote or consent of stockholders or disinterested directors, or otherwise. Additionally, nothing in this Article VI shall limit the ability of the Corporation, in its discretion, to indemnify or advance expenses to persons whom the Corporation is not obligated to indemnify or advance expenses pursuant to this Article VI. The Board of Directors of the Corporation shall have the power to delegate to such officer or other person as the Board of Directors shall specify the determination of whether indemnification shall be given to any person pursuant to this Section 6.3.

SECTION 6.4: Indemnification Contracts. The Board of Directors is authorized to cause the Corporation to enter into indemnification contracts with any director, officer, employee or agent of the Corporation, or any person serving at the request of the Corporation as a director, officer, employee or agent of another corporation, partnership, joint venture, trust or other enterprise, including employee benefit plans, providing indemnification rights to such person. Such rights may be greater than those provided in this Article VI.

SECTION 6.5: Continuation of Indemnification. The rights to indemnification and to advancement of expenses provided by, or granted pursuant to, this Article VI shall continue notwithstanding that the person has ceased to be a Covered Person and shall inure to the benefit of his or her estate, heirs, executors, administrators, legatees and distributees; *provided, however*, that the Corporation shall indemnify any such person seeking indemnity in connection with a proceeding (or part thereof) initiated by such person only if such proceeding (or part thereof) was authorized by the Board of Directors of the Corporation.

SECTION 6.6: Effect of Amendment or Repeal. The provisions of this Article VI shall constitute a contract between the Corporation, on the one hand, and, on the other hand, each individual who serves or has served as a Covered Person (whether before or after the adoption of these Bylaws), in consideration of such person's performance of such services, and pursuant to this Article VI, the Corporation intends to be legally bound to each such current or former Covered Person. With respect to current and former Covered Persons, the rights conferred under this Article VI are present contractual rights and such rights are fully vested, and shall be deemed to have vested fully, immediately upon adoption of these Bylaws. With respect to any Covered Persons who commence service following adoption of these bylaws, the rights conferred under this Article VI shall be present contractual rights, and such rights shall fully vest, and be deemed to have vested fully, immediately upon such Covered Person's service in the capacity which is subject to the benefits of this Article VI.

ARTICLE VII.

NOTICES

SECTION 7.1: Notice.

(a) General. Except as otherwise specifically provided herein or required by law, all notices required to be given pursuant to these Bylaws shall be in writing and may in every instance be effectively given by hand delivery (including use of a delivery service), by depositing such notice in the mail, postage prepaid, or by sending such notice by prepaid overnight express courier or facsimile. Any such notice shall be addressed to the person to whom notice is to be given at such person's address or facsimile number, as the case may be, as it appears on the records of the Corporation. The notice shall be deemed given

(i) in the case of hand delivery, when received by the person to whom notice is to be given or by any person accepting such notice on behalf of such person;

(ii) in the case of delivery by mail, upon deposit in the United States mail, postage prepaid, directed to the person to whom notice is being given at such person's address as it appears on the records of the Corporation;

(iii) in the case of delivery by overnight express courier, on the first business day after such notice is dispatched; and

(iv) in the case of delivery via facsimile, when directed to the person to whom notice is to be given or by any person accepting such notice on behalf of such person.

SECTION 7.2: Waiver of Notice. Whenever notice is required to be given under any provision of these Bylaws, a written waiver of notice, signed by the person entitled to notice, or a waiver by electronic transmission by the person entitled to notice, whether before or after the time stated therein, shall be deemed equivalent to notice. Attendance of a person at a meeting shall constitute a waiver of notice of such meeting, except when the person attends a meeting for the express purpose of objecting at the beginning of the meeting to the transaction of any business because the meeting is not lawfully called or convened. Neither the business to be transacted at, nor the purpose of, any regular or special meeting of the stockholders, directors or members of a committee of directors need be specified in any written waiver of notice or any waiver by electronic transmission.

ARTICLE VIII.

INTERESTED DIRECTORS

SECTION 8.1: Interested Directors; Quorum. No contract or transaction between the Corporation and one or more of its directors or officers, or between the Corporation and any other corporation, partnership, association or other organization in which one or more of its directors or officers are directors or officers, or have a financial interest, shall be void or voidable solely for this reason, or solely because the director or officer is present at or participates in the meeting of the Board of Directors or committee thereof that authorizes the contract or transaction, or solely because his, her or their votes are counted for such purpose, if:

> (i) the material facts as to his, her or their relationship or interest and as to the contract or transaction are disclosed or are known to the Board of Directors or the committee, and the Board of Directors or committee in good faith authorizes the contract or transaction by the affirmative votes of a majority of the disinterested directors, even though the disinterested directors be less than a quorum;

> (ii) the material facts as to his, her or their relationship or interest and as to the contract or transaction are disclosed or are known to the stockholders entitled to vote thereon, and the contract or transaction is specifically approved in good faith by vote of the stockholders; or

> (iii) the contract or transaction is fair as to the Corporation as of the time it is authorized, approved or ratified by the Board of Directors, a committee thereof, or the stockholders. Common or interested directors may be counted in determining the presence of a quorum at a meeting of the Board of Directors or of a committee which authorizes the contract or transaction.

ARTICLE IX.

MISCELLANEOUS

SECTION 9.1: Fiscal Year. The fiscal year of the Corporation shall be determined by resolution of the Board of Directors.

SECTION 9.2: Seal. The Board of Directors may provide for a corporate seal, which shall have the name of the Corporation inscribed thereon and shall otherwise be in such form as may be approved from time to time by the Board of Directors.

SECTION 9.3: Form of Records. Any records maintained by the Corporation in the regular course of its business, including its stock ledger, books of account and minute books, may be kept on, or by means of, or be in the form of, any information storage device or method provided that the records so kept can be converted into clearly legible paper form within a reasonable time. The Corporation shall so convert any records so kept upon the request of any person entitled to inspect such records pursuant to any provision of the Delaware General Corporation Law.

SECTION 9.4: Reliance Upon Books and Records. A member of the Board of Directors, or a member of any committee designated by the Board of Directors shall, in the performance of his or her duties, be fully protected in relying in good faith upon records of the Corporation and upon such information, opinions, reports or statements presented to the Corporation by any of the Corporation's officers or employees, or committees of the Board of Directors, or by any other person as to matters the member reasonably believes are within such other person's professional or expert competence and who has been selected with reasonable care by or on behalf of the Corporation.

SECTION 9.5: Certificate of Incorporation Governs. In the event of any conflict between the provisions of the Corporation's Certificate of Incorporation and Bylaws, the provisions of the Certificate of Incorporation shall govern.

SECTION 9.6: Severability. If any provision of these Bylaws shall be held to be invalid, illegal, unenforceable or in conflict with the provisions of the Corporation's Certificate of Incorporation, then such provision shall nonetheless be enforced to the maximum extent possible consistent with such holding and the remaining provisions of these Bylaws (including without limitation, all portions of any section of these Bylaws containing any such provision held to be invalid, illegal, unenforceable or in conflict with the Certificate of Incorporation, that are not themselves invalid, illegal, unenforceable or in conflict with the Certificate of Incorporation) shall remain in full force and effect.

ARTICLE X.

AMENDMENT

SECTION 10.1: Amendments. Subject to Section 6.6 of these Bylaws, stockholders of the Corporation holding at least a majority of the Corporation's outstanding voting stock shall have the power to adopt, amend or repeal Bylaws. To the extent provided in the Corporation's Certificate of Incorporation, the Board of Directors of the Corporation shall also have the power to adopt, amend or repeal Bylaws of the Corporation.

CERTIFICATION OF BYLAWS OF EBAY INC.

(a Delaware Corporation)

KNOW ALL BY THESE PRESENTS:

I, Michael R. Jacobson, certify that I am Secretary of eBay Inc., a Delaware corporation (the "*Company*"), that I am duly authorized to make and deliver this certification, that the attached Bylaws are a true and correct copy of the Bylaws of the Company in effect as of the date of this certificate.

Dated: April 27, 2012

/s/ Michael R. Jacobson
Michael R. Jacobson, Secretary

7. Business Law Glossary

BUSINESS LAW GLOSSARY

Abatement: Reduction.

Abnormal use: A defense to products liability actions by which a defendant argues it is not responsible for harm caused by the product because the plaintiff used the product for an unforeseeable purpose.

Acceptance: Agreeing to the terms of an offer.

Accord and satisfaction: Accepting performance, or a substitute for performance, as adequate.

Acquisition: Gaining of possession or control over a company.

Actual authority: The powers actually granted to an agent by the principal.

Actual malice: The standard of proof required of public figures in a defamation case. The public figure must show that the defendant knew the statement was false or acted with reckless disregard as to whether the statement was false or not.

Actus reus: Latin for "guilty act." Actions that constitute a crime when done with the appropriate state of mind (*mens rea*).

Adjudication: The exercise of judicial power by an administrative agency. Adjudication usually deals with disputes between the agency and individuals or business entities.

Ad litem: "For the purposes of the suit."

Administrative Procedure Act: The federal law that establishes the procedure for rulemaking and adjudication by federal administrative agencies.

Affidavit: A written statement of facts given under oath.

Agent: A person who is authorized to act for another person.

Alternative dispute resolution: Any means of settling disputes without litigation.

Amendatory: Supplemental, additional.

Answer: A written pleading filed by a defendant to respond to a complaint filed by a plaintiff in a lawsuit.

Antenuptial agreements: A pre-marital contract in which the parties agree on issues like the disposition of property after death or dissolution of the marriage.

Anticipatory breach: Informing a party that a contract will be breached before the breach takes place.

Apparent Authority: The reasonable assumption that an agent is allowed to act for a principal under given circumstances.

Appellant: The party who files an appeal of a court decision.

Appellee: The party responding to an appeal filed by the other party.

Arbitration: A method of alternative dispute resolution in which the parties present their case to one or more neutral parties, called arbitrators, who issue a binding decision on the parties.

Arbitration clause: A clause in a written agreement requiring the parties to resolve disputes between them through the arbitration process.

Arraignment: A court proceeding calling a party to court to answer a criminal charge.

Articles of incorporation: The document filed with the state for the formation of a corporation.

Articles of organization: The document filed with the state for the formation of a limited liability company.

Assumption of risk: A defense to tort liability in which a defendant argues it is not liable because the plaintiff knew and accepted the risks of an activity.

Attenuate: To lessen or weaken.

At-will employment: An employment relationship under which the employer or employee may end the relationship at any time.

Authentication: Formal proof of a security agreement, such as a signed document.

Author: In copyright law, the creator of a copyrightable work.

Automatic stay: An order from the Bankruptcy Court that stops all collection efforts against a debtor. The automatic stay goes into effect as soon as a bankruptcy case is filed.

Award: The final decision of the arbitrator in an arbitration proceeding.

Beyond a reasonable doubt: Standard of proof for a criminal conviction. "Reasonable doubt" is when jurors are not convinced of the defendant's guilt, or when they believe there is a reasonable possibility that the defendant is not guilty.

Binding mediation: A method of alternative dispute resolution in which the parties attempt mediation, but if they do not reach an agreement, they agree to follow a binding decision issued by the mediator.

Board of directors: Individuals elected to act as representatives of shareholders in running a corporation.

Board of governors: Individuals elected to act as representatives of members in running a limited liability company.

Bona fide occupational qualification: An employment qualification, related to an essential job duty, that employers may consider in making decisions about hiring and retention of employees.

Bond: A written promise to pay money. In securities law, long-term, interest bearing debt instruments, backed by the assets of the issuer.

Brief: A written legal argument submitted to the court.

Burden of proof: The amount of proof needed to prove one's case.

By-laws: The rules and regulations adopted to govern the operation of a corporation.

Cabinet: The most senior appointed officers of the executive branch of government, nominated by the President and confirmed by the Senate.

Capacity: The legal ability to make a contract.

Capitation: A tax levy that is a fixed sum per person, without regard to any other factors.

Cartel: A combination of sellers or producers of a product who join together to control production or price.

Causation: The causing or producing of an effect.

Cause of action: Fact(s) that enable a party to bring legal action against another party.

Cause-in-fact: The action that caused an injured party's injury. It is also referred to as but-for causation.

C corporation: A corporation that is subject to the federal corporate income tax. All for-profit corporations are C corporations, unless they qualify as an S corporation.

Certification mark: A type of trademark that certifies some characteristic of a product, such as the place of origin, method of manufacture, quality, or material.

Certiorari: A higher court's acceptance of a case from a lower court for review.

Chancellor: The judge presiding over a court of chancery, or equity.

Civil claim: A lawsuit to remedy a private wrong

Civil penalty: A fine assessed for a violation of a statute or regulation. A civil penalty is not considered to be punishment for a crime.

Class action: A lawsuit in which a single person or a small group of people represents the interests of a larger group.

Collateral: Property or goods used to guarantee payment of an obligation.

Collective bargaining: The process through which unions negotiate terms of employment with employers on behalf of the employees.

Collective bargaining agreement: The agreed-upon contract between union employees and the employer.

Collective mark: A type of trademark that shows membership in a group, or that identifies the goods or services offered by the members of the group.

Common carrier: A business that offers its services to the public for transportation of people, goods, or messages.

Common law: Law developed through court decisions over time rather than through constitutions or codes.

Common market: A geographic group of countries that seek to eliminate trade barriers among themselves and promote free movement of capital and labor within the member countries.

Comparative negligence: A doctrine under which a plaintiff's recovery of damages may be reduced by the amount of negligence attributed to the plaintiff.

Compensatory damages: A sum of money awarded to the injured party in a lawsuit to compensate for expenses incurred as a result of the injuries.

Complaint: The first document filed with a court by a party that claims legal rights against another party.

Concealment: The act of refraining from disclosure, especially an act by which one prevents or hinders the discovery of something.

Conflagration: A great destructive burning or fire.

Consideration: A bargained for exchange; a legal detriment.

Constitutionality: Whether a law or government action agrees with the Constitution.

Consumer product: For purposes of the Fair Packaging and Labeling Act, a product customarily produced or distributed for sale through retail sales for consumption by individuals, or use by individuals for personal care or household services.

Contributory negligence: A doctrine under which a plaintiff may be barred from recovering damages because the plaintiff was partially at fault for the accident or injury.

Convention: In international law, an agreement among several nations.

Convicted: Being found guilty of a crime.

Conviction: The declaration of guilt for a criminal charge.

Cooperative federalism: The collective cooperative interaction of state, local, and federal governments to solve common problems.

Corporate promoter: A person who solicits investors for a corporation before it is formed.

Corporation: A legal entity formed under the laws of a state to do business.

Counterclaim: A claim asserted by the defendant against the plaintiff in a lawsuit.

Counteroffer: A response to an offer that proposes different or additional terms.

Court of Exchequer: A trial level court which existed until 1873. Its jurisdiction was subsequently turned over to the Exchequer Division and then the Queen's Bench Division of the High Court of Justice.

Creditor: A person who owes money. In bankruptcy law, the "debtor" is the person or entity that files a bankruptcy petition.

Cross examination: Examination of a witness that has already testified in a court proceeding, conducted by the other side.

Crowdfunding: Funding a project or venture by soliciting money from a large number of people, usually via internet solicitation.

Customs duty: A tax paid on imported items based on the country of origin and the item's description.

Customs union: A free trade area that also adopts a common external tariff.

Damages: Money compensation awarded to the injured party in a lawsuit.

Debenture: A bond backed only by the general credit and financial reputation of the company issuing the bond.

Debtor: A person to whom money is owed. In bankruptcy law, a "creditor" has or may have a claim against the debtor's property.

Debtor in possession: A Chapter 11 bankruptcy debtor over the term of the Chapter 11 process.

Deed: A document that evidences a transfer of real estate. All transfers or conveyances of real estate must be in writing.

Defamation: A false statement that damages the other party's reputation.

Default judgment: A binding judgment entered by a court if the defendant does not respond to the plaintiff's complaint.

Defendant: The party accused in a legal action. The party who responds to a lawsuit initiated by another party; the defendant is the party whom the plaintiff alleges engaged in a tort.

De minimis: Small, or trivial. From the Latin maxim *de minimis non curat lex* (the law does not concern itself with trifles).

Demurrer: A demurrer is a means of attacking a party's pleading. In essence, the attacker argues that the pleading need not be answered because it is insufficient or defective in some manner. There are a variety of different demurrers, some of which are still recognized. The modern equivalent of a general demurrer is a request for dismissal under Federal Rule of Civil Procedure 12 (b) (6). A request under 12 (b) (6) alleges that the opposing party fails to state a claim for which relief can be granted.

Deposition: The process of receiving and recording the sworn testimony of a party or witness during discovery.

Derivative work: A work based on another work. Examples of derivative works include adaptations or sequels.

Design defect: A defect in the design of the product that makes the product dangerous or useless.

Detour: An agent's minor deviation from the principal's business for personal reasons.

Direct examination: Examination of a witness by the party that called the witness to testify

Directed verdict: A ruling in a lawsuit entered by the trial judge after a determination that a reasonable jury could not reach a different conclusion.

Disability insurance: A type of insurance providing income protection to individuals who become disabled and cannot work for a long period of time.

Discharge: A debt is discharged when the debtor is no longer liable for paying it.

Discovery: The process by which the parties to a lawsuit obtain information from each other and from witnesses.

Disparate impact: The effect of a neutral practice that is non-discriminatory in intention, but disproportionately affects individuals of a protected class.

Disparate treatment: Intentional, unequal treatment of an employee on the basis of a protected class by an employer.

Disposable income: Income to a bankrupt debtor that is beyond what the debtor needs for the maintenance or support of herself and her dependents or for payments to operate her business.

Diversity jurisdiction: A federal court case with parties from different states or with a foreign party

Divestiture: A court order to a defendant to rid itself of property, securities, or other assets to prevent a monopoly or restraint of trade.

Dividends: The distribution of profits to shareholders or members.

Document requests: A written request for documents, electronically stored information, or other items issued during discovery to an opposing party.

Durable power of attorney: A power of attorney that remains effective even if the principal becomes incapacitated.

Duress: 1. Inducing an agreement by means of a threat or wrongful act. 2. Threats of harm or other pressure that force a person to commit a criminal act against his will.

Easement: The right to use or cross land, without the right to possess the land.

Economic strikers: Striking union workers seeking to obtain an economic benefit for the workers.

Electronically stored information (ESI): Data or information that is stored in electronic format, including documents, emails, voice mails, tweets, blogs, social media posts, files, and other records.

Elements: The parts of a crime or legal action that must be proven.

Employee: A person working for another person or a business firm for pay.

Employee benefits: Non-cash compensation and services provided to employees by employers.

Enacted laws: Laws adopted by a legislative or administrative body

Enumerated powers: Specific identified powers reserved only for the federal government.

Exclusionary Rule: A rule that prohibits illegally obtained evidence from being used in court.

Execution: An order allowing the seizure another person's property to enforce a money judgment.

Executory contracts: An agreement that is not yet fully performed on both sides.

Exempt: Protected from being taken by creditors, unless the owner agrees. State and federal law both list certain items of real and personal property that are exempt.

Expectation damages: The monetary value of the benefit that would have been received if the contract had been performed as agreed.

Express authority: Actions and tasks that the principal specifically assigns to an agent.

Family and medical leave: An unpaid leave from work taken by an employee for family and medical reasons.

Federal question jurisdiction: A case with alleged violations of the U.S. Constitution, federal laws, or federal treaties.

Federal Register: A daily publication containing documents and orders issued by Executive Branch agencies.

Federalism: A governmental system that shares power between national and state governments

Felony: A crime punishable by a sentence of incarceration for more than one year, or by death.

Fiduciary/fiduciary duty: A fiduciary is a person required to act for the benefit of another person. A fiduciary owes the other person the duties of good faith, trust, confidence, and candor.

Fifth Amendment privilege: The rule set out in the Fifth Amendment to the U.S. Constitution that no person "shall be compelled in any criminal case to be a witness against himself." The privilege applies in any type of proceeding, so that a person may decline to answer questions if her answer could lead to criminal charges.

First sale: A defense to an action for copyright and patent infringement. A person who lawfully acquires a copyright or patent protected item may resell that item without violating the copyright or patent.

Foreseeability: The foreseeability of the consequences of a defendant's actions depend on the balancing between the likelihood of risk and the magnitude of damages flowing therefrom.

Franchise: A franchise is a type of agreement that lets one party have access to another's proprietary knowledge, processes, and trademarks in order to sell a product or provide a service.

Fraudulent misrepresentation: A false statement made with the intention to induce the other person's reliance on the statement.

Free trade area: Countries that negotiate a free trade agreement to reduce or eliminate customs duties and other trade barriers between themselves.

Frolic: An agent's significant deviation from the principal's business for personal reasons.

Full warranty: Under the Magnuson-Moss Warranty Act, a warranty that obliges the seller of a product to remedy a defective product within a reasonable time. If the defect cannot be remedied after a reasonable number of attempts, the seller must replace it, or refund the price paid.

General damages: The harm that normally flows form a breach of contract.

General partner: In a limited partnership, the party who operates the business.

General warranty deed: A deed that guarantees that the grantor of real estate has good title to the property.

Grand jury: A panel of citizens who examine accusations in a criminal case to determine if the case should go forward.

Grantor: A person who transfer ownership of property to another.

Habeas corpus: A proceeding brought to challenge the legality of a person's confinement.

Health care power of attorney: A power of attorney that allows another to make health care decisions when the principal is unable to make those choices.

Homicide: The taking of another person's life.

Identification: A collector must disclose that he is trying to collect a debt when contacting the debtor.

Implied authority: The agent's power to do whatever is necessary to accomplish specific responsibilities assigned by the principal.

Incontestable: A trademark that is immune from legal challenge to its validity.

Indemnification: Reimbursing another party for financial losses or damages, or an agreement to indemnify against losses or damages.

Indemnify: To insure or secure another party against a future loss or liability.

Independent contractors: Workers with a high level of independence who are in business for themselves.

In forma pauperis: "In the manner of a pauper"; being excused from paying court costs and fees.

Injunction: A court order for a party to do or not to do a specific thing.

Insider trading: A corporate insider's use of nonpublic information to trade the shares of a company.

Insolvent: Inability to pay debts as they become due.

Intentional interference with contractual relations: The tort that occurs when a person intentionally harms the plaintiff's contractual or business relationship.

Intentional interference with prospective economic advantage: The tort that occurs when a person intentionally harms the plaintiff's business relationship that was likely to have economic benefit for the plaintiff.

Intentional tort: A civil wrong causing harm to another that results from a party's intentional act.

Interrogatories: A written set of questions served by a party to a lawsuit to an opposing party during discovery. The responding party prepares written answers under oath.

Invasion: An encroachment upon the rights of another.

Issue of first impression: Refers to the first time a question of law is considered for determination by a court.

Joint and several liability: Liability that applies both to a group and to the individual members of the group personally.

Joint tenants: Two or more co-owners of real estate who take an undivided interest in the property. A joint tenant may not sell his interest in the property without the permission of the other joint tenant.

Judgment notwithstanding the verdict (JNOV): A judgment entered by the trial judge which reverses a jury verdict because the judge finds that there was no factual basis for the verdict or it was contrary to law.

Judicial arbitration: Arbitration that is required by a statute, court, court rule, or regulation, but is not binding on the parties.

Judicial review: A court's review of an administrative agency's factual or legal findings.

Jurisdiction: 1. The legal power to hear a case. 2. The geographic territory over which authority is exercised (such as, a state or county).

Labor certification: A statement from the Department of Labor indicating that there are insufficient U.S. workers who are qualified and available to perform a particular job, and that employment of a foreign worker for the job will not negatively affect U.S. workers.

Labor union: An organized association of workers in the same trade that is formed for the purpose of representing the members' interests regarding wages, benefits, and working conditions.

Landlord: A person who leases real estate to another.

Last clear chance: A doctrine usually associated with negligence law which places liability for an injury on the person with the last opportunity to avoid the accident by exercising reasonable care; it is not applied in every jurisdiction.

Lease: A contract giving a person or company the right to occupy real estate for a limited time.

Levy: The act of taking property to satisfy a judgment.

Libel: A written false statement that damages another person's reputation.

Lien: A claim on someone else's property that is made to enforce a debt.

Lien creditor: A person who claims a lien on someone else's property.

Limitation of liability: A contract clause which restricts the amount of damages a party may recover from the other party in the event of a lawsuit.

Limited liability company: A hybrid business organization that combines the liability protection for owners of a corporation, with the pass-through taxation of a partnership. Identified by the initials "LLC."

Limited liability partnership: A partnership in which partners are not personally liable for partnership debts or obligations. Identified by the initials "LLP."

Limited partners: A partner in a limited partnership who receives a share of the profits, but whose personal liability for partnership debts is limited to her investment in the limited partnership.

Limited partnership: A type of partnership in which one or more of the partners (the limited partners) is liable only to the extent of the amount of money that he has invested.

Limited warranty: Under the Magnuson-Moss Warranty Act, a warranty that does not meet the requirements of a full warranty. Limited warranties must be clearly labelled as "limited."

Limited warranty deed: A deed that guarantees that nothing the grantor has done while she owned the property affects the title to the property.

Liquidated damages: A contract clause that specifies a predetermined amount of money that must be paid as damages if a party breaches the contract.

Litigation: The process of resolving a dispute through a lawsuit initiated in the court system.

Living will: A document that shows a person's choices for end-of-life care when he is unable to indicate those preferences.

Lockout: A temporary work stoppage implemented by the employer.

Long-arm statute: A statute providing for jurisdiction over a nonresident defendant who has had contacts with the territory in which the statute is in effect.

Manufacturing defect: A product defect that occurs in the manufacturing process due to poor workmanship or poor quality materials.

Material breach: A breach of contract that deprives the non-breaching party of the value of the contract.

Material misrepresentation: A misrepresentation of a fact that would induce a reasonable person to make an agreement.

Maternity leave: A period of absence from work for a female employee for the purpose of giving birth and taking care of an infant child.

Mediation: A method of alternative dispute resolution in which the parties work with a neutral third party, a mediator, in an attempt to reach a settlement.

Mediation-arbitration: A method of alternative dispute resolution in which the parties attempt to mediate the case, and if they do not resolve the dispute, the dispute is then submitted to arbitration.

Medicaid: A federal-state cooperative program providing medical care to low-income individuals. The program is administered by the states in compliance with federal criteria, and is funded jointly by the state and federal governments.

Member: The owner, or one of the owners, of a limited liability company.

Mens rea: Latin for "guilty mind." The mental state of a person committing the criminal act (*actus reus*).

Merchant: Under Article 2 of the U.C.C., a person who regularly deals in goods of a kind.

Merger: The combining or uniting of two companies.

Metadata: Information about electronic files describing how, when, and by whom a particular set of data was collected, and how the data is formatted.

Minimum contacts: A nonresident defendant's forum-state connections, such as business activity or actions foreseeably leading to business activity, that are substantial enough to bring the defendant within the forum-state court's personal jurisdiction without offending traditional notions of fair play and substantial justice.

Minimum wage: The lowest wage permitted by law to be paid to workers.

Mini-trial: A method of alternative dispute resolution in which the parties present their arguments to a third party who issues an advisory opinion.

Minor breach: A breach of contract that allows the non-breaching party to have the benefits of the agreement.

Misclassification: When an employer incorrectly classifies an employee as an independent contractor.

Misdemeanor: A crime punishable by a fine or imprisonment of no more than one year.

Misrepresentation: The act of making a false or misleading statement about something, usually with the intent to deceive.

Modification: A defense to products liability by which the defendant argues it should not be liable for the defective product because the plaintiff modified the product.

Monopoly: Control over a market by one company or individual.

Moral rights: The right to be identified as the author of a copyrighted work, and the right to prevent unauthorized publication, display, modification, or distortion of a work. Moral rights are recognized mostly in European law.

Mortgage: The use of real estate as collateral for a debt.

Motion: A request to the judge to make a decision on an issue in a lawsuit.

Motion to dismiss: A party's request to end a legal action.

Navigable waters: A body of water used, or capable of being used, for commerce. The term includes the tributaries of such bodies of water.

Necessity: A defense to a criminal charge that says that the defendant acted in an emergency situation not of her own creation to prevent a harm greater than the harm caused by her actions.

Negligence: The failure to act as a reasonably prudent person would act in the same circumstances.

Negligence per se: A doctrine under which negligence is proven through the defendant's violation of a statute or regulation designed to prevent the type of injury that occurred.

Negotiation: A method of alternative dispute resolution in which the parties, either with or without their attorneys, work to reach a resolution.

Nolle prosequi: A formal declaration that a prosecutor or plaintiff will "no longer prosecute" a particular case.

Non-profit corporation: A business organization formed to serve some public purpose, rather than to make a profit for investors.

Note: An unconditional written promise to pay money.

Nuisance: A condition, activity, or situation that interferes with the use or enjoyment of a person's property.

Offer: A proposal to make a contract.

Offeree: The person to whom an offer is made.

Offeror: The person who makes an offer.

Office action: An examiner's communication with the applicant for a patent, usually giving reasons why the application is denied.

Operating agreement: The rules and regulations adopted to govern the operation of a limited liability company.

Option contract: Agreement that allows a party to buy something for a given price at a later date.

Oral argument: Spoken presentation of arguments to the appeals court by attorneys for the parties appearing in person.

OSHA: The Occupational Safety and Health Administration, which implements and enforces workplace safety rules.

Overtime pay: Additional compensation paid to workers for hours worked in excess of forty hours per week.

Parol evidence: Oral or verbal evidence. In contract law, "parol evidence" refers to evidence of agreements outside of the written agreement. Parol evidence is generally not admissible when it would alter or contradict the terms of a written agreement.

Partnership: An association of two or more persons for the purpose of carrying on a business for profit.

Party: Plaintiff or defendant in a court case

Paternity leave: An absence from work provided to male employees upon the birth of a child.

Perfection: Filing of a security interest paperwork with the government to provide notice of the creditor's right to the security.

Personal jurisdiction: Power of a court over the defendant in a case.

Personal property: Any property other than real estate. Also called "personalty."

Petition: In bankruptcy law, the documents that ask the court for relief under the Bankruptcy Act.

Piercing the corporate veil: The legal process by which corporate shareholders or LLC members may be held liable for the debts or obligations of a corporation or LLC.

Plaintiff: The party who files a complaint to initiate a lawsuit against another party; the injured party who seeks compensation from a tortfeasor.

Plea agreement: Agreement in a criminal case between prosecutor and defendant by which defendant agrees to plead guilty to a particular charge in return for some deal from the prosecutor.

Pleadings: Documents filed with the court by the parties to a lawsuit. Pleadings include the complaint, answer, and counterclaims.

Ponzi scheme: A fraudulent investment scheme in which money contributed by investors is used to pay people who made a prior investment. Usually, money is not invested in any revenue-producing enterprise, or if it is, the enterprise does not generate expected revenue.

Power of attorney: A document by which a principal gives an agent authority to perform specified acts on behalf of the principal.

Precedent: An earlier court decision regarded as a guide to be considered in similar, subsequent cases

Preemption: The principle that federal law can supersede state law or regulation.

Preponderance of the evidence: More than half of the evidence

Principal: A person who authorizes another to act on her behalf.

Probable cause: An objective and fact-based belief that a person has committed a crime or that there is evidence of a crime in a specific place.

Probation: A criminal sentence in which the defendant is not imprisoned, but is allowed to remain free, subject to certain conditions.

Product misuse: A defense to products liability in which the defendant argues the plaintiff used the product for an abnormal purpose.

Products liability: A manufacturer or seller's liability for a defective product created by the manufacturer and sold to the public.

Prosecutor: A public official who starts legal proceedings against another, usually for a crime.

Protected class: A personal characteristic that cannot be targeted for discrimination.

Proximate cause: The main or legal cause of an injury. The type of cause which in the natural and continuous sequence unbroken by any new independent cause produces an event, and without which the injury would not have occurred.

Public benefit corporation: A corporation that has a public or social purpose in addition to the purpose of earning a profit for shareholders.

Public domain: Work that cannot be copyrighted. An old copyright may have expired, or the author or owner of the work has made an explicit designation that the work is public domain. The term also refers to U.S. Government works that cannot be copyrighted.

Publicly-traded companies: A company whose stock is freely traded among members of the general public.

Puffery: Minor exaggeration of fact when selling goods.

Punitive damages: A sum of money awarded to the injured party in a lawsuit to punish the wrongdoer for his actions.

Purchase money security interests: A security interest in property that is purchased by means of the debt, such as a car purchase loan secured by the car itself.

Pyramid scheme: Business model based on making payments to members for enrolling new members, instead of providing a return on investment or products and services.

Quantum meruit: An equitable doctrine that allows a party to recover the actual value of goods and services rendered, even in the absence of an enforceable contract. The goal is to prevent unjust enrichment of a party.

Quitclaim deed: A deed that gives the grantee all of the grantor's interest in property. A quitclaim deed does not guarantee title.

Ratify: Accepting or confirming a prior act.

Real estate: Land, structures permanently attached to land, and legal interests in land.

Reasonable accommodation: A modification or adjustment to enable people with disabilities to perform job duties.

Reasonable person: The legal standard by which a person's conduct is measured in a negligence action. A party must act as a reasonable person would act in the same circumstances.

Receiver: A person appointed by a bankruptcy court to oversee a business.

Redeem/redemption: A foreclosed mortgage may be redeemed and the borrower may regain rights to the property if the borrower pays the full amount of the balance on the mortgage.

Reformation: Rewriting a contract to conform to the terms of the parties' agreement.

Reliance: Dependence or trust by a person, especially when combined with action based on that dependence or trust.

Reliance damages: The amount that the non-breaching party spent to perform the contract, in reliance on the other party's performance.

Remand: The result when an appellate court sends a case back to the trial court for further proceedings.

Renunciation: Termination of an agency agreement by the agent.

Replevin: A court order, or writ, deciding who is entitled to physical possession of particular personal property. Replevin does not decide who the legal owner of the property is, only who is entitled to possess it.

Requests for admission: A written set of questions or statements served by a party to a lawsuit on an opposing party or witness during discovery in an effort to determine agreed-upon facts. The responding party must deny or admit each statement in writing.

Res ipsa loquitur: A principle by which negligence may be presumed where the defendant had exclusive control of the situation and it is the type of incident that would not normally occur without negligence on the defendant's part.

Rescission: Cancellation of an agreement. The parties to the agreement are put back to where they were before the contract was made.

Restitution: Payment to a victim in compensation for a loss. Restitution is usually ordered as a part of a civil or criminal penalty.

Restitution damages: Damages awarded when there was no legally enforceable contract.

Reversionary interest: An interest in real estate that will give the holder ownership of the property in the future, when a certain event happens.

Revocation: Termination of an agency agreement by the principal.

Right to work laws: Laws prohibiting agreements between employers and unions that require workers to join the union or pay union dues or fees.

Rule absolute: A rule which commands that an order be forthwith enforced.

Sarbanes-Oxley Act: A federal law that protects investors from fraudulent accounting practices.

Scope of authority: The amount of power granted to an agent under a specific agency agreement.

Scope of employment: An act of a servant done with the intention to perform it as a part of or incident to a service on account of which he is employed.

S corporation: A corporation that meets certain qualifications and that has chosen to be taxed as a partnership.

Secondary meaning: A special meaning that attaches to a descriptive mark through use and advertising.

Security: An instrument that evidences an ownership right in a company, such as stock, or that is evidence of a debt or obligation (bonds, debentures, or notes).

Separation of powers: Giving legislative, executive, and judicial powers of government to separate bodies of the government.

Service mark: Something that is used to identify the source or origin of services. Some of the things that may be a servicemark include words, sounds, symbols, devices, logos, or phrases.

Severance agreement: A contract between an employer and employee detailing the rights and responsibilities of both parties after job termination.

Share: One of a number of equal parts into which the stock of a corporation is divided.

Shareholder: The owner of all or part of a corporation.

Sherman Act: A federal statute, passed in 1890, that prohibits direct or indirect interference with the freely competitive interstate production and distribution of goods. This Act was amended by the Clayton Act in 1914.

Sick leave: An absence from work when an employee is sick.

Slander: A spoken false statement that damages another person's reputation.

Sole proprietorship: An unincorporated business owned entirely by one person.

Special damages: Damages that occur due to the special circumstances of a particular contract.

Specific performance: An order from the court to do what the contract obligates the person to do.

Springing power of attorney: A power of attorney that becomes effective when the principal becomes incapacitated (it "springs" into effect).

Stare decisis: The doctrine that requires a court to follow earlier judicial decisions when the same points arise again.

Statute of Frauds: A law that states that certain types of contract are not enforceable unless they are in writing.

Statutes: Written laws passed by a legislative body.

Statutory damages: Damages that are fixed by statute. They are awarded without considering what the actual loss was.

Stayed sentence: A sentence that the court imposes, but delays the requirement that the defendant comply with it immediately. For example, a stayed prison sentence will allow the defendant to remain free as long as he remains law abiding and complies with the conditions of probation.

Stock: A proportional part of the capital of a corporation. Stock grants its owner the right to vote on the management of the corporation.

Strict Liability: 1. The imposition of liability on a party without a showing of fault. 2. In criminal law, a crime that does not have require proof of a guilty state of mind.

Strike: A collective effort of union employees to refuse to work in order to persuade the employer to negotiate or accept contract terms.

Subject matter jurisdiction: The authority of a court to decide a case of a particular type.

Sufficient contacts: Enough connection between a non-resident defendant with the state where a legal case is filed to give that court personal jurisdiction over that defendant.

Summary judgment: A judgment entered by the court deciding the case in favor of one party or the other based on application of the law to the available evidence, but without a full trial. Summary judgment is granted only when there is no genuine issue of material fact.

Summary jury trial: A method of alternative dispute resolution in which the parties engage in a short mock trial and a jury issues a non-binding verdict. The purpose is to encourage the parties to settle the case based on the verdict result.

Supreme court: The highest appellate court in a jurisdiction. In New York, the state trial court.

Suspended sentence: A criminal sentence that the defendant is not required to serve immediately.

Tenant: A person who rents real estate from another.

Tenants in common: Two or more co-owners of real estate who take an undivided interest in the property. A tenant in common may sell her interest in the property without the permission of the other tenant.

Termination: When an employee is fired from his or her job.

Title VII: A section of the Civil Rights Act of 1964 prohibiting employment discrimination on the basis of sex, race, color, national origin, and religion.

Tort: A lawsuit brought by an injured party seeking compensation from the party who performed an act that caused the harm.

Tortfeasor: An individual who commits a wrongful act that injures another person.

Trade libel: A defamatory statement about the quality of a business's services or products. It is also referred to as product disparagement.

Trademark: Something that is used to identify the source or origin of goods. Some of the things that may be a trademark include words, sounds, symbols, devices, logos, or phrases.

Trade name: The name under which a business operates.

Transferred intent: Shifting intent from the crime the defendant originally intended to commit to the crime that actually was committed.

Trap and trace device: means to capture the origination and routing information for email messages.

Trespass: An unlawful act against the person or property of another. The term is usually used to mean entry onto another person's property without the permission of the owner.

Trustee: A person appointed to hold or manage property for another. In bankruptcy law, a person appointed to oversee the case.

Ultra vires: An action outside the legal ability of an entity to perform.

Uncodified law: Rules taken from custom and precedent rather than statutes.

Unemployment compensation: Insurance benefits paid by the government to individuals who are out of work.

Unfair labor practice strikers: Union workers who are striking to protest an unfair labor practice by the employer.

Unlawful detainer: A type of legal action claiming that a tenant no longer has the right to remain on a property.

Unsecured: A debt is unsecured if there is no collateral guaranteeing the debt. Most credit cards are unsecured.

Validation notice: A notice to a debtor from a collector providing information on the debt, including the total and the creditor, as well as how to contest the debt.

Venue: The residence of defendant or place where most events leading to a legal claim took place.

Vested right: A right that is unconditional, that cannot be taken away from a party.

Vicarious liability: A principal's legal responsibility for the action or inaction of its agent while the agent was working on behalf of the principal.

Voir dire: The process of questioning potential jurors to determine if they are qualified to serve on the jury.

Warrant: Written authority to conduct a search or to seize property or arrest a person.

Warranty: A promise or guarantee to a consumer.

Warranty of merchantability: A promise from the manufacturer that the product is in good working order and can safely be used for the purposes stated on the label.

Well-pleaded complaint: An original or initial pleading that sufficiently sets forth a claim for relief—by including the grounds for the court's jurisdiction, the basis for the relief claimed, and a demand for judgment—so that a defendant may draft an answer that is responsive to the issues presented. A well-pleaded complaint must raise a controlling issue of federal law for a federal court to have federal-question jurisdiction over the lawsuit.

Whistleblower: An employee who reports her employer's wrongdoing to the government or to law enforcement.

Work for hire: A work that was either created by an employee within the scope of her employment, or that was commissioned for a special purpose with the written agreement that it would be work-for-hire. Copyright for a work-for-hire automatically vests in the employer or person who commissioned the work.

Work permit: Authorization from U.S. Citizenship and Immigration Services allowing individuals living in the United States under non-work visas to work in the U.S.

Workers' compensation: A type of insurance providing benefits to employees who are injured on the job.

Writ of certiorari: Permission to have a case heard by the U.S. Supreme Court that is given by the Court in response to a petition by the appealing party.

Writ of error: An order by an appellate court directing the trial court to produce the record of the case it is reviewing.

Writ of mandamus: A writ requiring a lower court or government official to perform some duty or act.

Index

A

ACCEPTANCE OF OFFER
Contracts, this index

ACCOUNTANTS AND AUDITORS
Sarbanes-Oxley Act (SOX), 388, 389

ADMINISTRATIVE AGENCIES
Independent agencies, 9, 421

ADMINISTRATIVE LAW
    Generally, 415 et seq.
Administrative Procedure Act (APA)
    Generally, 416–418
  Comments from public, 416
  Major rules, 417
  Notice of proposed rulemaking, 416
  Purpose, 416
Chevron deference to agency interpretation, 14, 15
Congressional disapproval of new regulation, 417
Effective date of new rules, 417
Federal Register, 416
Judicial challenges to final regulations, 418

ADMISSIONS
Requests for admissions in civil actions, 79

ADVERTISING AND MARKETING
Deceptive Trade Practices, this index
Environmental claims (Green Guide), 424
Factual claims, 422
Medications, 419

Offer to enter contract, 142, 143
Regulatory regimes, 419–425

AFFIRMATIVE ACTION
Generally, 367–368

AGENCY
    Generally, 317–344
Actual and apparent authority, 333
Control by principal, 323
Creation of relationship, 318
Duties and liabilities, 321–323
Employment, this index
Express and implied authority, 332
Fiduciary duty, scope of, 320, 323
Frolics, 332, 333
Good faith and fair dealing, 324
Indemnification, 325
Intent of parties, 318
Operation of law, termination of agreement, 338
Power of Attorney, this index
Principal and agent, 317
Principal's duties to agent, 323
Ratification, 320
Renunciation and revocation, 338
Scope of authority, 331, 332
Scope of relationship, 318
Termination of relationship, 337
Verbal agreements, 318
Vicarious liability, 339

ALTERNATIVE DISPUTE RESOLUTION
Generally, 73, 87
Arbitration, 91–95
Mediation, 89–91
Other kinds of ADR, 95, 96
Summary jury trials, 96

ANTENUPTIAL AGREEMENTS
Generally, 158

ANTITRUST LAWS
Generally, 392–400
Cartels, 392
Clayton Act, 398–400
Horizontal restraints, 395
Mergers and acquisitions, 398–400
Monopolies, 395, 396
Penalties for violations, 396
Per se violations, 395
Price discrimination, 398
Rule of reason approach, 395
Sherman Act, 392–398
Vertical integration, 398

APPEALS
Arbitration awards, 91
Available remedies, 87
Briefs, 86
Certiorari petitions, 52, 87
Civil actions, 22, 84–87
Criminal prosecutions, 49
Oral argument, 86
Record of trial court proceedings, 86
Supreme Court appeals, 87

ARBITRATION
Generally, 91–95
Appeals from awards, 91
Award, 91
Contract clause, 92
Employment contracts, 93
Finality of decision, 91
Judicial arbitration, 96
Mediation-arbitration, 96
Mini-trial, 96

B

BANKRUPTCY
Generally, 208–219
Automatic stay, 211
Chapter 7 liquidation
    Generally, 212–215
    Credit counseling, 213
    Discharge of debt, 213–215
    Exempt property, 212
    Means test, 213
    Noncooperation with trustee, 213
Chapter 9 (municipalities), 215
Chapter 11 reorganization
    Generally, 216, 217
    Collective bargaining agreements, 217
    Confirmation of plan, 217
    Creditor participation, 217
    Debtor in possession, 216
    Disclosure statement, 216
    Impaired claims, 217
    Plan of reorganization, 216
    Small businesses, 217
Chapter 12 (family farmers and commercial fishers), 217
Chapter 13 (wage earner's plan), 218, 219
Chapter 15 (crossing international borders), 219, 220
Corporations, 133
Credit counseling, 215
Debtor in possession, 216
Executory contracts, 211
Filing petition, 211
Historical background, 208
Meeting of creditors, 211
Receivership distinguished, 220

Stay, automatic, 211
Student loans, 213
Trustees, 211
Types of bankruptcy cases, 212

BRANCHES OF GOVERNMENT
    Generally, 2–10
Executive branch
    Generally, 5–7
  Cabinet, 5, 9
  Executive orders, 7
  Independent agencies, 9, 421
  President, 5
  Treaties, 7
  Veto power, 7
Judicial branch
    Generally, 7–12
  Appointment of federal judges, 10
  Article III courts, 7
  Constitutionality of laws, power to determine, 10, 11
  Courts, this index
  Federal jurisdiction, 10
  Federal questions, 10
Legislative branch
    Generally, 2–5
  Enumerated powers, 2
  House of Representatives, 5
  Powers, 5
  Senate, 5

BRIBERY
International business ethics, 34, 36

BURDEN OF PROOF
Civil actions, 46
Criminal prosecutions, 49, 50

BUSINESS FORMS
    Generally, 105–140
Corporations, this index
Formation of business, 121–123
Limited Liability Companies, this index
Partnerships, this index
Sole proprietorships, 106, 107, 121
Unincorporated businesses, 105–111

BUSINESS RELATIONSHIPS
    Generally, 385–414
Antitrust Laws, this index
Business-to-business issues, 391 et seq.
Corporations, this index
Imports and Exports, this index
Investor relations, 385–391
Real Property, this index
Sourcing and transportation issues, 400–411

C

CASE LAW
    Generally, 16, 17
Effect of later cases on earlier cases, 65
Format of decisions, 59
Legal analysis, 59 et seq.
Precedent, 16
Reading cases, 60–63
Rule of the case, 63–65
Stare decisis, 16

CIVIL ACTIONS
    Generally, 46, 74 et seq.
Admissions, requests for, 79, 80
Answer, 47, 75
Appeals, 48, 49, 85–87
Burden of proof, 46
Cause of action, 46, 47
Commencement, 46
Complaint, 46, 74
Counterclaims, 75
Default judgment, 78
Depositions, 79
Directed verdict, 84
Discovery, 47, 78–81
Document requests, 80
Electronically stored information (ESI), 80

Instructions to jury, 84
Interrogatories, 79
Judgment notwithstanding the verdict (JNOV) motion, 84, 85
Juries and jurors
    Generally, 48
  Instructions to jury, 84
  Voir dire of potential jurors, 84
Litigation process, 88
Motion practice, 47, 82
Motion to dismiss, 47, 75
Negotiation and settlement, 88, 89
New trial motion, 85
Parties, 46, 74
Pleadings, 74, 75
Post-trial motions, 84, 85
Preponderance of evidence, 47
Service of process, 75
Standard of proof, 46
Summary judgment, 82
Trial, elements and order of proceedings, 47, 82–84

COLLEGES AND UNIVERSITIES
Affirmative action, 368

COMMON LAW
    Generally, 1, 16–17
Case Law, this index

CONGRESS
Legislative branch. Branches of Government, this index

CONSIDERATION
Contracts, this index

CONSTITUTIONAL LAW
    Generally, 1, 2, 12
Bill of Rights, 12
Branches of Government, this index
First Amendment, this index
Search and seizure. Criminal Law, this index

Separation of powers, 1
State constitutions, 12
Supremacy Clause, 2, 11

CONSUMER PROTECTION
    Generally, 426–430
Consumer Financial Protection Bureau, 434–436
Cooling off period, door-to-door sales, 427, 428
Labeling and packaging, 425, 426
Lemon laws, 249
Plain language requirements, 428
Product safety, 429
Recall of dangerous products, 429
Sales transactions, 427
Telemarketing, 427
Unconscionable contracts, 428, 429
Warranties, 429, 430

CONTRACTS
    Generally, 141–193
Acceptance of offer
    Generally, 148–150
  Counteroffers, 147
  Meeting of the minds, 149
  Performance as acceptance, 150
  Silence, 149
  Time limits, 149
Accord and satisfaction defense, 170
Anticipatory breach, 169
Attorney's fees, 177
Breach of contract, 168–170
Capacity to contract, 154, 155
Conditions, 167
Consideration
    Generally, 150–154
  Adequacy, 151
  Disproportionate values, 151
  Forbearance, 152
  Legal detriment, 150
  Moral obligation, 151

Sufficiency, 153
Consumer Protection, this index
Cultural issues, 98, 99
Duress, 166
Duty of good faith, 166, 167
Elements, 141–157
Enforcement, 159
Expectation damages, 171
Formation, 157–159
Fraudulent misrepresentations, 160, 161
General and special damages, 171
Genuineness of assent, 166
Impossibility defense, 170
Intellectual property, licensing agreements, 309
Interest damages, 177
Interference with contract, 178
Legality, 155–157
Liquidated damages, 175–178
Litigation costs, 177
Material and minor breaches, 168, 169
Misrepresentations, 160–162
Mistake, mutual and unilateral, 162–165
Mitigation of damages, 177
Money damages, 171
Negotiations, 96–98
Offer
    Generally, 142–147
    Advertisements, 143, 144
    Counteroffers, 147
    Legal requirements, 142
    Option contracts, 147
    Revocation, 145
Online contracts, 186
Option contracts, 147
Performance, 166 et seq.
Promissory estoppel, 153, 154
Quantum meruit, 176
Reformation, 162

Reliance damages, 172
Remedies for breach, 171 et seq.
Restitution damages, 175
Sale of goods. Uniform Commercial Code, this index
Scrivener's error, 165
Specific performance, 175
Statute of frauds, 157–159
Undue influence, 165, 166
Uniform Commercial Code, this index
Written vs. oral, 157

COPYRIGHT
    Generally, 268–280
Access to copyrighted work, 304
Application for registration, 274
Authorship, 270, 271
Berne Convention, 301–303
Bundle of rights, 268
Creation of work, 269
Creative commons licensing, 275
Damages for infringement, 305
Defenses to infringement action, 305
Denial of application, 274
Derivative works, 270
Direct and indirect copying, 304
Duration of protection, 268, 275, 276
Electronic searching, 277
Excluded works, 271
Expiration, 269
Expiration of copyright, 275
Fair use, 276–280
Federal law, exclusivity, 300
First sale doctrine, 306
Historical background, 268
Infringement, 274–276, 303–305
Injunctive relief, 305
Innocent infringement, 272
Non-copyrightable works and parts of work, 270

Notice of copyright, 272
Original works, 269
Protecting copyrights, 274
Proving copyright, 272
Public domain, 274
Qualifying for protection, 269
Registration, 273, 274
Substantial similarity, 304
Tangible means of expression, 271
Technological changes, 310, 311
Trademark distinguished, 280
Work for hire, 270

CORPORATIONS

Generally, 114–117
Articles of incorporation, 115, 118
Bankruptcy, 133
Board of directors, 125
Business judgment rule, 386
Buy-sell agreements, 125
By-laws, 124, 125
C corporations, 116
Corporate powers, 124
Criminal liability (corporate)
    Generally, 476–481
  Acts of employees, 477, 478
  Confiscation of property, 481
  Dissolution, involuntary, 481
  Fines and restitution, 480
  Probation, 481
  Sentencing, 480, 481
Death of key member, 134
Dissolution, 130–134, 481
Dividends, 114, 115
Duty of loyalty and care, 386
Duty of transparency, 386
Filing obligations, 123
Formalities, 124, 125
Formation, 122
Investor relations, 385–391
Involuntary dissolution, 133, 134
Management, ongoing, 124 et seq.
Meetings, 126
Mergers and acquisitions, 132, 133
Non-profit corporations, 119, 120
Officers, 128
Personal jurisdiction, sufficiency of contacts, 53–57
Piercing the corporate veil, 128–130
Professional practices, 120
Promoters, 122
Public benefit corporations, 119, 120
Publicly traded companies, 127
S corporations, 117
Sarbanes-Oxley Act (SOX), this index
Securities Regulation, this index
Shareholders
    Generally, 114, 128
  C corporations, 116
  Functions, 128
  Limited personal liability, 118
  S corporations, 117
Succession planning, 131, 132
Tax obligations, 123
Ultra vires acts, 124
Voluntary dissolution, 130, 131
Voting rights, 115

COURTS

Bankruptcy courts, 210
Federal court system
    Generally, 52 et seq.
  Diversity or federal question jurisdiction, 57
Judicial branch. Branches of Government, this index
Jurisdiction, this index

CREDIT REPORTING

Debtor and Creditor, this index

CRIMINAL LAW
    Generally, 46, 49, 451–488
Actus reas, 452, 455, 456
Appeals, 51
Arraignment, 50
Attempts, 466, 467
Beyond reasonable doubt, 49, 452
Burden of proof, 49
Business crimes, 451, 469
Conspiracy, 468, 469
Conviction, 49, 50
Corporate criminal liability, 476–481
Cruel and unusual punishment, 462
Duress defense, 453
Embezzlement, 472, 473
Exclusionary rule, 462
Felonies, 49, 465
Fraud, 469–471
General intent, 452, 454
Grand jury, 50
Homicide, 453
Inchoate crimes, 465–468
Insider trading, 473–476
Jury instructions, 49
Mens rea, 452–455
Misdemeanors, 49, 465
Necessity defense, 453
Plea agreements, 50, 51
Ponzi schemes, 470
Pre-trial release, 50
Preliminary hearing, 50
Presumption of innocence, 50
Probable cause, 460
Probation, 464, 481
Prosecutors, 49
Search and seizure (Fourth Amendment)
    Generally, 458–465
  Exclusionary rule, 462
  Probable cause, 460
  Warrantless searches, 462
  What constitutes search, 458
Search warrants, 458–462
Sentencing
    Generally, 51, 462, 465
  Corporate offenders, 480
  Grossly disproportionate sentences, 462
  Guidelines, 464
  Stayed sentence, 465
  Suspended sentence, 464
Solicitation to commit crime, 467
Specific intent, 454
State of mind, 452
Strict liability, 452, 455
Suspended sentence, 464
Transferred intent, 453
Trial, elements and order of proceedings, 50, 51
Warrantless searches, 462

D

DAMAGES
Compensatory damages, 258
Contract remedies, 171–178
Copyright infringement, 303–305
Negligence claims, 233, 258
Patent infringement, 306, 307
Punitive damages, 259
Trade secret violations, 307

DEBTOR AND CREDITOR
    Generally, 195 et seq.
Bankruptcy, this index
Equal Credit Opportunity Act (ECOA), 197
Fair credit reporting
    Generally, 201
  Credit scores, 201
  Damages for violations, 201
  Disputed information, 201

Fair debt collection practices
    Generally, 199
    Compliance areas for debt collectors, 200
    Harassment, 200
    Identification requirements, 200
    Statutory damages, 200
    Validation notice, 200
Mortgage foreclosure, 207, 208
Receivership, 220, 221
Regulation Z disclosures, 196, 197
Rescission rights under TILA, 197
Truth in Lending Act (TILA), 196–199

DECEPTIVE TRADE PRACTICES
Disparagement, 424
Endorsements, 422
Factual claims, 424
FTC jurisdiction, 421–423
Material representations, 422
State law, 424, 425

DEFAMATION
    Generally, 238
Actual malice, 241, 242
Libel and slander, 239
Public *vs.* private figures, 241, 242
Trade libel, 243
Truth as defense, 240

DEFAULT JUDGMENT
Civil actions, 78

DEPOSITIONS
Civil actions, 79

DISABILITY INSURANCE
Generally, 366, 367

DISCOVERY
Civil actions, 47, 78, 79

DISCRIMINATION
Employment, this index

DISPUTE RESOLUTION
    Generally, 73–104
Alternative Dispute Resolution, this index
Avoiding disputes, 96

DODD-FRANK
Financial regulatory reform, 434

DRAM SHOP ACTS
Bartender and bar owner liability, 229

DURESS
Contracts, 166

E

EMBEZZLEMENT
Generally, 472, 473

EMPLOYMENT
    Generally, 345–384
Affirmative action, 367, 368
Age discrimination, 360–363
Agent distinguished from employee, 318
Anti-discrimination laws, 355 et seq.
Arbitration clauses in employment contracts, 93
At-will employment, 346
Bona fide occupational qualification (BFOQ), 356
Circumstantial evidence of discrimination, 359
Collective bargaining
    Generally, 375–377
    Chapter 11 reorganization, 216
Disability discrimination, 363
Disability insurance, 366, 367
Disparate treatment and disparate impact (Title VII violations), 356–360
Employee handbooks, 346
Employment relationship, 345–351
Family and medical leave, 353
Health insurance, 352
Hiring and retention, negligent, 330, 331

Holidays, 354
Immigration and employment
    Generally, 369–374
    Employment Authorization Document, 369
    I-9 form, 369–371
    Labor certification, 374
    Permanent resident status, 369
    Temporary work visas, 374
    Visa categories, 374
    Work permits, 374
Independent contractor, classification and misclassification, 347–351
International business ethics, 34
Jury service, 355
Labor unions, 374–377
Lockouts, 377
Malfeasance, employer liability, 327
Mandated benefits, 352
Maternity/paternity leave, 353
Minimum wage, 352
Negligence
    Employer's vicarious liability, 325–327
    Hiring and retention, 330, 331
Overtime pay, 352
Paid time off (PTO), 353
Protected classes, 355
Right to work laws, 377
Safe workplace requirements (OSHA), 363–365
Severance pay, 355
Sexual harassment, 357
Sick leave, 353
Strikes, 376
Termination of employment, 355, 368
Title VII (Civil Rights Act of 1964), 356–360
Unemployment compensation, 369
Unfair labor practices, 376
Vacation leave, 354
Visas. Immigration and employment, above
Wages and benefits, 352–355
WARN Act, plant closures or mass layoffs, 369
Workers' compensation, 365, 366

ENVIRONMENTAL PROTECTION
    Generally, 436
Air quality, 438, 439
Comprehensive Environmental Response, Compensation, and Liability Act (CERCLA), 442
Cooperative federalism, 437
Federal and state laws, 437
Federal Insecticide, Fungicide and Rodenticide Act (FIFRA), 443
Navigable waters, 439, 440
Pesticides, 443
Resource Conservation and Recovery Act (RCRA), 441
Toxic Substances Control Act (TSCA), 442, 443
Waste management, 441, 442
Water quality, 439, 440
Wetlands, 439, 440

ETHICS
    Generally, 23–39
Business ethics, 23
International business ethics, 34, 36
Internet, 37–39
Sarbanes-Oxley Act (SOX), 32, 33
Stakeholders, 23–25
Voluntary standards, 29

EXECUTIVE BRANCH
Branches of Government, this index

EXPORTS
Imports and Exports, this index

F

FEDERAL COURTS
Courts, this index

FEDERALISM
Generally, 1

FINANCE
Bonds and notes, 434
Consumer Financial Protection Bureau, 434–436
Crowdfunding, 434
Debentures, 434
Dodd-Frank, 434

FIRST AMENDMENT
Commercial speech, 419
Trademarks, 286, 287

FORECLOSURE
Mortgages, 207, 208

FOREIGN LAW
International Law, this index

FOREIGN RELATIONS
Federal powers, 10

FORMATION OF BUSINESS
Generally, 121–123

FRANCHISES
Generally, 121

FRAUDULENT MISREPRESENTATIONS
Contracts, 160–162
Criminal offenses, 469–471
Mail fraud and wire fraud, 470
Torts, 236, 237

G

GOOD SAMARITAN LAWS
Generally, 233

GOVERNMENT ORGANIZATION
Branches of Organization, this index

I

IMMIGRATION
Employment, this index

IMPORTS AND EXPORTS
Audits of import records, 408
Common markets, 410
Customs duties, 404, 405
Customs unions, 410
Free trade areas, 409, 410
Harmonized tariff schedule, 404–408
NAFTA, 409
Trading areas, 409–411

INJUNCTIONS
Generally, 48
Intellectual property, 305

INTELLECTUAL PROPERTY
Generally, 267 et seq.
Copyright, this index
Federal and state protection, 300
International protection, 301–303
Licensing and licensing agreements, 307–310
Owner's responsibility for protecting, 304, 305
Patents, this index
Technical intellectual property, protection of, 311
Technological changes, 310, 311
Trade Secrets, this index
Trademarks, this index

INTERNATIONAL LAW
Bijuridical systems, 58
Chapter 15 bankruptcy, 219, 220
Civil law, 58
Foreign legal systems, 58, 59
Imports and Exports, this index
Intellectual property protection, 301–303
Islamic law, 59
Sources of law, 17

INTERNET
Intellectual property, enforcement challenges, 310, 311
Online contracts, 186

Online ethics, 37–39
Online resources, acceptable use, 39
Privacy concerns, 37

INTERROGATORIES
Civil actions, 79

INVESTORS
Securities Regulation, this index

J

JOINT AND SEVERAL LIABILITY
Partnerships, 108

JUDICIAL BRANCH
Branches of Government, this index

JURIES AND JURORS
Civil Actions, this index
Jury service by employees, 355

JURISDICTION
Generally, 7, 53 et seq.
Federal question jurisdiction, 10, 57
Personal jurisdiction, 53
State and federal jurisdiction, 53–57
Subject matter jurisdiction, 53

L

LABELING AND PACKAGING
Consumer products, 425, 426
State law, 426

LABOR LAWS
Employment, this index

LEGAL ANALYSIS
Case Law, this index

LEGAL STRUCTURE
Branches of Government, this index

LEGISLATIVE BRANCH
Branches of Government, this index

LIBEL AND SLANDER
Defamation, this index

LICENSING
Intellectual property, 307–310

LIMITED LIABILITY COMPANIES
Generally, 118, 119
Articles of organization, 118
Filing obligations, 123
Operating agreement, 124, 125
Powers, 124
Tax obligations, 123
Tax treatment, 118

LIQUIDATED DAMAGES
Contract clauses, 175–178

LITIGATION
Civil Actions, this index

M

MAIL FRAUD
Generally, 470

MALPRACTICE
Professional malpractice, 233, 234

MEDIATION
Generally, 89–91
Binding mediation, 96
Mediation-arbitration, 96

MERGERS AND ACQUISITIONS
Generally, 132, 133, 398–400

MISREPRESENTATIONS
Fraudulent Misrepresentations, this index

MISTAKE
Contracts, mutual and unilateral mistakes, 162–165

MORTGAGES
Foreclosure, 207, 208

MUNICIPALITIES
Chapter 9 bankruptcy, 215, 216

N

NEGLIGENCE
Generally, 228–235
But for causation, 230
Causation, 229, 230
Comparative and contributory negligence, 253
Damages, 233, 258
Defenses, 235
Duty of reasonable care
Generally, 228, 229
Breach of duty, 229
Employment, this index
Foreseeability, 256
Intervening events, 230, 232
Negligence per se, 235
Products Liability, this index
Professional malpractice, 233, 234
Proximate cause, 230
Reasonable person standard, 228
Res ipsa loquitur, 234, 235

NEGOTIATION
Civil actions, 96–98
Contract negotiation, 96–98

O

OFFER
Contracts, this index

P

PARTNERSHIPS
Generally, 107–114
Death of key member or partner, 134
Formation, 120
Joint and several liability, 108
Limited liability partnerships, 112
Limited partnerships, 112–114
Professional practices, 120
Uniform Partnership Act, 109

PATENTS
Generally, 293–298
Abstract ideas, 294
Application process, 297, 298
Design patents, 295
First sale doctrine, 306
Infringement, 306, 307
Non-patentable things, 294
Paris Convention, 301–303
Plant patents, 294, 295
Protecting patents, 294, 301
Requirements, 293–295
Software, 311
Utility patents, 293, 295

PONZI SCHEMES
Generally, 470

POWER OF ATTORNEY
Generally, 319
Attorney in fact, 319
Durable power of attorney, 320
General and special powers, 319
Health care power of attorney, 319
Living wills distinguished, 319, 320
Springing power of attorney, 320

PREEMPTION
Federal *vs.* state law, 426
Toxic substances regulation, 442

PRESIDENT
Executive branch. Branches of Government, this index

PRIVACY
Internet, privacy concerns, 37

PRODUCT DISPARAGEMENT
Generally, 243

PRODUCTS LIABILITY
Generally, 228, 244
Abnormal uses, 256, 257
Assumption of risk, 251, 252
Comparative fault, 253
Defenses, 251
Design defects, 249
Failure-to-warn defects, 248
Manufacturing defects, 248
Misuse of product, 256, 257
Modification/substantial change defense, 255
Negligence, 245
Packaging, improper, 248
Strict liability, 245
Warranties, 246–248

PROFESSIONAL PRACTICES
Generally, 120

R

RECEIVERSHIP
Generally, 219
Bankruptcy distinguished, 220

REGULATIONS
Administrative Law, this index
Sources of law, 12–17

REGULATORY REGIMES
Generally, 415–449
Administrative Law, this index
Advertising and Marketing, this index
Consumer Protection, this index
Deceptive Trade Practices, this index
Environmental Protection, this index
Labeling and packaging, 425, 426

REPLEVIN
Generally, 205

RULEMAKING
Administrative Law, this index

S

SALE OF GOODS
Uniform Commercial Code, this index

SARBANES-OXLEY ACT (SOX)
Generally, 32, 386–388, 433, 434
Accountants and auditors, 388, 389
Criminal penalties, 391
Director responsibilities, 126
Financial reporting, 389, 390
Internal controls, 391, 392

SECURED TRANSACTIONS
Uniform Commercial Code, this index

SECURITIES REGULATION
Bonds, 434
Crowdfunding, 434
Debentures, 434
Dodd-Frank, 434
Financial reports, 430
Insider trading, 430, 473–476
Investment Advisers Act, 433
Investment Company Act, 433
Investor protection, 386, 430–436
JOBS Act, 434
Sarbanes-Oxley Act (SOX), this index
SEC enforcement authority, 430
SEC Rule 10b-5, 387, 432, 433
Securities Act of 1933, 431
Securities Exchange Act of 1934, 432
State laws, 436
Trust Indenture Act, 432

SENTENCING
Criminal Law, this index

SEPARATION OF POWERS
Generally, 1

SERVICE OF PROCESS
Commencement of civil action, 75

SETTLEMENT
Negotiation and settlement, 88, 89

SHAREHOLDERS
Corporations, this index

SOFTWARE
Patent protection, 311

SOLE PROPRIETORSHIPS
Generally, 106, 107, 121

SOURCES OF LAW
Generally, 12–17
Common law/case law, 1, 16–17
Constitution, 13
Enacted laws, 12
Hierarchy of laws, 12
Regulations, 14
Statutes, 13
Treaties and international law, 17
Uncodified law, 16

STARE DECISIS
Generally, 16

STATUTE OF FRAUDS
Contracts, 157–159
UCC Article 2, 182

STATUTES
Generally, 13
Agency interpretation, Chevron deference, 14, 15

STRICT LIABILITY
Criminal offenses, 452, 455
Products liability, 245
Torts, 243

SUMMARY JUDGMENT
Generally, 82

SUMMONS
Service on defendant in civil action, 75

T

TARIFFS
Harmonized tariff schedule, 404–408

TELEMARKETING
Consumer protection, 427

TORTS
Generally, 227–266
Categories, 228
Comparative fault, 253
Contract torts, 178, 179
Damages, 228
Defamation, this index
Defined, 227
Fraudulent misrepresentation, 236, 237
Hazardous activities, strict liability, 243
Intentional torts, 236–242
Interference with contractual relations, 178, 237
Interference with prospective business advantage, 238
Negligence, this index
Parties, 227
Product disparagement, 243
Products Liability, this index
Punitive damages, 259
Strict liability, 243
Tortfeasors, 227
Trade libel, 243
Types of torts, 228, 244

TRADE LIBEL
Generally, 243

TRADE PRACTICES
Deceptive Trade Practices, this index

TRADE RELATIONSHIPS
Imports and Exports, this index

TRADE SECRETS
Generally, 298

Confidentiality agreements, 300, 301
Damages and injunctive relief, 307
Defending Trade Secrets Act of 2016 (DTSA), 299
Misappropriation, 307
Protecting trade secrets, 300, 301
State law, 300

TRADEMARKS
Generally, 280
Applications, 287
Certification marks, 284
Classic fair use, 292
Collective marks, 284, 285
Copyright distinguished, 280
Denial of application, 288
Dilution, 289, 290
Distinctiveness, 289
Fair use, 292
Famous marks, 289, 290
Federal and state law, 286
First Amendment concerns, 286, 287
Functions, 280–282
Generic marks, 283, 284
Incontestable marks, 284
Infringement, 305, 306
Intent to use registration, 287
Likelihood of confusion, 281, 305
Nominative fair use, 292
Office action, 288
Paris Convention, 301–303
Protecting trademark, 290–292, 300
Registered marks, 286
Registration procedure, 282
Secondary meaning, 282
Service marks, 284
TM symbol, use of, 287
Trade dress, 285, 286
Trade names, 281

TRANSPORTATION
Risk and costs, 400

TREATIES
Intellectual property protection, 301–303
Presidential powers, 5
Sources of law, 17

TRIAL
Civil actions, 47, 48, 82
Criminal prosecutions, 51

TRUTH IN LENDING ACT (TILA)
Generally, 196–200

TYPES OF BUSINESSES
Business Forms, this index
Corporations, this index
Franchises, 121
Limited liability companies, 118, 119
Partnerships, this index
Unincorporated businesses, 105–111

U

UNDUE INFLUENCE
Voidable contracts, 165, 166

UNEMPLOYMENT COMPENSATION
Generally, 369

UNIFORM COMMERCIAL CODE
Sale of goods (Article 2)
    Generally, 179–185
  Disclaimers, 185
  Formation of contract, 182
  Performance of contract, 183
  Puffery, 184
  Risk of loss, 401
  Statute of frauds, 182
  Trade terms, UCC and Incoterm, 402, 403
  Warranties, express and implied, 183, 184
Secured transactions (Article 9)
    Generally, 201

Attachment of security interest, 202
Authentication of agreement, 202
Collateral, 201, 202
Financing statement, 203–205
Perfection of security interest, 202, 203
Purchase money security interests in consumer goods, 203
Repossession of collateral, 205
Sale of repossessed collateral, 205
Termination statement, 205

UNINCORPORATED BUSINESSES
Generally, 105–111

V

VENUE
Generally, 57, 58

W

WARRANTIES
Consumer protection, 429
Products liability, 246
UCC Article 2, 179–184

WHISTLEBLOWERS
Protections for, 435

WIRE FRAUD
Generally, 470

WITNESSES
Civil cases, 48, 84, 85
Criminal prosecutions, 49
Cross-examination, 48
Direct examination, 48

WORKERS' COMPENSATION
Generally, 365, 366

WRONGFUL DEATH
Generally, 233